Information Security Management

HANDBOOK

4TH EDITION
VOLUME 2

OTHER AUERBACH PUBLICATIONS

A Standard for Auditing Computer Applications
Martin Krist
ISBN: 0-8493-9983-1

Analyzing Business Information Systems
Shouhong Wang
ISBN: 0-8493-9240-3

Broadband Networking
James Trulove, Editor
ISBN: 0-8493-9821-5

Communications Systems Management Handbook, 6th Edition
Anura Gurugé and
Lisa M. Lindgren, Editors
ISBN: 0-8493-9826-6

Computer Telephony Integration
William Yarberry, Jr.
ISBN: 0-8493-9995-5

Data Management Handbook 3rd Edition
Sanjiv Purba, Editor
ISBN: 0-8493-9832-0

Electronic Messaging
Nancy Cox, Editor
ISBN: 0-8493-9825-8

Enterprise Operations Management Handbook, 2nd Edition
Steve F. Blanding, Editor
ISBN: 0-8493-9824-X

Enterprise Systems Architectures
Andersen Consulting
ISBN: 0-8493-9836-3

Enterprise Systems Integration
John Wyzalek, Editor
ISBN: 0-8493-9837-1

Healthcare Information Systems
Phillip L. Davidson, Editor
ISBN: 0-8493-9963-7

Information Security Architecture
Jan Tudor Killmeyer
ISBN: 0-8493-9988-2

Information Security Management Handbook, 4th Edition, Volume 2
Harold F. Tipton and Micki Krause, Editors
ISBN: 0-8493-0800-3

IS Management Handbook, 7th Edition
Carol V. Brown, Editor
ISBN: 0-8493-9820-7

Information Technology Control and Audit
Frederick Gallegos, Sandra Allen-Senft, and Daniel P. Manson
ISBN: 0-8493-9994-7

Internet Management
Jessica Keyes, Editor
ISBN: 0-8493-9987-4

Local Area Network Handbook, 6th Edition
John P. Slone, Editor
ISBN: 0-8493-9838-X

Multi-Operating System Networking: Living with UNIX, NetWare, and NT
Raj Rajagopal, Editor
ISBN: 0-8493-9831-2

The Network Manager's Handbook, 3rd Edition
John Lusa, Editor
ISBN: 0-8493-9841-X

Project Management
Paul C. Tinnirello, Editor
ISBN: 0-8493-9998-X

Effective Use of Teams in IT Audits,
Martin Krist
ISBN: 0-8493-9828-2

Systems Development Handbook, 4th Edition
Paul C. Tinnirello, Editor
ISBN: 0-8493-9822-3

AUERBACH PUBLICATIONS

www.auerbach-publications.com
TO Order: Call: 1-800-272-7737 • Fax: 1-800-374-3401
E-mail: orders@crcpress.com

Information Security Management

H A N D B O O K

4TH EDITION
VOLUME 2

Harold F. Tipton
Micki Krause

EDITORS

AUERBACH

Boca Raton   London   New York   Washington, D.C.

Chapter 6, "Packet Sniffers and Network Monitors; Chapter 17, "Introduction to Encryption;" Chapter 18, "Three New Models for the Application of Cryptography;" and Chapter 23, "An Introduction to Hostile Code and Its Control" © Lucent Technologies. All rights reserved. Chapter 8, "IPSec Virtual Private Networks;" and Chapter 20, "Message Authentication;" © INS. All rights reserved.

Library of Congress Cataloging-in-Publication Data

Information security management handbook / Harold F. Tipton, Micki Hrause, editors.—4th ed.
    p. cm.
    Includes bibliographical references and index.
    ISBN 0-8493-0800-3 (alk. paper)
    1. Computer security — Management — Handbooks, manuals, etc. 2. Data protection—Handbooks, manuals, etc. I. Tipton, Harold F. II. Hrause, Micki. III. Title: Handbook of information security 1999.
QA76.9.A25H36 1999a
6589.0558—dc21   99-42823
                                                CIP

Visit the Auerbach Publications Web site at www.auerbach-publications.com

© 2001 by CRC Press LLC
Auerbach is an imprint of CRC Press LLC

No claim to original U.S. Government works
International Standard Book Number 0-8493-0800-3
Library of Congress Card Number 99-42823
Printed in the United States of America   3 4 5 6 7 8 9 0
Printed on acid-free paper

Contributors

CHRISTINA BIRD, PH.D, CISSP, *Senior Security Analyst, Counterpane Internet Security, San Jose, California*

STEVE BLANDING, *Regional Director of Technology, Arthur Andersen LLP, Houston, Texas*

MICHAEL J. CORBY, *Vice President, Netigy Corp., San Francisco, California*

Eran Feigenbaum, *Manager, PricewaterhouseCoopers LLP, Los Angeles, California*

BRYAN FISH, *Network Systems Consultant, Lucent Technologies, Dallas, Texas*

STEPHEN FRIED, *Senior Manager, Global Risk Assessment and Secure Business Solutions, Lucent Technologies, Warren, New Jersey*

CHRIS HARE, CISSP, ACE, *Systems Auditor, Internal Audit, Nortel, Ottawa, Ontario, Canada*

JAY HEISER, CISSP, *Senior Security Consultant, Lucent NetworkCare, Washington, D.C.*

CARL B. JACKSON, CISSP, *Director, Global Security Practice, Netigy Corp., San Francisco, California*

MOLLY KHEHNKE, CISSP, *Computer Security Analyst, Lockheed Martin Energy Systems, Inc., Oak Ridge, Tennessee*

BRYAN T. KOCH, CISSP, *Principal Security Architect, Guardent, Inc., St. Paul, Minnesota*

ROSS LEO, CISSP, CBCP, *Director, Information Assurance & Security, Omitron, Inc., Houston, Texas*

BRUCE LOBREE, CISSP, *Security Manager, Oracle Business Online, Redwood Shores, California*

JEFF LOWDER, *Chief, Network Security Element, United States Air Force Academy, Colorado Springs, Colorado*

DOUGLAS C. MERRILL, PH.D., *Senior Manager, PricewaterhouseCoopers LLP, Los Angeles, California*

WILLIAM HUGH MURRAY, *Executive Consultant, Deloitte and Touche LLP, New Canaan, Connecticut*

SATNAM PUREWAL, B.SC., CISSP, *Manager, PricewaterhouseCoopers LLP, Seattle, Washington*

SEAN SCANLON, *e-Architect, fcgDoghouse, Huntington Beach, California*

KEN SHAURETTE, CISSP, CISA, *Information Systems Security Staff Advisor, American Family Institute, Madison, Wisconsin*

SANFORD SHERIZEN, PH.D., CISSP, *President, Data Security Systems, Inc., Natick, Massachusetts*

ED SKOUDIS, *Account Manager and Technical Director, Global Integrity, Howell, New Jersey*

BILL STACKPOLE, CISSP, *Managing Consultant, InfoSec Practice, Predictive Systems, Santa Cruz, California*

JAMES S. TILLER, CISSP, *Senior Security Architect, Belenos, Inc., Tampa, Florida*

GEORGE WADE, *Senior Manager, Lucent Technologies, Murray Hill, New Jersey*

Contents

Contents

Contents

Introduction

TECHNOLOGY IS GROWING AT A FEVERISH PACE. Consequently, the challenges facing the information security professional are mounting rapidly. For that reason, we are pleased to bring you Volume 2 of the 4th edition of the *Information Security Management Handbook*, with all new chapters that address emerging trends, new concepts, and security methodologies for evolving technologies. In this manner, we maintain our commitment to be a current, every-day reference for information security practitioners, as well as network and systems administrators.

In addition, we continue to align the contents of the handbook with the Information Security Common Body of Knowledge (CBK), in order to provide information security professionals with enabling material with which to conduct the rigorous review required to prepare for the Certified Information Systems Security professional certification examination. CISSP certification examinations and CBK seminars, both offered by the International Information Systems Security Certification Consortium (ISC)², are given globally and in high demand.

Preparing for the examination requires an enormous effort due to the need for not only a deep understanding, but also an application, of the topics contained in the CBK. This series of handbooks is recognized as some of the most important references used by candidates preparing for the CISSP certification examination — in particular because the chapters are authored by individuals who typically make their living in this profession. Likewise, the books are used routinely by professionals and practitioners who regularly apply the practical information contained herein.

Moreover, faced with the continuing proliferation of computer viruses and worms and the ongoing threat of malicious hackers exploiting the security vulnerabilities of open network protocols, the diligent Chief Executive Officer with fiduciary responsibilities for the protection of corporate assets, is compelled to hire the best qualified security staff. Consequently — and now more than ever — the CISSP is a prerequisite for employment.

The tables of contents for this and future editions of the handbook are purposely arranged to correspond to the domains of the CISSP certification examination. One or more chapters of each book address specific CBK topics because of the broad scope of the information security field. With this edition of the *Information Security Management Handbook*, we feature only new topics to ensure that we keep current as the field propels ahead.

HAL TIPTON
MICKI KRAUSE
October 2000

Domain 1
Access Control Systems and Methodology

A FUNDAMENTAL TENET OF INFORMATION SECURITY IS CONTROLLING ACCESS TO THE CRITICAL RESOURCES THAT REQUIRE PROTECTION. The essence of access control is that permissions are assigned to individuals, system objects, or processes that are authorized to access only those specific resources required to perform their role.

Some access control methodologies utilize certain characteristics associated with its user (e.g., what a person knows, what a person possesses, or what a person is) and range from a simple user identifier and fixed password, to hardware password generators, to technologically advanced biometric devices (e.g., retinal scanners or fingerprint readers).

Access controls can be implemented at various points in a system configuration, including the host operating system, database, or application layer. And in some instances — especially at the database or application layer — the lack of vendor-provided controls requires the imposition of access controls by third-party products. In other instances, access controls are invoked administratively or procedurally, as is the case with segregation of duties.

Access control management models can be architectured in a centralized model, a decentralized model, or a hybrid model. To ease the burden of access control administration, many organizations attempt to implement reduced or single sign-on. The chapters in this domain address the various methods that can be utilized to accomplish control of authorized access to information resources.

Chapter 1
Single Sign-on

Ross Leo

CORPORATIONS EVERYWHERE HAVE MADE THE FUNCTIONAL SHIFT FROM THE MAINFRAME-CENTERED DATA PROCESSING ENVIRONMENT TO THE CLIENT/SERVER CONFIGURATION. With this conversion have come new economies, a greater variety of operational options, and a new set of challenges. In the mainframe-centric installation, systems management was often the administrative twin of the computing complex itself: the components of the system were confined to one area, as were those who performed the administration of the system. In the distributed client/server arrangement, those who manage the systems are again arranged in a similar fashion. This distributed infrastructure has complicated operations, even to the extent of making the simple act of logging in more difficult.

Users need access to many different systems and applications to accomplish their work. Getting them set up to do this simply and easily is frequently time-consuming, requiring coordination between several individuals across multiple systems. In the mainframe environment, switching between these systems and applications meant returning to a main menu and making a new selection. In the client/server world, this can mean logging in to an entirely different system. New loginid, new password, and both very likely different than the ones used for the previous system — the user is inundated with these, and the problem of keeping them un-confused to prevent failed log-in attempts. It was because of this and related problems that the concept of the **Single Sign-on**, or SSO, was born.

EVOLUTION

Given the diversity of computing platforms, operating systems, and access control software (and the many loginids and passwords that go with them), having the capability to log on to multiple systems once and simultaneously through a single transaction would seem an answer to a prayer. Such a prayer is one offered by users and access control administrators everywhere. When the concept arose of a method to accomplish this, it became clear that integrating it with the different forms of system access control would pose a daunting challenge with many hurdles.

0-8493-0800-3/00/$0.00+$.50
© 2001 by CRC Press LLC

In the days when applications software ran on a single platform, such as the early days of the mainframe, there was by default only a single login that users had to perform. Whether the application was batch oriented or interactive, the user had only a single loginid and password combination to remember. When the time came for changing passwords, the user could often make up his own. The worst thing to face was the random password generator software implemented by some companies that served up number/letter combinations. Even then, there was only one of them.

The next step was the addition of multiple computers of the same type on the same network. While these machines did not always communicate with each other, the user had to access more than one of them to fulfill all data requirements. Multiple systems, even of the same type, often had different rules of use. Different groups within the Data Processing Department often controlled these disparate systems and sometimes completely separate organizations with the same company. Of course, the user had to have a different loginid and password for each one, although each system was reachable from the same terminal.

Then, the so-called "departmental computer" appeared. These smaller, less powerful processors served specific groups in the company to run unique applications specific to that department. Examples include materials management, accounting and finance applications, centralized word-processing, and shop-floor applications. Given the limited needs of these areas, and the fact that they frequently communicated electronically internal to themselves, tying these systems together on the same network was unnecessary. This state of affairs did not last long.

It soon became obvious that tying these systems together, and allowing them to communicate with each other over the network would speed up the information flow from one area to another. Instead of having to wait until the last week of the month to get a report through internal mail, purchasing records could be reconciled weekly with inventory records for materials received the same week from batched reports sent to Purchasing. This next phase in the process of information flow did not last long either.

As systems became less and less batch oriented and more interactive, and business pressures to record the movement of goods, services, and money mounted, more rapid access was demanded. Users in one area needed direct access to information in another. There was just one problem with this scenario — and it was not a small one.

Computers have nearly always come in predominantly two different flavors: the general-purpose machines and specific-use machines. Initially called "business processing systems" and "scientific and engineering systems", these computers began the divergence from a single protocol and single operating system that continues today. For a single user to have access to both often required two separate networks because each ran on a different protocol. This of course meant two different terminals on that user's desk. That all the systems came from the same manufacturer was immaterial: the systems could not be combined on the same wire or workstation.

The next stage in the evolution was to hook in various types of adapters, multiple screen "windowed" displays, protocol converters, etc. These devices sometimes eliminated the second terminal. Then came the now-ubiquitous personal computer, or "PC" as it was first called when it was introduced by IBM on August 12, 1981. Within a few short years, adapters appeared that permitted this indispensable device to connect and display information from nearly every type of larger host computer then in service. Another godsend had hit the end user!

This evolution has continued to the present day. Most proprietary protocols have gone the way of the woolly Mammoth, and have resolved down to a precious few, nearly all of them speaking TCP/IP in some form. This convergence is extremely significant: the basic method of linking all these different computing platforms together with a common protocol on the same wire exists.

The advent of Microsoft Windows pushed this convergence one very large step further. Just as protocols had come together, so too the capability of displaying sessions with the different computers was materializing. With refinement, the graphical user interface ("GUI" — same as gooey) enabled simultaneous displays from different hosts. Once virtual memory became a reality on the PC, this pushed this envelope further still by permitting simultaneous active displays and processing.

Users were getting capabilities they had wanted and needed for years. Now impossible tasks with impossible deadlines were rendered normal, even routine. But despite all the progress that had been made, the real issue had yet to be addressed. True to form, users were grateful for all the new toys and the ease of use they promised … until they woke up and found that none of these innovations fixed the thing they had complained most and loudest about: multiple loginids and passwords.

So what is single sign-on?

WHAT SINGLE SIGN-ON IS: THE BEGINNING

Beginning nearly 50 years ago, system designers realized that a method of tracking interaction with computer systems was needed, and so a form of identification — the loginid — was conceived. Almost simultaneously with this came the password — that sometimes arcane companion to the loginid that authenticates, or confirms the identity of, the user. And for most of the past five decades, a single loginid and its associated password was sufficient to assist the user in gaining access to virtually all the computing power then available, and to all the applications and systems that user was likely to use. Yes, those were the days… simple, straightforward, and easy to administer. And now they are all but gone, much like the club moss, the vacuum tube, and MS/DOS (perhaps).

Today's environment is more distributed in terms of both geography and platform. Although some will dispute, the attributes differentiating one operating system from another are being obscured by both network access and graphical user interfaces (the ubiquitous GUI). Because not every developer has chosen to offer his or her particular application on every computing platform (and networks have evolved to the point of being seemingly oblivious to this diversity), users now have access to a broader range of tools spread across more platforms, more transparently than at any time in the past. And yet all is not paradise.

Along with this wealth of power and utility comes the same requirement as before: to identify and authenticate the user. But now this must be done across all these various systems and platforms, and (no surprise) they all have differing mechanisms to accomplish this. The result is that users now have multiple loginids, each with its own unique password, quite probably governed by its equally unique set of rules. The CISSP knows that users complain bitterly about this situation, and will often attempt to circumvent it by whatever means necessary. To avoid this, the CISSP had to find a solution. To facilitate this, and take advantage of a marketing opportunity, software vendors saw a vital need, and thus the single sign-on (SSO) was conceived to address these issues.

Exhibit 1-1 shows where SSO was featured in the overall security program when it first appeared. As an access control method, SSO addressed important needs across multiple platforms (user identification and authentication). It was frequently regarded as a "user convenience" that was difficult and costly to implement, and of questionable value in terms of its contribution to the overall information protection and control structure.

THE ESSENTIAL PROBLEM

In simplest terms, too many loginids and passwords, and a host of other user access administration issues. With complex management structures requiring a geographically dispersed matrix approach to oversee employee work, distributed and often very different systems are necessary to meet operational objectives and reporting requirements.

In the days of largely mainframe-oriented systems, a problem of this sort was virtually nonexistent. Standards were made and enforcement was not complex. In these days, such conditions carry the same mandate for the establishment and enforcement of various system standards. Now, however, such conditions, and the systems arising in them, are of themselves not naturally conducive to this.

Traditional IT Security

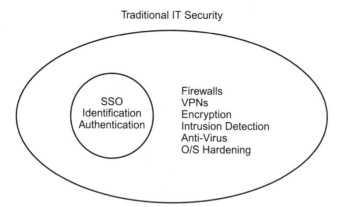

Exhibit 1-1. Single sign-on: in the beginning.

As mentioned above, such systems have different built-in systems for tracking user activity. The basic concepts are similar: audit trail, access control rule sets, Access Control Lists (ACLs), parameters governing system privilege levels, etc. In the end, it becomes apparent that one set of rules and standards, while sound in theory, may be exceedingly difficult to implement across all platforms without creating unmanageable complexity. It is however the "Holy Grail" that enterprise-level user administrators seek.

Despite the seeming simplicity of this problem, it represents only the tip of a range of problems associated with user administration. Such problems exist wherever the controlling access of users to resources is enforced: local in-house, remote WAN nodes, remote dial-in, and Web-based access.

As compared with Exhibit 1-1, Exhibit 1-2 illustrates how SSO has evolved into a broader scope product with greater functionality. Once considered merely a "user convenience," SSO has been more tightly integrated with other, more traditional security products and capabilities. This evolution has improved SSO's image measurably, but has not simplified its implementation.

In addition to the problem mentioned above, the need for this type of capability manifests itself in a variety of ways, some of which include:

1. As the number of entry points increases (Internet included), there is a need to implement improved and auditable security controls.
2. The management of large numbers of workstations is dictating that some control be placed over how they are used to avoid viruses, limit user-introduced problems, minimize help desk resources, etc.
3. As workstations have become electronic assistants, there has likewise arisen a need for end users to be able to use various workstations along their work path to reach their electronic desktop.

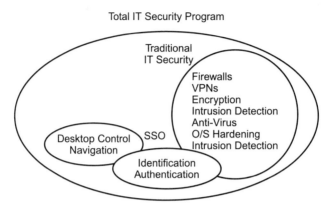

Exhibit 1-2. The evolution of SSO.

4. The proliferation of applications has made getting to all the information that is required too difficult, too cumbersome, or too time-consuming, even after passwords are automated.
5. The administration of security needs to move from an application focus to a global focus to improve compliance with industry guidelines and to increase efficiency.

MECHANISMS

The mechanisms used to implement SSO have varied over time. One method uses the Kerberos product to authenticate users and resources to each other through a "ticketing" system; tickets being the vehicle through which authorization to systems and resources is granted. Another method has been shells and scripting: primary authentication to the shell, which then initiated various platform-specific scripts to activate account and resource access on the target platforms.

For those organizations not wanting to expend the time and effort involved with a Kerberos implementation, the final solution was likely to be a variation of the shell-and-script approach. This had several drawbacks. It did not remove the need to set up user accounts individually on each platform. It also did not provide password synchronization or other management features. Shell-and-scripting was a half-step at best, and although it simplified user login, that was about the extent of the automation it facilitated. That was "then."

Today, different configuration approaches and options are available when implementing an SSO platform, and the drawbacks of the previous attempts have largely been well-addressed. Regardless, from the security engineering perspective, the design and objectives (i.e., the problem one is trying to solve) for the implementation plan must be evaluated in a risk analysis, and then mitigated as warranted. In the case of SSO, the operational concerns should also be evaluated, as discussed below.

One form of implementation allows one login session, which concludes with the user being actively connected to the full range of their authorized resources until logout. This type of configuration allows for reauthentication based on time (every … minutes or hours) or can be event driven (i.e., system boundary crossing).

One concern with this configuration is resource utilization. This is because a lot of network traffic is generated during login, directory/ACL accesses are performed, and several application/system sessions are established. This level of activity will degrade overall system performance substantially, especially if several users engage their login attempts simultaneously. Prevention of session loss (due to inactivity timeouts) would likely require an occasional "ping" to prevent this, if the feature itself cannot be deactivated. This too consumes resources with additional network traffic.

The other major concern with this approach would be that "open sessions" would exist, regardless of whether the user is active in a given application or not. This might make possible "session stealing" should the data stream be invaded, penetrated or rerouted.

Another potential configuration would perform the initial identification/authentication to the network service, but would not initialize access to a specific system or application until the user explicitly requests it (i.e., double-click the related desktop icon). This would reduce the network traffic level, and would invoke new sessions only when requested. The periodic reauthentication would still apply.

What Single Sign-on Provides

SSO products have moved beyond simple end-user authentication and password management to more complex issues that include addressing the centralized administration of endpoint systems, the administration of end users through a role-based view that allows large populations of end users to be affected by a single system administration change (e.g., adding a new application to all office workers), and the monitoring of end users' usage of sensitive applications.

The next section describes many of the capabilities and features that an ideal single sign-on product might offer. Some of the items that mention cost refer expressly to the point being made, and not to the software performing the function. The life-cycle cost of a product such as that discussed here can and does vary widely from one installation to the next. The extent of such variation is based on many factors, and is well beyond the scope of this discussion.

A major concern with applying the SSO product to achieve the potential economies is raised when consideration is given to the cost of the product, and comparing it to the cost of how things were done pre-SSO, and contrasting this with the cost of how things will be done post-SSO, the cost of putting SSO in, and all other dollars expended in the course of project completion.

By comparing the before-and-after expenditures, the ROI (return on investment) for installing the SSO can be calculated and used as part of the justification for the project. It is recommended that this be done using equivalent formulas, constraints, and investment/ROI objectives the enterprise applies when considering any project. When the analysis and results are presented (assuming they favor this undertaking), the audience will have better insight into the soundness of the investment in terms of real costs and real value contribution. Such insight fosters endorsement, and favors greater acceptance of what will likely be a substantial cost and lengthy implementation timeline.

Regardless, it is reasonably accurate to say that this technology is neither cheap to acquire nor to maintain. In addition, as with any problem-solution set, the question must be asked, "Is this problem worth the price of the solution?" The next section discusses some of the features to assist in making such a decision.

Internal Capability Foundation

Having GUI-based central administration offers the potential for simplified user management, and thus possibly substantial cost-savings in reduced training, reduced administrative effort, and lower life-cycle cost for user management. This would have beneath it a logging capability that, based on some DBMS engine and a set of report generation tools, would enhance and streamline the data reduction process for activity reporting and forensic analysis derived through the SSO product.

The basic support structure must include direct (standard customary login) and Web-based access. This would be standard, especially now that the Internet has become so prolific and also since an increasing number of applications are using some form of Web-enabled/aware interface. This means that the SSO implementation would necessarily limit the scope or depth of the login process to make remote access practical, whether direct dial-up or via the Web.

One aspect of concern is the intrusiveness of the implementation. Intrusiveness is the extent to which the operating environment must be modified to accommodate the functionality of the product. Another is the retrofitting of legacy systems and applications. Installation of the SSO product on the various platforms in the enterprise would generally be done through APIs to minimize the level of custom code.

Not surprisingly, most SSO solutions vendors developed their product with the retrofit of legacy systems in mind. For example, the Platinum Technologies (now CA) product AutoSecure SSO supported RACF, ACF2, and TopSecret — all of which are access control applications born and bred in the legacy systems world. It also supports Windows NT, Novell, and TCP/IP network-supported systems. Thus, it covers the range from present day to legacy.

General Characteristics

The right SSO product should provide all the required features and sustain itself in an enterprise production environment. Products that operate in an open systems distributed computing environment, complete with parallel network servers, are better positioned to address enterprise needs than more narrow NOS-based SSO products.

It is obvious then that SSO products must be able to support a fairly broad array of systems, devices, and interfaces if the promise of this technology is to be realized. Given that, it is clear some environments will require greater modification than others; that is, the SSO configuration is more complex and modifies the operating environment to a greater extent. Information derived through the following questions will assist in pre-implementation analysis:

1. Is the SSO nonintrusive; that is, can it manage access to all applications, without a need to change the applications in any way?
2. Does the SSO product dictate a single common logon and password across all applications?
3. What workstations are supported by the SSO product?
4. On what operating systems can SSO network servers operate?
5. What physical identification technologies are supported (e.g., Secure-ID card)?
6. Are dial-up end users supported?
7. Is Internet access supported? If so, are authentication and encryption enforced?
8. Can the SSO desktop optionally replace the standard desktop to more closely control the usage of particular workstations (e.g., in the production area)?
9. Can passwords be automatically captured the first time an end user uses an endpoint application under the SSO product's control?
10. Can the look of the SSO desktop be replaced with a custom site-specific desktop look?
11. How will the SSO work with the PKI framework already installed?

End-User Management Facilities

These features and options include the normal suite of functions for account creation, password management, etc. The performance of end-user identification and authentication is obvious. Password management includes all the normal features: password aging, histories, and syntax rules. To complete the picture, support for the wide variety of token-type devices (Secure-ID cards), biometric devices, and the like should be considered, especially if remote end users are going to be using the SSO product. At the very least, optional modules providing this support should exist and be available.

Some additional attributes that should be available are:

- *Role-based privileges:* this functionality makes it possible to administer a limited number of roles that are in turn shared by a large population of end users. This would not necessarily have any effect on individual users working outside the authority scope of that role.
- *Desktop control:* this allows the native desktop to be replaced by an SSO-managed desktop, thereby preventing end users from using the workstation in such a way as to create support problems (e.g., introducing unauthorized software). This capability is particularly important in areas where workstations are shared by end users (e.g., production floor).
- *Application authorization:* this ensures that any launched application is registered and cleared by the SSO product and records are kept of individual application usage.
- *Mobile user support:* this capability allows end users to reach their desktop, independent of their location or the workstation they are using. It should also include configuring the workstation to access the proper domain server and bringing the individual's preferences to the workstation before launching applications.

Application Management Facilities

Application management in the context of SSO refers to the treatment of an application in a manner similar to how it manages or treats users. As shown in Figure 1-2, the evolved state of SSO has moved beyond the simplistic identification/authentication of users, and now encompasses certain aspects of application management. This management capability relates to the appearance of user desktops and navigation through application menus and interfaces rather than with the maintenance and upgrading of application functionality.

Context management ensures that when multiple sessions that relate to a common subject are simultaneously active, each session is automatically updated when another related session changes position (e.g., in a health-care setting, the lab and pharmacy sessions must be on the same patient if the clinician is to avoid mixing two patients' records when reaching a clinical decision).

Application monitoring is particularly useful when it is desirable to monitor the usage of particular rows of information in an application that is not programmed to provide that type of information (e.g., access to particular constituents' records in a government setting).

Application positioning is a feature that relates to personalized yet centrally controlled desktops. This allows configuration of an end-user startup script to open an application (possibly chosen from a set of options) on initialization, and specify even what screen is loaded.

One other feature that binds applications together is application fusing. This allows applications to operate in unison such that the end user is only aware of a single session. The view to the end user can range from a simple automated switching between applications up to and including creating an entirely new view for the end user.

Endpoint Management Facilities

Endpoint administration is an essential component of an SSO product because, without it, administration is forced to input the same information twice; once in the SSO and once in the endpoint each time a change is made to the SSO database. Two methods of input into the endpoint should be supported: (1) API-based agents to update endpoint systems that support an API, and (2) session animation agents to update endpoint systems that do not support an API. Services provided by the SSO to accomplish this administrative goal should include:

- *Access control:* this is the vehicle used by end users to gain access to applications and, based on each application's capabilities, to define to the application the end user's privileges within it. Both API-based and session-based applications should be supported.
- *Audit services:* these should be made available through an API to endpoint applications that wish to publish information into the SSO product's logging system.
- *Session encryption:* this feature ensures information is protected from disclosure and tampering as it moves between applications and end users. This capability should be a requirement in situations where sensitive applications only offer cleartext facilities.

Mobile Users

The capability for end users to use any available workstation to reach information sources is mandatory in environments where end users are expected to function in a number of different locations. Such users would include traveling employees, health care providers (mobile nurses, physicians, and technicians), consultants, and sales staff. In the highly mobile workforce of today's world, it is unlikely that a product not offering this feature would be successful.

Another possible feature would facilitate workstation sharing; that is, the sharing of the device by multiple simultaneous users, each one with their own active session separate from all others. This capability would entail the use of a form of screen swapping so that loginids and passwords would not be shared. When the first user finishes his session, rather than logout, he locks the session, a hot-key combination switches to the next open login screen, and the second user initiates his session, etc.

When investigating the potential needs in this regard, the questions to ask yourself and the vendors of such products should include:

1. Can a workstation in a common area be shared by many end users (e.g., production floor)?
2. If someone wants to use a workstation already in use by another end user, can the SSO product gracefully close the existing end user's applications (including closing open documents) and turn control over to the new end user?
3. Can end users adjust the organization of their desktop, and if so, does it travel with them, independent of the workstation they use?
4. Can individual applications preferences travel with the end user to other workstations (e.g., MS Word preferences)?
5. Can the set of available applications be configured to vary based on the entry point of the end user into the network?
6. If a Novell end user is logging in at a workstation that is assigned to a different Novell domain, how does the end user get back to his or her domain?
7. Given that Windows 95 and Windows NT rely on a locally stored password for authentication, what happens when the end user logs onto another workstation?
8. Is the date and time of the last successful sign-on shown at the time the end user signs on to highlight unauthorized sign-ons?
9. Is the name of the logged in end user prominently displayed to avoid inadvertent use of workstations by other end users?

Authentication

Authentication ensures that users are who are who they claim to be. It also ensures that all processes and transactions are initiated only by authorized end users. User authentication couples the loginid and the password, providing an identifier for the user, a mechanism for assigning access privileges, and an auditing "marker" for the system against which to track all activity, such as file accesses, process initiation, and other actions (e.g., attempted logons). Thus, through the process of authentication, one has the means to control and track the "who" and the "what."

The SSO products take this process and enable it to be used for additional services that enhance and extend the applications of the log-inid/password combination. Some of these applications provide a convenience for the user that also improves security: the ability to lock the workstation just before stepping away briefly means the user is more likely to do it, rather than leave his workstation open for abuse by another. Some are extensions of audit tools: display of last login attempt, and log entry of all sign-ons. These features are certainly not unique to SSO, but they extend and enhance its functionality, and thus make it more user friendly.

As part of a Public Key Infrastructure (PKI) installation, the SSO should have the capability to support digital certificate authentication. Through a variety of methods (token, password input, biometrics possibly), the SSO supplies a digital certificate for the user that the system then uses as both an authenticator and an access privilege "license" in a fashion similar to the Kerberos ticket. The vital point here is not how this functionality is actually performed (that is another lengthy discussion), but that the SSO supports and integrates with a PKI, and that it uses widely recognized standards in doing so.

It should noted, however, that any SSO product that offers less than the standard suite of features obtainable through the more common access control programs should *not* be considered. Such a product may be offered as an alternative to the more richly featured SSO products on the premise that "simpler is better." Simpler is not better in this case because it means reduced effectiveness.

To know whether the candidates measure up, an inquiry should be made regarding these aspects:

1. Is authentication done at a network server or in the workstation?
2. Is authentication done with a proven and accepted standard (e.g., Kerberos)?
3. Are all sign-on attempts logged?
4. After a site-specified number of failed sign-on attempts, can all future sign-on attempts be unconditionally rejected?
5. Is an inactivity timer available to lock or close the desktop when there is a lack of activity for a period of time?
6. Can the desktop be easily locked or closed when someone leaves a workstation (e.g., depression of single key)?
7. Is the date and time of the last successful sign-on shown at the time the end user signs on to highlight unauthorized sign-ons?

Encryption

Encryption ensures that information that flows between the end users and the security server(s) and endpoint applications they access is not intercepted through spying, line-tapping, or some other method of eavesdropping. Many SSO products encrypt traffic between the end user and the security server but let cleartext pass between the end user and the endpoint applications, causing a potential security gap to exist. Some products by default encrypt all traffic between workstation and server, some do not, and still others provide this feature as an option that is selectable at installation.

Each installation is different in its environment and requirements. The same holds true when it comes to risks and vulnerabilities. Points to cover that address this include:

- Is all traffic between the workstation and the SSO server encrypted?
- Can the SSO product provide encryption all the way to the endpoint applications (e.g., computer room) without requiring changes to the endpoint applications?
- Is the data stream encrypted using an accepted and proven standard algorithm (e.g., DES, Triple DES, IDEA, AES, or other)?

Access Control

End users should only be presented with the applications they are authorized to access. Activities required to launch these applications should be carefully evaluated because many SSO products assume that only API-based endpoint applications can participate, or that the SSO is the owner of a single password that all endpoint applications must comply with. These activities include automatically inputting and updating application passwords when they expire.

Exhibit 1-3 shows how the SSO facilitates automatic login and acquisition of all resources to which a user is authorized. The user logs into the authentication server (centrally positioned on the network). This then validates the user and his access rights. The server then sends out the validated credentials and activates the required scripts to log the user in and attach his resources to the initiated session.

While it is certainly true that automatically generated passwords might make the user's life easier, current best practice is to allow users to create and use their own passwords. Along with this should be a rule set governing the syntax of those passwords; for example, no dictionary words, a combination of numbers and letters, a mixture of case among the letters, no repetition within a certain number of password generations, proscribed use of special characters (#, $, &, ?, %, etc.), and other rules. The SSO

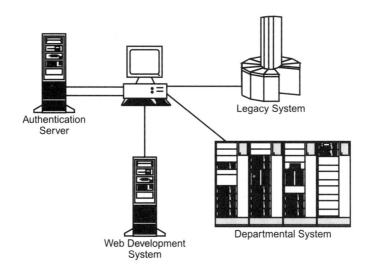

Exhibit 1-3. Automated login.

should support this function across all intended interfaces to systems and applications.

Exhibit 1-4 shows how the SSO facilitates login over the World Wide Web (WWW) by making use of cookies — small information packets shipped back and forth over the Web. The user logs into the initial Web server (1), which then activates an agent that retrieves the user's credentials from the credentials server (2). This server is similar in function to a name server or an LDAP server, except that this device provides authorization and access privileges information specifically. The cookie is then built and stored in the user's machine (3), and is used to revalidate the user each time a page transition is made.

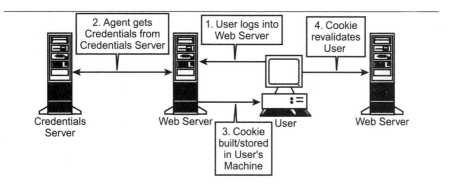

Exhibit 1-4. SSO: Web with cookies.

This process is similar to verification of application-level privileges inside a DBMS. While moving within the database system, each time the user accesses a new region or transaction, access privileges must be reverified to ensure correct authorization. Page transitions on the Web equate to new regions or transactions within the DBMS.

In this area, the following points should be covered:

1. Can all applications, regardless of platform, be nonintrusively supported (i.e., without changing them, either extensively or at all)?
2. What types of adapters are available to mechanize the application launching process without having to adjust the individual applications? Are API-based, OLE-based, DDE-based, scripting-based, and session-simulation adapters available?
3. Are all application activations and deactivations logged?
4. When application passwords expire, does the SSO product automatically generate new expired one-time passwords or are users able to select and enter their own choices?
5. When an application is activated, can information be used to navigate to the proper position in the application (e.g., order entry application is positioned to the order entry screen)?
6. Can the application activation procedure be hidden from the end user or does the end user have to see the mechanized process as it progresses?
7. Are inactivity timers available to terminate an application when there is a lack of activity for a period of time?

Application Control

Application control limits end users' use of applications in such a way that only particular screens within a given application are visible, only specific records can be requested, and particular uses of the applications can be recorded for audit purposes, transparently to the endpoint applications so no changes are needed to the applications involved.

As a way in which user navigation is controlled, this is another feature that can assist with enhancing the overall security posture of an installation. Again, this would be as an adjunct feature — not the key method. The determination of the usefulness of this capability can be made through the following questions.

1. Can applets be incorporated into the desktop's presentation space (e.g., list of major accounts)?
2. Can applet information (e.g., particular account) be used to navigate to the proper position within an application (e.g., list of orders outstanding for a particular customer)?

3. Can each application's view be adjusted to show only the information that is appropriate for a particular end user?
4. Can the SSO product log end users' activities inside applications (e.g., which accounts have been accessed)?
5. Can application screens be enhanced with new capabilities without having to change the applications themselves (e.g., additional validation of input as it is captured)?
6. Can the SSO product log attempt to reach areas of applications that go beyond permitted areas (e.g., confidential patient information)?
7. Can multiple applications be fused into a single end-user session to eliminate the need for end users to learn each application?
8. Can applications be automatically coordinated such that end-user movement in one application (e.g., billing) automatically repositions subordinate application sessions (e.g., current orders, accounts receivable)?

Administration

The centralized administration capabilities offered by the SSO are — if not the main attraction — the "Holy Grail" mentioned earlier. The management (creation, modification, deletion) of user accounts and resource profiles through an SSO product can streamline and simplify this function within an organization or enterprise. The power of the administration tools is key because the cost of administering a large population of end users can easily overshadow the cost of the SSO product itself.

The product analysis should take the following attributes into consideration:

1. Does the SSO product allow for the central administration of all endpoint systems? (That is, changes to the central administration database are automatically reflected in endpoint systems.)
2. Is administration done at an "end-user" or a "role within the enterprise" level? (This is a critical element because an end-user focus can result in disproportional administration effort.)
3. Does each workstation have to be individually installed? If so, what is the estimated time required?
4. Can end users' roles in the organization be easily changed (to deal with people that perform mixed roles)?
5. Is the desktop automatically adjusted if the end user's roles are changed, or does the desktop view have to be adjusted manually?
6. Can an administrator see a list of active end users by application?
7. Can an administrator access all granted passwords to specific endpoint applications?
8. Does the product gracefully deal with network server failures?

Services for Desktop-Aware Applications

In cases where it is possible to modify existing endpoint applications, the ability for them to cooperatively share responsibilities with the desktop is very attractive. What is required is a published desktop API and associated services.

The circumstance can and does arise where the end user wants to customize a standard product in the enterprise suite for his own use in a way that affects only him and does not change the basic application itself. Such customization may include display formats, scripts, and processes relating to specific tasks the individual user wants or needs to use in conjunction with the server-supplied application. Through the supplied API, the user can make the custom changes necessary without impediment, and this allows other users to proceed without affecting them or their workstations.

In such cases, the user wanting the changes may require specific access and other controls to lock out other users. An example might be one where the user requiring the changes works on sensitive or restricted information, and others in the same area do not, and are not permitted access to such. This then may necessitate the use of access controls embedded in the scripts used to change his desktop to meet his additional security needs.

That being the case, the API should provide the capability to access the SSO, and perform the access/privilege checking, without the user (the one making the localized changes) having any direct access to the SSO access/privilege database. This should likewise be true to facilitate the logging of access attempts, transactions, and data access authorizations to track the use of the local workstation. To determine the existence of this facility in the SSO, questions should be asked regarding such services, APIs, and related capabilities, such as

1. Can desktop-aware applications interrogate end-user permissions managed by the SSO product?
2. Can desktop-aware applications make use the SSO product's logging facilities for their own use?
3. Do API services exist that enable desktop customization?
4. Do these APIs facilitate this without compromising overall system integrity by providing "back-door" access to the resident security information database?

Reliability and Performance

Given that an SSO product is, by necessity, positioned between the end users and the applications they need access to get their jobs done, it has a very high visibility within the enterprise and any unexpected reliability or performance problems can have serious consequences. This issue points directly back at the original business case made to justify the product.

Concerns with regard to reliability and performance generally focus on the additional layering of one software upon another ("yet another layer"), the interfaces between the SSO and other access control programs it touches, the complexity of these interactions, etc. One aspect of concern is the increased latency introduced by this new layer. The time from power-on to login screen has steadily increased over the years, and the addition of the SSO may increase it yet again. This can exacerbate user frustration.

The question of reliability arises when considering the interaction between the SSO and the other security frontends. The complexity of the interfaces, if very great, may lead to increased service problems; the more complex the code, the more likely failure is to result more frequently. This may manifest itself by passwords and changes in them losing synchronization, not being reliably passed, or privilege assignment files not being updated uniformly or rapidly. Such problems as these call into question whether SSO was such a good idea, even if it truly was. Complex code is costly to maintain, and the SSO is nothing if not complex. Even the best programming can be rendered ineffective, or worse yet counterproductive, if it is not implemented properly.

An SSO product requires more of this type of attention than most because of its feature-rich complexity. It is clear that the goal of the sso is access control, and in that regard achieves the same goals of confidentiality, integrity, and availability as any other access control system does. SSO products are designed to provide more functionality, but in so doing can adversely affect the environments in which they are installed. If they do, the impacts will most likely appear against factors of reliability, integrity, and performance; and if large enough, the impacts will negate the benefits the SSO provides elsewhere.

REQUIREMENTS

This section presents the contents of a requirements document that the Georgia Area RACF Users Group (GARUG) put together regarding things they would like to see in an SSO application.

Objectives

The focus of this list is to present a set of functional requirements for the design and development of a trusted single sign-on and security administration product. It is the intention that this be used by security practitioners to determine the effectiveness of the security products they may be reviewing.

It contains many requirements that experienced security users feel are very important to the successful protection of multi-platform systems. It also contains several functional requirements that may not be immediately available at this time. Having said that, the list can be used as a research and development tool because the requirements are being espoused by experienced, working security practitioners in response to real-world problems.

This topic was brought to the forefront by many in the professional security community, and the GARUG members that prepared this list in response. This is not a cookbook to use in the search for security products. In many ways, this list is visionary, which is to say that many of the requirements stated here do not exist. But just because they do not exist now does not deter their inclusion now. As one member noted, "If we don't ask for it, we won't get it."

Functional Requirements

The following is a listing of the functional requirements of an ideal security product on the market. The list also includes many features that security practitioners want to see included in future products. The requirements are broken down in four major categories: security administration management, identification and authorization, access control, and data integrity/confidentiality/encryption. Under each category the requirements are listed in most critical to least critical order.

Assumptions

There are three general assumptions that follow throughout this document.

1. All loginids are unique; no two loginids can be the same. This prevents two users from having the same loginid.
2. The vendor should provide the requisite software to provide functionality on all supported platforms.
3. All vendor products are changing. All products will have to work with various unlike platforms.

Security Administration Management

Single Point of Administration. All administration of the product should be done from a single point. This enables an administrator to provide support for the product from any one platform device.

Ability to Group Users. The product should enable the grouping of like users where possible. These groups should be handled the same way individual users are handled. This will enable more efficient administration of access authority.

Ability to Enforce Enterprise/Global Security Rules. The product should provide the ability to enforce security rules over the entire enterprise, regardless of platform. This will ensure consistent security over resources on all protected platforms.

Audit Trail. All changes, modifications, additions, and deletions should be logged. This ensures that all security changes are recorded for review at a later time.

Ability to Recreate. Information logged by the system should be able to be used to "backout" changes to the security system. Example: used to recreate deleted resources or users. This enables mass changes to be "backed out" of production or enables mass additions or changes to be made based on logged information.

Ability to Trace Access. The product should enable the administrator to be able to traced access to systems, regardless of system or platform.

Scoping and Decentralization of Control. The product should be able to support the creation of spans of control so that administrators can be excluded from or included in certain security control areas within the overall security setup. This enables an administrator to decentralize the administration of security functions based on the groups, nodes, domains, and enterprises over which the decentralized administrator has control.

Administration for Multiple Platforms. The product should provide for the administration of the product for any of the supported platforms. This enables the administrator to support the product for any platform of his or her choice.

Synchronization Across All Entities. The product should be synchronizing security data across all entities and all platforms. This ensures that all security decisions are made with up-to-date security information.

Real-Time and Batch Update. All changes should be made online/real-time. The ability to batch changes together is also important to enable easy loading or changing of large numbers of security resources or users.

Common Control Language Across All Platforms. The product should feature a common control language across all serviced platforms so that administrators do not have to learn and use different commands on different platforms.

One Single Product. The product should be a single product — not a compendium of several associated products. Modularity for the sake of platform-to-platform compatibility is acceptable and favored.

Flexible Cost. The cost of the product should be reasonable. Several cost scenarios should be considered, such as per seat, CPU, site licensing, and MIPS pricing. Pricing should include disaster recovery scenarios.

Physical Terminal/Node/Address Control. The product should have the ability to restrict or control access on the basis of a terminal, node, or network address. This ability will enable users to provide access control by physical location.

Release Independent/Backward Compatible. All releases of the product should be backward compatible or release independent. Features of new releases should coexist with current features and not require a total reinstallation of the product. This ensures that the time and effort previously invested in the prior release of the product is not lost when a new release is installed.

Software Release Distribution. New releases of the product should be distributed via the network from a single distribution server of the administrator's choice. This enables an administrator to upgrade the product on any platform without physically moving from platform to platform.

Ability to Do Phased Implementation. The product should support a phased implementation to enable administrators to implement the product on individual platforms without affecting other platforms. This will enable installation on a platform-by-platform basis if desired.

Ability to Interface with Application/Database/Network Security. The product should be able to interface with existing application, database, or network security by way of standard security interfaces. This will ensure that the product will mesh with security products already installed.

SQL Reporting. The product should have the ability to use SQL query and reporting tools to produce security setup reports/queries. This feature will enable easy access to security information for administrators.

Ability to Create Security Extract Files. The product should have a feature to produce an extract file of the security structure and the logging/violation records. This enables the administrator to write his or her own reporting systems via SAS or any other language.

Usage Counter per Application/Node/Domain/Enterprise. The product should include an internal counter to maintain the usage count of each application, domain, or enterprise. This enables an administrator to determine which applications, nodes, domains, or enterprises are being used and to what extent they are being used.

Test Facility. The product should include a test facility to enable administrators to test security changes before placing them into production. This ensures that all security changes are fully tested before being placed into production.

Ability to Tag Enterprise/Domain/Node/Application. The product should be able to add a notation or "tag" an enterprise/domain/node/application in order to provide the administrator with a way identify the entity. This enables the administrator to denote the tagged entity and possibly perform extra or nonstandard operations on the entity based on that tag.

Platform Inquiries. The product should support inquiries to the secured platforms regarding the security setup, violations, and other logged events. This will enable an administrator to inquire on security information without having to signon/logon.

Customize in Real-Time. It is important to have a feature that enables the customization of selected features (those features for which customization is allowed) without reinitializing the product. This feature will ensure that the product is available for 24-hour, seven-day-a-week processing.

GUI Interface. The product should provide a user interface via a Windows-like user interface. The interface may vary slightly between platforms (i.e., Windows, OS/2, X-windows, etc.) but should retain the same functionality. This facilitates operating consistency and lowers operator and user training requirements.

User Defined Fields. The product should have a number of user customizable/user-defined fields. This enables a user to provide for informational needs that are specific to his or her organization.

Identification and Authorization

Support RACF Pass Ticket Technology. The product should support IBM's RACF Pass Ticket technology, ensuring that the product can reside in an environment using Pass Ticket technology to provide security identification and authorization.

Support Password Rules (i.e. Aging, Syntax, etc.). All common password rules should be supported:

- use or non-use of passwords
- password length rules
- password aging rules
- password change intervals
- password syntax rules
- password expiration warning message
- Save previous passwords
- Password uniqueness rules
- Limited number of logons after a password expires
- Customer-defined rules

Logging of All Activity Including Origin/Destination/Application/Platform.
All activity should be logged, or able to be logged, for all activities. The logging should include the origin of the logged item or action, the destination, the application involved, and the platform involved. This enables the administrator to provide a concise map of all activity on the enterprise. The degree of logging should be controlled by the administrator.

Single Revoke/Resume for All Platforms. The product should support a single revoke or resume of a loginid, regardless of the platform. This ensures that users can be revoked or resumed with only one command from one source or platform.

Support a Standard Primary loginid Format. The administrator should define all common loginid syntax rules. The product should include features to translate unlike loginids from different platforms so that they can be serviced. This enables the product to handle loginids from systems that support different loginid syntax that cannot be supported natively.

Auto Revoke after X Attempts. Users should be revoked from system access after a specified number of invalid attempts. This threshold should set by the administrator. This ensures that invalid users are prevented from retrying sign-ons indefinitely.

Capture Point of Origin Information, Including Caller ID/Phone Number for Dial-in Access. The product should be able to capture telephone caller ID (ANI) information if needed. This will provide an administrator increased information that can be acted upon manually or via an exit to provide increased security for chosen ports.

Authorization Server Should be Portable (Multi-platform). The product should provide for the authentication server to reside on any platform that the product can control. This provides needed portability if there is a need to move the authentication server to another platform for any reason.

Single Point of Authorization. All authorizations should be made a single point (i.e., an authentication server). The product should not need to go to several versions of the product on several platforms to gain the needed access to a resource. This provides not only a single point of administration for the product, but also reduced network security traffic.

Support User Exits/Options. The product should support the addition of user exits, options, or application programming interfaces (APIs) that could be attached to the base product at strategically identified points of operation. The points would include sign-on, sign-off, resource access check, etc. The enables an administrator or essential technical support personnel to add exit/option code to the package to provide for specific security needs above and beyond the scope of the package.

Insure loginid Uniqueness. The product should ensure that all loginids are unique; no two loginids can be the same. This prevents two users from having the same loginid.

Source Sign-on Support. The product should support sign-ons from a variety of sources. These sources should include LAN/WAN, workstations, portables (laptops and notebooks), dial-in, and dumb terminals. This would ensure that all potential login sources are enabled to provide login capability, and facilitate support for legacy systems.

Customizable Messages. The product should support the use of customized security messages. The will enable an administrator to customize messages to fit the needs of his or her organization.

Access Control

Support Smart Card Tokens. The product should support the use of the common smart card security tokens (i.e., SecurID cards) to enable their use on any platform. The enables the administrator to provide for increased security measures where they are needed for access to the systems.

Ability to Support Scripting — Session Manager Menus. The product should support the use of session manager scripting. This enables the use of a session manager script in those sites and instances where they are needed or required.

Privileges at the Group and System Level. The product should support administration privileges at a group level (based on span of control) or on the system level. This enables the product to be administered by several administrators without the administrators' authority overlapping.

Default Protection Unless Specified. The product should provide for the protection of all resources and entities as the default unless the opposite of protection for only those resources profiled is specified. The enables each organization to determine the best way to install the product based on their own security needs.

Support Masking/Generics. The product should support security profiles containing generic characters that enable the product to make security decisions based on groups of resources as opposed to individual security profiles. The enables the administrator to provide security profiles over many like-named resources with the minimum amount of administration.

Allow Delegation Within Power of Authority. The product should allow an administrator to delegate security administration authority to others at the discretion of the administrator within his or her span of authority. An administrator would have the ability to give some of his or her security authority to another administrator for backup purposes.

Data Integrity/Confidentiality/Encryption

No Cleartext Passwords (Net or DB) — Dumb Terminal Exception. At no time should any password be available on the network or in the security database in clear, human-readable form. The only exception is the use of dumb terminals where the terminal does not support encryption techniques. This will ensure the integrity of the users' passwords in all cases with the exception of dumb terminals.

Option to Have One or Distributed Security DBs. The product should support the option of having a single security database or several distributed security databases on different platforms. This enables an administrator to use a distributed database on a platform that may be sensitive to increased activity rather than a single security database. The administrator will control who can and if they can update distributed databases.

Inactive User Time-out. All users who are inactive for a set period during a session should be timed out and signed off of all sessions. This ensures that a user who becomes inactive for whatever reason does not compromise the security of the system by providing an open terminal to a system. This feature should be controlled by the administrator and have two layers:

- at the session manager/screen level
- at the application/platform level

Inactive User Revoke. All users who have not signed on within a set period should be revoked. This period should be configurable by the administrator. This will ensure that loginids are not valid if not used within a set period of time.

Ability to Back Up Security DBs to Choice of Platforms/Media. The product should be able to back up its security database to a choice of supported platforms or storage media. This enables the user to have a variety of destinations available for the security database backup.

Encryption Should be Commercial Standard (Presently DES). The encryption used in the product should be standard. That standard is presently DES but could change as new encryption standards are made. This will ensure that the product will be based on a tested, generally accepted encryption base.

Integrity of Security DB(s). The database used by the product to store security information and parameters should be protected from changes via any source other than the product itself. Generic file edit tools should not be able to view or update the security database.

Optional Application Data Encryption. The product should provide the optional ability to interface to encrypted application data if the encryption techniques are provided. This enables the product to interact with encrypted data from exiting applications.

Failsoft Ability. The product should have the ability to perform at a degraded degree without access to the security database. This ability should rely on administrator input on an as needed basis to enable a user to sign-on, access resources, and sign-off. This enables the product to at least work in a degraded mode in an emergency in such a fashion that security is not compromised.

CONCLUSION

Single sign-on (SSO) can indeed be the answer to an array of user administration and access control problems. For the user, it *might* be a godsend. It is, however, not a straightforward or inexpensive solution. As with other so-called "enterprise security solutions," there remain the problems of scalability and phasing-in. There is generally no half-step to be taken in terms of how such a technology as this is rolled out. It is of course possible to limit it to a single platform, but that negates the whole point of doing SSO in the first place.

Like all solutions, SSO must have a real problem that it addresses. Initially regarded as a solution looking for a problem, SSO has broadened its scope to address more than simply the avalanche of loginids and passwords users seem to acquire in their systems travels. This greater functionality can provide much needed assistance and control in managing the user, his access rights, and the trail of activity left in his wake. This however comes at a cost.

Some significant observations made by others regarding SSO became apparent from an informal survey conducted by this author. The first is that it can be very expensive, based mostly on the scope of the implementation. The second is that it can be a solution looking for a problem; meaning that it sounds like a "really neat" technology (which it is) that proffers religion on some. This "religion" tends to be a real cause for concern in the manager or CIO over the IT function, for reasons that are well-understood. When the first conjoins with the second, the result is frequently substantial project scope creep — usually a very sad story with an unhappy ending in the IT world.

The third observation was more subtle, but more interesting. Although several vendors still offer an SSO product as an add-on, the trend appears to be more toward SSO slowly disappearing as a unique product. Instead, this capability is being included in platform or enterprise IT management solution software such as Tivoli (IBM) and Unicenter-TNG (Computer Associates). Given the fact that SSO products support most of the functions endemic to PKI, the other likelihood in the author's opinion is that SSO will be subsumed into the enterprise PKI solution, and thus become a "feature" rather than a "product."

It does seem certain that this technology will continue to mature and improve, and eventually become more widely used. As more and more experience is gained in implementation endeavors, the files of "lessons learned" will grow large with many painful implementation horror stories. Such stories often arise from "bad products badly constructed." Just as often, they arise from poorly managed implementation projects. SSO will suffer, and has, from the same bad rap — partially deserved, partially not. The point here is: do your homework, select the right tool for the right job, plan your work carefully, and execute thoroughly. It will probably still be difficult, but one might actually get the results one wants.

In the mystical and arcane practice of Information Security, many different tools and technologies have acquired that rarified and undeserved status known as "panacea." In virtually no case has any one of these fully lived up to this unreasonable expectation, and the family of products providing the function known as "single sign-on" is no exception.

Chapter 2

Centralized Authentication Services (RADIUS, TACACS, DIAMETER)

Bill Stackpole

GOT THE TELECOMMUTER, MOBILE WORKFORCE, VPN, MULTI-PLATFORM, DIAL-IN USER AUTHENTICATION BLUES? Need a centralized method for controlling and auditing external accesses to your network? Then RADIUS, TACACS, or DIAMETER may be just what you have been looking for. Flexible, inexpensive, and easy to implement, these centralized authentication servers improve remote access security and reduce the time and effort required to manage remote access server (RAS) clients.

RADIUS, TACACS, and DIAMETER are classified as authentication, authorization, and accounting (AAA) servers. The Internet Engineering Task Force (IETF) chartered an AAA Working Group in 1998 to develop the authentication, authorization, and accounting requirements for network access. The goal was to produce a base protocol that supported a number of different network access models, including traditional dial-in network access servers (NAS), Mobile-IP, and roaming operations (ROAMOPS). The group was to build upon the work of existing access providers like Livingston Enterprises.

Livingston Enterprises originally developed RADIUS (Remote Authentication Dial-in User Service) for their line of network access servers (NAS) to assist timeshare and Internet service providers with billing information consolidation and connection configuration. Livingston based RADIUS on the IETF distributed security model and actively promoted it through the IETF Network Access Server Requirements Working Group in the early 1990s. The client/server design was created to be open and extensible so it could be easily adapted to work with other third-party products. At this writing, RADIUS version 2 was a proposed IETF standard managed by the RADIUS Working Group.

The origin of the Terminal Access Controller Access Control System (TACACS) daemon used in the early days of ARPANET is unknown. Cisco Systems adopted the protocol to support AAA services on its products in the early 1990s. Cisco extended the protocol to enhance security and support additional types of authentication requests and response codes. They named the new protocol TACACS+. The current version of the TACACS specification is a proposed IETF Standard (RFC 1492) managed by the Network Working Group. It was developed with the assistance of Cisco Systems.

Pat Calhoun (Sun Laboratories) and Allan Rubens (Ascend Communications) proposed the DIAMETER AAA framework as a draft standard to the IETF in 1998. The name DIAMETER is not an acronym but rather a play on the RADIUS name. DIAMETER was designed from the ground up to support roaming applications and to overcoming the extension limitations of the RADIUS and TACACS protocols. It provides the base protocols required to support any number of AAA extensions, including NAS, Mobile-IP, host, application, and Web-based requirements. At this writing, DIAMETER consisted of eight IETF draft proposals, authored by twelve different contributors from Sun, Microsoft, Cisco, Nortel, and others. Pat Calhoun continues to coordinate the DIAMETER effort.

AAA 101: KEY FEATURES OF AN AAA SERVICE

The key features of a centralized AAA service include (1) a distributed (client/server) security model, (2) authenticated transactions, (3) flexible authentication mechanisms, and (4) an extensible protocol. Distributed security separates the authentication process from the communications process, making it possible to consolidate user authentication information into a single centralized database. The network access devices (i.e., a NAS) are the clients. They pass user information to an AAA server and act upon the response(s) the server returns. The servers receive user connection requests, authenticate the user, and return to the client NAS the configuration information required to deliver services to the user. The returned information may include transport and protocol parameters, additional authentication requirements (i.e., callback, SecureID), authorization directives (i.e., services allowed, filters to apply), and accounting requirements (Exhibit 2-1).

Transmissions between the client and server are authenticated to ensure the integrity of the transactions. Sensitive information (e.g., passwords) is encrypted using a shared secret key to ensure confidentiality and prevent passwords and other authentication information from being monitored or captured during transmission. This is particularly important when the data travels across public carrier (e.g., WAN) links.

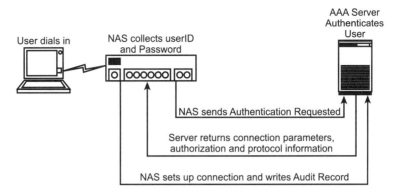

Exhibit 2-1. Key features of a centralized AAA service.

AAA servers can support a variety of authentication mechanisms. This flexibility is a key AAA feature. User access can be authenticated using PAP (Password Authentication Protocol), CHAP (Challenge Handshake Authentication Protocol), the standard UNIX login process, or the server can act as a proxy and forward the authentication to other mechanisms like a Microsoft domain controller, a Novell NDS server, or a SecureID ACE server. Some AAA server implementations use additional mechanisms like calling number identification (caller ID) and callback to further secure connections.

Because technology changes so rapidly, AAA servers are designed with extensible protocols. RADIUS, DIAMETER, and TACACS use variable-length attribute values designed to support any number of new parameters without disturbing existing implementations of the protocol. DIAMETER's framework approach provides additional extensibility by standardizing a transport mechanism (framework) that can support any number of customized AAA modules.

From a management perspective, AAA servers provide some significant advantages:

- reduced user setup and maintenance times because users are maintained on a single host
- fewer configuration errors because formats are similar across multiple access devices
- less security administrator training requirements because there is only one system syntax to learn
- better auditing because all login and authentication requests come through a single system
- reduced help desk calls because the user interface is consistent across all access methods
- quicker proliferation of access information because information only needs to be replicated to a limited number of AAA servers

- enhanced security support through the use of additional authentication mechanisms (i.e., SecureID)
- extensible design makes it easy to add new devices without disturbing existing configurations

RADIUS: REMOTE AUTHENTICATION DIAL-IN USER SERVICE

RADIUS is by far the most popular AAA service in use today. Its popularity can be attributed to Livingston's decision to open the distribution of the RADIUS source code. Users were quick to port the service across multiple platforms and add customized features, many of which Livingston incorporated as standard features in later releases. Today, versions of the RADIUS server are available for every major operating system from both freeware and commercial sources, and the RADIUS client comes standard on NAS products from every major vendor.

A basic RADIUS server implementation references two configuration files. The client configuration file contains the address of the client and the shared secret used to authenticate transactions. The user file contains the user identification and authentication information (e.g., user ID and password) as well as connection and authorization parameters. Parameters are passed between the client and server using a simple five-field format encapsulated into a single UDP packet. The brevity of the format and the efficiency of the UDP protocol (no connection overhead) allow the server to handle large volumes of requests efficiently. However, the format and protocol also have a downside. They do not lend themselves well to some of today's diverse access requirements (i.e., ROAMOPS), and retransmissions are a problem in heavy load or failed node scenarios.

Putting the AA in RADIUS: Authentications and Authorizations

RADIUS has eight standard transaction types: access-request, access-accept, access-reject, accounting-request, accounting-response, access-challenge, status-server, and status-client. Authentication is accomplished by decrypting a NAS access-request packet, authenticating the NAS source, and validating the access-request parameters against the user file. The server then returns one of three authentication responses: access-accept, access-reject, or access-challenge. The latter is a request for additional authentication information such as a one-time password from a token or a callback identifier.

Authorization is not a separate function in the RADIUS protocol but simply part of an authentication reply. When a RADIUS server validates an access request, it returns to the NAS client all the connection attributes specified in the user file. These usually include the data link (i.e., PPP, SLIP) and network (i.e., TCP/IP, IPX) specifications, but may also include vendor-specific authorization parameters. One such mechanism automatically initiates a Telnet or rlogin session to a specified host. Other methods include forcing the port to a specific IP address with limited connectivity, or applying a routing filter to the access port.

The Third A: Well, Sometimes Anyway!

Accounting is a separate function in RADIUS and not all clients implement it. If the NAS client is configured to use RADIUS accounting, it will generate an Accounting-Start packet once the user has been authenticated, and an Accounting-Stop packet when the user disconnects. The Accounting-Start packet describes the type of service the NAS is delivering, the port being used, and user being serviced. The Accounting-Stop packet duplicates the Start packet information and adds session information such as elapsed time, bytes inputs and outputs, disconnect reason, etc.

Forward Thinking and Other Gee-whiz Capabilities

A RADIUS server can act as a proxy for client requests, forwarding them to servers in other authentication domains. Forwarding can be based on a number of criteria, including a named or number domain. This is particularly useful when a single modem pool is shared across departments or organizations. Entities are not required to share authentication data; each can maintain their own RADIUS server and service proxied requests from the server at the modem pool. RADIUS can proxy both authentication and accounting requests. The relationship between proxies can be distributed (one-to-many) or hierarchical (many-to-one), and requests can be forwarded multiple times. For example, in Exhibit 2-2, it is perfectly permissible for the "master" server to forward a request to the user's regional server for processing.

Most RADIUS clients have the ability to query a secondary RADIUS server for redundancy purposes, although this is not required. The advantage is continued access when the primary server is offline. The disadvantage is the increase in administration required to synchronize data between the servers.

Most RADIUS servers have a built-in database connectivity component. This allows accounting records to be written directly into a database for billing and reporting purposes. This is preferable to processing a flat text accounting "detail" file. Some server implementations also include database access for authentication purposes. Novell's implementation queries NDS, NT versions query the PDC, and several vendors are working on LDAP connectivity.

It Does Not Get Any Easier than This. Or Does It?

When implementing RADIUS, it is important to remember that the source code is both open and extensible. The way each AAA, proxy, and database function is implemented varies considerably from vendor to vendor. When

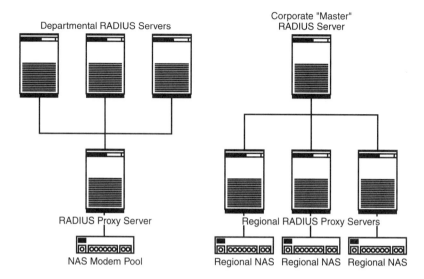

Exhibit 2-2. "Master" server forwards a request on to the user's regional server for processing.

planning a RADIUS implementation, it is best to define one's functional requirements first and then choose NAS components and server software that support them. Here are a few factors to consider:

- *What accesses need to be authenticated?* External accesses via modem pools and VPN servers are essential, but internal accesses to critical systems and security control devices (i.e., routers, firewalls) should also be considered.
- *What protocols need to be supported?* RADIUS can return configuration information at the data link, network, and transport levels. Vendor documentation as well as the RADIUS RFCs and standard dictionary file are good sources of information for evaluating these parameters.
- *What services are required?* Some RADIUS implementations require support for services like Telnet, rlogin, and third-party authentication (i.e., SecureID), which often require additional components and expertise to implement.
- *Is proxy or redundancy required?* When NAS devices are shared across management or security domains, proxy servers are usually required and it is necessary to determine the proxy relationships in advance. Redundancy for system reliability and accessibility is also an important consideration because not all clients implement this feature.

Other considerations might include:

- authorization, accounting, and database access requirements
- interfaces to authentication information in NDS, X.500, or PDC databases

- the RADIUS capabilities of existing clients
- support for third-party Mobile-IP providers like iPass
- secure connection support (i.e., L2TP, PPTP)

Client setup for RADIUS is straightforward. The client must be configured with the IP address of the server(s), the shared secret (encryption key), and the IP port numbers of the authentication and accounting services (the defaults are 1645 and 1646, respectively). Additional settings may be required by the vendor.

The RADIUS server setup consists of the server software installation and three configuration files:

1. The dictionary file is composed of a series of Attribute/Value pairs the server uses to parse requests and generate responses. The standard dictionary file supplied with most server software contains the attributes and values found in the RADIUS RFCs. One may need to add vendor-specific attributes, depending upon one's NAS selection. If any modifications are made, double-check that none of the attribute Names or Values are duplicated.
2. The client file is a flat text file containing the information the server requires to authenticate RADIUS clients. The format is the client name or IP address, followed by the shared secret. If names are used, the server must be configured for name resolution (i.e., DNS). Requirements for the length and format of the shared secret vary, but most UNIX implementations are eight characters or less. There is no limitation on the number of clients a server can support.
3. The user file is also a flat text file. It stores authentication and authorization information for all RADIUS users. To be authenticated, a user must have a profile consisting of three parts: the *username*, a list of authentication *check items,* and a list of *reply items.* A typical entry would look like the one displayed in Exhibit 2-3. The first line contains the user's name and a list of check items separated by commas. In this example, John is restricted to using one NAS device (the one at 10.100.1.1). The remaining lines contain reply items. Reply items are separated by commas at the end of each line. String values are put in quotes. The final line in this example contains an authorization parameter that applies a packet filter to this user's access.

The check and reply items contained in the user file are as diverse as the implementations, but a couple of conventions are fairly common. Username prefixes are commonly used for proxy requests. For example, usernames with the prefix CS/ would be forwarded to the computer science RADIUS server for authentication. Username suffixes are commonly used to designate different access types. For example, a user name with a %vpn suffix would indicate that this access was via a virtual private network (VPN). This makes it possible for a single RADIUS server to authenticate

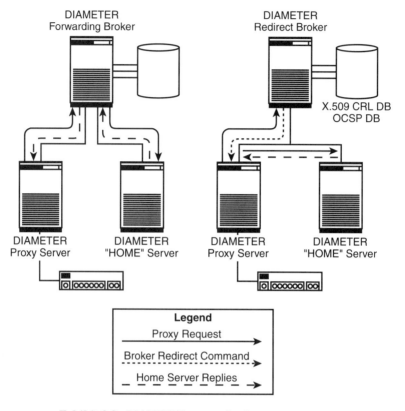

Exhibit 2-3. DIAMETER uses a broker proxy server.

users for multiple NAS devices or provide different reply values for different types of accesses on the same NAS.

The DEFAULT user parameter is commonly used to pass authentication to another process. If the username is not found in the user file, the DEFAULT user parameters are used to transfer the validation to another mechanism. On UNIX, this is typically the */etc/passwd* file. On NT, it can be the local user database or a domain controller. Using secondary authentication mechanisms has the advantage of expanding the check items RADIUS can use. For example, UNIX and NT groups can be check as well as account activation and date and time restriction.

Implementations that use a common NAS type or one server for each NAS type have fairly uncomplicated user files, but user file contents can quickly become quite convoluted when NAS devices and access methods are mixed. This not only adds complexity to the management of the server, but also requires more sophistication on the part of users.

Stumbling Blocks, Complexities, and Other RADIUS Limitations

RADIUS works well for remote access authentication but is not suitable for host or application authentication. Web servers may be the first exception. Adding a RADIUS client to a Web server provides a secure method for authenticating users across open networks. RADIUS provides only basic accounting facilities with no facilities for monitoring nailed-up circuits or system events. User-based rather than device-based connection parameters are another major limitation of RADIUS. When a single RADIUS server manages several different types of NAS devices, user administration is considerably more complex. Standard RADIUS authentication does not provide facilities for checking a user's group membership, restricting access by date or time of day, or expiring a user's account on a given date. To provide these capabilities, the RADIUS server must be associated with a secondary authentication service.

Overall, RADIUS is an efficient, flexible, and well-supported AAA service that works best when associated with a secondary authentication service like NDS or NT where additional account restrictions can be applied. The adoption of RADIUS version 2 as an IETF standard will certainly ensure its continued success and importance as a good general-purpose authentication, authorization, and accounting service.

TACACS: TERMINAL ACCESS CONTROLLER ACCESS CONTROL SYSTEM

What is commonly referred to today as TACACS actually represents two evolutions of the protocol. The original TACACS, developed in the early ARPANet days, had very limited functionality and used the UDP transport. In the early 1990s, the protocol was extended to include additional functionality and the transport changed to TCP. To maintain backward compatibility, the original functions were included as subsets of the extended functions. The new protocol was dubbed XTACACS (Extended TACACS). Virtually all current TACACS daemons are based on the extended protocol as described in RFC1492.

Cisco Systems adopted TACACS for its AAA architecture and further enhanced the product by separating the authentication, authorization, and accounting functions and adding encryption to all NAS-server transmissions. Cisco also improved the extensibility of TACACS by permitting arbitrary length and content parameters for authentication exchanges. Cisco called their version TACACS+, but in reality, TACACS+ bares no resemblance to the original TACACS and packet formats are not backward compatible. Some server implementations support both formats for compatibility purposes. The remainder of this section is based on TACACS+ because it is the proposed IETF standard.

TACACS+ servers use a single configuration file to control server options, define users and attribute/value (AV) pairs, and control authentication and authorization actions. The options section specifies the settings of the service's operation parameters, the shared secret key, and the accounting file name. The remainder of the file is a series of user and group definitions used to control authentication and authorization actions. The format is *"user = username"* or *"group = groupname,"* followed by one or more AV pairs inside curly brackets.

The client initiates a TCP session and passes a series of AV pairs to the server using a standard header format followed by a variable length parameter field. The header contains the service request type (authentication, authorization, or accounting) and is sent in the clear. The entire parameter field is encrypted for confidentiality. TACACS' variable parameter field provides for extensibility and site-specific customization, while the TCP protocol ensures reliable delivery. However, the format and protocol also increase communications overhead, which can impact the server's performance under heavy load.

A 1: TACACS Authentication

TACACS authentication has three packet types: Start, Continue, and Reply. The client begins the authentication with a Start packet that describes the type of authentication to be performed. For simple authentication types like PAP, the packet may also contain the user ID and password. The server responses with a Reply. Additional information, if required, is passed with client Continue and server Reply packets. Transactions include login (by privilege level) and password change using various authentication protocols (i.e., CHAP, PAP, PPP, etc.). Like RADIUS, a successful TACACS authentication returns attribute-value (AV) pairs for connection configuration. These can include authorization parameters or they can be fetched separately.

A 2: TACACS Authorization

Authorization functions in TACACS consist of Request and Response AV pairs used to:

- permit or deny certain commands, addresses, services or protocols
- set user privilege level
- invoke input and output packet filters
- set access control lists (ACLs)
- invoke callback actions
- assign a specific network address

Functions can be returned as part of an authentication transaction or an authorization-specific request.

A 3: TACACS Accounting

TACACS accounting functions use a format similar to authorization functions. Accounting functions include Start, Stop, More, and Watchdog. The Watchdog function is used to validate TCP sessions when data is not sent for extended periods of time. In addition to the standard accounting data supported by RADIUS, TACACS has an event logging capability that can record system level changes in access rights or privilege. The reason for the event as well as the traffic totals associated with it can also be logged.

Take Another Look (and Other Cool Capabilities)

TACACS authentication and authorization processes are considerably enhanced by two special capabilities: recursive lookup and callout. Recursive lookup allows connection, authentication, and authorization information to be spread across multiple entries. AV pairs are first looked up in the user entry. Unresolved pairs are then looked up in the group entry (if the user is a member of a group) and finally assigned the default value (if one is specified). TACACS+ permits groups to be embedded in other groups, so recursive lookups can be configured to encompass any number of connection requirements. TACACS+ also supports a callout capability that permits the execution of user-supplied programs. Callout can be used to dynamically alter the authentication and authorization processes to accommodate any number of requirements; a considerably more versatile approach than RADIUS' static configurations. Callout can be used to interface TACACS+ with third-party authentication mechanisms (i.e., Kerberos and SecureID), pull parameters from a directory or database, or write audit and accounting records.

TACACS, like RADIUS, can be configured to use redundant servers and because TACACS uses a reliable transport (TCP), it also has the ability to detect failed nodes. Unlike RADIUS, TACACS cannot be configured to proxy NAS requests, which limits its usefulness in large-scale and cross-domain applications.

Cisco, Cisco, Cisco: Implementing TACACS

There are a number of TACACS server implementations available, including two freeware versions for UNIX, a Netware port, and two commercial versions for NT, but the client implementations are Cisco, Cisco, Cisco. Cisco freely distributes the TACACS and TACACS+ source code, so features and functionality vary considerably from one implementation to another. CiscoSecure is generally considered the most robust of the commercial implementations and even supports RADIUS functions. Once again, be sure to define functional requirements before selecting NAS components and server software. If your shop is Cisco-centric, TACACS is going to work well; if not, one might want to consider a server product with both RADIUS and TACACS+ capabilities.

Client setup for TACACS on Cisco devices requires an understanding of Cisco's AAA implementation. The AAA function must be enabled for any of the TACACS configuration commands to work. The client must be configured with the IP address of the server(s) and the shared secret encryption key. A typical configuration would look like this:

```
aaa new-model
tacacs-server key <your key here>
tacacs-server host <your primary TACACS server
          IP address here >
tacacs-server host <your secondary TACACS server
          IP address here >
```

followed by port-specific configurations. Different versions of Cisco IOS support different TACACS settings. Other NAS vendors support a limited subset of TACACS+ commands.

TACACS server setup consists of the server software installation and editing the options, authentication, and authorization entries in the configuration files. Comments may be placed anywhere in the file using a pound sign (#) to start the line. In the following example, Jane represents a dial-in support contractor, Bill a user with multiple access methods, and Dick an IT staff member with special NAS access.

```
# The default authentication method will use the
          local UNIX
# password file, default authorization will be
          permitted for
# users without explicit entries and accounting
          records will be
# written to the /var/adm/tacacs file.
default authentication = file /etc/passwd
default authorization = permit
accounting file = /var/adm/tacacs

# Contractors, vendors, etc.
user = jane {
    name = "Jane Smith"
    global = cleartext "Jane'sPassword"
    expires = "May 10 2000"
    service=ppp
    protocol=ip {
        addr=10.200.10.64
        inacl=101
        outacl=102
    }
}
```

```
# Employees with "special" requirements
user = bill {
    name="Bill Jones"
    arap = cleartext "Apple_ARAP_Password"
    pap = cleartext "PC_PAP_Password"
    default service = permit
}

user = dick {
    name="Dick Brown"
    member = itstaff
    # Use the service parameters from the default user
    default service = permit
    # Permit Dick to access the exec command using
connection access list 4
    service = exec {
        acl = 4
    }
    # Permit Dick to use the telnet command
to everywhere but 10.101.10.1
    cmd = telnet {
        deny 10\.101\.10\.1
        permit .*
    }
}

# Standard Employees use these entries
user = DEFAULT {
    service = ppp {
        # Disconnect if idle for 5 minutes
        idletime = 5
        # Set maximum connect time to one hour
        timeout = 60
    }
    protocol = ip {
        addr-pool=hqnas
    }
}

# Group Entries
group = itstaff {
    # Staff uses a special password file
    login = file /etc/itstaff_passwds
}
```

Jane's entry sets her password to "Jane'sPassword" for all authentication types, requires her to use PPP, forces her to a known IP, and applies both inbound and outbound extended IP access control lists (a.k.a. IP filters). It also contains an account expiration date so the account can be easily enabled and disabled. Bill's entry establishes different passwords for

Apple and PAP logins, and assigns his connection the default service parameters. Dick's entry grants him access to the NAS executive commands, including Telnet, but restricts their use by applying a standard IP access control list and an explicit **deny** to the host at 10.101.10.1. Bill and Dick's entries also demonstrate TACACS' recursive lookup feature. The server first looks at user entry for a password, then checks for a group entry. Bill is not a member of any group, so the default authentication method is applied. Dick, however, is a member of "itstaff," so the server validates the group name and looks for a password in the group entry. It finds the **login** entry and authenticates Dick using the /etc/itstaff_passwds file. The default user entry contains AV pairs specifying the use of PPP with an idle timeout of five minutes and a maximum session time of one hour.

In this example, the UNIX /etc/password and /etc/group files are used for authentication, but the use of other mechanisms is possible. Novell implementations use NDS, NT versions use the domain controller, and CiscoSecure support LDAP and several SQL compatible databases.

Proxyless, Problems, and Pitfalls: TACACS limitations

The principle limitation of TACACS+ may well be its lack of use. While TACACS+ is a versatile and robust protocol, it has few server implementations and even fewer NAS implementations. Outside of Cisco, this author was unable to find any custom extensions to the protocol or any vendor-specific AV pairs. Additionally, TACACS' scalability and performance are an issue. Unlike RADIUS' single-packet UDP design, TACACS uses multiple queries over TCP to establish connections, thus incurring overhead that can severely impact performance. TACACS+ servers have no ability to proxy requests so they cannot be configured in a hierarchy to support authentication across multiple domains. CiscoSecure scalability relies on regional servers and database replication to scale across multiple domains. While viable, the approach assumes a single management domain, which may not always be the case.

Overall, TACACS+ is a reliable and highly extensible protocol with existing support for Cisco's implementation of NAS-based VPNs. Its "outcalls" capability provides a fairly straightforward way to customize the AAA functions and add support for third-party products. Although TACACS+ supports more authentication parameters than RADIUS, it still works best when associated with a secondary authentication service like NDS or an NT domain. The adoption of TACACS+ as an IETF standard and its easy extensibility should improve its adoption by other NAS manufactures. Until then, TACACS+ remains a solid AAA solution for Cisco-centric environments.

DIAMETER: TWICE RADIUS?

DIAMETER is a highly extensible AAA framework capable of supporting any number of authentication, authorization, or accounting schemes and connection types. The protocol is divided into two distinct parts: the Base Protocol and the Extensions. The DIAMETER Base Protocol defines the message format, transport, error reporting, and security services used by all DIAMETER extensions. DIAMETER Extensions are modules designed to conduct specific types of authentication, authorization, or accounting transactions (i.e., NAS, Mobile-IP, ROAMOPS, and EAP). The current IETF draft contains definitions for NAS requests, Mobile-IP, secure proxy, strong security, and accounting, but any number of other extensions are possible.

DIAMETER is built upon the RADIUS protocol but has been augmented to overcome inherent RADIUS limitations. Although the two protocols do not share a common data unit (PDU), there are sufficient similarities to make the migration from RADIUS to DIAMETER easier. DIAMETER, like RADIUS, uses a UDP transport but in a peer-to-peer rather than client/server configuration. This allows servers to initiate requests and handle transmission errors locally. DIAMETER uses reliable transport extensions to reduce retransmissions, improve failed node detection, and reduce node congestion. These enhancements reduce latency and significantly improve server performance in high-density NAS and hierarchical proxy configurations. Additional improvements include:

- full support for roaming
- cross-domain, broker-based authentication
- full support for the Extensible Authentication Protocol (EAP)
- vendor-defined attributes-value pairs (AVPs) and commands
- enhanced security functionality with replay attack protections and confidentiality for individual AVPs

There Is Nothing Like a Good Foundation

The DIAMETER Base Protocol consists of a fixed-length (96 byte) header and two or more attribute-value pairs (AVPs). The header contains the message type, option flags, version number, and message length, followed by three transport reliability parameters (see Exhibit 2-4).

AVPs are the key to DIAMETER's extensibility. They carry all DIAMETER commands, connection parameters, and authentication, authorization, accounting, and security data. AVPs consist of a fixed-length header and a variable-length data field. A single DIAMETER message can carry any number

Exhibit 2-4. DIAMETER Base Protocol packet format.

Type – Flags – Version	Message Length
Node Identifier	
Next Send	Next Received
AVPs . . .	

of AVPs, up to the maximum UDP packet size of 8192 bytes. Two AVPs in each DIAMETER message are mandatory. They contain the message Command Code and the sender's IP address or host name. The message type or the Extension in use defines the remaining AVPs. DIAMETER reserves the first header byte and the first 256 AVPs for RADIUS backward compatibility.

A Is for the Way You Authenticate Me

The specifics of a DIAMETER authentication transaction are governed by the Extension in use, but they all follow a similar pattern. The client (i.e., a NAS) issues an authentication request to the server containing the AA-Request Command, a session-ID, and the client's address and host name followed by the user's name and password and a state value.

The session-ID uniquely identifies this connection and overcomes the problem in RADIUS with duplicate connection identifiers in high-density installations. Each connection has its own unique session with the server. The session is maintained for the duration of the connection and all transactions related to the connection use the same session-ID. The state AVP is used to track the state of multiple transaction authentication schemes such as CHAP or SecureID.

The server validates the user's credentials and returns an AA-Answer packet containing either a Failed-AVP or the accompanying Result-Code AVP or the authorized AVPs for the service being provided (i.e., PPP parameters, IP parameters, routing parameters, etc.). If the server is not the HOME server for this user, it will forward (proxy) the request.

Proxy on Steroids!

DIAMETER supports multiple proxy configurations, including the two RADIUS models and two additional Broker models. In the hierarchical model, the DIAMETER server forwards the request directly to the user's HOME server using a session-based connection. This approach provides several advantages over the standard RADIUS implementation. Because the proxy connection is managed separately from the client connection, failed node and packet retransmissions are handled more efficiently and the hop can be secured with enhanced security like IPSec. Under RADIUS the first server in the authentication chain must know the CHAP shared secret, but DIAMETER's proxy scheme permits the authentication to take place at the HOME server. As robust as DIAMETER's hierarchical model is, it still is not suitable for many roaming applications.

DIAMETER uses a Broker proxy server to support roaming across multiple management domains. Brokers are employed to reduce the amount of configuration information that needs to be shared between ISPs within a roaming consortium. The Broker provides a simple message routing function. In

Exhibit 2-5. A typical entry.

User Name	Attribute = Value
john	Password = "1secret9," NAS-IP-Address = 10.100.1.1
	Service-Type = Framed-User,
	Framed-Protocol = PPP,
	Framed-IP-Address = 10.200.10.1,
	Framed-IP-Netmask = 255.255.255.0,
	Filter-Id = "firewall"

DIAMETER, two routing functions are provided: either the Broker forwards the message to the HOME server or provides the keys and certificates required for the proxy server to communicate directly with the HOME server (see Exhibit 2-5).

A Two Brute: DIAMETER Authorization

Authorization transactions can be combined with authentication requests or conducted separately. The specifics of the transaction are governed by the Extension in use but follow the same pattern and use the same commands as authentications. Authorization requests must take place over an existing session; they cannot be used to initiate sessions but they can be forwarded using a DIAMETER proxy.

Accounting for Everything

DIAMETER significantly improves upon the accounting capabilities of RADIUS and TACACS+ by adding event monitoring, periodic reporting, real-time record transfer, and support for the ROAMOPS Accounting Data Interchange Format (ADIF). DIAMETER accounting is authorization-server directed. Instructions regarding how the client is to generate accounting records is passed to the client as part of the authorization process. Additionally, DIAMETER accounting servers can force a client to send current accounting data. This is particularly useful for connection troubleshooting or to capture accounting data when an accounting server experiences a crash. Client writes and server polls are fully supported by both DIAMETER proxy models.

For efficiency, records are normally batch transferred but for applications like ROAMOPS where credit limit checks or fraud detection are required, records can be generated in real-time. DIAMETER improves upon standard connect and disconnect accounting with a periodic reporting capability that is particularly useful for monitoring usage on nailed-up circuits. DIAMETER also has an event accounting capability like TACACS+ that is useful for recording service-related events like failed nodes and server reboots.

Security, Standards, and Other Sexy Stuff

Support for strong security is a standard part of the DIAMETER Base Protocol. Many applications, like ROAMOPS and Mobile-IP, require sensitive connection information to be transferred across multiple domains. Hop-by-hop security is inadequate for these applications because data is subject to exposure at each interim hop. DIAMETER's Strong Proxy Extension overcomes the problem by encrypting sensitive data in S/MIME objects and encapsulating them in standard AVPs.

Got the telecommuter, mobile workforce, VPN, multi-platform, dial-in user authentication blues? One does not need to! AAA server solutions like RADIUS, TACACS, and DIAMETER can chase those blues away. With a little careful planning and a few hours of configuration, one can increase security, reduce administration time, and consolidate one's remote access venues into a single, centralized, flexible, and scalable solution. That should put a smile on one's face.

Domain 2
Telecommuni-
cations
and Network
Security

THIS DOMAIN CONTINUES TO ENCOMPASS A MULTITUDE OF TOPICS BECAUSE THE COMPUTING ENVIRONMENT EXTENDS BEYOND THE MAINFRAME TO THE NETWORK AND NETWORKED NETWORKS. For information security professionals to secure the network, they must have a good understanding of the various communications protocols, their vulnerabilities, and the mechanisms that are available to be deployed to improve network security.

Implementing security services in a layered communications architecture is a complex endeavor. Regardless, organizations are forced to extend beyond their own perimeters by way of connections to trading partners, suppliers, customers, and the public at large. And each connection must be secured to some degree.

Further, the pressure to do E-business has led most organizations to carve out their presence on the Web. Security vendors have made available network security vis-à-vis firewalls, encryption, virtual private networks, etc. The challenge for the information security professional is to know which strategies will be sufficiently robust, interoperable, and scalable, as well as which products fit a long-term network security strategy.

In this domain, new chapters address security at multiple layers within the network as well as the requirements to secure the Internet, intranet, and extranet environment.

Chapter 3
E-mail Security

Bruce A. Lobree

WHEN THE FIRST TELEGRAPH MESSAGE WAS FINALLY SENT, THE START OF THE ELECTRONIC COMMUNICATIONS AGE WAS BORN. Then about 50 years ago, people working on a mainframe computer left messages or put a file in someone else's directory on a Direct Access Storage Device (DASD) drive, and so the first electronic messaging system was born. Although most believe that electronic mail, or e-mail as it is called today, was started with the ARPA net, that is not the case. Electronic communication has been around for a much longer period than that, and securing that information has always been and will always be a major issue for both government and commercial facilities as well as the individual user.

When Western Telegraph started telegraphing money from point to point, this represented the beginnings of electronic transfers of funds via a certified system. Banks later began connecting their mainframe computers with simple point-to-point connections via SNA networks to enhance communications and actual funds transfers. This enabled individual operators to communicate with each other across platforms and systems enabling expedited operations and greater efficiencies at reduced operating costs.

When computer systems started to "talk" to each other, there was an explosion of development in communications between computer users and their respective systems. The need for connectivity grew as fast as the interest in it was developed by the corporate world. The Internet, which was originally developed for military and university use, was quickly pulled into this communications systems with its redundant facilities and fail-safe design, and was a natural place for electronic mail to grow toward.

Today (see Exhibit 3-1), e-mail, electronic chat rooms, and data transfers are happening at speeds that make even the most forward-thinking people wonder how far it will go. Hooking up networks for multiple-protocol communications is mandatory for any business to be successful. Electronic mail must cross multiple platforms and travel through many networks for it to go from one point to another. Each time it moves between networks and connections, this represents another point where it can be intercepted, modified, copied, or in worst-case scenario stopped altogether.

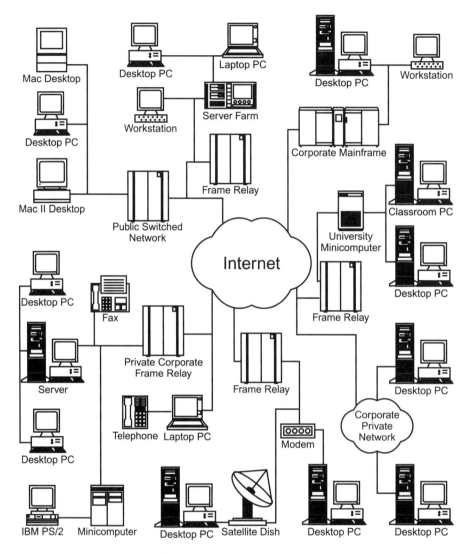

Exhibit 3-1. Internet connectivity.

Chat rooms on the Internet are really modified e-mail sites that allow multiple parties to read the mail simultaneously, similar to looking at a note stuck on a bulletin board. These services allow users to "post" a message to a board that allows several people to view it at once. This type of communication represents a whole new level of risk. There is controlling who has access to the site, where the site is hosted, how people gain access to the site, and many other issues that are created by any type of shared communications. The best example of a chat room is a conference call that has a publicly available phone number that can be looked up in any phone book. The difference is that when someone joins the conference, the phone usually has a tone indicating the arrival of a new individual or group. With many chat rooms, no such protocol exists and users may not know who is watching or listening to any particular session if there is no specific user authentication method in use.

Today, e-mail is a trusted form of corporate communications that just about every major government and corporation in the world are using. Internal networks move communications in cleartext with sometimes little to no authentication. These business-critical messages are moved across public phone lines that are utilized for internal communications. This traffic in most cases is never even questioned as to authenticity and data can be listened to and intercepted.

Messages are presumed to be from the original author although there is no certificate or signature verifying it. By today's standards, e-mail has become a de facto trusted type of communications that is considered legal and binding in many cases. Even today, for a document to be considered legal and binding, it must contain a third-party certificate of authenticity, or some form of binding notary. However, in the case of e-mail, people consider this a form of electronic signature although it is so easy to change the senders' names without much effort. It is possible for the most untrained person to quickly figure out how to change their identity in the message and the recipient quickly gets information that may cause major damage, both financially or reputationally.

What makes matters even worse is the sue-happy attitude that is prevalent in the United States and is quickly spreading around the globe. There have already been several cases that have tested these waters and proven fatal to the recipient of the message as well as the falsified sender. These cases have taken to task system administrators to prove where electronic information has come from and where it went. Questions like who actually sent it, when was it sent, and how can one prove it, became impossible to answer without auditing tools being in place that cover entire networks with long-term report or audit data retention.

Today, e-mail traffic is sharing communications lines with voice, video, audio, and just about anything else that can be moved through wire and fiber optics. Despite the best frame relay systems, tied to the cleanest wires with the best filters, there is still going to be bleed over of communications in most wired types of systems (note that the author has seen fiber-optic lines tapped). This is not as much an issue in fiber optic as it is in copper wire. System administrators must watch for capacity issues and failures. They must be able to determine how much traffic will flow and when are the time-critical paths for information. For example, as a system administrator, one cannot take down a mail server during regular business times. However, with a global network, what is business time, and when is traffic flow needed the most? These and many other questions must be asked before any mail system can be implemented, serviced, and relied upon by the specified user community.

Once the system administrator has answered all their questions about number of users, and the amount of disk space to be allocated to each user for the storage of e-mail, a system requirement can be put together. Now the administrative procedures can be completed and the configuration of the system can be put together. The administrator needs to figure out how to protect it without impacting the operational functionality of the system. The amount of security applied to any system will directly impact the operational functionality and speed at which the system can function.

Protection of the mail server becomes even more important as the data that moves through it becomes more and more mission critical. There is also the issue of protecting internal services from the mail server that may be handling traffic that contains viruses and Trojan horses. Viruses and Trojan horses as simple attachments to mail can be the cause for anything from simple annoyances or unwanted screen displays, all the way to complete destruction of computing facilities. Executives expect their mail to be "clean" of any type of malicious type of attachment. They expect the mail to always be delivered and always come from where the "FROM" in the message box states it came from.

The author notes that no virus can hurt any system until it is activated today. This may change as new programs are written in the future. This means that if a virus is going to do anything, the person receiving it via mail must open the mail message and then attempt to view or run the attachment. Simply receiving a message with an attached virus will not do anything to an individual's system. This hoax about a virus that will harm one's machine in this fashion is urban legend in this author's opinion.

Cookies or applets received over the Internet are a completely different subject matter that is not be discussed here. Users, however, must be aware of them and know how to deal with them. From a certain perspective, these can be considered a form of mail; however, by traditional definition, they are not.

TYPES OF MAIL SERVICES

Ever since that first message was sent across a wire using electricity, humanity has been coming up with better ways to communicate and faster ways to move that data in greater volume in smaller space. The first mainframe mail was based on simple SNA protocols and only used ASCII formatted text. The author contends that it was probably something as simple as a person leaving a note in another person's directory (like a Post-It on your computer monitor). Today, there is IP-based traffic that is moved through many types of networks using many different systems of communications and carries multiple fonts, graphics, and sound and other messages as attachments to the original message.

With all the different types of mail systems that exist on all the different types of operating systems, choosing which e-mail service to use is like picking a car. The only environment that utilizes one primary mail type is Mac OS. However, even in this environment, one can use Netscape or Eudora to read and create mail. With the advent of Internet mail, the possibility of integration of e-mail types has become enormous. Putting multiple mail servers of differing types on the same network is now a networking and security nightmare that must be overcome.

Sendmail

Originally developed by Eric Allman in 1981, Sendmail is a standard product that is used across multiple systems. Regardless of what e-mail program is used to create e-mail, any mail that goes beyond the local site is generally routed via a mail transport agent. Given the number of "hops" any given Internet mail message takes to reach its destination, it is likely that every piece of Internet e-mail is handled by a Sendmail server somewhere along it's route.

The commercially available version of Sendmail began in 1997 when Eric Allman and Greg Olson formed Sendmail, Inc. The company still continues to enhance and release the product with source code and the right to modify and redistribute. The new commercial product line focuses on cost-effectiveness with Web-based administration and management tools, and automated binary installation.

Sendmail is used by most Internet service providers (ISPs) and shipped as the standard solution by all major UNIX vendors, including Sun, HP, IBM, DEC, SGI, SCO, and others. This makes the Sendmail application very important in today's Internet operations.

The Sendmail program was connected to the ARPAnet, and was home to the INGRES project. Another machine was home to the Berkeley UNIX project and had recently started using UUCP. Software existed to move mail within ARPAnet, INGRES, and BerkNet, but none existed to move mail between these networks. For this reason, Sendmail was created to connect the individual mail programs with a common protocol.

The first Sendmail program was shipped with version 4.1c of the Berkeley Software Distribution or BSD (the first version of Berkeley UNIX to include TCP/IP). From that first release to the present (with one long gap between 1982 and 1990), Sendmail was continuously improved by its authors. Today, version 8 is a major rewrite that includes many bug fixes and significant enhancements that take this application far beyond its original conception.

Other people and companies have worked on their versions of the Sendmail programs and injected a number of improvements, such as support for database management (dbm) files and separate rewriting of headers and envelopes. As time and usage of this application have continued, many of the original problems with the application and other related functions have been repaired or replaced with more efficient working utilities.

Today, there are major offshoots from many vendors that have modified Sendmail to suit their particular needs. Sun Microsystems has made many modifications and enhancements to Sendmail, including support for Network Information Service (NIS) and NIS+ maps. Hewlett-Packard also contributed many fine enhancements, including 8BITMIME (multi-purpose Internet mail extensions that worked with 8-bit machines limited naming controls, which do not exist in the UNIX environment) support.

This explosion of Sendmail versions led to a great deal of confusion. Solutions to problems that work for one version of Sendmail fail miserably with others. Beyond this, configuration files are not portable, and some features cannot be shared. Misconfiguration occurs as administrators work with differing types of products, thus creating further problems with control and security.

Version 8.7 of Sendmail introduced multicharacter options and macro names, new interactive commands. Many of the new fixes resolved the problems and limitations of earlier releases. More importantly, V8.7 has officially adopted most of the good features from IDA, KJS, Sun, and HP's Sendmail, and kept abreast of the latest standards from the Internet Engineering Task Force (IETF). Sendmail is a much more developed and user-friendly tool that has an international following and complies with much needed e-mail standards.

From that basic architecture, there are many programs today that allow users to read mail — Eudora, MSmail, Lotus Notes, and Netscape Mail are some of the more common ones. The less familiar ones are BatiMail or Easymail for UNIX, and others. These products will take an electronically formatted message and display it on the screen after it has been written and sent from another location. This allows humans to read, write, and send electronic mail using linked computers systems.

Protecting E-mail

Protecting e-mail is no easy task and every administrator will have his own interpretation as to what constitutes strong protection of communication. The author contends that strong protection is only that protection needed to keep the information secured for as long as it has value. If the information will be forever critical to the organization's operation, then it will need to be protected at layer two (the data-link level) of the IP stack.

This will need to be done in a location that will not be accessible to outsiders, except by specific approval and with proper authentication.

The other side of that coin is when the information has a very short valued life. An example would be that the data becomes useless once is has been received. In this case, the information does not need to be protected any longer than it takes for it to be transmitted. The actual transmission time and speed at which this occurs may be enough to ensure security. The author assumes that this type of mail will not be sent on a regular basis or at predetermined times. Mail that is sent on a scheduled basis or very often is easier to identify and intercept than mail sent out at random times. Thieves have learned that credit card companies send out their plastic on a specific date of every month and know when to look for it; this same logic can be applied to electronic mail as well.

Which ever side one's data is on, it is this author's conviction that all data should be protected to one level of effort or one layer of communication below what is determined to be needed to ensure sufficient security. This will ensure that should one's system ever be compromised, it will not be due to a flaw in one's mail service, and the source of the problem will be determined to have come from elsewhere. The assumption is that the hardware or tapes that hold the data will be physically accessible. Therefore, it is incumbent on the data to be able to protect itself to a level that will not allow the needed data to be compromised.

The lowest level of protection is the same as the highest level of weakness. If one protects the physical layer (layer 1 of the IP stack) within a facility, but does not encrypt communications, then when one's data crosses public phone lines, it is exposed to inspection or interception by outside sources.

When the time comes to actually develop the security model for a mail system, the security person will need to look at the entire system. This means that one must include all the communications that are under one's control, as well as that which is not. This will include public phone lines, third-party communications systems, and everything else that is not under one's physical and logical control.

IDENTIFYING THE MAILER

Marion just received an electronic message from her boss via e-mail. Marion knows this because in the "FROM" section is her boss' name. Marion absolutely knows this because who could possibly copy the boss' name into their own mailbox for the purpose of transmitting a false identity? The answer: anyone who goes into their preferences and changes the identity of the user and then restarts their specific mail application.

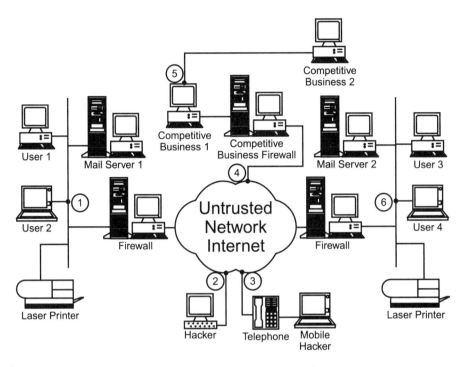

Exhibit 3-2. Unsecured network.

Whether talking about physical mail or electronic mail, the issue of authentication is an important subject. Authenticating the source of the communication and securing the information while in transit is critical to the overall security and reliability of the information being sent. In the physical world, a letter sent in a sealed, certified, bonded envelope with no openings is much safer and more reliable than a postcard with a mass mail stamp on it. So it goes with electronic mail as well.

Spoofing or faking an ID in mail is a fairly easy thing to do. Thankfully, not too many people know how to do it yet, and most will not consider it. To understand all the points of risk, one needs to understand how mail is actually sent. Not just what program has been implemented — but also the physical architecture of what is happening when one sends it.

In Exhibit 3-2, there are several points of intercept where a message can be infiltrated. Each point of contact represents another point of interception and risk. This includes the sender's PC which may store an original copy of the message in the sent box.

Network Architecture for Mail

User 1 wants to send an e-mail to User 4. If user 4 is connected to their network, then the mail will travel directly from User 1 to User 4 if all systems between the two users are functioning correctly. If User 4 is not connected, then the mail will be stored on User 4's mail server for later pickup. If any mail server in the path is not functioning correctly, the message may stop in transit until such time as it can be retransmitted, depending on the configuration of the particular mail servers.

For mail to go from one user to another, it will go through User 1's mail server. Then it will be routed out through the corporate firewall and off to User 4's firewall via the magic of IP addressing. For the purpose of this chapter, one assumes that all of the routing protocols and configuration parameters have been properly configured to go from point User 1 to point User 4. As a user, it is presumed that one's mail is sent across a wire that is connected from one point to another with no intercepting points. The truth is that it is multiple wires with many connections and many points of intercept exist, even in the simplest of mail systems.

With the structure of our communications systems being what it is today, and the nature of the environment and conditions under which people work, that assumption is dangerously wrong. With the use of electronic frame relay connections, multi-server connections, intelligent routers and bridges, a message crosses many places where it could be tapped into by intruders or fail in transmission all together.

Bad E-mail Scenario

One scenario that has played out many times and continues today looks like this (see Exhibit 3-2):

1. User 1 writes and sends a message to User 4.
2. The message leaves User 1's mailbox and goes to the mail server, where it is recorded and readied for transmission by having the proper Internet packet information added to its header.
3. Then the mail server transmits the data out onto the Internet through the corporate firewall.
4. A hacker who is listening to the Internet traffic copies the data as it moves across a shared link using a sniffer (an NT workstation in promiscuous mode will do the same thing).
5. Your competition is actively monitoring the Internet with a sniffer and also sees your traffic and copies it onto their own network.
6. Unbeknownst to your competition, they have been hacked into and now share that data with a third party without even knowing about it.
7. The mail arrives at the recipient's firewall where it is inspected (recorded maybe) and sent onto the mail server.
8. The recipient goes out and gathers his mail and downloads it to his local machine without deleting the message from the mail server.

This message has now been shared with at least three people who can openly read it and has been copied onto at least two other points where it can be retrieved at a later date. There are well-known court cases where this model has been utilized to get old copies of mail traffic that have not been properly deleted and then became a focal point in the case.

As a security officer, it will be your job to determine the points of weakness and also the points of data gathering, potentially, even after the fact. How will one protect these areas; who has access to them; and how are they maintained are all questions that must be answered. To be able to do that, one needs to understand how e-mail works and what its intended use really was yesterday and how it is used today.

This form of communication was originally intended to just link users for the purpose of communicating simple items. It is the author's belief that the original creators of e-mail never initially intended for it to be used in so many different ways for so many different types of communications and information protocols.

Intercept point 1 in Exhibit 3-2 represents the biggest and most common weakness. In 1998, the Federal Bureau of Investigation reported that most intercepted mail and computer problems were created internally to the company. This means that one's risk by internal employees is greater than outside forces. The author does not advocate paranoia internally, but common sense and good practice. Properly filtering traffic through routers and bridges and basic network protection and monitoring of systems should greatly reduce this problem.

Intercept points 2 through 4 all share the same risk — the Internet. Although this is considered by some to be a known form of communications, it is not a secure one. It is a well-known fact that communications can be listened in on and recorded by anyone with the most basic of tools. Data can be retransmitted, copied, or just stopped, depending on the intent of the hacker or intruder.

Intercept points 5 and 6 are tougher to spot and there may be no way to have knowledge of or about if they are compromised. This scenario has an intruder listening from an unknown point that one has no way of seeing. This is to say, one cannot monitor the network they are connected to or may not see their connection on one's monitoring systems. The recipient does not know about them and is as blind to their presence as you are. Although this may be one of the most unlikely problems, it will be the most difficult to resolve. The author contends that the worst-case scenario is when the recipients' mail is intercepted inside their own network, and they do not know about a problem.

It is now the job of the security officer to come up with a solution — not only to protect the mail, but to also be able to determine if and when that system of communications is working properly. It is also the security officer's responsibility to be able to quickly identify when a system has been compromised and what it will take to return it to a protected state. This requires continuous monitoring and ongoing auditing of all related systems.

HOW E-MAIL WORKS

The basic principle behind e-mail and its functionality is to send an electronic piece of information from one place to another with as little interference as possible. Today's e-mail has to be implemented very carefully and utilize controls that are well-defined to meet the clients need and at the same time protect the communications efficiently.

Today, there are some general mail terms that one must understand when discussing e-mail. They are Multipurpose Internet Mail Extensions (MIME), which was standardized with RFC 822 that defines the mail header and type of mail content; and RFC 1521, which is designed to provide facilities to include multiple objects in a single message, to represent body text in character sets other than US-ASCII, to represent formatted multi-font text messages, to represent nontextual material such as images and audio fragments, and generally to facilitate later extensions defining new types of Internet mail for use by cooperating mail agents.

Then there is the Internet Message Access Protocol (IMAP) format of mail messages that is on the rise. This is a method of accessing electronic mail or bulletin board data. Finally, there is POP, which in some places means Point of Presence (when dealing with an Internet provider); but for the purpose of this book means Post Office Protocol.

IP Traffic Control

Before going any further with the explanation of e-mail and how to protect it, the reader needs to understand the TCP/IP protocol. Although to many this may seem like a simple concept, it may be new to others. In short, the TCP/IP protocol is broken into five layers (see Exhibit 3-3). Each layer of the stack has a specific purpose and performs a specific function in the movement of data. The layers the author is concerned about are layers three and above (the network layer). Layers one and two require physical access to the connections and therefore become more difficult to compromise.

TCP/IP Five-Layer Stack:

1. The e-mail program sends the e-mail document down the protocol stack to the transport layer.
2. The transport layer attaches its own header to the file and sends the document to the network layer.

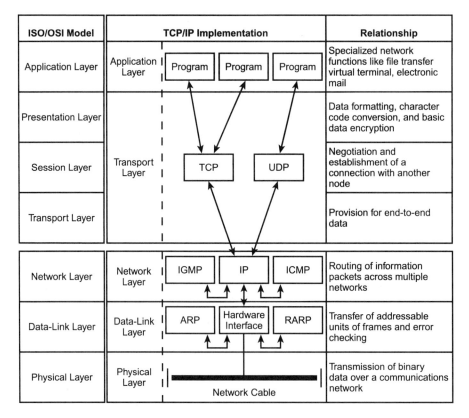

Exhibit 3-3. The five layers of the TCP/IP protocol.

3. The network layer breaks the data frames into packets, attaches additional header information to the packet, and sends the packets down to the data-link layer.
4. The data-link layer sends the packets to the physical layer.
5. The physical layer transmits the file across the network as a series of electrical bursts.
6. The electrical bursts pass through computers, routers, repeaters, and other network equipment between the transmitting computer and the receiving computer. Each computer checks the packet address and sends the packet onward to its destination.
7. At the destination computer, the physical layer passes the packets back to the data-link layer.
8. The data-link layer passes the information back to the network layer.
9. The network layer puts the physical information back together into a packet, verifies the address within the packet header, and verifies that the computer is the packet's destination. If the computer is the

packet's destination, the network layer passes the packet upward to the transport layer.

10. The transport layer, together with the network layer, puts together all the file's transmitted pieces and passes the information up to the application layer.
11. At the application layer, the e-mail program displays the data to the user.

The purpose of understanding how data is moved by the TCP/IP protocol is to understand all the different places that one's data can be copied, corrupted, or modified by an outsider. Due to the complexity of this potential for intrusion, critical data needs to be encrypted and or digitally signed. This is done so that the recipient knows who sent, and can validate the authenticity of, a message that they receive.

Encryption and digital signatures need to authenticate the mail from layer two (the data-link layer) up, at a minimum in this author's opinion. Below that level will require physical access; if one's physical security is good, this should not be an area of issue or concern.

Multipurpose Internet Mail Extensions (MIME)

Multipurpose Internet Mail Extensions (MIME) is usually one of the formats available for use with POP or e-mail clients (Pine, Eudora), Usenet News clients (WinVN, NewsWatcher), and WWW clients (Netscape, MS-IE). MIME extends the format of Internet mail.

STD 11, RFC 822, defines a message representation protocol specifying considerable detail about US-ASCII message headers, and leaves the message content, or message body, as flat US-ASCII text. This set of documents, collectively called the Multipurpose Internet Mail Extensions, or MIME, redefines the format of messages to allow:

- textual message bodies in character sets other than US-ASCII
- an extensible set of different formats for nontextual message bodies
- multi-part message bodies
- textual header information in character sets other than US-ASCII

These documents are based on earlier work documented in RFC 934, STD 11, and RFC 1049; however, it extends and revises them to be more inclusive. Because RFC 822 said so little about message bodies, these documents are largely not a revision of RFC 822 but are new requirements that allow mail to contain a broader type of data and data format.

The initial document specifies the various headers used to describe the structure of MIME messages. The second document, RFC 2046, defines the general structure of the MIME media typing system and also defines an initial set of media types. The third document, RFC 2047, describes extensions to RFC 822 to allow non-US-ASCII text data in Internet mail header fields. The fourth document, RFC 2048, specifies various Internet Assigned Numbers Authority (IANA) registration procedures for MIME-related facilities. The fifth and final document, RFC 2049, describes the MIME conformance criteria as well as providing some illustrative examples of MIME message formats, acknowledgments, and the bibliography.

Since its publication in 1982, RFC 822 has defined the standard format of textual mail messages on the Internet. Its success has been such that the RFC 822 format has been adopted, wholly or partially, well beyond the confines of the Internet and the Internet SMTP transport defined by RFC 821. As the format has seen wider use, a number of limitations have been found to be increasingly restrictive for the user community.

RFC 822 was intended to specify a format for text messages. As such, nontextual messages, such as multimedia messages that might include audio or images, are simply not mentioned. Even in the case of text, however, RFC 822 is inadequate for the needs of mail users whose languages require the use of character sets with far greater size than US-ASCII. Because RFC 822 does not specify mechanisms for mail containing audio, video, Asian language text, or even text in most European and Middle Eastern languages, additional specifications were needed, thus forcing other RFCs to include the other types of data.

One of the notable limitations of RFC 821/822 based mail systems is the fact that they limit the contents of electronic mail messages to relatively short lines (i.e., 1000 characters or less) of seven-bit US-ASCII. This forces users to convert any nontextual data that they may wish to send into seven-bit bytes representable as printable US-ASCII characters before invoking a local mail user agent (UA). The UA is another name for the program with which people send and receive their individual mail.

The limitations of RFC 822 mail becomes even more apparent as gateways were being designed to allow for the exchange of mail messages between RFC 822 hosts and X.400 hosts. The X.400 requirement also specifies mechanisms for the inclusion of nontextual material within electronic mail messages. The current standards for the mapping of X.400 messages to RFC 822 messages specify either that X.400 nontextual material must be converted to (not encoded in) IA5Text format, or that they must be discarded from the mail message, notifying the RFC 822 user that discarding has occurred. This is clearly undesirable, as information that a user may wish to receive is then potentially lost if the original transmission is not recorded appropriately. Although a user agent may not have the capability of dealing with the nontextual material, the user might have some mechanism external to the UA that can extract useful information from the material after the message is received by the hosting computer.

There are several mechanisms that combine to solve some of these problems without introducing any serious incompatibilities with the existing world of RFC 822 mail, including:

- *A MIME-Version header field,* which uses a version number to declare a message to be in conformance with MIME. This field allows mail processing agents to distinguish between such messages and those generated by older or nonconforming software, which are presumed to lack such a field.
- *A Content-Type header field,* generalized from RFC 1049, which can be used to specify the media type and subtype of data in the body of a message and to fully specify the native representation (canonical form) of such data.
- *A Content-Transfer-Encoding header field,* which can be used to specify both the encoding transformations that were applied to the body and the domain of the result. Encoding transformations other than the identity transformation are usually applied to data to allow it to pass through mail transport mechanisms that may have data or character set limitations.
- Two additional header fields that can be used to further describe the data in a body include the *Content-ID* and *Content-Description header fields.*

All of the header fields defined are subject to the general syntactic rules for header fields specified in RFC 822. In particular, all these header fields except for Content-Disposition can include RFC 822 comments, which have no semantic contents and should be ignored during MIME processing.

Internet Message Access Protocol (IMAP)

IMAP is the acronym for Internet Message Access Protocol. This is a method of accessing electronic mail or bulletin board messages that are kept on a (possibly shared) mail server. In other words, it permits a "client" e-mail program to access remote message stores as if they were local. For example, e-mail stored on an IMAP server can be manipulated from a desktop computer at home, a workstation at the office, and a notebook computer while traveling to different physical locations using different equipment. This is done without the need to transfer messages or files back and forth between these computers.

The ability of IMAP to access messages (both new and saved) from more than one computer has become extremely important as reliance on electronic messaging and use of multiple computers increase. However, this functionality should not be taken for granted and can be a real security risk if the IMAP server is not appropriately secured.

The IMAP includes operations for creating, deleting, and renaming mailboxes; checking for new messages; permanently removing messages; setting and clearing flags; server-based RFC-822 and MIME, and searching; and selective fetching of message attributes, texts, and portions thereof.

IMAP was originally developed in 1986 at Stanford University. However, it did not command the attention of mainstream e-mail vendors until a decade later. It is still not as well-known as earlier and less-capable alternatives such as using POP mail. This is rapidly changing, as articles in the trade press and the implementation of the IMAP are becoming more and more commonplace in the business world.

Post Office Protocol (POP)

The Post Office Protocol, version 3 (POP-3) is used to pick up e-mail across a network. Not all computer systems that use e-mail are connected to the Internet 24 hours a day, 7 days a week. Some users dial into a service provider on an as-needed basis. Others may be connected to a LAN with a permanent connection but may not always be powered on (not logged into the network). Other systems may simply not have the available resources to run a full e-mail server. Mail servers may be shielded from direct connection to the Internet by a firewall security system, or it may be against organization policy to have mail delivered directly to user systems. In the case where e-mail must be directly mailed to users, the e-mail is sent to a central e-mail server where it is held for pickup when the user connects at a later time. POP-3 allows a user to logon to an e-mail post office system across the network and validates the user by ID and password. Then it will allow mail to be downloaded, and optionally allow the user to delete the mail from the server.

The widely used POP works best when one has only a single computer. POP e-mail was designed to support "offline" message access to increase network usability and efficiency. This means that messages can be downloaded and then deleted from the mail server if so configured. This mode of access is not compatible with access from multiple computers because it tends to sprinkle messages across all of the computers used for mail access. Thus, unless all of those machines share a common file system, the offline mode of access that is using POP effectively ties the user to one computer for message storage and manipulation. POP further complicates access by placing user-specific information in several locations as the data is stored as well.

The pop3d command is a POP-3 server and supports the POP-3 remote mail access protocol. Also, it accepts commands on its standard input and responds on its standard output. One normally invokes the pop3d command with the inetd daemon with those descriptors attached to a remote client connection.

The pop3d command works with the existing mail infrastructure consisting of sendmail and bellmail.

```
Net::POP3 - Post Office Protocol 3 Client class
            (RFC1081)
```

IMAP is a server for the POP and IMAP mail protocols. POP allows a "post office" machine to collect mail for users and have that mail downloaded to the user's local machine for reading. IMAP provides the functionality of POP, and allows a user to read mail on a remote machine without moving it to the user's local mailbox.

The popd server implements POP, as described in RFC1081 and RFC1082. Basically, the server listens on the TCP port named pop for connections. When it receives a connection request from a client, it performs the following functions:

- checks for client authentication by searching the POP password file in /usr/spool/pop
- sends the client any mail messages it is holding for the client (the server holds the messages in /usr/spool/pop)
- for historical reasons, the MH POP defaults to using the port named pop (port 109) instead of its newly assigned port named pop3 (port 110)

To determine which port MH POP, check the value of the POPSERVICE configuration option. One can display the POPSERVICE configuration option by issuing any MH command with the -help option. To find the port number, look in the /etc/services file for the service port name assigned to the POPSERVICE configuration option. The port number appears beside the service port name.

The POP database contains the following entry for each POP subscriber:

```
name::primary_file:encrypted_passwd::
            user@<client_address>::::0
```

The fields represent the following:

- name — the POP subscriber's username
- primary_file — the mail drop for the POP subscriber (relative to the POP directory)
- encrypted_passwd — the POP subscriber's password generated by popwrd(8)
- user@<client_address> — the remote user allowed to make remote POP (RPOP) connections

This database is an ASCII file and each field within each POP subscriber's entry is separated from the next by a colon. Each POP subscriber is separated from the next by a new line. If the password field is null, then no password is valid; therefore, always check to see that a password is required to further enhance the security of your mail services.

To add a new POP subscriber, edit the file by adding a line such as the following:

```
bruce:: bruce::::::0i
```

Then, use popwrd to set the password for the POP subscriber. To allow POP subscribers to access their maildrops without supplying a password (by using privileged ports), fill in the network address field, as in:

```
bruce:: bruce::: bruce@filteringisim.edu::::0
```

which permits "bruce@filteringisim.edu" to access the maildrop for the POP subscriber "bruce." Multiple network addresses can be specified by separating them with commas, as in:

```
bruce::bruce:9X5/m4yWHvhCc::bruce@filteringisim.edu,
        bruce@rsch.isim.edu::::
```

To disable a POP subscriber from receiving mail, set the primary file name to the empty string. To prevent a POP subscriber from picking up mail, set the encrypted password to "*" and set the network address to the empty string. This file resides in home directory of the login "pop." Because of the encrypted passwords, it can and does have general read permission.

Encryption and Authentication

Having determined what your e-mail needs are, one will have to determine how and when one will need to protect the information being sent. The "when" part is fairly straightforward, as this is set by corporate policy. If the security officer does not have the proper documentation and description of the controls that will need to be in place for electronic data transfer, then now is the time to put it together, as later will be too late. Suffice it to say that this author presumes that all the proper detail exists already. This needs to be done so the security officer will be able to determine the classification of the information that he or she will be working with for traffic to move successfully.

Encryption is a process whereby the sender and the receiver will share an encryption and decryption key that will protect the data from someone reading the data while it is in transit. This will also protect the data when it is backed up on tape or when it is temporarily stored on a mail server. This is not to say that encryption cannot be broken — it can, and has been done to several levels. What is being said is that the encryption used will protect the information long enough that the data is no longer of value to the person who intercepts it or has value to anyone else. This is important to remember, to ensure that too much encryption is not used while, at the same time, enough is used to sufficiently protect the data.

Authentication is meant to verify the sender to the recipient. When the sender sends the message to the other party, they electronically sign the document that verifies to the person receiving the document the authenticity of it. It also verifies what the person sent is what the person received. It does not however protect the data while in transit, which is a distinct difference from encryption and is often a misconception on the part of the general user community.

Encryption

There are many books outlining encryption methodology and the tools that are available for this function. Therefore, this chapter does not go into great detail about the tools. However, the weaknesses as well as the strengths of such methods are discussed. All statements are those of the author and therefore are arguable; however, they are not conditional.

All mail can be seen at multiple points during its transmission. Whether it be from the sendmail server across the Internet, via a firewall to another corporation's firewall, or to their sendmail server, all mail will have multiple hops when it transits from sender to recipient. Every point in that transmission process is a point where the data can be intercepted, copied, modified, or deleted completely.

There are three basic types of encryption generally available today. They are private key (symmetric or single key) encryption, pretty good privacy (PGP) or public key encryption, and privacy enhanced mail (PEM). Each of these types of protection systems has strengths and flaws. However, fundamentally they all work the same way and if properly configured and used will sufficiently protect one's information (maybe).

Encryption takes the message that can be sent, turns it into unreadable text, and transmits it across a network where it is decrypted for the reader. This is a greatly simplified explanation of what occurs and does not contain nearly the detail needed to understand this functionality. Security professionals should understand the inner workings of encryption and how and when to best apply it to their environment. More importantly, they must understand the methods of encryption and decryption and the level at which encryption occurs.

Private key encryption is the least secure method of sending and receiving messages. This is due to a dependency on the preliminary setup that involves the sharing of keys between parties. It requires that these keys be transmitted either electronically or physically on a disk to the other party and that every person who communicates with this person potentially has a separate key. The person who supplies the encryption key must then manage them so that two different recipients of data do not share keys and data is not improperly encrypted before transmission. With each new mail recipient the user has, there could potentially be two more encryption keys to manage.

This being the problem that it is, today there is public key encryption available. This type of encryption is better known as pretty good privacy (or PGP). The basic model for this system is to maintain a public key on a server that everyone has access. User 1, on the other hand, protects his private key so that he is the only one who can decrypt the message that is encrypted with his public key. The reverse is also true in that if a person has User 1's public key, and User 1 encrypts using his private key, then only a person with User 1's public key will be able to decrypt the message. The flaw here is that potentially anyone could have User 1's public key and could decrypt his message if they manage to intercept it.

With this method, the user can use the second party's public key to encrypt the private (single or symmetric) key and thereby transmit the key to the person in a secured fashion. Now users are using both the PGP technology and the private key technology. This is still a complicated method. To make it easy, everyone should have a public key that they maintain in a public place for anyone to pick up. Then they encrypt the message to the recipient and only the recipient can decrypt the message. The original recipient then gets the original sender's public key and uses that to send the reply.

As a user, PGP is the easiest form of encryption to use. User 1 simply stores a public key on a public server. This server can be accessed by anyone and if the key is ever changed, User 1's decryption will not work and User 1 will know that something is amiss. For the system administrator, it is merely a matter of maintaining the public key server and keeping it properly secured.

There are several different algorithms that can be applied to this type of technology. If the reader would like to know more about how to build the keys or development of these systems, there are several books available that thoroughly describe them.

Digital Certificates

Like a written signature, the purpose of a digital signature is to guarantee that the individual sending the message really is who he or she claims to be. Digital signatures are especially important for electronic commerce and are a key component of most authentication schemes. A digital signature is an attachment to an electronic message used for security purposes. The most common use of a digital certificate is to verify that a user sending a message is who he or she claims to be, and to provide the receiver with the means to encode a reply.

The actual signature is a quantity associated with a message that only someone with knowledge of an entity's private key could have generated, but which can be verified through knowledge of that entity's public key. In plain terms, this means that an e-mail message will have a verifiable number generated and attached to it that can be authenticated by the recipient.

Digital signatures perform three very important functions:

1. *Integrity:* A digital signature allows the recipient of a given file or message to detect whether that file or message has been modified.
2. *Authentication:* A digital signature makes it possible to verify cryptographically the identity of the person who signed a given message.
3. *Nonrepudiation:* A digital signature prevents the sender of a message from later claiming that they did not send the message.

The process of generating a digital signature for a particular document type involves two steps. First, the sender uses a one-way hash function to generate a message digest. This hash function can take a message of any length and return a fixed-length (e.g., 128 bits) number (the message digest). The characteristics that make this kind of function valuable are fairly obvious. With a given message, it is easy to compute the associated message digest. It is difficult to determine the message from the message digest, and it is difficult to find another message for which the function would produce the same message digest.

Second, the sender uses its private key to encrypt the message digest. Thus, to sign something, in this context, means to create a message digest and encrypt it with a private key.

The receiver of a message can verify that message via a comparable two-step process:

1. Apply the same one-way hash function that the sender used to the body of the received message. This will result in a message digest.
2. Use the sender's public key to decrypt the received message digest.

If the newly computed message digest matches the one that was transmitted, the message was not altered in transit, and the receiver can be certain that it came from the expected sender. If, on the other hand, the number does not match, then something is amiss and the recipient should be suspect of the message and its content.

The particular intent of a message digest, on the other hand, is to protect against human tampering by relying on functions that are computationally infeasible to spoof. A message digest should also be much longer than a simple checksum so that any given message may be assumed to result in a unique value. To be effective, digital signatures must be unforgeable; this means that the value cannot be easily replaced, modified, or copied.

A digital signature is formed by encrypting a message digest using the private key of a public key encryption pair. A later decryption using the corresponding public key guarantees that the signature could only have been generated by the holder of the private key. The message digest uniquely identifies the e-mail message that was signed. Support for digital signatures could be added to the Flexible Image Transport System, or FITS, by defining a FITS extension format to contain the digital signature certificates, or perhaps by simply embedding them in an appended FITS table extension.

There is a trade-off between the error detection capability of these algorithms and their speed. The overhead of a digital signature can be prohibitive for multi-megabyte files, but may be essential for certain purposes (e.g., archival storage) in the future. The checksum defined by this proposal provides a way to verify FITS data against likely random errors. On the other hand, a full digital signature may be required to protect the same data against systematic errors, especially human tampering.

An individual wishing to send a digitally signed message applies for a digital certificate from a certificate authority (CA). The CA issues an encrypted digital certificate containing the applicant's public key and a variety of other identification information. The CA makes its own public key readily available through print publicity or perhaps on the Internet.

The recipient of an encrypted digital certificate uses the CA's public key to decode the digital certificate attached to the message. Then they verify it as issued by the CA and obtain the sender's public key and identification information held within the certificate. With this information, the recipient can verify the owner of a public key.

A certificate authority is a trusted third-party organization or company that issues digital certificates used to verify the owner of a public key and create public-private key pairs. The role of the CA in this process is to guarantee that the individual granted the unique certificate is who he or she claims to be. Usually, this means that the CA has an arrangement with a financial institution, such as a credit card company, which provides it with information to confirm an individual's claimed identity. CAs are a critical component in data security and electronic commerce because they guarantee that the two parties exchanging information are really who they claim to be.

The most widely used standard for digital certificates is X.509. X.509 is actually an ITU Recommendation, which means that has not yet been officially defined or approved. As a result, companies have implemented the standard in different ways. For example, both Netscape and Microsoft use X.509 certificates to implement SSL in their Web servers and browsers. However, an X.509 certificate generated by Netscape may not be readable by Microsoft products, and vice versa.

Secure Sockets Layer (SSL)

Short for Secure Sockets Layer, SSL is a protocol developed by Netscape for transmitting private documents via the Internet. SSL works using a private key to encrypt data that is transferred over the SSL connection. Both Netscape Navigator and Internet Explorer support SSL, and many Web sites use the protocol to obtain confidential user information, such as credit card numbers. By convention, Web pages that require an SSL connection start with https: instead of http:.

The other protocol for transmitting data securely over the World Wide Web is Secure HTTP (S-HTTP). Whereas SSL creates a secure connection between a client and a server, over which any amount of data can be sent securely, S-HTTP is designed to securely transmit individual messages. SSL and S-HTTP, therefore, can be seen as complementary rather than competing technologies. Both protocols have been approved by the Internet Engineering Task Force (IETF) as a standard.

However, fully understanding what SSL is means that one must also understand HTTP (HyperText Transfer Protocol), the underlying protocol used by the World Wide Web (WWW). HTTP defines how messages are formatted and transmitted, and what actions Web servers and browsers should take in response to various commands. For example, when one enters a URL in the browser, this actually sends an HTTP command to the Web server directing it to fetch and transmit the requested Web page.

HTTP is called a stateless protocol because each command is executed independently, without any knowledge of the commands that came before it. This is the main reason why it is difficult to implement Web sites that react intelligently to user input. This shortcoming of HTTP is being addressed in a number of new technologies, including ActiveX, Java, JavaScript, and cookies.

S-HTTP is an extension to the HTTP protocol to support sending data securely over the World Wide Web. Not all Web browsers and servers support S-HTTP and, in the United States and other countries, there are laws controlling the exportation of encryption that can impact this functionality as well. Another technology for transmitting secure communications over the World Wide Web — Secure Sockets Layer (SSL) — is more prevalent. However, SSL and S-HTTP have very different designs and goals, so it is possible to use the two protocols together. Whereas SSL is designed to establish a secure connection between two computers, S-HTTP is designed to send individual messages securely.

The other main standard that controls how the World Wide Web works is HTML, which covers how Web pages are formatted and displayed.

Good Mail Scenario

Combining everything discussed thus far and a few practical principles involved in networking, one now has the ability to put together a much more secure mail system. This will allow one to authenticate internal and external mail users. The internal requirements will only add one server and a router/filter outside the firewall, and the external requirements will require that there be a publicly available certificate authority (CA) for the world to access.

Now a system has been created that will allow users to segregate internally encrypted messages from externally. Each person will have two public keys to maintain:

- one that resides on the internally installed public key server
- one that resides on the external public key server

The private part of the public key pair will be a privately held key that the user will use to decrypt all incoming messages. Outside the firewall resides a server that will specifically handle all mail and will scan it for viruses and to be sure that all inbound mail is properly encrypted. If it is not, it will forward the message to a separate server that will authenticate the message to a specific user and will then scan and forward it after it has been properly accepted.

Now as we walk through the model of sending a message, no matter who intercepts it, or where it may be copied while in transit, the only place it can be understood will be at the final location of the keys. This method of PGP will not only secure the message, but it will act like a digital certificate in that the user will know limited information about the sender. If a digital signature is added to the model, then the recipient will know the source of the encryption session key. This will include the source of the digital signature and the senders' authentication information sufficiently enough to ensure that they are who they say they are.

There are many other components not discussed above that should be in place; these are outlined in the following steps. For more information, there are many books on router protocol and systems security that can be obtained at the local library.

Mail Sent Securely. The following steps break down the path with which a secure message can be sent (see Exhibit 3-4). This is a recommended method of securing all one's internal and external mail.

1. Before sending or receiving any messages, the author of the message gets a private encryption key from his private network.
2. Then the author places two public keys out on the networks. One is placed on his internal key ring and the second is placed on a public key ring. The purpose of this is to keep his internal mail private and still be able to use public-private key encryption of messages. This will also allow the author to separate mail traffic relevant to its origin.

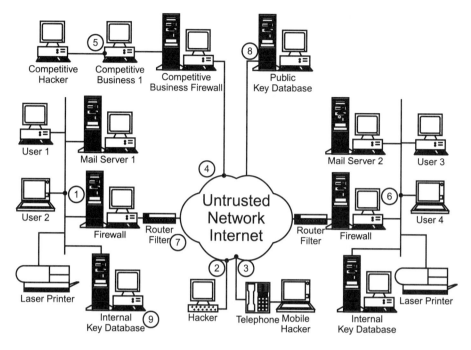

Exhibit 3-4. Secured network.

3. The author of an e-mail message logs on to his personal network and is also authenticated by the mail server via usage of a password to get ready to send electronic mail.

4. They the author composes the message using his personal mail utility that has been preconfigured with the following settings.
   a. all messages will be sent with a digital signature
   b. all messages will have receipt notice automatically sent
   c. private key encryption will be automatically utilized

5. The author signs and sends the document to a secure server. The message is encrypted and digitally signed before it leaves the author's machine.

6. The author's mail server is connected to the network with hardware-level encrypting routers that protect all internal communications. Note that the latency created by hardware-level encryption is nominal enough that most users will not notice a delay in transmission of data which is any different than already occurs.

7. The mail server determines whether the traffic is internal or external and forwards appropriately. This particular message is determined to be outbound and is therefore sent to the firewall and out to the Internet via an automated hardware encryption device.

8. In front of the firewall on the recipient's end is a hardware device that decrypts the traffic at layer three, but leaves it encrypted and signed as it was originally sent. Loss of this level of encryption is noted by the author. However, unless the outside recipient of this message has the proper hardware to decrypt the message, this level of protection will impede the communications and the recipient will not be able to read the message.

9. The message travels over the Internet. At this point, any interception that records the transmission will not assist another party in obtaining the information. To do so, they will have to:
   a. be in the line of traffic at the proper time to intercept the message
   b. have the decryption tools with which the message was encrypted
   c. have a copy or method of recreating the digital certificate if they want to modify the message and retransmit it

10. The message is then received by the recipient's firewall and allowed in based on the addressing of the message.

11. The firewall forwards the message to a mail server that quickly scans the message for viruses (this will slow down mail traffic considerably in a high traffic environment). To determine if this level of security is needed, one must determine the damage a virus or Trojan horse can do to the individual or systems to which the individual is connected.

12. The message is stored on the mail server until the recipient logs on to the network and authenticates himself to that particular server. The mail server is password protected and all data contained there will also be encrypted.

13. The mail recipient goes out to the appropriate public key server (internal for internal users and off the public key for external users) and retrieves the sender's public key before trying to open the sender's message.

14. The mail server then forwards the message to the individual user, who then opens the message after it is decrypted and verifies the signature based matching message digests.

15. Notification of receipt is automatically created and transmitted back to the original author via a reverse process that will include the recipient's signature.

The author recognizes that in a perfect world, the level of encryption that is used would not be breakable by brute force or other type of attack. The certificate and signature that are used cannot be copied or recreated. However, this is not true; it is believed that with 128-bit encryption, with an attached digital signature, the message's information will be secure enough that it will take longer to decrypt than the information would be viable or useful.

This methodology will slow down the communication of all e-mail. The return is the increased security that is placed on the message itself. There are several layers of protection and validation that show that the message is authentic. The sender and the recipient both know who the message is from and to whom it is being sent, and both parties have confirmation of receipt.

If senders are not concerned about protecting the content of their individual messages, then the encryption part could be skipped, thereby speeding up the process of delivery. It is this author's opinion that digital signatures should always be used to authenticate any business-related or personal message to another party.

CONCLUSION

From the beginning of time, people have tried to communicate over long distances — efficiently and effectively. The biggest concern then and today is that the message sent is the message received and that the enemy (e.g., corporate competition) does not intercept a message.

From the time that the first electronic message was sent to today's megabit communications systems, people have been trying to figure out new ways to copy, intercept, or just disrupt that messaging system. The value of getting one's data is proportionately equal to the value that data has if private, and is far greater if in the corporate world.

Our challenge in today's world of computer communications — voice, video, and audio communications — is to protect it: to make sure that when it is transmitted from one specific medium to another it is received in a fashion that the recipient will be able to hear it, read it, or see it. Both the author and the recipient are confident enough that the communications are secure and reliable enough that they do not have to worry about the message not getting to where it should.

Setting up a system of checks and balances to verify transmission, to authenticate users, to authenticate messages and protect them from prying eyes becomes the task at hand for the systems administrator and the security officer. Effective implementation of encryption, digital certificates, and configuration of mail servers placed in the proper areas of a network are all components of making this happen efficiently enough that users will not try to bypass the controls.

The security officer is responsible for the information in the corporation, and becomes a security consultant by default when the architecture of a mail system is to be built. The security officer will be asked how to, when to, and where to implement security, all the while keeping in mind that one must inflict as little impact on the user community as possible. The security officer will be asked to come up with solutions to control access to e-mail and for authentication methods.

To be able to do this, the security officer needs to understand the protocols that drive e-mail, as well as the corporate standards for classification and protecting information and the associated policies. If the policies do not exist, the security officer will need to write them. Then once they are written, one will need to get executive management to accept those polices and enforce them. The security officer will also need to make sure that all employees know and understand those standards and know how to follow them.

Most importantly, whenever something does not feel or look write, question it. Remember that even if something looks as if it is put together perfectly, one should verify it and test it. If everything tests out correctly and the messages are sent in a protected format, with a digital signature of some kind, and there is enough redundancy for high availability and disaster recovery, then all one has left to do is listen to the user community complain about the latency of the system and the complexity of successfully sending messages.

Chapter 4

Integrity and Security of ATM

Steve Blanding

ATM (ASYNCHRONOUS TRANSFER MODE) IS A RAPIDLY GROWING AND QUICKLY MATURING, WIDE AREA NETWORK TECHNOLOGY. Many vendors, public carriers, private corporations, and government agencies are delivering ATM services in their product offerings today. The popularity of ATM has been driven by several industry developments over the past decade, including:

- the growing interest in merging telecommunication and information technology (IT) networking services
- the increasing demand for World Wide Web services

ATM is now considered the wide area network transport protocol of choice for broadband communications because of its ability to handle much larger data volumes when compared to other transport technologies. The demand for increased bandwidth has emerged as a result of the explosive growth of the World Wide Web and the trend toward the convergence of information networking and telecommunications.

The purpose of this chapter is to describe the key integrity and security attributes of ATM. The design and architectural design of ATM provide a basis for its integrity. However, because of its power and flexibility, opportunities for poorly controlled implementation of ATM also exists. The unique characteristics of ATM must be used to design a cost-effective ATM broadband transport network to meet Quality of Service (QoS) requirements under both normal and congested network conditions. The business case for ATM is reviewed first, followed by an analysis of transport service, control, signaling, traffic management, and network restoration.

THE BUSINESS CASE FOR ATM: COMPUTERS AND NETWORKING

There are three possible sectors that might use ATM technology in the computer and networking industry: ATM for the desktop, ATM for LANs, and ATM for WANs. In general, ATM is winning the biggest place as a wide area networking solution, but there are serious challenges from existing and emerging LAN switching products (e.g., Fast Ethernet and Gigabit Ethernet) in the LAN and desktop environments.

The PC Desktop

Because of its cost, ATM is not currently perceived as an attractive option for the desktop environment when compared with existing and emerging technologies. Cost is not the only factor to consider when evaluating the use of ATM for the desktop. For example, most desktop applications today do not include the real-time multimedia for which ATM may be particularly suited. This increases the challenge of how to effectively bring ATM to the desktop. To overcome this challenge, the potential cost savings from eliminating private branch exchanges (PBXs) must be offset by the cost of upgrading every desktop with a new ATM network interface card.

To be competitive, ATM must be more cost affordable than switched Ethernet, which is regarded as the current standard in the industry. The most attractive approach would involve a solution that allows ATM to run over existing Ethernet. This approach would ignore higher-layer Ethernet protocols, reusing only the existing physical media, such as cabling and the Ethernet adapter. By adopting this solution, the need for any hardware upgrades to the desktop would be eliminated, requiring that workstation software be upgraded to include ATM signaling protocol, QoS, and flow control functionality.

LANs and WANs

The use of ATM technology for LANs will not become a widespread reality until application requirements force the traffic demand consistently into the gigabit-per-second range. The integration of voice, data, and video into a physical LAN would require the use of an ATM-type solution to meet the desired performance requirements. Currently, switched Ethernet and Gigabit Ethernet LANs are cost-effective solutions used to support most high traffic-intensive, client/server-based LAN applications.

The growth of high-demand WAN applications has driven the need for ATM as the transport technology solution of choice for wide area networking applications. Existing WAN transport technologies, such as Fiber Distributed Data Interface (FDDI), cannot support new applications that demand a QoS greater than FDDI's capability to deliver. ATM is considered the transport technology of choice although it is more expensive than FDDI and other similar transport solutions.

The recent explosive growth of the World Wide Web has also placed increased demands on higher bandwidth, wide area networks. As the Internet becomes a greater source of video- and multimedia-based applications, the requirement for a more robust underlying transport infrastructure such as ATM becomes increasingly imperative. The design features of ATM and its explicit rate flow control functionality provide a basis to meet the increasing demands of the Internet.

THE BUSINESS CASE FOR ATM: TELECOMMUNICATIONS

The emerging broadband services provide the greatest incentive for the use of ATM in the telecommunications industry. Those services that require megabit-per-second speed bandwidth to meet QoS requirements are referred to as broadband services. These services can be divided into three major classes:

1. enterprise information networking services such as LAN interconnection and LAN emulation
2. video and image distribution services, including video on demand, interactive TV, multimedia applications, cable television, and home shopping services
3. high-speed data services, including frame relay services, switched multimegabit data service, ATM cell relay services, gigabit data service, and circuit emulation services

These emerging services would initially be supported by broadband ATM networks through permanent virtual connections (PVCs), which do not require processing functions, call control, or signaling. Switched virtual connection (SVC) service capabilities could be added as signaling standards are developed during the evolution of the network.

CHARACTERISTICS AND COMPONENTS OF ATM

ATM transmits information through uniform cells in a connection-oriented manner through the use of high-speed, integrated multiplexing and switching technology. This section describes the new characteristics of ATM, as opposed to synchronous transfer mode (STM), which includes bandwidth on demand, separation between path assignment and capacity assignment, higher operations and maintenance bandwidth, and nonhierarchical path and multiplexing structure.

Where ATM has been adopted by the International Telecommunication Union as the core transport technology, both narrowband and emerging broadband services will be supported by a Broadband Integrated Service Digital Network (B-ISDN). The telecommunication network infrastructure will continue to utilize ATM capability as demand for capacity increases. Different virtual channels (VCs) or virtual paths (VPs) with different QoS requirements are used within the same physical network to carry ATM services, control, signaling, and operations and maintenance messages in order to maximize savings in this B-ISDN environment. To accomplish this, the integrated ATM transport model contains one service intelligent layer and two-layered transport networks. A control transport network and a service transport network make up the two-layered transport network. These correspond, respectively, to the control plan and user plan, and are coordinated by plane management and layer management systems.

B-ISDN Transport Network

The B-ISDN signal protocol reference model consists of three layers: physical, ATM, and ATM adaptation layer (AAL). The ATM transport platform is formed by the physical and ATM layers. The physical layer uses SONET standards and the AAL layer is a service-dependent layer. The SONET layer provides protection switching capability to ATM cells (when needed) while carrying the cells in a high-speed and transparent manner. Public network carriers have deployed SONET around the world for the last decade because of its cost-effective network architecture. The ATM layer provides, as its major function, fast multiplexing and routing for data transfer based on the header information. Two sublayers — the virtual path (VP) and virtual channel (VC) — make up the ATM layer. The unidirectional communication capability for the transport of ATM cells is described as the VC. Two types of VC are available: (1) permanent VC, which identifies the end-to-end connection established through provisioning, and (2) switched VC, which identifies the end-to-end connection established via near-real-time call setup.

A set of different VCs having the same source and destination can be accommodated by a VP. While VCs can be managed by users with ATM terminals, VPs are managed by network systems. To illustrate, a leased circuit may be used to connect a customer to another customer location using a VP and also be connected via a switched service using another VP to a central office. Several VCs for WAN and video conferencing traffic may be accommodated by each VP.

Virtual channel identifiers (VCIs) and virtual path identifiers (VPIs) are used to identify VCs and VPs, respectively. VCIs and VPIs are assigned on a per-link basis in large networks. As a result, intermediate ATM switches on an end-to-end VP or VC must be used to provide translation of the VPI or VCI.

Digital signals are provided by a SONET physical link bit stream. Multiple digital paths, such as Synchronous Transport Signal 3c (STS-3c), STS-12c, or STS-48c, may be included in a bit stream. STM using a hierarchical TSI concept is the switching method used for SONET's STS paths. A nonhierarchical ATM switching concept is the switching method used for VPs and VCs. Network rerouting through physical network reconfiguration is performed by STM, and network rerouting using logical network reconfiguration through update of the routing table is performed by ATM.

Physical Path versus Virtual Path

The different characteristics of the corresponding path structures for SONET's STS paths (STM) and ATM VPs/VCs (ATM) result in the use of completely different switching principles. A physical path structure is used for the STS path and a logical path structure is used for the VP/VC path. A hierarchical structure with a fixed capacity for each physical path is characteristic of the physical path concept of the SONET STM system.

To illustrate, VT1.5s, with a capacity of 1.728 Mbps each, are multiplexed to an STS-1 and then to STS-12, and STS-48 with other multiplexed streams for optical transport over fiber. As a result, for each hierarchy of signals, a SONET transport node may equip a variety of switching equipment. The VP transport system is physically nonhierarchical, with a multiplexing structure that provides for a simplified nodal system design. Its capacity can be varied in a range from zero (for protection) up to the line rate, or STS-Nc, depending on the application.

Channel Format

ATM switching is performed on a cell-by-cell basis based on routing information in the cell header. This is in contrast to the time slot channel format used in STM networks. Channels in ATM networks consist of a set of fixed-size cells and are identified through the channel indicator in the cell header.

The major function of the ATM layer is to provide fast multiplexing and routing for data transfer. This is based on information included in the 5-byte header part of the ATM cell. The remainder of the cell consists of a 48-byte payload. Other information contained in the header is used to (1) establish priority for the cell, (2) indicate the type of information contained in the cell payload, (3) facilitate header error control and cell delineation functions, and (4) assist in controlling the flow of traffic at the user-network interface (UNI).

Within the ATM layer, facility bandwidth is allocated as needed because ATM cells are independently labeled and transmitted on demand. This allocation is performed without the fixed hierarchical channel rates required for STM networks. Both constant and variable bit-rate services are supported at a broad range of bit rates because ATM cells are sent either periodically or in bursts (randomly). Call control, bandwidth management, and processing capabilities are not required through the permanent or semipermanent connections at the VP layer. Permanent, semipermanent, and switched connections are supported at the VC layer; however, switched connections do require the signaling system to support its establishment, tear-down, and capacity management.

Adaptation Layer

The function of adapting services onto the ATM layer protocol is performed by the ATM adaptation layer (AAL). The functional requirements of a service are linked by the AAL to the ATM transport, which is characterized as generic and service independent. AAL can be terminated in the network or used by customer premise equipment (CPE) having ATM capability, depending on the service.

There are four basic AAL service models or classes defined by the ATM Forum, a group created by four computer and communications companies in 1991 to supplement the work of the ANSI standards group. These classes — Class A, B, C, and D — are defined based on the distinctions of three parameters: delay, bit rates, and connection modes. Class A identifies connection-oriented services with constant bit rates (CBRs) such as voice service. Within this class, the timing of the bit rates at the source and receiver are related. Connected-oriented services with variable bit rates (VBRs), and related source and receiver timing, are represented by Class B. These services are characterized as real-time, such as VBR video. Class C defines bursty connection-oriented services with variable bit rates that do not require a timing relationship between the source and the receiver. Connection-oriented data services such as file transfer and X.25 are examples of Class C service. Connectionless services similar to Class C are defined as Class D service. Switched multimegabit data service is an example of Class D service.

Available bit rate (ABR) and unspecified bit rate (UBR) are potential new ATM service classes within the AAL. ABR provides variable data rates based on whatever is available through its use of the end-to-end flow control system and is primarily used in LAN and TCP/IP environments. UBR, on the other hand, does not require the specification of a required bit rate, and cells are transported by the network whenever the network bandwidth is available.

Three types of AAL are also identified, which are in current use. These are AAL Type 1, Type 3/4, and Type 5. CBR applications are carried by AAL Type 1, which has an available cell payload of 47 bytes for data. The transparent transport of a synchronous DS1 through the asynchronous ATM network is an example of an application carried by AAL Type 1. Error-free transmission of VBR information is designed to be carried by AAL Type 3/4, which has an available payload of 44 bytes. Connectionless SMDS applications are carried by this AAL type. AAL Type 5, with an available cell payload of 48 bytes for data, is designed for supporting VBR data transfer with minimal overhead. Frame Relay Service and user network signaling messages are transported over ATM using AAL Type 5. Other types of AAL include a null AAL and proprietary AALs for special applications. Null AALs are used to provide the basic capabilities of ATM switching and transport directly.

Comparing STM and ATM

STM and ATM use widely different switching concepts and methods. The major difference is that the path structure for STM is physical and hierarchical, whereas the structure for ATM is logical and nonhierarchical, due to its corresponding path multiplexing structure. With STM, the path capacity hierarchy is much more limited than with ATM. A relatively complex control system is required for ATM because of increased flexibility of bandwidth on demand, bandwidth allocation, and transmission system efficiency over the STM method. Network rerouting with STM may be slower than with ATM because rerouting requires physical switch reconfiguration as STM physically switches the signals.

BROADBAND SIGNALING TRANSPORT NETWORKS

Future broadband signaling needs must be addressed with a new, switched broadband service solution. These requirements demand a signaling network infrastructure that is much faster, more flexible, and more scalable than the older Signaling System #7 (SS7) signaling network solution. These new broadband signaling requirements can best be met through the implementation of an ATM signaling transport infrastructure. This section introduces the role of ATM technology in broadband signaling and potential ATM signaling network architectures.

New signaling requirements must be addressed in the areas of network services, intelligent networks, mobility management, mobility services, broadband services, and multimedia services. Broadband signaling enhancements needed to meet these requirements include: (1) increased signaling link speeds and processing capabilities, (2) increased service functionality, such as version identification, mediation, billing, mobility management, quality-of-service, traffic descriptors, and message flow control, (3) separate call control from connection control, and (4) reduced operational costs for services and signaling.

The Role of ATM in Broadband Signaling

The ATM signaling network has more flexibility in establishing connections and allocating needed bandwidth on demand when compared to the older SS7 signaling network solution. ATM is better suited to accommodate signaling traffic growth and stringent delay requirements due to flexible connection and bandwidth management capabilities. The ATM network is attractive for supporting services with unpredictable or unexpected traffic patterns because of its bandwidth-on-demand feature. The bandwidth allocation for each ATM signaling connection can be 173 cells per second, up to approximately 1.5 Mbps, depending on the service or application being supported. Applications such as new broadband multimedia and Personal Communication Service (PCS) can best be addressed by an ATM signaling solution.

ATM Signaling

The family of protocols used for call and connection setup is referred to as signaling. The set of protocols used for call and connection setup over ATM interfaces is called ATM signaling. The North American and international standards groups have specified two ATM signaling design philosophies. These architectures are designed for public networks and for enterprise networks, which is called Private Network-to-Network Interface or Private Network Node Interface (PNNI). The different natures of public and enterprise networks have resulted in the different signaling network design philosophies between public and enterprise networks. Network size, stability frequency, nodal complexity, and intelligent residence are the major differences between the public networks and enterprise networks. An interoffice network is generally on the order of up to several hundred nodes in public networks. As a result, a cautious, long planning process for node additions and deletions is required. In contrast, frequent node addition and deletion is expected in an enterprise network containing thousands, or tens of thousands, of nodes. Within the public network node, the network transport, control, and management capabilities are much more complex, reliable, and expensive than in the enterprise network. Thus, intelligent capabilities reside in customer premise equipment within enterprise networks, whereas intelligence in the public networks is designed primarily in the network nodes.

Enterprise ATM Signaling Approach. A TCP/IP-like structure and hierarchical routing philosophy form the foundation of enterprise ATM network routing and signaling as specified in the Private Network Node Interface (PNNI) by the ATM Forum. The PNNI protocol allows the ATM enterprise network to be scaled to a large network, contains signaling for SVCs, and includes dynamic routing capabilities. This hierarchical, link-state routing protocol performs two roles: (1) to distribute topology information between switches and clusters of switches used to compute routing paths from the source node through the network and (2) to use the signaling protocol to establish point-to-point and point-to-multi-point connections across the ATM network and to enable dynamic alternative rerouting in the event of a link failure.

The topology distribution function has the ability to automatically configure itself in networks where the address structure reflects the topology using a hierarchical mechanism to ensure network scalability. A connection's requested bandwidth and QoS must be supported by the path, which is based on parameters such as available bit rate, cell loss ratio, cell transfer delay, and maximum cell rate. Because the service transport path is established by signaling path tracing, the routing path for signaling and the routing path for service data are the same under the PNNI routing protocol.

The dynamic alternative rerouting function allows for reestablishment of the connection over a different route without manual intervention if a connection goes down. This signaling protocol is based on user-network interface (UNI) signaling with additional features that support crankback, source routing, and alternate routing of call setup requests when there has been a connection setup failure.

Public ATM Signaling Approach. Public signaling has developed in two major areas: the evolution of the signaling user ports and the evolution of the signaling transport in the broadband environment. Broadband signaling transport architectures and protocols are used within the ATM environment to provide reliable signaling transport while also making efficient use of the ATM broadband capabilities in support of new, vastly expanded signaling capabilities. Benefits of using an ATM transport network to carry the signaling and control messages include simplification of existing signaling transport protocols, shorter control and signaling message delays, and reliability enhancement via the self-healing capability at the VP level. Possible broadband signaling transport architectures include retention of signal transfer points (STPs) and the adoption of a fully distributed signaling transport architecture supporting the associated signaling mode only.

ATM NETWORK TRAFFIC MANAGEMENT

The primary role of network traffic management (NTM) is to protect the network and the end system from congestion in order to achieve network performance objectives while promoting the efficient use of network resources. The power and flexibility of bandwidth management and connection establishment in the ATM network has made it attractive for supporting a variety of services with different QoS requirements under a single transport platform. However, these powerful advantages could become disadvantages in a high-speed ATM network when it becomes congested. Many variables must be managed within an ATM network — bandwidth, burstiness, delay time, and cell loss. In addition, many cells have various traffic characteristics or quality requirements that require calls to compete for the same network resources.

Functions and Objectives

The ATM network traffic management facility consists of two major components: proactive ATM network traffic control and reactive ATM network congestion control. The set of actions taken by the network to avoid congested conditions is ATM network traffic control. The set of actions taken by the network to minimize intensity, spread, and duration of congestion, where these actions are triggered by congestion in one or more network elements, is ATM network congestion control. The objective is to make the ATM network operationally effective. To accomplish this objective, traffic carried on the ATM network must be managed and controlled effectively while taking advantage of ATM's unique characteristics with a minimum of problems for users and the network when the network is under stress. The control of ATM network traffic is fundamentally related to the ability of the network to provide appropriately differentiated QoS for network applications.

Three sets of NTM functions are needed to provide the required QoS to customers:

1. *NTM surveillance functions* are used to gather network usage and traffic performance data to detect overloads as indicated by measures of congestion (MOC).
2. *Measures of congestion (MOC)* are defined at the ATM level based on measures such as cell loss, buffer fill, utilization, and other criteria.
3. *NTM control functions* are used to regulate or reroute traffic flow to improve traffic performance during overloads and failures in the network.

Effective management of ATM network traffic must address how users define their particular traffic characteristics so that a network can recognize and use them to monitor traffic. Other key issues include how the network avoids congestion, how the network reacts to network congestion to minimize effects, and how the network measures traffic to determine if the cell can be accepted or if congestion control should be triggered. The most important issue to be addressed is how quality-of-services is defined at the ATM layer.

The complexity of ATM traffic management design is driven by unique characteristics of ATM networks. These include the high-speed transmission speeds, which limit the available time for message processing at immediate nodes and result in a large number of cells outstanding in the network. Also, the traffic characteristics of various B-ISDN services are not well-understood and the VBR source generates traffic at significantly different rates with very different QoS requirements.

The following sections describe ATM network traffic and congestion control functions. The objectives of these control functions are:

- to obtain the optimum set of ATM layer traffic controls and congestion controls to minimize network and end-system complexity while maximizing network utilization

- to support a set of ATM layer QoS classes sufficient for all planned B-ISDN services
- to not rely on AAL protocols that are B-ISDN service specific, nor on higher-layer protocols that are application specific

ATM Network Traffic Control

The set of actions taken by the network to avoid congested conditions is called network traffic control. This set of actions, performed proactively as network conditions dynamically change, includes connection admission control, usage and network parameter control, traffic shaping, feedback control, and network resource management.

Connection Admission Control. The set of actions taken by the network at the call setup phase to determine whether a virtual channel connection (VCC) or a virtual path connection (VPC) can be accepted is called connection admission control (CAC). Acceptance of a connection request is only made when sufficient resources are available to establish the connection through the entire network at its required QoS. The agreed QoS of existing connections must also be maintained. CAC also applies during a call renegotiation of the connection parameters of an existing call. The information derived from the traffic contract is used by the CAC to determine the traffic parameters needed by usage parameter control (UPC), routing and allocation of network resources, and whether the connection can be accepted.

Negotiation of the traffic characteristics of the ATM connections can be made using the network at its connection establishment phase. Renegotiation of these characteristics may be made during the lifetime of the connection at the request of the user.

Usage/Network Parameter Control. The set of actions taken by the network to monitor and control traffic is defined as usage parameter control (UPC) and network parameter control (NPC). These actions are performed at the user-network interface (UNI) and the network-network interface (NNI), respectively. UPC and NPC detect violations of negotiated parameters and take appropriate action to maintain the QoS of already established connections. These violations can be characterized as either intentional or unintentional acts.

The functions performed by UPC/NPC at the connection level include connection release. In addition, UPC/NPC functions can also be performed at the cell level. These functions include cell passing, cell rescheduling, cell tagging, and cell discarding. Cell rescheduling occurs when traffic shaping and UPC are combined. Cell tagging takes place when a violation is detected. Cell passing and cell rescheduling are performed on cells that are identified by UPC/NPC as conforming. If UPC identifies the cell as nonconforming to at least one element of the traffic contract, then cell tagging and cell discarding are performed.

The UPC/NPC function uses algorithms to carry out its actions. The algorithms are designed to ensure that user traffic complies with the agreed parameters on a real-time basis. To accomplish this, the algorithms must have the capability of detecting any illegal traffic situation, must have selectivity over the range of checked parameters, must exhibit rapid response time to parameter violations, and must possess simplicity for implementation. The algorithm design must also consider the accuracy of the UPC/NPC. UPC/NPC should be capable of enforcing a PCR at least 1 percent larger than the PCR used for the cell conformance evaluation for peak cell rate control.

Traffic Shaping. The mechanism that alters the traffic characteristics of a stream of cells on a VCC or a VPC is called traffic shaping. This function occurs at the source ATM endpoint. Cell sequence integrity on an ATM connection must be maintained through traffic shaping. Burst length limiting and peak cell rate reduction are examples of traffic shaping. Traffic shaping can be used in conjunction with suitable UPC functions as an option. The acceptable QoS negotiated at call setup must be attained, however, with the additional delay caused by the traffic shaping function. Customer equipment or terminals can also use traffic shaping to ensure that the traffic generated by the source or at the UNI is conforming to the traffic contract.

For typical applications, cells are generated at the peak rate during the active period and not at all during the silent period. At the time of connection, the amount of bandwidth reserved is between the average rate and the peak rate. Cells must be buffered before they enter the network so that the departure rate is less than the peak arrival rate of cells. This is the purpose of traffic shaping. Delay-sensitive services or applications, such as signaling, would not be appropriate for the use of traffic shaping.

As indicated previously, traffic can be reshaped at the entrance of the network. At this point, resources would be allocated in order to respect both the CDV and the fixed nodal processing delay allocated to the network. Two other options for traffic shaping are also available. One option is to dimension the network to accommodate the input CDV and provide for traffic shaping at the output. The other option is to dimension the network both to accommodate the input CDV and comply with the output CDV without any traffic shaping.

Feedback Control. The set of actions taken by the network and by users to regulate the traffic submitted to ATM connections according to the state of network elements is known as feedback control. The coordination of available network resource and user traffic volume for the purpose of avoiding network congestion is the responsibility of the feedback control mechanism.

Network Resource Management. Resource management is defined as the process of allocating network resources to separate traffic flows according to service characteristics. Network resource management is heavily dependent on the role of VPCs. One objective of using VPCs is to reduce the requirement of establishing individual VCCs by reserving capacity. By making simple connection admission decisions at nodes where VPCs are terminated, individual VPCs can be established. The trade-off between increased capacity costs and reduced control costs determines the strategies for reservation of capacity on VPCs. The performances of the consecutive VPCs used by a VCC and how it is handled in virtual channel connection-related functions determine the peer-to-peer network performance on a given VCC.

The basic control feature for implementation of advanced applications, such as ATM protection switching and bandwidth on demand, is VP bandwidth control. There are two major advantages of VP bandwidth control: (1) reduction of the required VP bandwidth, and (2) bandwidth granularity. The bandwidth of a VP can be precisely tailored to meet the demand with no restriction due to path hierarchy. Much higher utilization of the link capacity can be achieved when compared with digital, physical-path bandwidth control in STM networks.

ATM Network Congestion Control

The state of network elements and components (e.g., hubs, switches, routers, etc.) where the network cannot meet the negotiated network performance objectives for the established connections is called network congestion. The set of actions taken by the ATM network to minimize the intensity, spread, and duration of congestion is defined as ATM network congestion control. Network congestion does not include instances where buffer overflow causes cell losses but still meets the negotiated QoS.

Network congestion is caused by unpredictable statistical fluctuations of traffic flows under normal conditions or just simply having the network come under fault conditions. Both software faults and hardware failures can result in fault conditions. The unattended rerouting of network traffic, resulting in the exhaustion of some particular subset of network resources, is typically caused by software faults. Network restoration procedures are used to overcome or correct hardware failures. These procedures can include restoration or shifting of network resources from unaffected traffic areas or connections within an ATM network. Congestion measurement and congestion control mechanisms are the two major areas that make up the ATM network congestion control system.

Measure of Congestion. Performance parameters, such as percentage of cells discarded (cell loss ratio) or the percentage of ATM modules in the ATM NT that are congested, are used to define measures of congestion of an ATM network element (NE). ATM switching fabric, intraswitching links, and modules associated with interfaces are ATM modules within an ATM NE. ATM module measures of congestion include buffer occupancy, utilization, and cell loss ratio.

Buffer occupancy is defined as the number of cells in the buffer at a sampling time, divided by the cell capacity of the buffer. Utilization is defined as the number of cells actually transmitted during the sample interval, divided by the cell capacity of the module during the sampling interval. The cell loss ratio is defined as the number of cells dropped during the sampling interval, divided by the number of cells received during the sampling interval.

Congestion Control Functions. Recovery from network congestion occurs through the implementation of two processes. In the first method, low-priority cells are selectively discarded during the congestion. This method allows for the network to still meet network performance objectives for aggregate and high-priority flows. In the second method, an explicit forward congestion indication (EFCI) threshold is used to notify end users to lower their access rates. In other words, an EFCI is used as a congestion notification mechanism to assist the network in avoiding and recovering from a congested state.

Traffic control indication can also be performed by EFCI. When a network element begins to reach an impending state of congestion, an EFCI value may be set in the cell header for examination by the destination customer premise equipment (CPE). A state in which the network is operating around its maximum capacity level is defined as an impending congested state. Controls can be programmed into the CPE that would implement protocols to lower the cell rate of the connection during congestion or impending congestion.

Currently, three types of congestion control mechanisms can be used in ATM networks. These mechanisms include link-by-link credit-based congestion control, end-to-end rate-based congestion control, and priority control and selective cell discard. These congestion control methods can be used collectively within an ATM network; the most popular method is to use the priority control and selective discard method in conjunction with either the rate-based congestion control or credit-based congestion control.

The mechanism based on credits allocated to the node is called credit-based congestion control. This is performed on a link-by-link basis requiring that each virtual channel (VC) have a credit before a data cell can be sent. As a result, credits are consistently sent to the upstream node to maintain a continuous flow of data when cells are transmitted on a VC.

The other congestion control mechanism that utilizes an approach that is adaptive to network load conditions is called rate-based congestion control. This control mechanism adjusts the access rate based on end-to-end or segmented network status information. The ATM node notifies the traffic sources to adjust their rates based on feedback received from the network. The traffic source slows the rate at which it transmits data to the network upon receiving a congestion notification.

The simplest congestion control mechanism is the priority control and selective cell discard mechanism. Users can generate different priority traffic flows by using the cell loss priority (CLP), bit, allowing a congested network element to selectively discard cells with low priority. This mechanism allows for maximum protection of network performance for high-priority cells. For example, assume CLP=0 is assigned for low-priority flow, CLP=1 is assigned for high-priority flow, and CLP=0+1 is assigned for multiplexed flow. Network elements may selectively discard cells of the CLP=1 flow and still meet network performance objectives on both the CLP=0 and CLP=0+1 flow. The Cell Loss Ratio objective for CLP=0 cells should be greater than or equal to the CLR objective for the CLP=1 flow for any specified ATM connection.

ATM Network Restoration Controls

Network restoration is one of greatest area of control concerns in an ATM network. Loss of high-speed, high-capacity ATM broadband services due to disasters or catastrophic failures would be devastating to customers dependent on those services. While this area is one of most significant areas that must be addressed, providing protection against broadband network failures could be very expensive due to the high costs associated with transport equipment and the requirement for advanced control capability. An extremely important challenge in today's emerging ATM network environment is providing for an acceptable level of survivability while maintaining reasonable network operating costs. Growing technological advancements will have a major impact on the challenges of maintaining this critical balance.

Currently, there are three types of network protection and restoration schemes that can be utilized to minimize the effects of broadband ATM services when a network failure occurs. These control mechanisms include protection switching, rerouting, and self-healing. The term "network restoration" refers to the rerouting of new and existing connections around the failure area when a network failure occurs.

Protection Switching. The establishment of a preassigned replacement connection using equipment but without a network management control function is called protection switching. ATM protection switching systems can use one of two different design approaches: one based on fault

97

management and the other based on signaling capability. The design of the fault management system is independent of the routing design for the working system. The signaling capability design uses the existing routing capability to implement the protection switching function. This design can minimize development costs but may only be applicable to some particular networks using the same signaling messaging system.

Rerouting. The establishment of a replacement connection by the network management control connection is defined as rerouting. The replacement connection is routed depending on network resources available at the time the connection failure occurs. An example of rerouting is the centralized control DCS network restoration. Network protection mechanisms developed for automatic protection switching or for self-healing can also be used for network rerouting. As a result, network rerouting is generally considered as either centralized control automatic protection switching or as self-healing.

Self-healing. The establishment of a replacement connection by a network without utilizing a network management control function is called self-healing. In the self-healing technique, the replacement connection is found by the network elements (NE) and rerouted depending on network resources available at the time a connection failure occurs.

SUMMARY

This chapter has reviewed the major integrity and security areas associated with ATM transport network technology. These areas — transport service, control, and signaling, traffic management, and network restoration — form the foundation required for building and maintaining a well-controlled ATM network. The design and infrastructure of ATM must be able to support a large-scale, high-speed, high-capacity network while providing an appropriae multi-grade QoS requirement. The cost of ATM must also be balanced with performance and recoverability, which is a significant challenge to ATM network designers. Continuing technological changes and increasing demands for higher speeds and bandwidth will introduce new challenges for maintaining integrity and security of the ATM network environment.

Chapter 5
An Introduction to Secure Remote Access

Christina M. Bird

IN THE LAST DECADE, THE PROBLEM OF ESTABLISHING AND CONTROLLING REMOTE ACCESS TO CORPORATE NETWORKS HAS BECOME ONE OF THE MOST DIFFICULT ISSUES FACING NETWORK ADMINISTRATORS AND INFORMATION SECURITY PROFESSIONALS. As information-based businesses become a larger and larger fraction of the global economy, the nature of "business" itself changes. "Work" used to take place in a well-defined location — such as a factory, an office, or a store — at well-defined times, between relatively organized hierarchies of employees. But now, "work" happens everywhere: all over the world, around the clock, between employees, consultants, vendors, and customer representatives. An employee can be productive working with a personal computer and a modem in his living room, without an assembly line, a filing cabinet, or a manager in sight.

The Internet's broad acceptance as a communications tool in business and personal life has introduced the concept of remote access to a new group of computer users. They expect the speed and simplicity of Internet access to translate to their work environment as well. Traveling employees want their private network connectivity to work as seamlessly from their hotel room as if they were in their home office. This increases the demand for reliable and efficient corporate remote access systems, often within organizations for whom networking is tangential at best to the core business.

The explosion of computer users within a private network — now encompassing not only corporate employees in the office, but also telecommuters, consultants, business partners, and clients — makes the design and implementation of secure remote access even tougher. In the simplest local area networks (LANs), all users have unrestricted access to all resources on the network. Sometimes, granular access control is provided at the host computer level, by restricting log-in privileges. But in most real-world environments, access to different kinds of data — such as accounting, human resources, or research & development — must be restricted to limited groups of people. These restrictions may be provided by physically isolating resources on the network or through logical mechanisms (including router access control lists and stricter firewall technologies). Physical isolation, in particular, offers considerable protection to network resources, and sometimes develops without the result of a deliberate network security strategy.

Connections to remote employees, consultants, branch offices, and business partner networks make communications between and within a company extremely efficient; but they expose corporate networks and sensitive data to a wide, potentially untrusted population of users, and a new level of vulnerability. Allowing non-employees to use confidential information creates stringent requirements for data classification and access control. Managing a network infrastructure to enforce a corporate security policy for non-employees is a new challenge for most network administrators and security managers. Security policy must be tailored to facilitate the organization's reasonable business requirements for remote access. At the same time, policies and procedures help minimize the chances that improved connectivity will translate into compromise of data confidentiality, integrity, and availability on the corporate network.

Similarly, branch offices and customer support groups also demand cost-effective, robust, and secure network connections.

This chapter discusses general design goals for a corporate remote access architecture, common remote access implementations, and the use of the Internet to provide secure remote access through the use of virtual private networks (VPNs).

SECURITY GOALS FOR REMOTE ACCESS

All remote access systems are designed to establish connectivity to privately maintained computer resources, subject to appropriate security policies, for legitimate users and sites located away from the main corporate campus. Many such systems exist, each with its own set of strengths and weaknesses. However, in a network environment in which the protection of confidentiality, data integrity, and availability is paramount, a secure remote access system possesses the following features:

- reliable authentication of users and systems
- easy to manage, granular control of access to particular computer systems, files, and other network resources
- protection of confidential data
- logging and auditing of system utilization

- transparent reproduction of the workplace environment
- connectivity to a maximum number of remote users and locations
- minimal costs for equipment, network connectivity, and support

Reliable Authentication of Remote Users/Hosts

It seems obvious, but it is worth emphasizing that the main difference between computer users in the office and remote users is that remote users are not there. Even in a small organization, with minimal security requirements, many informal authentication processes take place throughout the day. Co-workers recognize each other, and have an understanding about who is supposed to be using particular systems throughout the office. Similarly, they may provide a rudimentary access control mechanism, if they pay attention to who is going in and out of the company's server room.

In corporations with higher security requirements, the physical presence of an employee or a computer provides many opportunities — technological and otherwise — for identification, authentication, and access control mechanisms to be employed throughout the campus. These include security guards, photographic employee ID cards, keyless entry to secured areas, among many other tools.

When users are not physically present, the problem of accurate identification and authentication becomes paramount. The identity of network users is the basis for assignment of all system access privileges that will be granted over a remote connection. When the network user is a traveling salesman 1500 miles away from corporate headquarters, accessing internal price lists and databases — a branch office housing a company's research and development organization — or a business partner with potential competitive interest in the company, reliable verification of identity allows a security administrator to grant access on a need-to-know basis within the network. If an attacker can present a seemingly legitimate identity, then that attacker can gain all of the access privileges that go along with it.

A secure remote access system supports a variety of strong authentication mechanisms for human users, and digital certificates to verify identities of machines and gateways for branch offices and business partners.

Granular Access Control

A good remote access system provides flexible control over the network systems and resources that may be accessed by an off-site user. Administrators must have fine-grain control to grant access for all appropriate business purposes while denying access for everything else. This allows management of a variety of access policies based on trust relationships with different types of users (employees, third-party contractors, etc.). The access control system must be flexible enough to support the organization's security requirements and easily modified when policies or personnel change. The remote access system should scale gracefully and enable the company to implement more complex policies as access requirements evolve.

Access control systems can be composed of a variety of mechanisms, including network-based access control lists, static routes, and host system- and application-based access filters. Administrative interfaces can support templates and user groups, machines, and networks to help manage multiple access policies. These controls can be provided, to varying degrees, by firewalls, routers, remote access servers, and authentication servers. They can be deployed at the perimeter of a network as well as internally, if security policy so demands.

The introduction of the remote access system should not be disruptive to the security infrastructure already in place in the corporate network. If an organization has already implemented user- or directory-based security controls (e.g., based on Novell's Netware Directory Service or Windows NT domains), a remote access system that integrates with those controls will leverage the company's investment and experience.

Protection of Confidential Data

Remote access systems that use public or semi-private network infrastructure (including the Internet and the public telephone network) provide lots of opportunities for private data to fall into unexpected hands. The Internet is the most widely known public network, but it is hardly the only one. Even private Frame Relay connections and remote dial-up subscription services (offered by many telecommunications providers) transport data from a variety of locations and organizations on the same physical circuits. Frame Relay sniffers are commodity network devices allowing network administrators to examine traffic over private virtual circuits, and allow a surprising amount of eavesdropping between purportedly secure connections. Reports of packet leaks on these systems are relatively common on security mailing lists like *BUGTRAQ* and *Firewall-Wizards*.

Threats that are commonly acknowledged on the Internet also apply to other large networks and network services. Thus, even on nominally private remote access systems — modem banks and telephone lines, cable modem connections, Frame Relay circuits — security-conscious managers will use equipment that performs strong encryption and per-packet authentication.

Logging and Auditing of System Utilization

Strong authentication, encryption, and access control are important mechanisms for the protection of corporate data. But sooner or later, every network experiences accidental or deliberate disruptions, from system failures (either hardware or software), human error, or attack. Keeping detailed logs of system utilization helps to troubleshoot system failures.

If troubleshooting demonstrates that a network problem was deliberately caused, audit information is critical for tracking down the perpetrator. One's corporate security policy is only as good as one's ability to associate users with individual actions on the remote access system — if one cannot tell who did what, then one cannot tell who is breaking the rules.

Unfortunately, most remote access equipment performs rudimentary logging, at best. In most cases, call level auditing — storing username, start time, and duration of call — is recorded, but there is little information available about what the remote user is actually *doing*. If the corporate environment requires more stringent audit trails, one will probably have to design custom audit systems.

Transparent Reproduction of the Workplace Environment

For telecommuters and road warriors, remote access should provide the same level of connectivity and functionality that they would enjoy if they were physically in their office. Branch offices should have the same access to corporate headquarters networks as the central campus. If the internal network is freely accessible to employees at work, then remote employees will expect the same degree of access. If the internal network is subject to physical or logical security constraints, then the remote access system should enable those constraints to be enforced. If full functionality is not available to remote systems, priority must be given to the most business-critical resources and applications, or people will not use it.

Providing transparent connectivity can be more challenging than it sounds. Even within a small organization, personal work habits differ widely from employee to employee, and predicting how those differences might affect use of remote access is problematic. For example, consider access to data files stored on a UNIX file server. Employees with UNIX workstations use the Network File Service (NFS) protocol to access those files. NFS requires its own particular set of network connections, server configurations, and security settings in order to function properly. Employees with Windows-based workstations probably use the Server Message Bus (SMB) protocol to access the same files. SMB requires its own set of configuration files and security tuning. If the corporate remote access system fails to transport NFS and SMB traffic as expected, or does not handle them at all, remote employees will be forced to change their day-to-day work processes.

Connectivity to Remote Users and Locations

A robust and cost-effective remote access system supports connections over a variety of mechanisms, including telephone lines, persistent private network connections, dial-on-demand network connections, and the Internet. This allows the remote access architecture to maintain its usefulness as network infrastructure evolves, whether or not all connectivity mechanisms are being used at any given time.

Support for multiple styles of connectivity builds a framework for access into the corporate network from a variety of locations: hotels, homes, branch offices, business partners, and client sites, domestic or international. This flexibility also simplifies the task of adding redundancy and performance tuning capabilities to the system.

The majority of currently deployed remote access systems, at least for employee and client-to-server remote connectivity, utilize TCP/IP as their network protocol. A smaller fraction continues to require support for IPX, NetBIOS/NetBEUI, and other LAN protocols; even fewer support SNA, DEC-Net, and older services. TCP/IP offers the advantage of support within most modern computer operating systems; most corporate applications either use TCP/IP as their network protocol, or allow their traffic to be encapsulated over TCP/IP networks. This chapter concentrates on TCP/IP-based remote access and its particular set of security concerns.

Minimize Costs

A good remote access solution will minimize the costs of hardware, network utilization, and support personnel. Note, of course, that the determination of appropriate expenditures for remote access, reasonable return on investment, and appropriate personnel budgets differs from organization to organization, and depends on factors including sensitivity to loss of resources, corporate expertise in network and security design, and possible regulatory issues depending on industry.

In any remote access implementation, the single highest contribution to overall cost is incurred through payments for persistent circuits, be they telephone capacity, private network connections, or access to the Internet. Business requirements will dictate the required combination of circuit types, typically based on the expected locations of remote users, the number of LAN-to-LAN connections required, and expectations for throughput and simultaneous connections. One-time charges for equipment, software, and installation are rarely primary differentiators between remote access architectures, especially in a high-security environment. However, to fairly judge between remote access options, as well as to plan for future growth, consider the following components in any cost estimates:

- one-time hardware and software costs
- installation charges
- maintenance and upgrade costs
- network and telephone circuits
- personnel required for installation and day-to-day administration

Not all remote access architectures will meet an organization's business requirements with a minimum of money and effort, so planning in the initial stages is critical.

At the time of this writing, Internet access for individuals is relatively inexpensive, especially compared to the cost of long-distance telephone charges. As long as home Internet access cost is based on a monthly flat fee rather than per-use calculations, use of the Internet to provide individual remote access, especially for traveling employees, will remain economically compelling. Depending on an organization's overall Internet strategy, replacing private network connections between branch offices and headquarters with secured Internet connections may result in savings of one third to one half over the course of a couple of years. This huge drop in cost for remote access is often the primary motivation for the evaluation of secure virtual private networks as a corporate remote access infrastructure. But note that if an organization does not already have technical staff experienced in the deployment of Internet networks and security systems, the perceived savings in terms of ongoing circuit costs can easily be lost in the attempt to hire and train administrative personnel.

It is the security architect's responsibility to evaluate remote access infrastructures in light of these requirements. Remote access equipment and service providers will provide information on the performance of their equipment, expected administrative and maintenance requirements, and pricing. Review pricing on telephone and network connectivity regularly; the telecommunications market changes rapidly and access costs are extremely sensitive to a variety of factors, including geography, volume of voice/data communications, and the likelihood of corporate mergers.

A good remote access system is scalable, cost-effective, and easy to support. Scalability issues include increasing capacity on the remote access servers (the gateways into the private network), through hardware and software enhancements; increasing network bandwidth (data or telephone lines) into the private network; and maintaining staff to support the infrastructure and the remote users. If the system will be used to provide mission-critical connectivity, then it needs to be designed with reliable, measurable throughput and redundancy from the earliest stages of deployment. Backup methods of remote access will be required from *every* location at which mission-critical connections will originate.

Remember that not every remote access system necessarily possesses (or requires) each of these attributes. Within any given corporate environment, security decisions are based on preexisting policies, perceived threat, potential losses, and regulatory requirements — and remote access decisions, like all else, will be specific to a particular organization and its networking requirements. An organization supporting a team of 30 to 40 traveling sales staff, with a relatively constant employee population, has minimal requirements for flexibility and scalability — especially since the remote users are all trusted employees and only one security policy applies. A large organization with multiple locations, five or six business partners, and a sizable population of consultants probably requires different levels of remote access. Employee turnover and changing business conditions also demand increased manageability from the remote access servers, which will probably need to enforce multiple security policies and access control requirements simultaneously.

REMOTE ACCESS MECHANISMS

Remote access architectures fall into three general categories: (1) remote user access via analog modems and the public telephone network; (2) access via dedicated network connections, persistent or on-demand; and (3) access via public network infrastructures such as the Internet.

Telephones. Telephones and analog modems have been providing remote access to computer resources for the last two decades. A user, typically at home or in a hotel room, connects her computer to a standard telephone outlet, and establishes a point-to-point connection to a network access server (NAS) at the corporate location. The NAS is responsible for performing user authentication, access control, and accounting, as well as maintaining connectivity while the phone connection is live. This model benefits from low end-user cost (phone charges are typically very low for local calls, and usually covered by the employer for long-distance tolls) and familiarity. Modems are generally easy to use, at least in locations with pervasive access to phone lines. Modem-based connectivity is more limiting if remote access is required from business locations, which may not be willing to allow essentially unrestricted outbound access from their facilities.

But disadvantages are plentiful. Not all telephone systems are created equal. In areas with older phone networks, electrical interference or loss of signal may prevent the remote computer from establishing a reliable connection to the NAS. Even after a connection is established, some network applications (particularly time-sensitive services such as multimedia packages and applications that are sensitive to network latency) may fail if the rate of data throughput is low. These issues are nearly impossible to resolve or control from corporate headquarters.

Modem technology changes rapidly, requiring frequent and potentially expensive maintenance of equipment. And network access servers are popular targets for hostile action because they provide a single point of entrance to the private network — a gateway that is frequently poorly protected.

Dedicated Network Connections. Branch office connectivity — network connections for remote corporate locations — and business partner connections are frequently met using dedicated private network circuits. Dedicated network connections are offered by most of the major telecommunications providers. They are generally deemed to be the safest way of connecting multiple locations because the only network traffic they carry "belongs" to the same organization.

Private network connections fall into two categories: dedicated circuits and Frame Relay circuits. Dedicated circuits are the most private, as they provide an isolated physical circuit for their subscribers (hence, the name). The only data on a dedicated link belongs to the subscribing organization. An attacker can subvert a dedicated circuit infrastructure only by attacking the telecommunications provider itself. This offers substantial protection. But remember that telco attacks are the oldest in the hacker lexicon — most mechanisms that facilitate access to voice lines work on data circuits as well because the physical infrastructure is the same. For high-security environments, such as financial institutions, strong authentication and encryption are required even over private network connections.

Frame Relay connections provide private bandwidth over a shared physical infrastructure by encapsulating traffic in frames. The frame header contains addressing information to get the traffic to its destination reliably. But the use of shared physical circuitry reduces the security of Frame Relay connections relative to dedicated circuits. Packet leak between frame circuits is well-documented, and devices that eavesdrop on Frame Relay circuits are expensive but readily available. To mitigate these risks, many vendors provide Frame Relay-specific hardware that encrypts packet payload, protecting it against leaks and sniffing, but leaving the frame headers alone.

The security of private network connections comes at a price, of course — subscription rates for private connections are typically two to five times higher than connections to the Internet, although discounts for high volume use can be significant. Deployment in isolated areas is challenging if telecommunications providers fail to provide the required equipment in those areas.

Internet-based Remote Access. The most cost-effective way to provide access into a corporate network is to take advantage of shared network infrastructure whenever feasible. The Internet provides ubiquitous, easy-to-use, inexpensive connectivity. However, important network reliability and security issues must be addressed.

Internet-based remote user connectivity and wide area networks are much less expensive than in-house modem banks and dedicated network circuits, both in terms of direct charges and in equipment maintenance and ongoing support. Most importantly, ISPs manage modems and dial-in servers, reducing the support load and upgrade costs on the corporate network/telecommunications group.

Of course, securing private network communications over the Internet is a paramount consideration. Most TCP/IP protocols are designed to carry data in cleartext, making communications vulnerable to eavesdropping attacks. Lack of IP authentication mechanisms facilitates session hijacking and unauthorized data modification (while data is in transit). A corporate presence on the Internet may open private computer resources to denial-of-service attacks, thereby reducing system availability. Ongoing development of next-generation Internet protocols, especially IPSec, will address many of these issues. IPSec adds per-packet authentication, payload verification, and encryption mechanisms to traditional IP. Until it becomes broadly implemented, private security systems must explicitly protect sensitive traffic against these attacks.

Internet connectivity may be significantly less reliable than dedicated network links. Troubleshooting Internet problems can be frustrating, especially if an organization has typically managed its wide area network connections in-house. The lack of any centralized authority on the Internet means that resolving service issues, including packet loss, higher than expected latency, and loss of packet exchange between backbone Internet providers, can be time-consuming. Recognizing this concern, many of the national Internet service providers are beginning to offer "business class" Internet connectivity, which provides service level agreements and improved monitoring tools (at a greater cost) for business-critical connections.

Given mechanisms to ensure some minimum level of connectivity and throughput, depending on business requirements, VPN technology can be used to improve the security of Internet-based remote access. For the purposes of this discussion, a VPN is a group of two or more privately owned and managed computer systems that communicates "securely" over a public network (see Exhibit 5-1).

Security features differ from implementation to implementation, but most security experts agree that VPNs include encryption of data, strong authentication of remote users and hosts, and mechanisms for hiding or masking information about the private network topology from potential attackers on the public network. Data in transmission is encrypted between the remote node and the corporate server, preserving data confidentiality and integrity. Digital signatures verify that data has not been modified. Remote users and hosts are subject to strong authentication and authorization mechanisms, including one-time password generators and digital certificates. These help to guarantee that only appropriate personnel can access and modify corporate data. VPNs can prevent private network addresses from being propagated over the public network, thus hiding potential target machines from attackers attempting to disrupt service.

In most cases, VPN technology is deployed over the Internet (see Exhibit 5-2), but there are other situations in which VPNs can greatly

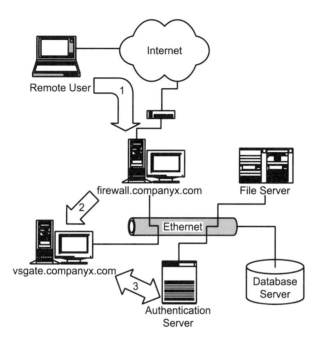

Exhibit 5-1. Remote user VPN.

enhance the security of remote access. An organization may have employees working at a business partner location or a client site, with a dedicated private network circuit back to the home campus. The organization may choose to employ a VPN application to connect its own employees back into their home network — protecting sensitive data from potential eavesdropping on the business partner network. In general, whenever a connection is built between a private network and an entity over which the organization has no administrative or managerial control, VPN technology provides valuable protection against data compromise and loss of system integrity.

When properly implemented, VPNs provide granular access control, accountability, predictability, and robustness at least equal to that provided by modem-based access or Frame Relay circuits. In many cases, because network security has been a consideration throughout the design of VPN products, they provide a higher level of control, auditing capability, and flexibility than any other remote access technology.

VIRTUAL PRIVATE NETWORKS

The term "virtual private network" is used to mean many different things. Many different products are marketed as VPNs, but offer widely varying functionality. In the most general sense, a VPN allows remote sites

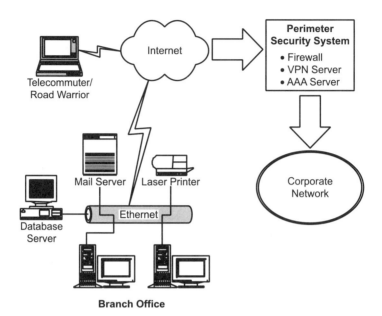

Exhibit 5-2. Intranet WAN over VPN.

to communicate as if their networks were directly connected. VPNs also enable multiple independent networks to operate over a common infrastructure. The VPN is implemented as part of the system's networking. That is, ordinary programs like Web servers and e-mail clients see no difference between connections across a physical network and connections across a VPN.

VPN technologies fall into a variety of categories, each designed to address distinct sets of concerns. VPNs designed for secure remote access implement cryptographic technology to ensure the confidentiality, authenticity, and integrity of traffic carried on the VPN. These are sometimes referred to as secure VPNs or crypto VPNs. In this context, private suggests confidentiality, and has specific security implications: namely, that the data will be encoded so as to be unreadable, and unmodified, by unauthorized parties.

Some VPN products are aimed at network service providers. These service providers — including AT&T, UUNET, and MCI/Sprint, to name only a few — built and maintain large telecommunications networks, using infrastructure technologies like Frame Relay and ATM. The telecom providers manage large IP networks based on this private infrastructure. For them, the ability to manage multiple IP networks using a single infrastructure might be called a VPN. Some network equipment vendors offer products for this purpose and call them VPNs.

When a network service provider offers this kind of service to an enterprise customer, it is marketed as equivalent to a private, leased-line network in terms of security and performance. The fact that it is implemented over an ATM or Frame Relay infrastructure does not matter to the customer, and is rarely made apparent. These so-called VPN products are designed for maintenance of telecom infrastructure, not for encapsulating private traffic over public networks like the Internet, and are therefore addressing a different problem. In this context, the private aspect of a VPN refers only to network routing and traffic management. It does not imply the use of security mechanisms such as encryption or strong authentication.

Adding further confusion to the plethora of definitions, many telecommunications providers offer subscription dial-up services to corporate customers. These services are billed as "private network access" to the enterprise computer network. They are less expensive for the organization to manage and maintain than in-house access servers because the telecom provider owns the telephone circuits and network access equipment.

But let the buyer beware. Although the providers tout the security and privacy of the subscription services, the technological mechanisms provided to help guarantee privacy are often minimal. The private network points-of-presence in metropolitan areas that provide local telephone access to the corporate network are typically co-located with the provider's Internet access equipment, sometimes running over the same physical infrastructure. Thus, the security risks are often equivalent to using a bare-bones Internet connection for corporate access, often without much ability for customers to monitor security configurations and network utilization. Two years ago, the services did not encrypt private traffic. After much criticism, service providers are beginning to deploy cryptographic equipment to remedy this weakness.

Prospective customers are well-advised to question providers on the security and accounting within their service. The security considerations that apply to applications and hardware employed within an organization apply to network service providers as well, and are often far more difficult to evaluate. Only someone familiar with a company's security environment and expectations can determine whether or not they are supported by a particular service provider's capabilities.

SELECTING A REMOTE ACCESS SYSTEM

For organizations with small, relatively stable groups of remote users (whether employees or branch offices), the cost benefits of VPN deployment are probably minimal relative to the traditional remote access methods. However, for dynamic user populations, complex security policies, and expanding business partnerships, VPN technology can simplify management and reduce expenses:

- VPNs enable traveling employees to access the corporate network over the Internet. By using remote sites' existing Internet connections where available, and by dialing into a local ISP for individual access, expensive long-distance charges can be avoided.
- VPNs allow employees working at customer sites, business partners, hotels, and other untrusted locations to access a corporate network safely over dedicated, private connections.
- VPNs allow an organization to provide customer support to clients using the Internet, while minimizing risks to the client's computer networks.

For complex security environments, requiring the simultaneous support of multiple levels of access to corporate servers, VPNs are ideal. Most VPN systems interoperate with a variety of perimeter security devices, such as firewalls. VPNs can utilize many different central authentication and auditing servers, simplifying management of the remote user population. Authentication, authorization, and accounting (AAA) servers can also provide granular assignment of access to internal systems. Of course, all this flexibility requires careful design and testing — but the benefits of the initial learning curve and implementation effort are enormous.

Despite the flexibility and cost advantages of using VPNs, they may not be appropriate in some situations; for example:

1. VPNs reduce costs by leveraging existing Internet connections. If remote users, branch offices, or business partners lack adequate access to the Internet, then this advantage is lost.
2. If the required applications rely on non-IP traffic, such as SNA or IPX, then the VPNs are more complex. Either the VPN clients and servers must support the non-IP protocols, or IP gateways (translation devices) must be included in the design. The cost and complexity of maintaining gateways in one's network must be weighed against alternatives like dedicated Frame Relay circuits, which can support a variety of non-IP communications.
3. In some industries and within some organizations, the use of the Internet for transmission of private data is forbidden. For example, the federal Health Care Finance Administration does not allow the Internet to be used for transmission of patient identifiable Medicare data (at the time of this writing). However, even within a private network, highly sensitive data in transmission may be best protected through the use of cryptographic VPN technology, especially bulk encryption of data and strong authentication/digital certificates.

REMOTE ACCESS POLICY

A formal security policy sets the goals and ground rules for all of the technical, financial, and logistical decisions involved in solving the remote access problem (and in the day-to-day management of all IT resources).

Computer security policies generally form only a subset of an organization's overall security framework; other areas include employee identification mechanisms, access to sensitive corporate locations and resources, hiring and termination procedures, etc.

Few information security managers or auditors believe that their organizations have well-documented policy. Configurations, resources, and executive philosophy change so regularly that maintaining up-to-date documentation can be prohibitive. But the most effective security policies define expectations for the use of computing resources within the company, and for the behavior of users, operations staff, and managers on those computer systems. They are built on the consensus of system administrators, executives, and legal and regulatory authorities within the organization. Most importantly, they have clear management support and are enforced fairly and evenly throughout the employee population.

Although the anatomy of a security policy varies from company to company, it typically includes several components.

- A concisely stated *purpose* defines the security issue under discussion and introduces the rest of the document.
- The *scope* states the intended audience for the policy, as well as the chain of oversight and authority for enforcement.
- The *introduction* provides background information for the policy, and its cultural, technical, and economic motivators.
- *Usage expectations* include the responsibilities and privileges with regard to the resource under discussion. This section should include an explicit statement of the corporate ownership of the resource.
- The final component covers *system auditing and violation of policy*: an explicit statement of an employee's right to privacy on corporate systems, appropriate use of ongoing system monitoring, and disciplinary action should a violation be detected.

Within the context of remote access, the scope needs to address which employees qualify for remote access to the corporate network. It may be tempting to give access to everyone who is a "trusted" user of the local network. However, need ought to be justified on a case-by-case basis, to help minimize the risk of inappropriate access.

A sample remote access policy is included in Exhibit 5-3.

Another important issue related to security policy and enforcement is ongoing, end-user education. Remote users require specific training, dealing with the appropriate use of remote connectivity; awareness of computer security risks in homes, hotels, and customer locations, especially related to unauthorized use and disclosure of confidential information; and the consequences of security breaches within the remote access system.

Exhibit 5-3. Sample remote access policy.

Purpose of Policy: To define expectations for use of the corporate remote access server (including access via the modem bank and access via the Internet); to establish policies for accounting and auditing of remote access use; and to determine the chain of responsibility for misuse of the remote access privilege.

Intended Audience: This document is provided as a guideline to all employees requesting access to corporate network computing resources from non-corporate locations.

Introduction: Company X provides access to its corporate computing environment for telecommuters and traveling employees. This remote connectivity provides convenient access into the business network and facilitates long-distance work. But it also introduces risk to corporate systems: risk of inappropriate access, unauthorized data modification, and loss of confidentiality if security is compromised. For this reason, Company X provides the following standards for use of the remote access system.

All use of the Company X remote access system implies knowledge of and compliance with this policy.

Requirements for Remote Access: An employee requesting remote access to the Company X computer network must complete the *Remote Access Agreement*, available on the internal Web server or from the Human Resources group. The form includes the following information: employee's name and log-in ID; job title, organizational unit, and direct manager; justification for the remote access; and a copy of remote user responsibilities. After completing the form, and acknowledging acceptance of the usage policy, the employee must obtain the manager's signature and send the form to the Help Desk.

NO access will be granted unless all fields are complete.

The Human Resources group will be responsible for annually reviewing ongoing remote access for employees. This review verifies that the person is still employed by Company X and that their role still qualifies them for use of the remote access system. Human Resources is also responsible for informing the IT/Operations group of employee terminations within one working day of the effective date of termination.

IT/Operations is responsible for maintaining the modem-based and Internet-based remote access systems; maintaining the user authentication and authorization servers; and auditing use of the remote access system (recording start and end times of access and user IDs for chargeback accounting to the appropriate organizational units).

Remote access users are held ultimately responsible for the use of their system accounts. The user must protect the integrity of Company X resources by safeguarding modem telephone numbers, log-in processes and startup scripts; by maintaining their strong authentication tokens in their own possession at all times; and by NOT connecting their remote computers to other private networks at the same time that the Company X connection is active. [This provision does not include private networks maintained solely by the employee within their own home, so long as the home network does not contain independent connections to the Internet or other private (corporate) environments.] Use of another employee's authentication token, or loan of a personal token to another individual, is strictly forbidden.

Exhibit 5-3. Sample remote access policy. (continued)

Unspecified actions that may compromise the security of Company X computer resources are also forbidden. IT/Operations will maintain ongoing network monitoring to verify that the remote access system is being used appropriately. Any employee who suspects that the remote access system is being misused is required to report the misuse to the Help Desk immediately.

Violation of this policy will result in disciplinary action, up to and including termination of employment or criminal prosecution.

Chapter 6
Packet Sniffers and Network Monitors
James S. Tiller
Bryan D. Fish

COMMUNICATIONS TAKE PLACE IN FORMS THAT RANGE FROM SIMPLE VOICE CONVERSATIONS TO COMPLICATED MANIPULATIONS OF LIGHT. Each type of communication is based on two basic principles: wave theory and particle theory. In essence, communication can be established by the use of either, frequently in concert with a carrier or medium to provide transmission. An example is the human voice. The result of wave communications using the air as the signal-carrying medium is that two people can talk to each other. However, the atmosphere is a common medium, and anyone close enough to receive the same waves can intercept and surreptitiously listen to the discussion. For computer communications, the process is exponentially more complicated; the medium and type may change several times as the data is moved from one point to another. Nevertheless, computer communications are vulnerable in the same way that a conversation can be overheard. As communications are established, several vulnerabilities in the accessibility of the communication will exist in some form or another. The ability to intercept communications is governed by the type of communication and the medium that is employed. Given the proper time, resources, and environmental conditions, any communication — regardless of the type or medium employed — can be intercepted.

In the realm of computer communications, sniffers and network monitors are two tools that function by intercepting data for processing. Operated by a legitimate administrator, a network monitor can be extremely helpful in analyzing network activities. By analyzing various properties of the intercepted communications, an administrator can collect information used to diagnose or detect network performance issues. Such a tool can be used to isolate router problems, poorly configured network devices, system errors, and general network activity to assist in the determination of network design. In dark contrast, a sniffer can be a powerful tool to enable an attacker to obtain information from network communications. Passwords, e-mail, documents, procedures for performing functions, and application information are only a few examples of the information obtainable with a sniffer. The unauthorized use of a network sniffer, analyzer, or monitor represents a fundamental risk to the security of information.

This is an article in two parts. Part one introduces the concepts of data interception in the computer-networking environment. It provides a foundation for understanding and identifying those properties that make communications susceptible to interception. Part two addresses a means for evaluating the severity of such vulnerabilities. It goes on to discuss the process of communications interception with real-world examples. Primarily, this article addresses the incredible security implications and threats that surround the issues of data interception. Finally, it presents techniques for mitigating the risks associated with the various vulnerabilities of communications.

FUNCTIONAL ASPECTS OF SNIFFERS

Network monitors and sniffers are equivalent in nature, and the terms are used interchangeably. In many circles, however, a network monitor is a device or system that collects statistics about the network. Although the content of the communication is available for interpretation, it is typically ignored in lieu of various measurements and statistics. These metrics are used to scrutinize the fundamental health of the network.

On the other hand, a sniffer is a system or device that collects data from various forms of communications with the simple goal of obtaining the data and traffic patterns, which can be used for dark purposes. To alleviate any interpretation issues, the term *sniffer* best fits the overall goal of explaining the security aspects of data interception.

The essence of a sniffer is quite simple; the variations of sniffers and their capabilities are determined by the network topology, media type, and access point. Sniffers simply collect data that is made available to them. If placed in the correct area of a network, they can collect very sensitive types of data. Their ability to collect data can vary depending on the topology and the complexity of the implementation, and is ultimately governed by the communications medium.

For computer communications, a sniffer can exist on a crucial point of the network, such as a gateway, allowing it to collect information from several areas that use the gateway. Alternatively, a sniffer can be placed on a single system to collect specific information relative to that system only.

Topologies, Media, and Location

There are several forms of network topologies, and each can use different media for physical communication.

Asynchronous Transfer Mode (ATM), Ethernet, Token Ring, and X.25 are examples of common network topologies that are used to control the transmission of data. Each uses some form of data unit packaging that is referred to as a frame or cell, and represents a manageable portion of the communication.

Coax, fiber, twisted-pair wire, and microwave are a few examples of computer communications media that can provide the foundation for the specific topology to transmit data units.

The location of a sniffer is a defining factor in the amount and type of information collected. The importance of location is relative to the topology and media being used. The topology defines the logical organization of systems on a network and how data is negotiated between them. The medium being utilized can assist in determining the environment simply based on its location. A basic example of this logical deduction is a simple Ethernet network spread across multiple floors in a building with a connection to the Internet. Ethernet is the topology at each floor and typically uses CAT5 cabling. Fiber cables can be used to connect each floor, possibly using FDDI as the topology. Finally, the connections to the Internet typically consists of a serial connection using a V.35 cable. Using this deduction, it is safe to say that a sniffer with serial capabilities (logically and physically) placed at the Internet router can collect every packet to and from the Internet. It is also feasible to collect all the data between the floors if access to the FDDI network is obtained.

It is necessary to understand the relationship of the topology to the location and the environment, which can be affected by the medium. The medium being used is relevant in various circumstances, but this is inherently related to the location. Exhibit 6-1 explains in graphical format the relationship between the location of the sniffer, the topology, and the medium being used.

There are three buckets on the left of a scale at varying distances from the axis point, or moment. Bucket A, the furthest from the axis, represents the weight that the sniffer's *location* carries in the success of the attack and the complexity of implementing a sniffer into the environment. Bucket A, therefore, provides greater leverage in the calculation of success relative to the difficulty of integration. Nearly equally important is the **topology,** represented by bucket B. Closer to the axis point, where the leverage is the least, is the **medium** represented by bucket C. Bucket C clearly has less impact on the calculation than the other two buckets.

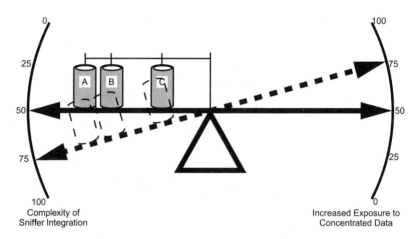

Exhibit 6-1. Location, topology, media, and their relationship to the complexity of the sniffer-based attack and the information collected.

Adding weight to a bucket is analogous to changing the value of the characteristic it represents. As the difficulty of the location, topology, or medium increases, more weight is added to the bucket. For example, medium bucket C may be empty if CAT5 is the available medium. The commonality of CAT5 and the ease of interacting with it without detection represents a level of simplicity. However, if a serial cable is intersected, the odds of detection are high and the availability of the medium in a large environment is limited; therefore, the bucket may be full. As the sophistication of each area is amplified, more weight is added to the corresponding bucket, increasing the complexity of the attack but enhancing the effectiveness of the assault.

This example attempts to convey the relationship between these key variables and the information collected by a sniffer. With further study, it is possible to move the buckets around on the bar to vary the impact each has on the scale.

How Sniffers Work

As one would imagine, there are virtually unlimited forms of sniffers, as each one must work in a different way to collect information from the target medium. For example, a sniffer designed for Ethernet would be nearly useless in collecting data from microwave towers.

However, the volume of security risks and vulnerabilities with common communications seems to focus on standard network topologies. Typically, Ethernet is the target topology for Local Area Networks (LANs) and serial is the target topology for Wide Area Networks (WANs).

Ethernet Networks. The most common among typical networks are Ethernet topologies, and IEEE 802.3, both of which are based on the same principle of Carrier-Sensing Multiple Access with Collision Detection (CSMA/CD) technology. Of the forms of communication in use today, Ethernet is one of the most susceptible to security breaches by the use of a sniffer. This is true for two primary reasons: installation base and communication type.

CSMA/CD is analogous to a conference call with several participants. Each person has the opportunity to speak if no one else is talking and if the participant has something to say. In the event two or more people on the conference call start talking at the same time, there is a short time during which everyone is silent, waiting to see whether to continue. Once the pause is over and someone starts talking without interruption, everyone on the call can hear the speaker. To complete the analogy, the speaker is addressing only one individual in the group, and that individual is identified by name at the beginning of the sentence.

Computers operating in an Ethernet environment interact in very much the same way. When a system needs to transmit data, it waits for an opportunity when no other system is transmitting. In the event two systems inject data onto the network at the same time, the electrical signals collide on the wire. This collision forces both systems to wait for an undetermined amount of time before retransmitting. The segment in which a group of systems participates is sometimes referred to as a collision domain, because all of the systems on the segment see the collisions. Also, just as the telephone was a common medium for the conference call participants, the physical network is a shared medium. Therefore, any system on a shared network segment is privy to all of the communications on that particular segment.

As data traverses a network, all of the devices on the network can see the data and act on certain properties of that data to provide communication services. A sniffer can reside at key locations on that network and inspect the details of that same data stream.

Ethernet is based on a Media Access Control (MAC) address, typically 48 bits assigned to the Network Interface Card (NIC). This address uniquely identifies a particular Ethernet interface. Every Ethernet data frame contains the destination station's MAC address. As data is sent across the network, it is seen by every station on that segment. When a station receives a frame, it checks to see whether the destination MAC address of that frame is its own. As detailed in Exhibit 6-2, if the destination MAC address defined in the frame is that of the system, the data is absorbed and processed. If not, the frame is ignored and dropped.

Promiscuous Mode. A typical sniffer operates in promiscuous mode. Promiscuous mode is a state in which the NIC accepts all frames, regardless of the destination MAC address of the frame. This is further detailed by Exhibit 6-3. The ability to support promiscuous mode is a prerequisite for

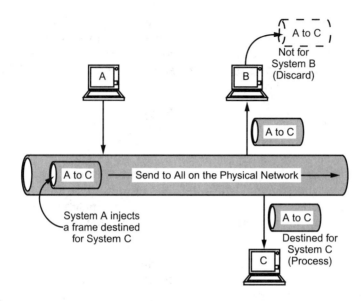

Exhibit 6-2. Standard Ethernet operations.

a NIC to be used as a sniffer, as this allows it to capture and retain all of the frames that traverse the network.

For software-based sniffers, the installed NIC must support promiscuous mode to capture all of the data on the segment. If a software-based sniffer is installed and the NIC does not support promiscuous mode, the

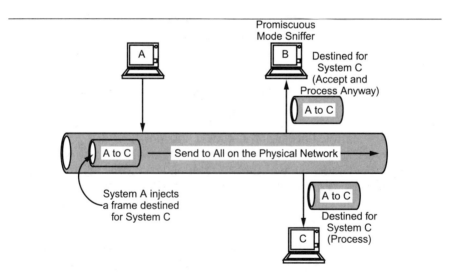

Exhibit 6-3. Promiscuous operations.

sniffer will collect only information sent directly to the system on which it is installed. This happens because the system's NIC only retains frames with its own MAC address.

For hardware-based sniffers — dedicated equipment whose sole purpose is to collect all data — the installed NIC must support promiscuous mode to be effective. The implementation of a hardware-based sniffer without the ability to operate in promiscuous mode would be nearly useless in-as-much as the device does not participate in normal network communications.

There is an aspect of Ethernet that addresses the situation in which a system does not know the destination MAC address, or needs to communicate with all the systems of the network. A broadcast occurs when a system simply injects a frame that every other system will process. An interesting aspect of broadcasts is that a sniffer can operate in nonpromiscuous mode and still receive broadcasts from other segments. Although this information is typically not sensitive, an attacker can use the information to learn additional information about the network.

Wide Area Networks. Wide area network communications typify the relationship between topology, transmission medium, and location as compared with the level of access. In a typical Ethernet environment, nearly any network jack in the corner of a room can provide adequate access to the network for the sniffer to do its job. However, in some infrastructures, location can be a crucial factor in determining the effectiveness of a sniffer.

For WAN communications the topology is much simpler. As a focal point device, such as a router, processes data, the information is placed into a new frame and forwarded to a corresponding endpoint. Because all traffic is multiplexed into a single data stream, the location of the device can provide amazing access to network activities. Exhibit 6-4 illustrates a common implementation of WAN connectivity. However, the location is sensitive and not easily accessed without authorization.

One way the sniffer can gain access to the data stream is through a probe. A probe is an optional feature on some Channel Service Unit/Data Service Unit (CSU/DSU) devices; it is a device that provides connectivity between the Customer Premise Equipment (CPE), such as a router, and the demarcation point of the serial line. As illustrated in Exhibit 6-5, a probe is implemented to capture all the frames that traverse the CSU/DSU.

Another way that the sniffer can gain access to the data stream is through a "Y" cable. A "Y" cable is connected between the CSU/DSU and the CPE. This is the most common location for a "Y" cable because of the complicated characteristics of the actual connection to the service provider's network, or local loop. Between the CSU/DSU and the CPE, a "Y" cable functions just like a normal cable. The third connector on the "Y"

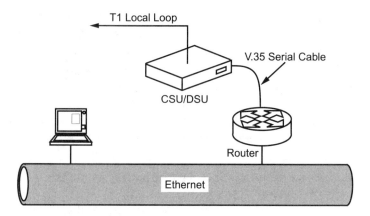

Exhibit 6-4. Common WAN connection.

cable is free and can be attached to a sniffer. Once a "Y" cable is installed, each frame is electrically copied to the sniffer where it is absorbed and processed without disturbing the original data stream (see Exhibit 6-6). Unlike a probe, the sniffer installed with a "Y" cable must be configured for the topology being used. Serial communication can be provided by several framing formats, including Point-to-Point Protocol (PPP), High-Level Data Link Control (HDLC), and frame relay encapsulation. Once the sniffer is configured for the framing format of the topology — much as an Ethernet sniffer is configured for Ethernet frames — it can collect data from the communication stream.

Other Communication Formats. Microwave communications are typically associated with line-of-sight implementations. Each endpoint has a

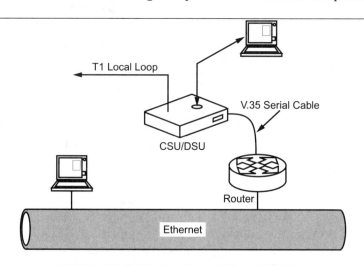

Exhibit 6-5. Sniffer probe used in a CSU/DSU.

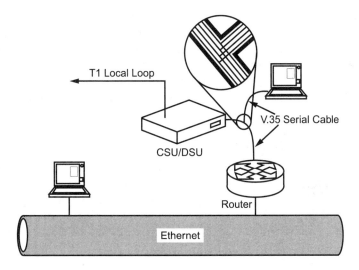

T1 Local Loop

V.35 Serial Cable

CSU/DSU

Router

Ethernet

Exhibit 6-6. "Y" cable installation.

clear, unobstructed focal path to the other. Microwave is a powerful carrier that can be precisely focused to reduce unauthorized interaction. However, as shown in Exhibit 6-7, the microwaves can wash around the receiving dish, or simply pass through the dish itself. In either event, a sniffer can be placed behind one of the endpoint microwave dishes to receive some of the signal. In some cases, all the of the signal is available but weak, but it can be amplified prior to processing.

Wireless communications devices, such as cellular phones or wireless home telephones, are extremely susceptible to interception. These devices must transmit their signal through the air to a receiving station. Even though the location of the receiving station is fixed, the wireless device itself is mobile. Thus, signal transmission cannot rely on a line of sight,

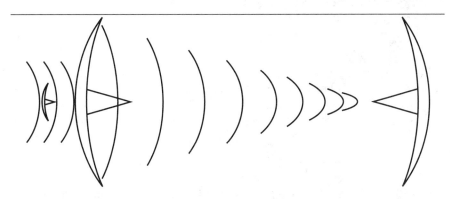

Exhibit 6-7. Microwave interception.

because a direct signal such as this would have to traverse a variety of paths during the course of a transmission. So, to enable wireless devices to communicate with the receiving station, they must broadcast their signal across a wide enough space to ensure that the device on the other end will receive some of the signal. Because the signal travels across such a wide area, an eavesdropper would have little trouble placing a device in a location that would receive the signal.

SECURITY CONSIDERATIONS

Communication interception by unauthorized individuals represents the core concern for many aspects of information security. For information to remain private, the participants must be confident that the data is not being shared with others. However, this simple concept of communication protection is nearly impossible. All communications — especially those that utilize shared network links — have to be assumed to have a vulnerability to unauthorized interception and dissemination.

The availability of software-based sniffers is astounding. Combine the availability of free software with the fact that most modern NICs support promiscuous mode operations, and data interception becomes an expected occurrence rather than a novelty. Anyone with a PC, a connection to a network, and some basic, freely available software can wreak havoc on the security infrastructure.

The use of a sniffer as an attack tool is quite common, and the efforts of the attacker can be extremely fruitful. Even with limited access to remote networks that may receive only basic traffic and broadcasts, information about the infrastructure can be obtained to determine the next phase of the attack.

From an attacker's perspective, a sniffer serves one essential purpose: to eavesdrop on electronic conversations and gain access to information that would not otherwise be available. The attacker can use this electronic eavesdropper for a variety of attacks.

CIA

As elements of what is probably the most recognized acronym in the security industry, confidentiality, integrity, and availability (CIA) constitute the foundation of information security. Each one of these categories represents a vast collection of related information security concepts and practices.

Confidentiality corresponds to such concepts as privacy through the application of encryption in communications technology. Confidentiality typically involves ensuring that only authorized people have access to information. Integrity encompasses several aspects of data security that are to ensure that information has not had unauthorized modifications. The main objective of integrity is ensuring that data remains in the condition that was intended by the owner. In communications, the goal of integrity is to ensure that the data received has not been altered. The goal of availability is to ensure that information remains accessible to authorized users. Availability services do not attempt to distinguish between authorized and unauthorized users, but rely on other services to make that distinction. Availability services are designed to simply provide for the accessibility of the mechanisms and communication channels used to access information.

CIA embodies the core information security concepts that can be used to discuss the effectiveness of a sniffer. Sniffers can be used to attack these critical information properties directly, or to attack the mechanisms employed to guarantee these properties. An example of these mechanisms is authentication. Authentication is the process of verifying the identity of a user or resource so that a level of trust or access can be granted. Authentication also deals with verifying the source of a piece of information to establish the validity of that information. Authentication includes several processes and technologies to ultimately determine privileged access. Given the type of information exchange inherent in authentication, it has become a focal point for sniffer attacks. If an attacker obtains a password for a valid user name, other security controls may be rendered useless. This is also true for confidentiality and the application of encryption. If an attacker obtains the key being used to protect the data, it would be trivial to decrypt the data and obtain the information within.

Sniffer attacks expose any weakness in security technology and the application of that technology. As information is collected, various levels of vulnerabilities are exposed and acted upon to advance the attack. The goal of an attack may vary, but all of the core components of the security infrastructure must be functioning to reduce the risks.

This is highlighted by the interrelationship between the facets of CIA and the observation that, as one aspect fails, it may assist the attack in other areas. The goal of an attack may be attained if poor password protection is exploited or weak passwords are used that lead to the exposure of an encryption key. That key may have been used during a previous session that was collected by the sniffer. In that decrypted data may be instructions for a critical process that the attacker wishes to affect. The attacker can then utilize portions of data collected to reproduce the information, encrypt it, and retransmit it in a manner that produces the desired results.

Without adequate security, an attacker armed with a sniffer is limited only by his imagination. As security is added, the options available to the attacker are reduced but not eliminated. As more and more security is applied, the ingenuity and patience of the attacker is tested but not broken.

The only real protection from a sniffer attack is not allowing one on the network.

Attack Methodologies

In various scenarios, a sniffer can be a formidable form of attack. If placed in the right location, a sniffer can be used to obtain proprietary information, or it can be used to gain information helpful in formulating a greater attack. In either case, information on a network can be used against the systems of that network.

There are many caveats regarding the level of success a sniffer can enjoy in a particular environment. Location is an obvious example. If the sniffer is placed in an area that is not privy to secret information, only limited data will be collected. Clearly, location and environment can have an impact on the type and amount of useful information captured. Therefore, attackers focus on specific concentrated areas of network activity in highly segmented networks.

Risks to Confidentiality. Confidentiality addresses issues of appropriate information disclosure. For information to remain confidential, systems and processes must ensure that unauthorized individuals are unable to access private information. The confidentiality implications introduced by a sniffer are clear. By surreptitiously absorbing conversations buried in network traffic, the attacker can obtain unauthorized information without employing conventional tactics. This contradicts the very definition of confidentiality.

Information security revolves around data and the protection of that data. Much of the information being shared, stored, or processed over computer networks is considered private by many of its owners. Confidentiality is fundamental to the majority of practicing information security professionals.

Encryption has been the obvious enabler for private exchanges, and its use dates back to Roman communications. Interestingly enough, computer communications are just now starting to implement encryption for confidentiality in communication domains that have traditionally been the most susceptible to sniffer attacks. Internal network communications, such as those within a LAN and WAN, do not utilize robust protection suites to ensure that data is not being shared with unauthorized individuals within the company. Terminal access emulation to a centralized AS/400 system is a prime example. Many companies have hundreds of employees accessing private data on centralized systems at banks, hospitals, insurance companies, financial firms, and government agencies. If the communication were to encroach onto an untrusted network, such as the Internet, encryption and data authentication techniques would not be questioned. Recently, the protection that has been normally afforded to external means of communication is being adopted for internal use be cause of the substantial risks that sniffers embody.

A properly placed sniffer would be privy to volumes of data, some of which may be open to direct interpretation. Internet services are commonly associated with the protection of basic private communications. However, at any point at which data is relayed from one system to another, its exposure must be questioned.

Ironically, the implementation of encryption can hinder the ultimate privacy. In a scenrio in which poor communication encryption techniques are in use, the communication participants become overly trusting of the confidentiality of those communications. In reality, however, an attacker has leveraged a vulnerability in that weak encryption mechanism and is collecting raw data from the network. This example conveys the importance of properly implemented confidentiality protection suites. Confidentiality must be supported by tested and verified communication techniques that have considered an attack from many directions. This results in standards, guidelines, and best practices for establishing a trusted session with a remote system such that the data is afforded confidentiality. IPSec, PGP, SSL, SSH, ISAKMP, PKI, S/MIME are only a few of the technologies that exist to ensure confidentiality on some level — either directly or by collateral effect. A sniffer can be employed to inspect every aspect of a communication setup, processing, and completion, allowing attackers to operate on the collected data at their own leisure offline. This aspect of an offline attack on confidentiality requires intensely robust communication standards to establish an encrypted session. If the standard or implementation is weak or harbors vulnerabilities, an attacker will defeat it.

Vulnerable Authentication Processes. Authentication deals with verification of the identity of a user, resource, or source of information and is a critical component of protecting the confidentiality, integrity, and availability of information. When one entity agrees to interact with another in electronic communications, there is an implicit trust that both parties will operate within the bounds of acceptable behavior. That trust is based on the fact that each entity believes that the other entity is, in fact, who it claims to be. Authentication mechanisms provide systems and users on a communication network with a reliable means for validating electronic claims of identity. Secure communications will not take place without proper authentication on the front end.

Trust is powerful in computer networking. If a user is trusted to perform a certain operation or process, she will be granted access to the system resources necessary to perform that function. Similarly, if a person is trusted in a communication session, the recipient of that person's messages will most likely believe what is being said. Trust, then, must be heavily guarded, and should not be granted without stringent proof of identity. Authentication mechanisms exist to provide that proof of identity.

Because authentication mechanisms govern trust, they are ripe targets for attack. If an attacker can defeat an authentication mechanism, he can virtually assume the identity of a trusted individual and immediately gain access to all of the resources and functions available to that individual. Even if the attacker gains access to a restricted user-level account, this is a huge first step that will likely lead to further penetration.

Sniffers provide an attacker with a means to defeat authentication mechanisms. The most straightforward example is a password sniffer. If authentication is based on a shared secret such as a password, then a candidate that demonstrates knowledge of that password will be authenticated and granted access to the system. This does a good job of guarding trust — until that shared secret is compromised. If an attacker learns the secret, he can present himself to the system for authentication and provide the correct password when prompted. This will earn him the trust of the system and access to the information resources inside.

Password sniffing is an obvious activity that can have an instant impact on security. Unless robust security measures are taken, passwords can be easily collected from a network. Most passwords are hashed or encrypted to protect them from sniffer-based attacks, but some services that are still heavily relied on do not protect the password. File Transfer Protocol (FTP), Telnet, and Hyper-Text Transfer Protocol (HTTP) are good examples of protocols that treat private information, such as usernames and passwords, as standard information and transmit them in the clear. This presents a significant threat to authentication processes on the network.

Communication Integrity. Integrity addresses inappropriate changes to the state of information. For the integrity of information to remain intact, systems and processes must ensure that an unauthorized individual cannot surreptitiously alter or delete that information. The implications of a sniffer on information integrity are not as clear-cut as those for confidentiality or authentication.

Sniffers are passive devices. However, by definition, an action is required to compromise the integrity of information. Sniffers and the information they procure are not always inherently valuable. The actions taken based on that information provide the real value either to an attacker or to an administrator. Sniffers, for example, can be used as part of a coordinated attack to capture and manipulate information and resubmit it, hence compromising its integrity. It is the sniffer's ability to capture the information in these coordinated attacks that allows the integrity of information to be attacked.

Session initiation provides an example. Essential information, such as protocol handshakes, format agreement, and authentication data, must be exchanged among the participants in order to establish the communication session. Although the attack is complicated, an attacker could use a sniffer to capture the initialization process, modify it, and use it later to falsify authentication. If the attacker is able to resend the personalized setup information to the original destination, the destination may believe that this is a legitimate session initialization request and allow the session to be established. In the event the captured data was from a privileged user, the copied credentials used for the attack could provide extensive access.

As with communications integrity, the threat of the sniffer from an availability standpoint is not direct. Because sniffers are passive devices, they typically do not insert even a single bit into the communication stream. Given this nature, a sniffer is poorly equipped to mount any form of denial of service (DoS) attack, the common name for attacks on resource availability. However, the sniffer can be used to provide important information to a would-be DoS attacker, such as addresses of key hosts and network services or the presence server software versions known to be vulnerable to DoS attacks. The attacker can use this information to mount a successful DoS attack against the resource, compromising its availability.

While the primary target of a sniffer attack will not be the availability of information resources, the results of the attack can provide information useful in subsequent attacks on resource availability.

Growth Over Time. Information collected by the attacker may not be valuable in and of itself. Rather, that information can be used in a learning process, enabling the attacker to gain access to the information or systems that are the ultimate targets.

An attacker can use a sniffer to learn useful pieces of information about the network, such as addresses of interesting devices, services and applications running on the various systems, and types of system activity. Each of these examples and many others can be combined into a mass of information that allows the attacker to form a more complete picture of the target environment and that ultimately assists in finding other vulnerabilities. Even in a well-secured environment, the introduction of a sniffer can amount to death by a thousand cuts. Information gathering can be quite dangerous, as seemingly innocuous bits of data are collected over time. The skilled attacker can use these bits of data to mount an effective attack against the network.

Attack Types

There are several types of sniffer attacks. These attacks are distinguishable by the network they target. The following sections describe the various types of attacks.

LAN Based. As discussed throughout this chapter, LAN-based attacks represent the most common and easiest to perform attacks, and can reveal an amazing amount of private information. The proliferation of LAN sniffer attacks has produced several unique tools that can be employed by an attacker to obtain very specific data that pertains to the target environment. As a result of the commonality of Ethernet, tools were quickly developed to provide information about the status of the network. As people became aware of their simplicity and availability and the relative inability to detect their presence, these tools became a desired form of attack.

There are nearly infinite ways to implement a sniffer on a LAN. The level and value of the data collected is directly related to the location of the sniffer, network infrastructure, and other system vulnerabilities. As an example, it is certainly feasible that the attacker can learn a password to gain access to network systems from sniffing on a remote segment. Some network devices are configured by HTTP access, which does not directly support the protection of private information. As an administrator accesses the device, the attacker can easily obtain the necessary information to modify the configuration at a later time to allow greater access in the future.

Given the availability of sniffing tools, the properties of Ethernet, and the amount of unprotected ports in an office, what may appear to be a dormant system could actually be collecting vital information. One common method of LAN-based sniffer attack is the use of an inconspicuous, seemingly harmless system. A laptop can easily fit under a desk, on a bookshelf, in a box, or in the open; anywhere that network access can be obtained is a valid location. An attacker can install the laptop after hours and collect it the next evening. The batteries may be exhausted by the next evening, but the target time is early morning when everyone is logging in and performing a great deal of session establishment. The attacker is likely to obtain many passwords and other useful fragments of information during this time.

Another aspect of LAN attacks is that the system performing the collection does not have to participate as a member of the network. To further explain, if a network is running TCP/IP as the protocol, the sniffer system does not need an IP addresses. As a matter of fact, it is highly desirable by the attacker not to obtain an IP address or interact with other network systems. Since the sniffer is interested only in Layer 2 activities (i.e., frames, cells, or the actual packages defined by the topology) any interaction with the Layer 3, or protocol layer, could alert systems and administrators to the existence of an unauthorized system. Clearly, the fact that sniffers can operate autonomously increases the respect for the security implications of such a device.

WAN-Based. Unlike a sniffer on a LAN, WAN-based attacks can collect information as it is sent from one remote network to another. A common

WAN topology is Frame Relay (FR) encapsulation. The ability of an attacker to access an FR cloud or group of configured circuits is limited, but the amount of information gained through such access is large.

There are three basic methods for obtaining data from a WAN, each growing in complexity but capable of collecting large amounts of private data. The first is access to the serial link between the router and the CSU/DSU, which was detailed earlier. Second, access to the carrier system would provide access not only to the target WAN but could conceivably allow the collection of data from other networks as well. This scenario is directly related to the security posture of the chosen carrier. It can be generally assumed that access to the carrier's system is limited and properly authenticated; however, it is not unheard of to find otherwise. The final form of access is to gather information from the digital line providing the Layer 1 connectivity. This can be accomplished, for example, with a fiber tap. The ability to access the provider's line is highly complicated and requires specialized tools in the proper location. This type of attack represents a typically accepted vulnerability, as the complexity of the attack reduces the risk associated with the threat. That is, if an attacker has the capability to intercept communications at this level, other means of access are more than likely available to the attacker.

Gateway Based. A gateway is a computer or device that provides access to other networks. It can be a simple router providing access to another local network, a firewall providing access to the Internet, or a switch providing Virtual Local Area Network (VLAN) segmentation to several networks. Nevertheless, a gateway is a focal point for network-to-network communications.

Installing a sniffer on a gateway allows the attacker to obtain information relative to internetworking activities, and in today's networked environments, many services are accessed on remote networks. By collecting data routed through a gateway, an attacker will obtain a great deal of data, with a high probability of finding valuable information within that data.

For example, Internet access is common and considered a necessity for doing business. E-mail is a fundamental aspect of Internet business activities. A sniffer installed on a gateway could simply collect all information associated with port 25 (SMTP). This would provide the attacker with volumes of surreptitiously gained email information.

Another dangerous aspect of gateway-based attacks is simple neglect of the security of the gateway itself. A painful example is Internet router security. In the past few years, firewalls have become standard issue for Internet connectivity. However, in some implementations, the router that provides the connection to the Internet on the outside of the firewall is ignored. Granted, the internal network is afforded some degree of security from general attacks from the Internet, but the router can be compromised to gather information about the internal network indirectly. In some cases, this can be catastrophic. If a router is compromised, a privileged user's password could be obtained from the user's activities on the Internet. There is a strong possibility that this password is the same as that used for internal services, giving the attacker access to the inside network.

There are several scenarios of gateway-based sniffer attacks, each with varying degrees of impact. However, they all represent enormous potential to the attacker.

Server -Based. Previously, the merits of traffic focal points as good sniffer locations were discussed. Given the type and amount of information that passes in and out of network servers, they become a focal point for sensitive information. Server-based sniffers take advantage of this observation, and target the information that flows in and out of the server. In this way, sniffers can provide ample amounts of information about the services being offered on the system and provide access to crucial information. The danger is that the attacker can isolate specific traffic that is relative to the particular system.

Common server-based sniffers operate much like normal sniffers in non-promiscuous mode, capturing data from the NIC as information is passed into the operating system. An attacker can accomplish this type of sniffing with either of two basic methods: installing a sniffer, or using an existing one provided by the operating system.

It is well known that the majority of today's systems can be considered insecure, and most have various vulnerabilities for a number of reasons. Some of these vulnerabilities allow an attacker to obtain privileged access to the system. Having gained access, an attacker may choose to install a sniffer to gather more information as it is sent to the server. A good example is servers that frequently process requests to add users of various services. Free e-mail services are common on the Internet, and in the event that users' passwords are gathered when they enroll, their e-mail will be completely accessible by an attacker.

By employing the system's existing utilities, an attacker needs only the necessary permissions to operate the sniffer. An example is tcpdump, described in detail later, which can be used by one user to view the activities of other users on the system. Improperly configured UNIX systems are especially vulnerable to these utility attacks because of the inherent nature of the multiuser operating environment.

SNIFFER COUNTERMEASURES

A sniffer can be a powerful tool for an attacker. However, there are techniques that reduce the effectiveness of these attacks and eliminate the greater part of the risk. Many of these techniques are commonplace and currently exist as standards, while others require more activity on the part of the user.

In general, sniffer countermeasures address two facets of the attacker's approach: the ability to actually capture traffic, and the ability to use that information for dark purposes. Many countermeasures address the first approach, and attempt to prevent the sniffer from seeing traffic at all. Other countermeasures take steps to ensure that data extracted by the sniffer will not yield any useful information to the attacker. The following sections discuss examples of both of these types of countermeasures.

Security Policy

Security policy defines the overall security posture of a network. Security policy is typically used to state an organization's position on particular network security issues. These policy statements are backed up by specific standards and guidelines that provide details on how an organization is to achieve its stated posture. Every organization should have a security policy that addresses its overall approach to security. A good security policy should address several areas that affect an attacker's ability to launch a sniffer-based attack.

Given physical access to the facility, it is easy to install a sniffer on most networks. Provisions in the security policy should limit the ability of an attacker to gain physical access to a facility. Denial of physical access to a network severely restricts an attacker's ability to install and operate a sniffer. Assuming an attacker does have physical access to a facility, provisions in the security policy should ensure that it is nontrivial to find an active but unused network port. A good security policy should also thoroughly address host security issues. Strong host security can prevent an attacker from installing sniffer software on a host already attached to the network. This closes down yet another avenue of approach for an attacker to install and operate a sniffer. Furthermore, policies that address the security of network devices help to deter gateway, LAN, and WAN attacks.

Policy should also clearly define the roles and responsibilities of the administrators that will have access to network sniffers. Because sniffing traffic for network analysis can easily lead to the compromise of confidential information, discretion should be exercised in granting access to sniffers and their output.

The following sections address point solutions that help to dilute the effectiveness of a sniffer-based attack. Security policy standards and guidelines should outline the specific use of these techniques.

Strong Authentication

It has been shown how password-based authentication can be exploited with the use of a sniffer. Stronger authentication schemes can be employed to render password-sniffing attacks useless. Password-sniffing attacks are successful, assuming that the attacker can use the sniffed password again to authenticate to a system. Strong authentication mechanisms ensure that the data seen on the network cannot be used again for later authentication. This defeats the password sniffer by rendering the data it captures useless.

Although certain strong authentication schemes can help to defeat against password sniffers, they are not generally effective against all sniffer attacks. For example, an attacker sniffing the network to determine the version of Sendmail running on the mail server would not be deterred by a strong authentication scheme.

Encryption

Sniffer attacks are based on a fundamental security flaw in many types of electronic communications. The endpoints of a conversation may be extremely secure, but the communications channel itself is typically wide open, as many networks are not designed to protect information in transit. Encryption can be used to protect that information as it traverses various networks between the endpoints.

The process of encryption combines the original message, or plaintext, with a secret key to produce ciphertext. The definition of encryption provides that the ciphertext is not intelligible by an eavesdropper. Furthermore, without the secret key, it is not feasible for the eavesdropper to recover the plaintext from the ciphertext. These properties provide assurance that the ciphertext can be sent to the recipient without fear of compromise by an eavesdropper. Assuming the intended recipient also knows the secret key, she can decrypt the ciphertext to recover the plaintext, and read the original message. Encryption is useful in protecting data in transit, because the ciphertext can be viewed by an eavesdropper, but is ultimately useless to an attacker.

Encryption protects the data in transit, but does not restrict the attacker's ability to intercept the communication. Therefore, the cryptographic protocols and algorithms in use must themselves be resistant to attack. themselves. The encryption algorithm — the mathematical recipe for transforming plaintext into ciphertext — must be strong enough to prevent the attacker from decrypting the information without knowledge of the key. Weak encryption algorithms can be broken through a variety of cryptanalytic techniques. The cryptographic protocols — the rules that govern the use of cryptography in the communication process — must ensure that the attacker cannot deduce the encryption key from information made available during the conversation. Weak encryption provides no real security, only a false sense of confidence in the users of the system.

Switched Network Environments

Ethernet sniffers are by far the most commonly encountered sniffers in the wild. One of the reasons for this is that Ethernet is based on a shared segment. It is this shared-segment principle that allows a sniffer to be effective in an Ethernet environment; the sniffer can listen to all of the traffic within the collision domain.

Switches are used in many environments to control the flow of data through the network. This improves overall network performance through a virtual increase in bandwidth. Switches achieve this result by segmenting network traffic, which reduces the number of stations in an Ethernet collision domain. The fundamentals of Ethernet allow a sniffer to listen to traffic within a single collision domain. Therefore, by reducing the number of stations in a collision domain, switches also limit the amount of network traffic seen by the sniffer.

In most cases, servers reside on dedicated switched segments that are separate from the workstation switched networks. This will prevent a sniffer from seeing certain types of traffic. With the reduced cost of switches over the past few years, however, many organizations have implemented switches to provide a dedicated segment to each workstation. A sniffer in these totally switched environments can receive only broadcasts and information destined directly for it, missing out on all of the other network conversations taking place. Clearly, this is not a desirable situation for an attacker attempting to launch a sniffer-based attack.

Sniffers are usually deployed to improve network performance. The fact that sniffers heighten the security of the network is often a secondary consideration or may not have been considered at all. This is one of those rare cases in which the classic security/functionality paradox does not apply. In this case, an increase in functionality and performance on the network actually leads to improved security as a side effect.

Detecting Sniffers

The sniffer most commonly found in the wild is a software sniffer running on a workstation with a promiscuous Ethernet interface. Because sniffing is a passive activity, it is conceptually impossible for an administrator to directly detect such a sniffer on the network. It may be possible, however, to deduce the presence of a sniffer based on other information available within the environment. L0pht Heavy Industries has developed a tool that can deduce, with fairly high accuracy, when a machine on the network is operating its NIC in promiscuous mode. This tool is known as AntiSniff.

It is not generally possible to determine directly whether a machine is operating as a packet sniffer. AntiSniff uses deduction to form a conclusion about a particular machine and is quite accurate. Rather than querying directly to detect a sniffer, AntiSniff looks at various side effects exhibited by the operation of a sniffer. AntiSniff conducts three tests to gather information about the hosts on the network.

Most operating systems exhibit some unique quirks when operating an interface in promiscuous mode. For example, the TCP/IP stack in most early Linux kernels did not handle packets properly when operating in promiscuous mode. Under normal operation, the kernel behaves properly. When the stack receives a packet, it checks to see whether destination MAC address is its own. If it is, the packet moves up to the next layer of the stack, which checks to see whether the destination IP address is its own. If it is, the packet is processed by the local system. However, in promiscuous mode, a small bug in the code produces abnormal results. In promiscuous mode, when the packet is received, the MAC address is ignored, and the packet is handed up the stack. The stack verifies the destination IP address and reacts accordingly. If the address is its own, it processes the packet. If not, the stack drops the packet. Either way, the packet is copied to the sniffer software.

There is a flaw, however, in this logic. Suppose station A is suspected of operating in promiscuous mode. AntiSniff crafts a packet, a ping for example, with a destination of station B's MAC address, but with station A's IP address. When station B receives the packet, it will drop it because the destination IP address does not match. When station A receives the packet, it will accept it because it is in promiscuous mode, so it will grab the packet regardless of the destination MAC address. Then, the IP stack checks the destination IP address. Because it matches its own, station A's IP stack processes the packet and responds to the ping. Under nonpromiscuous mode, station A would have dropped the packet, because the destination MAC address was not its own. The only way the packet would have made it up the stack for processing is if the interface happened to be in promiscuous mode. When AntiSniff receives the ping reply, it can deduce that station A is operating in promiscuous mode.

This quirk is specific to early Linux kernels, but other operating systems exhibit their own quirks. The first AntiSniff test exercises the conditions that uncover those quirks in the various operating systems, with the intent to gain some insight as to whether the machine is operating in promiscuous mode.

Many sniffer-based attacks will perform a reverse-DNS query on the IP addresses it sees, in an attempt to maximize the amount of information it gleans from the network. The second AntiSniff test baits the alleged sniffer with packets destined for a nonexistent IP address and waits to see whether the machine does a reverse-DNS lookup on that address. If it does, chances are that it is operating as a sniffer.

A typical machine will take a substantial performance hit when operating its NIC in promiscuous mode. The final AntiSniff test floods the network with packets in an attempt to degrade the performance of a promiscuous machine. During this window of time, AntiSniff attempts to locate machines suffering from a significant performance hit and deduces that they are likely running in promiscuous mode.

AntiSniff is a powerful tool, because it gives the network administrator the ability to detect machines that are operating as sniffers. This enables the administrator to disable the sniffer capability and examine the hosts for further evidence of compromise by an attacker. AntiSniff is the first tool of its kind, one that can be a powerful countermeasure for the network administrator.

TOOLS OF THE TRADE

Sniffers and their ability to intercept network traffic make for an interesting conceptual discussion. However, the concept is not useful in the trenches of the internetworking battlefield until it is realized as a working tool. The power of a sniffer, in fact, has been incarnated in various hardware- and software-based tools. These tools can be organized into two general categories: those that provide a useful service to a legitimate network administrator, and those that provide an attacker with an easily operated, highly specialized attack tool. It should be noted that an operational tool that sees the entirety of network traffic can just as easily be used for dark purposes. The following sections describe several examples of both the operational tools and the specialized attack tools.

Operational Tools

Sniffer operational tools are quite useful to the network administrator. By capturing traffic directly from the network, the tool provides the administrator with data that can be analyzed to discern valuable information about the network. Network administrators use operational tools to sniff traffic and learn more about how the network is behaving. Typically, an administrator is not interested in the contents of the traffic, only in the characteristics of the traffic that relate to network operation.

There are three primary types of operational tools, or utilities that can be used for network monitoring or unauthorized activities. On the lower end of the scale are raw packet collectors — simple utilities that obtain various specifics about the communication but do not typically absorb the user data. These tools allow the user to see the communication characteristics for analysis, rather than providing the exact packet contents. For example, the operator can view the manner in which systems are communicating and the services being used throughout the network. Raw packet collectors are useful for determining basic communication properties, allowing the observer to draw certain deductions about the communication. The second, more common, type of tool is the application sniffer. These are applications that can be loaded on a PC, providing several layers of information to the operator. Everything from frame information to user data is collected and presented in a clear manner that facilitates easy interpretation. Typically, extended tools are provided for analyzing the data to determine trends in the communication. The last type of tool is dedicated sniffer equipment. Highly flexible and powerful, such equipment can be attached to many types of networks to collect data. Each topology and associated protocol that is supported by the device is augmented with analyzing functionality that assists in determining the status of the network. These tools provide powerful access at the most fundamental levels of communication. This blurs the line between network administration and unauthorized access to network traffic. Sniffers should be treated as powerful tools with tremendous potential for harm and good. Access to network sniffers should be tightly controlled to prevent individuals from crossing over that line.

Raw Packet Collectors. There are several variations of raw packet collectors, most of which are associated with UNIX systems. One example is tcpdump, a utility built into most variations of UNIX. It essentially makes a copy of everything seen by the kernel's TCP/IP protocol stack. It performs a basic level of packet decode, and displays key values from the packets in a tabular format. Included in the display is information such as the packet's timestamp, source host and port, destination host and port, protocol type, and packet size.

Snoop, similar to tcpdump, is another of the more popular utilities used in UNIX. These utilities do not wrap a graphical interface around their functionality, nor do they provide extended analytical information as part of their native feature set. The format used to store data is quite basic, however, and can be exported into other applications for trend analysis.

These tools can be very dangerous because they are easily operated, widely available, and can be started and stopped automatically. As with most advanced systems, separate processes can be started and placed in the background; they remain undetected while they collect vital information and statistics.

Application Sniffers. There are several commercial-grade products that are available to provide collection, analysis, and trend computations along with unprecedented access to user data. The most common operate on Microsoft platforms because of the market share Microsoft currently enjoys. Many examples exist, but Etherpeek, Sniffer, and Microsoft's own, NetMon are very common. Be assured there are hundreds of others, and some are even proprietary to certain organizations.

Each supports customizable filters, allowing the user to be selective about the type of packets saved by the application. With filters enabled, the promiscuous interface continues to capture every packet it sees, but the sniffer itself retains only those packets that match the filters. This allows a user to be selective and retain only those packets that meet certain criteria. This can be very helpful, both in network troubleshooting and launching attacks, as it significantly reduces the size of the packet capture while isolating specific communications that have known weaknesses or information. If either an administrator or an attacker is looking for something particular, having a much smaller data set is clearly an advantage.

By default, many application products display a summary listing of the packets as they are captured and retained. Typically, more information is available through packet decode capabilities, which allow the user to drill down into individual packets to see the contents of various protocol fields. The legitimate network administrator will typically stop at the protocol level, as this usually provides sufficient information to perform network troubleshooting and analysis. Packet decodes, however, also contain the packet's data payload, providing access to the contents of the communications. Access to this information might provide the attacker with the information he is looking for.

In addition to the ability to display vital detailed information about captured packets, many packages perform a variety of statistical analyses across the entire capture. This can be a powerful tool for the attacker to identify core systems and determine application flow. An example is an attacker that has enough access to get a sniffer on the network but is unaware of the location or applications that will allow him to obtain the desired information. By capturing data and applying statistical analysis, application servers can be identified, and their use, by volume or time of day, can be compared with typical business practices. The next time the sniffer is enabled, it can be focused on what appears to have the desired data to assist in expanding the attack.

Microsoft's NetMon runs as a service and can be configured to answer to polls from a central Microsoft server running the network monitor administrator. This allows an administrator to strategically place sniffers throughout the network environment and have them all report packet captures back to a central server. Although it is a powerful feature for the network administrator, the ability to query a remote NetMon sniffer also presents security concerns. For example, if an attacker cannot gain physical access to the network he wishes to sniff but learns that NetMon is running, he may be able to attack the NetMon service itself, causing it to report its sniffer capture back to the attacker rather than to the legitimate administrative server. It is relatively simple to identify a machine running NetMon. An NBTSTAT –A/-a <IP/Name> command will provide a list of NetBIOS tags of the remote system. If a system tag of [BEh] is discovered, it indicates that the NetMon service is running on the remote system. Once this has been discovered, a sophisticated attacker can take advantage of the service and begin collecting information on a network that was previously inaccessible.

Dedicated Sniffer Equipment. Network General's Sniffer is the most recognized version of this type of tool; its existence is actually responsible for the term sniffer. It is a portable device built to perform a single function: sniffing network traffic. Dedicated devices are quite powerful and have the ability to monitor larger traffic flows than could be accomplished with a PC-based sniffer. Additionally, dedicated devices have built-in interfaces for various media and topology types, making them flexible enough to be used in virtually any environment. This flexibility, while powerful, comes with a large price tag, so much so that dedicated equipment is not seen often in the wild.

Dedicated equipment supports advanced customizable filters, allowing the user to prune the traffic stream for particular types of packets. The sniffer is primarily geared toward capturing traffic, and allows the user to export the capture data to another machine for in-depth analysis.

Attack-Specific Tools

Staging a successful attack with an operational tool is often more an art than a science. Although there are many factors that determine the attacker's ability to capture network traffic, that is only half of the battle. The attacker must be able to find the proverbial needle in the haystack of packets provided by the sniffer. The attacker must understand internetworking protocols to decipher much of the information and must have a sound strategy for wading through the millions of packets that a sniffer might return.

Recent trends in computer hacking have seen the rise of scripted attacks and attacker toolkits. The Internet itself has facilitated the proliferation of hacking tools and techniques from the few to the many. Very few of the people who label themselves "hackers" actually understand the anatomy of the attacks they wage. Most simply download an exploit script, point it at a target, and pull the trigger. Simplifying the attack process into a suite of user-friendly software tools opens up the door to a whole new class of attacker.

Sniffer-based attacks have not escaped this trend. It can be argued that the information delivered by a sniffer does not provide any real value. It is what the attacker does with this information that ultimately determines the success of the sniffer-based attack. If this is true, then a sniffer in the hands of an unskilled attacker is probably of no use. Enter the attack-specific sniffer tool. Some of the talented few that understand how a sniffer's output can be used to launch attacks have bundled that knowledge and methodology into software packages.

These software packages are essentially all-in-one attack tools that leverage the information produced by a sniffer to automatically launch an attack. The following sections present several examples of these attack-specific sniffer tools.

L0pht Crack Scanner. The L0pht Crack Scanner is produced by L0pht Heavy Industries, a talented group of programmers that specialize in security tools that operate on both sides of the network security battlefield. This tool is a password sniffer that exposes usernames and passwords in a Microsoft networking environment. L0pht Crack Scanner targets Microsoft's authentication processes, which uses mild algorithms to protect passwords from disclosure as they are sent across the network. This tool underscores the complementary role that a sniffer plays in many types of network attacks. The L0pht Crack Scanner combines a sniffer with a protocol vulnerability to attack the network, with drastic results.

The scanner capitalizes on several weaknesses in the authentication process to break the protection suites used, providing the attacker with usernames and passwords from the network. The individuals at L0pht have developed an algorithm to successfully perform cryptanalysis and recover the cleartext passwords associated with usernames.

The L0pht Crack Scanner uses a built-in sniffer to monitor the network, looking for authentication traffic. When the sniffer recognizes specific traffic, the packets are captured and the scanner applies L0pht's cryptanalysis routine and produces the password for the attacker.

PPTP Scanner. Microsoft's Point-to-Point Tunneling Protocol (PPTP) is a protocol designed to provide tunneled, encrypted communications. It has been proved that the encryption used in PPTP can be broken with simple cryptanalysis of the protocol. This cryptanalysis has been translated into a methodology for recovering traffic from a PPTP session.

PPTP Scanner combines a sniffer with a weakness in the design of the PPTP protocol, exposing and exercising a serious vulnerability. This vulnerability, when exercised, allows for the recovery of plaintext from an encrypted session.

PPTP Scanner is the incarnation of the PPTP cryptanalysis methodology. The Scanner uses built-in sniffer software to monitor network traffic, looking for a PPTP session. When PPTP traffic is recognized, the packets are captured and stored for analysis. The Scanner applies the cryptanalytic methodology, and recovers the plaintext traffic for the attacker.

Previously, we have discussed the use of encryption to protect network traffic from sniffer-based attacks was discussed. The ease with which the L0pht Crack Scanner and PPTP Scanner do their dirty work underscores an important point. Simply encrypting traffic before sending it across the network affords only limited protection. For this technique to provide any real security, the encryption algorithms and protocols chosen must be strong and resistant to attack.

Hunt. Hunt, an automated session hijack utility, is another example of a sniffer with a built-in attack capability. Hunt operates by examining network traffic flow for certain signatures — distinct traffic patterns that indicate a particular event or condition. When Hunt recognizes a signature for traffic it can work with, it springs into action. When Hunt goes active, it knocks one station offline, and assumes its identity in the ongoing TCP session. In this manner, Hunt hijacks the TCP session for itself, giving the operator access to an established connection that can be used to further explore the target system.

This capability can be quite useful to an attacker, especially if Hunt hijacks a privileged session. Consider the following example. If Hunt detects the traffic signature for a Telnet session that it can hijack, it will knock the originating station offline and resume the session itself. This gives the Hunt operator instant command-line access to the system. The attacker will be able to access the system as the original user, which could be anyone from a plain user to a system administrator.

CONCLUSION

Network sniffers exist primarily to assist network administrators in analyzing and troubleshooting their networks. These devices take advantage of certain characteristics of electronic communications to provide a window of observation into the network. This window provides the operator with a clear view into the details of network traffic flow.

In the hands of an attacker, a network sniffer can be used to learn many types of information. This information can range from basic operational characteristics of the network itself to highly sensitive information about the company or individuals that use the network. The amount and significance of the information learned through a sniffer-based attack is dependant on certain characteristics of the network and the attacker's ability to introduce a sniffer. The type of media employed, the topology of the network, and the location of the sniffer are key factors that combine to determine the amount and type of information seen by the sniffer.

Information security practitioners are committed to the pursuit of confidentiality, integrity, and availability of resources, and information in computing and electronic communications. Sniffers represent significant challenges in each of these arenas. As sniffer capabilities have progressed, so have the attacks that can be launched with a sniffer. The past few years have seen the evolution of easy-to-use sniffer tools that can be exercised by attackers of all skill levels to wage war against computing environments and electronic communications. As attackers have increased their capabilities, so have network administrators seeking to protect themselves against these attacks. The security community has responded with a myriad of techniques and technologies that can be employed to diminish the success of the sniffer-based attack.

As with most competitive environments, security professionals and system attackers continue to raise the bar for one another, constantly driving the other side to expand and improve its capabilities. This creates a seemingly endless chess match, in which both sides must constantly adjust their strategy to respond to the moves made by the other. As security professionals continue to improve the underlying security of computing and communications systems, attackers will respond by finding new ways to attack these systems. Similarly, as attackers continue to find new vulnerabilities in computer systems, networks, and communications protocols, the security community will respond with countermeasures to combat these risks.

Chapter 7
Enclaves: The Enterprise as an Extranet

Bryan T. Koch

EVEN IN THE MOST SECURE ORGANIZATIONS, INFORMATION SECURITY THREATS AND VULNERABILITIES ARE INCREASING OVER TIME. Vulnerabilities are increasing with the complexity of internal infrastructures; complex structures have more single points of failure, and this in turn increases the risk of multiple simultaneous failures. Organizations are adopting new, untried, and partially tested products at ever-increasing rates. Vendors and internal developers alike are relearning the security lessons of the past — one at a time, painful lesson by painful lesson.

Given the rapid rate of change in organizations, minor or incremental improvements in security can be offset or undermined by "organizational entropy." The introduction of local area networks (LANs) and personal computers (PCs) years ago changed the security landscape, but many security organizations continued to function using centralized control models that have little relationship to the current organizational or technical infrastructures. The Internet has brought new threats to the traditional set of organizational security controls. The success of the Internet model has created a push for electronic commerce (E-commerce) and electronic business (E-business) initiatives involving both the Internet itself and the more widespread use of Internet Protocol (IP)-based extranets (private business-to-business networks).

Sophisticated, effective, and easy-to-use attack tools are widely available on the Internet. The Internet has implicitly linked competing organizations with each other, and linked these organizations to communities that are opposed to security controls of any kind. There is no reason to assume that attack tools developed in the Internet cannot or will not be used within an organization.

External threats are more easily perceived than internal threats, while surveys and studies continue to show that the majority of security problems are internal. With all of this as context, the need for a new security paradigm is clear.

The time has come to apply the lessons learned in Internet and extranet environments to one's own organization. This article proposes to apply Internet/extranet security architectural concepts to internal networks by creating protected *enclaves* within organizations. Access between enclaves and the enterprise is managed by *network guardians*. Within enclaves, the security objective is to apply traditional controls consistently and well. Outside of enclaves, current practice (i.e., security controls at variance with formal security policies) is tolerated (one has no choice). This restructuring can reduce some types of network security threats by orders of magnitude. Other threats remain and these must be addressed through traditional security analysis and controls, or accepted as part of normal risk/reward trade-offs.

SECURITY CONTEXT

Security policies, procedures, and technologies are supposed to combine to yield acceptable risk levels for enterprise systems. However, the nature of security threats, and the probability that they can be successfully deployed against enterprise systems, have changed. This is partly a result of the diffusion of computer technology and computer networking into enterprises, and partly a result of the Internet.

For larger and older organizations, security policies were developed to address security vulnerabilities and threats in legacy mainframe environments. Legacy policies have been supplemented to address newer threats such as computer viruses, remote access, and e-mail. In this author's experience, it is rare for current policy frameworks to effectively address network-based threats. LANs and PCs were the first steps in what has become a marathon of increasing complexity and inter-relatedness; intranet (internal networks and applications based on IP), extranet, and Internet initiatives are the most common examples of this.

The Internet has brought network technology to millions. It is an enabling infrastructure for emerging E-business and E-commerce environments. It has a darker side, however, because it also:

- serves as a "proving ground" for tools and procedures that test for and exploit security vulnerabilities in systems
- serves as a distribution medium for these tools and procedures
- links potential users of these tools with anonymously available repositories

Partly because it began as an "open" network, and partly due to the explosion of commercial use, the Internet has also been the proving ground for security architectures, tools, and procedures to protect information in the Internet's high-threat environment. Examples of the tools that have emerged from this environment include firewalls, virtual private networks, and layered physical architectures. These tools have been extended from the Internet into extranets.

In many sectors — most recently telecommunications, finance, and health care — organizations are growing primarily through mergers and acquisitions. Integration of many new organizations per year is challenging enough on its own. It is made more complicated by external network connectivity (dial-in for customers and employees, outbound Internet services, electronic commerce applications, and the like) within acquired organizations. It is further complicated by the need to integrate dissimilar infrastructure components (e-mail, calendaring, and scheduling; enterprise resource planning (ERP); and human resources (HR) tools). The easiest solution — to wait for the dust to settle and perform long-term planning — is simply not possible in today's "at the speed of business" climate.

An alternative solution, the one discussed here, is to accept the realities of the business and technical contexts, and to create a "network security master plan" based on the new realities of the internal threat environment. One must begin to treat enterprise networks as if they were an extranet or the Internet and secure them accordingly.

THE ONE BIG NETWORK PARADIGM

Network architects today are being tasked with the creation of an integrated network environment. One network architect described this as a mandate to "connect everything to everything else, with complete transparency." The author refers to this as the One Big Network paradigm. In this author's experience, some network architects aim to keep security at arm's length — "we build it, you secure it, and we don't have to talk to each other." This is untenable in the current security context of rapid growth from mergers and acquisitions.

One Big Network is a seductive vision to network designers, network users, and business executives alike. One Big Network will — in theory — allow new and better business interactions with suppliers, with business customers, and with end-consumers. Everyone connected to One Big Network can — in theory — reap great benefits at minimal infrastructure cost. Electronic business-to-business and electronic-commerce will be — in theory — ubiquitous.

However, one critical element has been left out of this brave new world: security. Despite more than a decade of networking and personal computers, many organizational security policies continue to target the legacy environment, not the network as a whole. These policies assume that it is possible to secure stand-alone "systems" or "applications" as if they have an existence independent of the rest of the enterprise. They assume that attackers will target applications rather than the network infrastructure that links the various parts of the distributed application together. Today's automated attack tools target the network as a whole to identify and attack weak applications and systems, and then use these systems for further attacks.

One Big Network changes another aspect of the enterprise risk/reward equation: it globalizes risks that had previously been local. In the past, a business unit could elect to enter into an outsource agreement for its applications, secure in the knowledge that the risks related to the agreement affected it alone. With One Big Network, the risk paradigm changes. It is difficult, indeed inappropriate, for business unit management to make decisions about risk/reward trade-offs when the risks are global while the benefits are local.

Finally, One Big Network assumes consistent controls and the loyalty of employees and others who are given access. Study after study, and survey after survey, confirm that neither assumption is viable.

NETWORK SECURITY AND THE ONE BIG NETWORK PARADIGM

It is possible that there was a time when One Big Network could be adequately secured. If it ever existed, that day is long past. Today's networks are dramatically bigger, much more diverse, run many more applications, connect more divergent organizations, in a more hostile environment where the "bad guys" have better tools than ever before. The author believes that it is not possible to secure, to any reasonable level of confidence, any enterprise network for any large organization where the network is managed as a single "flat" network with "any-to-any" connectivity.

In an environment with no effective internal network security controls, each network node creates a threat against every other node. (In mathematical terms, where there are n network nodes, the number of threats is approximately n^2.) Where the organization is also on the Internet without a firewall, the effective number of threats becomes essentially infinite (see Exhibit 7-1).

Effective enterprise security architecture must augment its traditional, applications-based toolkit with *network-based tools* aimed at addressing network-based threats.

INTERNET SECURITY ARCHITECTURE ELEMENTS

How does one design differently for Internet and extranet than one did for enterprises? What are Internet/extranet security engineering principles?

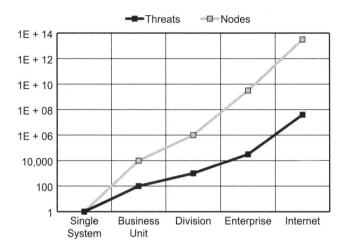

Exhibit 7-1. Network threats (log scale).

- *Simplicity.* Complexity is the enemy of security. Complex systems have more components, more single points of failure, more points at which failures can cascade upon one another, and are more difficult to certify as "known good" (even when built from known good components, which is rare in and of itself).
- *Prioritization and valuation.* Internet security systems know what they aim to protect. The sensitivity and vulnerability of each element is understood, both on its own and in combination with other elements of the design.
- *Deny by default, allow by policy.* Internet security architectures begin with the premise that all traffic is to be denied. Only traffic that is explicitly required to perform the mission is enabled, and this through defined, documented, and analyzed pathways and mechanisms.
- *Defense in depth, layered protection.* Mistakes happen. New flaws are discovered. Flaws previously believed to be insignificant become important when exploits are published. The Internet security architecture must, to a reasonable degree of confidence, fail in ways that result in continued security of the overall system; the failure (or misconfiguration) of a single component should not result in security exposures for the entire site.
- *End-to-end, path-by-path analysis.* Internet security engineering looks at all components, both on the enterprise side and on the remote side of every transaction. Failure or compromise of any component can undermine the security of the entire system. Potential weak points must be understood and, if possible, managed. Residual risks must be understood, both by the enterprise and by its business partners and customers.

- *Encryption.* In all Internet models, and most extranet models, the security of the underlying network is not assumed. As a result, some mechanism — encryption — is needed to preserve the confidentiality of data sent between the remote users and enterprise servers.
- *Conscious choice, not organic growth.* Internet security architectures are formally created through software and security engineering activities; they do not "just happen."

THE ENCLAVE APPROACH

This article proposes to treat the enterprise as an extranet. The extranet model invokes an architecture that has security as its first objective. It means identifying what an enterprise genuinely cares about: what it lives or dies by. It identifies critical and securable components and isolates them into protected *enclaves.* Access between enclaves and the enterprise is managed by *network guardians.* Within enclaves, the security objective is to apply traditional controls consistently and well. Outside of enclaves, current practice (i.e., security controls at variance with formal security policies), while not encouraged, is acknowledged as reality. This restructuring can reduce some types of network security threats by orders of magnitude. Taken to the extreme, all business-unit-to-business-unit interactions pass through enclaves (see Exhibit 7-2).

ENCLAVES

The enclaves proposed here are designed to contain high-value securable elements. Securable elements are systems for which security controls consistent with organizational security objectives can be successfully designed, deployed, operated, and maintained at any desired level of confidence. By contrast, nonsecurable elements might be semi-autonomous business units, new acquisitions, test labs, and desktops (as used by tele-

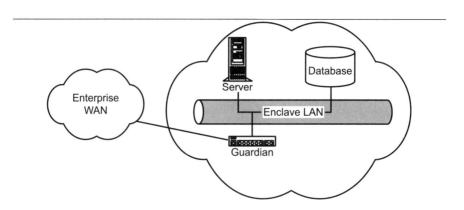

Exhibit 7-2. Relationship of an enclave to the enterprise.

commuters, developers, and business partners) — elements for which the cost, time, or effort required to secure them exceeds their value to the enterprise.

Within a secure enclave, every system and network component will have security arrangements that comply with the enterprise security policy and industry standards of due care. At enclave boundaries, security assurance will be provided by network guardians whose rule sets and operational characteristics can be enforced and audited. In other words, there is some level of assurance that comes from being part of an enclave. This greatly simplifies the security requirements that are imposed on client/server architectures and their supporting applications programming interfaces (APIs). Between enclaves, security assurance will be provided by the application of cryptographic technology and protocols.

Enclave membership is earned, not inherited. Enclave networks may need to be created from the ground up, with existing systems shifted onto enclave networks when their security arrangements have been adequately examined.

Enclaves could potentially contain the elements listed below:

1. mainframes
2. application servers
3. database servers
4. network gateways
5. PKI certificate authority and registration authorities
6. network infrastructure components (domain name and time servers)
7. directories
8. windows "domain controllers"
9. approved intranet web servers
10. managed network components
11. Internet proxy servers

All these are shared and securable to a high degree of confidence.

NETWORK GUARDIANS

Network guardians mediate and control traffic flow into and out of enclaves. Network guardians can be implemented initially using network routers. The routers will isolate enclave local area network traffic from LANs used for other purposes (development systems, for example, and user desktops) within the same physical space. This restricts the ability of user desktops and other low-assurance systems to monitor traffic between remote enclave users and the enclave. (Users will still have the ability to intercept traffic on their own LAN segment, although the use of switching network hubs can reduce the opportunity for this exposure as well.)

The next step in the deployment of network guardians is the addition of access control lists (ACLs) to guardian routers. The purpose of the ACLs is similar to the functionality of "border routers" in Internet firewalls — screening incoming traffic for validity (anti-spoofing), screening the destination addresses of traffic within the enclave, and to the extent possible, restricting enclave services visible to the remainder of the enterprise to the set of intended services.

Decisions to implement higher levels of assurance for specific enclaves or specific enclave-to-enclave or enclave-to-user communications can be made based on later risk assessments. Today and for the near future, simple subnet isolation will suffice.

ENCLAVE BENEFITS

Adopting an enclave approach reduces network-based security risks by orders of magnitude. The basic reason is that in the modern enterprise, the number of nodes (n) is very large, growing, and highly volatile. The number of enclaves (e) will be a small, stable number. With enclaves, overall risk is on the order of $n \times e$, compared with $n \times n$ without enclaves. For large n, $n \times e$ is much smaller than $n \times n$.

Business units can operate with greater degrees of autonomy than they might otherwise be allowed, because the only data they will be placing at risk is their own data on their own networks. Enclaves allow the realignment of risk with reward. This gives business units greater internal design freedom.

Because they require documentation and formalization of network data flows, the presence of enclaves can lead to improved network efficiency and scalability. Enclaves enforce an organization's existing security policies, at a network level, so by their nature they tend to reduce questionable, dubious, and erroneous network traffic and provide better accounting for allowed traffic flows. This aids capacity planning and disaster planning functions.

By formalizing relationships between protected systems and the remainder of the enterprise, enclaves can allow faster connections to business partners. (One of the significant sources of delay this author has seen in setting up extranets to potential business partners is collecting information about the exact nature of network traffic, required to configure network routers and firewalls. The same delay is often seen in setting up connectivity to newly acquired business units.)

Finally, enclaves allow for easier allocation of scarce security resources where they can do the most good. It is far easier to improve the security of enclave-based systems by, say, 50 percent, than it is to improve the overall security of all desktop systems in the enterprise by a similar amount, given a fixed resource allocation.

LIMITATIONS OF ENCLAVES

Enclaves protect only the systems in them; and by definition, they exclude the vast majority of the systems on the enterprise network and all external systems. Some other mechanism is needed to protect data in transit between low-assurance (desktops, external business partner) systems and the high-assurance systems within the enclaves. The solution is a set of confidentiality and authentication services provided by encryption. Providing an overall umbrella for encryption and authentication services is one role of public key infrastructures (PKIs).

From a practical perspective, management is difficult enough for externally focused network guardians (those protecting Internet and extranet connectivity). Products allowing support of an enterprisewide set of firewalls are just beginning to emerge. Recent publicity regarding Internet security events has increased executive awareness of security issues, without increasing the pool of trained network security professionals, so staffing for an enclave migration may be difficult.

Risks remain, and there are limitations. Many new applications are not "firewall friendly" (e.g., Java, CORBA, video, network management). Enclaves may not be compatible with legacy systems. Application security is just as important — perhaps more important than previously — because people connect to the application. Applications, therefore, should be designed securely. Misuse by authorized individuals is still possible in this paradigm, but the enclave system controls the path they use. Enclave architecture is aimed at network-based attacks, and it can be strengthened by integrating virtual private networks (VPNs) and switching network hubs.

IMPLEMENTATION OF ENCLAVES

Enclaves represent a fundamental shift in enterprise network architecture. Stated differently, they re-apply the lessons of the Internet to the enterprise. Re-architecting cannot happen overnight. It cannot be done on a cookie-cutter, by-the-book basis. The author's often-stated belief is that "security architecture" is a verb; it describes a *process*, rather than a destination. How can an organization apply the enclave approach to its network security problems? In a word, planning. In a few more words, information gathering, planning, prototyping, deployment, and refinement. These stages are described more fully below.

INFORMATION GATHERING

Information is the core of any enclave implementation project. The outcome of the information-gathering phase is essentially an inventory of critical systems with a reasonably good idea of the sensitivity and criticality of these systems. Some readers will be fortunate enough to work for organizations that already have information systems inventories from the business continuity planning process, or from recent Year 2000 activities. A few will actually have accurate and complete information. The rest will have to continue on with their research activities.

The enterprise must identify candidate systems for enclave membership and the security objectives for candidates. A starting rule-of-thumb would be that no desktop systems, and no external systems, are candidates for enclave membership; all other systems are initially candidates. Systems containing business-critical, business-sensitive, legally protected, or highly visible information are candidates for enclave membership. Systems managed by demonstrably competent administration groups, to defined security standards, are candidates.

External connections and relationships, via dial-up, dedicated, or Internet paths, must be discovered, documented, and inventoried.

The existing enterprise network infrastructure is often poorly understood and even less well-documented. Part of the information-gathering process is to improve this situation and provide a firm foundation for realistic enclave planning.

PLANNING

The planning process begins with the selection of an enclave planning group. Suggested membership includes senior staff from the following organizations: information security (with an emphasis on network security and business continuity specialists), network engineering, firewall management, mainframe network operations, distributed systems or client/server operations, E-commerce planning, and any outsource partners from these organizations. Supplementing this group would be technically well-informed representative from enterprise business units.

The planning group's next objective is to determine the scope of its activity, answering a set of questions including at least:

- Is one enclave sufficient, or is more than one a better fit with the organization?
- Where will the enclaves be located?
- Who will manage them?
- What level of protection is needed within each enclave?
- What is the simplest representative sample of an enclave that could be created within the current organization?

The purpose of these questions is to apply standard engineering practices to the challenge of carving out a secure enclave from the broader enterprise, and to use the outcome of these practices to make a case to enterprise management for the deployment of enclaves.

Depending on organizational readiness, the planning phase can last as little as a month or as long as a year, involving anywhere from days to years of effort.

PROTOTYPING

Enclaves are not new; they have been a feature of classified government environments since the beginning of computer technology (although typically within a single classification level or compartment). They are the basis of essentially all secure Internet electronic commerce work. However, the application of enclave architectures to network security needs of large organizations is, if not new, at least not widely discussed in the professional literature. Further, as seen in Internet and extranet environments generally, significant misunderstandings can often delay deployment efforts, and efforts to avoid these delays lead either to downward functionality adjustments, or acceptance of additional security risks, or both.

As a result, prudence dictates that any attempt to deploy enclaves within an enterprise be done in a stepwise fashion, compatible with the organization's current configuration and change control processes. The author recommends that organizations considering the deployment of the enclave architecture first evaluate this architecture in a prototype or laboratory environment. One option for doing this is an organizational test environment. Another option is the selection of a single business unit, district, or regional office.

Along with the selection of a locale and systems under evaluation, the enterprise must develop evaluation criteria: what does the organization expect to learn from the prototype environment, and how can the organization capture and capitalize on learning experiences?

DEPLOYMENT

After the successful completion of a prototype comes general deployment. The actual deployment architecture and schedule depends on factors too numerous to mention in any detail here. The list includes:

- *The number of enclaves.* (The author has worked in environments with as few as one and as many as a hundred, potential enclaves.)
- *Organizational readiness.* Some parts of the enterprise will be more accepting of the enclave architecture than others. Early adopters exist in every enterprise, as do more conservative elements. The deployment plan should make use of early adopters and apply the lessons learned in these early deployments to sway or encourage more change-resistant organizations.
- *Targets of opportunity.* The acquisition of new business units through mergers and acquisitions may well present targets of opportunity for early deployment of the enclave architecture.

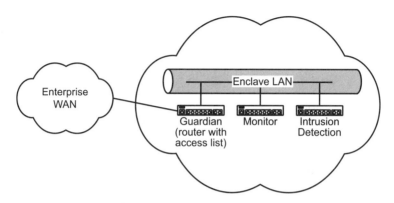

Exhibit 7-3. Initial enclave guardian configuration.

REFINEMENT

The enclave architecture is a concept and a process. Both will change over time: partly through organizational experience and partly through the changing technical and organizational infrastructure within which they are deployed.

One major opportunity for refinement is the composition and nature of the network guardians. Initially, this author expects network guardians to consist simply of already-existing network routers, supplemented with network monitoring or intrusion detection systems. The router will initially be configured with a minimal set of controls, perhaps just anti-spoofing filtering and as much source and destination filtering as can be reasonably considered. The network monitoring system will allow the implementers to quickly learn about "typical" traffic patterns, which can then be configured into the router. The intrusion detection system looks for known attack patterns and alerts network administrators when they are found (see Exhibit 7-3).

In a later refinement, the router may well be supplemented with a firewall, with configuration rules derived from the network monitoring results, constrained by emerging organizational policies regarding authorized traffic (see Exhibit 7-4).

Still later, where the organization has more than one enclave, encrypted tunnels might be established between enclaves, with selective encryption of traffic from other sources (desktops, for example, or selected business partners) into enclaves. This is illustrated in Exhibit 7-5.

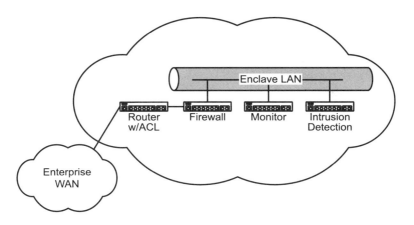

Exhibit 7-4. Enclave with firewall guardian.

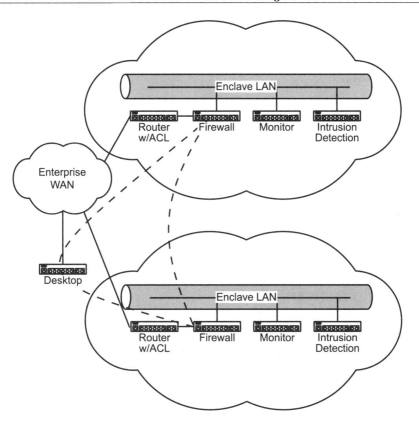

Exhibit 7-5. Enclaves with encrypted paths (dashed lines).

CONCLUSION

The enterprise-as-extranet methodology gives business units greater internal design freedom without a negative security impact on the rest of the corporation. It can allow greater network efficiency and better network disaster planning because it identifies critical elements and the pathways to them. It establishes security triage. The net results are global threat reduction by orders of magnitude and improved, effective real-world security.

Chapter 8
IPSec Virtual Private Networks

James S. Tiller

THE INTERNET HAS GRADUATED FROM SIMPLE SHARING OF E-MAIL TO BUSINESS-CRITICAL APPLICATIONS THAT INVOLVE INCREDIBLE AMOUNTS OF PRIVATE INFORMATION. The need to protect sensitive data over an untrusted medium has led to the creation of virtual private networks (VPNs). A VPN is the combination of tunneling, encryption, authentication, access control, and auditing technologies and services used to transport traffic over the Internet or any network that uses the TCP/IP protocol suite to communicate.

This chapter:

- introduces the IPSec standard and the RFCs that make up VPN technology
- introduces the protocols of the IPSec suite and key management
- provides a technical explanation of the IPSec communication technology
- discusses implementation considerations and current examples
- discusses the future of IPSec VPNs and the industry's support for growth of the standard

HISTORY

In 1994, the Internet Architecture Board (IAB) issued a report on "Security in the Internet Architecture" (Request For Comment [RFC] 1636). The report stated the general consensus that the Internet needs more and better security due to the inherent security weaknesses in the TCP/IP protocol suite, and it identified key areas for security improvements. The IAB also mandated that the same security functions become an integral part of the next generation of the IP protocol, IPv6. So, from the beginning, this evolving standard will continually be compatible with future generations of IP and network communication technology.

VPN infancy started in 1995 with the AIAG (Automotive Industry Action Group), a nonprofit association of North American vehicle manufacturers and suppliers, and their creation of the ANX (Automotive Network eXchange) project. The project was spawned to fulfill a need for a TCP/IP network comprised of trading partners, certified service providers, and network exchange points. The requirement demanded efficient and secure electronic communications among subscribers, with only a single connection over unsecured channels. As this technology grew, it became recognized as a solution for any organization wishing to provide secure communications with partners, clients, or any remote network. However, the growth and acceptance had been stymied by the lack of standards and product support issues.

In today's market, VPN adoption has grown enormously as an alternative to private networks. Much of this has been due to many performance improvements and the enhancement of the set of standards. VPN connections must be possible between any two or more types of systems. This can be further defined in three groups:

1. client to gateway
2. gateway to gateway
3. client to client

This process of broad communication support is only possible with detailed standards. IPSec (IP Security protocol) is an ever-growing standard to provide encrypted communications over IP. Its acceptance and robustness has fortified IPSec as the VPN technology standard for the foreseeable future. There are several RFCs that define IPSec, and currently there are over 40 Internet Engineering Task Force (IETF) RFC drafts that address various aspects of the standard's flexibility and growth.

BUILDING BLOCKS OF A STANDARD

The IPSec standard is used to provide privacy and authentication services at the IP layer. Several RFCs are used to describe this protocol suite. The interrelationship and organization of the documents are important to understand to become aware of the development process of the overall standard.

As Exhibit 8-1 shows, there are seven groups of documents that allow for the association of separate aspects of the IPSec protocol suite to be developed independently while a functioning relationship is attained and managed.

The Architecture is the main description document that covers the overall technology concepts and security considerations. It provides the access point for an initial understanding of the IPSec protocol suite.

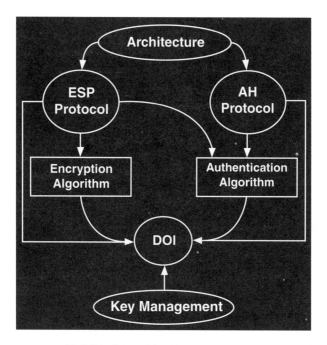

Exhibit 8-1. IETF IPSec DOI model.

The ESP (Encapsulating Security Payload) protocol (RFC 2406) and AH (Authentication Header) protocol (RFC 2402) document groups detail the packet formats and the default standards for packet structure that include implementation algorithms.

The Encryption Algorithm documents are a set of documents that detail the use of various encryption techniques utilized for the ESP. Examples of documents include DES (Data Encryption Standard RFC 1829) and Triple DES (draft-simpson-desx-02) algorithms and their application in the encryption of the data.

The Authentication Algorithms are a group of documents describing the process and technologies used to provide an authentication mechanism for the AH and ESP Protocols. Examples would be HMAC-MD5 (RFC 2403) and HMAC-SHA-1 (RFC 2404).

All of these documents specify values that must be consolidated and defined for cohesiveness into the DOI, or Domain of Interpretation (RFC 2407). The DOI document is part of the IANA assigned numbers mechanism and is a constant for many standards. It provides the central repository for values for the other documents to relate to each other. The DOI contains parameters that are required for the other portions of the protocol to ensure that the definitions are consistent.

The final group is Key Management, which details and tracks the standards that define key management schemes. Examples of the documents in this group are the Internet Security Association and Key Management Protocol (ISAKMP) and public key infrastructure (PKI). This chapter unveils each of these protocols and the technology behind each that makes it the standard of choice in VPNs.

INTRODUCTION OF FUNCTION

IPSec is a suite of protocols used to protect information, authenticate communications, control access, and provide nonrepudiation. Of this suite there are two protocols that are the driving elements:

1. Authentication Header (AH)
2. Encapsulating Security Payload (ESP)

AH was designed for integrity, authentication, sequence integrity (replay resistance), and nonrepudiation — but not for confidentiality for which the ESP was designed. There are various applications where the use of only an AH is required or stipulated. In applications where confidentiality is not required or not sanctioned by government encryption restrictions, an AH can be employed to ensure integrity, which in itself can be a powerful foe to potential attackers. This type of implementation does not protect the information from dissemination but will allow for verification of the integrity of the information and authentication of the originator. AH also provides protection for the IP header preceding it and selected options. The AH includes the following fields:

- IP Version
- Header Length
- Packet Length
- Identification
- Protocol
- Source and Destination Addresses
- Selected Options

The remainder of the IP header is not used in authentication with AH security protocol. ESP authentication does not cover any IP headers that precede it.

The ESP protocol provides encryption as well as some of the services of the AH. These two protocols can be used separately or combined to obtain the level of service required for a particular application or environmental structure. The ESP authenticating properties are limited compared to the AH due to the non-inclusion of the IP header information in the authentication process. However, ESP can be more than sufficient if only the upper layer protocols need to be authenticated. The application of only ESP to provide authentication, integrity, and confidentiality to the upper layers will increase efficiency over the encapsulation of ESP in the AH. Although authentication and confidentiality are both optional operations, one of the security protocols must be implemented. It is possible to establish communications with just authentication and without encryption or null encryption (RFC 2410). An added feature of the ESP is payload padding, which conceals the size of the packet being transmitted and further protects the characteristics of the communication.

The authenticating process of these protocols is necessary to create a security association (SA), the foundation of an IPSec VPN. An SA is built from the authentication provided by the AH or ESP Protocol and becomes the primary function of key management to establish and maintain the SA between systems. Once the SA is achieved, the transport of data may commence.

UNDERSTANDING THE FOUNDATION

Security associations are the infrastructure of IPSec. Of all the portions of IPSec protocol suite, the SA is the focal point for vendor integration and the accomplishment of heterogeneous virtual private networks. SAs are common among all IPSec implementations and must be supported to be IPSec compliant. An SA is nearly synonymous with VPN, but the term "VPN" is used much more loosely. SAs also exist in other security protocols. As described later, much of the key management used with IPSec VPNs is existing technology without specifics defining the underlying security protocol, allowing the key management to support other forms of VPN technology that use SAs.

SAs are simplex in nature in that two SAs are required for authenticated, confidential, bi-directional communications between systems. Each SA can be defined by three components:

- security parameter index (SPI)
- destination IP address
- security protocol identifier (AH or ESP)

An SPI is a 32-bit value used to distinguish among different SAs terminating at the same destination and using the same IPSec protocol. This data allows for the multiplexing of SAs to a single gateway. Interestingly, the destination IP address can be unicast, multicast, or broadcast; however, the standard for managing SAs currently applies to unicast applications or point-to-point SAs. Many vendors will use several SAs to accomplish a point-to-multipoint environment.

The final identification — the security protocol identifier — is the security protocol being utilized for that SA. Note that only one security protocol can be used for communications provided by a single SA. In the event that the communication requires authentication and confidentiality by use of both the AH and ESP security protocols, two or more SAs must be created and added to the traffic stream.

Finding the Gateway

Prior to any communication, it is necessary for a map to be constructed and shared among the community of VPN devices. This acts to provide information regarding where to forward data based on the required ultimate destination. A map can contain several pieces of data that exist to provide connection point information for a specific network and to assist the key management process. A map typically will contain a set of IP addresses that define a system, network, or groups of each that are accessible by way of a gateway's IP address.

An example of a map that specifies how to get to network 10.1.0.0 by a tunnel to 251.111.27.111 and use a shared secret with key management, might look like:

```
begin static-map
target "10.1.0.0/255.255.0.0"
mode "ISAKMP-Shared"
tunnel "251.111.27.111"
end
```

Depending on the vendor implemented, keying information and type may be included in the map. A shared secret or password may be associated with a particular destination. An example is a system that wishes to communicate with a remote network via VPN and needs to know the remote gateway's IP address and the expected authentication type when communication is initiated. To accomplish this, the map may contain mathematical representations of the shared secret in the map to properly match the secret with the destination gateway. A sample of this is a Diffie–Hellman key, explained in detail later in this article 87-10-29.

MODES OF COMMUNICATION

The type of operation for IPSec connectivity is directly related to the role the system is playing in the VPN or the SA status. There are two modes of operation, as shown in Exhibit 8-2, for IPSec VPNs: transport mode and tunnel mode.

Transport mode is used to protect upper layer protocols and only affects the data in the IP packet. A more dramatic method, tunnel mode, encapsulates the entire IP packet to tunnel the communications in a secured communication.

Transport mode is established when the endpoint is a host, or when communications are terminated at the endpoints. If the gateway in gateway-to-host communications was to use transport mode, it would act as a

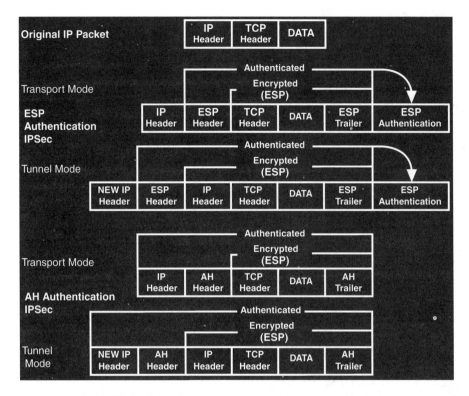

Exhibit 8-2. Tunnel and transport mode packet structure.

host system, which can be acceptable for direct protocols to that gateway. Otherwise, tunnel mode is required for gateway services to provide access to internal systems.

Transport Mode

In transport mode, the IP packet contains the security protocol (AH or ESP) located after the original IP header and options and before any upper layer protocols contained in the packet, such as TCP and UDP. When ESP is utilized for the security protocol, the protection, or hash, is only applied to the upper layer protocols contained in the packet. The IP header information and options are not utilized in the authentication process. Therefore, the originating IP address cannot be verified for integrity against the data. With the use of AH as the security protocol, the protection is extended forward into the IP header to provide integrity of the entire packet by use of portions of the original IP header in the hashing process.

Tunnel Mode

Tunnel mode is established for gateway services and is fundamentally an IP tunnel with authentication and encryption. This is the most common mode of operation. Tunnel mode is required for gateway-to-gateway and host-to-gateway communications. Tunnel mode communications have two sets of IP headers — inside and outside.

The outside IP header contains the destination IP address of the VPN gateway. The inside IP header contains the destination IP address of the final system behind the VPN gateway. The security protocol appears after the outer IP header and before the inside IP header. As with transport mode, extended portions of the IP header are utilized with AH that are not included with ESP authentication, ultimately providing integrity only of the inside IP header and payload.

The inside IP header's TTL (Time To Live) is decreased by one by the encapsulating system to represent the hop count as it passes through the gateway. However, if the gateway is the encapsulating system, as when NAT is implemented for internal hosts, the inside IP header is not modified. In the event the TTL is modified, the checksum must be recreated by IPSec and used to replace the original to reflect the change, maintaining IP packet integrity.

During the creation of the outside IP header, most of the entries and options of the inside header are mapped to the outside. One of these is ToS (Type of Service) which is currently available in IPv4.

PROTECTING AND VERIFYING DATA

The AH and ESP protocols can provide authentication or integrity for the data, and the ESP can provide encryption support for the data. The security protocol's header contains the necessary information for the accompanying packet. Exhibit 8-3 shows each header's format.

Authentication and Integrity

Security protocols provide authentication and integrity of the packet by use of a message digest of the accompanying data. By definition, the security protocols must use HMAC-MD5 or HMAC-SHA-1 for hashing functions to meet the minimum requirements of the standard. The security protocol uses a hashing algorithm to produce a unique code that represents the original data that was hashed and reduces the result into a reasonably sized element called a digest. The original message contained in the packet accompanying the hash can be hashed by the recipient and then compared to the original delivered by the source. By comparing the hashed results, it is possible to determine if the data was modified in transit. If they match, then the message was not modified. If the message hash does not match, then the data has been altered from the time it was hashed. Exhibit 8-4 shows the communication flow and comparison of the hash digest.

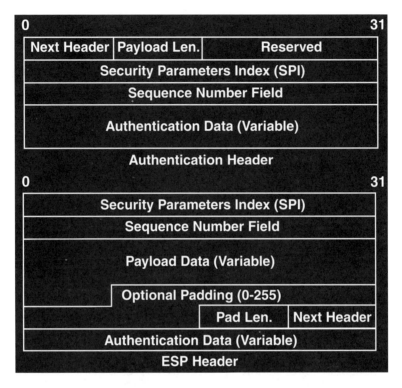

Exhibit 8-3. AH and ESP header format.

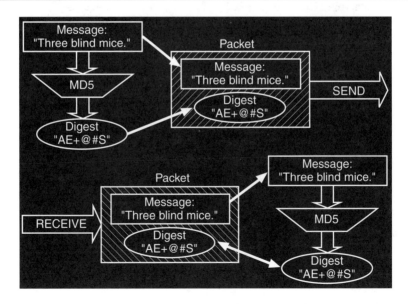

Exhibit 8-4. Message digest flow.

Confidentiality and Encryption

The two modes of operation effect the implementation of the ESP and the process of encrypting portions of the data being communicated. There is a separate RFC defining each form of encryption and the implementation of encryption for the ESP and the application in the two modes of communication. The standard requires that DES be the default encryption of the ESP. However, many forms of encryption technologies with varying degrees of strength can be applied to the standard. The current list is relatively limited due to the performance issues of high-strength algorithms and the processing required. With the advent of dedicated hardware for encryption processes and the advances in small, strong encryption algorithms such as ECC (Elliptic Curve Cryptosystems), the increase of VPN performance and confidentiality is inevitable.

In transport mode, the data of the original packet is encrypted and becomes the ESP. In tunnel mode, the entire original packet is encrypted and placed into a new IP packet in which the data portion is the ESP containing the original encrypted packet.

MANAGING CONNECTIONS

As mentioned earlier, SAs furnish the primary purpose of the IPSec protocol suite and the relationship between gateways and hosts. Several layers of application and standards provide the means for controlling, managing, and tracking SAs.

Various applications may require the unification of services, demanding combined SAs to accomplish the required transport. An example would be an application that requires authentication and confidentiality by utilizing AH and ESP and requires that further groups of SAs provide hierarchical communication. This process is called a SA Bundle, which can provide a layered effect of communications. SA bundles can be utilized by applications in two formats: fine granularity and coarse granularity.

Fine granularity is the assignment of SAs for each communication process. Data transmitted over a single SA is protected by a single security protocol. The data is protected by an AH or ESP, but not both because SAs can have only one security protocol.

Coarse granularity is the combination of services from several applications or systems into a group or portion of a SA bundle. This affords the communication two levels of protection by way of more than one SA.

Exhibit 8-5 conveys the complexity of SAs, and the options available become apparent considering that SAs in a SA bundle can terminate at different locations.

Consider the example of a host on the Internet that established a tunnel-mode SA with a gateway and a transport-mode SA to the final destination

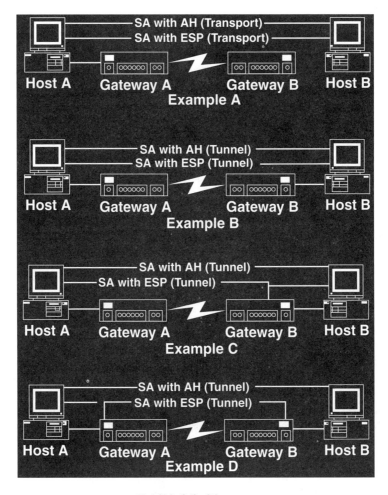

Exhibit 8-5. SA types.

internal host behind the gateway. This implementation affords the protection of communications over an untrusted medium and further protection once on the internal network for point-to-point secured communications. It also requires an SA bundle that terminates at different destinations.

There are two implementations of SA Bundles:

1. transport adjacency
2. iterated tunneling

Transport adjacency is applying more than one security protocol to the same IP datagram without implementing tunnel mode for communications. Using both AH and ESP provides a single level of protection and no nesting of communications since the endpoint of the communication is the final

171

destination. This application of transport adjacency is applied when transport mode is implemented for communication between two hosts, each behind a gateway. (See Exhibit 8-5: Example A.)

In contrast, iterated tunneling is the application of multiple layers of security protocols within a tunnel-mode SA(s). This allows for multiple layers of nesting since each SA can originate or terminate at different points in the communication stream. There are three occurrences of iterated tunneling:

- endpoints of each SA are identical
- one of the endpoints of the SAs is identical
- neither endpoint of the SAs is identical

Identical endpoints can refer to tunnel-mode communications between two hosts behind a set of gateways where SAs terminate at the hosts and AH (or ESP) is contained in an ESP providing the tunnel. (See Exhibit 8-5: Example B.)

With only one of the endpoints being identical, an SA can be established between the host and gateway and between the host and an internal host behind the gateway. This was used earlier as an example of one of the applications of SA Bundling. (See Exhibit 8-5: Example C.)

In the event of neither SA terminating at the same point, an SA can be established between two gateways and between two hosts behind the gateways. This application provides multi-layered nesting and communication protection. An example of this application is a VPN between two gateways that provide Tunnel mode operations for their corresponding networks to communicate. Hosts on each network are provided secured communication based on client-to-client SAs. This provides for several layers of authentication and data protection. (See Exhibit 8-5: Example D.)

ESTABLISHING A VPN

Now that the components of a VPN have been defined, it is necessary to discuss the form that they create when combined. To be IPSec compliant, four implementation types are required of the VPN. Each type is merely a combination of options and protocols with varying SA control. The four detailed here are only the required formats, and vendors are encouraged to build on the four basic models.

The VPNs shown in Exhibit 8-6 can use either security protocol. The mode of operation is defined by the role of the endpoint — except in client-to-client communications, which can be transport or tunnel mode.

In Example A, two hosts can establish secure peer communications over the Internet. Example B illustrates a typical gateway-to-gateway VPN with the VPN terminating at the gateways to provide connectivity for internal

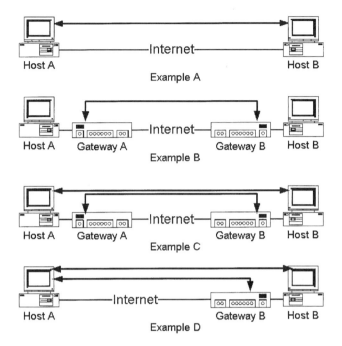

Exhibit 8-6. VPN types.

hosts. Example C combines Examples A and B to allow secure communications from host to host in an existing gateway-to-gateway VPN. Example D details the situation when a remote host connects to an ISP, receives an IP address, and then establishes a VPN with the destination network's gateway. A tunnel is established to the gateway, and then a tunnel or transport-mode communication is established to the internal system. In this example, it is necessary for the remote system to apply the transport header prior to the tunnel header. Also, it will be necessary for the gateway to allow IPSec connectivity and key management protocols from the Internet to the internal system.

KEEPING TRACK

Security associations and the variances of their applications can become complicated; levels of security, security protocol implementation, nesting, and SA Bundling all conspire to inhibit interoperability and to decrease management capabilities. To ensure compatibility, fundamental objectives are defined to enable coherent management and control of SAs. There are two primary groups of information, or databases, that are required to be maintained by any system participating in a IPSec VPN Security Policy Database (SPD) and Security Association Database (SAD).

The SPD is concerned with the status, service, or character provided by the SA and the relationships provided. The SAD is used to maintain the parameters of each active association. There are a minimum of two of each database — one for tracking inbound and another for outbound communications.

Communication Policies

The SPD is a security association management constructed to enforce a policy in the IPSec environment. Consequently, an essential element of SA processing is an underlying security policy that specifies what services are to be offered to IP datagrams and in what fashion they are implemented. SPD is consulted for all IP and IPSec communications, inbound and outbound, and therefore is associated with an interface. An interface that provides IPSec, and ultimately is associated with an SPD, is called a "black" interface. An interface where IPSec is not being performed is called a "red" interface and no data is encrypted for this network by that gateway. The number of SPDs and SADs are directly related to the number of black and red interfaces being supported by the gateway. The SPD must control traffic that is IPSec based and traffic that is not IPSec related. There are three modes of this operation:

1. forward and do not apply IPSec
2. discard packet
3. forward and apply IPSec

In the policy, or database, it is possible to configure traffic that is only IPSec to be forwarded, hence providing a basic firewall function by allowing only IPSec protocol packets into the black interface. A combination will allow multi-tunneling, a term that applies to gateways and hosts. It allows the system to discriminate and forward traffic based on destination, which ultimately determines if the data is encrypted or not. An example is to allow basic browsing from a host on the Internet while providing a secured connection to a remote gateway on the same connection. A remote user may dial an ISP and establish a VPN with the home office to get their mail. While receiving the mail, the user is free to access services on the Internet using the local ISP connection to the Internet.

If IPSec is to be applied to the packet, the SPD policy entry will specify a SA or SA bundle to be employed. Within the specification are the IPSec protocols, mode of operation, encryption algorithms, and any nesting requirements.

A *selector* is used to apply traffic to a policy. A security policy may determine several SAs be applied for an application in a defined order, and the parameters of this bundled operation must be detailed in the SPD. An example policy entry may specify that all matching traffic be protected by an ESP using DES, nested inside an AH using SHA-1. Each selector is employed to associate the policy to SAD entries.

The policies in the SPD are maintained in an ordered list. Each policy is associated with one or more selectors. Selectors define the IP traffic that characterizes the policy. Selectors have several parameters that define the communication to policy association, including:

- destination IP address
- source IP address
- name
- data sensitivity
- transport protocol
- source and destination TCP ports

Destination address may be unicast, multicast, broadcast, range of addresses, or a wildcard address. Broadcast, range, and wildcard addresses are used to support more than one destination using the same SA. The destination address defined in the selector is not the destination that is used to define an SA in the SAD (SPI, destination IP address, and IPSec protocol). The destination from the SA identifier is used as the packet arrives to identify the packet in the SAD. The destination address within the selector is obtained from the encapsulating IP header. Once the packet has been processed by the SA and un-encapsulated, its selector is identified by the IP address and associated to the proper policy in the inbound SPD. This issue does not exist in transport mode because only one IP header exists. The source IP address can be any of the types allowed by the destination IP address field.

There are two sets of names that can be included in the Name field: User ID and System Name.

User ID can be a user string associated with a fully qualified domain name (FQDN), as with person@company.com. Another accepted form of user identification is X.500 distinguished name. An example of this type of name could be: C=US,O=Company,OU=Finance,CN=Person. System name can be a FQDN, box.company.com, or an X.500 distinguished name.

Data sensitivity defines the level of security applied to that packet. This is required for all systems implemented in an environment that uses data labels for information security flow.

Transport protocol and port are obtained from the header. These values may not be available because of the ESP header or not mapped due to options being utilized in the originating IP header.

Security Association Control

The SPD is policy driven and is concerned with system relationships. However, the SAD is responsible for each SA in the communications defined by the SPD. Each SA has an entry in the SAD. The SA entries in the

SAD are indexed by the three SA properties: destination IP address, IPSec protocol, and SPI. The SAD database contains nine parameters for processing IPSec protocols and the associated SA:

- sequence number counter for outbound communications
- sequence number overflow counter that sets an option flag to prevent further communications utilizing the specific SA
- a 32-bit anti-replay window that is used to identify the packet for that point in time traversing the SA and provides the means to identify that packet for future reference
- lifetime of the SA that is determined by a byte count or time frame, or a combination of the two
- the algorithm used in the AH
- the algorithm used in the authenticating the ESP
- the algorithm used in the encryption of the ESP
- IPSec mode of operation: transport or tunnel mode
- path MTU (PMTU) (this is data that is required for ICMP data over a SA)

Each of these parameters is referenced in the SPD for assignment to policies and applications. The SAD is responsible for the lifetime of the SA, which is defined in the security policy. There are two lifetime settings for each SA: soft lifetime and hard lifetime.

Soft lifetime determines a point when to initiate the process to create a replacement SA. This is typical for rekeying procedures. Hard lifetime is the point where the SA expires. If a replacement SA has not been established, the communications will discontinue.

PROVIDING MULTI-LAYERED SECURITY FLOW

There are many systems that institute multi-layered security (MLS), or data labeling, to provide granularity of security based on the data and the systems it may traverse while on the network. This model of operation can be referred to as Mandatory Access Control (MAC). An example of this security model is the Bell–LaPadula model, designed to protect against the unauthorized transmission of sensitive information. Because the data itself is tagged for review while in transit, several layers of security can be applied. Other forms of security models such as Discretionary Access Control (DAC) that may employ access control lists or filters are not sufficient to support multi-layer security. The AH and ESP can be combined to provide the necessary security policy that may be required for MLS systems working in a MAC environment.

This is accomplished by using the authenticating properties of the AH security protocol to bind security mappings in the original IP header to the payload. Using the AH in this manner allows the authentication of the data against the header. Currently, IPv4 does not validate the payload with the header. The sensitivity of the data is assumed only by default of the header.

To accomplish this process each SA, or SA Bundle, must be discernable from other levels of secured information being transmitted. An example is: "SENSITIVE" labeled data will be mapped to a SA or a SA Bundle, while "CLASSIFIED" labeled data will be mapped to others. The SAD and SPD contain a parameter called *Sensitivity Information* that can be accessed by various implementations to ensure that the data being transferred is afforded the proper encryption level and forwarded to the associated SAs.

There are two forms of processing when MAC is implemented:

1. inbound operation
2. outbound operation

When a packet is received and passed to the IPSec functions, the MLS must verify the sensitivity information level prior to passing the datagram to upper layer protocols or forwarding. The sensitivity information level is then bound to the associated SA and stored in the SPD to properly apply policies for that level of secured data.

Outbound requirements of the MLS are to ensure that the selection of a SA, or SA Bundle, is appropriate for the sensitivity of the data, as defined in the policy. The data for this operation is contained in the SAD and SPD, which is modified by defined policies and the previous inbound operations.

Implementations of this process are vendor driven. Defining the level of encryption, type of authentication, key management scheme, and other security-related parameters associated with a data label are available for vendors to implement. The mechanism for defining policies that can be applied is accessible and vendors are beginning to become aware of these options as comfort and maturity of the IPSec standard are realized.

A KEY POINT

Key management is an important aspect of IPSec or any encrypted communication that uses keys to provide information confidentiality and integrity. Key management and the protocols utilized are implemented to set up, maintain, and control secure relationships and ultimately the VPN between systems. During key management, there are several layers of system insurance prior to the establishment of an SA, and there are several mechanisms used to accommodate these processes.

KEY HISTORY

Key management is far from obvious definition, and lackadaisical conversation with interchanged acronyms only adds to the perceived misunderstandings. The following is an outline of the different protocols that are used to get keys and data from one system to another.

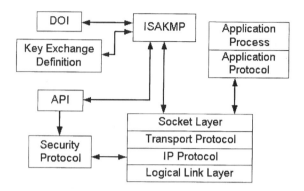

Exhibit 8-7. ISAKMP structure.

The Internet Security Association and Key Management Protocol (ISAKMP) (RFC 2408) defines the procedures for authenticating a communicating peer and key generation techniques. All of these are necessary to establish and maintain an SA in an Internet environment. ISAKMP defines payloads for exchanging key and authentication data. As shown Exhibit 8-7, these formats provide a consistent framework that is independent of the encryption algorithm, authentication mechanism being implemented, and security protocol, such as IPSec.

The Internet Key Exchange (IKE) protocol (RFC 2409) is a hybrid containing three primary, existing protocols that are combined to provide an IPSec-specific key management platform. The three protocols are:

1. ISAKMP
2. Oakley
3. SKEME (Secure Key Exchange Mechanism)

Different portions of each of these protocols work in conjunction to securely provide keying information specifically for the IETF IPSec DOI. The terms IKE and ISAKMP are used interchangeably with various vendors, and many use ISAKMP to describe the keying function. While this is correct, ISAKMP addresses the procedures and not the technical operations as they pertain to IPSec. IKE is the term that best represents the IPSec implementation of key management.

Public Key Infrastructure (PKI) is a suite of protocols that provide several areas of secure communication based on trust and digital certificates. PKI integrates digital certificates, public key cryptography, and certificate authorities into a total, enterprisewide network security architecture that can be utilized by IPSec.

IPSec IKE

As described earlier, IKE is a combination of several existing key management protocols that are combined to provide a specific key management system. IKE is considerably complicated, and several variations are available in the establishment of trust and providing keying material.

Oakley and ISAKMP protocols, which are included in IKE, each define separate methods of establishing an authenticated key exchange between systems. Oakley defines *modes* of operation to build a secure relationship path, and ISAKMP defines *phases* to accomplish much the same process in a hierarchical format. The relationship between these two is represented by IKE with different exchanges as modes, which operate in one of two phases. Implementing multiple phases may add overhead in processing, resulting in performance degradation, but several advantages can be realized. Some of these are:

- first phase creation assisted by second phase
- first phas key material used in second phase
- first phase trust used for second phase

The first phase session can be disbursed among several second phase operations to provide the construction of new ISAKMP security associations (ISA for purposes of clarity in this document) without the renegotiation process between the peers. This allows for the first phase of subsequent ISAs to be preempted via communications in the second phase.

Another benefit is that the first phase process can provide security services for the second phase in the form of encryption keying material. However, if the first phase does not meet the requirements of the second phase, no data can be exchanged or provided from the first to the second phase.

With the first phase providing peer identification, the second phase may provide the creation of the security protocol SAs without the concern for authentication of the peer. If the first phase were not available, each new SA would need to authenticate the peer system. This function of the first phase is an important feature for IPSec communications. Once peers are authenticated by means of certificates or shared secret, all communications of the second phase and internal to the IPSec SAs are authorized for transport. The remaining authentication is for access control. By this point, the trusted communication has been established at a higher level.

PHASES AND MODES

Phase one takes place when the two ISAKMP peers establish a secure, authenticated channel with which to communicate. Each system is verified and authenticated against its peer to allow for future communications.

Phase two exists to provide keying information and material to assist in the establishment of SAs for an IPSec communication.

Within phase one, there are two modes of operation defined in IKE: main mode and aggressive mode. Each of these accomplishes a phase one secure exchange, and these two modes only exist in phase one. Within phase two, there are two modes: quick mode and new group mode.

Quick Mode is used to establish SAs on behalf of the underlying security protocol. New Group Mode is designated as a phase two mode only because it must exist in phase two; however, the service provided by New Group Mode is to benefit phase one operations. As described earlier, one of the advantages of a two-phase approach is that the second phase can be used to provide additional ISAs, which eliminates the reauthorization of the peers.

Phase one is initiated using ISAKMP-defined cookies. The initiator cookie (I-cookie) and responder cookie (R-cookie) are used to establish an ISA, which provides end-to-end authenticated communications. That is, ISAKMP communications are bi-directional and, once established, either peer may initiate a Quick mode to establish SA communications for the security protocol. The order of the cookies is crucial for future second phase operations. A single ISA can be used for many second phase operations, and each second phase operation can be used for several SAs or SA Bundles. Main Mode and Aggressive Mode each use Diffie-Hellman keying material to provide authentication services.

While Main Mode must be implemented, Aggressive Mode is not required. Main Mode provides several messages to authenticate. The first two messages determine a communication policy; the next two messages exchange Diffie–Hellman public data; and the last two messages authenticate the Diffie–Hellman Exchange. Aggressive Mode is an option available to vendors and developers that provides much more information with fewer messages and acknowledgements. The first two messages in Aggressive Mode determine a communication policy and exchange Diffie–Hellman public data. In addition, a second message authenticates the responder, thus completing the negotiation.

Phase two is much simpler in nature in that it provides keying material for the initiation of SAs for the security protocol. This is the point where key management is utilized to maintain the SAs for IPSec communications. The second phase has one mode designed to support IPSec: Quick Mode. Quick Mode verifies and establishes the keying process for the creation of SAs. Not related directly to IPSec SAs is the New Group Mode of operation; New Group provides services for phase one for the creation of additional ISAs.

SYSTEM TRUST ESTABLISHMENT

The first step in establishing communications is verification of the remote system. There are three primary forms of authenticating a remote system:

1. shared secret
2. certificate
3. public/private key

Of these methods, shared secret is currently used widely due to the relatively slow integration of Certificate Authority (CA) systems and the ease of implementation. However, shared secret is not scalable and can become unmanageable very quickly due to the fact that there can be a separate secret for each communication. Public and private key use is employed in combination with Diffie–Hellman to authenticate and provide keying material. During the system authentication process, hashing algorithms are utilized to protect the authenticating shared secret as it is forwarded over untrusted networks. This process of using hashing to authenticate is nearly identical to the authentication process of an AH security protocol. However, the message — in this case a password — is not sent with the digest. The map previously shared or configured with participating systems will contain the necessary data to be compared to the hash.

An example of this process is a system, called system A, that requires a VPN to a remote system, called system B. By means of a preconfigured map, system A knows to sends its hashed shared secret to system B to access a network supported by system B. System B will hash the expected shared secret and compare it to the hash received from system A. If the two hashes match, an authenticated trust relationship is established.

Certificates are a different process of trust establishment. Each device is issued a certificate from a CA. When a remote system requests communication establishment, it will present its certificate. The recipient will query the CA to validate the certificate. The trust is established between the two systems by means of an ultimate trust relationship with the CA and the authenticating system. Seeing that certificates can be made public and are centrally controlled, there is no need to attempt to hash or encrypt the certificate.

KEY SHARING

Once the two systems are confident of each other's identity, the process of sharing or swapping keys must take place to provide encryption for future communications. The mechanisms that can be utilized to provide keying are related to the type of encryption to be utilized for the ESP. There are two basic forms of keys: symmetrical and asymmetrical.

Symmetrical key encryption occurs when the same key is used for the encryption of information into human unintelligible data (or cipher text) and the decryption of that cipher text into the original information format. If the key used in symmetrical encryption is not carefully shared with the participating individuals, an attacker can obtain the key, decrypt the data, view or alter the information, encrypt the data with the stolen key, and forward it to the final destination. This process is defined as a man-in-the-middle attack and, if properly executed, can affect data confidentiality and integrity, rendering the valid participants in the communication oblivious to the exposure and the possible modification of the information.

Asymmetrical keys consist of a key-pair that is mathematically related and generated by a complicated formula. The concept of asymmetrical comes from the fact that the encryption is one way with either of the key-pair, and data that is encrypted with one key can only be decrypted with the other key of the pair. Asymmetrical key encryption is incredibly popular and can be used to enhance the process of symmetrical key sharing. Also, with the use of two keys, digital signatures have evolved and the concept of trust has matured to certificates, which contribute to a more secure relationship.

ONE KEY

Symmetrical keys are an example of DES encryption, where the same keying information is used to encrypt and decrypt the data. However, to establish communications with a remote system, the key must be made available to the recipient for decryption purposes. In early cases, this may have been a phone call, e-mail, fax, or some form of nonrelated communication medium. However, none of these options are secure or can communicate strong encryption keys that require a sophisticated key that is nearly impossible to convey in a password or phrase.

In 1976, two mathematicians, Bailey W. Diffie at Berkeley and Martin E. Hellman at Stanford, defined the Diffie–Hellman agreement protocol (also known as exponential key agreement) and published it in a paper entitled, "New Directions in Cryptography." The protocol allows two autonomous systems to exchange a secret key over an untrusted network without any prior secrets. Diffie and Hellman postulated that the generation of a key could be accomplished by fundamental relationships between prime numbers. Some years later, Ron Rivest, Adi Shamir, and Leonard Adelman, who developed the RSA Public and Private key cryptosystem based on large prime numbers, further developed the Diffie–Hellman formula (i.e., the nuts and bolts of the protocol). This allowed communication of a symmetrical key without transmitting the actual key, but rather a mathematical portion or fingerprint.

An example of this process is system A and system B requires keying material for the DES encryption for the ESP to establish a SA. Each system

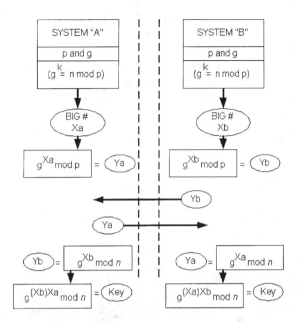

Exhibit 8-8. Diffie-Hellman exchange protocol.

acquires the Diffie–Hellman parameters, a large prime number p and a base number g, which must be smaller than $p - 1$. The generator, g, is a number that represents every number between 1 and p to the power of k. Therefore, the relationship is $g^k =$ n mod p.

Both of these numbers must be hardcoded or retrieved from a remote system. Each system then generates a number X, which must be less than $p - 2$. The number X is typically created by a random string of characters entered by a user or a passphrase that can be combined with date and time to create a unique number. The hardcoded numbers will not be exceeded because most, if not all, applications employ a limit on the input.

As shown in Exhibit 8-8, a new key is generated with these numbers, g^xmod p. The result Y, or fingerprint, is then shared between the systems over the untrusted network. The formula is then exercised again using the shared data from the other system and the Diffie–Hellman parameters. The results will be mathematically equivalent and can be used to generate a symmetrical key. If each system executes this process successfully, they will have matching symmetrical keys without transmitting the key itself. The Diffie–Hellman protocol was finally patented in 1980 (U.S. Patent 4200770) and is such a strong protocol that there are currently 128 other patents that reference Diffie–Hellman.

To complicate matters, Diffie–Hellman is vulnerable to man-in-the-middle attacks because the peers are not authenticated using Diffie-Hellman.

The process is built on the trust established prior to keying material creation. To provide added authentication properties within the Diffie-Hellman procedure, the Station-to-Station (STS) protocol was created. Diffie, Oorschot, and Wiener completed STS in 1992 by allowing the two parties to authenticate themselves to each other by the use of digital signatures created by a public and private key relationship.

An example of this process, as shown in Exhibit 8-9, transpires when each system is provided a public and private key-pair. System A will encrypt the Y value (in this case Ya) with the private key. When system B receives the signature, it can only be decrypted with the system A public key. The only plausible result is that system A encrypted the Ya value authenticating system A. The STS protocol allows for the use of certificates to further authorize the public key of system A to ensure that the man-in-the-middle has not compromised the key-pair integrity.

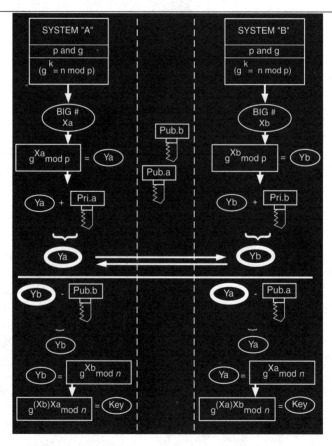

Exhibit 8-9. Diffie–Hellman exchange protocol with STS.

Many Keys

Asymmetrical keys, such as PGP (Pretty Good Privacy) and RSA, can be used to share the keying information. Asymmetrical keys were specifically designed to have one of the keys in a pair published. A sender of data can obtain the public key of the preferred recipient to encrypt data that can only be decrypted by the holder of the corresponding private key. The application of asymmetrical keys in the sharing of information does not require the protection of the public key in transit over an untrusted network.

KEY ESTABLISHMENT

IPSec standard mandates that key management must support two forms of key establishment: manual and automatic.

The other IPSec protocols (AH and ESP) are not typically affected by the type of key management. However, there may be issues with implementing anti-replay options, and the level of authentication can be related to the key management process supported. Indeed, key management can also be related to the ultimate security of the communication. If the key is compromised, the communication can be endangered of attack. To thwart the eventuality of such an attack, there are re-keying mechanisms that attempt to ensure that if a key is compromised its validity is limited either by time, amount of data encrypted, or a combination of both.

Manual Keying

Manual key management requires that an administrator provide the keying material and necessary security association information for communications. Manual techniques are practical for small environments with limited numbers of gateways and hosts. Manual key management does not scale to include many sites in a meshed or partially meshed environment. An example is a company with five sites throughout North America. This organization wants to use the Internet for communications, and each office site must be able to communicate directly with any other office site. If each VPN relationship had a unique key, the number of keys can be calculated by the formula $n(n - 1)/2$, where n is the number of sites. In this example, the number of keys is 10. Apply this formula to 25 sites (i.e., five times the number of sites in the previous example) and the number of keys skyrockets to 300, not 50. In reality, the management is more difficult than it may appear by the examples. Each device must be configured, and the keys must be shared with all corresponding systems. The use of manual keying conspires to reduce the flexibility and options of IPSec. Anti-replay, on-demand re-keying, and session-specific key management are not available in manual key creation.

Automatic Keying

Automatic key management responds to the limited manual process and provides for widespread, automated deployment of keys. The goal of the IPSec is to build off existing Internet standards to accommodate a fluid approach to interoperability. As described earlier, the IPSec default automated key management is IKE, a hybrid based in ISAKMP. However, based on the structure of the standard, any automatic key management can be employed. Automated key management, when instituted, may create several keys for a single SA. There are various reasons for this, including:

- encryption algorithm requires more than one key
- authentication algorithm requires more than one key
- encryption and authentication are used for a single SA
- re-keying

The encryption and authentication algorithms' use of multiple keys, or if both algorithms are used, then multiple keys will need to be generated for the SA. An example of this would be if Triple-DES is used to encrypt the data. There are several types of applications of Triple-DES (DES-EEE3, DES-EDE3, and DES-EEE2) and each uses more than one key (DES-EEE2 uses two keys, one of which is used twice).

The process of re-keying is to protect future data transmissions in the event a key is compromised. This process requires the rebuilding of an existing SA. The concept of re-keying during data transmission provides a relatively unpredictable communication flow. Being unpredictable is considered a valuable security method against an attacker.

Automatic key management can provide two primary methods of key provisioning:

- multiple string
- single string

Multiple strings are passed to the corresponding system in the SA for each key and for each type. For example, the use of Triple-DES for the ESP will require more than one key to be generated for a single type of algorithm, in this case, the encryption algorithm. The recipient will receive a string of data representing a single key; once the transfer has been acknowledged, the next string representing another key will be transmitted.

In contrast, the single string method sends all the required keys in a single string. As one might imagine, this requires a stringent set of rules for management. Great attention is necessary to ensure that the systems involved properly map the corresponding bits to the same key strings for the SA being established. To ensure that IPSec-compliant systems properly map the bit to keys, the string is read from the left, highest bit order first for the encryption key(s) and the remaining string is used for the authentication. The number of bits used is determined by the encryption algorithm and the number of keys required for the encryption being utilized for that SA.

TECHNOLOGY TURNED MAINSTREAM

VPNs are making a huge impact on the way communications are viewed. They are also providing ample fodder for administrators and managers to have seemingly endless discussions about various applications. On one side are the possible money savings, and the other are implementation issues. There are several areas of serious concern:

- performance
- interoperability
- scalability
- flexibility

Performance

Performance of data flow is typically the most common concern, and IPSec is very processor intensive. The performance costs of IPSec are the encryption being performed, integrity checking, packet handling based on policies, and forwarding, all of which become apparent in the form of latency and reduced throughput. IPSec VPNs over the Internet increase the latency in the communication that conspires with the processing costs to discourage VPN as a solution for transport-sensitive applications. Process time for authentication, key management, and integrity verification will produce delay issues with SA establishment, authentication, and IPSec SA maintenance. Each of these results in poor initialization response and, ultimately, disgruntled users.

The application of existing hardware encryption technology to IPSec vendor products has allowed these solutions to be considered more closely by prospective clients wishing to seize the monetary savings associated with the technology. The creation of a key and its subsequent use in the encryption process can be offloaded onto a dedicated processor that is designed specifically for these operations. Until the application of hardware encryption for IPSec, all data was managed through software computation that was also responsible for many other operations that may be running on the gateway.

Hardware encryption has released IPSec VPN technology into the realm of viable communication solutions. Unfortunately, the client operating system participating in a VPN is still responsible for the IPSec process. Publicly available mobile systems that provide hardware-based encryption for IPSec communications are becoming available, but are sometime away from being standard issue for remote users.

Interoperability

Interoperability is a current issue that will soon become antiquated as vendors recognize the need to become fully IPSec compliant — or consumers will not implement their product based simply on its incompatibility. Shared secret and ISAKMP key management protocol are typically allowing multi-vendor interoperability. As Certificate Authorities and the technology that supports them become fully adopted technology, they will only add to the cross-platform integration. However, complex and large VPNs will not be manageable using different vendor products in the near future. Given the complexity, recentness of the IPSec standard, the and the various interpretations of that standard, time to complete interoperability seems great.

Scalability

Scalability is obtained by the addition of equipment and bandwidth. Some vendors have created products focused on remote access for roaming users, while others have concentrated on network-to-network connectivity without much attention to remote users. The current ability to scale the solution will be directly related to the service required. The standard supporting the technology allows for great flexibility in the addition of services. It will be more common to find limitations in equipment configurations than in the standard as it pertains to growth capabilities. Scalability ushers in a wave of varying issues, including:

- authentication
- management
- performance

Authentication can be provided by a number of processes, although the primary focus has been on RADIUS (Remote Access Dial-In User Security), Certificates, and forms of two factor authentication. Each of these can be applied to several supporting databases. RADIUS is supported by nearly every common authenticating system from Microsoft Windows NT to NetWare's NDS. Authentication, when implemented properly, should not become a scalability issue for many implementations, because the goal is to integrate the process with existing or planned enterprise authenticating services.

A more interesting aspect of IPSec vendor implementations and the scalability issues that might arise is management. As detailed earlier, certain implementations do not scale, due to the shear physics of shared secrets and manual key management. In the event of the addition of equipment or increased bandwidth to support remote applications, the management will need to take multiplicity into consideration. Currently, VPN management of remote users and networks leaves a great deal to be desired. As vendors and organizations become more acquainted with what can be accomplished, sophisticated management capabilities will become increasingly available.

Performance is an obvious issue when considering the increase of an implementation. Typically, performance is the driving reason, followed by support for increased numbers. Both of these issues are volatile and inter-related with the hardware technology driving the implementation. Performance capabilities can be controlled by the limitation of supported SAs on a particular system — a direct limitation in scalability. A type of requested encryption might not be available on the encryption processor currently available. Forcing the calculation of encryption onto the operating system ultimately limits the performance. A limitation may resonate in the form of added equipment to accomplish the link between the IPSec equipment and the authenticating database. When users authenticate, the granularity of control over the capabilities of that user may be directly related to the form of authentication. The desired form of authentication may have limitations in various environments due to restrictions in various types of authenticating databases. Upgrade issues, service pack variations, user limitations, and protocol requirements also combine to limit growth of the solution.

THE MARKET FOR VPN

Several distinct qualities of VPN are driving the investigation by many organizations to implement VPN as a business interchange technology. VPNs attempt to resolve a variety of current technological limitations that represent themselves as costs in equipment and support or solutions where none had existed prior. Three areas that can be improved by VPNs are:

- remote user access and remote office connectivity
- extranet partner connectivity
- internal departmental security

Remote Access

Providing remote users access via a dial-up connection can become a costly service for any organization to provide. Organizations must consider costs for:

- telephone lines
- terminating equipment
- long-distance
- calling card
- 800/877 number support

Telephone connections must be increased to support the number of proposed simultaneous users that will be dialing in for connectivity to the network. Another cost that is rolled up into the telephone line charge is the possible need for equipment to allow the addition of telephone lines to an existing system. Terminating equipment, such as modem pools, can become expenses that are immediate savings once VPN is utilized. Long-distance charges, calling cards that are supplied to roaming users, and toll-free lines require initial capital and continuous financial support. In reality, an organization employing conventional remote access services is nothing more than a service provider for their employees. Taking this into consideration, many organizations tend to overlook the use of the Internet connection by the remote users. As the number of simultaneous users access the network, the more bandwidth is utilized for the existing Internet service.

The cost savings are realized by redirecting funds, originally to support telephone communications, in an Internet service provider (ISP) and its ability to support a greater area of access points and technology. This allows an organization to eliminate support for all direct connectivity and focus on a single connection and technology for all data exchange — ultimately saving money. With the company access point becoming a single point of entry, access controls, authenticating mechanisms, security policies, and system redundancy is focused and common among all types of access regardless of the originator's communication technology.

The advent of high-speed Internet connectivity by means of cable-modems and ADSL (Asynchronous Digital Subscriber Line) is an example of how VPN becomes an enabler to facilitate the need for high-speed, individual remote access where none existed before. Existing remote access technologies are generally limited to 128K ISDN (Integrated Services Digital Network), or more typically, 56K modem access. Given the inherent properties of the Internet and IPSec functioning at the network layer, the communication technology utilized to access the Internet only needs to be supported at the immediate connection point to establish an IP session with the ISP. Using the Internet as a backbone for encrypted communications allows for equal IP functionality with increased performance and security over conventional remote access technology.

Currently, cable-modem and ADSL services are expanding from the home-user market into the business industry for remote office support. A typical remote office will have a small Frame Relay connection to the home office. Any Internet traffic from the remote office is usually forwarded to the home office's Internet connection, where access controls can be centrally managed and Internet connection costs are eliminated at the remote office. However, as the number of remote offices and the distances increase, so does the financial investment. Each Frame Relay connection, PVC (Permanent Virtual Circuit), has costs associated with it. Committed Information Rate (CIR), Port speed (e.g., 128K), and sometimes a connection fee add to the overall investment. A PVC is required for any connection; so as remote offices demand direct communication to their peers, a PVC will need to be added to support this decentralized communication. Currently within the United States, the cost of Frame Relay is very low and typically outweighs the cost of an ISP and Internet connectivity. As the distance increases and moves beyond the United States, the costs can increase exponentially and will typically call for more than one telecommunications vendor. With VPN technology, a local connection to the Internet can be established. Adding connectivity to peers is accomplished by configuration modifications; this allows the customer to control communications without the inclusion of the carrier in the transformation.

The current stability of remote, tier three and lower ISPs is an unknown variable. The arguable service associated with multiple and international ISP connectivity has become the Achilles' heel for VPN acceptance for business-critical and time-critical services. As the reach of tier one and tier two ISPs increases, they will be able to provide contiguous connectivity over the Internet to remote locations using an arsenal of available technologies.

Extranet Access

The single, most advantageous characteristic of VPNs is to provide protected and controlled communication with partnering organizations. Years ago, prior to VPN becoming a catchword, corporations were beginning to feel the need for dedicated Internet access. The dedicated access is becoming utilized for business purposes, whereas before it was viewed as a service for employees and research requirements.

The Internet provides the ultimate bridge between networks that was relatively nonexistent before VPN technology. Preceding VPNs, a corporation needing to access a partner's site was typically provided a Frame Relay connection to a common Frame Relay cloud where all the partners claimed access. Other options were ISDN and dial-on-demand routing. As this requirement grows, several limitations begin to surface. Security issues, partner support, controlling access, disallowing unwanted interchange between partners, and connectivity support for partners without supported access technologies all conspire to expose the huge advantages of VPNs over the Internet. Utilizing VPNs, an organization can maintain a high granularity of control over the connectivity per partner or per user on a partner network.

Internal Protection

As firewalls became more predominant as protection against the Internet, they were increasingly being utilized for internal segmentation of departmental entities. The need for protecting vital departments within an organization originally spawned this concept of using firewalls internally. As the number of departments increase, the management, complexity, and cost of the firewalls increase as well. Also, any attacker with access to the protected network can easily obtain sensitive information due to the fact that the firewall applies only perimeter security.

VLANs (Virtual Local Area Networks) with access control lists became a minimized replacement for conventional firewalls. However, the same security issue remained, in that the perimeter security was controlled and left the internal network open for attack.

As IPSec became accepted as a viable secure communication technology and applied in MAC environments, it also became the replacement for other protection technologies. Combined with strategically placed firewalls, VPN over internal networks allows secure connectivity between hosts. IPSec encryption, authentication, and access control provide protection for data between departments and within a department.

CONSIDERATION FOR VPN IMPLEMENTATION

The benefits of VPN technology can be realized in varying degrees depending on the application and the requirements it has been applied to. Considering the incredible growth in technology, the advantages will only increase. Nevertheless, the understandable concerns with performance, reliability, scalability, and implementation issues must be investigated.

System Requirements

The first step is determining the foreseeable amount of traffic and its patterns to ascertain the adjacent system requirements or augmentations. In the event that existing equipment is providing all or a portion of the service the VPN is replacing, the costs can be compared to discover initial savings in the framework of money, performance, or functionality.

Security Policy

It will be necessary to determine if the VPN technology and how it is planned to be implemented meets the current security policy. In case the security policy does not address the area of remote access, or in the event a policy or remote access does not exist, a policy must address the security requirements of the organization and its relationship with the service provided by VPN technology.

Application Performance

As previously discussed, performance is the primary reason VPN technology is not the solution for many organizations. It will be necessary to determine the speed at which an application can execute the essential processes. This is related to the type of data within the VPN. Live traffic or user sessions are incredibly sensitive to any latency in the communication. Pilot tests and load simulation should be considered strongly prior to large-scale VPN deployment or replacement of exiting services and equipment.

Data replication or transient activity that is not associated with human or application time sensitivity is a candidate for VPN connectivity. The application's resistance to latency must be measured to determine the minimum requirements for the VPN. This is not to convey that VPNs are only good for replication traffic and cannot support user applications. It is necessary to determine the application needs and verify the requirements to properly gauge the performance provisioning of the VPN. The performance "window" will allow the proper selection of equipment to meet the needs of the proposed solution; otherwise, the equipment and application may present poor results compared to the expected or planned results. Or, more importantly, the acquired equipment is under-worked or does not scale in the direction needed for a particular organization's growth path. Each of these results in poor investment realization and make it much more difficult to persuade management to use VPN again.

Training

User and administrator training are an important part of the implementation process. It is necessary to evaluate a vendor's product from the point of the users, as well as evaluating the other attributes of the product. In the event the user experience is poor, it will reach management and ultimately weigh heavily on the administrators and security practitioners. It is necessary to understand the user intervention that is required in the every-day process of application use. Comprehending the user knowledge requirements will allow for the creation of a training curriculum that best represents what the users are required to accomplish to operate the VPN as per the security policy.

FUTURE OF IPSec VPNs

Like it or not, VPN is here to stay. IP version 6 (IPv6) has the IPSec entrenched in its very foundation; and as the Internet grows, Ipv6 will become more prevalent. The current technological direction of typical networks will become the next goals for IPSec; specifically, Quality of Service (QoS). ATM was practically invented to accommodate the vast array of communication technologies at high speeds; but to do it efficiently, it must control who gets in and out of the network.

Ethernet Type of Service (ToS) (802.1p) allows for three bits of data in the frame to be used to add ToS information and then be mapped into ATM cells. IP version 4, currently applied, has support for a ToS field in the IP Header similar to Ethernet 802.1p; it provides three bits for extended information. Currently, techniques are being applied to map QoS information from one medium to another. This is very exciting for service organizations that will be able sell end-to-end QoS. As the IPSec standard grows and current TCP/IP applications and networks begin to support the existing IP ToS field, IPSec will quickly conform to the requirements.

The IETF and other participants, in the form of RFCs, are continually addressing the issues that currently exist with IPSec. Packet sizes are typically increased due to the added headers and sometimes trailer information associated with IPSec. The result is increased possibility of packet fragmentation. IPSec addresses fragmentation and packet loss; the overhead of these processes are the largest concern.

IPSec can only be applied to the TCP/IP protocol. Therefore, multi-protocol networks and environments that employ IPX/SPX, NetBEUI, and others will not take direct advantage of the IPSec VPN. To allow non-TCP/IP protocols to communicate over a an IPSec VPN, an IP gateway must be implemented to encapsulate the original protocol into an IP packet and then be forwarded to the IPSec gateway. IP gateways have been in use for some time and are proven technology. For several organizations that cannot eliminate non-TCP/IP protocols and wish to implement IPSec as the VPN of choice, a protocol gateway is imminent.

As is obvious, performance is crucial to IPSec VPN capabilities and cost. As encryption algorithms become increasingly sophisticated and hardware support for those algorithms become readily available, this current limitation will be surpassed.

Another perceived limitation of IPSec is the encryption export and import restrictions of encryption. There are countries that the United States places restrictions on to hinder the ability of those countries to encrypt possibly harmful information into the United States. In 1996, the International Traffic in Arms Regulation (ITAR) governing the export of cryptography was reconditioned. Responsibility for cryptography exports was transferred to the Department of Commerce from the Department of State. However, the Department of Justice is now part of the export review process. In addition, the National Security Agency (NSA) remains the final arbiter of whether to grant encryption products export licenses.

The NSA staff is assigned to the Commerce Department and many other federal agencies that deal with encryption policy and standards. This includes the State Department, Justice Department, National Institute for Standards and Technology (NIST), and the Federal Communications Commission. As one can imagine, the laws governing the export of encryption are complicated and are under constant revision. Several countries are completely denied access to encrypted communications to the United States; other countries have limitations due to government relationships and political posture. The current list of (as of this writing) embargoed countries include:

- Syria
- Iran
- Iraq
- North Korea
- Libya
- Cuba
- Sudan
- Serbia

As one reads the list of countries, it is easy to determine why the United States is reluctant to allow encrypted communications with these countries. Past wars, conflict of interests, and terrorism are the primary ingredients to become exiled by the United States.

Similar rosters exist for other countries that have the United States listed as "unfriendly," due to their perception of communication with the United States.

As one can certainly see, the concept of encryption export and import laws is vague, complex, and constantly in litigation. In the event a VPN is required for international communication, it will be necessary to obtain the latest information available to properly implement the communication as per the current laws.

CONCLUSION

VPN technology, based on IPSec, will become more prevalent in our every day existence. The technology is in its infancy; the standards and support for them are growing everyday. Security engineers will see an interesting change in how security is implemented and maintained on a daily basis. It will generate new types of policies and firewall solutions — router support for VPN will skyrocket.

This technology will finally confront encryption export and import laws forcing the hand of many countries. Currently, there are several issues with export and import restrictions that affect how organizations deploy VPN technology. As VPNs become more prevalent in international communications, governments will be forced to expedite the process. With organizations sharing information, services, and product, the global economy will force computer security to become the primary focus for many companies.

For VPNs, latency is the center for concern and, once hardware solutions and algorithms collaborate to enhance overall system performance, the technology will become truly accepted. Once this point is reached, every packet on every network will be encrypted. Browsers, e-mail clients, and the like will have VPN software embedded, and only authenticated communications will be allowed. Clear Internet traffic will be material for campfire stories. It is a good time to be in security.

Domain 3
Security
Management
Practices

SECURITY MANAGEMENT EMBODIES THE ADMINISTRATIVE AND PROCEDURAL INFRASTRUCTURE FOR THE SUPPORT OF INFORMATION PROTECTION. It encompasses risk management, policy development, and security education. The results of a diligent business risk management program establish the foundation for the information security program. Following on the risk assessment, security policies provide the management direction for the protection of information assets; security awareness programs communicate to the corporate community at large, the value that management places on its assets; and how each employee can play a role in its protection.

Information security is a business issue. A well-managed information security program ensures that technology is implemented to support the business priorities for the protection of assets and that the cost and extent of protection is commensurate with the value of the information.

The new chapters in this domain delve into the myriad of tools and techniques that are applied within the organization, to provide an adequate standard of due care.

Chapter 9
Penetration Testing
Stephen Fried

THIS CHAPTER PROVIDES A GENERAL INTRODUCTION TO THE SUBJECT OF PENETRATION TESTING AND PROVIDES THE SECURITY PROFESSIONAL WITH THE BACKGROUND NEEDED TO UNDERSTAND THIS SPECIAL AREA OF SECURITY ANALYSIS. Penetration testing can be a valuable tool for understanding and improving the security of a computer or network. However, it can also be used to exploit system weaknesses and attack systems and steal valuable information. By understanding the need for penetration testing, and the issues and processes surrounding its use, a security professional will be better able to use penetration testing as a standard part of the analysis toolkit.

This article presents penetration testing in terms of its use, application, and process. It is not intended as an in-depth guide to specific techniques that can be used to test penetration-specific systems. Penetration testing is an art that takes a great deal of skill and practice to do effectively. If not done correctly and carefully, the penetration test can be deemed invalid (at best) and, in the worst case, actually damage the target systems. If the security professional is unfamiliar with penetration testing tools and techniques, it is best to hire or contract someone with a great deal of experience in this area to advise and educate the security staff of an organization.

WHAT IS PENETRATION TESTING?

Penetration testing is defined as a formalized set of procedures designed to bypass the security controls of a system or organization for the purpose of testing that system's or organization's resistance to such an attack. Penetration testing is performed to uncover the security weaknesses of a system and to determine the ways in which the system can be compromised by a potential attacker. Penetration testing can take several forms (which will be discussed later) but, in general, a test consists of a series of "attacks" against a target. The success or failure of the attacks, and how the target reacts to each attack, will determine the outcome of the test.

The overall purpose of a penetration test is to determine the subject's ability to withstand an attack by a hostile intruder. As such, the tester will be using the tricks and techniques a real-life attacker might use. This simulated attack strategy allows the subject to discover and mitigate its security weak spots before a real attacker discovers them.

The reason penetration testing exists is that organizations need to determine the effectiveness of their security measures. The fact that they want tests performed indicates that they believe there might be (or want to discover) some deficiency in their security. However, while the testing itself might uncover problems in the organization's security, the tester should attempt to discover and explain the underlying cause of the lapses in security that allowed the test to succeed. Simply stating that the tester was able to walk out of a building with sensitive information is not sufficient. The tester should explain that the lapse was due to inadequate attention by the guard on duty or a lack of guard staff training that would enable them to recognize valuable or sensitive information.

There are three basic requirements for a penetration test. First, the test must have a defined goal and that goal should be clearly documented. The more specific the goal, the easier it will be to recognize the success or failure of the test. A goal such as "break into the XYZ corporate network," while certainly attainable, is not as precise as "break into XYZ's corporate network from the Internet and gain access to the research department's file server." Each test should have a single goal. If the tester wishes to test several aspects of security at a business or site, several separate tests should be performed. This will enable the tester to more clearly distinguish between successful tests and unsuccessful attempts.

The test should have a limited time period in which it is to be performed. The methodology in most penetration testing is to simulate the types of attacks that will be experienced in the real world. It is reasonable to assume that an attacker will expend a finite amount of time and energy trying to penetrate a site. That time may range from one day to one year or beyond; but after that time is reached, the attacker will give up. In addition, the information being protected may have a finite useful "lifetime." The penetration test should acknowledge and accept this fact. Thus, part of the goal statement for the test should include a time limit that is considered reasonable based on the type of system targeted, the expected level of the threat, and the lifetime of the information.

Finally, the test should have the approval of the management of the organization that is the subject of the test. This is extremely important, as only the organization's management has the authority to permit this type of activity on its network and information systems.

TERMINOLOGY

There are several terms associated with penetration testing. These terms are used throughout this chapter to describe penetration testing and the people and events involved in a penetration test.

The *tester* is the person or group who is performing the penetration test. The purpose of the tester is to plan and execute the penetration test and analyze the results for management. In many cases, the tester will be a member of the company or organization that is the subject of the test. However, a company may hire an outside firm to conduct the penetration test if it does not have the personnel or the expertise to do it itself.

An *attacker* is a real-life version of a tester. However, where the tester works with a company to improve its security, the attacker works against a company to steal information or resources.

An *attack* is the series of activities performed by the tester in an attempt to circumvent the security controls of a particular target. The attack may consist of physical, procedural, or electronic methods.

The *subject* of the test is the organization upon whom the penetration test is being performed. The subject can be an entire company or it can be a smaller organizational unit within that company.

A *target* of a penetration test is the system or organization that is being subjected to a particular attack at any given time. The target may or may not be aware that it is being tested. In either case, the target will have a set of defenses it presents to the outside world to protect itself against intrusion. It is those defenses that the penetration test is designed to test. A full penetration test usually consists of a number of attacks against a number of different targets.

Management is the term used to describe the leadership of an organization involved in the penetration test. There may be several levels of management involved in any testing effort, including the management of the specific areas of the company being tested, as well as the upper management of the company as a whole. The specific levels of management involved in the penetration testing effort will have a direct impact on the scope of the test. In all cases, however, it is assumed that the tester is working on behalf of (and sponsored by) at least one level of management within the company.

The *penetration test* (or more simply the *test*) is the actual performance of a simulated attack on the target.

WHY TEST?

There are several reasons why an organization will want a penetration test performed on its systems or operations. The first (and most prevalent) is to determine the effectiveness of the security controls the organization has put into place. These controls may be technical in nature, affecting the computers, network, and information systems of the organization. They may be operational in nature, pertaining to the processes and procedures a company has in place to control and secure information. Finally, they may be physical in nature. The tester may be trying to determine the effectiveness of the physical security a site or company has in place. In all cases, the goal of the tester will be to determine if the existing controls are sufficient by trying to get around them.

The tester may also be attempting to determine the vulnerability an organization has to a particular threat. Each system, process, or organization has a particular set of threats to which it feels it is vulnerable. Ideally, the organization will have taken steps to reduce its exposure to those threats. The role of the tester is to determine the effectiveness of these countermeasures and to identify areas for improvement or areas where additional countermeasures are required. The tester may also wish to determine whether the set of threats the organization has identified is valid and whether or not there are other threats against which the organization might wish to defend itself.

A penetration test can sometimes be used to bolster a company's position in the marketplace. A test, executed by a reputable company and indicating that the subject's environment withstood the tester's best efforts, can be used to give prospective customers the appearance that the subject's environment is secure. The word "*appearance*" is important here because a penetration test cannot examine all possible aspects of the subject's environment if it is even moderate in size. In addition, the security state of an enterprise is constantly changing as new technology replaces old, configurations change, and business needs evolve. The "environment" the tester examines may be very different from the one the customer will be a part of. If a penetration test is used as proof of the security of a particular environment for marketing purposes, the customer should insist on knowing the details, methodology, and results of the test.

A penetration test can be used to alert the corporation's upper management to the security threat that may exist in its systems or operations. While the general knowledge that security weaknesses exist in a system, or specific knowledge of particular threats and vulnerabilities may exist among the technical staff, this message may not always be transmitted to management. As a result, management may not fully understand or appreciate the magnitude of the security problem. A well-executed penetration test can systematically uncover vulnerabilities that management was unaware existed. The presentation of concrete evidence of security problems, along with an analysis of the damage those problems can cause to the company, can be an effective wake-up call to management and spur them into paying more attention to information security issues. A side effect of this wake-up call may be that once management understands the nature of the threat and the magnitude to which the company is vulnerable, it may be more willing to expend money and resources to address not only the security problems uncovered by the test but also ancillary security areas needing additional attention by the company. These ancillary issues may include a general security awareness program or the need for more funding for security technology. A penetration test that uncovers moderate or serious problems in a company's security can be effectively used to justify the time and expense required to implement effective security programs and countermeasures.

TYPES OF PENETRATION TESTING

The typical image of a penetration test is that of a team of high-tech computer experts sitting in a small room attacking a company's network for days on end or crawling through the ventilation shafts to get into the company's "secret room." While this may be a glamorous image to use in the movies, in reality the penetration test works in a variety of different (and very nonglamorous) ways.

The first type of testing involves the physical infrastructure of the subject. Very often, the most vulnerable parts of a company are not found in the technology of its information network or the access controls found in its databases. Security problems can be found in the way the subject handles its physical security. The penetration tester will seek to exploit these physical weaknesses. For example, does the building provide adequate access control? Does the building have security guards, and do the guards check people as they enter or leave a building? If intruders are able to walk unchecked into a company's building, they will be able to gain physical access to the information they seek. A good test is to try to walk into a building during the morning when everyone is arriving to work. Try to get in the middle of a crowd of people to see if the guard is adequately checking the badges of those entering the building.

Once inside, check if sensitive areas of the building are locked or otherwise protected by physical barriers. Are file cabinets locked when not in use? How difficult is it to get into the communications closet where all the telephone and network communication links terminate? Can a person walk into employee office areas unaccompanied and unquestioned? All the secure and sensitive areas of a building should be protected against unauthorized entry. If they are not, the tester will be able to gain unrestricted access to sensitive company information.

While the physical test includes examining protections against unauthorized entry, the penetration test might also examine the effectiveness of controls prohibiting unauthorized exit. Does the company check for theft of sensitive materials when employees exit the facility? Are laptop computers or other portable devices registered and checked when entering and exiting the building? Are security guards trained not only on what types of equipment and information to look for, but also on how equipment can be hidden or masked and why this procedure is important?

Another type of testing examines the operational aspects of an organization. Whereas physical testing investigates physical access to company computers, networks, or facilities, operational testing attempts to determine the effectiveness of the operational procedures of an organization by attempting to bypass those procedures. For example, if the company's help desk requires each user to give personal or secret information before help can be rendered, can the tester bypass those controls by telling a particularly believable "sob story" to the technician answering the call? If the policy of the company is to "scramble" or demagnetize disks before disposal, are these procedures followed? If not, what sensitive information will the tester find on disposed disks and computers? If a company has strict policies concerning the authority and process required to initiate ID or password changes to a system, can someone simply claiming to have the proper authority (without any actual proof of that authority) cause an ID to be created, removed, or changed? All these are attacks against the operational processes a company may have, and all of these techniques have been used successfully in the past to gain entry into computers or gain access to sensitive information.

The final type of penetration test is the electronic test. Electronic testing consists of attacks on the computer systems, networks, or communications facilities of an organization. This can be accomplished either manually or through the use of automated tools. The goal of electronic testing is to determine if the subject's internal systems are vulnerable to an attack through the data network or communications facilities used by the subject.

Depending on the scope and parameters of a particular test, a tester may use one, two, or all three types of tests. If the goal of the test is to gain access to a particular computer system, the tester may attempt a physical penetration to gain access to the computer's console or try an electronic test to attack the machine over the network. If the goal of the test is to see if unauthorized personnel can obtain valuable research data, the tester may use operational testing to see if the information is tracked or logged when accessed or copied and determine who reviews those access logs. The tester may then switch to electronic penetration to gain access to the computers where the information is stored.

WHAT ALLOWS PENETRATION TESTING TO WORK?

There are several general reasons why penetration tests are successful. Many of them are in the operational area; however, security problems can arise due to deficiencies in any of the three testing areas.

A large number of security problems arise due to a lack of awareness on the part of a company's employees of the company's policies and procedures regarding information security and protection. If employees and contractors of a company do not know the proper procedures for handling proprietary or sensitive information, they are much more likely to allow that information to be left unprotected. If employees are unaware of the company policies on discussing sensitive company information, they will often volunteer (sometimes unknowingly) information about their company's future sales, marketing, or research plans simply by being asked the right set of questions. The tester will exploit this lack of awareness and modify the testing procedure to account for the fact that the policies are not well-known.

In many cases, the subjects of the test will be very familiar with the company's policies and the procedures for handling information. Despite this, however, penetration testing works because often people do not adhere to standardized procedures defined by the company's policies. Although the policies may say that system logs should be reviewed daily, most administrators are too busy to bother. Good administrative and security practices require that system configurations should be checked periodically to detect tampering, but this rarely happens. Most security policies indicate minimum complexities and maximum time limits for password, but many systems do not enforce these policies. Once the tester knows about these security procedural lapses, they become easy to exploit.

Many companies have disjointed operational procedures. The processes in use by one organization within a company may often conflict with the processes used by another organization. Do the procedures used by one application to authenticate users complement the procedures used by other applications, or are there different standards in use by different applications? Is the access security of one area of a company's network lower than that of another part of the network? Are log files and audit records reviewed uniformly for all systems and services, or are some systems monitored more closely than others? All these are examples of a lack of coordination between organizations and processes. These examples can be exploited by the tester and used to get closer to the goal of the test. A tester needs only to target the area with the lower authentication standards, the lower access security, or the lower audit review procedures in order to advance the test.

Many penetration tests succeed because people often do not pay adequate attention to the situations and circumstances in which they find themselves. The hacker's art of social engineering relies heavily on this fact. Social engineering is a con game used by intruders to trick people who know secrets into revealing them. People who take great care in protecting information when at work (locking it up or encrypting sensitive data, for example) suddenly forget about those procedures when asked by an acquaintance at a party to talk about their work. Employees who follow strict user authentication and system change control procedures suddenly "forget" all about them when they get a call from the "Vice President of Such and Such" needing something done "right away." Does the "Vice President" himself usually call the technical support line with problems? Probably not, but people do not question the need for information, do not challenge requests for access to sensitive information even if the person asking for it does not clearly have a need to access that data, and do not compare the immediate circumstances with normal patterns of behavior.

Many companies rely on a single source for enabling an employee to prove identity, and often that source has no built-in protection. Most companies assign employee identification (ID) numbers to their associates. That number enables access to many services the company has to offer, yet is displayed openly on employee badges and freely given when requested. The successful tester might determine a method for obtaining or generating a valid employee ID number in order to impersonate a valid employee.

Many hackers rely on the anonymity that large organizations provide. Once a company grows beyond a few hundred employees, it becomes increasingly difficult for anyone to know all employees by sight or by voice. Thus, the IT and HR staff of the company need to rely on other methods of user authentication, such as passwords, key cards, or the above-mentioned employee ID number. Under such a system, employees become anonymous entities, identified only by their ID number or their password. This makes it easier to assume the identity of a legitimate employee or to use social engineering to trick people into divulging information. Once the tester is able to hide within the anonymous structure of the organization, the fear of discovery is reduced and the tester will be in a much better position to continue to test.

Another contributor to the successful completion of most penetration tests is the simple fact that most system administrators do not keep their systems up to date with the latest security patches and fixes for the systems under their control. A vast majority of system break-ins occur as a result of exploitation of known vulnerabilities — vulnerabilities that could have easily been eliminated by the application of a system patch, configuration change, or procedural change. The fact that system operators continue to let systems fall behind in security configuration means that testers will continuously succeed in penetrating their systems.

The tools available for performing a penetration test are becoming more sophisticated and more widely distributed. This has allowed even the novice hacker to pick up highly sophisticated tools for exploiting system weaknesses and applying them without requiring any technical background in how the tool works. Often these tools can try hundreds of vulnerabilities on a system at one time. As new holes are found, the hacker tools exploit them faster than the software companies can release fixes, making life even more miserable for the poor administrator who has to keep pace. Eventually, the administrator will miss something, and that something is usually the one hole that a tester can use to gain entry into a system.

BASIC ATTACK STRATEGIES

Every security professional who performs a penetration test will approach the task somewhat differently, and the actual steps used by the tester will vary from engagement to engagement. However, there are several basic strategies that can be said to be common across most testing situations.

First, do not rely on a single method of attack. Different situations call for different attacks. If the tester is evaluating the physical security of a location, the tester may try one method of getting in the building; for example walking in the middle of a crowd during the morning inrush of people. If that does not work, try following the cleaning people into a side door. If that does not work, try something else. The same method holds true for electronic attacks. If one attack does not work (or the system is not susceptible to that attack), try another.

Choose the path of least resistance. Most real attackers will try the easiest route to valuable information, so the penetration tester should use this method as well. If the test is attempting to penetrate a company's network, the company's firewall might not be the best place to begin the attack (unless, of course, the firewall was the stated target of the test) because that is where all the security attention will be focused. Try to attack lesser-guarded areas of a system. Look for alternate entry points; for example, connections to a company's business partners, analog dial-up services, modems connected to desktops, etc. Modern corporate networks have many more connection points than just the firewall, so use them to the fullest advantage.

Feel free to break the rules. Most security vulnerabilities are discovered because someone has expanded the limits of a system's capabilities to the point where it breaks, thus revealing a weak spot in the system. Unfortunately, most users and administrators concentrate on making their systems conform to the stated policies of the organization. Processes work well when everyone follows the rules, but can have unpredictable results when those rules are broken or ignored. Therefore, when performing a test attack, use an extremely long password; enter a thousand-byte URL into a Web site; sign someone else's name into a visitors log; try anything that represents abnormality or nonconformance to a system or process. Real attackers will not follow the rules of the subject system or organization — nor should the tester.

Do not rely exclusively on high-tech, automated attacks. While these tools may seem more "glamorous" (and certainly easier) to use they may not always reveal the most effective method of entering a system. There are a number of "low-tech" attacks that, while not as technically advanced, may reveal important vulnerabilities and should not be overlooked. Social engineering is a prime example of this type of approach. The only tools required to begin a social engineering attack are the tester's voice, a telephone, and the ability to talk to people. Yet despite the simplicity of the method (or, perhaps, because of it), social engineering is incredibly effective as a method of obtaining valuable information.

"Dumpster diving" can also be an effective low-tech tool. Dumpster diving is a term used to describe the act of searching through the trash of the subject in an attempt to find valuable information. Typical information found in most Dumpsters includes old system printouts, password lists, employee personnel information, drafts of reports, and old fax transmissions. While not nearly as glamorous as running a port scan on a subject's computer, it also does not require any of the technical skill that port scanning requires. Nor does it involve the personal interaction required of social engineering, making it an effective tool for testers who may not be highly skilled in interpersonal communications.

One of the primary aims of the penetration tester is to avoid detection. The basic tenet of penetration testing is that information can be obtained from a subject without his or her knowledge or consent. If a tester is caught in the act of testing, this means, by definition, that the subject's defenses against that particular attack scenario are adequate. Likewise, the tester should avoid leaving "fingerprints" that can be used to detect or trace an attack. These fingerprints include evidence that the tester has been working in and around a system. The fingerprints can be physical (e.g., missing reports, large photocopying bills) or they can be virtual (e.g., system logs detailing access by the tester, or door access controls logging entry and exit into a building). In either case, fingerprints can be detected and detection can lead to a failure of the test.

Do not damage or destroy anything on a system unless the destruction of information is defined as part of the test and approved (in writing) by management. The purpose of a penetration test is to uncover flaws and weaknesses in a system or process, — not to destroy information. The actual destruction of company information not only deprives the company of its (potentially valuable) intellectual property, but it may also be construed as unethical behavior and subject the tester to disciplinary or legal action. If the management of the organization wishes the tester to demonstrate actual destruction of information as part of the test, the tester should be sure to document the requirement and get written approval of the management involved in the test. Of course, in the attempt to "not leave fingerprints," the tester might wish to alter the system logs to cover the tester's tracks. Whether or not this is acceptable is an issue that the tester should discuss with the subject's management before the test begins.

Do not pass up opportunities for small incremental progress. Most penetration testing involves the application of many tools and techniques in order to be successful. Many of these techniques will not completely expose a weakness in an organization or point to a failure of an organization's security. However, each of these techniques may move the tester closer and closer to the final goal of the test. By looking for a single weakness or vulnerability that will completely expose the organization's security, the tester may overlook many important, smaller weaknesses that, when combined, are just as important. Real-life attackers can have infinite patience; so should the tester.

Finally, be prepared to switch tactics. Not every test will work, and not every technique will be successful. Most penetration testers have a standard "toolkit" of techniques that work on most systems. However, different systems are susceptible to different attacks and may call for different testing measures. The tester should be prepared to switch to another method if the current one is not working. If an electronic attack is not yielding the expected results, switch to a physical or operational attack. If attempts to circumvent a company's network connectivity are not working, try accessing the network through the company's dial-up connections. The attack that worked last time may not be successful this time, even if the subject is the same company. This may either be because something has changed in the target's environment or the target has (hopefully) learned itslesson from the last test. Finally, unplanned opportunities may present themselves during a test. Even an unsuccessful penetration attempt may expose the possibility that other types of attack may be more successful. By remaining flexible and willing to switch tactics, the tester is in a much better position to discover system weaknesses.

PLANNING THE TEST

Before any penetration testing can take place, a clear testing plan must be prepared. The test plan will outline the goals and objectives of the test, detail the parameters of the testing process, and describe the expectations of both the testing team and the management of the target organization.

The most important part of planning any penetration test is the involvement of the management of the target organization. Penetration testing without management approval, in addition to being unethical, can reasonably be considered "espionage" and is illegal in most jurisdictions. The tester should fully document the testing engagement in detail and get the written approval from management before proceeding. If the testing team is part of the subject organization, it is important that the management of that organization knows about the team's efforts and approves of them. If the testing team is outside the organizational structure and is performing the test "for hire" the permission of management to perform the test should be included as part of the contract between the testing organization and the target organization. In all cases, be sure that the management that approves the test has the authority to give such approval. Penetration testing involves attacks on the security infrastructure of an organization. This type of action should not be approved or undertaken by someone who does not clearly have the authority to do so.

By definition, penetration testing involves the use of simulated attacks on a system or organization with the intent of penetrating that system or organization. This type of activity will, by necessity, require that someone in the subject organization be aware of the testing. Make sure that those with a need to know about the test do, in fact, know of the activity. However, keep the list of people aware of the test to an absolute minimum. If too many people know about the test, the activities and operations of the target may be altered (intentionally or unintentionally) and negate the results of the testing effort. This alteration of behavior to fit expectations is known as the Hawthorne effect (named after a famous study at Western Electric's Hawthorne factory whose employees, upon discovering that their behavior was being studied, altered their behavior to fit the patterns they believed the testers wanted to see.)

Finally, during the course of the test, many of the activities the tester will perform are the very same ones that real-life attackers will use to penetrate systems. If the staff of the target organization discovers these activities, they may (rightly) mistake the test for a real attack and catch the "attacker" in the act. By making sure that appropriate management personnel are aware of the testing activities, the tester will be able to validate the legitimacy of the test.

An important ethical note to consider is that the act of penetration testing involves intentionally breaking the rules of the subject organization in order to determine its security weaknesses. This requires the tester to use many of the same tools and methods that real-life attackers use. However, real hackers sometime break the law or engage in highly questionable behavior in order to carry out their attacks. The security professional performing the penetration test is expected to draw the line between bypassing a company's security procedures and systems and actually breaking the law. These distinctions should be discussed with management prior to the commencement of the test, and discussed again if any ethical or legal problems arise during the execution of the test.

Once management has agreed to allow a penetration test, the parameters of the test must be established. The testing parameters will determine the type of test to be performed, the goals of the tests, and the operating boundaries that will define how the test is run. The primary decision is to determine precisely what is being tested. This definition can range from broad ("test the ability to break into the company's network") to extremely specific ("determine the risk of loss of technical information about XYZ's latest product"). In general, more specific testing definitions are preferred, as it becomes easier to determine the success or failure of the test. In the case of the second example, if the tester is able to produce a copy of the technical specifications, the test clearly succeeded. In the case of the first example, does the act of logging in to a networked system constitute success, or does the tester need to produce actual data taken from the network? Thus, the specific criteria for success or failure should be clearly defined.

The penetration test plan should have a defined time limit. The time length of the test should be related to the amount of time a real adversary can be expected to attempt to penetrate the system and also the reasonable lifetime of the information itself. If the data being attacked has an effective lifetime of two months, a penetration test can be said to succeed if it successfully obtains that data within a two-month window.

The test plan should also explain any limits placed on the test by either the testing team or management. If there are ethical considerations that limit the amount of "damage" the team is willing to perform, or if there are areas of the system or operation that the tester is prohibited from accessing (perhaps for legal or contractual reasons), these must be clearly explained in the test plan. Again, the testers will attempt to act as real-life attackers and attackers do not follow any rules. If management wants the testers to follow certain rules, these must be clearly defined. The test plan should also set forth the procedures and effects of "getting caught" during the test. What defines "getting caught" and how that affects the test should also be described in the plan.

Once the basic parameters of the test have been defined, the test plan should focus on the "scenario" for the test. The scenario is the position the tester will assume within the company for the duration of the test. For example, if the test is attempting to determine the level of threat from company insiders (employees, contractors, temporary employees, etc.), the tester may be given a temporary job within the company. If the test is designed to determine the level of external threat to the organization, the tester will assume the position of an "outsider." The scenario will also define the overall goal of the test. Is the purpose of the test a simple penetration of the company's computers or facilities? Is the subject worried about loss of intellectual property via physical or electronic attacks? Are they worried about vandalism to their Web site, fraud in their electronic commerce systems, or protection against denial-of-service attacks? All these factors help to determine the test scenario and are extremely important in order for the tester to plan and execute an effective attack.

PERFORMING THE TEST

Once all the planning has been completed, the test scenarios have been established, and the tester has determined the testing methodology, it is time to perform the test. In many aspects, the execution of a penetration test plan can be compared to the execution of a military campaign. In such a campaign, there are three distinct phases: reconnaissance, attack, and (optionally) occupation.

During the reconnaissance phase (often called the "discovery" phase) the tester will generally survey the "scene" of the test. If the tester is planning a physical penetration, the reconnaissance stage will consist of examining the proposed location for any weaknesses or vulnerabilities. The tester should look for any noticeable patterns in the way the site operates. Do people come and go at regular intervals? If there are guard services, how closely do they examine people entering and leaving the site? Do they make rounds of the premises after normal business hours, and are those rounds conducted at regular times? Are different areas of the site occupied at different times? Do people seem to all know one another, or do they seem to be strangers to each other. The goal of physical surveillance is to become as completely familiar with the target location as possible and to establish the repeatable patterns in the site's behavior. Understanding those patterns and blending into them can be an important part of the test.

If an electronic test is being performed, the tester will use the reconnaissance phase to learn as much about the target environment as possible. This will involve a number of mapping and surveillance techniques. However, because the tester cannot physically observe the target location, electronic probing of the environment must be used. The tester will start by developing an electronic "map" of the target system or network. How is the network laid out? What are the main access points, and what type of equipment runs the network? Are the various hosts identifiable, and what operating systems or platforms are they running? What other networks connect to this one? Is dial-in service available to get into the network, and is dial-out service available to get outside?

Reconnaissance does not always have to take the form of direct surveillance of the subject's environment. It can also be gathered in other ways that are more indirect. For example, some good places to learn about the subject are:

- former or disgruntled employees
- local computer shows
- local computer club meetings
- employee lists, organization structures
- job application handouts and tours
- vendors who deliver food and beverages to the site

All this information will assist the tester in determining the best type of attack(s) to use based on the platforms and service available. For each environment (physical or electronic), platform, or service found during the reconnaissance phase, there will be known attacks or exploits that the tester can use. There may also be new attacks that have not yet made it into public forums. The tester must rely on the experience gained in previous tests and the knowledge of current events in the field of information security to keep abreast of possible avenues of attack.

The tester should determine (at least preliminarily) the basic methods of attack to use, the possible countermeasures that may be encountered, and the responses that may be used to those countermeasures.

The next step is the actual attack on the target environment. The attack will consist of exploiting the weaknesses found in the reconnaissance phase to gain entry to the site or system and to bypass any controls or restrictions that may be in place. If the tester has done a thorough job during the reconnaissance phase, the attack phase becomes much easier.

Timing during the attack phase can be critical. There may be times when the tester has the luxury of time to execute an attack, and this provides the greatest flexibility to search, test, and adjust to the environment as it unfolds. However, in many cases, an abundance of time is not available. This may be the case if the tester is attempting to enter a building in between guard rounds, attempting to gather information from files during the owner's lunch hour, or has tripped a known alarm and is attempting to complete the attack before the system's intrusion response interval (the amount of time between the recognition of a penetration and the initiation of the response or countermeasure) is reached. The tester should have a good idea of how long a particular attack should take to perform and have a reasonable expectation that it can be performed in the time available (barring any unexpected complications).

If, during an attack, the tester gains entry into a new computer or network, the tester may elect to move into the occupation phase of the attack. Occupation is the term used to indicate that the tester has established the target as a base of operations. This may be because the tester wants to spend more time in the target gathering information or monitoring the state of the target, or the tester may want to use the target as a base for launching attacks against other targets. The occupation phase presents perhaps the greatest danger to the tester, because the tester will be exposed to detection for the duration of the time he or she is resident in the target environment. If the tester chooses to enter the occupation phase, steps should be taken to make the tester's presence undetectable to the greatest extent possible.

It is important to note that a typical penetration test may repeat the reconnaissance/attack/occupation cycle many times before the completion of the test. As each new attack is prepared and launched, the tester must react to the attack results and decide whether to move on to the next step of the test plan, or abandon the current attack and begin the reconnaissance for another type of attack. Through the repeated and methodical application of this cycle the tester will eventually complete the test.

Each of the two basic test types — physical and electronic — has different tools and methodologies. Knowledge of the strengths and weaknesses of each type will be of tremendous help during the execution of the penetration test. For example, physical penetrations generally do not require an in-depth knowledge of technical information. While they may require some specialized technical experience (bypassing alarm systems, for example), physical penetrations require skills in the area of operations security, building and site operations, human nature, and social interaction.

The "tools" used during a physical penetration vary with each tester, but generally fall into two general areas: abuse of protection systems and abuse of social interaction. Examples of abuse of protection systems include walking past inattentive security guards, piggybacking (following someone through an access-controlled door), accessing a file room that is accidentally unlocked, falsifying an information request, or picking up and copying information left openly on desks. Protection systems are established to protect the target from typical and normal threats. Knowledge of the operational procedures of the target will enable the tester to develop possible test scenarios to test those operations in the face of both normal and abnormal threats.

Lack of security awareness on the part of the victim can play a large part in any successful physical penetration test. If people are unaware of the value of the information they possess, they are less likely to protect it properly. Lack of awareness of the policies and procedures for storing and handling sensitive information is abundant in many companies. The penetration tester can exploit this in order to gain access to information that should otherwise be unavailable.

Finally, social engineering is perhaps the ultimate tool for effective penetration testing. Social engineering exploits vulnerabilities in the physical and process controls, adds the element of "insider" assistance, and combines it with the lack of awareness on the part of the subject that they have actually contributed to the penetration. When done properly, social engineering can provide a formidable attack strategy.

Electronic penetrations, on the other hand, generally require more in-depth technical knowledge than do physical penetrations. In the case of many real-life attackers, this knowledge can be their own or "borrowed" from somebody else. In recent years, the technical abilities of many new attackers seem to have decreased, while the high availability of penetration

216

and attack tools on the Internet, along with the sophistication of those tools, has increased. Thus, it has become relatively simple for someone without a great deal of technical knowledge to "borrow" the knowledge of the tool's developer and inflict considerable damage on a target. There are, however, still a large number of technically advanced attackers out there with the skill to launch a successful attack against a system.

The tools used in an electronic attack are generally those that provide automated analysis or attack features. For example, many freely available host and network security analysis tools provide the tester with an automated method for discovering a system's vulnerabilities. These are vulnerabilities that the skilled tester may be able to find manually, but the use of automated tools provides much greater efficiency. Likewise, tools like port scanners (that tell the tester what ports are in use on a target host), network "sniffers" (that record traffic on a network for later analysis), and "war dialers" (that systematically dial phone numbers to discover accessible modems) provide the tester with a wealth of knowledge about weaknesses in the target system and possible avenues the tester should take to exploit those weaknesses.

When conducting electronic tests there, are three basic areas to exploit: the operating system, the system configuration, and the relationship the system has to other systems. Attacks against the operating system exploit bugs or holes in the platform that have not yet been patched by the administrator or the manufacturer of the platform. Attacks against the system configuration seek to exploit the natural tendency of overworked administrators not to keep up with the latest system releases and to overlook such routine tasks as checking system logs, eliminating unused accounts, or improper configuration of system elements. Finally, the tester can exploit the relationship a system has with respect other systems to which it connects. Does it have a trust relationship with a target system? Can the tester establish administrative rights on the target machine through another machine? In many cases, a successful penetration test will result not from directly attacking the target machine, but from first successfully attacking systems that have some sort of "relationship" to the target machine.

REPORTING RESULTS

The final step in a penetration test is to report the findings of the test to management. The overall purpose and tone of the report should actually be set at the beginning of the engagement with management's statement of their expectation of the test process and outcome. In effect, what the tester is asked to look for will determine, in part, the report that is produced. If the tester is asked to examine a company's overall physical security, the report will reflect a broad overview of the various security measures the company uses at its locations. If the tester is asked to evaluate the controls surrounding a particular computer system, the report will most likely contain a detailed analysis of that machine.

The report produced as a result of a penetration test contains extremely sensitive information about the vulnerabilities the subject has and the exact attacks that can be used to exploit those vulnerabilities. The penetration tester should take great care to ensure that the report is only distributed to those within the management of the target who have a need-to-know. The report should be marked with the company's highest sensitivity label. In the case of particularly sensitive or classified information, there may be several versions of the report, with each version containing only information about a particular functional area.

The final report should provide management with a replay of the test engagement in documented form. Everything that happened during the test should be documented. This provides management with a list of the vulnerabilities of the target and allows them to assess the methods used to protect against future attacks.

First, the initial goals of the test should be documented. This will assist anyone who was not part of the original decision-making process is becoming familiar with the purpose and intent of the testing exercise. Next, the methodology used during the test should be described. This will include information about the types of attacks used, the success or failure of those attacks, and the level of difficulty and resistance the tester experienced during the test. While providing too much technical detail about the precise methods used may be overly revealing and (in some cases) dangerous, the general methods and procedures used by the testing team should be included in the report. This can be an important tool for management to get a sense of how easy or difficult it was for the testing team to penetrate the system. If countermeasures are to be put in place, they will need to be measured for cost-effectiveness against the value of the target and the vulnerabilities found by the tester. If the test revealed that a successful attack would cost the attacker U.S. $10 million, the company might not feel the need for additional security in that area. However, if the methodology and procedures show that an attack can be launched from the Internet for the price of a home computer and an Internet connection, the company might want to put more resources into securing the target.

The final report should also list the information found during the test. This should include information about what was found, where it was found, how it was found, and the difficulty the tester had in finding it. This information is important to give management a sense of the depth and breadth of the security problems uncovered by the test. If the list of items found is only one or two items long, it might not trigger a large response (unless, of course, the test was only looking for those one or two items). However, if the list is several pages long, it might spur management into making dramatic improvements in the company's security policies and procedures.

The report should give an overall summary of the security of the target in comparison with some known quantity for analysis. For example, the test might find that 10 percent of the passwords on the subject's computers were easily guessed. However, previous research or the tester's own experience might show that the average computer on the Internet or other clients contains 30 percent easily guessed passwords. Thus, the company is actually doing better than the industry norm. However, if the report shows that 25 percent of the guards in the company's buildings did not check for employee badges during the test, that would most likely be considered high and be cause for further action.

The report should also compare the initial goals of the test to the final result. Did the test satisfy the requirements set forth by management? Were the results expected or unexpected, and to what degree? Did the test reveal problems in the targeted area, or were problems found in other unrelated areas? Was the cost or complexity of the tests in alignment with the original expectations of management?

Finally, the report should also contain recommendations for improvement of the subject's security. The recommendations should be based on the findings of the penetration test and include not only the areas covered by the test, but ancillary areas might help improve the security of the tested areas. For example, inconsistent system configuration might indicate a need for a more stringent change control process. A successful social engineering attempt that allowed the tester to obtain a password from the company's help desk might lead to better user authentication requirements.

CONCLUSION

Although it seems to parallel the activities of real attackers, penetration testing, in fact, serves to alert the owners of computer and networks to the real dangers present in their systems. Other risk analysis activities, such as automated port scanning, war dialing, and audit log reviews, tend to point out the theoretical vulnerabilities that might exist in a system. The owner of a computer will look at the output from one of these activities and see a list of holes and weak spots in a system without getting a good sense of the actual threat these holes represent. An effective penetration test, however, will show that same system owner the actual damage that can occur if those holes are not addressed. It brings to the forefront the techniques that can be used to gain access to a system or site and makes clear the areas that need further attention. By applying the proper penetration testing techniques (in addition to the standard risk analysis and mitigation strategies), the security professional can provide a complete security picture of the subject's enterprise.

Chapter 10
The Building Blocks of Information Security

Ken M. Shaurette

INFORMATION SECURITY IS NOT JUST ABOUT TECHNOLOGICAL CONTROLS. SECURITY CANNOT BE ACHIEVED SOLELY THROUGH THE APPLICATION OF SOFTWARE OR HARDWARE. Any attempt to implement technology controls without considering the cultural and social attitudes of the corporation is a formula for disaster. The best approach to effective security is a layered approach that encompasses both technological and nontechnological safeguards. Ideally, these safeguards should be used to achieve an acceptable level of protection while enhancing business productivity. While the concept may sound simple, the challenge is to strike a balance between being too restrictive (overly cautious) or too open (not cautious enough).

Security technology alone cannot eliminate all exposures. Security managers must integrate themselves with existing corporate support systems. Together with their peers, they will develop the security policies, standards, procedures, and guidelines that form the foundation for security activities. This approach will ensure that security becomes a function of the corporation — not an obstacle to business.

A successful layered approach must look at all aspects of security. A layered approach concentrating on technology alone becomes like a house of cards. Without a foundation based on solid policies, the security infrastructure is just cards standing side by side, with each technology becoming a separate card in the house. Adding an extra card (technology layer) to the house (overall security) does not necessarily make the house stronger.

Without security policies, standards, procedures, and guidelines, there is no general security framework or foundation. Policies define the behavior that is allowed or not allowed. They are short because they do not explain how to achieve compliance; such is the purpose of procedures and

0-8493-0800-3/00/$0.00+$.50
© 2001 by CRC Press LLC

guidelines. Corporate policy seldom changes because it does not tie to technology, people, or specific processes. Policy establishes technology selection and how it will be configured and implemented. Policies are the consensus between people, especially important between all layers of corporate management. Policy can ensure that the Security Manager and his or her peers apply security technology with the proper emphasis and return on investment for the good of the business as a whole.

In most security audits or reviews, checking, maybe even testing, an organization's security policies, standards, procedures, and guidelines is often listed as the first element in assessing security risk. It is easy to see the published hard-copy policy; but to ensure that policy is practiced, it is necessary to observe the workplace in order to evaluate what is really in operation. Lack of general awareness or compliance with a security policy usually indicates a policy that was not developed with the participation of other company management.

Whether the organization is global or local, there is still expectation of levels of due diligence. As a spin on the golden rule: "Compute unto others as you would want them to compute unto you."

Define the Scope: Objective

"The first duty of a human is to assume the right functional relationship to society — more briefly, to find your real job, and do it."

— Charlotte Perkins Gilman

Define Security Domain

Every organization has a different perspective on what is within the domain of its Information Security department.

- Does the Information Security domain include both electronic and non-electronic information, printed versus the bytes stored on a computer?
- Does the Information Security department report to IS and have responsibility for only information policies, not telephone, copier, fax, and mail use?
- Does physical security and contingency planning fall into the Information Security Manager's domain?
- Is the Security Manager's responsibility corporate, regional, national, or global?

Information Security's mission statement must support the corporation's business objective. Very often, one can find a security mission stated something like:

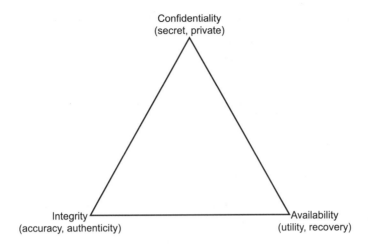

Exhibit 10-1. Basic security triad.

> The mission of the Information Security department is to protect the information assets, the information systems, and networks that deliver the information, from damage resulting from failures of confidentiality, integrity, and availability (CIA) (see Exhibit 10-1).

This mission is quite specific to Information Security and a specific department. A mission like this is a prime reason why defining the Security Manager's domain is critical to the success of policy formation.

Would the mission be more positive and clear by being tied to the business objectives with something like:

> Security's objective is to enhance the productivity of the business by reducing probability of loss through the design and implementation of policies, standards, procedures, and guidelines that enhance the protection of business assets.

Notice how this mission statement does not limit itself to "information." It does not limit the responsibilities to only computer systems and their processing of information. In addition, it ties the success of the mission to the business. It still provides the flexibility to define assets and assign owners to them for accountability. It is important to understand the objectives that security is going to deliver for the business. Exhibit 10-2 outlines some sample objectives.

What will be in the Security Manager's domain: physical security, contingency planning, telephones, copiers, faxes, or mail (especially e-mail)? These technologies process information too, so would they be covered by Information Security Policy? How far reaching will the Security Manager's responsibilities be: corporate, global, national, regional, or local? Is it the

Exhibit 10-2. Questions to help determine security philosophy.

- Do users have expectations relating to security?
- Is it possible to lose customers if security is too restrictive, not restrictive enough, or if controls and policy are so unreasonable that functionality is impaired?
- Is there a history for lost availability or monetary loss from security incidents in the past? What was the cost to the business?
- Who is the primary enemy — employees or outsiders?
- How much confidential information is online, and how is it accessed? What would be the loss if the information was compromised or stolen?
- Is it important to layer security controls for different parts of the organization?
- Are dangerous services that increase vulnerabilities supported by the organization? Is it required that networks and systems meet a security baseline?
- What security guidelines, procedures, regulations, or laws must be met?
- Is there a conflict between business objectives and security?
- Confidentiality, integrity, and availability: how crucial is each to the overall operation?
- Consider business needs and economic reality. What meets due diligence for like companies, the security industry, for this information in other environments?

Security Manager's responsibility to enforce compliance? Is contingency planning or business continuity planning (BCP) a function of physical security? Once the domain has been clearly defined, it becomes easy for responsible areas to form and begin to create their specific policies, standards, procedures, and guidelines.

Traditionally, organizations would refer to different departments for the responsibility of security on such things as telephones, copiers, faxes, or mail. An organization would have to climb quite high in the organizational structure — executive VP, COO, CEO — to find the common management point in the organizational structure where a person responsible for the security of all the disparate resources would come together for central accountability.

Hint: Policies written with the term "electronic" can cover e-mail, (electronic mail), EDI (electronic data interchange), or all the other "E-words" that are becoming popular (i.e., E-commerce, E-marketing, and E-business). Policies not using the term "electronic" can refer to information regardless of technology, storage media, or transportation methods.

In that regard, what used to be called datasecurity, today is referred to as information security. Information security often considers the security of data, information in both electronic and non-electronic forms. The role of the Information Security Manager has either expanded or information security personnel have begun assuming responsibilities in areas that are often not clearly defined. Some organizations are recognizing the difficulty of separating information dealing with technology from non-technology. With that in mind, Corporate Security Officer (CSO) type positions are being created (other possible name: Chief Security Officer). These positions can be scoped to have responsibility for security, regardless of technology, and across the entire enterprise regardless of geography. This would not necessarily mean that all of the impacted areas report to this position, but this position would provide the enterprise or corporate vision of information security. It would coordinate the security accomplishments for the good of the entire organization, crossing domains and departments. Define "information"; what does it not include?

For years, security purists have argued for information security to report high in the organization as well as not necessarily within the information services (IS) division. Some organizations accomplished this by creating executive-level security positions reporting to the president, COO, or CEO. In differing ways, more organizations are finally making strides to at least put the "corporate" or "enterprise" spin on addressing the security issues of the organization, not just the issues (policy) of IS. An appointment of security personnel with accountability across the organization is a start. Giving them top management and line management support across the organization remains critical to their success, regardless of how high they report in the organization. An executive VP of information security will fail if the position is only a token position. On the other hand, the flunky of information security can be successful if everyone from top down is behind him and the concept of corporate information security.

In this structure, traditional areas can remain responsible for their parts of security and policy definition, their cards in the house, but a corporate entity coordinates the security efforts and brings it all together. That corporate entity is tasked with providing the corporate security vision and could report high in the organization, which is probably the best, or it could be assigned corporate responsibility by executive management. Total and very visual support by all management is obviously critical for success.

Sample roles and responsibilities for this structure include:

- The protection and safety department would continue to contract for guards, handle building access control, ID cards, and other physical building controls, including computer rooms.
- The telecommunications department is still be accountable for the security of phone systems and helps with establishment of policy addressing phone-mail and use of company telephones, probably including fax.
- A corporate mail department deals with internal and external mail, possibly including e-mail.

- IS has accountability for computer-based information processing systems and assists with the establishment of standards for use of them or policy dealing with information processing.
- The corporate legal department would help to ensure that policy meets regulations from a legal perspective and that proper wording makes them enforceable.
- A corporate compliance department can insure that regulatory and legislative concerns are addressed, such as the federal sentencing guidelines.
- Human resources (HR) is still a critical area in identifying employee policies and works closely with the Corporate Security Officer (CSO) on all policies, standards, procedures, and guidelines, as well as proper enforcement.
- The CSO works with all areas to provide high-level security expertise, coordinate and establish employee security awareness, security education programs, along with publication and communication of the security policies, standards, procedures, and guidelines.

SECURITY PHILOSOPHY

> No gain is possible without attendant outlay, but there will be no profit if the outlay exceeds the receipts.
>
> — Plautus

Return on Investment (ROI): What is the basis for security philosophy?

Security is often expected to provide a return on investment (ROI) to justify expenditures. How often is it possible for information security to generate a direct ROI? Which is more expensive, recover from an incident or prevent the incident in the first place? Computer security is often an intangible process. In many instances, the level of security is not evident until a catastrophe happens, at which time the lack of security is all too painfully evident.

Information security should be viewed in terms of the processes and goals of the business. Business risk is different from security risk, but poor security can put the business at risk, or make it risky doing business.

Example

- Would a wise company provide banking services, transmitting credit card numbers and account balances using an unsecured Internet connection? A properly secured infrastructure using encryption or certificates for nonrepudiation can provide the company with a business opportunity that it would not otherwise be likely to engage in. In that situation, the security is an integral part of that business opportunity, minimizing the business risk.

- How can a security manager justify control procedures over program changes or over developers with update access to production data? Assume that 20 percent of problems result from program errors or incorrect updates to data. Maybe inadequately tested code in a program is transferred to production. If controls can reduce the errors and resulting rework to say 10 percent, the payback would be only a few months. In a company that sells its programming services based on quality, this would directly relate to potential business opportunity and increased contracts.
- What about customer privacy? A Harris Poll showed that 53 percent of American adults are concerned about privacy threats from corporations. People have stated in surveys that they would rather do business with a company they feel is going to protect the privacy of their information. Increased business opportunity exists for the company that can show that it protects customer privacy better than its competition, even if it only generates the perception of better. Perception is 90 percent reality. Being able to show how the company enforces sound security policies, standards, and procedures would provide the business advantage.

    Although a mission statement may no longer refer directly to confidentiality, integrity, and availability, the security department cannot ignore CIA (see Exhibit 10-1). As discussed, the base security philosophy must now help improve business productivity. The real life situation is that we can never provide 100 percent security. We can, however, reduce the probability of loss or taking reasonable measures of due diligence consistent with industry norms for how like companies are dealing with like information. Going that extra step ahead to lead the industry can create business opportunity and minimize business risk.

To meet the security business objective, a better order for this triad is probably AIC, but that does not stir as much intrigue as CIA. Studies show AIC to be better matched to the order of priority for many security managers.

WHY?

- *Availability:* A corporation gathers endless amounts of information and in order to effectively produce product, that information must be available and usable when needed. This includes the concept of utility, or that the information must have the quality or condition of being useful. Just being available is not sufficient.
- *Integrity:* For the information to have any value and in order to produce quality product, the data must be protected against unauthorized or inadvertent modification. Its integrity must be of the highest quality and original. If the authenticity of the information is in doubt or compromised, the integrity is still jeopardized.

- *Confidentiality:* The privacy of customer information is becoming more and more important, if not to the corporation, to the customer. Legislation could one day mandate minimum protections for specific pieces of information like health records, credit card numbers, and bank account numbers. Ensuring that only the proper people have access to the information needed to perform their job or that they have been authorized to access it is often the last concern because it can impede business productivity.

MANAGEMENT MYTHS OF SECURITY

1. Security technology will solve all the problems.

Buy the software; now the company is secure. Management has signed the purchase order and the software has arrived. Is management's job finished and the company now secure? Management has done their due diligence, right? Wrong! Remember, software and security technologies are only a piece of the overall security program.

Management must have a concept or philosophy regarding how it wants to address information security, recognizing that technology and software are not 100 percent effective and are not going to magically eliminate all security problems. Does the security software restrict any access to a resource, provide everyone access, or just audit the access until someone steps forward with resources that need to be protected? The security job is not done once the software is installed or the technology is chosen.

Management support for proper security software implementation, configuration, continued maintenance, and the research and development of new security technologies is critical.

2. I have written the policy, so now we are done.

If policies or standards are written but never implemented, or not followed, not enforced, or enforced inconsistently it is worse than not having them at all. Federal Sentencing Guidelines require consistent application of policy and standards.

In an excerpt from the Federal Sentencing Guidelines, it states:

> The standards must have been consistently enforced through appropriate disciplinary mechanisms, including as appropriate, discipline of individuals responsible for the failure to detect an offense. Adequate discipline of individuals responsible for an offense is a necessary component of enforcement; however, the form of discipline that will be appropriate will be case specific.

Management must recognize that policy and standards implementation should be defined as a specific project receiving continued management support. They may not have understood that there is a cost associated with implementing policy and thought this was only a policy development effort.

Strict enforcement of policy and standards must become a way of life in business. Corporate policy-making bodies should consider adherence to them a condition of employment. Never adopt a policy unless there is a good prospect that it will be followed. Make protecting the confidentiality, integrity, and availability of information "The Law."

3. Publish policy and standards and everyone will comply.

Not only is the job not done once the policy is written, but ensuring that every employee, customer, vendor, constituent, or stockholder knows and understands policy is essential. Training them and keeping records of the training on company policy are critical. Just publishing the policy does not encourage anyone to comply with it.

Simply training people or making them aware (security awareness) is also not sufficient; all one gets is shallow or superficial security. There needs to be motivation to carry out policy; only penalizing people for poor security does not always create positive motivation and is a militaristic attitude. Even child psychologists recommend positive reinforcement.

Security awareness alone can have a negative effect by teaching people how to avoid security in their work. Everyone knows it just slows them down, and they hate it anyway, especially if only penalties are associated with it. Positive reinforcement calls for rewards when people show actions and attitudes toward very good security. Do not eliminate penalties for poor security, but do not let them be the only motivator. Once rewards and penalties are identified, education can include how to achieve the rewards and avoid the penalties, just as for other work motivation. This requires an effectively applied security line item in salary and performance reviews and real rewards and penalties.

4. Follow the vendor's approach: it is the best way to make an organization secure.

An organization's goals should be to build the fences as high as it can. Protect everything; implement every feature of that new software. The organization has paid for those functions and the vendor must know the best way to implement them.

Often, an organization might be inclined to take a generic security product and fail to tailor it to fit its business objectives. Everyone can name an operating system that is not quite as secure as one would like it to be using the vendor defaults. The vendor's approach may go against organization security philosophy. The product may come out of the box with limited security, open architecture, but the company security philosophy is to allow only access as appropriate, or vice versa.

Should one put all one's eggs in one basket or build one's house all from the same deck of cards? Does using only one security solution from a single vendor open vulnerability to the security architecture? Think about using the best-of-class solution from multiple vendors; this way, one's security architecture is not easily blueprinted by outsiders.

BUILDING THE BRIDGE: SECURITY CONTROLS REACH FOR BUSINESS NEEDS

An information security infrastructure is like a bridge built between the user with a business need to access information and at the other end of the bridge the information they wish to access. Creating gates between the end user and the data are the controls (technology) providing security protection or defining specific paths to the information. Forming the foundation for the security technology to be implemented are policies, standards, and procedures.

Guidelines are not required actions, but provide a map (suggestions of how to comply) or, like the railings of the bridge, help direct end users to their destination so they do not fall off the bridge. Just like the rails of a bridge, if the guidelines are not followed, it is still possible to fall off the bridge (not comply with policy and standards). The river represents unauthorized access, malicious elements (hackers), or unauthorized entities (disgruntled employees) that could affect the delivery of the payloads (information) across the bridge. The river (malicious access) is constantly flowing and often changing faster than security controls can be implemented. The security technology or software are locked gates, toll ways, or speed bumps on the bridge that control and audit the flow of traffic authorized to cross. Exposures or risks that have been accepted by management are represented by holes in the surface of the bridge that are not patched or are not covered by a security technology. Perhaps they are only covered with a see-through mesh, because ignorance is the only protection. The bigger the risk, the bigger the hole in the roadbed.

Build bridges that can get the organization from the "Wild Wild West" of the Internet to the future wars that are yet to be identified. William Hugh Murray of Deloitte and Touche once stated that one should build a solid infrastructure; the infrastructure should be a foundation that will last for 30 years. Work to build a bridge that will handle traffic for a long time and one will have the kind of infrastructure that can be depended upon for many years. Well-written and management-accepted policy should rarely change.

THE RIVER: UNDERSTANDING THE BUSINESS NEED

Understanding what one is protecting the business against is the first place to start. Too often, IS people will build a fantastic bridge — wide, double decked, all out of the best steel in the world — then they begin looking for a river to cross. This could also be called knowing the enemy or, in a more positive light to go with the business concept, understanding the business need.

If the Security Manager does not understand what objectives the end users of the information have, one will not know what is the best security philosophy to choose. One will not know whether availability is more important than integrity or confidentiality, nor which should get the primary focus. It will be difficult to leverage sufficient security technology with administrative procedures, policies, and standards. ROI will be impossible to guage. There will be no way of knowing what guidelines would help the end user follow policy or work best with the technology. Organizations often focus efforts on technical priorities that may not even be where the greatest exposures to the information are (see Exhibit 10-3). Problems for nonexistent exposures will be getting solved; a bridge will be getting erected across a dry river.

Exhibit 10-3.   Case study: bank of the world savings.

CASE STUDY:

The Bank of the World Savings (BOWS) organization is dealing daily with financial information. BOWS has security technology fully implemented for protecting information from manipulation by unauthorized people and from people stealing credit card numbers, etc. to the best of its technical ability. Assuming this is equivalent to what all other banks do, BOWS has probably accomplished a portion of its due diligence.

Because no technology can provide 100 percent security, what happens if a person does get by the security technology? BOWS can be damaged just as severely by bad publicity as from the actual loss incurred by circumvention of the technology. Unless the bank has created procedures and policies for damage control, its loss could be orders of magnitude larger in lost business than the original loss.

BOWS does not process information using Internet technology; therefore, the outside element is of less concern. However, the company does have a high employee turnover rate and provides remote access via dial-up and remote control software. No policy exists to require unique user IDs, nor are there any procedures to ensure that terminated employees are promptly removed from system access.

The perpetrator (a terminated employee) is angry with BOWS and wants to get back at the company. He would not even need to use the information for his own financial gain. He could simply publish his ability to penetrate BOWS' defenses and create a consumer scare. The direct loss from the incident was $0, but overall damage to business was likely mega-dollars when the consumer community found out about BOWS bad security practices.

LAYING THE ROADBED: POLICY AND STANDARDS

The roadbed consists of policy and standards. Security policy and standards must have muscle. They must include strong yet enforceable statements, clearly written with no room for interpretation, and most importantly must be reasonable and supported by all levels of management. Avoid long or complex policies. As a rule of thumb, no policy should be more than one page in length; a couple of short paragraphs is preferable. Use words in the policy like must, shall, and will. If a policy is something that will not be supported or it is not reasonable to expect someone to follow it to do their job, it should not be published. (See also Exhibit 10-5.) Include somewhere in policy documentation of the disciplinary measures for anyone who does not comply. Procedures and guidelines can provide detail explaining how personnel can comply. To be valid, policy and standards must be consistently enforced. More information on the structure of policy and standards is available later in this article.

Enforcement procedures are the edges of the roadbed. Noncompliance might result in falling off the bridge, which many can relate to being in trouble, especially if one cannot swim. Enforcement provides the boundaries to keep personnel on the proper road. A sample of a simple enforcement procedure for a security violation might be:

1. On the first occurrence, the employee will be informed and given a warning of the importance to comply with policy.
2. On the next occurrence, the employee's supervisor will be contacted. The supervisor will discuss the indiscretion with the employee.
3. Further violations of the same policy will result in disciplinary actions that might consist of suspension or possible termination, depending on the severity of the incident.

In any case, it might be necessary to publish a disclaimer stating that depending on the severity of the incident, disciplinary actions can result in termination. Remember that, to some degree, common sense must come into the decisions regarding how enforcement procedures should be applied, but they should always be consistently enforced. Also, emphasize the fact that it is all management's responsibility to enforce policy, not just the Security Manager's.

Start with the basics, create baselines, and build on them until one has a corporate infrastructure that can stand years and years of traffic. Policy and standards form the benchmarks or reference points for audits. They provide the basis of evidence that management has acted with due diligence, thus reducing their liability.

THE GATE KEEPERS: TECHNOLOGY

Technology is everywhere. In the simplest terms, the security technology consists of specific software that will provide for three basic elements of protection: authentication, accountability, and audit. Very specific standards provide the baselines for which technology is evaluated, purchased, and implemented. Technology provides the mechanism to enforce policies, standards, and procedures.

Authentication. Authentication is the process by which access is established and the system verifies that the end user requesting access to the information is who they claim to be. The process involves providing one's personal key at the locked gate to open it in order to be able to cross the bridge using the path guarded by that gate.

Accountability. Accountability is the process of assigning appropriate access and identification codes to users in order for them to access the information. Establishing audit trails is what establishes accountability.

An example of accountability in electronic commerce is the assignment of digital certificates that can provide varying levels of guaranteed accountability (trust). At the least trusted levels, the user has a credit card or cash to buy a certificate. At a middle degree of trust, there is more checking done to validate that the user really is the person who they claim to be. At the highest level of trust, an entity is willing to stand behind the accountability of the certificate assignment to make it legally binding. This would mean a signature document was signed in person with the registrant that assigns certificates for establishing the accountability.

Assigning a personal key to an individual who has provided beyond-doubt proof (DNA test) that they are who they say they are and that they have agreed to guard their key with their life and that any access by that key can only be by them.

Audit. This is the process, on which accountability depends that can verify using system events to show beyond a reasonable doubt, that specific activities, authorized or unauthorized, occurred in the system by a specific user identification at a given point in time. The information is available on request and used to report to management, internal and external auditors, and could be used as legal evidence in a criminal prosecution.

Having the necessary proof that the personal (authentication) key assigned (accountable) to Ken M. Shaurette was used to perform an unauthorized activity such as to modify the payroll system, adding bonus bucks to the salaries of all CISSP personnel.

PROVIDING TRANSPORTATION: COMMUNICATION

Communication is the #1 key to the success of any security infrastructure. Not only do policy, standards, procedures, and guidelines need to be communicated, but proper use and availability of the security technologies and processes also need to be communicated. Communications is like the racecar or the bus that gets the user across the bridge faster from their business need to the information on the other side. Arguably, the most important aspect of security is informing everyone that they have a responsibility for its effectiveness.

CERT estimates that 80 percent of network security intrusions are a result of users selecting and using passwords that are easy to guess and as such are easy to compromise. If users are unaware that bad password selection is a risk, what incentive is there to make better selections? If they knew of guidelines that could help them pick a more difficult password to compromise, would they not be more inclined to do so? If users are unaware that guidelines exist to help them, how can they follow them?

What makes up communications? Communications involves integrating the policy into the organization using a successful security-training program consisting of such things as:

- new employee orientations
- periodic newsletters
- intranet Web site
- electronic announcements (i.e., banners, e-mail)
- CBT course
- technology lunches, dinners
- informal user group forums
- regular company publications
- security awareness days
- ethics and appropriate use agreements signed annually

EXPERT VERSUS FOOL: IMPLEMENTATION RECOMMENDATIONS

Before beginning policy and standard development, understand that in an established organization, policy and standards may exist in different forms. There is probably official, de jure, less official, *de facto* and proprietary, no choice. Official is the law; they are formal and already accepted. Less official consists of things that get followed but are not necessarily published, but maybe should be. Proprietary are the items that are dictated by an operating system; for example, MVS has limitations of eight-character user IDs and eight-character passwords.

Be the Expert: Implementation Recommendations

Form a team or committee that gets the involvement and cooperation of others. If the policies, standards, procedures, and guidelines are to become enterprisewide, supported by every layer of management, and be reasonable and achievable, representation from all areas — both technology and non-technology — will go a long way toward meeting that goal. Only a team of the most wise and sage experts from all over the organization will know what may already exist and what might still be necessary.

As the security professional, efforts should be concentrated on providing high-level security expertise, coordination, recommendations, communication, and education in order to help the team come to a consensus. Be the engineer, not the builder; get the team to build the bridge.

Layering Security

Layer protection policies and standards. Support them with procedures and guidelines. Review and select security technology that can be standards. Create guidelines and procedures that help users comply with policy. Establishing policy and adequate standards provides the organization with control of its own destiny. Not doing so provides the potential for auditors (internal or external) or legal actions to set policy.

The following walks the reader through the layers outlined in Exhibit 10-4, from the top down.

Corporate Security Policy. This is the top layer of Exhibit 10-4. There should be as few policies as possible used to convey corporate attitude and the attitude from the top down. Policies will have very distinct characteristics. They should be short, enforceable, and seldom change. See Exhibit 10-5 for tips on writing security policy. Policy that gets in the way of business productivity will be ignored or eliminated. Corporate ethics are a form of policy at the top level. Proper use of computing resources or platforms is another example of high-level policy, such as the statement, "for business use only."

SAMPLE POLICY:
Information will be protected based on a need-to-know philosophy. Information will be classified and protected in a manner commensurate with its sensitivity, value, and criticality. Protection of information will apply regardless of the media where the information is stored (printed, electronic, etc.), the systems that process it (PC, mainframes, voice mail systems, etc.), or the transport mechanisms by which it is moved (fax, electronic mail, TCP/IP network, voice conversation, etc.).

Functional Standards

Functional standards (the second layer of Exhibit 10-4) are generally associated to a business area. The Loan department in a bank might have standards governing proper handling of certain loan information. For example, a loan department might have a standard with an associated procedure for the special handling of loans applied for by famous people, or executives of the company. Standards might require that information assigned sensitive classification levels is shredded, or an HR department

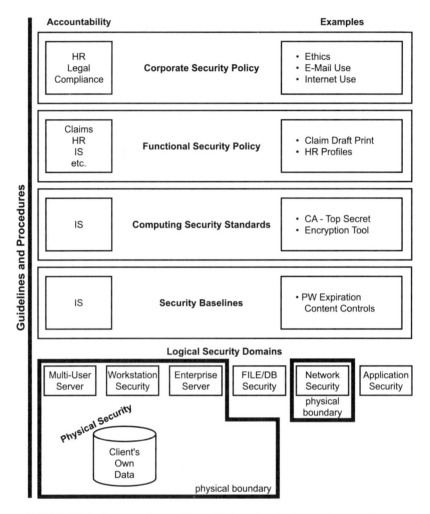

Exhibit 10-4. Layers of security: policies, standards, and procedures.

might require that employee profiles only be printed on secure printers, available and handled only by specific personnel. The Claims department in an insurance company may set standards that require the printing of claim checks on printers local to the office that is handling the claim.

Computing Policy

The computing policies (the third layer in Exhibit 10-4) are tied with technology. These standards establish computing environments such as identifying the standard security software for securing mainframe-computing environments (i.e., CA-Top Secret, RACF, or CA-ACF2), establishing an encryption standard (i.e., PGP, BLOWFISH, DES, 3DES) for every desktop/laptop, or

Exhibit 10-5. Tips on writing security policy.

- Make the policy easy to understand.
- Make it applicable. Does the policy really fit? Does it relate to what actually happens at the company? Does if fit the organizations culture?
- Make it do-able. Can the company still meet business objectives if the policy is implemented?
- Make it enforceable.
- Use a phased-in approach. Allow time for employees to read, digest, and respond to the policy.
- Be pro-active. State what must be done.
- Avoid absolutes; almost never say "never."
- Use wording such as "must," "will," or "shall" — not "would," "should," or "could."
- Meet business objectives. Allow the organization to identify an acceptable level of risk.
- Address all forms of information. (How were the machine names obtained)?
- Obtain appropriate management support.
- Conform. It is important that policy looks like other written company policies.
- Keep it short. Policies are shorter than procedures or practices, usually one or two pages in length maximum.
- What is to be protected?
- When does the policy take effect?
- Where within the organization does the policy reach? Remember the scope.
- To whom does the policy apply? Is there a limitation on the domain?
- Why was the policy developed?
- Who is responsible for enforcement?
- What are the ramifications of noncompliance?
- What, if any, deviations are allowed? If allowed, what are the deviation procedures?
- Are audit trails available and required?
- Who developed, approved, and authorized the policy?
- How will compliance be monitored?
- Are there only penalties for noncompliance, or are rewards available to motivate people toward good practices?
- Who has update and maintenance responsibility for the policies?
- How often will the policy be reviewed and updated if necessary?
- Are there documented approval procedures for new or updated policy?
- Is there an archive of policy, past to present? What was in effect last year at the time of the incident?
- What is the date of the last revision?

transmission of any sensitive information. Information services is most likely establishing the computing security standards that work with information owner requirements, and business needs.

Security Baselines

Security baselines (the fourth layer in Exhibit 10-4) can also be called the minimums. These are tied very closely to the operating environment and day-to-day functioning of the business. Some baselines might be password expiration intervals, password content controls (six characters must be one numeric or special character), and minimum length of user ID. Another might be requiring that every computing system perform authentication based on a personal identity code that will be assigned to each user and that they use their personal password or alternative authentication (token, biometrics) before access is granted to perform any activities. Audit would also be another baseline requirement.

Technology and Physical Security

Technology and physical security are the components making up the bottom layer of Exhibit 10-4. This is the technology, the security software or hardware, that makes up the various computing platforms that comprise the information processing environment. It is the specific security within an NOS, an application, firewalls for the network, database security, or any other specific technology that provides the actual controls that allow the organization to enforce baselines and standards. An application program may have the security checking that restricts the printing of employee profiles and claim checks or provides alerts and special handling controls for loans by special people.

Procedures and Guidelines

Procedures and guidelines cross all layers of the information security infrastructure, as illustrated in Exhibit 10-4. Guidelines are not required actions, but procedures could fall into either something that must be done or provide help in compliance with security policy, standards, and technology. The best policy and standard can have minimal value if people do not have guidelines to follow. Procedures go that next step in explaining the why and how of policy in the day-to-day business operation to help ensure proper implementation and continued compliance. Policy can only be concise if the guidelines and procedures provide sufficient explanation of how to achieve the business objective. Enforcement is usually spelled out in the form of a procedure; procedures would tell how to and why it is necessary to print to specific printers or handle certain loans in a special way. Guidelines are the hints and tips; for example, sharing one's password does not eliminate one's accountability; choose passwords that are not easily guessed and give sample techniques for password selection. Help personnel find the right path and they will follow it; reminders of the consequences are good incentives.

THE POLICE ARE COMING!

In conclusion, what are the measures that can be taken to protect the company or management from litigation? Security cannot provide 100 percent protection. There will be a need to accept some risk. Recognize due care methods to reduce and limit liability by minimizing how much risk must be accepted. Computer security is often an intangible process. In many instances, the level of security is not evident until a catastrophe happens, at which time the lack of security is all too painfully evident. Make the protection of corporate information assets "the law." Make adherence to policy and standards a condition of employment. Policy, standards, and procedures must become part of the corporation's living structure, not just a policy development effort. Information security's objective is to enhance the productivity of the business by reducing probability of loss through the design and implementation of policies, standards, procedures, and guidelines that enhance the protection of business assets.

- Information security is not just about technological controls such as software or hardware. Establishing policy and adequate standards provide an organization with control over its own destiny.
- Information security should be viewed in terms of the processes and goals of the business. Business risk is different than security risk, but poor security can put the business at risk; or make it risky doing business.
- Security must become a function of the corporation, and not viewed as an obstacle to business. Policies support the business; put them in business terminology.
- Form a team. Only a team of the most wise and sage experts from all over the organization will know what policy may already exist and what might still be necessary.
- There should be as few policies as possible used to convey corporate attitude and the attitude from the top down. Policies will have very distinct characteristics. They should be short, enforceable, and seldom altered. They must include strong yet enforceable statements, be clearly written with no room for interpretation, and most importantly, must be reasonable and supported by all levels of management. Use words in the policy like must, shall, and will.
- Policy can only be concise if the guidelines and procedures provide sufficient explanation of how to achieve the business objective.
- Test policy and standards; it is easy to know what is published, but is that what is really in operation?
- To be valid, policy and standards must be consistently enforced.
- Carefully define the Security Manager's domain, responsibility, and accountabilities. Clearly identify the scope of their job.
- Communication is the #1 key to the success of any security infrastructure.

> To defeat a strong enemy: Deploy forces to defend the strategic points;
> exercise vigilance in preparation, do not be indolent. Deeply investigate
> the true situation, secretly await their laxity. Wait until they leave their
> strongholds, then seize what they love.
>
> — Sun Tzu

Information security is a team effort; all members in an organization must support the business objectives; and information security is an important part of that objective.

Chapter 11

The Business Case for Information Security: Selling Management on the Protection of Vital Secrets and Products

Sanford Sherizen

IF THE WORLD WAS RATIONAL AND INDIVIDUALS AS WELL AS ORGANIZA-
TIONS ALWAYS OPERATED ON THAT BASIS, THIS CHAPTER WOULD NOT
HAVE TO BE WRITTEN. After all, who can argue with the need for protecting
vital secrets and products? Why would senior managers not understand
the need for spending adequate funds and other resources to protect their
own bottom line? Why not secure information as it flows throughout the
corporation and sometimes around the world?

Unfortunately, rationality is not something that one can safely assume
when it comes to the field of information security. Therefore, this chapter
is not only required, but it needs to be presented as a bilingual document,
that is, written in a way that reveals strategies by which senior managers
as well as information security professionals can maximize their specific
interests.

This chapter is based on over 20 years of experience in the field of information security, with a special concentration on consulting with senior- and

middle-level managers. The suggestions are based on successful projects and, if followed, can help other information security professionals achieve successful results with their management.

THE STATE OF INFORMATION SECURITY

Improving information security for an organization is a bit like an individual deciding to lose weight, to exercise, or to stopping smoking. Great expectations. Public declarations of good intentions. A projected starting date in the near future. And then the realization that this is a constant activity, never to end and never to be resolved without effort.

Why is it that there are so many computer crime and abuse problems at the same time that an increasing number of senior executives are declaring that information security is an absolute requirement in their organizations? This question is especially perplexing when one considers the great strides that have been made in the field of information security in allowing greater protection of assets. While the skill levels of the perpetrators have increased and the complexity of technology today leaves many exposures, one of the central issues for today's information security professional is nontechnical in nature. More and more, a challenge that many in the field face is how to inform, convince, influence, or in some other way "sell" their senior management on the need for improving information security practices.

This chapter looks at the information security–senior executive dialogue, offering the reasons why such exchanges often do not work well and suggesting ways to make this a successful discussion.

SENIOR MANAGEMENT VIEWS OF INFORMATION SECURITY

Information security practitioners need to understand two basic issues regarding their senior management. The first is that computer crime is only one of the many more immediate risks that executives face today. The second is that thinking and speaking in managerial terms is a key to even gaining their attention in order to present a business case for improvements.

To the average senior executive, information security may seem relatively easy — simply do not allow anyone who should not see certain information to see that information. Use the computer as a lock against those who would misuse their computer use. Use all of that money that has been given for information technology to come up with the entirely safe computer. Stop talking about risks and vulnerabilities and solve the problem. In other words, information security may be so complex that only simple answers can be applied from the non-practitioner's level.

Among all the risks that a manager must respond to, computer crime seems to fall into the sky-is-falling category. The lack of major problems with the Y2K issue has raised questions in some managerial and other circles as to whether the entire crisis was manufactured by the media and technical companies. Even given the extensive media coverage of major incidents, such as the Yahoo, etc. distributed denial-of-service attack, the attention of managers is quickly diverted as they move on to other, "more important issues." To managers, who are faced with making the expected profits for each quarter, information security is a maybe type of event. Even when computer crime happens in a particular organization, managers are given few risk figures that can indicate how much improvement in information security (X) will lead to how much prevention of crime (Y).

With certain notable exceptions, there are fundamental differences and perceptions between information security practitioners and senior executives. For example, how can information security professionals provide the type of cost-justification or return-on-investment (ROI) figures given the current limited types of tools? A risk analysis or similar approach to estimating risks, vulnerabilities, exposures, countermeasures, etc. is just not sufficient to convince a senior manager to accept large allocations of resources.

The most fundamental difference, however, is that senior executives now are the Chief Information Security Manager (or Chief Corporate Cop) of their organizations. What that quite literally means is that the executives — rather than the information security manager or the IS manager — now have legal and fiduciary responsibilities to provide adequate resources and support for information protection.

Liabilities are now a given fact of life for senior executives. Of particular importance, among the extensive variety of liability situations found in an advanced economy, is the adequacy of information protection. The adequacy of managerial response to information security challenges can be legally measured in terms of due care, due diligence, and similar measures that indicate what would be considered as a sufficient effort to protect their organization's informational assets. Unfortunately, as discussed, senior executives often do not know that they have this responsibility, or are unwilling to take the necessary steps to meet this responsibility. The responsibility for information security is owned by senior management, whether they want it or not and whether they understand its importance or not.

INFORMATION SECURITY VIEWS OF SENIOR MANAGEMENT

Just as there are misperceptions of information security, so information security practitioners often suffer from their misperceptions of management. At times, it is as if there are two quite different and quite unconnected views of the world.

In a study done several years ago, CEOs were asked how important information security was to their organization and whether they provided what they felt was adequate assistance to that activity. The results showed an overwhelming vote for the importance of information security as well as the majority of these executives providing sufficient resources. However, when the IS, audit, and information security managers were asked about their executives' views of security, they indicated that there was a large gap between rhetoric and reality. Information security was often mentioned, but the resources provided and the support given to information security programs often fell below necessary levels.

One of the often-stated laments of information security practitioners is how difficult it is to be truly heard by their executives. Information security can only work when senior management supports it, and that support can only occur when they can be convinced of the importance of information protection. Such support is required because, by the nature of its work, information security is a political activity that crosses departmental lines, chains of command, and even national boundaries.

Information security professionals must become more managerial in outlook, speech, and perspectives. What that means is that it is no longer sufficient to stress the technical aspects of information protection. Rather, the stress needs to be placed on how the information security function protects senior executives from major legal and public relations liabilities. Further, information security is an essential aspect of managing organizations today. Just as information is a strategic asset, so information protection is a strategic requirement. In essence, information security provides many contributions to an organization. The case to be made to management is the business case for information security.

THE MANY POSITIVE ROLES OF INFORMATION SECURITY

While people may realize that they play many roles in their work, it is worthwhile listing which of those roles apply to "selling information security." This discussion allows the information security practitioner to determine which of the work-related activities that he or she is involved in has implications for convincing senior management of the importance of that work and the need for senior management to provide sufficient resources in order to maximize the protection span of control.

One of the most important roles to learn is how to become an information security "marketeer." Marketing, selling, and translating technical, business, and legal concepts into "managerialeze" is a necessary skill for the field of information security today. What are you marketing or selling? You are clarifying for management that not only do you provide information protection but, at the same time, also provide such other valuable services as:

1. *Compliance enforcer and advisor.* As IT has grown in importance, so have the legalities that have to be met in order to be in compliance with laws and regulations. Legal considerations are ever-present today. This could include the discovery of a department using unauthorized copies of programs; internal employee theft that becomes public knowledge and creates opportunity for shareholder suits; a penetration from the outside that is used as a launching pad to attack other organizations and thus creating the possibility of a downstream liability issue; or any of the myriad ways that organizations get into legal problems.
   — **Benefit to management.** A major role of the information security professional is to assist management in making sure that the organization is in compliance with the law.
2. *Business enabler and company differentiator.* E-commerce has changed the entire nature of how organizations offer goods and services. The business enabler role of information security is to provide an organization with information security as a value-added way of providing ease of purchase as well as security and privacy of customer activities. Security has rapidly become the way by which organizations can provide customers with safe purchasing while offering the many advantages of e-commerce.
   — **Benefit to management.** Security becomes a way of differentiating organizations in a commercial setting by providing "free safety" in addition to the particular goods and services offered by other corporations. "Free safety" offers additional means of customer satisfaction, encouraging the perception of secure Web-based activities.
3. *Total quality management contributor.* Quality of products and services is related to information security in a quite direct fashion. The confidentiality, integrity, and availability of information that one seeks to provide allow an organization to provide customer service that is protected, personal, and convenient.
   — **Benefit to management.** By combining proper controls over processes, machines, and personnel, an organization is able to meet the often contradictory requirements of production as well as protection. Information security makes E-commerce possible, particularly in terms of the perceptions of customers that such purchasing is safe and reliable.
4. *"Peopleware" controller.* Peopleware is not the hardware or software of IT. It involves the human elements of the human-machine interface. Information security as well as the audit function serve as key functions in controlling the unauthorized behavior of people. Employees, customers, and clients need to be controlled in their use

of technology and information. The need-to-know and separation-of-duties concepts become of particular importance in the complex world of E-commerce. Peopleware are the elements of the control structure that allow certain access and usage as well as disallow what have been defined as unauthorized activities.

— **Benefit to management.** Managerial policies are translated into information security policies, programs, and practices. Authorized usage is structured, unauthorized usage is detected, and a variety of access control and similar measures offer protections over sensitive informational assets.

The many roles of information security are of clear benefit to commercial and governmental institutions. Yet, these critical contributions to managing complex technical environments tend not to be considered when managers view the need for information security. As a result, one of the most important roles of information security practitioners is to translate these contributions into a business case for the protection of vital information.

MAKING THE BUSINESS CASE FOR INFORMATION SECURITY

While there are many different ways to make the business case and many ways to "sell" information security, the emphasis of this section is on the common body of knowledge (CBK) and similar sources of explication or desired results. These are a highly important source of professional knowledge that can assist in informing senior executives regarding the importance of information security.

CBK, as well as other standards and requirements (such as the Common Criteria and the British Standards 7799), are milestones in the growth of the professional field of information security. These compendia of the best ways to evaluate security professionals as well as the adequacy of their organizations serve many purposes in working with senior management.

They offer information security professionals the ability to objectively recommend recognized outside templates for security improvements to their own organizations. These external bodies contain expert opinion and user feedback regarding information protection. Because they are international in scope, they offer a multinational company the ability to provide a multinational overview of security.

Further, these enunciations of information security serve as a means of measuring the adequacy of an organization's information security program and efforts. In reality, they serve as an indication of "good practices" and "state of knowledge" needed in today's IT environments. They also provide legal authorities with ways to measure or evaluate what are considered as appropriate, necessary, or useful for organizations in protecting information. A "good-faith effort" to secure information, a term used in the U.S. Federal

Sentencing Guidelines, becomes an essential legal indicator of an organization's level of effort, concern, and adequacy of security programs. Being measured against these standards and being found lax may cost an organization millions of dollars in penalties as well as other serious personal and organizational punishments. (For further information on the U.S. Sentencing Guidelines as they relate to information security, see the author's publication on the topic at http://www.computercrimestop.com/.)

MEETING THE INFORMATION SECURITY CHALLENGE

The many challenges of information security are technical, organizational, political, legal, and physical. For the information security professional, these challenges require new skills and new orientations. To be successful in "selling" information security to senior executives, information security practitioners should consider testing themselves on how well they are approaching these decision-makers.

One way to do such a self-evaluation is based on a set of questions used in forensic reviews of computer and other crimes. Investigators are interested in determining whether a particular person has motive, opportunity, and means (MOM). In an interesting twist, this same list of factors can be helpful in determining whether information security practitioners are seeking out the many ways to get the attention of their senior executives.

1. *Motivation.* Determine what motivates executives in their decisions. Understand the key concepts and terms they use. Establish a benefits approach to information security, stressing the advantages of securing information rather than emphasizing the risks and vulnerabilities. Find out what "marketeering" means in your organization, including what are the best messages, best media, and best communicators needed for this effort.
2. *Opportunity.* Ask what opportunities are available, or can be made, to meet with, be heard by, or gain access to senior executives. Create openings as a means to stress the safe computing message. Opportunities may mean presenting summaries of the current computer crime incidents in memos to management. An opportunity can be created when managers are asked for a statement to be used in user awareness training. Establish an Information Security Task Force, composed of representatives from many units, including management. This could be a useful vehicle for sending information security messages upward. Find out the auditor's perspectives on controls to see how these may reinforce the messages.
3. *Means.* The last factor is means. Create ways to get the message heard by management. Meeting may be direct or indirect. Gather clippings of current computer crime cases, particularly those found in organizations or industries similar to one's own. Do a literature

review of leading business, administrative, and industry publications, pulling out articles on computer crime problems and solutions. Work with an organization's attorneys in gathering information on the changing legal requirements around IT and security.

CONCLUSION

In the "good old days" of information security, security was relatively easy. Only skilled data processing people had the capability to operate in their environment. That, plus physical barriers, limited the type and number of people who could commit computer crimes.

Today's information security picture is far more complicated. The environment requires information security professionals to supplement their technical skills with a variety of "soft skills" such as managing, communicating, and stressing the business reasons for security objectives. The successful information security practitioner will learn these additional skills in order to be heard in the on-rush of challenges facing senior executives.

The technical challenges will certainly not go away. However, it is clear that the roles of information security will increase and the requirements to gain the acceptance of senior management will become more important.

Domain 4
Applications and Systems Development Security

WITH THE INCREASING DEPLOYMENT OF CLIENT/SERVER APPLICATIONS AND THE ADVENT OF INTERNET AND INTRANET APPLICATIONS, USER IDENTIFICATION AND AUTHENTICATION, AND DATA ACCESS CONTROLS ARE DISTRIBUTED THROUGHOUT THE MULTIPLE LAYERS OF A SYSTEM ARCHITECTURE. This decentralized security model differs greatly from the centrally controlled and managed mainframe environment.

The distributed system security architecture demands that protection mechanisms are embedded throughout. The chapters in this domain address the integration and unity of the controls within the application and database design. Further, the concept of the public key infrastructure is featured, which encompasses the policies, procedures, and robust administrative and technical controls required to support and secure scalable applications for potential deployment to millions of users.

Chapter 12
PeopleSoft Security
Satnam Purewal

SECURITY WITHIN AN ORGANIZATION'S INFORMATION SYSTEMS ENVIRONMENT IS GUIDED BY THE BUSINESS AND DRIVEN BY AVAILABLE TECHNOLOGY ENABLERS. Business processes, functional responsibilities, and user requirements drive security within an application. This chapter highlights security issues to consider in a PeopleSoft 7.5 client/server environment, including the network, operating system, database, and application components.

Within the PeopleSoft client/server environment, there are several layers of security that should be implemented to control logical access to PeopleSoft applications and data: network, operating system, database, and PeopleSoft application security. Network, operating system, and database security depend on the hardware and software selected for the environment (Windows NT, UNIX, and Sybase, respectively). User access to PeopleSoft functions is controlled within the PeopleSoft application.

1. Network security controls:
   a. who can log on to the network
   b. when they can log on (via restricted logon times)
   c. what files they can access (via file rights such as execute-only, read-only, read/write, no access, etc.)
2. Operating system security controls:
   a. who can log on to the operating system
   b. what commands can be issued
   c. what network services are available (controlled at the operating system level)
   d. what files/directories a user can access
   e. the level of access (read, write, delete)
3. Database security controls:
   a. who can log on to a database
   b. which tables or views users can access
   c. the commands users can execute to modify the data or the database
   d. who can perform database administration activities

4. PeopleSoft online security controls:
   a. who can sign-on to PeopleSoft (via operator IDs and passwords)
   b. when they can sign-on (via operator sign-on times)
   c. the panels users can access and the functions they can perform
   d. the processes users can run
   e. the data they can query/update

NETWORK SECURITY

The main function of network security is to control access to the network and its shared resources. It serves as the first line of defense against unauthorized access to the PeopleSoft application.

At the network security layer, it is important to implement login controls. PeopleSoft 7.5 delivers limited authentication controls. If third-party tools are not going to be used to enhance the PeopleSoft authentication process, then it is essential that the controls implemented on this layer are robust.

The network servers typically store critical application data like client-executable programs and management reports. PeopleSoft file server directories should be set up as read-only for only those individuals accessing the PeopleSoft application (i.e., access should not be read-only for everyone on the network). If executables are not protected, unauthorized users could inadvertently execute programs that result in a denial-of-service. For this reason, critical applications used to move data should be protected in a separate directory. Furthermore, the PeopleSoft directories containing sensitive report definitions should be protected by only granting read access to users who require access.

DATABASE MANAGEMENT SYSTEM SECURITY

The database management system contains all PeopleSoft data and object definitions. It is the repository where organizational information resides and is the source for reporting. Direct access to the database circumvents PeopleSoft application security and exposes important and confidential information.

All databases compatible with the PeopleSoft applications have their own security system. This security system is essential for ensuring the integrity and accuracy of the data when direct access to the database is granted.

To reduce the risk of unauthorized direct access to the database, the PeopleSoft access ID and password must be secured, and direct access to the database should be limited to the database administrators (DBAs).

The access ID represents the account that the application uses to connect to the underlying database in order to access PeopleSoft tables. For the access ID to update data in tables, the ID must have read/write access to all PeopleSoft tables (otherwise, each individual operator would have to be granted access to each individual table). To better understand the risk posed by the access ID, it helps to have an understanding of the PeopleSoft sign-on (or logon) process:

1. When PeopleSoft is launched on the user workstation, the application prompts for an operator ID and password. The ID and password input by the operator is passed to the database (or application server in three-tier environments).
2. The operator ID and password are validated against the PSOPRDEFN security table. If both are correct, the access ID and password are passed back to the workstation.
3. PeopleSoft disconnects from the DBMS and reconnects using the access ID and password. This gives PeopleSoft read/write access to all tables in the database.

The application has full access to all PeopleSoft tables, but the access granted to the individual operator is restricted by PeopleSoft application security (menu, process, query, object, and row-level security). Users with knowledge of the access ID and password could log on (e.g., via an ODBC connection) directly to the database, circumventing application security. The user would then have full access privileges to all tables and data, including the ability to drop or modify tables.

To mitigate this risk, the following guidelines related to the access ID and password should be followed:

- Procedures should be implemented for regularly changing the access ID password (e.g., every 30 days). At a minimum, the password must be changed anytime someone with knowledge of it leaves the organization.
- Ownership of the access ID and password should be assigned, preferably to a DBA. This person would be responsible for ensuring that the password is changed on a regular interval, and for selecting strong passwords. Only this person and a backup should know the password. However, the ID should never be used by the person to log on to the database.
- Each database instance should have its own unique access ID password. This reduces the risk that a compromised password could be used to gain unauthorized access to all instances.
- The access ID and password should not be hard-coded in cleartext into production scripts and programs. If a batch program requires it, store the ID and password in an encrypted file on the operating system and "point" to the file in the program.

- Other than DBAs and technical support personnel, no one should have or need a database ID and direct connectivity to the database (e.g., SQL tools).

OPERATING SYSTEM SECURITY

The operating system needs to be secured to prevent unauthorized changes to source, executable, and configuration files. PeopleSoft and database application files and instances reside on the operating system. Thus, it is critical that the operating system environment be secure to prevent unauthorized changes to source, executable, and configuration files.

PEOPLESOFT APPLICATION SECURITY

To understand PeopleSoft security, it is first essential to understand how users access PeopleSoft. To access the system, an operator ID is needed. The system will determine the level of access for which the user is authorized and allow the appropriate navigation to the panels.

Many organizations have users with similar access requirements. In these situations, an "operator class" can be created to facilitate the administration of similar access to multiple users. It is possible to assign multiple operator classes to users. When multiple operator classes are used, PeopleSoft determines the level of access in different ways for each component. The method of determining access is described below for each layer when there are multiple operator classes.

PeopleSoft controls access to the different layers of the application using operator classes and IDs. The term "operator profile" is used to refer, in general, to both operator IDs and classes. Operator profiles are used to control access to the different layers, which can be compared to an onion. Exhibit 12-1 shows these layers: Sign-on security, panel security, query security, row-level security, object security, field security, and process security. The outer layers (i.e., sign-on security and panel security) define broader access controls. Moving toward the center, security becomes defined at a more granular level.

The layers in Exhibit 12-1:

- Sign-on security provides the ability to set up individual operator IDs for all users, as well as the ability to control when these users can access the system.
- Panel security provides the ability to grant access to only the functions the user requires within the application.
- Query security controls the tables and data users can access when running queries.
- Row-level security defines the data that users can access through the panels they have been assigned.

The outer layers define access at a general level and
the inner circles define access at a more detailed level.

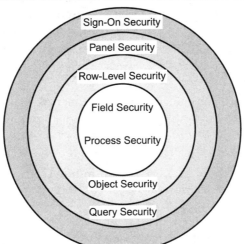

Exhibit 12-1. PeopleSoft security onion.

- Object security defines the objects that users can access through the tools authorized through panel security.
- Field security is the ability to restrict access to certain fields within a panel assigned to a user.
- Process security is used to restrict the ability to run jobs from the PeopleSoft application.

Sign-on Security

PeopleSoft sign-on security consists of assigning operator IDs and passwords for the purpose of user logon. An operator ID and the associated password can be one to eight characters in length. However, the delivered sign-on security does not provide much control for accessing the PeopleSoft application.

PeopleSoft (version 7.5 and earlier) modules are delivered with limited sign-on security capabilities. The standard features available in many applications are not available within PeopleSoft. For example, there is no way to limit the number of simultaneous sessions a user can initiate with an operator ID. There also are no controls over the types of passwords that can be chosen. For example, users can choose one-character passwords or they can set the password equal to their operator ID. Users with passwords equal to the operator ID do not have to enter passwords at logon. If these users are observed during the sign-on process, it is easy to determine their passwords.

Many organizations have help desks for the purpose of troubleshooting common problems. With PeopleSoft, password maintenance cannot be decentralized to the help desk without also granting the ability to maintain operator IDs. This means that the help desk would also have the ability to change a user's access as well as the password. Furthermore, it's not possible to force users to reset passwords during the initial sign-on or after a password reset by the security administrator.

There are no intrusion detection controls that make it possible to suspend operator IDs after specified violation thresholds are reached. Potentially, intruders using the brute-force method to enter the system will go undetected unless they are caught trying to gain access while at the workstation.

Organizations requiring more robust authentication controls should review third-party tools. Alternatively, PeopleSoft plans to introduce password management features in version 8.0.

Sign-on Times. A user's session times are controlled through the operator ID or the operator class(es). In either case, the default sign-on times are 24 hours a day and 7 days a week. If users will not be using the system on the weekend or in the evening, it is best to limit access to the known work hours.

If multiple operator classes are assigned to operator IDs, attention must be given to the sign-times. The user's start time will be the earliest time found in the list of assigned operator classes. Similarly, the user's end time will be the latest time found in the list of assigned operator classes.

Delivered IDs. PeopleSoft is delivered with operator IDs with the passwords set equal to the operator ID. These operator IDs should be deleted because they usually have full access to business panels and developer tools. If an organization wishes to keep the delivered operator IDs, the password should be changed immediately for each operator ID.

Delivered Operator Classes. PeopleSoft-delivered operator classes also have full access to a large number of functional and development menus and panels. For example, most of these operator classes have the ability to maintain panels and create new panels. These operator classes also have the ability to maintain security.

These classes should be deleted in order to prevent them from being assigned accidentally to users. This will prevent users from getting these operator classes assigned to their profile in error.

Panel Security

There are two ways to grant access to panels. The first way is to assign menus and panels directly to the operator ID. The second way is to assign menus/panels to an operator class and then assign the operator class to

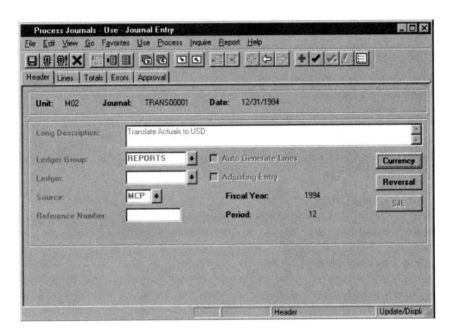

Exhibit 12-2. The PeopleSoft journal entry panel.

the operator ID. When multiple operator classes are assigned to a user, the menus granted to a user are determined by taking a union of all the menus and panels assigned from the list of operator classes assigned to the user. If a panel exists in more than one of the user's operator classes with different levels of access, the user is granted the greater access. This means if in one operator class the user has read-only access and in the other the user has update access, the user is granted update access. This capability allows user profiles to be built like building blocks. Operator classes should be created that reflect functional access. Operator classes should then be assigned according to the access the user needs.

Panel security is essentially column security. It controls access to the columns of data in the PeopleSoft tables. This is best described with an example. The PeopleSoft Journal Entry panel (see Exhibit 12-2) has many fields, including Unit, Journal, Date, Ledger, Long Description, Ledger Group, Ledger, Source, Reference Number, and Auto Generate Lines.

Exhibit 12-3 shows a subset of the columns in the table JRNL_HEADER. This table is accessible from the panel **Process Journals – Use – Journal Entry Headers** panel. The fields in this panel are only accessible by the user if they are displayed on the panel to which the user has access.

When access is granted to a panel, it is also necessary to assign *actions* that a user can perform through the panel. Exhibit 12-4 shows the actions that are

Exhibit 12-3. A subset of the columns in the table JRNL_HEADER.

Unit	Journal	Date	Long Descr	Ledger Grp	Ledger	Source	Ref No	Auto Gen
M02	TRANS0001	1994-12-31	Translate Actuals to USD	REPORTS		MCP		N
M02	TRANS0001	1995-12-31	Translate Actuals to USD	REPORTS		MCP		N
M02	TRANS0001	1996-01-01	Translate Actuals to USD	REPORTS		MCP		N
M04	0000005185	1995-12-27	Adjusting entries for unexpected Production Scrap - not to be repeated.	ACTUALS		ADJ		N
M04	0000005197	1998-03-13	Inventory Transactions	ACTUALS		INV	INV100	N
M04	0000005259	1998-03-19	Inventory Transactions	ACTUALS		INV	INV100	N
M04	0000005271	1998-01-31		BUDGETS		CFO		N
M04	0000005272	1998-01-01	Budget Journals	BUDGETS		CFO		N

Exhibit 12-4. Common actions in panels.

Action	Capability
Add	Ability to insert a new row
Update/Display	Ability to access present and future data
Update/Display All	Ability to access present, future, and historical data; updates to historical data are not permitted
Correction	Ability to access present, future, and historical data; updates to historical data are permitted

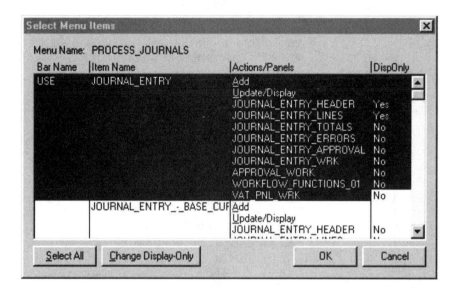

Exhibit 12-5. Assigning read-only access.

common to most panels. This table only shows a subset of all the actions that are available. Furthermore, not all of these actions are available on all panels.

From a security standpoint, correction access should be limited to select individuals in an organization because users with this authority have the ability to change historical information without maintaining an audit trail. As a result, the ability to change historical information could create questions about the integrity of the data. Correction should be used sparingly and only granted in the event that an appropriate process is established to record changes that are performed.

The naming convention of two of the actions (Update/Display, Update/Display All) is somewhat misleading. If a user is granted access to one or both of these actions, the user does not necessarily have update access. Update access also depends on the "Display Only" attribute associated with each panel. When a panel is assigned to an operator ID or operator class, the default access is update. If the user is to have read-only access to a panel, then this attribute must be set to "Y" for yes (see Exhibit 12-5 for an example). This diagram shows that the user has been assigned read-only access to the panels "JOURNAL_ENTRY_HEADER" and "JOURNAL_ENTRY_LINES." For the other highlighted panels, the user has been granted update capabilities.

The panels that fall under the menu group PeopleTools provide powerful authority (see Exhibit 12-6 for a list of PeopleTools menu items). These panels should only be granted to users who have a specific need in the production environment.

Exhibit 12-6. PeopleTools menu items.

APPLICATION DESIGNER
SECURITY ADMINISTRATOR
OBJECT SECURITY
APPLICATION REVIEWER
UTILITIES
IMPORT MANAGER
PROCESS SCHEDULER
EDI MANAGER
nVISION
REPORT BOOKS
TREE MANAGER
QUERY
APPLICATION ENGINE
MASS CHANGE
WORKFLOW ADMINISTRATOR
PROCESS MONITOR
TRANSLATE
CUBE MANAGER

Query Security

Users who are granted access to the **Query** tool will not have the capability to run any queries unless they are granted access to PeopleSoft tables. This is done by adding *Access Groups* to the user's operator ID or one of the operator classes in the user's profile. Access Groups are a way of grouping related tables for the purposes of granting query access.

Configuring query security is a three-step process:

1. Grant access to the **Query** tool.
2. Determine which tables a user can query against and assign **Access Groups**.
3. Set up the Query Profile.

Sensitive organizational and employee data is stored within the PeopleSoft application and can be viewed using the **Query** tool. The challenge in setting up query security is consistency. Many times, organizations will spend a great deal of effort restricting access to panels and then grant access to view all tables through query. This amounts to possible unauthorized access to an organization's information. To restrict access in query to the data accessible through the panels may not be possible using the PeopleSoft delivered access groups. It may be necessary to define new access groups to enable querying against only the tables a user has been authorized to view. Setting up customized access groups will facilitate an organization's objective to ensure consistency when authorizing access.

The **Query Profile** helps define the types of queries a user can run and whether the user can create queries. Exhibit 12-7 displays an example of a profile. Access to the Query tool grants users the ability to view information that resides within the PeopleSoft database tables. By allowing users to create ad hoc queries can require high levels of system resources in order to run complex queries. The Query Profile should be configured to reduce the risk of overly complex queries from being created without being tuned by the database administrators.

The Query Profile has several options to configure. In the **PS/Query Use** box, there are three options. If a user is not a trained query user, then access should be limited to *Only Allowed to run Queries.* Only the more experienced users should be given the authority to create queries. This will reduce the likelihood that resource intensive queries are executed.

Row-level Security

Panel security controls access to the tables and columns of data within the tables but a user will be able to access all data within the columns of the tables on the panel. To restrict user access to data on a panel, row-level security should be established. Access is granted to data using control fields. For example, in Exhibit 12-8 the control field is "Unit" (or Business Unit). If a user is assigned to only the M02 business unit, that user would only be able to see the first four lines of data.

Row-level security is implemented differently in HRMS and Financials.

Human Resource Management System (HRMS) Row-level Security. In HRMS, the modules are delivered with row-level security activated. The delivered row-level security is based on a Department Security Tree and is hierarchical (see Exhibit 12-9). In this example, if a user is granted access to ABC manufacturing department, then the user would have access to the ABC manufacturing department and all of the child nodes. If access is granted to the department Office of the Director Mfg, then the user would have access to the Office of the Director Mfg as well as Corporate Sales, Corporate Marketing, Corporate Admin/Finance, and Customer Services. It is also possible to grant access to the department Office of the Direct Mfg. and then deny access to a lower level department such as Corporate Marketing.

It is important to remember that the organizational tree and the security tree in HRMS need not be the same. In fact, they should not be the same. The organizational tree should reflect the organization today. The security tree will have historical nodes that may have been phased out. It is important to keep these trees in order to grant access to the associated data.

Financials Row-level Security. In the Financials application, row-level security is not configured in the modules when it is delivered. If row-level

263

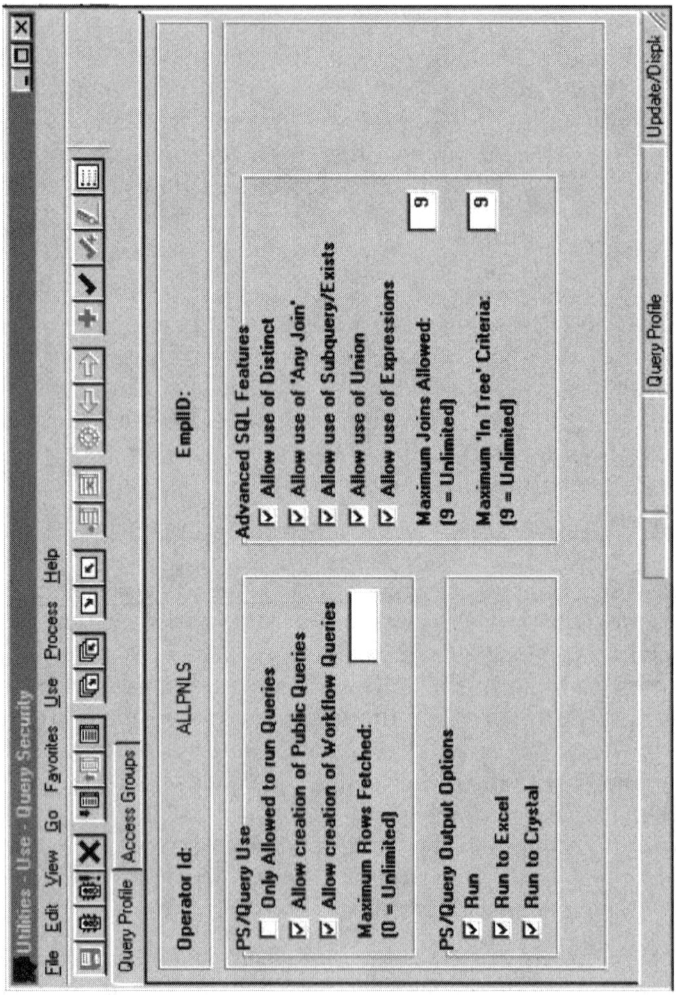

Exhibit 12-7. Query profile.

Exhibit 12-8. Row-level security.

Unit	Journal	Date	Ledger	Unit	Currency	Foreign Curr.	Debits	Credits
M02	AP00005168	1995-12-31	ACTUALS	M02	CAD	CAD	50000.00	50000.00
M02	BI00005216	1998-03-16	ACTUALS	M02	CAD	USD	10149.30	10149.30
M02	BI00005258	1998-03-18	ACTUALS	M02	CAD	USD	20298.60	20298.60
M02	TRANS00001	1995-12-31	REPORTS	M02	USD	USD	3470257761.27	3470257761.27
M04	0000005185	1995-12-27	ACTUALS	M04	USD	CAD	60362.91	60362.91
M04	0000005185	1995-12-27	ACTUALS	M04	USD	USD	6345.00	6345.00
M04	0000005197	1998-03-13	ACTUALS	M04	USD	USD	525145.27	525145.27
M04	0000005271	1998-01-31	BUDGETS	M04	USD	CAD	69075.08	69075.08

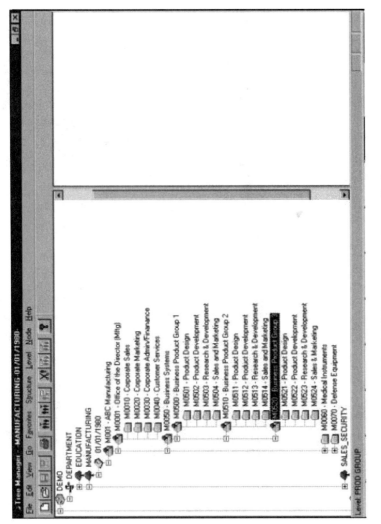

Exhibit 12-9. Department security tree.

security is desired, then it is necessary to first determine if row-level security will be implemented at the operator ID or operator class level. Next, it is necessary to determine the control fields that will be used to implement row-level security. The fields available for row-level security depend on the modules being implemented. Exhibit 12-10 shows which module the options are available in.

Exhibit 12-10. Modules of available options.

Field	Module
Business Unit	General Ledger
SetID	General Ledger
Ledger	General Ledger
Book	Asset Management
Project	Projects
Analysis Group	Projects
Pay Cycle	Accounts Payable

Object Security

In PeopleSoft, an object is defined as a menu, a panel, or a tree. For a complete list of objects, see Exhibit 12-11. By default, all objects are accessible to users with access to the appropriate tools. This should not always be the case. For example, it is not desirable for the security administrator to update the organization tree, nor is it appropriate for an HR supervisor to update the department security tree. This issue is resolved through object groups. Object groups are groups of objects with similar security privileges. Once an object is assigned to an object group, it is no longer accessible unless the object group is assigned to the user.

Exhibit 12-11. PeopleSoft objects.

Import Definitions (I)
Menu Definitions (M)
Panel Definitions (P)
Panel Group Definitions (G)
Record Definitions (R)
Trees (E)
Tree Structure Definitions (S)
Projects (J)
Translate Tables (X)
Query Definitions
Business Process Maps (U)
Business Processes (B)

APPLICATIONS AND SYSTEMS DEVELOPMENT SECURITY

In production, there should not be any access to development-type tools. For this reason, the usage of object security is limited in production. It is mainly used to protect trees. When users are granted access to the Tree Manager, the users have access to all the available trees. In production HRMS, this would mean access to the organization tree, the department security tree, and query security trees. In Financials, this means access to the query security trees and the reporting trees. To resolve this issue, object security is used to ensure that the users with access to Tree Manager are only able to view/update trees that are their responsibility.

Field Security

The PeopleSoft application is delivered with a standard set of menus and panels that provides the functionality required for users to perform their job functions. In delivering a standard set of menus and panels, there are occasions in which the access to data granted on a panel does not coincide with security requirements. For this reason, field-level security may need to be implemented to provide the appropriate level of security for the organization.

Field security can be implemented in two ways; either way, it is a customization that will affect future upgrades. The first option is to implement field security by attaching PeopleCode to the field at the table or panel level. This is complicated and not easy to track. Operator IDs or operator classes are hard-coded into the code. To maintain security on a long-term basis, the security administrator would require assistance from the developers.

The other option is to duplicate a panel, remove the sensitive field from the new panel, and secure access through panel security to these panels. This is the preferred method because it allows the security administrator control over which users have access to the field and it is also easier to track for future upgrades.

Process Security

For users to run jobs, it is necessary for them to have access to the panel from which the job can be executed. It is also necessary for the users to have the process group that contains the job assigned to their profile.

To simplify security administration, it is recommended that users be granted access to all process groups and access be maintained through panel security. This is only possible if the menus/panels do not contain jobs with varying levels of sensitivity. If there are multiple jobs on a panel and users do not require access to all jobs, then access can be granted to the panel and to the process group that gives access to only the jobs required.

SUMMARY

Within the PeopleSoft client/server environment, there are four main layers of security that should be implemented to control logical access to PeopleSoft applications: network, operating system, database, and application security. Network security is essential to control access to the network and the PeopleSoft applications and reports. Operating system security will control access to the operating system as well as shared services. Database security will control access to the database and the data within the database. Each layer serves a purpose and ignoring the layer could introduce unnecessary risks.

PeopleSoft application security has many layers. An organization can build security to the level of granularity required to meet corporate requirements. Sign-on security and panel security are essential for basic access. Without these layers, users are not able to access the system. Query security needs to be implemented in a manner that is consistent with the panel security. Users should not be able to view data through query that they cannot view through their authorized panels. The other component can be configured to the extent that is necessary to meet the organization's security policies.

Individuals responsible for implementing security need to first understand the organization's risk and the security requirements before they embark on designing PeopleSoft security. It is complex, but with planning it can be implemented effectively.

Chapter 13
World Wide Web Application Security

Sean Scanlon

DESIGNING, IMPLEMENTING, AND ADMINISTERING APPLICATION SECURITY ARCHITECTURES THAT ADDRESS AND RESOLVE USER IDENTIFICATION, AUTHENTICATION, AND DATA ACCESS CONTROLS, HAVE BECOME INCREASINGLY CHALLENGING AS TECHNOLOGIES TRANSITION FROM A MAINFRAME ARCHITECTURE, TO THE MULTIPLE-TIER CLIENT/SERVER MODELS, TO THE NEWEST WORLD WIDE WEB-BASED APPLICATION CONFIGURATIONS. Within the mainframe environment, software access control utilities are typically controlled by one or more security officers, who add, change, and delete rules to accommodate the organization's policy compliance. Within the n-tier client/server architecture, security officers or business application administrators typically share the responsibility for any number of mechanisms, to ensure the implementation and maintenance of controls. In the Web application environment, however, the *application user* is introduced as a co-owner of the administration process.

This chapter provides the reader with an appreciation for the intricacies of designing, implementing, and administering security and controls within Web applications, utilizing a commercial third-party package. The manuscript reflects a real-life scenario, whereby a company with the need to do E-business on the Web goes through an exercise to determine the cost/benefit and feasibility of building in security versus adding it on, including all of the considerations and decisions made along the way to implementation.

HISTORY OF WEB APPLICATIONS: THE NEED FOR CONTROLS

During the last decade or so, companies spent a great deal of time and effort building critical business applications utilizing client/server architectures. These applications were usually distributed to a set of controlled, internal users, usually accessed through internal company resources or dedicated, secured remote access solutions. Because of the limited set of users and respective privileges, security was built into the applications or provided by third-party utilities that were integrated with the application. Because of the centralized and limited nature of these applications,

0-8493-0800-3/00/$0.00+$.50
© 2001 by CRC Press LLC

Exhibit 13-1. Considerations for large Web-based application development.

- Authenticating and securing multiple applications, sometimes numbering in the hundreds
- Securing access to applications that access multiple systems, including legacy databases and applications
- Providing personalized Web content to users
- Providing single sign-on access to users accessing multiple applications, enhancing the user experience
- Supporting hundreds, thousands, and even millions of users
- Minimizing the burden on central IT staffs and facilitating administration of user accounts and privileges
- Allowing new customers to securely sign-up quickly and easily without requiring phone calls
- Scalability to support millions of users and transactions and the ability to grow to support unforeseen demand
- Flexibility to support new technologies while leveraging existing resources like legacy applications, directory servers, and other forms of user identification
- Integration with existing security solutions and other Internet security components

management of these solutions was handled by application administrators or a central IT security organization.

Now fast-forward to current trends, where the Web and Internet technologies are quickly becoming a key component for companies' critical business applications (see Exhibit 13-1). Companies are leveraging the Web to enhance communications with customers, vendors, subcontractors, suppliers, and partners, as well as utilizing technologies to reach new audiences and markets. But the same technologies that make the Web such an innovative platform for enhancing communication also dictates the necessity for detailed security planning. The Web has opened up communication to anyone in the world with a computer and a phone line. But the danger is that along with facilitating communication with new markets, customers, and vendors, there is the potential that anyone with a computer and phone line could now access information intended only for a select few.

For companies that have only a few small applications that are accessed by a small set of controlled users, the situation is fairly straightforward. Developers of each application can quickly use directory- or file-level security; if more granular security is required, the developers can embed security in each application housing user information and privileges in a security database. Again, within this scenario, management of a small set of users is less time-consuming and can be handled by a customer service group or the IT security department.

However, most companies are building large Web solutions, many times providing front-end applications to multiple legacy systems on the back end. These applications are accessed by a diverse and very large population of users, both internal and external to the organization. In these instances, one must move to a different mindset to support logon administration and access controls for hundreds, thousands, and potentially millions of users.

A modified paradigm for security is now a requirement for Web applications: accommodating larger numbers of users in a very noninvasive way. The importance of securing data has not changed; a sure way to lose customers is to have faulty security practices that allow customer information to be accessed by unauthorized outside parties. Further, malicious hackers can access company secrets and critical business data, potentially ruining a company's reputation. However, the new security challenge for organizations now becomes one of transitioning to electronic business by leveraging the Web, obtaining and retaining external constituents in the most customer-intimate and customer-friendly way, while maintaining the requirement for granular access controls and "least privilege."

HOW WEB APPLICATION SECURITY IT FITS INTO AN OVERALL INTERNET SECURITY STRATEGY

Brief Overall Description

Building a secure user management infrastructure is just one component of a complete Internet Security Architecture. While a discussion of a complete Internet Security Architecture (including network security) is beyond the scope of this chapter, it is important to understand the role played by a secure user management infrastructure. The following is a general overview of an overall security architecture (see Exhibit 13-2) and the components that a secure user management infrastructure can help address.

		Management	Security
End User		• Reporting/Statistics • User Administration • Delegation • Self-Management	• Identification • Authentication
Application		• Clustering • Policies & Profiles	• Access Controls • Content Filtering • Proxy Services
Data		• Fault Tolerance • Reporting/Statistics	• Encryption • Auditing
Network		• Fault Tolerance • Traffic Reporting • Intrusion Detection	• Authentication • Encryption • Auditing • Non-Repudiation

Exhibit 13-2. Internet Security Architecture.

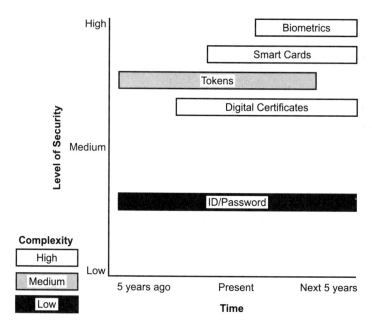

Exhibit 13-3. Authentication time chart.

Authentication

A wide range of authentication mechanisms are available for Web systems and applications. As the Internet matures, more complex and mature techniques will evolve (see Exhibit 13-3). With home-grown developed security solutions, this will potentially require rewriting applications and complicated migrations to new authentication techniques as they become available.

The implementation of a centralized user management architecture can help companies simplify the migration of new authentication techniques by removing the authentication of users from the Internet applications. As new techniques emerge, changes can be made to the user management infrastructure, while the applications themselves would not need major updates, or updates at all.

WHY A WEB APPLICATION AUTHENTICATION/ACCESS CONTROL ARCHITECTURE?

Before deciding whether or not it is necessary to implement a centralized authentication and access control architecture, it is helpful to compare the differences between developing user management solutions for each application and building a centralized infrastructure that is utilized by multiple applications.

Characteristics of decentralized authentication and access control include:

- low initial costs
- quick to develop and implement for small-scale projects
- each application requires its own security solution (developers must build security into each new application)
- user accounts are required for each application
- user must log in separately to each application
- accounts for users must be managed in multiple databases or directories
- privileges must be managed across multiple databases or directories
- inconsistent approach, as well as a lower security level, because common tasks are often done differently across multiple applications
- each system requires its own management procedures increasing administration costs and efforts
- custom solutions may not be scalable as users and transactions increase
- custom solutions may not be flexible enough to support new technologies and security identification schemes
- may utilize an existing directory services infrastructure

Characteristics of centralization authentication and access control include:

- higher start-up costs
- more upfront planning and design required
- a centralized security infrastructure is utilized across multiple applications and multiple Web server platforms
- a single account can be used for multiple applications
- users can log in one time and access multiple applications
- accounts for multiple applications can be managed in a single directory; administration of accounts can easily be distributed to customer service organizations
- privileges can be managed centrally and leveraged over multiple applications
- consistent approach to security, standards are easily developed and managed by a central group and then implemented in applications
- developers can focus on creating applications without having to focus on building security into each application
- scalable systems can be built to support new applications, which can leverage the existing infrastructure
- most centralized solutions are flexible enough to support new technologies; as new technologies and security identification schemes are introduced, they can be implemented independent of applications

Exhibit 13-4. Project phases.

Phase	Tasks
Project planning and initiation	• Develop project scope and objectives • Outline resources required for requirements and design phase • Roles and responsibilities
Requirements	• Develop business requirements • Develop technical requirements • Develop risk assessment • Develop contingency plans • Prioritize requirements and set selection criteria • Roles and responsibilities
Product strategy and selection	• Decide on centralized versus decentralized strategy • Make or buy • Product evaluation and testing • Product selection • License procurement
Design	• Server architecture • Network architecture • Directory services • Directory services strategy • Architecture • Schema • Development environment standards • Administrative responsibilities • Account • Infrastructure
Implementation	• Administrative tools development • Server Implementation • Directory services implementation • Integration
Testing	• Functionality • Performance • Scalability and failover • Testing strategies • Pilot test
Post-implementation	• Ongoing support

PROJECT OVERVIEW

Purpose

Because of the diverse nature of users, data, systems, and applications that can potentially be supported by the centralized user management infrastructure, it is important to ensure that detailed requirements and project plans are developed prior to product selection and implementation (see Exhibit 13-4). Upfront planning will help ensure that all business and

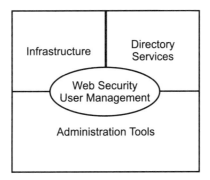

Exhibit 13-5. Web secure user management components.

technical requirements are identified and prioritized, potentially helping prevent serious schedule issues and cost overruns.

PROJECT PLANNING AND INITIATION

Project Components

There are three key components that make up developing an enterprise-wide Web security user management infrastructure (see Exhibit 13-5). While there is significant overlap between components, and each component will affect how the other components will be designed, breaking the project into components makes it more manageable.

Infrastructure. The infrastructure component involves defining the back-end networking and server components of the user management infrastructure, and how that infrastructure integrates into overall Web and legacy data system architecture.

Directory Services. The directory services component involves defining where the user information will be stored, what type of information will be stored, and how that information will be synchronized with other data systems.

Administration Tools. The administration tools component defines the processes and procedures that will be used to manage user information, delegation of administration, and business processes and rules. The administration tools component also involves developing the tools that are used to manage and maintain information.

Roles and Responsibilities

Security. The security department is responsible for ensuring that the requirements meet the overall company security policies and practices.

Security should also work closely with the business to help them identify business security requirements. Processes and procedures should be updated in support of the new architecture.

Business. The business is responsible for identifying the business requirements associated with the applications.

Application Developers. Application developers are responsible for identifying tool sets currently in place, information storage requirements, and other requirements associated with the development of the applications that will utilize the infrastructure.

Infrastructure Components. It is very important for the infrastructure and networking groups to be involved. Infrastructure for support of the hardware, webservers, and directory services. Networking group to ensure that the necessary network connections and bandwidth is available.

REQUIREMENTS

Define Business Requirements

Before evaluating the need for, selecting, and implementing a centralized security authentication infrastructure, it is critical to ensure that all business requirements are thoroughly identified and prioritized. This process is no different than building the business and security requirements for client/server and Internet applications. Identifying the business requirements will help identify the following key issues:

1. What existing security policies and processes are in place?
2. Is the cost of implementing a single centralized infrastructure warranted, or is it acceptable to implement decentralized security in each application?
3. What data and systems will users be accessing? What is the confidentiality of the data and systems being accessed?
4. What are the business security requirements for the data and systems being accessed? Are there regulations and legal issues regarding the information that dictate specific technologies or processes?
5. What type of applications will require security? Will users be accessing more than one application? Should they be allowed single sign-on access?
6. What type of auditing is required? Is it permissible to track user movements in the Web site?
7. Is user personalization required?
8. Is self-registration necessary, or are users required to contact a customer service organization to request a name and password?
9. Who will be responsible for administering privileges? Are there different administration requirements for different user groups?

10. What are the projected numbers of users?
11. Are there password management requirements?
12. Who will be accessing applications/data? Where are these users located? This information should be broken down into groups and categories if possible.
13. What are the various roles of people accessing the data? Roles define the application/data privileges users will have.
14. What is the timeframe and schedules for the applications that the infrastructure will support?
15. What are the cost constraints?

Define Technical Requirements

After defining the business requirements, it is important to understand the existing technical environment and requirements. This will help determine the size and scope of the solution required, what platforms need to be supported, and the development tools that need to be supported by the solution.

Identifying the technical requirements will help identify the following key issues:

1. What legacy systems need to be accessed?
2. What platforms need to be supported?
3. Is there an existing directory services infrastructure in place, or does a new one need to be implemented?
4. What Web development tools are utilized for applications?
5. What are the projected number of users and transactions?
6. How granular should access control be? Can users access an entire Web site or is specific security required for single pages, buttons, objects, and text?
7. What security identification techniques are required: account/password, biometrics, certificates, etc.? Will new techniques be migrated to as they are introduced?
8. Is new equipment required? Can it be supported?
9. What standards need to be supported?
10. Will existing applications be migrated to the new infrastructure, including client/server and legacy applications?
11. What are the cost constraints?

Risk Assessment

Risk assessment is an important part of determining the key security requirements (see Exhibit 13-6). While doing a detailed analysis of a security risk assessment is beyond the scope of this chapter, it is important to understand some of the key analyses that need to be done.

Exhibit 13-6. Risk assessment.

- What needs to be protected?
  — Data
  — Systems
- Who are the potential threats?
  — Internal
  — External
  — Unknown
- What are the potential impacts of a security compromise?
  — Financial
  — Legal
  — Regulatory
  — Reputation
- What are the realistic chances of the event occurring?
  — Attempt to determine the realistic chance of the event occurring
  — Verify that all requirements were identified

The benefits of risk assessment include ensuring that one does not spend hundreds of thousands of dollars to protect information that has little financial worth, as well as ensuring that a potential security compromise that could cause millions of dollars worth of damage, in both hard dollars and reputation, does not occur because one did not spend what in hindsight is an insignificant investment.

The most difficult part of developing the risk assessment is determining the potential impacts and the realistic chances of the event occurring. In some cases, it is very easy to identify the financial impacts, but careful analysis must be done to determine the potential legal, regulatory, and reputation impacts. While a security breach may not have a direct financial impact if user information is lost, if publicized on the front page of the business section, the damage caused to one's reputation and the effect that has on attracting new users could be devastating.

Sometimes, it can be very difficult to identify the potential chance of a breach occurring. Threats can come from many unforeseen directions and new attacks are constantly being developed. Steps should be taken to ensure that detailed processes, including monitoring and reviews of audit logs, are done on a regular basis. This can be helpful in identifying existing or potential threats and analyzing their chance of occurrence. Analysis of threats, new and existing, should be performed routinely.

Prioritization and Selection Criteria

After defining the business and technical requirements, it is important to ensure that the priorities are discussed and agreed upon. Each group should completely understand the priorities and requirements of the other groups. In many cases, requirements may be developed that are nice to have, but are not a priority for implementing the infrastructure. One question that should be asked is: is one willing to delay implementation for an extended amount of time to implement that requirement? For example, would the business group wait an extra six months to deliver the application so that it is personalized to the user, or are they willing to implement an initial version of the Web site and upgrade it in the future? By clearly understanding the priorities, developing selection criteria will be much easier and products can be separated and evaluated based on how well they meet key criteria and requirements.

Selection criteria should be based on the requirements identified and the priorities of all parties involved. A weight should be given to each selection criterion; as products are analyzed, a rating can be given to each selection criterion and then multiplied against the weight. While one product may meet more requirements, one may find that it does not meet the most important selection criterion and, therefore, is not the proper selection.

It is also important to revisit the requirements and their priorities on a regular basis. If the business requirements change during the middle of the product, it is important to understand those changes and evaluate whether or not the project is still moving in the right direction or whether modifications need to be made.

PRODUCT STRATEGY AND SELECTION

Selecting the Right Architecture

Selecting the right infrastructure includes determining whether centralized or decentralized architecture is more appropriate and whether to develop the solution in-house or purchase/implement a third-party solution.

Centralized or Decentralized. Before determining whether to make or buy, it is first important to understand if a centralized or decentralized infrastructure meets the organization's needs (see Exhibit 13-7). Based on the requirements and priorities identified above, it should become obvious as to whether or not the organization should implement a centralized or decentralized architecture. A general rule of thumb can be identified.

Make or Buy. If one has determined that a centralized architecture is required to meet one's needs, then it is realistic to expect that one will be purchasing and implementing a third-party solution. For large-scale Web sites, the costs associated with developing and maintaining a robust and scalable user management infrastructure quickly surpass the costs associated with purchasing, installing, and maintaining a third-party solution.

Exhibit 13-7. Centralized or decentralized characteristics.

Centralized	Decentralized
Multiple applications	Cost is a major issue
Supports large number of users	Small number of applications
Single sign-on access required	One authentication technique
Multiple authentication techniques	Minimal audit requirements
Large-scale growth projected	Manageable growth projected
Decentralized administration	Minimal administration requirements
Detailed audit requirements	

If it has been determined that a decentralized architecture is more appropriate, it is realistic to expect that one will be developing one's own security solutions for each Web application, or implementing a third-party solution on a small scale, without the planning and resources required to implement an enterprisewide solution.

Product Evaluation & Testing. Having made a decision to move forward with buying a third-party solution, now the real fun begins — ensuring that one selects the best product that will meet one's needs, and that can be implemented according to one's schedule.

Before beginning product evaluation and testing, review the requirements, prioritization, and selection criteria to ensure that they accurately reflect the organization's needs. A major determination when doing product evaluation and testing is to define the following:

What are the time constraints involved with implementing the solution? Are there time constraints involved? If so, that may limit the number of tools that one can evaluate or select products based on vendor demonstrations, product reviews, and customer references. Time constraints will also identify how long and detailed one can evaluate each product. It is important to understand that implementing a centralized architecture can be a time-consuming process and, therefore, detailed testing may not be possible. Top priorities should be focused on, with the evaluation of lower priorities based on vendor demonstrations and other resources.

- *Is there an in-house solution already in place?* If there is an in-house solution in place, or a directory services infrastructure that can be leveraged, this can help facilitate testing.
- *Is hands-on testing required?* If one is looking at building a large-scale solution supporting millions of users and transactions, one will probably want to spend some time installing and testing at least one tool prior to making a selection.
- *Are equipment and resources available?* While one might like to do detailed testing and evaluation, it is important to identify and locate

the appropriate resources. Hands-on testing may require bringing in outside consulting or contract resources to perform adequate tests. In many cases, it may be necessary to purchase equipment to perform the testing; and if simultaneous testing of multiple tools is going to occur, then each product should be installed separately.

Key points to doing product evaluation and testing include:

- To help facilitate installation and ensure proper installation, either the vendor or a service organization familiar with the product should be engaged. This will help minimize the lead time associated with installing and configuring the product.
- Multi-function team meetings, with participants from Systems Development, Information Security and Computer Resources, should occur on a regular basis, so that issues can be quickly identified and resolved by all stakeholders.
- If multiple products are being evaluated, each product should be evaluated separately and then compared against the other products. While one may find that both products meet a requirement, it may be that one product meets it better.

Product Selection. Product selection involves making a final selection of a product. A detailed summary report with recommendations should be created. The summary report should include:

- business requirements overview
- technical requirements overview
- risk assessment overview
- prioritization of requirements
- selection criteria
- evaluation process overview
- results of evaluation and testing
- risks associated with selection
- recommendations for moving forward

At this point, one should begin paying special attention to the risks associated with moving forward with the selected product and begin identifying contingency plans that need to be developed.

License Procurement. While selecting a product, it is important to understand the costs associated with implementing that product. If there are severe budget constraints, this may have a major impact on the products that can be implemented. Issues associated with purchasing the product include:

1. How many licenses are needed? This should be broken out by timeframes: immediate (3 months), short term (6 to 12 months), and long term (12 months+).

2. How is the product licensed? Is it a per-user license, site license? Are transaction fees involved? What are the maintenance costs of the licenses? Is there a yearly subscription fee for the software?
3. How are the components licensed? Is it necessary to purchase server licenses as well as user licenses? Are additional components required for the functionality required by the infrastructure?
4. If a directory is being implemented, can that be licensed as part of the purchase of the secure user management product? Are there limitations on how that directory can be used?
5. What type of, if any, implementation services are included in the price of the software? What are the rates for implementation services?
6. What type of technical support is included in the price of the software? Are there additional fees for the ongoing technical support that will be required to successfully maintain the product?

DESIGN

The requirements built for the product selection should be reevaluated at this stage, especially the technical requirements, to ensure that they are still valid. At this stage, it may be necessary to obtain design assistance from the vendor or one of its partner service organizations to ensure that the infrastructure is designed properly and will meet both immediate and future usage requirements. The design phase can be broken into the following components.

Server Infrastructure

The server infrastructure should be the first component analyzed.

- What is the existing server infrastructure for the Internet/intranet architecture?
- What components are required for the product? Do client agents need to be installed on the Web servers, directory servers, or other servers that will utilize the infrastructure?
- What servers are required? Are separate servers required for each component? Are multiple servers required for each component?
- What are the server sizing requirements? The vendor should be able to provide modeling tools and sizing requirements.
- What are the failover and redundancy requirements? What are the failover and redundancy capabilities of the application?
- What are the security requirements for the information stored in the directory/databases used by the application?

Network

The network should next be analyzed.

- What are the network and bandwidth requirements for the secure user management infrastructure?

- What is the existing Internet/intranet network design? Where are the firewalls located? Are traffic load balancers or other redundancy solutions in place?
- If the Internet servers are hosted remotely, what are the bandwidth capabilities between the remote site and one's internal data center?

Directory Services

The building of a complete directory infrastructure in support of a centralized architecture is beyond the scope of this chapter. It is important to note that the directory services are the heart and soul of one's centralized architecture. The directory service is responsible for storing user-related information, groups, rights and privileges, and any potential personalization information. Here is an overview of the steps that need to be addressed at this juncture.

Directory Services Strategy.

- What is the projected number of users?
- The projected number of users will have a major impact on the selection of a directory solution. One should break projections into timeframes: 1 month, 6 months, 1 year, and 2 years.
- Is there an existing directory service in place that can be utilized?
- Does the organization have an existing directory service that can be leveraged? Will this solution scale to meet long-term user projections? If not, can it be used in the short term while a long-term solution is being implemented? For example, the organization might already have a Windows NT domain infrastructure in place; but while this would be sufficient for five to 10,000 users, it cannot scale to meet the needs of 100,000 users.
- What type of authentication schemes will be utilized?
- Determining the type of authentication schemes to be utilized will help identify the type of directory service required. The directory requirements for basic account/password requirements, where one could get away with using a Windows NT domain infrastructure or maybe an SQL infrastructure, are much different than the requirements for a full-scale PKI infrastructure, for which one should be considering a more robust solution, like an LDAP directory service.

Directory Schema Design.

- What type of information needs to be stored?
- What are the namespace design considerations?
- Is only basic user account information being stored, or is additional information, like personal user information and customization features, required? Using a Windows NT domain infrastructure limits the type of information that can be stored about a user, but using an LDAP

or NDS infrastructure allows one to expand the directory schema and store additional information that can be used to personalize the information provided to a user.

- What are the administration requirements?
- What are the account creation and maintenance requirements?

Development Environment

Building a development environment for software development and testing involves development standards.

Development Standards. To take advantage of a centralized architecture, it is necessary to build development security processes and development standards. This will facilitate the design of security into applications and the development of applications (see Exhibit 13-8). The development security process should focus on helping the business and development team design the security required for each application. Exhibit 13-8 is a sample process created to help facilitate the design of security requirements for Web-based applications utilizing a centralized authentication tool.

Administrative Responsibilities

There are multiple components of administration for a secure user management infrastructure. There is administration of the users and groups that will be authenticated by the infrastructure; there is administration of the user management infrastructure itself; and there is the data security administration that is used to develop and implement the policies and rules used to protect information.

Account Administration. Understanding the administration of accounts and user information is very important in developing the directory services architecture. The hierarchy and organization of the directory will resemble how the management of users is delegated.

If self-administration and registration are required, this will impact the development of administrative tools.

Infrastructure Administration. As with the implementation of any enterprisewide solution, it is very important to understand the various infrastructure components, and how those will be administered, monitored, and maintained. With the Web globalizing applications and being "always on," the user management infrastructure will be the front door to many of the applications and commerce solutions that will require 24 × 7 availability and all the maintenance and escalation procedures that go along with a 24 × 7 infrastructure.

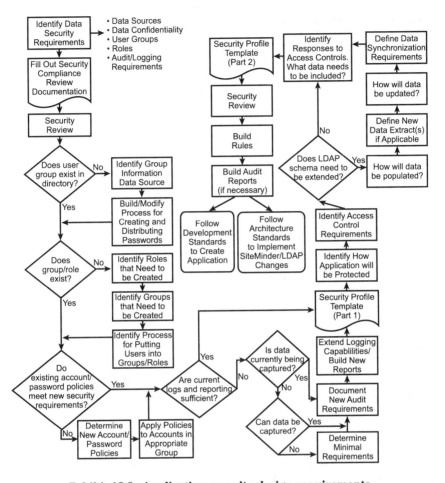

Exhibit 13-8. Application security design requirements.

Data Security Administration. A third set of administrators is required. The role of data security administrators is to work with data owners to determine how the information is to be protected, and then to develop the rules and policies that will be used by the management infrastructure and developers to protect the information.

TESTING

The testing of one's centralized architecture will resemble that of any other large-scale enterprisewide or client/server application. The overall test plan should include all the features listed in Exhibit 13-9.

287

Exhibit 13-9. Testing strategy examples.

Test	Purpose
Functionality	To ensure that the infrastructure is functioning properly. This would include testing rules and policies to ensure that they are interacting correctly with the directory services. If custom administrative tools are required for the management of the directory, this would also include detailed testing to ensure that these tools were secure and functioning properly.
Performance	Because the centralized infrastructure is the front end to multiple applications, it is important to do performance and scalability testing to ensure that the user management infrastructure does not become a bottleneck and adversely affect the performance and scalability of applications. Standard Internet performance testing tools and methods should be utilized.
Reliability and failover	An important part of maintaining 24 × 7 availability is built-in reliability, fault tolerance, and failover. Testing should occur to ensure that the architecture will continue to function despite hardware failures, network outages, and other common outages.
Security	Because one's user management infrastructure is ultimately a security tool, it is very important to ensure that the infrastructure itself is secure. Testing would mirror standard Internet and server security tests like intrusion detection, denial-of-service, password attacks, etc.
Pilot test	The purpose of the pilot is to ensure that the architecture is implemented effectively and to help identify and resolve any issues in a small, manageable environment. Because the user management architecture is really a tool used by applications, it is best to integrate the pilot testing of the infrastructure into the roll-out of another application. The pilot group should consist of the people who are going to be using the product. If it is targeted toward internal users, then the pilot end-user group should be internal users. If it is going to be the general internet population, one should attempt to identify a couple of best customers who are willing to participate in a pilot test/beta program. If the member services organization will be administering accounts, then they should be included as part of the pilot to ensure that that process has been implemented smoothly. The pilot test should focus on all aspects of the process, not just testing the technology. If there is a manual process associated with distributing the passwords, then this process needs to be tested as well. One would hate to go live and have thousands of people access accounts the first day only to find out that one has never validated that the mailroom could handle the additional load.

SUMMARY

This chapter is intended to orient the practitioner to the multiple issues requiring attention when an organization implements secure Web applications using third-party commercial software. Designing, implementing, and administering application security architectures, which address and resolve user identification, authentication, and data access controls, have become increasingly popular. In the Web application environment, the author introduces the complexity of *application user* as co-owner of the administration process.

This chapter reflects a real-life scenario, whereby a company with the need to do E-business on the Web, goes through an exercise to determine the cost/benefit and feasibility of building in security versus adding it on, including all of the considerations and decisions made along the way to implementation. For the readers' reference, several products were evaluated, including "getAccess" from EnCommerce and Netegrity's SiteMinder.

Chapter 14
Common System Design Flaws and Security Issues
William Hugh Murray

THIS CHAPTER IDENTIFIES AND DESCRIBES MANY OF THE COMMON ERRORS IN APPLICATION AND SYSTEM DESIGN AND IMPLEMENTATION. It explains the implications of these errors and makes recommendations for avoiding them. It treats unenforced restrictions, complexity, incomplete parameter checking and error handling, gratuitous functionality, escape mechanisms, and unsafe defaults, among others.

In his acceptance of the Turing Award, Ken Thompson reminded us that unless one writes a program oneself, one cannot completely trust it. Most people realize that while writing a program may be useful, even necessary, for trust, it is not sufficient. That is to say, even the most skilled and motivated programmers make errors. On the other hand, if one had to write every program that one uses, computers would not be very useful. It is important to learn to both write and recognize reliable code.

Historically, the computer security community has preferred to rely on controls that are external to the application. The community believed that such controls were more reliable, effective, and efficient. They are thought to be more reliable because fewer people have influence over them and those people are farther away from the application. They are thought to be more effective because they are more resistant to bypass. They are thought to be more efficient because they operate across and are shared by a number of applications.

Nonetheless, application controls have always been important. They are often more granular and specific than the environmental controls. It is usually more effective to say that those who can update the vendor name and address file cannot also approve invoices for payment than it is to say that Alice cannot see or modify Bob's data. While it sometimes happens that the

0-8493-0800-3/00/$0.00+$.50

privilege to update names and addresses maps to one data object and the ability to approve invoices maps to another data object, this is not always true. While it can always be true that the procedure to update names and addresses is in a different program from that to approve invoices, and while this may be coincidental, it usually requires intent and design.

However, in modern systems, the reliance on application controls goes up even more. While the application builder may have some idea of the environment in which his program will run, his ability to specify it and control it may be very low. Indeed, it is increasingly common for applications to be written in cross-platform languages. These languages make it difficult for the author to know whether his program will run in a single-user system or a multi-user system, a single application system or a multi-application system. While historically, one relied on the environment to protect the application from outside interference or contamination, in modern systems one must rely on the application to protect itself from its traffic. In distributed systems, environmental controls are far less reliable than in traditional systems. It has become common, not to say routine, for systems to be contaminated by applications.

The fast growth of the industry suggests that people with limited experience are writing many programs. It is difficult enough for them to write code that operates well when the environment and the inputs conform to their expectation, much less when they do not.

The history of controls in applications has not been very good. While programs built for the marketplace are pretty good, those built one-off specifically for an enterprise are often disastrous. What is worse, the same error types are manifesting themselves as seen 20 years ago. The fact that they get renamed, or even treated as novel, suggests that people are not taking advantage of the history. "Those who cannot remember the past, are condemned to repeat it."[1]

This chapter identifies and discusses some of the more common errors and their remedies in the hope that there will be more reliable programs in the future. While a number of illustrations are used to demonstrate how these errors are maliciously exploited, the reader is asked to keep in mind that most of the errors are problems per se.

UNENFORCED RESTRICTIONS

In the early days of computing, it was not unusual for program authors to respond to error reports from users by changing the documentation rather than changing the program. Instead of fixing the program such that a particular combination of otherwise legitimate input would not cause the program to fail, the programmers simply changed the documentation to say, "Do not enter this combination of inputs because it may cause unpredictable results." Usually, these results were so unpredictable that, while disruptive, they were not exploitable. Every now and then, the result was one that could be exploited for malicious purposes.

It is not unusual for the correct behavior of an application to depend on the input provided. It is sometimes the case that the program relies on the user to ensure the correct input. The program may tell the user to do A and not to do B. Having done so, the program then behaves as if the user will always do as he is told. For example, the programmer may know that putting alpha characters in a particular field intended to be numeric might cause the program to fail. The programmer might even place a caution on the screen or in the documentation that says, "Put only numeric characters in this field." What the programmer does not do is check the data or constrain the input such that the alpha data cannot cause an error.

Of course, in practice, it is rarely a single input that causes the application to fail. More often, it is a particular, even rare, combination of inputs that causes the failure. It often seems to the programmer as if such a rare combination will never occur and is not worth programming for.

COMPLEXITY

Complexity is not an error *per se.* However, it has always been one of the primary sources of error in computer programs. Complexity causes some errors and may be used to mask malice. Simplicity maximizes understanding and exposes malice.

Limiting the scope of a program is necessary but not sufficient for limiting its complexity and ensuring that its intent is obvious. The more one limits the scope of a program, the more obvious will be what it does. On the other hand, the more one limits the scope of all programs, the more programs one ends up with.

Human beings improve their understanding of complex things by subdividing them into smaller and simpler parts. The atomic unit of a computer program is an instruction. One way to think about programming is that it is the art of subdividing a program into its atomic instructions. If one were to reduce all programs to one instruction each, then all programs would be simple and easy to understand but there would be many programs and the relationship between them would be complex and difficult to comprehend.

Large programs may not necessarily be more complex than short ones. However, as a rule, the bigger a program is, the more difficult it is to comprehend. There is an upper bound to the size or scope of a computer program that can be comprehended by a human being. As the size of the program goes up, the number of people that can understand it approaches zero and the length of time required for that understanding approaches infinity. While one cannot say with confidence exactly where that transition is, neither is it necessary. Long before reaching that point, one can make program modules large enough to do useful work.

The issue is to strike a balance in which programs are large enough to do useful work and small enough to be easily understood. The comfort zone should be somewhere between and 10 and 50 verbs and between one complete function and a page.

Another measure of the complexity of a program is the total number of paths through it. A simple program has one path from its entry at the top to its exit at the bottom. Few programs look this way; most will have some iterative loops in them. However, the total number of paths may still be numbered in the low tens as long as these loops merely follow one another in sequence or embrace but do not cross. When paths begin to cross, the total number of possible paths escalates rapidly. Not only does it become more difficult to understand what each path does, it becomes difficult simply to know if a path is used (i.e., is necessary) at all.

INCOMPLETE PARAMETER CHECK AND ENFORCEMENT

Failure to check input parameters has caused application failures almost since the day one. In modern systems, the failure to check length is a major vulnerability. While modern databases are not terribly length sensitive, most systems are sensitive to input length to some degree or another.

A recent attack involved giving an e-mail attachment a name more than 64K in length. Rather than impose an arbitrary restriction, the designer had specified that the length be dynamically assigned. At lengths under 64K, the program worked fine; at lengths above that, the input overlaid program instructions. Not the programmer, the compiler, nor the tester asked what would happen for such a length. At least two separate implementations of the function failed in this manner.

Yes, there really are people out there that are stressing programs in this way. One might well argue that one should not need to check for a file name greater than 64K in length. Most file systems would not even accept such a length. Why would anyone do that? The answer is to see if it would cause an exploitable failure; the answer is that it did.

Many compilers for UNIX permit the programmer to allocate the size of the buffer statically, at execution time. This makes such an overrun more likely but improves performance. Dynamic allocation of the buffer is more likely to resist an accidental overrun but is not proof against attacks that deliberately use excessively long data fields.

These attacks are known generically as "buffer-overflow" attacks. More than a decade after this class of problem was identified, programs vulnerable to it continue to proliferate.

In addition to length, it is necessary to check code, data type, format, range, and for illegal characters. Many computers recognize more than one code type (e.g., numeric, alphabetic, ASCII, hexadecimal, or binary). Frequently, one of these may be encoded in another. For example, a binary number might be entered in either a numeric or alphanumeric field. The application program must ensure that the code values are legal in both code sets — the entry and display set and the storage set. Note that because modern database managers are very forgiving, the mere fact that the program continues to function may not mean that the data is correct. Data types (e.g., alpha, date, currency) must also be checked. The application itself and other programs that operate on the data may be very sensitive to the correctness of dates and currency formats. Data that is correct by code and data type may still not be valid. For example, a date of birth that is later than the date of death is not valid although it is a valid data type.

INCOMPLETE ERROR HANDLING

Closely related to the problem of parameter checking is that of error handling. Numbers of employee frauds have their roots in innocent errors that were not properly handled. The employee makes an innocent error; nothing happens. The employee pushes the envelope; still nothing. It begins to dawn on the employee that she could make the error in the direction of her own benefit — and still nothing would happen.

In traditional applications and environments, such conditions were dangerous enough. However, they were most likely to be seen by employees. Some employees might report the condition. In the modern network, it is not unusual for such conditions to be visible to the whole world. The greater the population that can see a system or application, the more attacks it is likely to experience. The more targets an attacker can see, the more likely he is to be successful, particularly if he is able to automate his attack.

It is not unusual for systems or applications to fail in unusual ways when errors are piled on errors. Programmers may fail to program or test to ensure that the program correctly handles even the first error, much less for successive ones. Attackers, on the other hand, are trying to create exploitable conditions; they will try all kinds of erroneous entries and then pile more errors on top of those. While this kind of attack may not do any damage at all, it can sometimes cause an error and occasionally cause an exploitable condition. As above, attackers may value their own time cheaply, may automate their attacks, and may be very patient.

TIME OF CHECK TO TIME OF USE (TOCTU)

Recently, a user of a Web mail service application noticed that he could "bookmark" his in-box and return to it directly in the future, even after shutting down and restarting his system, without going through logon again.

On a Friday afternoon, the user pointed this out to some friends. By Saturday, another user had recognized that one of the things that made this work was that his user identifier (UID), encoded in hexadecimal, was included in the universal record locator (URL) for his in-box page. That user wondered what would happen if someone else's UID was encoded in the same way and put into the URL. The reader should not be surprised to learn that it worked. By Sunday, someone had written a page to take an arbitrary UID encoded in ASCII, convert to hexadecimal, and go directly to the in-box of any user. Monday morning, the application was taken down.

The programmer had relied on the fact that the user was invited to logon before being told the URL of the in-box. That is, the programmer relied on the relationship between the time of the check and the time of use. The programmer assumes that a condition that is checked continues to be true. In this particular case, the result of the decision was stored in the URL, where it was vulnerable to both replay and interference. Like many of the problems discussed here, this one was first documented almost 30 years ago.

Now the story begins to illustrate another old problem.

INEFFECTIVE BINDING

Here, the problem can be described as ineffective binding. The programmer, having authenticated the user on the server, stores the result on the client. Said another way; the programmer stores privileged state in a place where he cannot rely on it and where he is vulnerable to replay.

Client/server systems seem to invite this error. In the formal client/server paradigm, servers are stateless. That is to say, a request from a client to a server is atomic; the client makes a request, the server answers and then forgets that it has done so.

To the extent that servers remember state, they become vulnerable to denial-of-service attacks. One such attack is called the Syn Flood Attack. The attacker requests a TCP session. The victim acknowledges the request and waits for the attacker to complete and use the session. Instead, the attacker requests yet another session. The victim system keeps allocating resources to the new sessions until it runs out.

Because the server cannot anticipate the number of clients, it cannot safely allocate resource to more than one client at a time. Therefore, all application state must be stored on the clients. The difficulty with this is that it is then vulnerable to interference or contamination on the part of the user or other applications on the same system. The server becomes vulnerable to the saving, replication, and replay of that state.

Therefore, at least to the extent that the state is privileged, it is essential that it be saved in such way as to protect the privilege and the server. Because the client cannot be relied on to preserve the state, the protection must rely on secret codes.

INADEQUATE GRANULARITY OF CONTROLS

Managers often find that they must give a user more authority than they wish or than the user needs because the controls or objects provided by the system or application are insufficiently granular. Stated another way, they are unable to enforce usual and normal separation of duties. For example, they might wish to assign duties in such a way that those who can set up accounts cannot process activity against those accounts, and vice versa. However, if the application design puts both capabilities into the same object (and provides no alternative control), then both individuals will have more discretion than management intends. It is not unusual to see applications in which all capabilities are bundled into a single object.

GRATUITOUS FUNCTIONALITY

A related, but even worse design or implementation error is the inclusion in the application of functionality that is not native or necessary to the intended use or application. Because security may depend on the system doing only what is intended, this is a major error and source of problems. In the presence of such functionality, not only will it be difficult to ensure that the user has only the appropriate application privileges but also that the user does not get something totally unrelated.

Recently, the implementer of an E-commerce Web server application did the unthinkable; he read the documentation. He found that the software included a script that could be used to display, copy, or edit any data object that was visible to the server. The script could be initiated from any browser connected to the server. He recognized that this script was not necessary for his use. Worse, its presence on his system put it at risk; anyone who knew the name of the script could exploit his system. He realized that all other users of the application knew the name of that script. It was decided to search servers already on the Net to see how many copies of this script could be found. It was reported that he stopped counting when he got to 100.

One form of this is to leave in the program hooks, scaffolding, or tools that were originally intended for testing purposes. Another is the inclusion of backdoors that enable the author of the program to bypass the controls. Yet another is the inclusion of utilities not related to the application. The more successful and sensitive the application, the greater the potential for these to be discovered and exploited by others. The more copies of the program in use, the bigger the problem and the more difficult the remedy.

One very serious form of gratuitous functionality is an escape mechanism.

ESCAPE MECHANISMS

One of the things that Ken Thompson pointed out is the difficulty maintaining the separation between data and procedure. One man's data is another man's program. For example, if one receives a file with a file name extension of .doc, one will understand that it is a document, that is, data to be operated on by a word processing program. Similarly, if one receives a file with .xls, one is expected to conclude that this is a spreadsheet, data to operated on by a spreadsheet program. However, many of these word processing and spreadsheet application programs have mechanisms built into them that permit their data to escape the environment in which the application runs. These programs facilitate the embedding of instructions, operating system commands, or even programs, in their data and provide a mechanism by which such instructions or commands can escape from the application and get themselves executed on behalf of the attacker but with the identity and privileges of the user.

One afternoon, the manager of product security for several divisions of a large computer company received a call from a colleague at a famous security consulting company. The colleague said that a design flaw had been discovered in one of the manager's products and that it was going to bring about the end of the world. It seems that many terminals had built into them an escape mechanism that would permit user A to send a message to user B that would not display but would rather be returned to the shared system looking as if it had originated with user B. The message might be a command, program, or script that would then be interpreted as if it had originated with user B and had all of user B's privileges.

The manager pointed out to his colleague that most buyers looked upon this "flaw" as a feature, were ready to pay extra for it, and might not consider a terminal that did not have it. The manager also pointed out that his product was only one of many on the market with the same feature and that his product enjoyed only a small share of the market. And, furthermore, there were already a million of these terminals in the market and that, no matter what was offered or done, they would likely be there five years hence. Needless to say, the sky did not fall and there are almost none of those terminals left in use today.

On another occasion, the manager received a call from another colleague in Austin, Texas. It seems that this colleague was working on a mainframe e-mail product. The e-mail product used a formatter produced by another of the manager's divisions. It seems that the formatter also contained an escape mechanism. When the exposure was described, the manager realized that the work required to write an exploit for this vulnerability was measured in minutes for some people and was only low tens of minutes for the manager.

The behavior of the formatter was changed so that the ability to use the escape mechanism could be controlled at program start time. This left the question of whether the control would default to "yes" so that all existing uses would continue to work, or to "no" so as to protect unsuspecting users. In fact, the default was set to the safe default. The result was that tens of thousands of uses of the formatter no longer worked, but the formatter itself was safe for the naïve user.

Often these mechanisms are legitimate, indeed even necessary. For example, MS Word for DOS, a single-user single-tasking system, required this mechanism to obtain information from the file system or to allow the user access to other facilities while retaining its own state. In modern systems, these mechanisms are less necessary. In a multi-application system, the user may simply "open a new window;" that is, start a new process.

Nonetheless, while less necessary, these features continue to proliferate. Recent instances appear in MS Outlook. The intent of the mechanisms is to permit compound documents to display with fidelity even in the preview window. However, they are being used to get malicious programs executed. All such mechanisms can be used to dupe a user into executing code on behalf of an attacker. However, the automation of these features makes it difficult for the user to resist, or even to recognize, the execution of such malicious programs.

They may be aggravated when the data is processed in an exceptional manner. Take, for example, so-called "Web mail." This application turns two-tier client/server e-mail into three-tier. The mail agent, instead of running as a client on the recipient's system, runs as a server between the mail server and the user. Instead of accessing his mail server using an application on his system, the user accesses it via this middleware server using his (thin-client) browser. If html tags are embedded in a message, the mail agent operating on the server, like any mail agent, will treat them as text. However, the browser, like any browser will, will treat these tags as tags to be interpreted.

In a recent attack, html tags were included in a text message and passed through the mail agent to the browser. The attacker used the html to "pop a window" labeled "....Mail Logon." If the user were duped into responding to this window with his identifier and password, it would then be broadcast into the network for the benefit of the attacker.

While experienced users would not be likely to respond to such an unexpected logon window, many other users would. Some of these attacks are so subtle that users cannot reasonably be expected to know about them or to resist their exploitation.

EXCESSIVE PRIVILEGE

Many multi-user, multi-application systems such as the IBM AS/400 and most implementations of UNIX contain a mechanism to permit a program to run with privileges and capabilities other than those assigned to the user.

The concept seems to be that such a capability would be used to provide access control more granular and more restrictive than would be provided by full access to the data object. While unable to access object A, the user would be able to access a program that was privileged to access object A but which would show the user a only a specified sub-set of object A.

However, in practice, it is often used to permit the application to operate with the privileges of the programmer or even those of the system manager. One difficulty of such use is manifest when the user manages to escape the application to the operating system but retain the more privileged state. Another manifests itself when a started process, subsystem, or daemon runs with excessive privilege. For example, the mail service may be set up to run with the privileges of the system manager rather than with a profile created for the purpose. An attacker who gains control of this application, for example by a buffer overflow or escape mechanism, now controls the system, not simply with the privileges required by the application or those of the user but with those of the system manager.

One might well argue that such a coincidence of a flawed program with excessive privilege is highly unlikely to occur. However, experience suggests that it is not only likely, but also common. One might further argue that the application programmer causes only part of this problem; the rest of it is the responsibility of the system programmer or system manager. However, in practice, it is common for the person installing the program to be fully privileged and to grant to the application program whatever privileges are requested.

FAILURE TO A PRIVILEGED STATE

Application programs will fail, often for reasons completely outside of their control, that of their programmers, or of their users. As a rule, such failures are relatively benign. Occasionally, the failure exposes their data or their environment.

It is easiest to understand this by comparing the possible failure modes. From a security point of view, the safest state for an application to fail to is a system halt. Of course, this is also the state that leaves the fewest options for the user and for system and application management. They will have to reinitialize the system, reload and restart the application. While this may be the safest state, it may not be the state with the lowest time to recovery. System operators often value short time to recovery more than long time to failure.

Alternatively, the application could fail to logon. For years, this was the failure mode of choice for the multi-user, multi-application systems of the time. The remedy for the user was to logon and start the application again. This was both safe and fairly orderly.

In more modern systems like Windows and UNIX, the failure mode of choice is for the application to fail to the operating system. In single-user, multi-application systems, this is fairly safe and orderly. It permits the user to use the operating system to recover the application and data. However, while still common in multi-user, multi-application systems, this failure mode is more dangerous. Indeed, it is so unsafe that crashing applications has become a favored manner of attacking systems that are intended to be application-only systems. Crash the application and the attacker may find himself looking at the operating system (command processor or graphical user interface [GUI]) with the identity and privileges of the person who started the application. In the worst case, this person is the system manager.

UNSAFE DEFAULTS

Even applications with appropriate controls often default to the unsafe setting of those controls. That is to say, when the application is first installed and until the installing user changes things, the system may be unsafely configured. A widespread example is audit trails. Management may be given control over whether the application records what it has done and seen. However, out-of-the-box, and before management intervenes, the journals default to "off." Similarly, management may be given control of the length of passwords. Again, out-of-the-box, password length may default to zero.

There are all kinds of good excuses as to why a system should default to unsafe conditions. These often relate to ease of installation. The rationale is that if the system initializes to safe settings, any error in the procedure may result in a deadlock situation in which the only remedy is to abort the installation and start over. The difficulty is that once the system is installed and running, the installer is often reluctant to make any changes that might interfere with it.

In some instances, it is not possible for designers or programmers to know what the safe defaults are because they do not know the environment or application. On the other hand, users may not understand the controls. This can be aggravated if the controls are complex and interact in subtle ways. One system had a control to ensure that users changed their passwords at maximum life. It had a separate control to ensure that it could not be changed to itself. To make this control work, it had a third control to set the minimum life of the password. A great deal of special knowledge was required to understand the interaction of these controls and their effective use.

EXCLUSIVE RELIANCE ON APPLICATION CONTROLS

The application designer frequently has a choice whether to rely on application program controls, file system controls, database manager controls, or some combination of these. Application programmers sometimes rely exclusively on controls in the application program. One advantage of this is that one may not need to enroll the user to the file system or database manager or to define the user's privileges and limitations to those systems. However, unless the application is tightly bound to these systems, either by a common operating system or by encryption, a vulnerability arises. It will be possible for the user or an attacker to access the file system or database manager directly. That is, it is possible to bypass the application controls. This problem often occurs when the application is developed in a single-system environment, where the application and file service or database manager run under a single operating system and are later distributed.

Note that the controls of the database manager are more reliable than those in the application. The control is more localized and it is protected from interference or bypass on the part of the user. On the other hand, it requires that the user be enrolled to the database manager and that the access control rules be administered.

This vulnerability to control bypass also arises in other contexts. For example, controls can be bypassed in single-user, multi-application systems with access control in the operating system rather than the file system. An attacker simply brings his own operating system in which he is fully privileged and uses that in *lieu* of the operating system in which he has no privileges.

RECOMMENDATIONS

The following recommendation should be considered when crafting and staging applications. By adhering to these recommendations, the programmer and the application manager can avoid many of the errors outlined in this chapter.

1. Enforce all restrictions that are relied on.
2. Check and restrict all parameters to the intended length and code type.
3. Prefer short and simple programs and program modules. Prefer programs with only one entry point at the top or beginning, and only one exit at the bottom or end.
4. Prefer reliance on well-tested common routines for both parameter checking and error correction. Consider the use of routines supplied with the database client. Parameter checking and error correcting code is difficult to design, write, and test. It is best assigned to master programmers.
5. Fail applications to the safest possible state. Prefer failing multi-user applications to a halt or to logon to a new instance of the application. Prefer failing single-user applications to a single-user operating system.

6. Limit applications to the least possible privileges. Prefer the privileges of the user. Otherwise, use a limited profile created and used only for the purpose. Never grant an application systemwide privileges. (Because the programmer cannot anticipate the environment in which the application may run and the system manager may not understand the risks, exceptions to this rule are extremely dangerous.)

7. Bind applications end-to-end to resist control bypass. Prefer a trusted single-system environment. Otherwise, use a trusted path (e.g., dedicated local connection, end-to-end encryption, or a carefully crafted combination of the two).

8. Include in an application user's privileges only that functionality essential to the use of the application. Consider dividing the application into multiple objects requiring separate authorization so as to facilitate involving multiple users in sensitive duties.

9. Controls should default to safe settings. Where the controls are complex or interact in subtle ways, provide scripts ("wizards"), or profiles.

10. Prefer localized controls close to the data (e.g., file system to application, database manager to file system).

11. Use cryptographic techniques to verify the integrity of the code and to resist bypass of the controls.

12. Prefer applications and other programs from known and trusted sources in tamper-evident packaging.

Note

1. George Santayana, *Reason in Common Sense.*

Chapter 15
Data Marts and Data Warehouses: Keys to the Future or Keys to the Kingdom?

M. E. Krehnke
D. K. Bradley

WHAT DO YOU THINK WHEN YOU HEAR THE TERM "DATA MART" OR "DATA WAREHOUSE"? CONVENIENCE? AVAILABILITY? CHOICES? CONFUSION FROM OVERWHELMING OPTIONS? POWER? SUCCESS? Organizational information, such as marketing statistics or customer preferences, when analyzed, can mean power and success in today's and future markets. If it is more convenient for a customer to do business with a "remembering" organization — one that retains and uses customer information (e.g., products used, sales trends, goals) and does not have to ask for the information twice — then that organization is more likely to retain and grow that customer's base.[1] There are even organizations whose purpose is to train business staff to acquire competitor's information through legal, but espionage-like techniques, calling it "corporate intelligence."[2]

DATA WAREHOUSES AND DATA MARTS: WHAT ARE THEY?

Data warehouses and data marts are increasingly perceived as vital organizational resources and — given the effort and funding required for their creation and maintenance, and their potential value to someone inside (or outside) the organization — they need to be understood, effectively used, and protected. Several years ago, one data warehouse proponent suggested a data warehouse's justification that includes support for

0-8493-0800-3/00/$0.00+$.50
© 2001 by CRC Press LLC

"merchandising, logistics, promotions, marketing and sales programs, asset management, cost containment, pricing, and product development," and equated the data warehouse with "corporate memory."[3]

The future looked (and still looks) bright for data warehouses, but there are significant implementation issues that need to be addressed, including scalability (size), data quality, and flexibility for use. These are the issues highlighted today in numerous journals and books — as opposed to several years ago when the process for creating a data warehouse and its justification were the primary topics of interest.

Data Warehouse and Data Mart Differences

Key differences between a data warehouse and data mart are size, content, user groups, development time, and amount of resources required to implement. A data warehouse (DW) is generally considered to be organizational in scope, containing key information from all divisions within a company, including marketing, sales, engineering, human resources, and finance, for a designated period of time. The users, historically, have been primarily managers or analysts (aka power users) who are collecting and analyzing data for planning and strategy decisions. Because of the magnitude of information contained in a DW, the time required for identifying what information should be contained in the warehouse, and then collecting, categorizing, indexing, and normalizing the data, is a significant commitment of resources, generally taking several years to implement.

A data mart (DM) is considered to be a lesser-scale data warehouse, often addressing the data needs of a division or an enterprise or addressing a specific concern (e.g., customer preferences) of a company. Because the amount and type of data are less varied, and the number of users who have to achieve concurrence on the pertinent business goals is fewer, the amount of time required to initiate a DM is less. Some components of a DM can be available for use within nine months to a year of initiation, depending on the design and scope of the project. If carefully planned and executed, it is possible for DMs of an enterprise to actually function as components of a (future) DW for the entire company. These DMs are linked together to form a DW via a method of categorization and indexing (i.e., metadata) and a means for accessing, assembling, and moving the data about the company (i.e., middleware software). It is important to carefully plan the decision support architecture, however, or the combination of DMs will result in expensive redundancy of data, with little or no reconciliation of data across the DMs. Multiple DMs within an organization cannot replace a well-planned DW.[4]

Data Warehouse and Data Mart Similarities

Key similarities between a DW and DM include the decisions required regarding the data before the first byte is ever put into place:

- What is the strategic plan for the organization with regard to the DW architecture and environment?
- What is the design/development/implementation process to be followed?
- What data will be included?
- How will the data be organized?
- How and when will the data be updated?

Following an established process and plan for DW development will help ensure that key steps are performed — in a timely and accurate manner by the appropriate individuals. (Unless noted otherwise, the concepts for DWs also apply to DMs.) The process involves the typical development steps of requirements gathering, design, construction, testing, and implementation.

The DW or DM is not an operational database and, as such, does not contain the business rules that can be applied to data before it is presented to the user by the original business application. Merely dumping all the operational data into the DW is not going to be effective or useful. Some data will be summarized or transformed, and other data may not be included. All data will have to be "scrubbed" to ensure that quality data is loaded into the DW. Careful data-related decisions must be made regarding the following:[5]

- business goals to be supported
- data associated with the business goals
- data characteristics (e.g., frequency, detail)
- time when transformation of codes is performed (e.g., when stored, accessed)
- schedule for data load, refresh, and update times
- size and scalability of the warehouse or mart

Business Goals Identification. The identification of the business goals to be supported will involve the groups who will be using the system. Because DWs are generally considered to be nonoperational decision support systems, they will contain select operational data. This data can be analyzed over time to identify pertinent trends or, as is the case with data mining, be used to identify some previously unknown relationship between elements that can be used to advance the organization's objectives. It is vital, however, that the DW be linked to, and supportive of, the strategic goals of the business.

Data Associated with Business Goals. The data associated with the identified business goals may be quantitative (e.g., dollar amount of sales) or qualitative (i.e., descriptive) in nature. DWs are not infinite in nature, and decisions must be made regarding the value of collecting, transforming, storing, and updating certain data to keep it more readily accessible for analysis.

Data Characteristics. Once the data has been identified, additional decisions regarding the number of years to be stored and the level of frequency to be stored have to be made. A related, tough decision is the level of detail. Are item sales needed: by customer, by sale, by season, by type of customer, or some other summary? Resources available are always going to be limited by some factor: funding, technology, or available support.

Data Transformation and Timing. Depending on the type of data and its format, additional decisions must be made regarding the type and timing of any transformations of the data for the warehouse. Business applications usually perform the transformations of data before they are viewed on the screen by the user or printed in a report, and the DW will not have an application to transform the data. As a result, users may not know that a certain code means engineering firm (for example) when they retrieve data about XYZ Company to perform an analysis. Therefore, the data must be transformed prior to its presentation, either before it is entered into the database for storage or before the user sees it.

Data Reloading and Updating. Depending on the type and quantity of data, the schedules for data reloading or data updating may require a significant amount of time. Decisions regarding the reload/update frequency will have to be made at the onset of the design because of the resources required for implementing and maintaining the process. A crucial decision to be made is: will data be reloaded en masse or will only changed data be loaded (updated)? A DW is nonoperational, so the frequency for reload/update should be lower than that required for an operational database containing the same or similar information. Longer reload and update times may impact users by limiting their access to the required information for key customer-related decisions and competition-beating actions. Data maintenance will be a substantial component of ongoing costs associated with the DW.

Size and Scalability. Over time, the physical size of the DW increases because the amount of data contained increases. The size of the database may impact the data updating or retrieval processes, which may impact the usage rate; as well, an increase in the number of users will also impact the retrieval process. Size may have a strongly negative impact on the cost, performance, availability, risk, and management of the DW. The ability of a DW to grow in size and functionality and not affect other critical factors is called scalability, and this capability relies heavily on the architecture and technologies to be used, which were agreed upon at the time the DW was designed.

DATA QUALITY

The quality of data in a DW is significant because it contains summarized data, addresses different audiences and functions than originally intended, and depends on other systems for its data. The time-worn phrase "garbage in, garbage out" is frequently applied to the concept of DW data. Suggested ways to address data quality include incorporating metadata into the data warehouse structure, handling content errors at load time, and setting users' expectations about data quality. In addition, "it is mandatory to track the relationships among data entities and the calculations used over time to ensure that essential referential integrity of the historical data is maintained."[6]

Metadata Incorporation into the DW Design

Metadata is considered to be the cornerstone of DW success and effective implementation. Metadata not only supports the user in the access and analysis of the data, but also supports the data quality of the data in the warehouse.

The creation of metadata regarding the DW helps the user define, access, and understand data needed for a particular analysis or exploration. It standardizes all organizational data elements (e.g., the customer number for marketing and finance organizations), and acts as a "blueprint" to guide the DW builders and users through the warehouse and to guide subsequent integration of later data sources.

Metadata for a DW generally includes the following[7]:

1. organizational business models and rules
2. data view definitions
3. data usage model
4. report dictionary
5. user profiles
6. physical and logical data models
7. source file data dictionaries
8. data element descriptions
9. data conversion rules

Standardization of Metadata Models

The importance of metadata to the usefulness of a DW is a concept mentioned by most of the authors reviewed. Metadata and its standardization are so significant that Microsoft has joined the Metadata Coalition (MDC) consortium. Microsoft turned its metadata model, the Open Information Model (OIM), over to the MDC for integration into the MDC Metadata Interchange Specification (MDIS). This standard will enable various vendors to exchange metadata among their tools and databases, and support proprietary metadata.[8] There are other vendors, however, that are reluctant to participate and are maintaining their own versions of metadata management.[9] But this present difference of opinions does not diminish the need for comprehensive metadata for a DW.

Setting User Expectations Regarding Data Quality

Metadata about the data transformations can indicate to the user the level of data quality that can be expected. Depending on the user, the availability of data may be more significant than the accuracy, and this may be the case for some DMs. But because the DW is intended to contain significant data that is maintained over the long term and can be used for trend analysis, data quality is vital to the organization's DW goals. In a "Report from the Trenches," Quinlan emphasizes the need to manage user expectations and identify potential hardships as well as benefits.[10] This consideration is frequently mentioned in discussions of requirements for a successful DW implementation.

Characteristics of data quality are[11]:

- *accuracy:* degree of agreement between a set of data values and a corresponding set of correct values
- *completeness:* degree to which values are present in the attributes that require them
- *consistency:* agreement or logical coherence among data that frees them from variation or contradiction
- *relatability:* agreement or logical coherence that permits rational correlation in comparison with other similar or like data
- *timeliness:* data item or multiple items that are provided at the time required or specified
- *uniqueness:* data values that are constrained to a set of distinct entries, each value being the only one of its kind
- *validity:* conformance of data values that are edited for acceptability, reducing the probability of error

DW USE

The proposed use of a DW will define the initial contents, and the initial tools and analysis techniques. Over time, as users become trained in its use and there is proven applicability to organizational objectives, the content of a DW generally expands and the number of users increases. Therefore, developers and management need to realize that it is not possible to create the "perfect warehouse." Users cannot foresee every decision that they are going to need to make and define the information they need to do so. Change is inevitable. Users become more adept at using the DW and want data in more detail than they did initially; users think of questions they had not considered initially; and business environments change and new information is needed to respond to the current marketplace or new organizational objectives.[12] This is why it is important to plan strategically for the DW environment.

Types of Users

DWs are prevalent today in the retailing, banking, insurance, and communications sectors; and these industries tend to be leaders in the use of business intelligence/data warehouse (BI/DW) applications, particularly in financial and sales/marketing applications.[13] Most organizations have a customer base that they want to maintain and grow (i.e., providing additional products or services to the same customer over time). The use of DWs and various data exploration and analysis techniques (such as data mining) can provide organizations with an extensive amount of valuable information regarding their present or potential customer base. This valuable information includes cross-selling and up-selling, fraud detection and compliance, potential lifetime customer value, market demand forecasting, customer retention/vulnerability, product affinity analysis, price optimization, risk management, and target market segmentation.

Techniques of Use

The data characteristics of the DW are significantly different from those of a transactional or operational database, presenting large volumes of summary data that address an extensive time period, which is updated on a periodic (rather than daily) basis. The availability of such data, covering multiple areas of a business enterprise over a long period of time, has significant value in organizational strategic marketing and planning. The availability of metadata enables a user to identify useful information for further analysis. If the data quality is high, the user will have confidence in the results.

The type of analysis performed is determined, in part, by the capabilities of the user and the availability of software to support the analysis. The usefulness of the data can be related to the frequency of updates and the level of detail provided in the DW. There are three general forms of study that can be performed on DW data[14]:

1. *analysis:* discovering new patterns and hypotheses for existing, unchanging data by running correlations, statistics, or a set of sorted reports
2. *monitoring:* automatic detection of matches or violations of patterns to provide a timely response to the change
3. *discovery:* interactive identification, a process of uncovering previously unknown relationships, patterns, and trends that would not necessarily be revealed by running correlations, statistics, or a set of sorted reports

The DW is more applicable for the "monitoring" and "discovery" techniques because the resources available are more fully utilized. It is possible that ad hoc analysis may be accepted in such a positive manner that scheduled reports are then performed as a result of that analysis, in which case the method changes from "discovery" to simply "analysis." However, the discovery of patterns (offline) can then be used to define a set of rules that will automatically identify the same patterns when compared with new, updated data online.

Data Mining. Data mining is a prevalent DW data analysis technique. It can be costly and time-consuming, because the software is expensive and may require considerable time for the analyst to become proficient. The benefits, however, can be quite remarkable. Data mining can be applied to a known situation with a concrete, direct question to pursue (i.e., reactive analysis) or to an unknown situation with no established parameters. The user is "seeking to identify unknown patterns and practices, detect covert/unexplained practices, and have the capability to expose organized activity (i.e., proactive invigilation)."[14]

Data mining is an iterative process, and additional sources can be introduced at any time during the process. It is most useful in exploratory analysis scenarios with no predetermined expectations as to the outcome. Data mining is not a single-source (product/technology) solution, and must be applied, as any tool, with the appropriate methodological approach. When using data mining, the analyst must consider:

- organizational requirements
- available data sources
- corporate policies and procedures

There are questions that have to be answered to determine if the data mining effort is worthwhile, including[15]:

1. Are sufficient data sources available to make the effort worthwhile?
2. Is the data accurate, well coded, and properly maintained for the analyst to produce reasonable results?
3. Is permission granted to access all of the data needed to perform the analysis?
4. Are static extractors of data sufficient?
5. Is there an understanding of what things are of interest or importance to set the problem boundaries?
6. Have hypothetical examples been discussed beforehand with the user of the analysis?
7. Are the target audience and the intent known (e.g., internal review, informational purposes, formal presentation, or official publication)?

Activities associated with data mining are[16]:

- *classification:* establishing a predefined set of labels for the records
- *estimation:* filling in missing values in a particular field
- *segmentation:* identification of subpopulations with similar behavior
- *description:* spotting any anomalous or "interesting" information

Data mining goals may be[17]:

- *predictive:* models (expressed as executable code) to perform some form of classification or estimation
- *descriptive:* informational by uncovering patterns and relationships

Data to be mined may be[17]:

- *structured:* fixed length, fixed format records with fields that contain numeric values, character codes, or short strings
- *unstructured:* word or phrase queries, combining data across multiple, diverse domains to identify unknown relationships

The data mining techniques (and products) to be used will depend on the type of data being mined and the end objectives of the activity.

Data Visualization. Data visualization is an effective data mining technique that enables the analyst and the recipients to discern relationships that may not be evident from a review of numerical data by abstracting the information from low-level detail into composite representations. Data visualization presents a "top-down view of the range of diversity represented in the data set on dimensions of interest."[18]

Data visualization results depend on the quality of data. "An ill-specified or preposterous model or a puny data set cannot be rescued by a graphic (or by calculation), no matter how clever or fancy. A silly theory means a silly graphic."[19] Data visualization tools can, however, support key principles of graphical excellence[20]:

- a well-designed presentation of interesting data through "substance, statistics, and design"
- communication of complex ideas with "clarity, precision, and efficiency"
- presentation of the "greatest number of ideas in the shortest time with the least ink in the smallest space"

Enterprise Information Portals. Extended use of the Internet and Web-based applications within an enterprise now supports a new form of access, data filtering, and data analysis: a personalized, corporate search engine — similar to the Internet personalized search engines (e.g., My Yahoo) — called a corporate portal, enterprise information portal, or business intelligence portal. This new tool provides multiple characteristics that would be beneficial to an individual seeking to acquire and analyze relevant information[21]:

- ease of use through a Web browser
- filtering out of irrelevant data
- integration of numerical and textual data
- capability of providing alerts when certain data events are triggered.

Enterprise information portals (EIPs) can be built from existing data warehouses or from the ground up through the use of Extensible Markup Language (XML). XML supports the integration of unstructured data resources (e.g., text documents, reports, e-mails, graphics, images, audio, and video) with structured data resources in relational and legacy databases.[22] Business benefits associated with the EIP are projected to include[23]:

- leverage of DW, Enterprise Resource Planning (ERP), and other IT systems
- transforming E-commerce business into "true" E-business
- easing reorganization, merger, and acquisition processes
- providing improved navigation and access capabilities

But it is emphasized that all of the design and implementation processes and procedures, network infrastructures, and data quality required for successful DWs s must be applied to ensure an EIP's potential for supporting enterprise operations and business success.

Results

The results of data mining can be very beneficial to an organization, and can support numerous objectives: customer-focused planning and actions, business intelligence, or even fraud discovery. Examples of industries and associated data mining uses presented in *Data Mining Solutions, Methods and Tools for Real-World Problems*[18] include:

- *pharmaceuticals:* research to fight disease and degenerative disorders by mapping the human genome
- *telecommunications:* customer profiling to provide better service
- *retail sales and marketing:* managing the market saturation of individual customers
- *financial market analysis:* managing investments in an unstable Asian banking market
- *banking and finance:* evaluation of customer credit policy and the reduction of delinquent and defaulted car loans
- *law enforcement and special investigative units:* use of financial reporting regulations and data to identify money-laundering activities and other financial crimes in the United States by companies

Other examples are cited repeatedly throughout data management journals, such as *DM Review*. The uses of data mining continue to expand as users become more skilled, and as the tools and techniques increase in options and capabilities.

RETURNS ON THE DW INVESTMENT

Careful consideration and planning are required before initiating a DW development and implementation activity. The resources required are substantial, although the benefits can surpass the costs many times.

Costs

The DW design and implementation activity is very labor intensive, and requires the involvement of numerous business staff (in addition to Information Technology staff) over the entire life cycle of the DW, in order for the project to be successful by responding to organizational information needs. Although technology costs over time tend to drop, while providing even greater capabilities, there is a significant investment in hardware and software. Administration of the DWs is an ongoing expense. Because DWs are not static and will continue to grow in terms of the years of data and the types of data maintained, additional data collection and quality control are required to ensure continued viability and usefulness of the corporate information resource.

Costs are incurred throughout the entire DW life cycle; some costs are one-time costs, others are recurrent costs. One-time costs and a likely percentage of the total DW budget (shown in parentheses) include[24]:

- *hardware:* disk storage (30%), processor costs (20%), network communication costs (10%)
- *software:* database management software (10%); access/analysis tools (6%); systems management tools: activity monitor (2%), data monitor (2%); integration and transformation(15%); interface creation, metadata creation and population (5%)

Cost estimates (cited above) are based on the implementation of a centralized (rather than distributed) DW, with use of an automated code generator for the integration and transformation layer.

Recurrent costs include[24]:

- refreshment of the data warehouse data from the operational environment (55%)
- maintenance and update of the DW and metadata infrastructure (3%)
- end-user training (6%)
- data warehouse administration — data verification of conformance to the enterprise data model (2%), monitoring (7%), archiving (1%), reor-

ganization/restructuring (1%); servicing DW requests for data (21%); capacity planning (1%); usage analysis (2%); and *security administration* (1%) [emphasis added]

The recurrent costs are almost exclusively associated with the administrative work required to keep the DW operational and responsive to the organization's needs. Additional resources may be required, however, to upgrade the hardware (e.g., more storage) or for the network to handle an unexpected increase in the volume of requests for DW information over time. It is common for the DW budget to grow an order of magnitude per year for the first two years that the DW is being implemented. After the first few years, the rate of growth slows to 30 or 40 percent growth per year.[24]

The resources that should be expended for any item will depend on the strategic goals that the DW is intended to support. Factors affecting the actual budget values include [24]:

- size of the organization
- amount of history to be maintained
- level of detail required
- sophistication of the end user
- competitive marketplace participant or not
- speed with which DW will be constructed
- construction of DW is manual or automated
- amount of summary data to be maintained
- creation of integration and transformation layer is manual or automated
- maintenance of the integration and transformation layer is manual or automated

MEASURES OF SUCCESS

The costs for a DW can be extraordinary. Bill Inmon shows multiple DMs costing in the tens of millions in the graphics in his article on metadata and DMs.[4] Despite the costs, William McKnight indicates that that a recent survey of DW users has shown a range of return on investment (ROI) for a three-year period between 1857 percent and 16,000 percent, with an average annual ROI of 401 percent.[25] However, Douglas Hackney cautions that the sample sets for some DW ROI surveys were self-selected and the methodology flawed. Hackney does say that there are other ROI measures that need to be considered: "pure financial ROI, opportunity cost, 'do nothing' cost and a 'functional ROI'. In the real world, your financial ROI may be 0 percent, but the overall return of all the measures can easily be over 100 percent."[26] So, the actual measures of success for the DW in an organization, and the quantitative or qualitative values obtained, will depend on the organization.

Internal customers and their focus should be considered when determining the objectives and performance measures for the DW ROI, including[25]:

- sales volume (sales and marketing)
- reduced expenses (operations)
- inventory management (operations)
- profits (executive management)
- market share (executive management)
- improved time to market (executive management)
- ability to identify new markets (executive management)

DWs respond to these objectives by bringing together, in a cohesive and manageable group, subject areas, data sources, user communities, business rules, and hardware architecture.

Expanding on the above metrics, other benefits that can significantly impact the organization's well-being and its success in the marketplace are[25]:

- reduced losses due to fraud detection
- reduced write-offs because of (previous) inadequate data to combat challenges from vendors and customers
- reduced overproduction of goods and commensurate inventory holding costs
- increased metrics on customer retention, targeted marketing and an increased customer base, promotion analysis programs with increased customer numbers and penetration, and lowering time to market

Mergers by companies in today's market provide an opportunity for cross-selling by identifying new, potential customers for the partners or by providing additional services that can be presented for consideration to existing customers. Responsiveness to customers' needs, such as speed (submitting offers to a customer prior to the customer making a decision) and precision (tailoring offerings to what is predicted the customer wants), can be facilitated with a well-designed and well-utilized DW. Associated actions can include the automatic initiation of marketing activity in response to known buying or attrition triggers, or tools that coordinate a "continuous customized communication's stream with customers." Data mining expands the potential beyond query-driven efforts by identifying previously unknown relationships that positively affect the customer base.[27]

MISTAKES TO AVOID

The Data Warehousing Institute conducted meetings with DW project managers and Information Systems executives in 1995 to identify the "ten mistakes to avoid for data warehousing managers" and created a booklet (Ten Mistakes Booklet) that is available from the institute.[28] Time has not changed the importance or the essence of the knowledge imparted through the experienced contributors. Although many authors have high-lighted one or more topics in their writings, this source is very succinct and comprehensive. The "Ten Data Warehousing Mistakes to Avoid" and a very brief explanation are noted below.[29]

1. *Starting with the wrong sponsorship chain.* Supporters of the DW must include an executive sponsor with funding and an intense interest in the effective use of information, a project "driver" who keeps the project moving in the right direction with input from appropriate sources, and the DW manager.

2. *Setting expectations that one cannot meet and frustrating executives at the moment of truth.* DWs contain a select portion of organizational information, often at a summary level. If DWs are portrayed as "the answer" to all questions, then users are going to be disappointed. User expectations must be managed.

3. *Engaging in politically-naïve behavior.* DWs are a tool to support managers. To say that DWs will "help managers make better deci-sions" can alienate potential supporters (who may have been per-forming well *without* a DW).

4. *Loading the warehouse with information just because it was available.* Extraneous data makes it more difficult to locate the essential infor-mation and slows down the retrieval and analysis process. The data selected for inclusion in the DW must support organizational strate-gic goals.

5. *Believing that the data warehousing database design is the same as the transactional database design.* DWs are intended to maintain and pro-vide access to selected information from operational (transactional) databases, generally covering long periods of time. The type of information contained in a DW will cross multiple divisions within the organization, and the source data may come from multiple data-bases and may be summarized or provided in detail. These charac-teristics (as well as the database objectives) are substantially differ-ent from those of operational or transactional databases.

6. *Choosing a data warehouse manager who is technology oriented rather than user oriented.* Data warehousing is a service business — not a storage business — and making clients angry is a near-perfect method of destroying a service business.

7. *Focusing on traditional internal record-oriented data and ignoring the potential value of external data and text, images, and — potentially — sound and video.* Expand the data warehouse beyond the usual data presentation options and include other vital presentation options. Users may ask: Where is the copy of the contract (image) that

explains the information behind the data? Where is the ad (image) that ran in that magazine? Where is the tape (audio or video) of the key competitor at a recent conference talking about its business strategy? Where is the recent product launch (video)? Being able to provide the required reference data will enhance the analysis that the data warehouse designers and sponsors endeavor to support.

8. *Delivering data with overlapping and confusing definitions.* Consensus on data definitions is mandatory, and this is difficult to attain because multiple departments may have different meanings for the same term (e.g., sales). Otherwise, users may not have confidence in the data they are acquiring. Even worse, they may acquire the wrong information, embarrass themselves, and blame the data warehouse.

9. *Believing the vendor's performance, capacity, and scalability promises.* Planning to address the present and future DW capacity in terms of data storage, user access, and data transfer is mandatory. Budgeting must include unforeseen difficulties and costs associated with less than adequate performance by a product.

10. *Believing that once the data warehouse is up and running, one's problems are finished.* Once they become familiar with the data warehouse and the process for acquiring and analyzing data, users are going to want additional and different types of data than that already contained in the DW. The DW project team must be maintained after the initial design and implementation takes place for on-going DW support and enhancement.

11. *Focusing on ad hoc data mining and periodic reporting.* (Believing there are only ten mistakes to avoid is also a mistake.) Sometimes, ad hoc reports are converted into regularly scheduled reports, but the recipients may not read the reports. Alert systems can be a better approach and make a DW mission-critical, by monitoring data flowing into the warehouse and informing key people with a need-to-know as soon as a critical event takes place.

Responsiveness to key business goals — high-quality data, metadata, and scalable architecture — is emphasized repeatedly by many DW authors, as noted in the next section on suggestions for DW implementation.

DW IMPLEMENTATION

Although the actual implementation of a DW will depend on the business goals to be supported and the type and number of users, there are general implementation considerations and measures of success that are applicable to many circumstances.

General Considerations

As expected, implementation suggestions are (basically) the opposite of the mistakes to avoid. There is some overlap in the suggestions noted because there are multiple authors cited. Suggestions include:

1. Understand the basic requirements.
2. Design a highly scalable solution.
3. Deliver the first piece of the solution into users' hands quickly.[30]
4. Support a business function that is directly related to the company's strategy; begin with the end in mind.
5. Involve the business functions from the project inception throughout its lifecycle.
6. Ensure executive sponsorship understands the DW value, particularly with respect to revenue enhancement that focuses on the customer.
7. Maintain executive sponsorship and interest throughout the project.[31]
8. Develop standards for data transformation, replication, stewardship, and naming.
9. Determine a cost-justification methodology, and charge users for data they request.
10. Allow sufficient time to implement the DW properly, and conduct a phased implementation.
11. Designate the authority for determining data sources and populating the metadata and DW data to Data Administration.
12. Monitor data usage and archive data that is rarely or never accessed.[5]
13. Budget resources for metadata creation. Make metadata population a metric for the development team.
14. Budget resources for metadata maintenance. Any change in the data requires a change in the metadata.
15. Ensure ease of access. Find and deploy tools that seamlessly integrate metadata.[32]
16. Monitor DW storage growth and data activity to implement reasonable capacity planning.
17. Monitor user access and analysis techniques to ensure that they optimize usage of the DW resources.
18. Tune the DW for performance based on usage patterns (e.g., selectively index data, partition data, create summarization, and create aggregations).
19. Support both business metadata and technical metadata.
20. Plan for the future. Ensure that interface between applications and the DW is as automated as possible. Data granularity allows for continuous DW tuning and reorganization, as required to meet user needs and organization strategic goals.

21. Consider the creation of an "exploration warehouse" for the "out-of-the-box thinkers" who may want to submit lengthy resource-consuming queries — if they become a regular request.[33]

Qualitative Measures of DW Implementation Success

In 1994, Sears, Roebuck and Co. (a leading U.S. retailer of apparel, home, and automotive products that operates 3000 department and specialty stores) implemented a DW to address organizational objectives. The eight (qualitative) measures of success presented below are based on the experiences associated with the Sears DW implementation.

1. *Regular implementation of new releases.* The DW and applications are evolving to meet business needs, adding functionality through a phased implementation process.
2. *Users will wait for promised system upgrades.* When phases will deliver the functionality that is promised, at the expected quality level and data integrity level, planned implementation schedules (and possibly slippage) will be tolerated.
3. *New applications use the DW to serve their data requirements.* Increased reliance on the DW provides consistency company-wide and is cost effective.
4. *Users and support staff will continue to be involved in the DW.* Users become reliant on the DW and the part it plays in the performance of their work responsibilities. Therefore, there needs to be a permanent DW staff to support the constantly changing DW and business environment. When product timeliness is crucial to profitability, then designated staff (such as the Sears Business Support Team) and the DW staff can provide additional, specialized support to meet user needs.
5. *The DW is used to identify new business opportunities.* As users become familiar with the DW, they will increasingly pursue new discovery opportunities.
6. *Special requests become the rule, not the exception.* The ability to handle special requests on a routine basis is an example of DW maturity and a positive leverage of DW resources.
7. *Ongoing user training.* New and advanced user training (e.g., troubleshooting techniques, sophisticated functionality) and the provision of updated documentation (highlighting new features) facilitate and enhance DW use in support of business objectives.
8. *Retirement of legacy systems.* Use of legacy systems containing duplicate information will decline. Retirement of legacy systems should follow a planned process, including verification of data accuracy, completeness, and timely posting, with advance notification to identified users for a smooth transition to the DW applications.[34]

DW SECURITY IMPLICATIONS

The benefits of the well-implemented and well-managed DW can be very significant to a company. The data is integrated into a single data source. There is considerable ease of data access that can be used for decision-making support, including trends identification and analysis, and problem-solving. There is overall better data quality and uniformity, and different views of the same data are reconciled. Analysis techniques may even uncover useful competitive information. But with this valuable warehouse of information and power comes substantial risk if the information is unavailable, destroyed, improperly altered, or disclosed to or acquired by a competitor.

There may be additional risks associated with a specific DW, depending on the organization's functions, its environment, and the resources available for the DW design, implementation, and maintenance — which must be determined on an individual basis — that are not addressed here. Consider the perspective that the risks will change over time as the DW receives increased use by more sophisticated internal and external users; supports more functions; and becomes more critical to organizational operations.

DW Design Review

Insofar as the literature unanimously exhorts the need for upper-management support and applicability to critical business missions, the importance of the system is significant before it is even implemented. Issues associated with availability, integrity, and confidentiality should be addressed in the system design, and plans should include options for scalability and growth in the future. The DW must be available to users when they need the information; its integrity must be established and maintained; and only those with a need-to-know must access the data. Management must be made aware of the security implications and requirements, and security should be built into the DW design.

DW Design is Compliant with Established Corporate Information Security Policy, Standards, Guidelines, and Procedures. During the design phase, certain decisions are being made regarding expected management functions to be supported by the DW: user population (quantity, type, and expertise level); associated network connectivity required; information to be contained in the initial phase of the DW; data modeling processes and associated data formats; and resources (e.g., hardware, software, staff, data) necessary to implement the design. This phase also has significant security implications. The DW design must support and comply with corporate information security policies, including:

- non-disclosure statements signed by employees when they are hired[35]

- installation and configuration of new hardware and software, according to established corporate policies, guidelines, and procedures
- documentation of acceptable use and associated organizational monitoring activities
- consistency with overall security architecture
- avoidance of liability for inadequately addressing security through "negligence, breach of fiduciary duty, failing to use the security measures found in other organizations in the same industry, failing to exercise due care expected from a computer professional, or failure to act after an 'actual notice' has taken place"[45]
- protection from prosecution regarding inappropriate information access by defining appropriate information security behavior by authorized users[46]

DW Data Access Rights Are Defined and modeled for the DW User Population. When determining the access requirements for the DW, your initial users may be a small subset of employees in one division. Over time, it will expand to employees throughout the entire organization, and may include selected subsets of subcontractors, vendors, suppliers, or other groups who are partnering with the organization for a specific purpose. Users will not have access to all DW information, and appropriate access and monitoring controls must be implemented. Areas of security concern and implementation regarding user access controls include:

- DW user roles' definition for access controls (e.g., role-based access controls)
- user access rights and responsibilities documentation
- development of user agreements specifying security responsibilities and procedures[35]
- definition of user groups and their authorized access to specific internal or external data
- user groups and their authorized levels of network connectivity and use definitions
- definition of procedures for review of system logs and other records generated by the software packages[37]

DW Data Content and Granularity Is Defined and Appropriately Implemented in the DW Design. Initially, the DW content may be internal organizational numerical data, limited to a particular department or division. As time passes, the amount and type of data is going to increase, and may include internal organizational textual data, images, and videos, and external data of various forms as well. In addition, the required granularity of the data may change. Users initially may be comfortable with summary data; but as their familiarity with the DW and the analysis tools increases, they are going to want more detailed data, with a higher level of granularity than originally provided. Decisions that affect data content and its integrity throughout the DW life cycle include:

- Data granularity (e.g., summary, detail, instance, atomic) is defined.
- Data transformation rules are documented for use in maintaining data integrity.
- Process is defined for maintaining all data transformation rules for the life of the system.

Data Sensitivity Is Defined and Associated with Appropriate Access Controls
Issues associated with data ownership, sensitivity, labeling, and need-to-know will need to be defined so that the data can be properly labeled, and access requirements (e.g., role-based access controls) can be assigned. Establishment of role-based access controls "is viewed as effective and efficient for general enterprise security" and would allow the organization to expand the DW access over time, and successfully manage a large number of users.[38] Actions required that define and establish the data access controls include:

- determination of user access control techniques, including the methods for user identification, authentication, and authorization
- assignment of users to specific groups with associated authority, capabilities, and privileges[38] for role-based access controls
- determination of database controls (e.g., table and data labeling, encryption)
- establishment of a process for granting access and for the documentation of specified user roles and authorized data access, and a process for preventing the circumvention of the granting of access controls
- establishment of a process for officially notifying the Database Administrator (or designated individual) when an individual's role changes and his or her access to data must be changed accordingly
- establishment of a process for periodically reviewing access controls, including role-based access controls to ensure that only individuals with specified clearances and need-to-know have access to sensitive information

Data Integrity and Data Inference Requirements Are Defined and Associated with Appropriate Access Controls. Data integrity will be reviewed when the data is transformed for the DW, but should be monitored on a periodic basis throughout the life cycle of the DW, in cooperation with the DW database administration staff. Data inference and aggregation may enable an individual to acquire information for which he or she has no need-to-know, based on the capability to acquire other information. "An inference presents a security breach if higher-classified information can be inferred from lower-classified information."[39]

Circumstances in which this action might occur through data aggregation or data association in the DW need to be identified and addressed through appropriate data access controls. Data access controls to prevent or reduce unauthorized access to information obtained through a data inference process (i.e., data aggregation or data association) can include[39]:

- *Appropriate labeling of information:* unclassified information is reclassified (or labeled at a higher level) to prevent unauthorized inferences by data aggregation or data association.
- *Query restriction:* all queries are dominated by the level of the user, and inappropriate queries are aborted or modified to include only authorized data.
- *Polyinstantiation:* multiple versions of the same information item are created to exist at different classification levels.
- *Auditing:* a history of user queries is analyzed to determine if the response to a new query might suggest an inference violation.
- *Toleration of limited inferences:* inferred information violations do not pose a serious threat, and the prevention of certain inferences may be unfeasible.

Operating System, Application, and Communications Security Requirements Are Defined. Many DWs are using a Web-based interface, which provides easy accessibility and significant risk. Depending on the location of the system, multiple security mechanisms will be required. Actions required to define the security requirements should be based on a risk analysis and include:

- determination of mechanisms to ensure operating system and application system availability and integrity (e.g., firewalls, intrusion detection systems)
- determination of any secure communication requirements (e.g., Secure Socket Layer, encryption)

Plans for Hardware Configuration and Backup Must Be Included in the DW Design. The creation of a DW as a separate, nonoperational function will result in a duplication of hardware resources, because the operational hardware is maintained separately. In examples of mature DW utilizations, a second DW is often created for power users for "exploratory research" because the complexity of their analysis requests would take too much time and resources away from the other general users of the initial DW. This is then (possibly) a third set of hardware that must be purchased, configured, maintained, administered, and protected. The hardware investment keeps increasing. Documentation and updating of hardware and backup configurations should be performed as necessary.

Plans for Software Distribution, Configuration, and Use Must Be Included in the DW Design. The creation of one or multiple DWs also means additional operating system, application, middleware, and security software. In addition, as the number of users increases, the number of licensed software copies must also increase. Users may not be able to install the software themselves and so technical support may need to be provided. Distribution activities should ensure that:

- users have authorized copies of all software
- technical support is provided for software installation, use, and troubleshooting to maintain licensing compliance and data integrity

Plans for Continuity of Operations and Disaster Recovery Must Be Included in the DW Design. Capabilities for hardware and software backup, continuity of operations, and disaster recovery options will also have to be considered. The DW is used to implement strategic business goals, and downtime must be limited. As more users integrate the DW data into their routine work performance, more users will be negatively impacted by its unavailability. Activities in support of operations continuity and disaster recovery should include:

- designations from the design team regarding the criticality of data and key functions
- creation of an alternative hardware list
- resource allocations for DW system backups and storage
- resource allocations for business continuity and disaster recovery plans

Plans for Routine Evaluation of the Impact Of Expanded Network Connectivity on Organizational Network Performance Must Be Included in the DW Design.
Over time, with the increased number of users and the increased amount and type of data being accessed in the DW and transmitted over the organizational network, network resources are going to be "stressed." Possible options for handling increased network loads will need to be discussed. Network upgrades may be required over the long term and this needs to be considered in the resource planning activities. Otherwise data availability and data integrity may be impacted at crucial management decision times — times when one wants the DW to stand out as the valuable resource it was intended to be. Changes in network configurations must be documented and comply with organizational security policies and procedures. Planning to address DW scalability and the ability of the network to respond favorably to growth should include:

- evaluation of proposed network configurations and the expected service to be provided by a given configuration against DW requirements [40]

- estimation of DW network requirements' impact on existing organizational network connectivity requirements and possible reduction in data availability or integrity
- consideration of network connectivity options and the effects on the implementation of security

DW Security Implementation Review

A security review must be conducted to ensure that all the DW components supporting information security that were defined during the design phase are accurately and consistently installed and configured. Testing must be performed to ensure that the security mechanisms and database processes perform in a reliable manner and that the security mechanisms enforce established access controls. Availability of data must be consistent with defined requirements. The information security professional, the database administrator, and the network administrator should work together to ensure that data confidentiality, integrity, and availability are addressed.

Monitor the Acquisition and Installation of DW Technology Components in Accordance with Established Corporate Security Policies. When acquired, the hardware and software DW components must be configured to support the corporate security policies and the data models defined during the design phase. During installation, the following actions should take place: (1) documentation of the hardware and software configurations; and (2) testing of the system before operational to ensure compliance with policies.

Review the Creation/Generation of Database Components for Security Concerns. A process should be established to ensure that data is properly labeled, access requirements are defined and configured, and all controls can be enforced. In cooperation with the design team, individuals responsible for security should perform a review of the database configurations for compliance with security policies and defined data access controls. Database processes must enforce the following data integrity principles[39]:

1. *Well-formed transactions:* transactions support the properties of correct-state transformation, serialization, failure atomicity, progress (transaction completion), entity integrity, and referential integrity.
2. *Least privilege:* programs and users are given the minimum access required to perform their jobs.
3. *Separation of duties:* events that affect the balance of assets are divided into separate tasks performed by different individuals.
4. *Reconstruction of events:* user accountability for actions and determination of actions are performed through a well-defined audit trail.
5. *Delegation of authority:* process for acquisition and distribution of privileges is well-defined and constrained.

6. *Reality checks:* cross-checks with an external reality are performed.
7. *Continuity of operations:* system operations are maintained at an appropriate level.

Review the Acquisition of DW Source Data. DW data is coming from other sources; ensure that all internal and external data sources are known and documented, and data use is authorized. If the data is external, ensure that appropriate compensation for the data (if applicable) has been made, and that access limitations (if applicable) are enforced.

Review testing. Configuration settings for the security mechanisms must be verified, documented, and protected from alteration. Testing to ensure that the security mechanisms are installed and functioning properly must be performed and documented prior to the DW becoming operational. A plan should also be established for the testing of security mechanisms throughout the life cycle of the DW, including the following situations:

- routine testing of security mechanisms on a scheduled basis
- hardware or software configurations of the DW are changed
- circumstances indicate that an unauthorized alteration may have occurred
- a security incident occurs or is suspected
- a security mechanism is not functioning properly

DW Operations

The DW is not a static database. Users and information are going to be periodically changing. The process of data acquisition, modeling, labeling, and insertion into the DW must follow the established procedures. Users must be trained in DW use and updated as processes or procedures change, depending on the data being made available to them. More users and more data mean additional demands will be placed on the organization's network, and performance must be monitored to ensure promised availability and data integrity. Security mechanisms must be monitored to ensure accurate and consistent performance. Backup and recovery procedures must also be implemented as defined to ensure data availability.

Participate as a Co-instructor in DW User Instruction/Training. Training will be required for users to fully utilize the DW. This is also an opportunity to present (and reinforce) applicable information security requirements and the user's responsibility to protect enterprise information and other areas of concern. Activities associated with this include:

- promotion of users' understanding of their responsibilities regarding data privacy and protection
- documentation of user responsibilities and nondisclosure agreements

Perform Network Monitoring for Performance. Document network performance against established baselines to ensure that data availability is being implemented as planned.

Perform Security Monitoring for Access Control Implementation. Review defined hardware and software configurations on a periodic basis to ensure no inappropriate changes have been made, particularly in a distributed DW environment. Security monitoring activities should include:

- review of user accesses to verify established controls are in place and operational, and no unauthorized access is being granted (e.g., individual with role X is being granted to higher level data associated with role Y)
- provision of the capability for the DW administrator to cancel a session or an ID, as might be needed to combat a possible attack[35]
- review of operating system and application systems to ensure no unauthorized changes have been made to the configurations

Perform Software Application and Security Patches in a Timely and Accurate Manner. All patches must be installed as soon as they are received and documented in the configuration information.

Perform Data and Software Backups and Archiving. As data and software are changed, backups must be performed as defined in the DW design. Maintaining backups of the current data and software configurations will support any required continuity of operations or disaster recovery activities. Backups must be stored offsite at a remote location so that they are not subject to the same threats. If any data is moved from the DW to remote storage because it is not currently used, then the data must be appropriately labeled, stored, and protected to ensure access in the event that the information is needed again.

Review DW Data and Metadata Integrity. DW data will be reloaded or updated on a periodic basis. Changes to the DW data may also require changes to the metadata. The data should be reviewed to determine that the updates are being performed on the established schedule, are being performed correctly, and the integrity of the data is being maintained.

DW Maintenance

DW maintenance is a significant activity, because the DW is an ever-changing environment, with new data and new users being added on a routine basis. All security-relevant changes to the DW environment must be reviewed, approved, and documented prior to implementation.

Review and Document the Updating of DW Hardware and Software. Over time, changes will be made to the hardware and software, as technology improves or patches are required in support of functions or security. Associated activities include:

- installation of all software patches in a timely manner and documentation of the software configuration
- maintenance of software backups and creation of new backups after software changes
- ensuring new users have authorized copies of the software
- ensuring that system backup and recovery procedures reflect the current importance of the DW to organizational operations. If DW criticality has increased over time with use, has the ability to respond to this new level of importance been changed accordingly?

Review the Extraction/Loading of Data Process and Frequency to Ensure Timeliness and Accuracy. The DW data that is to be updated will be extracted from a source system, transformed, and then loaded into the DW. The frequency with which this activity is performed will depend on the frequency with which the data changes, and the users' needs regarding accurate and complete data. The process required to *update* DW data takes significantly less time than that required to *reload* the entire DW database, but there has to be a mechanism for determining what data has been changed. This process needs to be reviewed, and adjusted as required, throughout the life cycle of the DW.

Scheduling/Performing Data Updates. Ensure that data updates are performed as scheduled and the data integrity is maintained.

DW Optimization

Once the DW is established within an organization, it is likely that there will be situations in which individuals or organizations are working to make the DW better (e.g., new data content and types), cheaper (e.g., more automated, less labor intensive), and faster (e.g., new analysis tools, better network connectivity and throughput). Optimization will result in changes, and changes need to be reviewed in light of their impact on security. All changes should be approved before being implemented and carefully documented.

Participate in User Refresher/Upgrade Training. Over time, additional data content areas are going to be added to the DW and new analysis tools may be added. Users will need to be trained in the new software and other DW changes. This training also presents an opportunity to present any new security requirements and procedures — and to review existing requirements and procedures associated with the DW.

Review and Update the Process for Extraction/Loading of Data. As new data requirements evolve for the DW, new data may be acquired. Appropriate procedures must be followed regarding the access, labeling, and maintenance of new data to maintain the DW reputation regarding data integrity and availability.

Review the Scheduling/Performance of Data Updates. Over time, users may require more frequent updates of certain data. Ensure that data updates are performed as scheduled and that data integrity is maintained.

Perform Network Monitoring for Performance. Document network performance against established baselines to ensure that data availability is being implemented as planned. An expanded number of users and increased demand for large volumes of data may require modifications to the network configuration or to the scheduling of data updates. Such modifications may reduce the network traffic load at certain times of the day, week, or month, and ensure that requirements for data availability and integrity are maintained.

Perform Security Monitoring for Access. The DW information can have substantial operational value or exchange value to a competitor or a disloyal employee, as well as to the authorized users. With the use of corporate "portals" of entry, all of the data may be available through one common interface — making the means and opportunity for "acquisition" of information more easily achieved. Implementation of access controls needs to be continually monitored and evaluated throughout the DW life cycle. The unauthorized acquisition or dissemination of business-sensitive information (such as privacy data, trade secrets, planning information, or financial data) could result in lost revenue, company embarrassment, or legal problems. Monitoring access controls should be a continual security procedure for the DW.

Database Analysis. Some existing DW data may not be used with the expected frequency and it may be moved to another storage location, creating space for data more in demand. Changes in DW data configurations and locations should be documented.

There may be additional risks associated with an actual DW, depending on the organization's functions, its environment, and the resources available for the DW design, implementation, and maintenance — which must be determined on an individual basis. But with careful planning and implementation, the DW will be a valuable resource for the organization and help the staff to meet its strategic goals — now and in the future.

CONCLUSION

The security section presented some of the security considerations that need to be addressed throughout the life cycle of the DW. One consideration not highlighted above is the amount of time and associated resources (including equipment and funding) necessary to implement DW security. Bill Inmon estimated Security Administration to be 1 percent of the total warehouse costs, with costs to double the first year and then grow 30 to 40 percent after that. Maintaining adequate security is a crucial DW and organizational concern. The value of the DW is going to increase over time, and more users are going to have access to the information. Appropriate resources must be allocated to the protection of the DW. The ROI to the organization can be very significant if the information is adequately protected. If the information is not protected, then someone else is getting the keys to the kingdom. Understanding the DW design and implementation process can enable security professionals to justify their involvement early on in the design process and throughout the DW life cycle, and empower them to make appropriate, timely security recommendations and accomplish their responsibilities successfully.

Notes

1. Peppers, Don and Rogers, Martha, Mass Customization: Listening to Customers, *DM Review*, 9(1), 16, January 1999.
2. Denning, Dorothy E., *Information Warfare and Security*, Addison-Wesley, Reading, MA, July 1999, 148.
3. Saylor, Michael, Data Warehouse on the Web, *DM Review*, 6(9), 22–26, October 1996.
4. Inman, Bill, Meta Data for the Data Mart Environment, *DM Review*, 9(4), 44, April 1999.
5. Adelman, Sid, The Data Warehouse Database Explosion, *DM Review*, 6(11), 41–43, December 1996.
6. Imhoff, Claudia and Geiger, Jonathan, Data Quality in the Data Warehouse, *DM Review*, 6(4), 55–58, April 1996.
7. Griggin, Jane, Information Strategy, *DM Review*, 6(11), 12, 18, December 1996.
8. Mimmo, Pieter R., Building Your Data Warehouse Right the First Time, *Data Warehousing: What Works*, Vol. 9, November 1999, The Data Warehouse Institute Web site: www.dw-institute.com.
9. King, Nelson, Metadata: Gold in the Hills, *Intelligent Enterprise*, 2(3), 12, February 16, 1999.
10. Quinlan, Tim, Report from the Trenches, *Database Programming & Design*, 9(12), 36–38, 40–42, 44–45, December 1996.
11. Hufford, Duane, Data Warehouse Quality, *DM Review*, 6(3), 31–34, March 1996.
12. Rudin, Ken, The Fallacy of Perfecting the Warehouse, *DM Review*, 9(4), 14, April 1999.
13. Burwen, Michael P., BI and DW: Crossing the Millennium, *DM Review*, 9(4), 12, April 1999.
14. Westphal, Christopher and Blaxton, Teresa, *Data Mining Solutions, Methods and Tools for Solving Real-World Problems*, Wiley Computer Publishing, New York, 1998, 68–69.
15. Westphal, Christopher and Blaxton, Teresa, *Data Mining Solutions, Methods and Tools for Solving Real-World Problems*, Wiley Computer Publishing, New York, 1998, 19–24.
16. Westphal, Christopher and Blaxton, Teresa, *Data Mining Solutions, Methods and Tools for Solving Real-World Problems*, Wiley Computer Publishing, New York, 1998, xiv–xv.
17. Westphal, Christopher and Blaxton, Teresa, *Data Mining Solutions, Methods and Tools for Solving Real-World Problems*, Wiley Computer Publishing, New York, 1998, xv.
18. Westphal, Christopher and Blaxton, Teresa, *Data Mining Solutions, Methods and Tools for Solving Real-World Problems*, Wiley Computer Publishing, New York, 1998, 35.
19. Tufte, Edward R., *The Visual Display of Quantitative Information*, Graphics Press, Cheshire, CT, 1983, 15.

20. Tufte, Edward R., *The Visual Display of Quantitative Information*, Graphics Press, Cheshire, CT, 1983, 51.
21. Osterfelt, Susan, Doorways to Data, *DM Review*, 9(4), April 1999.
22. Finkelstein, Clive, Enterprise Portals and XML, *DM Review*, 10(1), 21, January 2000.
23. Schroeck, Michael, Enterprise Information Portals, *DM Review*, 10(1), 22, January 2000.
24. Inmon, Bill, The Data Warehouse Budget, *DM Review*, 7(1), 12–13, January 1997.
25. McKnight, William, Data Warehouse Justification and ROI, *DM Review*, 9(10), 50–52, November 1999.
26. Hackney, Douglas, How About 0% ROI?, *DM Review*, 9(1), 88, January 1999.
27. Suther, Tim, Customer Relationship Management, *DM Review*, 9(1), 24, January 1999.
28. The Data Warehousing Institute (TDWI), 849-J Quince Orchard Boulevard, Gaithersburg, MD 20878, (301) 947-3730, www.dw-institute.com.
29. The Data Warehousing Institute, Data Warehousing: What Works?, Gaithersburg, MD, Publication Number 295104, 1995.
30. Rudin, Ken, The Fallacy of Perfecting the Warehouse, *DM Review*, 9(4), 14, April 1999.
31. Schroeck, Michael J., Data Warehouse Best Practices, *DM Review*, 9(1), 14. January 1999.
32. Hackney, Douglas, Metadata Maturity, *DM Review*, 6(3), 22, March 1996.
33. Inmon, Bill, Planning for a Healthy, Centralized Warehouse, Bill Inmon, *Teradata Review*, 2(1), 20–24, Spring 1999.
34. Steerman, Hank, Measuring Data Warehouse Success: Eight Signs You're on the Right Track, *Teradata Review*, 2(1), 12–17, Spring 1999.
35. Fites, Philip and Kratz, Martin, *Information Systems Security: A Practitioner's Reference,* International Thomson Computer Press, Boston, 10.
36. Wood, Charles C., *Information Security Policies Made Easy*, Baseline Software, Sausalito, CA, 6.
37. Wood, Charles C., *Information Security Policies Made Easy*, Baseline Software, Sausalito, CA, 5.
38. Murray, William, Enterprise Security Architecture, *Information Security Management Handbook*, 4th ed., Harold F. Tipton and Micki S. Krause, Eds., Auerbach, New York, 1999, chap. 13, 215–230.
39. Sandhu, Ravi S. and Jajodia, Sushil, Data Base Security Controls, *Handbook of Information Security Management*, Zella G. Ruthberg and Harold F. Tipton, Eds., Auerbach, Boston, 1993, chap. II-3-2, 481–499.
40. Kern, Harris et al., *Managing the New Enterprise*, Prentice-Hall, Sun SoftPress, NJ, 1996, 120.

Chapter 16
Mitigating E-business Security Risks: Public Key Infrastructures in the Real World

Douglas C. Merrill
Eran Feigenbaum

MANY ORGANIZATIONS WANT TO GET INVOLVED WITH ELECTRONIC COM-
MERCE — OR ARE BEING FORCED TO BECOME AN E-BUSINESS BY THEIR
COMPETITORS. The goal of this business decision is to realize bottom-line
benefits from their information technology investment, such as more efficient vendor interactions and improved asset management. Such benefits
have indeed been realized by organizations, but so have the associated
risks, especially those related to information security. Managed risk is a
good thing, but risk for its own sake, without proper management, can
drive a company out of existence. More and more corporate management
teams — even up to the board of directors level — are requiring evidence
that security risks are being managed. In fact, when asked about the
major stumbling blocks to widespread adoption of electronic business,
upper management pointed to a lack of security as a primary source of
hesitation.

An enterprisewide security architecture, including technology, appropriate security policies, and audit trails, can provide reasonable measures
of risk management to address senior management concerns about E-business opportunities. One technology involved in enterprisewide security
architectures is public key cryptography, often implemented in the form of
a public key infrastructure (PKI). This chapter describes several hands-on

examples of PKI, including business cases and implementation plans. The authors attempt to present detail from a very practical, hands-on approach, based on their experience implementing PKI and providing large-scale systems integration services. Several shortcuts are taken in the technical discussions to simplify or clarify points, while endeavoring to ensure that these did not detract from the overall message.

Although this chapter focuses on a technology — PKI — it is important to realize that large implementations involve organizational transformation. Many nontechnical aspects are integral to the success of a PKI implementation, including organizational governance, performance monitoring, stakeholder management, and process adjustment. Failing to consider these aspects greatly increases the risk of project failure, although many of these factors are outside the domain of information security. In the authors' experience, successful PKI implementations involve not only information security personnel, but also business unit leaders and senior executives to ensure that these nontechnical aspects are handled appropriately.

NETWORK SECURITY: THE PROBLEM

As more and more data is made network-accessible, security mechanisms must be put in place to ensure only authorized users access the data. An organization does not want its competitor to read, for example, its internal pricing and availability information. Security breaches often arise through failures in authentication. Authentication is the process of identifying an individual so that one can determine the individual's access privileges. To start my car, I must authenticate myself to my car. When I start my car, I have to "prove" that I have the required token — the car key — before my car will start. Without a key, it is difficult to start my car. However, a car key is a poor authentication mechanism — it is not that difficult to get my car keys, and hence be me, at least as far as my car is concerned. In the everyday world, there are several stronger authentication mechanisms, such as presenting one's driver's license with a picture. People are asked to present their driver's licenses at events ranging from getting on a plane to withdrawing large amounts of money from a bank. Each of these uses involves comparing the image on the license to one's appearance. This strengthens the authentication process by requiring two-factor authentication — an attacker must not only have my license, but he must also resemble me. In the electronic world, it is far more difficult to get strong authentication: a computer cannot, in general, check to be sure a person looks like the picture on their driver's license. Typically, a user is required to memorize a username and password. These username and password pairs must be stored in operating system-specific files, application tables, and the user's head (or desk). Any individual sitting at a keyboard that can produce a user's password is assumed to be that user.

Traditional implementations of this model, although useful, have several significant problems. When a new user is added, a new username must be generated and a new password stored on each of the relevant machines. This can be a significant effort. Additionally, when a user leaves the company, that user's access must be terminated. If there are several machines and databases, ensuring that users are completely removed is not easy. The authors' experience with PricewaterhouseCoopers LLP (PricewaterhouseCoopers) assessing security of large corporations suggests that users are often not removed when they leave, creating significant security vulnerabilities.

Additionally, many studies have shown that users pick amazingly poor passwords, especially when constrained to use a maximum of eight characters, as is often the case in operating system authentication. For example, a recent assessment of a FORTUNE 50 company found that almost 10 percent of users chose a variant of the company's logo as their password. Such practices often make it possible for an intruder to simply guess a valid password for a user and hence obtain access to all the data that user could (legitimately) view or alter.

Finally, even if a strong password is selected, the mechanics of network transmission make the password vulnerable. When the user enters a username and password, there must be some mechanism for getting the identification materials to the server itself. This can be done in a variety of ways. The most common method is to simply transmit the username and password across the network. However, this information can be intercepted during transmission using commonly available tools called "sniffers." A sniffer reads data as it passes across a network — data such as one's username and password. After reading the information, the culprit could use the stolen credentials to masquerade as the legitimate user, attaining access to any information that the legitimate user could access. To prevent sniffing of passwords, many systems use cryptography to hide the plaintext of the password before sending it across the network. In this event, an attacker can still sniff the password off the network, but cannot simply read its plaintext; rather, the attacker sees only the encrypted version. The attacker is not entirely blocked, however. There are publicly available tools to attack the encrypted passwords using dictionary words or brute-force guessing to get the plaintext password from the encrypted password. These attacks exploit the use of unchanging passwords and functions. Although this requires substantial effort, many demonstrated examples of accounts being compromised through this sort of attack are known.

These concerns — lack of updates after users leave, poor password selection, and the capability to sniff passwords off networks — make reliance on username and password pairs for remote identification to business-critical information unsatisfactory.

WHY CRYPTOGRAPHY IS USEFUL

Cryptography (from the Greek for "secret writing") provides techniques for ensuring data integrity and confidentiality during transport and for lessening the threat associated with traditional passwords. These techniques include codes, ciphers, and steganography. This chapter only considers ciphers; for information on other types of cryptography, one could read Bruce Schneier's *Applied Cryptography* or David Kahn's *The Codebreakers*. Ciphers use mathematics to transform plaintext into "ciphertext." It is very difficult to transform ciphertext back into plaintext without a special key. The key is distributed only to select individuals. Anyone who does not have the key cannot read or alter the data without significant effort. Hence, authentication becomes the question, "does this person have the expected key?" Additionally, the property that only a certain person (or set of people) has access to a key implies that only those individuals could have done anything to an object encrypted with that key. This so-called "nonrepudiation" provides assurance about an action that was performed, such as that the action was performed by John Doe, or at a certain time, etc.

There are two types of ciphers. The first method is called secret key cryptography. In secret key cryptography, a secret — a password — must be shared between sender and recipient in order for the recipient to decrypt the object. The best-known secret key cryptographic algorithm is the Data Encryption Standard (DES). Other methods include IDEA, RC4, Blowfish, and CAST. Secret key cryptography methods are, in general, very fast, because they use fairly simple mathematics, such as binary additions, bit shifts, and table lookups.

However, transporting the secret key from sender to recipient — or recipients — is very difficult. If four people must all have access to a particular encrypted object, the creator of the object must get the same key to each person in a safe manner. This is difficult enough. However, an even more difficult situation occurs when each of the four people must be able to communicate with each of the others without the remaining individuals being able to read the communication (see Exhibit 16-1). In this event, each pair of people must share a secret key known only to those two individuals. To accomplish this with four people requires that six keys be created and distributed. With ten people, the situation requires 45 key exchanges (see Exhibit 16-2). Also, if keys were compromised — such as would happen when a previously authorized person leaves the company — all the keys known to the departing employee must be changed. Again, in the four-person case, the departure requires three new key exchanges; nine are required in the ten-person case. Clearly, this will not work for large organizations with hundreds or thousands of employees.

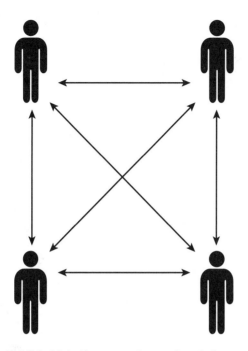

Exhibit 16-1. Four people require six keys.

In short, secret key cryptography has great power, employs fairly simple mathematics, and can quickly encrypt large volumes of data. However, its Achilles heel is the problem of key distribution and maintenance.

This Achilles heel led a group of mathematicians to develop a new paradigm for cryptography — asymmetric cryptography, also known as public key cryptography. Public key cryptography lessens the key distribution problem by splitting the encryption key into a public portion — which is given out to anyone — and a secret component that must be controlled by the user. The public and private keys, which jointly are called a key pair, are generated together and are related through complex mathematics. In the public key model, a sender looks up the recipient's public keys, typically stored in certificates, and encrypts the document using those public keys. No previous connection between sender and recipient is required, because only the recipient's public key is needed for secure transmission, and the certificates are stored in public databases. Only the private key that is associated with the public key can decrypt the document. The public and private keys can be stored as files, as entries in a database, or on a piece of hardware called a token. These tokens are often smart cards that look like credit cards but store user keys and are able to perform cryptographic computations far more quickly than general-purpose CPUs.

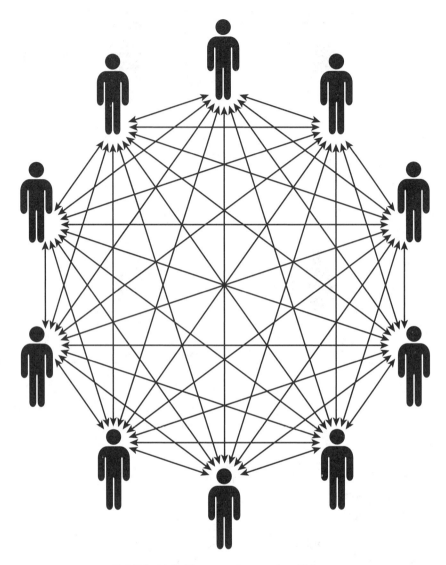

Exhibit 16-2. Ten people require 45 keys.

There are several public key cryptographic algorithms, including RSA, Diffie-Hellman, and Elliptic Curve cryptography. These algorithms relay on the assumption that there are mathematical problems that are easy to perform but difficult to do in reverse. To demonstrate this to yourself, calculate 11 squared (11^2). Now calculate the square root of 160. The square root is a bit more difficult, right? This is the extremely simplified idea behind public key cryptography. Encrypting a document to someone is akin to squaring a number, while decrypting it without the private key is somewhat like taking the square root. Each of the public key algorithms uses a different type of problem, but all rely on the assumption that the particular problem chosen is difficult to perform in reverse without the key.

Most public key algorithms have associated "signature" algorithms that can be used to ensure that a piece of data was sent by the owner of a private key and was unchanged in transit. These digital signature algorithms are commonly employed to ensure data integrity, but do not, in and of themselves, keep data confidential.

Public key cryptography can be employed to protect data confidentiality and integrity while it is being transported across the network. In fact, Secure Sockets Layer (SSL) is just that: a server's public key is used to create an encrypted tunnel across which World Wide Web (WWW) data is sent. SSL is commonly used for WWW sites that accept credit card information; in fact, the major browsers support SSL natively, as do most Web servers. Unfortunately, SSL does not address all the issues facing an organization that wants to open up its data to network access. By default, SSL authenticates only the server, not the client. However, an organization would want to provide its data only to the correct person; in other words, the whole point of this exercise is to ensure that the client is authenticated.

The SSL standards provide methods to authenticate not only the server, but also the client. Doing this requires having the client side generate a key pair and having the server check the client keys. However, how can the server know that the supposed client is not an imposter even if the client has a key pair? Additionally, even if a key does belong to a valid user, what happens when that user leaves the company, or when the user's key is compromised? Dealing with these situations requires a process called key revocation. Finally, if a user generates a key pair, and then uses that key pair to, for example, encrypt attachments to business-related electronic mail, the user's employer may be required by law to provide access to user data when served with a warrant. For an organization to be able to answer such a warrant, it must have "escrowed" a copy of the users' private keys — but how could the organization get a copy of the private key, since the user generated the pair?

Public key cryptography has a major advantage over secret key cryptography. Recall that secret key cryptography required that the sender and recipient share a secret key in advance. Public key cryptography does not require the sharing of a secret between sender and recipients, but is far slower than secret key cryptography, because the mathematics involved are far more difficult.

Although this simplifies key distribution, it does not solve the problem. Public key cryptography requires a way to ensure that John Doe's public key in fact belongs to him, not to an imposter. In other words, anyone could generate a key pair and assert that the public key belongs to the President of the United States. However, if one were to want to communicate with the President securely, one would need to ensure that the key was in fact his. This assurance requires that a trusted third party assert a particular public key does, in fact, belong to the supposed user. Providing this assurance requires additional elements, which, together make up a public key infrastructure (PKI).

The next section describes a complete solution that can provide data confidentiality and integrity protection for remote access to applications. Subsequent sections point out other advantages yielded by the development of a full-fledged infrastructure.

USING A PKI TO AUTHENTICATE TO AN APPLICATION

Let us first describe, at a high level, how a WWW-based application might employ a PKI to authenticate its users (see Exhibit 16-3). The user directs her WWW browser to the (secured) WWW server that connects to the application. The WWW page uses the form of SSL that requires both server and client authentication. The user must unlock her private key; this is done by entering a password that decrypts the private key. The server asks for the identity of the user, and looks up her public key in a database. After retrieving her public key, the server checks to be sure that the user is still authorized to access the application system, by checking to be sure that the user's key has not been revoked. Meanwhile, the client accesses the key database to get the public key for the server and checks to be sure it has not been revoked. Assuming that the keys are still valid, the server and client engage in mutual authentication.

There are several methods for mutual authentication. Regardless of approach, mutual authentication requires several steps; the major difference between methods is the order in which the steps occur. Exhibit 16-4 presents a simple method for clarity. First, the server generates a piece of random data, encrypts it with the client's public key, and signs it with its own private key. This encrypted and signed data is sent to the client, who checks the signature using the server's public key and decrypts the data. Only the client could have decrypted the data, because only the client has access to the user's private key; and only the server could have signed the data, because to sign the encrypted data, the server requires access to the server's private key. Hence, if the client can produce the decrypted data, the server can believe that the client has access to the user's private key. Similarly, if the client verifies the signature using the server's public key, the client is assured that the server signed the data. After decrypting the data, the client takes it, along with another piece of unique data, and encrypts both with the server's public key. The client then signs this piece of encrypted data and sends it off to the server. The server checks the

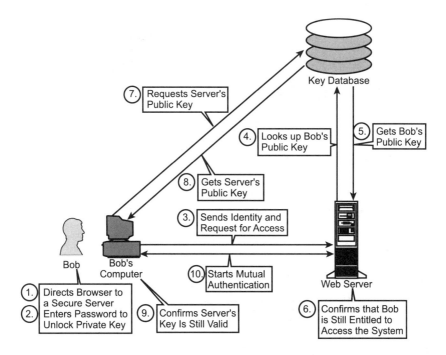

Key Database

7. Requests Server's Public Key

4. Looks up Bob's Public Key

5. Gets Bob's Public Key

8. Gets Server's Public Key

3. Sends Identity and Request for Access

Bob

Bob's Computer

10. Starts Mutual Authentication

Web Server

1. Directs Browser to a Secure Server

2. Enters Password to Unlock Private Key

9. Confirms Server's Key Is Still Valid

6. Confirms that Bob is Still Entitled to Access the System

Exhibit 16-3. Using a PKI to authenticate users.

signature, decrypts the data, checks to be sure the first piece of data is the same as what the server sent off before, and gathers the new piece of data. The server generates another random number, takes this new number along with the decrypted data received from the client, and encrypts both together. After signing this new piece of data, the resulting data is sent off to the client. Only the client can decrypt this data, and only the server could have signed it. This series of steps guarantees the identity of each party. After mutual authentication, the server sends a notice to the log server, including information such as the identity of the user, client location, and time.

Recall that public key cryptography is relatively slow; the time required to encrypt and decrypt data could interfere with the user experience. However, if the application used a secret key algorithm to encrypt the data passing over the connection, after the initial public key authentication, the data would be kept confidential to the two participants, but with a lower overhead. This is the purpose of the additional piece of random data in the second message sent by the server. This additional piece of random data will be used as a session key — a secret shared by client and server. Both client and server will use the session key to encrypt all network transactions in the current network connection using a secret key algorithm such as DES, IDEA, or RC4. The secret key algorithm provides confidentiality and

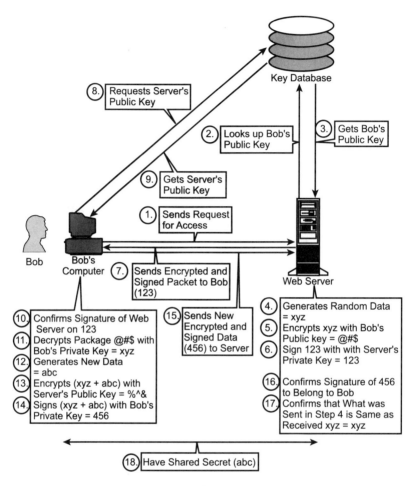

Exhibit 16-4. Mutual authentication.

integrity assurance for all data and queries as they traverse the network without the delay required by a public key algorithm. The public key algorithm handles key exchange and authentication. This combination of both a public key algorithm and a private key one offers the benefits of each.

How did these steps ensure that both client and server were authenticated? The client, after decrypting the data sent by the server, knows that the server was able to decrypt what the client sent, and hence knows that the server can access the server's private key. The server knows that the client has decrypted what it sent in the first step, and thus knows that the client has access to the user's private key. Both parties have authenticated the other, but no passwords have traversed the network, and no information that could be useful to an attacker has left the client or server machines.

Additionally, the server can pass the authentication through to the various application servers without resorting to insecure operating system-level trust relationships, as is often done in multi-system installations. In other words, a user might be able to leverage the public key authentication to not only the WWW-based application, but also other business applications. More details on this reduced sign-on functionality are provided in a later section.

COMPONENTS OF A PKI

The behavior described in the example above seemed very simple, but actually involved several different entities behind the scenes. As is so often the case, a lot of work must be done to make something seem simple. The entities involved here include a certificate authority, registration authorities, directory servers, various application programming interfaces and semi-custom development, third-party applications, and hardware. Some of these entities would be provided by a PKI vendor, such as the CA, RA, and a directory server, but other components would be acquired from other sources. Additionally, the policies that define the overall infrastructure and how the pieces interact with each other and the users are a central component. This section describes each component and tells why it is important to the overall desired behavior.

The basic element of a PKI is the certificate authority. One of the problems facing public key solutions is that anyone can generate a public key and claim to be anyone they like. For example, using publicly available tools, one can generate a public key belonging, supposedly, to the President of the United States. The public key will say that it belongs to the President, but it actually would belong to an imposter. It is important for a PKI to provide assurance that public keys actually belong to the person who is named in the public key. This is done via an external assurance link; to get a key pair, one demonstrates to a human that they are who they claim to be. For example, the user could, as part of the routine on the first day of employment, show his driver's license to the appropriate individual, known as a registration authority. The registration authority (RA) generates a key pair for the individual and tells the certificate authority (CA) to attest that the public key belongs to the individual. The CA does this attestation by signing the public key with the CA's private key. All users trust the CA. Because only the CA could access the CA's private key, and the private key is used to attest to the identity, all will believe that the user is in fact who the user claims to be. Thus, the CA (and associated RA) is required in order for the PKI to be useful, and any compromise of the CA's key is fatal for the entire PKI. CAs and RAs are usually part of the basic package bought from a PKI vendor. An abridged list of PKI vendors (in alphabetical order) includes Baltimore, Entrust Technologies, RSA Security, and Verisign.

When one user (or server) wants to send an encrypted object to another, the sender must get the recipient's public key. For large organizations, there can be thousands of public keys, stored as certificates signed by the CA. It does not make sense for every user to store all other certificates, due to storage constraints. Hence, a centralized storage site (or sites) must store the certificates. These sites are databases, usually accessed via the Lightweight Directory Access Protocol (LDAP), and normally called directory servers. A directory server will provide access throughout the enterprise to the certificates when an entity requires one. There are several vendors for LDAP directories, including Netscape, ICL, Novell, and Microsoft.

There are other roles for directory servers, including escrow of users' private keys. There are several reasons why an organization might need access to users' private keys. If an organization is served by a warrant, it may be required to provide access to encrypted objects. Achieving this usually involves having a separate copy of users' private keys; this copy is called an "escrowed" key. LDAP directories are usually used for escrow purposes. Obviously, these escrow databases must be extremely tightly secured, because access to a user's private key compromises all that user's correspondence and actions. Other reasons to store users' private keys include business continuity planning and compliance monitoring.

When a sender gets a recipient's public key, the sender cannot be sure that the recipient still works for the organization, and does not know if someone has somehow compromised that key pair. Human resources, however, will know that the recipient has left the organization and the user may know that the private key has been compromised. In either case, the certificate signed by the CA — and the associated private key — must be revoked. Key revocation is the process through which a key is declared invalid. Much as it makes little sense for clients to store all certificates, it is not sensible for clients to store all revoked certificates. Rather, a centralized database — called a certificate revocation list (CRL) — should be used to store revoked certificates. The CRL holds identifiers for all revoked certificates. Whenever an entity tries to use a certificate, it must check the CRL in order to ensure that the certificate is still valid; if an entity is presented a revoked certificate, it should log the event as a possible attack on the infrastructure. CRLs are often stored in LDAP databases, in data structures accessible through Online Certificate Status Processing (OCSP), or on centralized revocation servers, as in Valicert's Certificate Revocation Tree service. Some PKIs have ability to check CRLs, such as Entrust's Entelligence client, but most rely on custom software development to handle CRL checking. Additionally, even for PKIs supporting CRL checking, the capabilities do not provide access to other organization's CRLs — only a custom LDAP solution or a service such as, for example, Valicert's can provide this inter-organization (or inter-PKI) capability.

Off-the-shelf PKI tools are often insufficient to provide complete auditing, dual authentication, CRL checking, operating system integration, and application integration. To provide these services, custom development must be performed. Such development requires that the application and PKI both support application programming interfaces (APIs). The API is the language that the application talks and through which the application is extended. There are public APIs for directory servers, operating system authentication, CRL checking, and many more functions. It is very common for applications to support one or more APIs. Many PKI vendors have invested heavily in the creation of toolkits — notably, RSA Security, Entrust Technologies, and Baltimore.

For both performance and security reasons, hardware cryptographic support can be used as part of a PKI. The hardware support is used to generate and store keys and also to speed cryptographic operations. The CA and RAs will almost always require some sort of hardware support to generate and store keys. Potential devices include smart cards, PCMCIA cards, or external devices. An abridged list of manufactures includes Spyrus, BBN, Atalla, Schlumberger, and Rainbow. These devices can cost anywhere from a few dollars up to $5000, depending on model and functionality. They serve not only to increase the performance of CA encryption, but also to provide additional security for the CA private key, because it is difficult to extract the private key from a hardware device.

Normally, one would not employ a smart card on a CA but, if desired, user private keys can be stored on smart cards. Such smart cards may provide additional functionality, such as physical access to company premises. Employing a smart card provides higher security for the user's private key because there is (virtually) no way for the user's private key to be removed from the card, and all computations are performed on the card itself. The downside of smart cards is that each card user must be given both a card and a card reader. Note that additional readers are required anywhere a user wishes to employ the card. There are several card manufacturers, but only some cards work with some PKI selections. The card manufacturers include Spyrus, Litronic, Datakey, and GemPlus. In general, the cards cost approximately $100 per user, including both card and reader.

However, the most important element of a PKI is not a physical element at all, but rather the policies that guide design, implementation, and operation of the PKI. These policies are critical to the success of a PKI, yet are often given short shrift during implementation. The policies are called a "Certificate Practice Statement" (CPS). A CPS includes, among other things, direction about how users are to identify themselves to an RA in order to get their key pair; what the RA should do when a user loses his password (and hence cannot unlock his private key); and how keys should be escrowed, if at all. Additionally, the CPS covers areas such as backup policies for the directory servers, CA, and RA machines. There are several good CPS examples that serve as the starting point for an implementation. A critical element of the security of the entire system is the sanctity of the CA itself — the root key material, the software that signs certificate requests, and the OS security itself. Extremely serious attention must be paid to the operational policies — how the system is administered, background checks on the administrators, multiple-person control, etc. — of the CA server.

The technology that underpins a PKI is little different from that of other enterprisewide systems. The same concerns that would apply to, for example, a mission-critical database system should be applied to the PKI components. These concerns include business continuity planning, stress and load modeling, service-level agreements with any outsourced providers or contract support, etc. The CA software often runs either on Windows NT or one of the UNIX variants, depending on the CA vendor. The RA software is often a Windows 9x client. There are different architectures for a PKI. These architectures vary on, among other things, the number and location of CA and RA servers, the location, hierarchy, and replication settings of directory servers, and the "chain of trust" that carries from sub-CA servers (if any) back to the root CA server. Latency, load requirements, and the overall security policy should dictate the particular architecture employed by the PKI.

OTHER PKI BENEFITS: REDUCED SIGN-ON

There are other benefits of a PKI implementation — especially the promise of reduced sign-on for users. Many applications require several authentication steps. For example, a user may employ one username and password pair to log on to his local desktop, others to log on to the servers, and yet more to access the application and data itself. This creates a user interaction nightmare; how many usernames and passwords can a user remember? A common solution to this problem is to employ "trust" relationships between the servers supporting an application. This reduces the number of logins a user must perform, because logging into one trusted host provides access to all others. However, it also creates a significant security vulnerability; if an attacker can access one trusted machine, the attacker has full access to all of them. This point has been exploited many times during PricewaterhouseCoopers attack and penetration exercises. The "attackers" find a development machine, because development machines typically are less secure than production machines, and attack it. After compromising the development machine, the trust relationships allow access to the production machines. Hence, the trust relationships mean that the security of the entire system is dependent not on the most secure systems — the production servers — but rather on the least secure ones.

Even using a trust relationship does not entirely solve the user interaction problem; the user still has at least one operating system username and password pair to remember and another application username and password. PKI systems offer a promising solution to this problem. The major PKI vendors have produced connecting software that replaces most operating system authentication processes with a process that is close to the PKI authentication system described above.

The operating system authentication uses access to the user's private key, which is unlocked with a password. After unlocking the private key, it can be used in the PKI authentication process described above. Once the private key is unlocked, it remains unlocked for a configurable period of time. The user would unlock the private key when first used, which would typically be when logging in to the user's desktop system. Hence, if the servers and applications use the PKI authentication mechanism, the users will not need to reenter a password — they need unlock the private key only once. Each system or application can, if it desires, engage in authentication with the user's machine, but the user need not interact, because the private key is already unlocked. From the user's perspective, this is single sign-on, but without the loss of security provided by other partial solutions (such as trust relationships).

There are other authentications involved in day-to-day business operations. For example, many of us deal with legacy systems. These legacy systems have their own, often proprietary, authentication mechanisms. Third-party products provide connections between a PKI and these legacy applications. A username and password pair is stored in a protected database. When the user attempts to access the legacy application, a "proxy" application requests PKI-based authentication. After successfully authenticating the user — which may not require reentry of the user's PKI password — the server passes the legacy application the appropriate username and password and connects the client to the legacy application. The users need not remember the username and password for the legacy application because they are stored in the database. Because the users need not remember the password, the password can be as complicated as the legacy application will accept, thus making security compromise of the legacy application more difficult while still minimizing user interaction headaches.

Finally, user keys, as mentioned above, can be stored as files or on tokens, often called smart cards. When using a smart card, the user inserts the card into a reader attached to the desktop and authenticates to the card, which unlocks the private key. From then on, the card will answer challenges sent to it and issue them in turn, taking the part of the client machine in the example above. Smart cards can contain more than simply the user keys, although this is their main function. For example, a person's picture can be printed onto the smart card, thus providing a corporate identification badge. Magnetic stripes can be put on the back of the smart card and encoded with normal magnetic information. Additionally, smart card manufacturers can build proximity transmitters into their smart card. These techniques allow the same card that authenticates the user to the systems to allow the user access to the physical premises of the office. In this model, the PKI provides not only secure access to the entity's systems and applications with single sign-on, but also to physically secured areas of the entity. Such benefits are driving the increase in the use of smart cards for cryptographic security.

PKI IN OPERATION

With the background of how a PKI works and descriptions of its components, one can now walk through an end-to-end example of how a hypothetical organization might operate its PKI.

Imagine a company, DCMEF, Inc., which has a few thousand employees located primarily in southern California. DCMEF, Inc. makes widgets used in the manufacture of automobile air bags. DCMEF uses an ERP system for manufacturing planning and scheduling as well as for its general ledger and payables. It uses a shop-floor data management system to track the manufacturing process, and has a legacy system to maintain human resource-related information. Employees are required to wear badges at all times when in the facility, and these same picture badges unlock the various secured doors at the facility near the elevators and at the entrances to the shop floor via badge readers.

DCMEF implemented its PKI in 1999, using commercial products for CA and directory services. The CA is located in a separately secured data center, with a warm standby machine locked in a disaster recovery site in the Midwest. The warm standby machine does not have keying material. The emergency backup CA key is stored in a safety deposit box that requires the presence of two corporate officers or directors to access. The CA is administered by a specially cleared operations staff member who does not have access to the logging server, which ensures that that operations person cannot ask the CA to do anything (such as create certificates) without a third person seeing the event. The RA clients are scattered through human resources, but are activated with separate keys, not the HR representatives' normal day-to-day keys.

When new employees are hired, they are first put through a two-day orientation course. At this course, the employees fill out their benefits forms, tax information, and also sign the data security policy form. After signing the form, each employee is given individual access to a machine that uses cryptographic hardware support to generate a key pair for that user. The public half of the key pair is submitted to the organization's CA for certification by the human resources representative, who is serving as the RA, along with the new employee's role in the organization.

The CA checks to be sure that the certificate request is correctly formed and originated with the RA. Then, the CA creates and signs a certificate for the new employee, and returns the signed certificate to the human resources representative. The resulting certificate is stored on a smart card at that time, along with the private key. The private key is locked on the smart card with a PIN selected by the user (and known only to that user). DCMEF's CPS specifies a four-digit PIN, and prohibits use of common patterns like "1234" or "1111." Hence, each user selects four digits; those who select inappropriate PIN values are prompted to select again until their selection meets DCMEF policies.

A few last steps are required before the user is ready to go. First, a copy of each user's private key is encrypted with the public key of DCMEF's escrow agent and stored in the escrow database. Then, the HR representative activates the WWW-based program that stores the new employee's certificate in the directory server, along with the employee's phone number and other information, and adds the employee to the appropriate role entry in the authentication database server. After this step, other employees will be able to look up the new employee in the company electronic phone book, be able to encrypt e-mail to the new employee, and applications will be able to determine the information to which the employee should have access. After these few steps, the user is done generating key material.

The key generating machine is rebooted before the next new employee uses it. During this time, the new employee who is finished generating a key pair is taken over to a digital camera for an identification photograph. This photograph is printed onto the smart card, and the employee's identification number is stored on the magnetic strip on the back of the card to enable physical access to the appropriate parts of the building.

At this point, the new employees return to the orientation course, armed with their smart cards for building access loaded with credentials for authentication to the PKI. This entire process took less than 15 minutes per employee, with most of that spent typing in information.

The next portion of the orientation course is hands-on instruction on using the ERP modules. In a normal ERP implementation, users have to log on to their client workstation, to an ERP presentation server and, finally, to the application itself. In DCMEF, Inc., the users need only insert their smart cards into the readers attached to their workstations (via either the serial port or a USB port, in this case), and they are logged in transparently to their local machine and to every PKI-aware application — including the ERP system. When the employees insert their smart cards, they are prompted for the PIN to unlock their secret key. The remainder of the authentication to the client workstation is done automatically, in roughly the manner described above. When the user starts the ERP front-end application, it expects to be given a valid certificate for authentication purposes, and expects to be able to look that certificate up in an authorization database to select which ERP data this user's role can access. Hence, after the authentication process between ERP application server and user (with the smart card providing the user's credentials) completes, the user has full access to the appropriate ERP data. The major ERP packages are PKI-enabled using vendor toolkits and internal application-level controls. However, it is not always so easy to PKI-enable a legacy application, such as DCMEF's shop-floor data manager. In this case, DCMEF could have chosen to leave the legacy application entirely alone, but that would have meant users would need to remember a different username and password pair to gain access to the shop-floor information, and corporate security would need to manage a second set of user credentials. Instead, DCMEF decided to use a gateway approach to the legacy application. All network access to the shop-floor data manager system was removed, to be replaced by a single gateway in or out. This gateway ran customized proxy software that uses certificates to authenticate users. However, the proxy issues usernames and passwords that match the user's role to the shop-floor data manager. There are fewer roles than users, so it is easier to maintain a database of role-password pairs, and the shop-floor data manager itself does not know that anything has changed. The proxy application must be carefully designed and implemented, because it is now a single point of failure for the entire application, and the gateway machine should be hardened against attack.

The user credentials issued by HR expire in 24 months — this period was selected based on the average length of employment at DCMEF, Inc. Hence, every two years, users must renew their certificates. This is done via an automatic process; users visit an intranet WWW site and ask for renewal. This request is routed to human resources, which verifies that the person is still employed and is still in the same role. If appropriate, the HR representative approves the request, and the CA issues a new certificate — with the same public key — to the employee, and adds the old certificate to DCMEF's revocation list. If an employee leaves the company, HR revokes the user's certificate (and hence their access to applications) by asking the CA to add the certificate to the public revocation list. In DCMEF's architecture, a promoted user needs no new certificate, but HR must change the permissions associated with that certificate in the authorization database.

This example is not futuristic at all — everything mentioned here is easily achievable using commercial tools. The difficult portions of this example are related to DCMEF itself. HR, manufacturing, planning, and accounting use the PKI on a day-to-day basis. Each of these departments has its own needs and concerns that need to be addressed up-front, before implementation, and then training, user acceptance, and updates must include each department going forward. A successful PKI implementation will involve far more than corporate information security — it will involve all the stakeholders in the resulting product.

IMPLEMENTING A PKI: GETTING THERE FROM HERE

The technical component of building a PKI requires five logical steps:

1. The policies that govern the PKI, known as a Certificate Practice Statement (CPS), must be created.
2. The PKI that embodies the CPS must be initialized.
3. Users and administration staff must be trained.
4. Connections to secured systems that could circumvent the PKI must be ended.
5. Any other system integration work — such as integrating legacy applications with the PKI, using the PKI for operating system authentication, or connecting back-office systems including electronic mail or human resource systems to the PKI — must be done.

The fourth and fifth steps may not be appropriate for all organizations.

The times included here are based on the authors' experience in designing and building PKI systems, but will vary for each situation. Some of the variability comes from the size of clients; it requires more time to build a PKI for more users. Other variability derives from a lack of other standards; it is difficult to build a PKI if the organization supports neither Windows NT nor UNIX, for example. In any case, the numbers provided here offer a glimpse into the effort involved in implementing a PKI as part of an ERP implementation.

The first step is to create a CPS. Creating a CPS involves taking a commonly accepted framework, such as the National Automated Clearing House Association guidelines, PKIX-4, or the framework promulgated by Entrust Technologies, and adapting it to the needs of the particular organization. The adaptations involve modification of roles to fit organizational structures and differences in state and federal regulation. This step involves interviews and extensive study of the structure and the environment within which the organization falls. Additionally, the CPS specifies the vendor for the PKI as well as for any supporting hardware or software, such as smart cards or directories. Hence, building a CPS includes the analysis stage of the PKI selection. Building a CPS normally requires approximately three person-months, assuming that the organization has in place certain components, such as an electronic mail policy and Internet use policy, and results in a document that needs high-level approval, often including legal review.

The CPS drives the creation of the PKI, as described above. Once the CPS is complete, the selected PKI vendor and products must be acquired. This involves hardware acquisition for the CA, any RA stations, the directories, and secure logging servers, as well as any smart cards, readers, and other hardware cryptographic modules. Operating system and supporting software must be installed on all servers, along with current security-related operating system patches. The servers must all be hardened, as the security of the entire system will rely to some extent on their security. Additional traditional information security work, such as the creation of intrusion detection systems, is normally required in this phase. Many of the servers — especially the logging server — will require hardware support for the cryptographic operations they must perform; these cryptographic support modules must be installed on each server. Finally, with the pieces complete, the PKI can be installed.

Installing the PKI requires, first, generating a "root" key and using that root key to generate a CA key. This generation normally requires hardware support. The CA key is used to generate the RA keys that in turn generate all user public keys and associated private keys. The CA private key signs users' public keys, creating the certificates that are stored on the directory server. Additionally, the RA must generate certificates for each server that requires authentication. Each user and server certificate and the associated role — the user's job — must be entered into a directory server to support use of the PKI by, for example, secure electronic mail. The server keys must be installed in the hardware cryptographic support modules, where appropriate. Client-side software must be installed on each client to support use of the client-side certificates. Additionally, each client browser must be configured to accept the organization's CA key and to use the client's certificate. These steps, taken together, constitute the initialization of the PKI. The time required to initialize a PKI is largely driven by the number of certificates required. In a recent project involving 1000 certificates, ten applications, and widespread use of smart cards, the PKI initialization phase required approximately twelve person-months. Approximately two person-months of that time were spent solely on the installation of the smart cards and readers.

Training cannot be overlooked when installing large-scale systems such as a PKI. With the correct architecture, much of the PKI details are below users' awareness, which minimizes training requirements. However, the users have to be shown how to unlock their certificates, a process that replaces their login, and how to use any ancillary PKI services, such as secure e-mail and the directory. This training is usually done in groups of 15 to 30 and lasts approximately one to two hours, including hands-on time for the trainees.

After training is completed, users and system administration staff are ready to use the PKI. At this point, one can begin to employ the PKI itself.

This involves ensuring that any applications or servers that should employ the PKI cannot be reached without using the PKI. Achieving this goal often requires employing third-party network programs that interrupt normal network processing to require the PKI. Additionally, it may require making configuration changes to routers and operating systems to block back door entry into the applications and servers. Blocking these back-doors requires finding all connections to servers and applications; this is a non-trivial analysis effort that must be included in the project planning.

Finally, an organization may want to use the PKI to secure applications and other business processes. For example, organizations, as described above, may want to employ the PKI to provide single sign-on or legacy system authentication. This involves employing traditional systems integration methodologies — and leveraged software methodologies — to mate the PKI to these other applications using various application programming interfaces. Estimating this effort requires analysis and requirements assessment.

As outlined here, a work plan for creating a PKI would include five steps. The first step is to create a CPS. Then, the PKI is initialized. Third, user and administrator training must be performed. After training, the PKI connections must be enforced by cutting off extraneous connections. Finally, other system integration work, including custom development, is performed.

CONCLUSION

Security is an enabler for electronic business; without adequate security, senior management may not feel confident moving away from more expensive and slower traditional processes to more computer-intensive ones. Security designers must find usable solutions to organizational requirements for authentication, authorization, confidentiality, and integrity. Public key infrastructures offer a promising technology to serve as the foundation for E-business security designs. The technology itself has many components — certificate authorities, registration authorities, directory servers — but, even more importantly, requires careful policy and procedure implementation.

This chapter has described some of the basics of cryptography, both secret and public key cryptography, and has highlighted the technical and procedural requirements for a PKI. The authors have presented the five high-level steps that are required to implement a PKI, and have mentioned some vendors in each of the component areas. Obviously, in a chapter this brief, it is not possible to present an entire workplan for implementing a PKI — especially since the plans vary significantly from situation to situation. However, the authors have tried to give the reader a start toward such a plan by describing the critical factors that must be addressed, and showing how they all work together to provide an adequate return on investment.

Domain 5
Cryptography

THE SCIENCE AND APPLICATION OF CRYPTOGRAPHY ARE CHALLENGING ISSUES AND ARE AMONG THE MOST DIFFICULT FOR WHICH THE CISSP CERTIFICATION EXAMINATION CANDIDATE PREPARES. The terminology is complex and the concepts are far from intuitive. The chapters in this domain are written to assist the reader in appreciating the intricacies of encryption technologies.

From symmetric to asymmetric keys, to elliptical curve, from private key to public key, encryption methodologies enable the protection of information, at rest and while in transmission. This domain features new chapters that range from a comprehensive introduction to encryption to an explanation of the various methods that can be used to attack cryptosystems.

Chapter 17
Introduction to Encryption

Jay Heiser

THROUGHOUT RECORDED HISTORY, NEW FORMS OF COMMUNICATION HAVE BEEN PARALLELED BY DEVELOPMENTS IN CRYPTOGRAPHY, THE PRACTICE OF SECURING COMMUNICATIONS. Secret writing appeared soon after the development of writing itself — an Egyptian example from 1900 BC is known. During the Renaissance, the significance of the nation state and growth in diplomacy created a requirement for secret communication systems to support diplomatic missions located throughout Europe and the world. The high volume of encrypted messages, vulnerable to interception through slow and careless human couriers, encouraged the first organized attempts to systematically break secret communications. Several hundred years later, the widespread use of the telegraph, and especially the use of radio in World War I, forced the development of efficient and robust encryption techniques to protect the high volume of sensitive communications vulnerable to enemy surveillance. At the start of World War II, highly complex machines, such as the German Enigma, were routinely used to encipher communications. Despite the sophistication of these devices, commensurate developments in cryptanalysis, the systematic technique of determining the plain text content of an encrypted message, provided the Allies with regular access to highly sensitive German and Japanese communications.

The ubiquity of computers — and especially the growth of the Internet — has created a universal demand for secure high-volume, high-speed communications. Governments, businesses of all sizes, and even private individuals now have a routine need for protected Internet communications. Privacy is just one of the necessary services that cryptography is providing for E-commerce implementations. The burgeoning virtual world of online transactions has also created a demand for virtual trust mechanisms. Cryptological techniques, especially those associated with public key technology, enable highly secure identification mechanisms, digital signature, digital notary services, and a variety of trusted electronic transaction types to replace paper and human mechanisms.

HOW ENCRYPTION FAILS

Encryption has a history of dismal failures. Like any other human device, it can always be circumvented by humans; it is not a universal panacea to security problems. Having an understanding of how encryption implementations are attacked and how they fail is crucial in being able to successfully apply encryption.

CRYPTOGRAPHIC ATTACKS

Brute-force attack is the sequential testing of each possible key until the correct one is found. On average, the correct key will be found once half of the total key space has been tried. The only defense against a brute-force attack is to make the key space so huge that such an attack is *computationally infeasible* (i.e., theoretically possible, but not practical given the current cost/performance ratio of computers). As processing power has increased, the limits of computational infeasibility have been reduced, encouraging the use of longer keys. A 128-bit key space is an awesomely large number of keys — contemporary computing resources could not compute 2^{128} keys before the sun burned out.

Cryptanalysis is the systematic mathematical attempt to discover weaknesses in either cryptographic implementation or practice, and to use these weaknesses to decrypt messages. The idea of cryptanalytic attack is fascinating, and in some circumstances, the successes can be quite dramatic. In reality, more systems are breached through human failure. Several of the more common forms of cryptanalytic attack are described below.

A **ciphertext-only attack** is based purely on intercepted ciphertext. It is the most difficult because there are so few clues as to what has been encrypted, forcing the cryptanalyst to search for patterns within the ciphertext. The more ciphertext available for any given encryption key, the easier it is to find patterns facilitating cryptanalysis. To reduce the amount of ciphertext associated with specific keys, virtual private networks, which can exchange huge amounts of encrypted data, automatically change them regularly.

A **known plaintext attack** is based on knowledge of at least part of the plaintext message, which can furnish valuable clues in cracking the entire text. It is not unusual for an interceptor to be aware of some of a message's plaintext. The name of the sender or recipient, geographical names, standard headers and footers, and other context-dependent text may be assumed as part of many documents and messages. A **reasonable guess attack** is similar to a known plaintext attack.

Password cracking tools are a common example of reasonable guess techniques. Called a **dictionary attack**, they attempt to crack passwords by starting with words known to be common passwords. If that fails, they then attempt to try all of the words in a dictionary list supplied by the operator. Such automated attacks are effectively brute-force attacks on a limited subset of keys. L0phtcrack not only uses a dictionary attack but also exploits weaknesses in NT's password hashing implementation that were discovered through cryptanalysis, making it a highly efficient password guesser.

COMPROMISE OF KEY

In practice, most encryption failures are due to human weakness and sloppy practices. The human password used to access a security domain or crypto subsystem is often poorly chosen and easily guessable. Password guessing can be extraordinarily fruitful, but stolen passwords are also quite common. Theft may be accomplished through physical examination of an office; passwords are often stuck on the monitor or glued underneath the keyboard. Social engineering is the use of deception to elicit private information. A typical social engineering password theft involves the attacker phoning the victim, explaining that they are with the help desk and need the user's password to resolve a problem.

Passwords can also be stolen using a sniffer to capture them as they traverse the network. Older services, such as FTP and Telnet, send the user password and login across the network in plaintext. Automated attack tools that sniff Telnet and FTP passwords and save them are commonly found in compromised UNIX systems. NT passwords are hashed in a very weak fashion, and the L0phtcrack utility includes a function to collect crackable password hashes by sniffing login sessions.

If a system is compromised, there might be several passwords available on it for theft. Windows 95 and 98 systems use a very weak encryption method that is very easy to crack. Software that requires a password entry often leaves copies of the unencrypted passwords on the hard drive, either in temporary files or swap space, making them easy to find. Private keys are typically 1024 bits long, but are protected online by encrypting them with a human password that is usually easy to remember (or else it would be written down). Recent studies have shown that identifying an encrypted public key on a hard drive is relatively straightforward, because it has such a high level of entropy (high randomness) relative to other data. If a system with a private key on the hard drive is compromised, it must be assumed that a motivated attacker will be able to locate and decrypt the private key and would then be able to masquerade as the key holder.

Even if a workstation is not physically compromised, remote attacks are not difficult. If the system has an exploitable remote control application on it — either a legitimate one like PCAnywhere that might be poorly configured, or an overtly hostile backdoor application such as NetBus — then an attacker can capture the legitimate user's password. Once the attacker has a user's password, if the private key is accessible through software, the remote control attacker can create a message or document and sign it with the victim's private key, effectively appropriating their identity. A virus named Caligula is designed to steal encrypted keys from infected systems using PGP Mail, copying them back out to a site on the Internet where potential attackers can download them and attempt to decrypt them. Because software-based keys are so easily compromised, they should only be used for relatively low assurance applications, like routine business and personal mail. Legal and commercial transactions should be signed with a key stored in a protected and removable hardware device.

CREATING RELIABLE ENCRYPTION IS DIFFICULT

As should be clear from the wide variety of attacks, creating and using encryption is fraught with danger. Unsuccessful cryptosystems typically fail in one of four areas.

Algorithm Development

Modern encryption techniques derive their strength from having so many possible keys that a brute-force attack is infeasible. The key space (i.e., the potential population of keys) is a function of key size. A robust encryption implementation should not be breakable by exploiting weaknesses in the algorithm, which is the complex formula of transpositions and substitutions used to perform the data transformation. When designing algorithms, cryptologists assume that not only the algorithm, but even the encryption engine source code will be known to anyone attempting to break encrypted data. This represents a radical change from pre-computing era cryptography, in which the mechanics of the encryption engines were jealously guarded. The success of the American forces over the Japanese at the battle of Midway was facilitated by knowledge of the Japanese naval deployment, allowing American aviators to attack the larger Japanese fleet at the maximum possible range. American cryptanalysts had reverse-engineered the Japanese encryption machines, making it feasible to break their enciphered transmissions.

Suitable encryption algorithms are notoriously difficult to create. Even the best developers have had spectacular failures. History has shown that the creation and thorough testing of new encryption algorithms requires a team of highly qualified cryptologists. Experience has also shown that proprietary encryption techniques, which are common on PCs, usually fail when subjected to rigorous attack. At best, only a few thousand specialists can claim suitable expertise in the esoteric world of cryptology. Meanwhile, millions of Internet users need access to strong cryptologic technology. The only safe choice for the layperson is to choose encryption products based on standard algorithms that are widely recognized by experts as being appropriately resistant to cryptanalytic attack.

> Even worse, it doesn't do any good to have a bunch of random people examine the code; the only way to tell good cryptography from bad cryptography is to have it examined by experts. Analyzing cryptography is hard, and there are very few people in the world who can do it competently. Before an algorithm can really be considered secure, it needs to be examined by many experts over the course of years.
>
> — Bruce Schneier, CRYPTO-GRAM, September 15, 1999

Implementation

Creation of a robust encryption algorithm is just the first challenge in the development of an encryption product. The algorithm must be carefully implemented in hardware or software so that it performs correctly and is practical to use. Even when an algorithm is correctly implemented, the overall system security posture may be weakened by some other factor. Key generation is a weak spot. If an attacker discovers a pattern in key generation, it effectively reduces the total population of possible keys and greatly reduces the strength of the implementation. A recent example was the failure of one of the original implementations of Netscape's SSL, which used a predictable time-based technique for random number generation. When subjected to statistical analysis, few man-made devices can provide sufficiently random output.

Deplomyment

Lack of necessary encryption, due to a delayed or cancelled program, can cause as much damage as the use of a flawed system. For a cryptosystem to be successful, the chosen products must be provided to everyone who will be expected to use them.

Operation

Experience constantly demonstrates that people are the biggest concern, not technology. A successful encryption project requires clearly stated goals, which are formally referred to as policies, and clearly delineated user instructions or procedures. Highly sophisticated encryption projects, such as public key infrastructures, require detailed operational documents such as practice statements. Using encryption to meet organizational goals requires constant administrative vigilance over infrastructure and use of keys. Encryption technology will fail without user cooperation.

It turns out that the threat model commonly used by cryptosystem designers was wrong: most frauds were not caused by cryptanalysis or other technical attacks, but by implementation errors and management failures. This suggests that a paradigm shift is overdue in computer security; we look at some of the alternatives, and see some signs that this shift may be getting under way.

— Ross Anderson, "Why Cryptosystems Fail"
A United Kingdom-based study of failure modes
of encryption in banking applications

TYPES OF ENCRYPTION

Two basic types of encryption are used: symmetric and asymmetric. The traditional form is symmetric, in which a single secret key is used for both encryption and decryption. Asymmetric encryption uses a pair of mathematically related keys, commonly called the private key and the public key. It is not computationally feasible to derive the matching private key using the encrypted data and the public key. Public key encryption is the enabler for a wide variety of electronic transactions and is crucial for the implementation of E-commerce.

Symmetric Encryption

A symmetric algorithm is one that uses the same key for encryption and decryption. Symmetric algorithms are fast and relatively simple to implement. The primary disadvantage in using secret key encryption is actually keeping the key secret. In multi-party transactions, some secure mechanism is necessary in order to share or distribute the key so that only the appropriate parties have access to the secret key. Exhibit 17-1 lists the most common symmetric algorithms, all of which have proven acceptably resistant to cyryptanalytic attack in their current implementation.

Asymmetric (Public Key) Encryption

The concept of public key encryption represented a revolution in the applicability of computer-based security in 1976 when it was introduced in a journal article by Whitfield Diffie and Martin Hellman. This was quickly followed in 1978 with a practical implementation. Developed by Ron Rivest, Adi Shamir, and Len Adelman, their "RSA" scheme is still the only public key encryption algorithm in widespread use. Public key encryption uses one simple but powerful concept to enable an extraordinary variety of online trusted transactions: one party can verify that a second party holds a specific secret without having to know what that secret is. It is impossible to imagine what E-commerce would be without it. Many transaction types would be impossible or hopelessly difficult. Unlike secret key encryption, asymmetric encryption uses two keys, either one of which can be used to decrypt ciphertext encrypted with the corresponding key. In practice, one

Exhibit 17-1. Common symmetric algorithms.

Algorithm	Developer	Key Size (bits)	Characteristics
DES	IBM under U.S. government contract	56	Adopted as a U.S. federal standard in 1976 Most widely implemented encryption algorithm Increasing concern over resistance to brute-force attack
3DES	3 sequential applications of DES	112	Slow
IDEA	Developed in Switzerland by Xuejia Lai and James Massey	128	Published in 1991 Widely used in PGP Must be licensed for commercial use
Blowfish	Bruce Schneier	Up to 448	Published in 1993 Fast, compact, and flexible

key is referred to as the secret key, and is carefully protected by its owner, while the matching public key can be freely distributed. Data encrypted with the public key can only be decrypted by the holder of the private key. Likewise, if ciphertext can be successfully decrypted using the public key, it is proof that whoever encrypted the message used a specific private key.

Like symmetric algorithms, public key encryption implementations do not rely on the obscurity of their algorithm, but use key lengths that are so long that a brute-force attack is impossible. Asymmetric encryption keys are based on prime numbers, which limits the population of numbers that can be used as keys. To make it impractical for an attacker to derive the private key, even when ciphertext and the public key are known, RSA key length of 1024 bits has become the standard practice. This is roughly equivalent to an 80-bit symmetric key in resistance to a brute-force attack. Not only does public key encryption require a much longer key than symmetric encryption, it is also exponentially slower. It is so time-consuming that it is usually not practical to encrypt an entire data object. Instead, a one-time session key is randomly generated and used to encrypt the object with an efficient secret key algorithm. The asymmetric algorithm and the recipient's public key are then used to encrypt the session key so that it can only be decrypted with the recipient's private key.

Only a few asymmetric algorithms are in common use today. The Whitfield-Diffie algorithm is used for secure key exchange, and the digital signature algorithm (DSA) is used only for digital signature. Only two algorithms are currently used for encryption; RSA is by far the most widespread. *Elliptic curve* is a newer form of public key encryption that uses smaller key lengths and is less computationally intensive. This makes it ideal for smart cards, which have relatively slow processors. Because it is newer, and based on unproven mathematical concepts, elliptic curve encryption is sometimes considered riskier than RSA encryption. It is important to understand that RSA encryption, while apparently remaining unbroken in 20 years of use, has not been mathematically proven secure either. It is based on the intuitive belief that the process of factoring very large numbers cannot be simplified. Minor improvements in factoring, such as a technique called Quadratic Sieve, encouraged the increase in typical RSA key length from 512 to 1024 bits. A mathematical or technological breakthrough in factoring is unlikely, but it would quickly obsolete systems based on RSA technology.

Additional Cryptography Types

A hash algorithm is a one-way cryptographic function. When applied to a data object, it outputs a fixed-size output, often called a message digest. It is conceptually similar to a checksum, but is much more difficult to corrupt. To provide a tamper-proof fingerprint of a data object, it must be impossible to derive any information about the original object from its message digest. If the original data is altered and the hash algorithm is reapplied, the new message digest must provide no clue as to what the change in the data was. In other words, even a 1-bit change in the data must result in a dramatically different hash value.

The most widely used secure hash algorithm is MD5, published by Ron Rivest in 1992. Some authorities expect it to be obsolete shortly, suggesting that developments in computational speed might already have rendered it inadequate. SHA-1 outputs a longer hash than MD5. The U.S. federal government is promulgating SHA-1, and it is becoming increasingly common in commercial applications.

Steganography is the practice of hiding data. This differs from encryption, which makes intercepted data unusable, but does not attempt to conceal its presence. While most forms of security do not protect data by hiding it, the mere fact that someone has taken the trouble to encrypt it indicates that the data is probably valuable. The owner may prefer not to advertise the fact that sensitive data even exists. Traditional forms of steganography include invisible ink and microdots; cryptographic steganography uses data transformation routines to hide information within some other digital data.

Multimedia objects, such as bitmaps and audio or video files, are the traditional hiding places, although a steganographic file system was recently announced. Multimedia files are relatively large compared to textual documents, and quite a few bits can be changed without making differences that are discernable to human senses. As an example, this chapter can easily be secreted within a true color photograph suitable as a 1024 × 768 screen background. The desired storage object must be both large enough and complex enough to allow the data object to be hidden within it without making detectable changes to the appearance or sound of the object. This is an implementation issue; a secure steganography utility must evaluate the suitability of a storage object before allowing the transformation to occur. An object containing data secreted within it will have a different hash value than the original, but current implementations of steganography do not allow a direct human comparison between the original and modified file to show any detectible visual or audio changes.

While there are legitimate applications for cryptographic steganography, it is certainly a concern for corporations trying to control the outflow of proprietary data and for computer forensic investigators. Research is being conducted on techniques to identify the existence of steganographically hidden data, based on the hypotheses that specific steganography utilities leave characteristic patterns, or fingerprints. Most steganography utilities also provide an encryption option, so finding the hidden data does not mean that its confidentiality is immediately violated.

Digital watermarking is a communication security mechanism used to identify the source of a bitmap. It is most often used to protect intellectual property rights by allowing the owner of a multimedia object to prove that they were the original owners or creators of the object. Watermarking is similar to digital steganographic techniques in that the coded data is hidden in the least significant bits of some larger object.

CRYPTOGRAPHIC SERVICES

The most obvious use of encryption is to provide privacy, or confidentiality. Privacy can be applied in several contexts, depending on the specific protection needs of the data. Messages can be encrypted to provide protection from sniffing while being transmitted over a LAN or over the Internet. Encryption can also be used to protect the confidentiality of stored data that might be physically accessed by unauthorized parties.

Identification is accomplished in one of three ways, sometimes referred to as (1) something you know, (2) something you have, and (3) something you are. "Something you are" refers to biometric mechanisms, which are beyond the scope of this chapter, but the other two identification mechanisms are facilitated through encryption.

Passwords and passphrases are examples of "something you know" and they are normally protected cryptographically. The best practice is not to actually store phrases or passwords themselves, but to store their hash values. Each hash value has the same length, so they provide no clue as to the content or characteristics of the passphrase. The hash values can be further obfuscated through use of a *salt* value. On UNIX systems, for example, the first two letters of the user name are used as salt as part of the DE-based hash routine. The result is that different logins that happen to have the same password will be associated with different hash values, which greatly complicates brute-force attacks.

Encryption keys can also serve as "something you have." This can be done with either symmetric or asymmetric algorithms. If two people share a secret key, and one of them encrypts a known value, they can recognize the other as being the only one who can provide the same encrypted result. In practice, public key-based identification systems scale much better, and are becoming increasingly common. Identification keys are stored on magnetic media or within a smart card. Usually, they are encrypted themselves and must be unlocked by the entry of a PIN, password, or passphrase by their owner before they can be accessed.

Integrity is provided by hashing a document to create a message digest. The integrity of the object can be verified by deriving the hash sum again, and comparing that value to the original. This simple application of a cryptographic hash algorithm is useful only when the hash value is protected from change. In a transaction in which an object is transmitted from one party to another, simply tacking a message digest onto the end of the object is insufficient — the recipient would have no assurance that the original document had not been modified and a matching new message digest included.

Authorship and Integrity assurance is provided cryptographically by digital signature. To digitally sign a document using RSA encryption, a hash value of the original document is calculated, which the signer then encrypts with their private key. The digital signature can be verified by decrypting the signature value with the signer's public key, and comparing the result to the hash value of the object. If the values do not match, the original object is no longer intact or the public and private keys do not match; in either case, the validation fails. Even if proof of authorship is not a requirement, digital signature is a practical integrity assurance mechanism because it protects the message digest by encrypting it with the signer's public key.

Digital signature provides a high level of assurance that a specific private key was used to sign a document, but it cannot provide any assurance that the purported owner of that private key actually performed the signature operation. The appropriate level of trust for any particular digitally signed object is provided through organizational procedures that are based on formal written policy. Any organization using digital signature must determine what level of systemic rigor is necessary when signing and verifying objects. Because the signature itself can only prove which key was used to sign the document, but not who actually wielded that key, signature keys must be protected by authentication mechanisms. It is useless to verify a digital signature without having an acceptable level of trust that the public key actually belongs to the purported sender. Manual sharing of public keys is one way to be certain of their origin, but it is not practical for more than a few dozen correspondents. A third-party authentication service is the only practical way to support the trust needs of even a moderately sized organization, let alone the entire Internet.

A digital certificate provides third-party verification of the identity of a key holder. It takes the form of the keyholder's public key signed by the private key of a Certificate Authority (CA). This powerful concept makes it feasible to verify a digitally signed object sent by an unknown correspondent. The CA vouches for the identity of the certificate holder, and anyone with a trusted copy of the CA's public key can validate an individual's digital certificate. Once the authenticity of a certificate has been confirmed, the public key it contains can be used to validate the digital signature on an object from the certificate holder. E-mail applications that support digital signature and public key-based encryption typically include the sender's digital certificate whenever sending a message with a signed or encrypted object, making it easy for the sender to verify the message contents.

A Certificate Revocation List (CRL) is periodically published by some CAs to increase the level of trust associated with their certificates. Although digital certificates include an expiration date, it is often desirable to be able to cancel a certificate before it has expired. If a private key is compromised, a user account is cancelled, or a certificate holder is provided with a replacement certificate, then the original certificate is obsolete. Listing it on a CRL allows the CA to notify verifiers that the certificate issuer no longer considers it a valid certificate. CRLs increase the implementation and administration costs of a CA. Clients must access the revocation list over a network during verification, which increases the time required to validate a signature. Verification is impossible if the network or revocation list server is unavailable. Although their use can significantly increase the level of assurance provided by digital certificates, revocation implementations are rare.

It is not always practical to provide a digital certificate with every signed object, and high-assurance CAs need a CRL server. Directory service is a distributed database optimized for reading that can make both CRLs and certificates available on a wide area network (WAN) or the Internet. Most directory services are based on the X.500 standard and use the extensible format X.509 to store digital certificates.

Public key infrastructure (PKI) refers to the total system installed by an organization to support the distribution and use of digital certificates. A PKI encompasses both infrastructure and organizational process. Examples of organizational control mechanisms include certificate policies (CP) specifying the exact levels of assurance necessary for specific types of information, and practice statements specifying the mechanisms and procedures that will provide it. A PKI can provide any arbitrary level of assurance, based on the rigor of the authentication mechanisms and practices. The more effort an organization uses to verify a certificate applicant's identity, and the more secure the mechanisms used to protect that certificate holder's private key, the more trust that can be placed in an object signed by that certificate holder. Higher trust exacts a higher cost, so PKIs typically define a hierarchy of certificate trust levels allowing an optimal trade-off between efficiency and assurance.

Transactional Roles (Witnessing)

Commerce and law rely on a variety of transactions. Over thousands of years of civilization, conventions have been devised to provide the parties to these transactions with acceptable levels of assurance. The same transactions are desirable in the digital realm, but mechanisms requiring that a human mark a specific piece of paper need virtual replacements. Fortunately, trust can be increased using witnessing services that are enabled through public key encryption.

Nonrepudiation describes protection against the disavowal of a transaction by its initiator. Digital signature provides nonrepudiation by making it impossible for the owner of a private key to deny that his key was used to sign a specific object. The key holder can still claim that his private key had been stolen — the level of trust appropriate for any electronically signed document is dependent on the certificate policy. For example, a weak certificate policy may not require any authentication during the certificate request, making it relatively easy to steal someone's identity by obtaining a certificate in his or her name. A CP that requires a more robust vetting process before issuing a certificate, with private keys that can only be accessed through strong authentication mechanisms (such as biometrics), decreases the potential that a signer will repudiate a document.

A digital notary is a trusted third party that provides document signature authentication. The originator digitally signs a document and then registers it with a digital notary, who also signs it and then forwards it the final recipient. The recipient of a digitally notarized document verifies the signature of the notary, not the originator. A digital notary can follow much more stringent practices than is practical for an individual, and might also offer some form of monetary guarantee for documents that it notarizes. The slight inconvenience and cost of utilizing a digital notary allows a document originator to provide a higher level of assurance than they would be able to without using a trusted third party.

Timestamping is a transactional service that can be offered along with notarization, or it might be offered by an automated timestamp service that is both lower cost and lower assurance than a full notarization service. A timestamp service is a trusted third party guaranteeing the accuracy of their timestamps. Witnessing is desirable for digital object time verification because computer clocks are untrustworthy and easily manipulated through both hardware and software. Like a digitally notarized document, a timestamped document is digitally signed with the private key of the verification service and then forwarded to the recipient. Applications suitable for timestamping include employee or consultant digital time cards, performance data for service level agreements, telemetry or test data registration, and proposal submission.

Key exchange is a process in which two parties agree on a secret key known only to themselves. Some form of key exchange protocol is required in many forms of secure network connectivity, such as the initiation of a virtual private network connection. The Whitfield-Diffie algorithm is an especially convenient key exchange technique because it allows two parties to securely agree on a secret session key without having any prior relationship or need for a certificate infrastructure.

Key Recovery

Clashes between civil libertarians and the U.S. federal government have generated negative publicity on the subject of key escrow. Security practitioners should not let this political debate distract them from understanding that organizations have a legitimate need to protect their own data. Just as employers routinely keep extra keys to employee offices, desks, and safes, they are justified in their concern over digital keys. Very few organizations can afford to allow a single individual to exercise sole control over valuable corporate information. Key recovery is never required for data transmission keys because lost data can be immediately resent. However, if someone with the only key to stored encrypted data resigns is unavailable, or loses his key, then the organization loses that data permanently. Key recovery describes the ability to decrypt data without the permission or assistance of its owner. Organizations that use encryption to protect the privacy of stored data must understand the risk of key loss; and if key loss is unacceptable, their encryption policy should mandate key recovery or backup capabilities.

PUTTING IT INTO PRACTICE

Exhibit 17-2 provides an example process using both secret and public key cryptography to digitally sign and encrypt a message. Contemporary public key-based systems, such as e-mail and file encryption products, are complex hybrids using symmetric algorithms for privacy and the RSA public key algorithm to securely exchange keys. A hashing algorithm and the RSA public key algorithm provide digital signature. Starting in this case

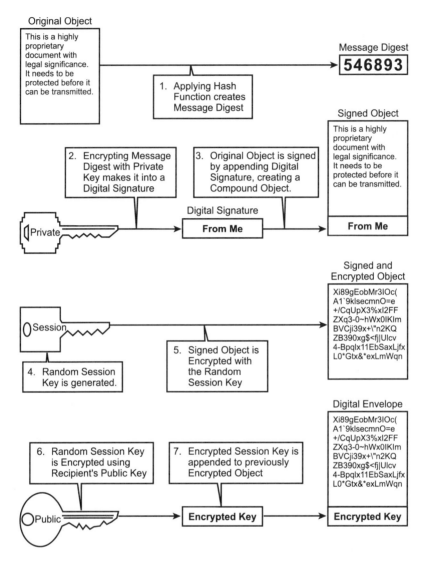

Exhibit 17-2. Using public key encryption to protect an object.

with a text file, the first step is to apply a cryptographic hash function to create a message digest (1). To protect this message digest from manipulation, and to turn it into a digital signature, it is encrypted with the private key of the signer (2). The signer's public key is highly sensitive stored information, and it must be protected with some sort of authentication mechanism. At a minimum, the key owner must enter a password to access the key. (While this is the most common protective mechanism for private keys, it is by far the weakest link in this entire multi-step process). After creating the digital signature, it is concatenated onto the original file, creating a signed object (3). In practice, a compound object like this normally has additional fields, such as information on the hash algorithm used, and possibly the digital certificate of the signer. At this point, the original object has been turned into a digitally signed object, suitable for transmission. This is effectively an unsealed digital envelope. If privacy is required, the original object and the digital signature must be encrypted.

Although it would be possible to encrypt the signed object using a public key algorithm, this would be extremely slow, and it would limit the potential distribution of the encrypted object. To increase efficiency and provide destination flexibility, the object is encrypted using a secret key algorithm. First, a one-time random session key is generated (4). The signed object is encrypted with a symmetric algorithm, using this session key as the secret key (5). Then the session key, which is relatively small, is encrypted using the public key of the recipient (6). In systems based on RSA algorithms, users normally have two pairs of public and private keys: one pair is used for digital signature and the other is used for session key encryption. If the object is going to be sent to multiple recipients, copies of the session key will be encrypted with each of their public keys. If the message is meant to be stored, one of the keys could be associated with a key recovery system or it might be encrypted for the supervisor of the signer. All of the encrypted copies of the session key are appended onto the encrypted object, effectively creating a sealed digital envelope. Again, in practice, this compound object is in a standardized format that includes information on the encryption algorithms, and mapping information between encrypted session keys and some sort of user identifier is included. A digital envelope standard from RSA called PKCS #7 is widely used. It can serve as either an unsealed (signed but not encrypted) or sealed (signed and encrypted) digital envelope.

The processes are reversed by the recipient. As shown in Exhibit 17-3, the encrypted session key must be decrypted using the recipient's private key (2) (which should be stored in encrypted form and accessed with a password). The decrypted session key is used to decrypt the data portion of the digital envelope (3), providing a new object consisting of the original data and a digital signature. Verification of the digital signature is a three-step process. First, a message digest is derived by performing a hash function on the original data object (5). Then the digital signature is decrypted using the signer's public key. If the decrypted digital signature does not have the same value as the computed hash value, then either the original object has been changed, or the public key used to verify the signature does not match the private key used to sign the object.

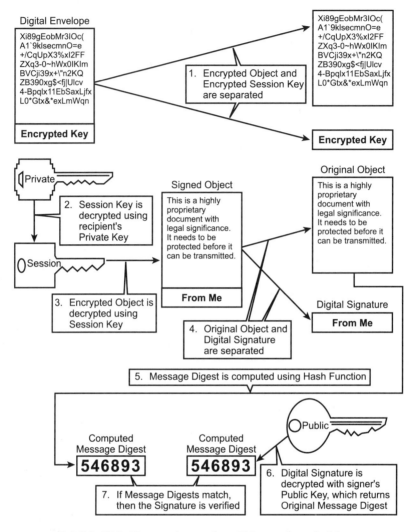

Exhibit 17-3. Decrypting and verifying a signed object.

CONCLUSION

This chapter is just a brief introduction to a fascinating and complex subject. Familiarity with encryption concepts has become mandatory for those seeking a career involving Internet technology (see Exhibit 17-4). Many online and printed resources are available to provide more detailed information on encryption technology and application. The "Annotated Bibliography" contains suggestions for readers interested in a more in-depth approach to this subject.

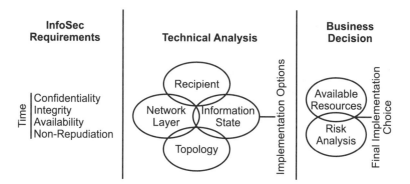

Exhibit 17-4. Encryption concepts.

Annotated Bibliography

Printed References

1. Dan and Lim, Eds., *Cryptography's Role in Securing the Information Society,* National Research Council. Although somewhat dated, this contains useful information not found in other sources on how specific industries apply encryption.
2. Diffie, W. and Hellman, M., New Directions in Cryptography, *IEEE Transactions on Information Theory,* November 1976. This is the first article on public key encryption to appear in an unclassified publication.
3. Kahn, David, *The Codebreakers; The Comprehensive History of Secret Communication from Ancient Times to the Internet.* Kahn's original 1969 tome was recently updated. It is an exhaustive reference that is considered the most authoritative historical guide to cryptography.
4. Marks, Leo, *Between Silk and Cyanide: A Codemaker's War 1941–1945.* A personal biography of a WWII British cryptographer. An entertaining book that should make crystal clear the importance of following proper procedures and maintaining good hygiene. The electronic cryptographic infrastructure can be broken down just like the manual infrastructure used in WWII for military and intelligence traffic. It dramatizes the dangers in making decisions about the use of encryption without properly understanding how it can be broken down.
5. Schneier, Bruce, *Applied Cryptography,* 2nd edition. Everyone involved in encryption in any fashion must have a copy of this comprehensive text. Schneier is brilliant not only in making complex mathematics accessible to the layperson, but he also has a tremendous grasp on the trust issues and the human social conventions replicated cryptographically in the virtual world.
6. Smith, Richard, *Internet Cryptography.* A basic text intended for non-programmers.
7. Stallings, William, *Cryptography and Network Security: Principles and Practice.* A comprehensive college textbook.

Online References

1. Anderson, Ross, Why Cryptosystems Fail, http://www.cl.cam.ac.uk/users/rja14/wcf.html.
2. Schneier, Bruce, Security Pitfalls in Cryptography, http://www.counterpane.com/pitfalls.html.
3. Schneier, Bruce, Why Cryptography Is Harder Than It Looks, http://www.counterpane.com/whycrypto.html.

4. PKCS documentation, http://www.rsa.com/rsalabs/pubs/PKCS/.

5. Ellis, J., The Story of Non-decret Encryption, CESG Report, 1987, http://www.cesg.gov.uk/ellisint.htm.

6. Johnson, N., Steganography, http://patriot.net/~johnson/html/neil/stegdoc/stegdoc.html, 1997.

7. M. Blaze, W. Diffie, R. Rivest, B. Schneier, T. Shimomura, E. Thompson, and M. Weiner, Minimal Key Lengths for Symmetric Ciphers to Provide Adequate Commercial Security, http://www.counterpane.com/keylength.html.

Chapter 18
Three New Models for the Application of Cryptography

Jay Heiser

APPLYING ENCRYPTION IS NOT EASY. False confidence placed in improperly applied security mechanisms can leave an organization at greater risk than before the flawed encryption project was started. It is also possible to err in the opposite direction. Overbuilt security systems cost too much money up-front, and the ongoing expense from unneeded maintenance and lost productivity continues forever. To help avoid costly misapplications of security technology, this chapter provides guidance in matching encryption implementations to security requirements. It assumes a basic understanding of cryptological concepts, and is intended for security officers, programmers, network integrators, system managers, Web architects, and other technology decision-makers involved with the creation of secure systems.

INTRODUCTION

The growing reliance on the Internet is increasing the demand for well-informed staff capable of building and managing security architectures. It is not just E-commerce that is generating a demand for encryption expertise. Personal e-mail needs to be protected, and employees demand secure remote access to their offices. Corporations hope to increase their productivity — without increasing risk — by electronically linking themselves to their business partners. Unfortunately, eager technologists have a tendency to purchase and install security products without fully understanding how those products address their security exposures. Because of the high cost of a security failure, requirements analysis and careful planning are crucial to the success of a system that relies on cryptological services. This chapter presents four different models, each providing a different understanding of the effective application of encryption technology. Descriptive models like these are devices that isolate salient aspects of the systems being analyzed. By artificially simplifying complex reality, the insight they provide helps match security and application requirements to appropriate encryption-based security architectures.

The first model analyzes how encryption implementations accommodate the needs of the encrypted data's recipient. The relationship between the encrypter and the decrypter has significant ramifications, both for the choice of technology and for the cryptographic services used. The second model describes how encryption applications differ based on their logical network layer. The choice of available encryption services varies from network layer to network layer. Somewhat less obviously, choice of network layer also affects who within the organization controls the encryption process. The third encryption application model is topological. It illustrates concepts usually described with terms such as end-to-end, host-to-host, and link-to-link. It provides an understanding of the scope of protection that can be provided when different devices within the network topology perform encryption. The final model is based on the operational state of data. The number of operational states in which data is cryptographically protected varies, depending on the form of encryption service chosen.

BUSINESS ANALYSIS

Before these descriptive models can be successfully applied, the data security requirements must be analyzed and defined. One of the classic disputes within the information security community is over the accuracy of quantitative risk analysis. Neither side disagrees that some form of numeric risk analysis providing an absolute measure of security posture would be desirable, and neither side disputes that choice of security countermeasures would be facilitated by an accounting analysis which could provide return on investment or at least a break-even analysis. The issue of contention is whether it is actually possible to quantify security implementations, given that human behavior can be quite random and very little data is available. Whether or not an individual prefers a quantitative or a qualitative analysis, some form of analysis must be performed to provide guidance on the appropriate resource expenditure for security countermeasures. It is not the purpose of this chapter to introduce the subject of risk management; however, a security architecture can only be optimized when the developer has a clear understanding of the security requirements of the data that requires protection.

The Data Criticality Matrix is helpful in comprehending and prioritizing an organization's information asset security categories. Exhibit 18-1 shows

Exhibit 18-1. Data Criticality Matrix.

	Confidentiality	Integrity	Availability	Nonrepudiation	Lifetime
Public Web page	Low	High	High	Low	NA
Unreleased earnings data	High	High	Medium	Low	2 weeks
Accounts receivable	High	High	Medium	High	5 years
Employee medical records	High	High	Low	Low	80 years

an example analysis for a corporation. This matrix includes five security requirements. The widely used CIA requirements of Confidentiality, Integrity, and Availability are supplemented with two additional requirements: Nonrepudiation and Time. The term "nonrepudiation" refers to the ability to prevent the denial of a transaction. If a firm submits a purchase order but then refuses to honor the purchase, claiming no knowledge of the original transaction, then the firm has repudiated it. In addition to privacy services, cryptography may be required to provide nonrepudiation services. The models in this chapter illustrate encryption options that include both services. The time requirements for data protection are important both in choosing appropriately strong encryption, and in ensuring that data is never left unprotected while it has value. This particular Data Criticality Matrix presents a simplified view of the lifetime requirement; in some cases, it may be useful to assign a specific lifetime to each of the first four security requirements, instead of assuming that confidentiality, integrity, availability, and nonrepudiation all must be supported to the same degree over the same period of time. Note that availability is usually not a service provided by encryption, although encryption applications have the potential to negatively affect availability. Encryption rarely improves availability, but if mission-critical encryption services fail, then availability requirements probably will not be met. (Use of a cryptographically based strong authentication system to prevent denial-of-service attacks would be an example of using encryption to increase availability.)

An economic analysis cannot be complete without an understanding of the available resources. Insufficient funds, lack of internal support, or poor staff skills can prevent the successful achievement of any project. While the four models below can be used to develop an ideal security architecture, they can also facilitate an understanding of the security ramifications of a resource-constrained project.

	Personal Encryption	**Workgroup Encryption**	**Transaction Encryption**
Recipient	Data Owner	Co-workers	Strangers
Concern	Privacy	Privacy	Establishment and Maintenance of Trust
Technical Concerns	Speed and Transparency	Speed and Transparency	Interoperability

Exhibit 18-2. Recipient model.

RECIPIENT MODEL

The choice of cryptographic function and implementation is driven by the relationship between the originator and the recipient. The recipient is the party — an individual, multiple individuals, or an organizational entity — consuming data that has cryptological services applied to it. The simplified diagram in Exhibit 18-2 presents three possible choices of recipient. In reality, the recipient model is a spectrum, encompassing everything from a well-known recipient to a recipient with no prior relationship to the originator. The recipient model provides guidance when choosing between an open standard product and a closed proprietary product, and it provides insight into the specific cryptographic services that will be needed.

Personal encryption is the use of cryptographic services on an individual basis, without the expectation of maintaining cryptographic protection when sharing data. Someone encrypting data for his own personal use has completely different priorities than someone encrypting data for others. In most cases, that someone is using personal encryption to maintain the confidentiality of data that is at risk of being physically accessed — especially on a laptop. In a corporate setting, personal encryption is legitimately used on workstations to provide an additional level of privacy beyond what can be provided by an operating environment's access controls — which can always be circumvented by an administrator. Personal encryption might also be used by corporate employees trying to hide data they are not authorized to have, and criminals concerned about law enforcement searches also use personal encryption. While individuals might want to use digital signature to provide assurance that they did indeed sign their own documents — especially if they have a high number of them — this use is rare. Increasingly, digital signature is used as an integrity control, even for files originated and stored locally. While few individuals currently use digital signature to protect files on their own workstation or laptop, the increasing proliferation of hostile code could make this use of personal encryption routine. Maintaining the confidentiality of personal information is the usual intent of individual encryption, but the technical concerns remain the same for any use of personal encryption. Individuals encrypting data for themselves place a high priority on speed and ease of use. Laptop users typically encrypt the entire hard drive, using an encryption product transparent to applications and almost transparent to users, requiring only the entry of a password at the start of a session. Standards and interoperability are not important for personal encryption, although use of unproven proprietary encryption algorithms should be avoided.

Workgroup encryption is the use of cryptological services to meet the confidentiality needs of a group of people who know each other personally and share data. As in the case of the individual, the group might be concerned that sensitive data is at risk of inappropriate viewing by system administrators. Encryption can even be used to implement a form of access control — everyone given a password has access to the encrypted data, but nobody else does. If the workgroup shares data but does not have a common server, encryption can help them share that data without having to rely on distributed access controls. The most significant issue with workgroup encryption is managing it. If the data has a long life, it is likely that the membership of the workgroup will change. New members need access to existing data, and members leaving the group may no longer be authorized for access after leaving. Constantly decrypting and reencrypting large amounts of data and then passing out new keys is inefficient. For a short-term project, it is feasible for group members to agree on a common secret key and use it to access sensitive data for the project duration. Groups and data with a longer life might find it easier to use an encryption system built on a session key that can be encrypted in turn with each group member's public key. Whether it is based on secret or public key encryption, workgroup encryption is similar to personal encryption, having the advantage of not being concerned with open standards or multivendor compatibility. Interoperability is provided by choosing a single product for all group members, either a stand-alone encryption utility, an application with encryption capabilities, or an operating environment with security services. Trust is a function of organizational and group membership and personal relationships. Because all the members of a workgroup are personally acquainted, no special digital efforts need be provided to enhance the level of trust.

Transactional encryption describes the use of cryptological services to protect data between originators and recipients who do not have a personal relationship capable of providing trust. It facilitates electronic transactions between unknown parties; E-commerce and Web storefronts are completely dependent on it. While confidentiality may be important, in many transactions the ability to establish identity and prevent repudiation is even more significant. To accept a transaction, the recipient must have an appropriate level of trust that the purported sender is the actual sender. The recipient must also have an appropriate level of confidence that the sender will not deny having initiated the transaction. Likewise, the sender often requires a level of assurance that the recipient cannot later deny having accepted it. If the value of the transaction is high, some form of nonrepudiation service may be necessary. Other cryptographic services that can be provided to increase the level of confidence include timestamp and digital notary service. Authentication mechanisms and nonrepudiation controls are all electronic attempts to replace human assurance mechanisms that are impossible, impractical, or easily subverted in a digital world. The technical characteristic distinguishing transactional encryption from workgroup or personal encryption is the significance of interoperability. Because the parties of a transaction often belong to different organizations and may not be controlled by the same authority, proprietary products cannot be used. The parties of the transaction might be using different platforms, and might have different applications to generate and process their transactions. Transactional encryption depends on the use of standards to provide interoperability. Not only must standard encryption algorithms be used, but they must be supported with standard data formats such as PKCS#7 and X.509.

NETWORK LAYER MODEL

The OSI seven-layer reference model is widely used to explain the hierarchical nature of network implementations. Services operating at a specific network layer communicate with corresponding services at the same layer through a network protocol. Services within a network stack communicate with higher and lower level services through interprocess communication mechanisms exposed to programmers as APIs. No actual network represents a pure implementation of the OSI seven-layer model, but every network has a hierarchical set of services that are effectively a subset of that model. Encryption services can be provided in any of the seven network layers, each with its own advantages and disadvantages. Use of the seven-layer model to describe existing network protocol stacks that grew up organically is more than a little subjective. Over the years, the mapping of the Internet protocol set into the model has slowly but surely changed. Today, it is accepted that the IP layer maps to the OSI network layer, and the TCP protocol maps to the OSI transport layer, although this understanding of exact correspondence is not universal. Likewise, the assignment of specific encryption protocols and services to specific network layers is somewhat arbitrary. The importance of this model to security

OSI Layer	Internet Protocol	Crypto Protocol	Crypto Function	Controlled by
Application	HTML	SET	Non-Repudiation / Integrity / Authentication / Privacy	Programmer
Presentation	MIME	S-MIME		User
		S-HTTP		
Session	HTTP	SSL		Webmaster
Transport	TCP	Proprietary VPNs		Network Administrator
Network	IP	IPSec		
Datalink	802.2	L2TP PPTP L2F		
Physical	Ethernet	Spread Spectrum		

Granularity ↑ / Transparency ↓

Exhibit 18-3. OSI model.

practitioners is in understanding how relative position within the network hierarchy affects the characteristics of cryptographic services. As illustrated in Exhibit 18-3, the higher up within the network hierarchy encryption is applied, the more granular its ability to access objects can be. The lower down encryption is provided, the greater the number of upper layer services that can transparently take advantage of it. Greater granularity means that upper layer encryption can offer more cryptographic functions. Services based on digital signature can only be provided in the upper layers. A simplified version of this layered model can be used to analyze a non-network environment. For the purposes of this discussion, stand-alone hosts are considered to have four layers: physical, session, presentation, and application.

The physical layer is the lowest layer, the silicon foundation upon which the entire network stack rests. Actually, providing encryption services at the physical layer is quite rare. In a network environment, several secure LANs have been developed using specialized Ethernet cards that perform encryption. Most of these systems actually operate at the data-link layer. Several specialized systems have been built for the defense and intelligence market that could possibly be considered to operate at the physical layer, but these systems are not found in the commercial market. The only common form of physical network layer encryption is spread spectrum, which scrambles transmissions across a wide range of constantly changing frequencies. Physical layer encryption products have been developed for stand-alone systems to protect the hard drive. The advantage of such a system is that it provides very high performance and is very difficult to circumvent. Furthermore, because it mimics the standard hardware interfaces, it is completely transparent to all system software and applications. Physical layer security is under control of the hardware administrator.

A great deal of development work is being done today at both the data-link and the network layer. Because they provide interoperability between hosts and network elements, and are completely transparent to network-based applications, these two layers are used for the implementation of VPNs. The data-link layer is used to support L2TP, PPTP, and L2F. Although many popular implementations of these link layer security services actually take advantage of the IPSec transport mode, the model still treats them as link layer services because they are providing interfaces at that layer. A major advantage of the link layer is that a single encryption service can support multiple transport protocols. For example, VPNs providing an interface at this layer can support TCP/IP and SPX/IPX traffic simultaneously. Organizations running both Novell and Internet protocols can use a single VPN without having to build and maintain a protocol gateway. The IPSec security protocol resides at the network layer. It is less flexible than the link layer security services, and only supports Internet protocols, but IPSec is still transparent to applications that use TCP or UDP. Whether implemented at the network or the link layer, in order to be considered a VPN, the interface must be completely transparent to network services, applications, and users. The disadvantage of this complete transparency is a low level of granularity. VPNs can provide identification and authentication either at the host level, or in the case of a remote access client, at the user level. In other words, remote access users can authenticate themselves to whatever host is at the other end of their VPN. Individual files are effectively invisible to a VPN security service, and no transactional services are provided by a VPN. Many proprietary VPN and remote access products are arguably implemented at the transport layer, although no standard defines a security service at this layer. Most transport layer encryption products are actually built as a shim on top of the existing transport layer. However, because they still support the existing transport interface — usually the socket interface — they should be treated as transport layer services. These VPN products are often implemented using protocols operating at higher network layers. Upper layer security services such as SSH and SOCKS are robust and proven, making them useful mechanisms for VPN implementations. The characteristic that determines if a security service is operating as a true VPN is not the layer at which the encryption service itself runs, but the interface layer at which security services are provided to existing upper layer applications; whatever is running under the hood is hidden from applications and not relevant to this model. VPNs are under the administrative control of the network administrator.

The session layer is not considered relevant for standard implementations of the Internet protocols; however, the Secure Socket Layer (SSL) service neatly fits into the definition of a session layer service. Applications capable of using SSL must be compiled with special SSL versions of the normal socket libraries. Network services compiled with support for SSL, such as S-HTTP, listen on specific ports for connection requests by compatible clients, like Web browsers. SSL is still too low in the network stack to provide transactional services. In common with a VPN, it provides session level privacy, and host-to-user, or host-to-host authentication at the session start. SSL does offer a higher level of control granularity than does a VPN. Applications capable of using SSL, such as Web browsers or mail clients, usually have the ability to use it as needed by alternating between connections to standard ports and connections to secured daemons running on SSL ports. This amount of granularity is adequate for electronic commerce applications that do not require digital signature. Note that the HTML designer does have the option of specifying URLs that invoke SSL, providing that person with indirect influence over the use of SSL. Whoever has write access to the Web server is the person who has the final say over which pages are protected with SSL. Sometimes, the user is provided with a choice between SSL-enabled Web pages or unsecured pages, but giving them this option is ultimately the prerogative of the Web master. A stand-alone system analogy to a session layer security service is a security service based on a file system. An encrypting file system is effectively a session layer service. It requires initial session identification and authentication, and then performs transparently in the background as a normal file system, transparent to applications. An encrypting file system is under the control of the system administrator.

Several commonly used Internet applications, such as Web browsers and mail clients, provide data representation services, which are presentation layer services. Presentation layer services operate at the granularity of an individual file. Presentation layer file operators are not aware of application-specific data formats, but are aware of more generalized data standards, especially those for text representation. Another example is FTP, which copies individual files while simultaneously providing text conversion such as EBCDIC to ASCII. In a non-networked environment, any generic application that operates on files can be considered a presentation layer service. This includes compression and file encryption utilities. Because it allows access to individual files, the presentation layer is the lowest layer that can provide transactional services, such as integrity verification and nonrepudiation. Generic network services that provide digital signature of files, such as PGP, S-MIME, and file system utilities, are not operating at the application level; they are at the presentation level. Presentation services are under control of the end user. Secure HTTP (S-HTTP) is another example of a presentation layer security service. It was intended to be used both for privacy and the digital signature of individual file objects. Secure HTTP was at one time in competition with SSL as the Web security mechanism of choice. SSL gained critical mass first, and is the only one of the two now being used. If it were available, S-HTTP would be under the control of the Web master, so Exhibit 18-3 represents it as being lower in the crypto protocol hierarchy than S-MIME.

Application layer services have access to the highest level of data granularity. Accessible objects may include application-specific file formats such as word processors or spreadsheets records, or even fields within a database. Application layer encryption is provided within an application and can only be applied to data compatible with that application. This makes application layer encryption completely nontransparent, but it also means that application encryption can provide all cryptographic services at any needed granularity. Application layer encryption services are normally proprietary to a specific application, although standard programming libraries are available. These include CAPI, the Java security libs, and BSAFE. Although it could arguably be considered a session layer protocol, SET (Secure Electronic Transaction) data formats are quite specific, so it more closely resembles an application layer protocol. It is intended to provide a complete system for electronic transaction processing, especially for credit card transactions, between merchants and financial institutions. Application layer encryption is under the control of the programmer. In many cases, the programmer allows the user the option of selectively taking advantage of encryption services, but it is always the programmer's prerogative to make security services mandatory.

TOPOLOGICAL MODEL

The topological model addresses the physical scope of a network cryptological implementation. It highlights the segments of the transmission path over which encryption is applied. Exhibit 18-4 illustrates the six most common spans of network encryption. The top half of the diagram, labeled "a," depicts an individual user on the Internet interacting with organizational servers. This user may be dialed into an ISP, be fully connected through a cable modem or DSL, or may be located within another organization's network. The bottom half of the diagram, labeled "b," depicts a user located at a partner organization or affiliated office. In case b, the security perimeter on the left side of the diagram is a firewall. In case a, it is the user's own PC. Note that the endpoints are always vulnerable because encryption services are always limited in their scope.

The term "end-to-end encryption" refers to the protection of data from the originating host all the way to the final destination host, with no unprotected transmission points. In a complex environment, end-to-end encryption is usually provided at the presentation or application layer. The top

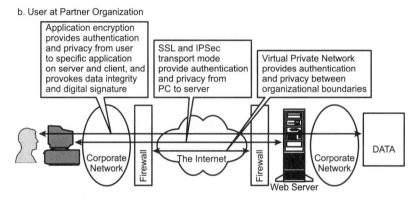

Exhibit 18-4. Topological model.

boxes in both "a" and "b" in Exhibit 18-4 illustrate a client taking advantage of encryption services to protect data directly between the user and the data server. As shown, the data might not be located on the Web server, but might be located on another server located several hops further interior from the firewall and Web server. SSL cannot provide protection beyond the Web server, but application or presentation layer encryption can. Full end-to-end protection could still be provided — even in the Web environment illustrated — if both the client and data server have applications supporting the same encryption protocols. This could even take the form of a Java applet. Although the applet would be served by the Web server, it would actually run within the Java virtual machine on the Web browser, providing cryptographic services for data shared between the client and the server, protecting it over all the interior and exterior network segments.

SSL and IPSec transport mode provide authentication and privacy between a workstation and a remote server. This is a sometimes referred to as host-to-host, or node-to-node. The two middle boxes in Exhibit 18-4 represent virtually identical situations. In b, the outgoing SSL session must transit a firewall, but it is common practice to allow this. On the server side, if the Web server is located inside a firewall, traffic on the port conventionally used by S-HTTP is allowed through the firewall to the IP address of the Web server. The SSL session provides privacy between the Web browser on the client machine and the Web server on the remote host. As in this example, if the Web server uses a back-end database instead of a local datastore, SSL cannot provide protection between the Web server and the database server (hopefully, this connection would be well-protected using noncryptographic countermeasures). SSL is somewhat limited in what it can provide, but its convenience makes it the most widely implemented form of network encryption. SSL is easy to implement; virtually all Web servers provide it as a standard capability, and it requires no programming skills. It does not necessarily provide end-to-end protection, but it does protect the transmission segment that is most vulnerable to outside attack.

Another form of host-to-host encryption is the virtual private network (VPN). As shown in both cases a and b in Exhibit 18-4 at least one of the hosts in a VPN is located on an organizational security boundary. This is usually, but not always, an Internet firewall. Unlike the previous example, where a and b were functionally identical in terms of security services, in the case of a VPN, b is distinct from a in that security services are not applied over the entire transmission path. A VPN is used to create an extension of the existing organizational security perimeter beyond that which is physically controlled by the organization. VPNs do not provide protect transmissions within the security perimeter that they extend. The VPN architecture is probably the more common use of the term "host-to-host." The term implies that cryptographic services are provided between two hosts, *at least one of which is not an endpoint.* Like SSL, a VPN provides host authentication and privacy. Depending on the implementation, it may or may not include additional integrity services. As shown in case a, VPN software is often used to support remote access users. In this scenario, the VPN represents only a temporary extension of the security perimeter. Case b shows an example of two remotely separated sites that are connected permanently or temporarily using a VPN. In this case, the user side represents a more complex configuration, with the user located on a network not necessarily directly contiguous with the security perimeter. In both a and b, the VPN is only providing services between security perimeters.

Link-to-link encryption is not illustrated. The term refers to the use of encryption to protect a single segment between two physically contiguous nodes. It is usually a hardware device operating at layer two. Such devices are used by financial firms to protect automatic teller machine transactions. Another common form of link-to-link encryption is the secure telephone unit (STU) used by the military. The most common use of link layer encryption services on the Internet is the protection of ATM or frame relay circuits using high-speed hardware devices.

INFORMATION STATE MODEL

It should be clear by now that no encryption architecture provides total protection. When data undergoes transition through processing, copying, or transmission, cryptographic security may be lost. When developing a security architecture, the complete data flow must be taken into account to ensure an appropriate level of protection whenever operations are performed on critical data. As shown in Exhibit 18-5, the number of states in which data is protected varies widely, depending on the choice of encryption service. The table is sorted from top to bottom in increasing order of the number of states in which protection is provided. SSL and VPNs are at the top of the chart because they only protect during one phase: the transmission phase. In contrast, application encryption can be designed to protect data during every state but one. Although systems have been researched, no commercially available product encrypts data while it is being processed. Data undergoing processing is vulnerable in a number of ways, including:

- The human entering or reading the data can remember it or write it down.
- Information on the screen is visible to shoulder surfers.
- Virtual memory can store the cleartext data on the hard drive's swap space.
- If the process crashes, the operating system may store a core dump file containing the cleartext data.

Outside of the processing phase, which can only be addressed through administrative and physical security countermeasures, encryption options are available to protect data wherever necessary.

Several different styles of automated encryption have been developed, relieving users of the responsibility of remembering to protect their data. Some products encrypt an entire hard drive or file system, while others allow configuration of specific directories and encrypt all files placed into them. After users correctly authenticates themselves to such an encryption system, files are automatically decrypted when accessed. The downside of this automated decryption is that whenever authenticated users access a file, the encryption protection is potentially lost. Critical data can be inadvertently stored in cleartext by transmitting it, backing it up, or copying it to another system. Protection can be maintained for an encrypted file system by treating the entire file system as a single object, dumping the raw data to backup storage. Depending on the implementation, it may be impossible to perform incremental backups or restore single files. Products that

Exhibit 18-5. Information state model.

	Encrypted During Processing	Automatically Encrypted on First Save	Sent Data Encrypted on Originating Host	Automatically Reencrypted after Use	Encrypted when Backed Up	Encrypted During Transmission	Data Encrypted on Receiving Host
SSL						✓	
VPN						✓	
Encrypting file system that automatically decrypts		✓	✓	✓			
Encryption utility			✓		✓	✓	✓
Encrypting file system without automatic decryption		✓	✓	✓	✓	✓	No key
E-mail encryption			✓	✓	✓	✓	✓
Application with built-in data encryption		Optional	✓	✓	✓	✓	✓

do not encrypt the directory listing, leaving the names of encrypted files in cleartext, offer more flexibility, but increase the risk that an intruder can gain information about the encrypted data. If the data can be copied without automatically decrypting it, then it can be backed up or transmitted without losing cryptographic protection. Although such data would be safely encrypted on a recipient's system, it probably would not be usable because the recipient would not have a key for it. It would rarely be appropriate for someone automatically encrypting data to share the key with someone else if that key provided access to one's entire personal information store. Automatic encryption is difficult in a workgroup scenario — at best, moving data between personal storage and group storage requires decryption and reencryption with a different key.

File encryption utilities, and this includes compression utilities with an encryption option (beware of proprietary encryption algorithms), are highly flexible, allowing a file or set of files to be encrypted with a unique key and maintaining protection of that data throughout copy and transmission phases. The disadvantage of encrypting a file with a utility is that the data owner must remember to manually encrypt the data, increasing the risk that sensitive information remains unencrypted. Unless the encryption utility has the ability to invoke the appropriate application, a plaintext version of the encrypted data file will have to be stored on disk before encrypted data can be accessed. The user who decrypts it will have to remember to reencrypt it. Even if the encryption utility directly invokes an application, nothing prevents the user from bypassing automated reencryption by saving the data from within the application, leaving a decrypted copy on disk. E-mail encryption services, such as PGP and S-MIME, leave data vulnerable at the ends. Unless the data is created completely within the e-mail application and is never used outside of a mail browser, cleartext can be left on the hard drive. Mail clients that support encryption protect both the message and any attachments. If cryptographic protection is applied to an outgoing message (usually a choice of signature, encryption, or both), and outgoing messages are stored, the stored copy will be encrypted. The recipient's copy will remain encrypted too, as long as it is stored within the mail system. As soon as an attachment is saved to the file system, it is automatically decrypted and stored in cleartext. Encrypting within an application is the most reliable way to prevent inappropriate storage of cleartext data. Depending on the application, the user may have no choice but to always use encryption. When optional encryption has been applied to data, normal practice is to always maintain that encryption until a keyholder explicitly removes it. On a modern windowing workstation, a user can still defeat automated reencryption by copying the data and pasting it into another application, and application encryption is often weakened by the tendency of application vendors to choose easily breakable proprietary encryption algorithms.

Several manufacturers have created complex encryption systems that attempt to provide encryption in every state and facilitate the secure sharing of that data. Analysis of these systems will show that they use combinations of the encryption types listed in the first column of Exhibit 18-5. Such a hybrid solution potentially overcomes the disadvantages of any single encryption type while providing the advantages of several. The Information State Model is useful in analyzing both the utility and the security of such a product.

PUTTING THE MODELS TO WORK

The successful use of encryption consists of applying it appropriately so that it provides the anticipated data protection. The models presented in this chapter are tools, helpful in the technical analysis of an encryption implementation. As shown in Exhibit 18-4, good implement choices are made by following a process. Analyzing the information security requirements is the first step. This consists of understanding what data must be protected, and its time and sensitivity requirements for confidentiality, integrity, availability, and nonrepudiation. Once the information security requirements are well-documented, technical analysis can take place. Some combination of the four encryption application models should be used to develop potential implementation options. These models overlap, and they may not all be useful in every situation — choose whichever one offers the most useful insight into any particular situation. After technical analysis is complete, a final implementation choice is made by returning to business analysis. Not every implementation option may be economically feasible. The most rigorous encryption solution will probably be the most expensive. The available resources will dictate which of the implementation options are possible. Risk analysis should be applied to those choices to ensure that they are appropriately secure. If insufficient resources are available to adequately offset risk, the conclusion of the analysis should be that it is inappropriate to undertake the project. Fortunately, given the wide range of encryption solutions available for Internet implementations today, most security practitioners should be able to find a solution that meets their information security requirements and fits within their budget.

Chapter 19
Methods of Attacking and Defending Cryptosystems
Joost Houwen

ENCRYPTION TECHNOLOGIES HAVE BEEN USED FOR THOUSANDS OF YEARS AND, THUS, BEING ABLE READ THE SECRETS THEY ARE PROTECTING HAS ALWAYS BEEN OF GREAT INTEREST. As the value of our secrets have increased, so have the technological innovations used to protect them. One of the key goals of those who want to keep secrets is to keep ahead of techniques used by their attackers. For today's IT systems, there is increased interest in safeguarding company and personal information, and therefore the use of cryptography is growing. Many software vendors have responded to these demands and are providing encryption functions, software, and hardware. Unfortunately, many of these products may not be providing the protection that the vendors are claiming or customers are expecting. Also, as with most crypto usage throughout history, people tend to defeat much of the protection afforded by the technology through misuse or inappropriate use. Therefore, the use of cryptography must be appropriate to the required goals and this strategy must be constantly reassessed. To use cryptography correctly, the weaknesses of systems must be understood.

This chapter reviews various historical, theoretical, and modern methods of attacking cryptographic systems. While some technical discussion is provided, this chapter is intended for a general information technology and security audience.

CRYPTOGRAPHY OVERVIEW

A brief overview of definitions and basic concepts is in order at this point. Generally, *cryptography* refers to the study of the techniques and methods used to hide data, while *encryption* is the process of disguising a message so that its meaning is not obvious. Similarly, decryption is the

0-8493-0800-3/00/$0.00+$.50
© 2001 by CRC Press LLC

reverse process of encryption. The original data is called *cleartext* or *plaintext,* while the encrypted data is called *ciphertext.* Sometimes, the words *encode/encipher* and *decode/decipher* are used in the place of *encrypt* and *decrypt.* A cryptographic algorithm is commonly called a *cipher. Cryptanalysis* is the science of breaking cryptography, thereby gaining knowledge about the plaintext. The amount of work required to break an encrypted message or mechanism is call the *work factor. Cryptology* refers to the combined disciplines of cryptography and cryptanalysis.

Cryptography is one of the tools used in information security to assist in ensuring the primary goals of confidentiality, integrity, authentication, and nonrepudiation.

Some of the things a cryptanalyst needs to be successful are:

- enough ciphertext
- full or partial plaintext
- known algorithm
- strong mathematical background
- creativity
- time, time, and more time for analysis
- large amounts of computing power

Motivations for a cryptanalyst to attack a cryptosystem include:

- financial gain, including credit card and banking information
- political or espionage
- interception or modification of e-mail
- covering up another attack
- revenge
- embarrassment of vendor (potentially to get them to fix problems)
- peer or open-source review
- fun/education (cryptographers learn from others' and their own mistakes)

It is important to review the basic types of commonly used ciphers and some historical examples of cryptosystems. The reader is strongly encouraged to review cryptography books, but especially Bruce Schneier's essential *Applied Cryptography* [1] and *Cryptography and Network Security* [2] by William Stallings.

CIPHER TYPES

Substitution Ciphers

A simple yet highly effective technique for hiding text is the use of substitution cipher, where each character is switched with another. There are several of these types of ciphers with which the reader should be familiar.

Monoalphabetic Ciphers. One way to create a substitution cipher is to switch around the alphabet used in the plaintext message. This could involve shifting the alphabet used by a few positions or something more complex. Perhaps the most famous example of such a cipher is the Caesar cipher, used by Julius Caesar to send secret messages. This cipher involves shifting each letter in the alphabet by three positions, so that "A" becomes "D," and "B" is replaced by "E," etc. While this may seems simple today, it is believed to have been very successful in ancient Rome. This is probably due, in large part, to the fact the even the ability to read was uncommon, and therefore writing was probably a code in itself.

A more modern example of the use of this type of cipher is the UNIX *crypt* utility, which uses the ROT13 algorithm. ROT13 shifts the alphabet 13 places, so that "A" is replaced by "N," "B" by "M," etc. Obviously, this cipher provides little protection and is mostly used for obscuration rather than encryption, although with a utility named *crypt*, some users may assume there is actually some real protection in place. Note that this utility should not be confused with the UNIX *crypt( )* software routine that is used in the encryption of passwords in the password file. This routine uses the repeated application of the DES algorithm to make decrypting these passwords extremely difficult.[3]

Polyalphabetic Ciphers. By using more than one substitution cipher (alphabet), one can obtain improved protection from a frequency analysis attack. These types of ciphers were successfully used in the American Civil War[4] and have been used in commercial word-processing software. Another example of this type of cipher is the Vigenère cipher, which uses 26 Caesar ciphers that are shifted. This cipher is interesting as well because it uses a keyword to encode and decode the text.

One-Time Pad

In 1917, Joseph Mauborgne and Gilbert Vernam invented the unbreakable cipher called a one-time pad. The concept is quite effective, yet really simple. Using a random set of characters as long as the message, it is possible to generate ciphertext that is also random and therefore unbreakable even by brute-force attacks. In practice, having — and protecting — shared suitably random data is difficult to manage but this technique has been successfully used for a variety of applications. It should be understood by the reader that a true, and thus unbreakable, one-time pad encryption scheme is essentially a theoretical concept as it is dependent on true random data, which is very difficult to obtain.

Transposition Cipher

This technique generates ciphertext by performing some form of permutation on plaintext characters. One example of this technique is to arrange the plaintext into a matrix and perform permutations on the columns.

The effectiveness of this technique is greatly enhanced by applying it multiple times.

Stream Cipher

When large amounts of data need to enciphered, a cipher must be used multiple times. To efficiently encode this data, a stream is required. A stream cipher uses a secret key and then accepts a stream of plaintext producing the required ciphertext.

Rotor Machines. Large numbers of computations using ciphers can be time-consuming and prone to errors. Therefore, in the 1920s, mechanical devices called rotors were developed. The rotors were mechanical wheels that performed the required substitutions automatically. One example of a rotor machine is the Enigma used by the Germans during World War II. The initial designs used three rotors and an operator plugboard. After the early models were broken by Polish cryptanalysts, the Germans improved the system only to have it broken by the British.

RC4. Another popular stream cipher is the Rivest Cipher #4 (RC4) developed by Ron Rivest for RSA.

Block Cipher

A block cipher takes a block of plaintext, a key, and produces a block of ciphertext. Current block ciphers produce ciphertext blocks that are the same size as the corresponding plaintext block.

DES. The Data Encryption Standard (DES) was developed by IBM for the United States National Institute of Standards and Technology (NIST) as Federal Information Processing Standard (FIPS) 46. Data is encrypted using a 56-bit key and eight parity bits with 64-bit blocks.

3DES. To improve the strength of DES-encrypted data, the algorithm can be applied in the triple DES form. In this algorithm, the DES algorithm is applied three times, either using two keys (112 bit) encrypt-decrypt-encrypt, or using three keys (168 bit) encrypt-encrypt-encrypt modes. Both forms of 3DES are considered much stronger than single DES. There have been no reports of breaking 3DES.

IDEA. The International Data Encryption Algorithm (IDEA) is another block cipher developed in Europe. This algorithm uses 128-bit keys to encrypt 64-bit data blocks. IDEA is used in Pretty Good Privacy (PGP) for data encryption.

TYPES OF KEYS

Most algorithms use some form of secret key to perform encryption functions. There are some differences in these keys that should be discussed.

1. **Private/Symmetric.** A private, or symmetric, key is a secret key that is shared between the sender and receiver of the messages. This key is usually the only key that can decipher the message.
2. **Public/Asymmetric.** A public, or asymmetric, key is one that is made publicly available and can be used to encrypt data that only the holder of the uniquely and mathematically related private key can decrypt.
3. **Data/Session.** A symmetric key, which may or may not be random or reused, is used for encrypting data. This key is often negotiated using standard protocols or sent in a protected manner using secret public or private keys.
4. **Key Encrypting.** Keys that are used to protect data encrypting keys. These keys are usually used only for key updates and not data encryption.
5. **Split Keys.** To protect against intentional or unintentional key disclosure, it is possible to create and distribute parts of larger keys which only together can be used for encryption or decryption.

SYMMETRIC KEY CRYPTOGRAPHY

Symmetric key cryptography refers to the use of a shared secret key that is used to encrypt and decrypt the plaintext. Hence, this method is sometimes referred to as secret key cryptography. In practice, this method is obviously dependent on the "secret" remaining so. In most cases, there needs to be a way that new and updated secret keys can be transferred. Some examples of symmetric key cryptography include DES, IDEA, and RC4.

ASYMMETRIC KEY CRYPTOGRAPHY

Asymmetric key cryptography refers to the use of public and private key pairs, and hence this method is commonly referred to as public key encryption. The public and private keys are mathematically related so that only the private key can be used to decrypt data encrypted with the public key. The public key can also be used to validate cryptographic signatures generated using the corresponding private key.

Examples of Public Key Cryptography

RSA. This algorithm was named after its inventors, Ron Rivest, Adi Shamir, and Leonard Adleman, and based on the difficulty in factoring large prime numbers. RSA is currently the most popular public key encryption algorithm and has been extensively cryptanalyzed. The algorithm can be used for both data encryption and digital signatures.

Elliptic Curve Cryptography (ECC). ECC utilizes the unique mathematical properties of elliptic curves to generate a unique key pair. To break the ECC cryptography, one must attack the "elliptic curve discrete logarithm problem." Some of the potential benefits of ECC are that it uses significantly shorter key lengths and that is well-suited for low bandwidth/CPU systems.

HASH ALGORITHMS

Hash or digest functions generate a fixed-length hash value from arbitrary-length data. This is usually a one-way process, so that it impossible to reconstruct the original data from the hash. More importantly, it is, in general, extremely difficult to obtain the same hash from two different data sources. Therefore, these types of functions are extremely useful for integrity checking and the creation of electronic signatures or fingerprints.

MD5

The Message Digest (MD) format is probably the most common hash function in use today. This function was developed by Ron Rivest at RSA, and is commonly used as a data integrity checking tool, such as in Tripwire and other products. MD5 generates a 128-bit hash.

SHA

The Secure Hash Algorithm (SHA) was developed by the NSA. The algorithm is used by PGP, and other products, to generate digital signatures. SHA produces a 160-bit hash.

STEGANOGRAPHY

Steganography is the practice used to conceal the existence of messages. That is different from encryption, which seeks to make the messages unintelligible to others.[5]

A detailed discussion of this topic is outside the scope of this chapter, but the reader should be aware that there are many techniques and software packages available that can be used to hide information in a variety of digital data.

KEY DISTRIBUTION

One of the fundamental problems with encryption technology is the distribution of keys. In the case of symmetric cryptography, a shared secret key must be securely transmitted to users. Even in the case of public key cryptography, getting private keys to users and keeping public keys up-to-date and protected remain difficult problems. There are a variety of key distribution and exchange methods that can be used. These range from manual paper delivery to fully automated key exchanges. The reader is advised to consult the references for further information.

KEY MANAGEMENT

Another important issue for information security professionals to consider is the need for proper key management. This is an area of cryptography that is often overlooked and there are many historical precedents in North America and other parts of the world. If an attacker can easily, or inexpensively, obtain cryptographic keys through people or unprotected systems, there is no need to break the cryptography the hard way.

PUBLIC VERSUS PROPRIETARY ALGORITHMS AND SYSTEMS

It is generally an accepted fact among cryptography experts that closed or proprietary cryptographic systems do not provide good security. The reason for this is that creating good cryptography is very difficult and even seasoned experts make mistakes. It is therefore believed that algorithms that have undergone intense public and expert scrutiny are far superior to proprietary ones.

CLASSIC ATTACKS

Attacks on cryptographic systems can be classified under the following threats:

- interception
- modification
- fabrication
- interruption

Also, there are both passive and active attacks. Passive attacks involve the listening-in, eavesdropping, or monitoring of information, which may lead to interception of unintended information or traffic analysis where information is inferred. This type of attack is usually difficult if not impossible to detect. However, active attacks involve actual modification of the information flow. This may include[6]:

- masquerade
- replay
- modification of messages
- denial of service

There are many historical precedents of great value to any security professional considering the use of cryptography. The reader is strongly encouraged to consult many of the excellent books listed in the bibliography, but especially the classic *The Codebreakers: The Story of Secret Writing* by David Kahn.[7]

STANDARD CRYPTANALYSIS

Cryptanalysis strives to break the encryption used to protect information, and to this end there are many techniques available to the modern cryptographer.

Reverse Engineering

Arguably, one of the simplest forms of attack on cryptographic systems is reverse engineering, whereby an encryption device (method, machine, or software) is obtained through other means and then deconstructed to learn how best to extract plaintext. In theory, if a well-designed crypto hardware system is obtained and even its algorithms are learned, it may still be impossible to obtain enough information to freely decrypt any other ciphertext.[8] During World War II, efforts to break the German Enigma encryption device were greatly aided when one of the units was obtained. Also, today when many software encryption packages that claim to be foolproof are analyzed by cryptographers and security professionals, they are frequently found to have serious bugs that undermine the system.

Guessing

Some encryption methods may be trivial for a trained cryptanalyst to decipher. Examples of this include simple substitutions or obfuscation techniques that are masquerading as encryption. A common example of this is the use of the logical XOR function, which when applied to some data will output seemingly random data, but in fact the plaintext is easily obtained. Another example of this is the Caesar cipher, where each letter of the alphabet is shifted by three places so that A becomes D, B becomes E, etc. These are types of cryptograms that commonly present in newspapers and puzzle books.

The *Principle of Easiest Work* states that one cannot expect the interceptor to choose the hard way to do something.[9]

Frequency Analysis

Many languages, especially English, contain words that repeatedly use the same patterns of letters. There have been numerous English letter frequency studies done that give an attacker a good starting point for attacking much ciphertext. For example, by knowing that the letters E, T, and R appear the most frequently in English text, an attacker can fairly quickly decrypt the ciphertext of most monoalphabetic and polyalphabetic substitution ciphers. Of course, critical to this type of attack is the ready supply of sufficient amounts of ciphertext from which to work. These types of frequency and patterns also appear in many other languages, but English appears particularly vulnerable. Monoalphabetic ciphers, such as the Caesar cipher, directly transpose the frequency distribution of the underlying message.

Brute Force

The process of repeatedly trying different keys in order to obtain the plaintext are referred to as brute-force techniques. Early ciphers were made stronger and stronger in order to prevent human "computers" from decoding secrets; but with the introduction of mechanical and electronic computing devices, many ciphers became no longer usable. Today, as computing power grows daily, it has become a race to improve the resistance, or work factor, to these types of attacks. This of course introduces a problem for applications that may need to protect data which may be of value for many years.

Ciphertext-Only Attack

The cryptanalyst is presented only with the unintelligible ciphertext, from which she tries to extract the plaintext. For example, by examining only the output of a simple substitution cipher, one is able to deduce patterns and ultimately the entire original plaintext message. This type of attack is aided when the attacker has multiple pieces of ciphertext generated from the same key.

Known Plaintext Attack

The cryptanalyst knows all or part of the contents of the ciphertext's original plaintext. For example, the format of an electronic fund transfer might be known except for the amount and account numbers. Therefore, the work factor to extract the desired information from the ciphertext is significantly reduced.

Chosen Plaintext Attack

In this type of attack, the cryptanalyst can generate ciphertext from arbitrary plaintext. This scenario occurs if the encryption algorithm is known. A good cryptographic algorithm will be resistant even to this type of attack.

Birthday Attack

One-way hash functions are used to generate unique output, although it is possible that another message could generate an identical hash. This instance is called a collision. Therefore, an attacker can dramatically reduce the work factor to duplicate the hash by simply searching for these "birthday" pairs.

Factoring Attacks

One of the possible attacks against RSA cryptography is to attempt to use the public key and factor the private key. The security of RSA depends on this being a difficult problem, and therefore takes significant computation.

Obviously, the greater the key length used, the more difficult the factoring becomes.

Replay Attack

An attacker may be able to intercept an encrypted "secret" message, such as a financial transaction, but may not be able to readily decrypt the message. If the systems are not providing adequate protection or validation, the attacker can now simply send the message again, and it will be processed again.

Man-in-the-Middle Attack

By interjecting oneself into the path of secure communications or key exchange, it possible to initiate a number of attacks. An example that is often given is the case of an online transaction. A customer connects to what is thought to be an online bookstore; but in fact, the attacker has hijacked the connection in order to monitor and interact with the data stream. The customer connects normally because the attacker simply forwards the data onto the bookstore, thereby intercepting all the desired data. Also, changes to the data stream can be made to suit the attacker's needs.

In the context of key exchange, this situation is potentially even more serious. If an attacker is able to intercept the key exchange, he may be able to use the key at will (if it is unprotected) or substitute his own key.

Dictionary Attacks

A special type of known-plaintext and brute-force attack can be used to guess the passwords on UNIX systems. UNIX systems generally use the *crypt( )* function to generate theoretically irreversible encrypted password hashes. The problem is that some users choose weak passwords that are based on real words. It is possible to use dictionaries containing thousands of words and to use this wel-known function until there is a match with the encoded password. This technique has proved immensely successful in attacking and compromising UNIX systems. Unfortunately, Windows NT systems are not immune from this type of attack. This is accomplished by obtaining a copy of the NT SAM file, which contains the encrypted passwords, and as in the case of UNIX, comparing combinations of dictionary words until a match is found. Again, this is a popular technique for attacking this kind of system.

Attacking Random Number Generators

Many encryption algorithms utilize random data to ensure that an attacker cannot easily recognize patterns to aid in cryptanalysis. Some examples of this include the generation of initialization vectors or SSL sessions. However, if these random number generators are not truly random, they are subject to attack. Furthermore, if the random number generation process or function is known, it may be possible to find weaknesses in its implementation. Many encryption implementations utilize pseudorandom number generators (PRNGs), which as the name the name suggests, attempt to generate numbers that are practically impossible to predict. The basis of these PRNGs is the initial random seed values, which obviously must be selected properly. In 1995, early versions of the Netscape Navigator software were found to have problems with the SSL communication security.[10] The graduate students who reverse-engineered the browser software determined that there was a problem with the seeding process used by the random number generator. This problem was corrected in later versions of the browser.

Inference

A simple and potential low-tech attack on encrypted communication can be via simple inference. Although the data being sent back and forth is unreadable to the interceptor, it is possible that the mere fact of this communication may mean there is some significant activity. A common example of this is the communication between military troops, where the sudden increase in traffic, although completely unreadable, may signal the start of an invasion or major campaign. Therefore, these types of communications are often padded so as not to show any increases or decreases in traffic. This example can easily be extended to the business world by considering a pending merger between two companies. The mere fact of increased traffic back and forth may signal the event to an attacker. Also, consider the case of encrypted electronic mail. While the message data is well-encrypted, the sender and recipient are usually plainly visible in the mail headers and message. In fact, the subject line of the message (e.g., merger proposal") may say it all.

MODERN ATTACKS

While classical attacks still apply and are highly effective against modern ciphers, there have been a number of recent cases of new and old cryptosystems failing.

Bypass

Perhaps one of the simplest attacks that has emerged, and arguably is not new, is to simply go around any crypto controls. This may be as simple as coercion of someone with access to the unencrypted data or by exploiting a flaw in the way the cipher is used. There are currently a number of PC encryption products on the market and the majority of these have been found to have bugs. The real difference in these products has been the ways in which the vendor has fixed, or not, the problem. A number of these products have been found to improperly save passwords for convenience or have back-door recovery mechanisms installed. These bugs were mostly exposed by curious users exploring how the programs work. Vendor responses have ranged from immediately issuing fixes to denying there is a problem.

Another common example is the case of a user who is using some type of encryption software that may be protecting valuable information or communication. An attacker could trick the user into running a Trojan horse program, which secretly installs a back-door program, such as BackOrifice on PCs. On a UNIX system, this attack may occur via an altered installation script run by the administrator. The administrator can now capture any information used on this system, including the crypto keys and passphrases. There have been several demonstrations of these types of attacks where the target was home finance software or PGP key-rings. The author believes that this form of attack will greatly increase as many more users begin regularly using e-mail encryption and Internet banking.

Operating System Flaws

The operating system running the crypto function can itself be the cause of problems. Most operating systems use some form of virtual memory to improve performance. This "memory" is usually stored on the system's hard disk in files that may be accessible. Encryption software may cache keys and plaintext while running, and this data may remain in the system's virtual memory. An attacker could remotely or physically obtain access to these files and therefore may have access to crypto keys and possibly even plaintext.

Memory Residue

Even if the crypto functions are not cached in virtual memory or on disk, many products still keep sensitive keys in the system memory. An attacker may be able to dump the system memory or force the system to crash, leaving data from memory exposed. Hard disks and other media may also have residual data that may reside on the system long after use.

Temporary Files

Many encryption software packages generate temporary files during processing and may accidentally leave plaintext on the system. Also, application packages such as word-processors leave many temporary files on the system, which may mean that even if the sensitive file is encrypted and there are no plaintext versions of the file, the application may have created plaintext temporary files. Even if temporary files have been removed, they usually can be easily recovered from the system disks.

Differential Power Analysis

In 1997, Anderson and Kuhn proposed inexpensive attacks against through which knowledgeable insiders and funded organizations could compromise the security of supposed tamper-resistant devices such as smart cards.[11] While technically not a crypto attack, these types of devices are routinely used to store and process cryptographic keys and provide other forms of assurance. Further work in this field has been done by Paul Kocher and Cryptographic Research, Inc. Basically, the problem is that statistical data may "leak" through the electrical activity of the device, which could compromise secret keys or PINs protected by it. The cost of mounting such an attack appears to be relatively low but it does require a high technical skill level. This excellent research teaches security professionals that new forms of high-security storage devices are highly effective but have to be used appropriately and that they do not provide *absolute* protection.

Parallel Computing

Modern personal computers, workstations, and servers are very powerful and are formidable cracking devices. For example, in *Internet Cryptography*,[12] Smith writes that a single workstation will break a 40-bit export crypto key, as those used by Web browsers, in about ten months. However, when 50 workstations are applied to this problem processing in parallel, the work factor is reduced to about six days. This type of attack was demonstrated in 1995 when students using a number of idle workstations managed to obtain the plaintext of an encrypted Web transaction.

Another example of this type of processing is *Crack* software, which can be used to brute-force guess UNIX passwords. The software can be enabled on multiple systems that will work cooperatively to guess the passwords.

Parallel computing has also become very popular in the scientific community due the fact that one can build a supercomputer using off-the-shelf hardware and software. For example, Sandia National Labs has constructed a massively parallel system called Cplant, which was ranked the 44th fastest among the world's 500 fastest supercomputers (http://www.wired.com/news/technology/0,1282,32706,00.html). Parallel computing techniques mean that even a moderately funded attacker, with sufficient time, can launch very effective and low-tech brute-force attacks against medium to high value ciphertext.

Distributed Computing

For a number of years, RSA Security has proposed a series of increasingly difficult computation problems. Most of the problems require the extraction of RSA encrypted messages and there is usually a small monetary award. Various developers of elliptic curve cryptography (ECC) have also organized such contests. The primary reason for holding these competitions is to test current minimum key lengths and obtain a sense of the "real-world" work factor.

Perhaps the most aggressive efforts have come from the Distributed.Net group, which has taken up many such challenges. The Distributed team consists of thousands of PCs, midrange, and high-end systems that collaboratively work on these computation problems. Other Internet groups have also formed and have spawned distributed computing rivalries. These coordinated efforts show that even inexpensive computing equipment can be used in a distributed or collaborative manner to decipher ciphertext.

DES Cracker

In 1977, Whitfield Diffie and Martin Hellman proposed the construction of a DES-cracking machine that could crack 56-bit DES keys in 20 hours. While the cost of such a device is high, it seemed well within the budgets of determined attackers. Then in 1994, Michael Weiner proposed a design for a device built from existing technology which could crack 56-bit DES keys in under four hours for a cost of U.S. $1 million. The cost of this theoretical device would of course be much less today if one considers the advances in the computer industry.

At the RSA Conferences held in 1997 and 1998, there were contests held to crack DES-encrypted messages. Both contests were won by distributed computing efforts. In 1998, the DES message was cracked in 39 days. Adding to these efforts was increased pressure from a variety of groups in the United States to lift restrictive crypto export regulations. The Electronic Freedom Foundation (EFF) sponsored a project to build a DES cracker. The intention of the project was to determine how cheap or how expensive it would be to build a DES cracker.

In the summer of 1998, the EFF DES cracker was completed, costing U.S.$210,000 and taking only 18 months to design, test, and build. The performance of the cracker was estimated at about five days per key. In July 1998, EFF announced to the world that it had easily won the RSA Security "DES Challenge II," taking less than three days to recover the secret message. In January 1999, EFF announced that in a collaboration with Distributed.Net, it had won the RSA Security "DES Challenge III," taking 22 hours to recover the plaintext. EFF announced that this "put the final nail into the Data Encryption Standard's coffin." EFF published detailed chip design, software, and implementation details and provided this information freely on the Internet.

RSA-155 (512bit) Factorization

In August 1999, researchers completed the factorization of the 155-digit (512-bit) RSA Challenge Number. The total time taken to complete the solution was around five to seven months without dedicating hardware. By comparison, RSA-140 was solved in nine weeks. The implications of this achievement in relatively short time may put RSA keys at risk from a determined adversary. In general, it means that 768- or 1024-bit RSA keys should be used as a minimum.

TWINKLE RSA Cracker

In summer 1999, Adi Shamir, co-inventor of the RSA algorithm, presented a design for The Weizmann Institute Key Locating Engine (TWINKLE), which processes the "sieving" required for factoring large numbers. The device would cost about U.S.$5000 and provide processing equivalent to 100 to 1000 PCs. If built, this device could be used similarly to the EFF DES Cracker device. This device is targeted at 512-bit RSA keys, so it reinforces the benefits of using of 768- or 1024-bit, or greater keys.

Key Recovery and Escrow

Organizations implementing cryptographic systems usually require some way to recover data encrypted with keys that have been lost. A common example of this type of system is a public key infrastructure, where each private (and public) key is stored on the Certificate Authority, which is protected by a root key(s). Obviously, access to such a system has to be tightly controlled and monitored to prevent a compromise of all the organization's keys. Usually, only the private data encrypting, but not signing, keys are "escrowed."

In many nations, governments are concerned about the use of cryptography for illegal purposes. Traditional surveillance becomes difficult when the targets are using encryption to protect communications. To this end, some nations have attempted to pursue strict crypto regulation, including requirements for key escrow for law enforcement.

In general, key recovery and escrow implementations could cause problems because they are there to allow access to all encrypted data. While a more thorough discussion of this topic is beyond the scope of this chapter, the reader is encouraged to consult the report entitled "The Risks of Key Recovery, Key Escrow, & Trusted Third Party Encryption," which was published in 1997 by an Ad Hoc Group of Cryptographers and Computer Scientists. Also, Whitfield Diffie and Susan Landau's *Privacy on the Line* is essential reading on the topic.

PROTECTING CRYPTOSYSTEMS

Creating effective cryptographic systems requires balancing business protection needs with technical constraints. It is critical that these technologies be included as part of an effective and holistic protection solution. It is not enough to simply implement encryption and assume all risks have been addressed. For example, just because an e-mail system is using message encryption, it does not necessarily mean that e-mail is secure, or even any better than plaintext. When considering a protection system, not only must one look at and test the underlying processes, but one must also look for ways around the solutions and address these risks appropriately. It is vital to understand that crypto solutions can be dangerous because they can easily lead to a false sense of information security.

Design, Analysis, and Testing

Fundamental to the successful implementation of a cryptosystem are thorough design, analysis, and testing methodologies. The implementation cryptography is probably one of the most difficult and most poorly understood IT fields. Information technology and security professionals must fully understand that cryptographic solutions that are simply dropped into place are doomed to failure.

It is generally recommended that proprietary cryptographic systems are problematic and usually end up being not quite what they appear to be. The best algorithms are those that have undergone rigorous public scrutiny by crypto experts. Just because a cryptographer cannot break his or her own algorithm, this does not mean that this is a safe algorithm. As Bruce Schneier points out in "Security Pitfalls in Cryptography," the output from a poor cryptographic system is very difficult to differentiate from a good one.

Smith[13] suggests that preferred crypto algorithms should have the following properties:

- no reliance on algorithm secrecy
- explicitly designed for encryption
- available for analysis
- subject to analysis
- no practical weaknesses

When designing systems that use cryptography, it is also important to build in proper redundancies and compensating controls, because it is entirely possible that the algorithms or implementation may fail at some point in the future or at the hands of a determined attacker.

Selecting Appropriate Key Lengths

Although proper design, algorithm selection, and implementation are critical factors for a cryptosystem, the selection of key lengths is also very important. Security professionals and their IT peers often associate the number of "bits" a product uses with the measure of its level of protection. As Bruce Schneier so precisely puts it in his paper "Security Pitfalls in Cryptography": "…reality isn't that simple. Longer keys don't always mean more security."[14] As stated earlier, the cryptographic functions are but part of the security strategy. Once all the components and vulnerabilities of a encryption strategy have been reviewed and addressed, one can start to consider key lengths.

In theory, the greater the key length, the more difficult the encryption is to break. However, in practice, there are performance and practical concerns that limit the key lengths to be used. In general, the following factors will determine what key sizes are used:

- value of the asset it is protecting (compare to cost to break it)
- length of time it needs protecting (minutes, hours, years, centuries)
- determination of attacker (individual, corporate, government)
- performance criteria (seconds versus minutes to encrypt/decrypt)

Therefore, high value data that needs to protected for a long time, such as trade secrets, requires long key lengths. Whereas, a stock transaction may only be of value for a few seconds, and therefore is well-protected with shorter key lengths. Obviously, it is usually better to err toward longer key sizes than shorter. It is fairly common to see recommendations of symmetric key lengths, such as for 3DES or IDEA, of 112 to 128 bits, while 1024- to 2048-bit lengths are common for asymmetric keys, such as for RSA encryption.

Random Number Generators

As discussed earlier, random number generators are critical to effective cryptosystems. Hardware-based RNG are generally believed to be the best, but more costly form of implementation. These devices are generally based on random physical events, and therefore should generate data that is nearly impossible to predict.

Software RNGs obviously require additional operating system protection, but also protection from covert channel analysis. For example, systems that use system clocks may allow an attacker access to this information via other means, such as remote system statistics or network time protocols. Bruce Schneier has identified software random number generators as being a common vulnerability among crypto implementations [SOURCE], and to that end has made an excellent free PRNG available, with source code, to anyone. This PRNG has undergone rigorous independent review.

Source Code Review

Even if standard and publicly scrutinized algorithms and methods are used in an application, this does not guarantee that the application will work as expected. Even open-source algorithms are difficult to implement correctly because there are many nuances (e.g., cipher modes in DES and proper random number generation) that the programmer may not understand.

Also, as discussed in previous sections, many commercial encryption packages have sloppy coding errors such as leaving plaintext temporary files unprotected. Cryptographic application source code should be independently reviewed to ensure that it actually does what is expected.

Vendor Assurances

Vendor assurances are easy to find. Many products claim that their data or communications are encrypted or are secure; however, unless they provide any specific details, it usually turns out that this protection is not really there or is really just "obfuscation" at work. There are some industry evaluations and standards that may assist in selecting a product. Some examples are the Federal Information Processing Standards (FIPS), the Common Criteria evaluations, ICSA, and some information security publications.

New Algorithms

Advanced Encryption Algorithm (AES). NIST is currently reviewing submissions for replacement algorithms for DES. There have been a number of submissions made for the Advanced Encryption Standard (AES) and the process is currently, as of November 1st, 1999, in Round Two discussions. The Round Two finalists include:

- MARS (IBM)
- RC6TM (RSA Laboratories)
- RIJNDAEL (Joan Daemen, Vincent Rijmen)
- Serpent (Ross Anderson, Eli Biham, Lars Knudsen)
- Twofish (Bruce Schneier, John Kelsey, Doug Whiting, David Wagner, Chris Hall, Niels Ferguson)

The development and public review process has proven very interesting, showing the power of public review of cryptographic algorithms.

CONCLUSION

The appropriate use of cryptography is critical to modern information security, but it has been shown that even the best defenses can fail. It is critical to understand that cryptography, while providing excellent protection, can also lead to serious problems if the whole system is not considered. Ultimately, practitioners must understand not only the details of the crypto products they are using, but what they are in fact protecting, why these controls are necessary, and who they are protecting these assets against.

Notes

1. Schneier, Bruce, *Applied Cryptography*, ,19 .
2. Stallings, William, *Cryptography and Network Security; Principles and Practice,* , 19 .
3. Spafford, , *Practical UNIX and Internet Security,* , 19 .

4. Schneier, Bruce, *Applied Cryptography,* , 19 , 11.
5. Stallings, William, *Cryptography and Network Security: Principles and Practices,* 19 , 26.
6. Stallings, William, *Cryptography and Network Security: Principles and Practice,* , 19 , 7–9.
7. Kahn, David, *The Codebreakers: The Story of Secret Writing,* , 19 .
8. Smith, Richard, *Internet Cryptography,* 19 , 95.
9. Pfleeger, , *The Principle of Easiest Work,* 19 , 71.
10. Smith, Richard, *Internet Cryptography,* , 19 , 91.
11. Anderson, Ross and Kuhn, Markus, Low Cost Attacks on Tamper Resistant Devices, *Security Protocols, 5th Int. Workshop,* 1997.
12. Smith, Richard E., *Internet Cryptography,* , 19 .
13. Smith, Richard E., *Internet Cryptography,* , 19 , 52.
14. Schneier, Bruce, *Security Pitfalls in Cryptography,* http://www.counterpane.com/pitfalls.html.

Chapter 20
Message Authentication
James S. Tiller

FOR CENTURIES, VARIOUS FORMS OF ENCRYPTION HAVE PROVIDED CONFIDENTIALITY OF INFORMATION AND HAVE BECOME AN INTEGRAL COMPONENT OF COMPUTER COMMUNICATION TECHNOLOGY. Early encryption techniques were based on shared knowledge between the communication participants. Confidentiality and basic authentication were established by the fact that each participant must know a common secret to encrypt or decrypt the communication, or as with very early encryption technology, the diameter of a stick.

The complexity of communication technology has increased the sophistication of attacks and has intensified the vulnerabilities confronting data. The enhancement of communication technology inherently provides tools for attacking other communications. Therefore, mechanisms are employed to reduce the new vulnerabilities that are introduced by new communication technology. The mechanisms utilized to ensure confidentiality, authentication, and integrity are built on the understanding that encryption alone, or simply applied to the data, will not suffice any longer. The need to ensure that the information is from the purported sender, that it was not changed or viewed in transit, and to provide a process to validate these concerns is, in part, the responsibility of message authentication.

This chapter describes the technology of message authentication, its application in various communication environments, and the security considerations of those types of implementations.

HISTORY OF MESSAGE AUTHENTICATION

An encrypted message could typically be trusted for several reasons. First and foremost, the validity of the message content was established by the knowledge that the sender had the appropriate shared information to produce the encrypted message. An extension of this type of assumed assurance was also recognized by the possession of the encrypting device.

An example is the World War II German Enigma, a diabolically complex encryption machine that used three or four wheels to produce ciphertext as an operator typed in a message. The Enigma was closely guarded; if it fell into the enemy's possession, the process of deciphering any captured encrypted messages would become much less complex. The example of the Enigma demonstrates that possession of a device in combination with the secret code for a specific message provided insurance that the message contents received were genuine and authenticated.

As the growth of communication technology embraced computers, the process of encryption moved away from complex and rare mechanical devices to programs that provided algorithms for encryption. The mechanical algorithm of wheels and electrical conduits was replaced by software that could be loaded onto computers, which are readily available, to provide encryption. As algorithms were developed, many became open to the public for inspection and verification for use as a standard. Once the algorithm was exposed, the power of protection was in the key that was combined with the clear message and fed into the algorithm to produce ciphertext.

WHY AUTHENTICATE A MESSAGE?

The ability of a recipient to trust the content of a message is placed squarely on the trust of the communication medium and the expectation that it came from the correct source. As one would imagine, this example of open communication is not suitable for information exchange and is unacceptable for confidential or any form of valuable data.

There are several types of attacks on communications that range from imposters posing as valid participants replaying or redelivering outdated information, to data modification in transit.

Communication technology has eliminated the basic level of interaction between individuals. For two people talking in a room, it can be assured — to a degree — that the information from one individual has not been altered prior to meeting the listener's ears. It can be also assumed that the person that is seen talking is the originator of the voice that is being heard. This example is basic, assumed, and never questioned — it is trusted. However, the same type of communication over an alternate medium must be closely scrutinized due to the massive numbers of vulnerabilities to which the session is exposed.

Computers have added several layers of complexity to the trusting process and the Internet has introduced some very interesting vulnerabilities. With a theoretically unlimited amount of people on a single network, the options of attacks are similarly unlimited. As soon as a message takes advantage of the Internet for a communication medium, all bets are off without layers of protection.

How are senders sure that what they send will be the same at the intended recipient? How can senders be sure that the recipients are who they claim to be? The same questions hold true for the recipients and the question of initiator identity.

TECHNOLOGY OVERVIEW

It is virtually impossible to describe message authentication without discussing encryption. Message authentication is nothing more than a form of cryptography and, in certain implementations, takes advantage of encryption algorithms.

Hash Function

Hash functions are computational functions that take a variable-length input of data and produce a fixed-length result that can be used as a finger-print to represent the original data. Therefore, if the hashes of two messages are identical it can be reasonably assumed that the messages are identical, as well. However, there are caveats to this assumption, which are discussed later.

Hashing information to produce a fingerprint will allow the integrity of the transmitted data to be verified. To illustrate the process, Alice creates the message "Mary loves basketball," and hashes it to produce a smaller, fixed-length message digest, "a012f7." Alice transmits the original message and the hash to Bob. Bob hashes the message from Alice and compares his result with the hash received with the original message from Alice. If the two hashes match, it can be assumed that the message was not altered in transit. If the message was changed after Alice sent it and before Bob received it, Bob's hash will not match, resulting in discovering the loss of message integrity. This example is further detailed in Exhibit 20-1.

In the example, a message from Alice in cleartext is used as input for a hash function. The result is a message digest that is a much smaller, fixed-length value unique to the original cleartext message. The message digest is attached to the original cleartext message and sent to the recipient, Bob. At this point, the message and the hash value are in the clear and vulnerable to attack. When Bob receives the message he separates the message from the digest and hashes the message using the same hash function Alice used. Once the hash process is complete, Bob compares his message digest result with the one included with the original message from Alice. If the two match, the message was not modified in transit.

The caveat to the example illustrated is that an attacker using the same hashing algorithm could simply intercept the message and digest, create a new message and corresponding message digest, and forward it on to the original recipient. The type of attack, known as the "man in the middle,"

Hashing and Sending

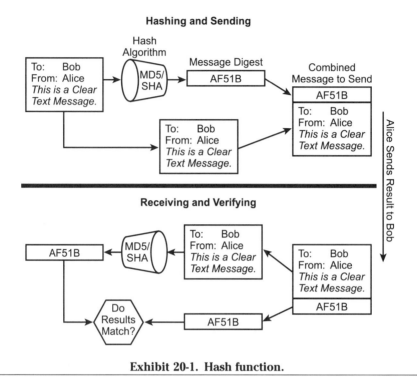

Exhibit 20-1. Hash function.

described here is the driving reason why message authentication is used as a component in overall message protection techniques.

Encryption

Encryption, simply stated, is the conversion of plaintext into unintelligible ciphe-text. Typically, this is achieved with the use of a key and an algorithm. The key is combined with the plaintext and computed with a specific algorithm.

There are two primary types of encryption keys: symmetrical and asymmetrical.

Symmetrical. Symmetrical keys, as shown in Exhibit 20-2, are used for both encryption and decryption of the same data. It is necessary for all the communication participants to have the same key to perform the encryption and decryption. This is also referred to as a shared secret.

In the example, Alice creates a message that is input into an encryption algorithm that uses a unique key to convert the clear message into unintelligible ciphertext. The encrypted result is sent to Bob, who has obtained the same key through a previous mechanism called "out-of-band" messaging. Bob can now decrypt the ciphertext by providing the key and the

Sending and Encrypting

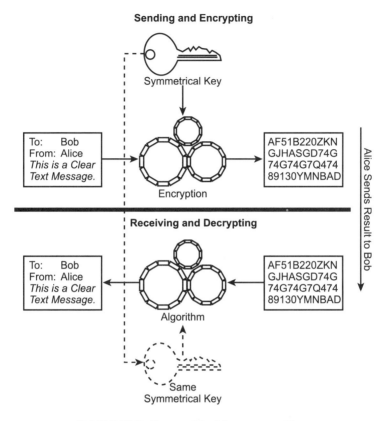

Exhibit 20-2. Symmetrical key encryption.

encrypted data as input for the encryption algorithm. The result is the original plaintext message from Alice.

Asymmetrical. To further accentuate authentication by means of encryption, the technology of public key cryptography, or asymmetrical keys, can be leveraged to provide message authentication and confidentiality.

Alice and Bob each maintain a private and public key pair that is mathematically related. The private key is well-protected and is typically passphrase protected. The public key of the pair is provided to anyone who wants it and wishes to send an encrypted message to the owner of the key pair.

An example of public key cryptography, as shown in Exhibit 20-3, is that Alice could encrypt a message with Bob's public key and send the cyphertext to Bob. Because Bob is the only one with the matching private key, he would be the only recipient who could decrypt the message. However, this interaction only provides confidentiality and not authentication

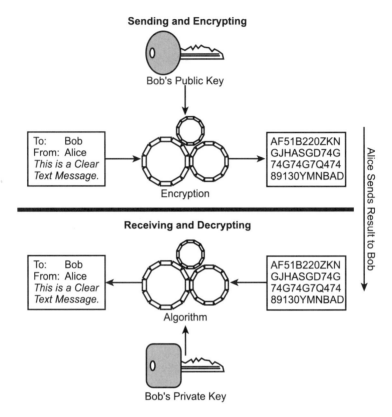

Exhibit 20-3. Asymmetrical key encryption.

because anyone could use Bob's public key to encrypt a message and claim to be Alice.

As illustrated in Exhibit 20-3, the encryption process is very similar to normal symmetrical encryption. A message is combined with a key and processed by an algorithm to construct ciphertext. However, the key being used in the encryption cannot be used for decryption. As detailed in the example, Alice encrypts the data with the public key and sends the result to Bob. Bob uses the corresponding private key to decrypt the information.

To provide authentication, Alice can use her private key to encrypt a message digest generated from the original message, then use Bob's public key to encrypt the original cleartext message, and send it with the encrypted message digest. When Bob receives the message, he can use his private key to decrypt the message. The output can then be verified using Alice's public key to decrypt the message authentication that Alice encrypted with her private key. The process of encrypting information

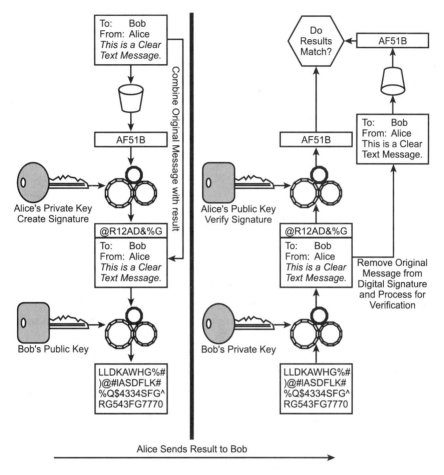

Exhibit 20-4. Digital signature with the use of hash functions.

with a private key to allow the recipient to authenticate the sender is called digital signature. An example of this process is detailed in Exhibit 20-4.

The illustration conveys a typical application of digital signature. There are several techniques of creating digital signatures; however, the method detailed in the exhibit represents the use of a hash algorithm. Alice generates a message for Bob and creates a message digest with a hash function. Alice then encrypts the message digest with her private key. By encrypting the digest with her private key, Alice reduces the system load created by the processor-intensive encryption algorithm and provides an authenticator. The encrypted message digest is attached to the original cleartext message and encrypted using Bob's public key. The example includes the encrypted digest with the original message for the final encryption, but this is not necessary. The final result is sent to Bob. The entire package is decrypted with Bob's private key — ensuring recipient authentication. The result is the cleartext message and an encrypted digest. Bob decrypts the digest with Alice's public key, which authenticates the sender. The result is the original hash created by Alice that is compared to the hash Bob created using the cleartext message. If the two match, the message content has been authenticated along with the communication participants.

Digital signatures are based on the management of public and private keys and their use in the communication. The process of key management and digital signatures has evolved into certificates. Certificates, simply stated, are public keys digitally signed by a trusted Certificate Authority. This provides comfort in the knowledge that the public key being used to establish encrypted communications is owned by the proper person or organization.

Message Authentication Code

Message Authentication Code (MAC) with DES is the combination of encryption and hashing. As illustrated in Exhibit 20-5, as data is fed into a hashing algorithm, a key is introduced into the process.

MAC is very similar to encryption but the MAC is designed to be irreversible, like a standard hash function. Because of the computational properties

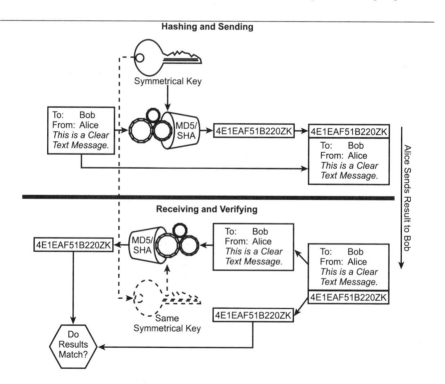

Exhibit 20-5. Message Authentication Code.

of the MAC process, and the inability to reverse the encryption designed into the process, MACs are much less vulnerable to attacks than encryption with the same key length. However, this does not prevent an attacker from forging a new message and MAC.

MAC ensures data integrity like a message digest but adds limited layers of authentication because the recipient would have to have the shared secret to produce the same MAC to validate the message.

The illustration of a message authentication code function appears very similar to symmetrical encryption; however, the process is based on compressing the data into a smaller fixed length that is not designed for decryption. A message is passed into the algorithm, such as DES-CBC, and a symmetrical key is introduced. The result is much like that of a standard message digest, but the key is required to reproduce the digest for verification.

THE NEED FOR AUTHENTICATION

As data is shared across networks — networks that are trusted or not — the opportunities for undesirables to interact with the session are numerous. Of the attacks that communications are vulnerable to, message authentication, in general application, addresses only a portion of the attacks. Message authentication is used as a tool to combine various communication-specific data that can be verified by the valid parties for each message received. Message authentication alone is not an appropriate countermeasure; but when combined with unique session values, it can protect against four basic categories of attacks:

1. masquerading
2. content modification
3. sequence manipulation
4. submission modification

To thwart these vulnerabilities inherent in communications, hash functions can be used to create message digests that contain information for origination authentication and timing of the communications. Typically, time-sensitive random information, or a nonce, is provided during the initialization of the session. The nonce can be input with the data in the hashing process or used as key material to further identify the peer during communications. Also, sequence numbers and timestamps can be generated and hashed for communications that require consistent session interaction — not like that of non-time-sensitive data such as e-mail. The process of authentication, verification through the use of a nonce, and the creation of a key for MAC computations provides an authenticated constant throughout the communication.

Masquerading

The process of masquerading as a valid participant in a network communication is a type of attack. This attack includes the creation of messages from a fraudulent source that appears to come from an authorized origin. Masquerading can also represent the acknowledgment of a message by an attacker in place of the original recipient. False acknowledgment or denial of receipt could complicate nonrepudiation issues. The nonce that may have been used in the hash or the creation of a symmetrical key assists in the identification of the remote system or user during the communication. However, to accommodate origin authentication, there must be an agreement on a key prior to communication. This is commonly achieved by a pre-shared secret or certificate that can be used to authenticate the initial messages and create specific data for protecting the remainder of the communication.

Content Modification

Content modification is when the attacker intercepts a message, changes the content, and then forwards it to the original recipient. This type of attack is quite severe in that it can manifest itself in many ways, depending on the environment.

Sequence Manipulation

Sequence modification is the process of inserting, deleting, or reordering datagrams. This type of attack can have several types of effects on the communication process, depending on the type of data and communication standard. The primary result is denial-of-service. Destruction of data or confusion of the communication can also result.

Submission Modification

Timing modification appears in the form of delay or replay. Both of these attacks can be quite damaging. An example is session establishment. In the event that the protocol is vulnerable to replay, an attacker could use the existence of a valid session establishment to gain unauthorized access.

Message authentication is a procedure to verify that the message received is from the intended source and has not been modified or made susceptible to the previously outlined attacks.

AUTHENTICATION FOUNDATION

To authenticate a message, an authenticator must be produced that can be used later by the recipient to authenticate the message. An authenticator is a primitive, reduction, or representation of the primary message to be authenticated. There are three general concepts in producing an authenticator.

Encryption

With encryption, the ciphertext becomes the authenticator. This is related to the trust relationship discussed earlier by assuming the partner has the appropriate secret and has protected it accordingly.

Consider typical encrypted communications: a message sent from Alice to Bob encrypted with a shared secret. If the secret's integrity is maintained, confidentiality is assured by the fact that no unauthorized entities have the shared secret.

Bob can be assured that the message is valid because the key is secret and an attacker without the key would be unable to modify the ciphertext in a manner to make the desired modifications to the original plaintext message.

Message Digest

As briefly described above, hashing is a function that produces a unique fixed-length value that serves as the authenticator for the communication. Hash functions are one-way, in that the creation of the hash is quite simple, but the reverse is infeasible. A well-constructed hash function should be collision resistant. A collision is when two different messages produce the same result or digest. For a function to take a variable length of data and produce a much smaller fixed-length result, it is mathematically feasible to experience collisions. However, a well-defined algorithm with a large result should have a high resistance to collisions.

Hash functions are used to provide message integrity. It can be argued that encryption can provide much of the same integrity. An example is an attacker could not change an encrypted message to modify the resulting cleartext. However, hash functions are much faster than encryption processes and can be utilized to enhance performance while maintaining integrity. Additionally, the message digest can be made public without revealing the original message.

Message Authentication Code

Message authentication code with DES is a function that uses a secret key to produce a unique fixed-length value that serves as the authenticator. This is much like a hash algorithm but provides the added protection by use of a key. The resulting MAC is appended to the original message prior to sending the data. MAC is similar to encryption but cannot be reversed and does not directly provide any authentication process because both parties share the same secret key.

HASH PROCESS

As mentioned, a hash function is a one-way computation that accepts a variable-length input and produces a fixed-length result. The hash function calculates each bit in a message; therefore, if any portion of the original message changes, the resulting hash will be completely different.

Function Overview

A hash function must meet several requirements to be used for message authentication. The function must:

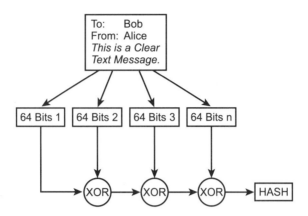

Exhibit 20-6. Simple hash function example.

- be able to accept any size data input
- produce a fixed-length output
- be relatively easy to execute, using limited resources
- make it computationally impractical to derive a message from the digest (one-way property)
- make it computationally impractical to create a message digest that is equal to a message digest created from different information (collision resistance)

Hash functions accommodate these requirements by a set of basic principles. A message is processed in a sequence of blocks, as shown in Exhibit 20-6. The size of the blocks is determined by the hash function. The function addresses each block one at a time and produces parity for each bit. Addressing each bit provides the message digest with the unique property that dramatic changes will occur if a single bit is modified in the original message.

As detailed in Exhibit 20-6, the message is separated into specific portions. Each portion is XOR with the next portion, resulting in a value the same size of the original portions, not their combined value. As each result is processed, it is combined with the next portion until the entire message has been sent through the function. The final result is a value the size of the original portions that were created and a fixed-length value is obtained.

MESSAGE AUTHENTICATION CODES AND PROCESSES

Message authentication code with DES is applying an authentication process with a key. MACs are created using a symmetrical key so the intended recipient or the bearer of the key can only verify the MAC. A plain hash function can be intercepted and replaced or brute-force attacked to determine collisions that can be of use to the attacker. With MACs, the addition of a key complicates the attack due to the secret key used in its computation.

There are four modes of DES that can be utilized:

1. block cipherbased
2. hash functionbased
3. stream cipherbased
4. unconditionally secure

Block Cipher-based Mode

Block cipher-based message authentication can be derived from block cipher algorithms. A commonly used version is DES-CBC-MAC, which simply put is DES encryption based on the Cipher Block Chaining (CBC) mode of block cipher to create a MAC. A very common form of MAC is Data Authentication Algorithm (DAA), which is based on DES. The process uses the CBC mode of operation of DES with a zero initialization vector. As illustrated in Exhibit 20-7, the message is grouped into contiguous blocks of 64 bits; the last group is padded on the right with zeros to attain the 64-bit requirement. Each block is fed into the DES algorithm with a key to produce a 64-bit Data Authentication Code (DAC). The resulting DAC is XOR with the next 64 bits of data is then fed again into the DES algorithm. This process continues until the last block, and returns the final MAC.

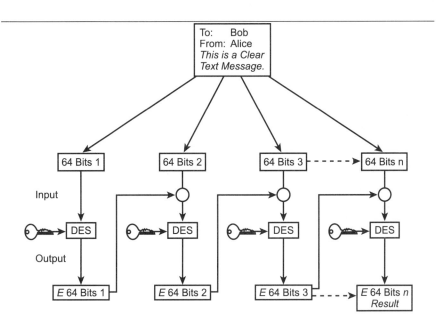

Exhibit 20-7. MAC Based on DES CBC.

A block cipher is a type of symmetric key encryption algorithm that accepts a fixed block of plaintext to produce ciphertext of the same length — a linear relationship. There are four primary modes of operation on which the block ciphers can be based:

1. Electronic Code Book (ECB)
2. Cipher Block Chaining (CBC)
3. Cipher Feedback (CFB)
4. Output Feedback (OFB)

Electronic Code Book (ECB). Electronic Code Book mode accepts each block of plaintext and encrypts it independently of previous block cipher results. The weakness in ECB is that identical input blocks will produce identical cipher results of the same length. Interestingly, this is a fundamental encryption flaw that affected the Enigma. For each input, there was a corresponding output of the same length. The "step" of the last wheel in an Enigma could be derived from determinations in ciphertext patterns.

Cipher Block Chaining (CBC). With CBC mode, each block result of ciphertext is exclusively OR'ed (XOR) with the previous calculated block, and then encrypted. Any patterns in plaintext will not be transferred to the cipher due to the XOR process with the previous block.

Cipher Feedback (CFB). Similar to CBC, CFB executes an XOR between the plaintext and the previous calculated block of data. However, prior to being XOR'ed with the plaintext, the previous block is encrypted. The amount of the previous block to be used (the feedback) can be reduced and not utilized as the entire feedback value. If the full feedback value is used and two cipher blocks are identical, the output of the following operation will be identical. Therefore, any patterns in the message will be revealed.

Output Feedback (OFB). Output Feedback is similar to CFB in that the result is encrypted and XOR'ed with the plaintext. However, the creation of the feedback is generated independently of the ciphertext and plaintext processes. A sequence of blocks is encrypted with the previous block, the result is then XOR'ed with the plaintext.

Hash Function-based Mode

Hash Function-based message authentication code (HMAC) uses a key in combination with hash functions to produce a checksum of the message. RFC 2104 defines that HMAC can be used with any iterative cryptographic hash function (e.g., MD5, SHA-1) in combination with a secret shared key. The cryptographic strength of HMAC depends on the properties of the underlying hash function.

The definition of HMAC requires a cryptographic hash function and a secret key. The hash function is where data is hashed by iterating a basic compression function on blocks of data, typically 64 bytes in each block. The symmetrical key to be used can be any length up to the block size of the hash function. If the key is longer than the hash block size, the key is hashed and the result is used as the key for the HMAC function.

This process is very similar to the DES-CBC-MAC discussed above; however, the use of the DES algorithm is significantly slower than most hashing functions, such as MD5 and SHA-1.

HMAC is a process of combining existing cryptographic functions and a keyed process. The modularity of the standard toward the type of cryptographic function that can be used in the process has become the point of acceptance and popularity. The standards treat the hash function as a variable that can consist of any hash algorithm. The benefits are that legacy, or existing hash implementations can be used in the process and the hash function can be easily replaced without affecting the process. The latter example represents an enormous security advantage. In the event the hash algorithm is compromised, a new one can be immediately implemented.

There are several steps to the production of a HMAC; these are graphically represented in Exhibit 20-8. The first step is to determine the key length requested and compare it to the block size of the hash being implemented. As described above, if the key is longer than the block size it is

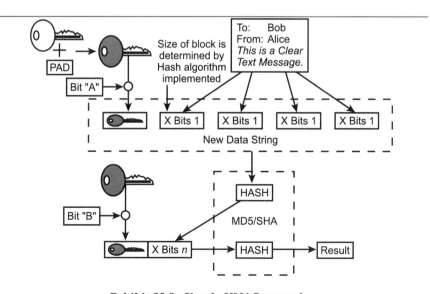

Exhibit 20-8. Simple HMAC example.

hashed, the result will match the block size defined by the hash. In the event the key is smaller, it is padded with zeros to accommodate the required block size.

Once the key is defined, it is XOR'ed with a string of predefined bits "A" to create a new key that is combined with the message. The new message is hashed according to the function defined (see Exhibit 20-6). The hash function result is combined with the result of XOR the key with another defined set of bits "B." The new combination of the second key instance and the hash results are hashed again to create the final result.

Stream Cipher-based Mode

A stream cipher is a symmetric key algorithm that operates on small units of plaintext, typically bits. When data is encrypted with a stream cipher, the transformation of the plaintext into ciphertext is dependant on when the bits were merged during the encryption. The algorithm creates a keystream that is combined with the plaintext. The keystream can be independent of the plaintext and ciphertext (typically referred to as a synchronous cipher), or it can depend on the data and the encryption (typically referred to as self-synchronizing cipher).

Unconditionally Secure Mode

Unconditional stream cipher is based on the theoretical aspects of the properties of a one-time pad. A one-time pad uses a string of random bits to create the keystream that is the same length as the plaintext message. The keystream is combined with the plaintext to produce the ciphertext. This method of employing a random key is very desirable for communication security because it is considered unbreakable by brute force. Security at this level comes with an equally high price: key management. Each key is the same size and length as the message it was used to encrypt, and each message is encrypted with a new key.

MESSAGE AUTHENTICATION OVER ENCRYPTION

Why use message authentication (e.g., hash functions and message authentication codes) when encryption seems to meet all the requirements provided by message authentication techniques? Following are brief examples and reasoning to support the use of message authentication over encryption.

Speed

Cryptographic hash functions, such as MD5 and SHA-1, execute much faster and use less system resources than typical encryption algorithms. In the event that a message only needs to be authenticated, the process of encrypting the entire message, such as a document or large file, is not entirely logical and consumes valuable system resources.

The reasoning of reducing load on a system holds true for digital signatures. If Alice needs to send a document to Bob that is not necessarily confidential but may contain important instructions, authentication is paramount. However, encrypting the entire document with Alice's private key is simply overkill. Hashing the document will produce a very small rendition of the original message, which then can be encrypted with her private key. The much smaller object encrypts quickly and provides ample authentication and abundant message integrity.

Limited Restrictions

No export restrictions on cryptographic functions are defined. Currently, the laws enforcing import and export restrictions in the international community are complicated and constantly changing. Basically, these laws are to control the level of technology and intellectual property of one country from another. Message authentication releases the communication participants from these restrictions.

Application Issues

There are applications where the same message is broadcast to several destinations. One system is elected as the communication monitor and verifies the message authentication on behalf of the other systems. If there is a violation, the monitoring system alerts the other systems.

Simple Network Management Protocol (SNMP) is an example where command messages can be forged or modified in transit. With the application of MAC, or HMAC, a password can be implemented to act as a key to allow a degree of authentication and message authentication. Each system in the community is configured with a password that can be combined with the data during the hash process and verified upon receipt. Because all the members are configured with the same password, the data can be hashed with the locally configured password and verified. It can also be forged at the destination.

System Operation

In the event that one of a communication pair is overburdened, the process of decryption would be overwhelming. Authentication can be executed in random intervals to ensure authentication with limited resources. Given the hashing process is much less intensive than encryption, periodical hashing and comparisons will consume fewer system cycles.

Code Checksum

Application authentication is achieved by adding the checksum to the program. While the program itself may be open to modification, the checksum can be verified at run-time to ensure that the code is in the original format and should produce the expected results. Otherwise, an attacker could have constructed a malicious activity to surreptitiously operate while the original application was running. It can be argued that if an attacker can modify the code, the checksum should pose little resistance because it can be simply regenerated also. Given the typically small size of checksums, it is typically published on several Web pages or included in an e-mail. In other words, an attacker would have to modify every existence of the checksum to ensure that the recipient would inadvertently verify the modified application. If encryption was utilized, the program would have to decrypt at each run-time, consuming time and resources. This is very important for systems that provide security functions, such as firewalls, routers, and VPN access gateways.

An example of the need for code protection can be illustrated by the heavy reliance on the Internet for obtaining software, updates, or patches. In early computing, systems patches and software were mailed to the recipient as the result of a direct request, or as a registered system user. As communication technology advanced, Bulletin Board Systems (BBS) could be directly accessed with modems to obtain the necessary data. In both of these examples, a fair amount of trust in the validity of the downloaded code is assumed.

In comparison, the complexity of the Internet is hidden from the user by a simple browser that is used to access the required files. The data presented in a Web page can come from dozens of different sources residing on many different servers throughout the Internet. There are few methods to absolutely guarantee that the file being downloaded is from a trusted source. To add to the complexity, mirrors can be established to provide a wider range of data sources to the Internet community. However, the security of a mirrored site must be questioned. The primary site may have extensive security precautions, but a mirror site may not. An attacker could modify the code on an alternate download location. When the code is finally obtained, a checksum can be validated to ensure that the code obtained is the code the creator intended for receipt.

Utilization of Existing Resources

There is available installed technology designed for DES encryption processes. The use of DEC-CBC-MAC can take advantage of existing technology to increase performance and support the requirements of the communication. The DES encryption standard has been available for quite some time. There are many legacy systems that have hardware designed specifically for DES encryption. As more advanced encryption becomes available and new standards evolve, the older hardware solutions can be utilized to enhance the message authentication process.

SECURITY CONSIDERATIONS

The strength of any message authentication function, such as a MAC or HASH, is determined by two primary factors:

- one-way property
- collision resistance

One-way property is the ability of the hash to produce a message digest that cannot be used to determine the original message. This is one of the most significant aspects of message authentication algorithms. If a message authentication algorithm is compromised and a weakness is discovered, the result could have a detrimental effect on various forms of communication.

MD4 is an example of a function's poor one-way property. Within MD4, the data is padded to obtain a length divisible by 512, plus 448. A 64-bit value that defines the original message's length is appended to the padded message. The result is separated into 512-bit blocks and hashed using three distinct rounds of computation. Weaknesses were quickly discovered if the first or last rounds were not processed. However, it was later discovered that without the last round, the original message could be derived. MD4 had several computation flaws that proved the function had limited one-way capabilities.

Collision resistance is the most considered security aspect of message authentication functions. A collision is typically defined as when two different messages have the same hash result. In the event that a hash function has a collision vulnerability, such as MD2, a new message can be generated and used to replace the original in a communication, and the hash will remain valid. The combination of the original hash and the known vulnerability will provide the attacker with enough information to produce an alternative message that will produce the same checksum. An example is the hash algorithm MD2. It was created for 8-bit computers in the late 1980s and uses 16-bit blocks of the message against which to execute the hash. MD2 produces a 16-bit checksum prior to passing through the hash function. If this checksum is omitted, the production of a collision would be trivial. MD4 was subject to weak collision resistance as well, and it was proven that collisions could be produced in less than a minute on a simple personal computer.

The concept of a collision is a fundamental issue concerning probabilities. Take, for example, a hash function that produces an n-bit digest. If one is looking for a result of x, it can be assumed that one would have to try 2^n input possibilities. This type of brute-force attack is based on a surprising outcome referred to as the "Birthday paradox": What is the least number of people in a group that can provide the probability, greater than half, that at least two people will have the same birthday?

If there are 365 days per year, and if the number of people exceeds 365, there will be a successful collision. If the number of people in the group is less than 365, then the number of possibilities is 365^n, where n is the number of people in a group. For those still wondering, the number of people, assuming there is a collision, is 23. This is a very small number; but when calculated against the number of possibilities that any two people's birthdays match, one sees that there are 253 possibilities. This is simply calculated as $n(n-1)/2$, which results in the probability of $P(365, 23) = 0.5073$, or greater than one-half.

The birthday paradox states that given a random integer with a constant value between 1 and n, what is the selection of the number of permutations (the number of people required to meet 0.5 probability) that will result in a collision?

Given a fixed-length output that can represent an infinite amount of variation, it is necessary to understand the importance of a robust algorithm. It is also necessary for the algorithm to produce a relatively large result that remains manageable.

However, as certificates and other public key cryptography is utilized, message authentication processes will not be exposed to direct attack. The use of a HASH to accommodate a digital signature process is based on the ownership and trust of a private key; the HASH, while important, is only a step in a much more complicated process.

CONCLUSION

Communication technology has provided several avenues for unauthorized interaction with communications requiring the need to address security in ways previously unanalyzed. Message authentication provides a means to thwart various forms of attack and can enhance other aspects of communication security. A message "fingerprint" can be created in several ways, ranging from simple bit parity functions (hash) to utilization of encryption algorithms (DES-CBC-MAC) to complicated hybrids (HMAC). This fingerprint cannot only be used to ensure message integrity, but also given the inherent process of message reduction, it lends itself to authentication and signature processes.

Message authentication is a broad activity that employs several types of technology in various applications to achieve timely, secure communications. The combinations of the application of these technologies are virtually limitless and, as advancements in cryptography, cryptanalysis, and overall communication technology are realized, message authentication will most certainly remain an interesting process.

Domain 6
Security
Architecture
and Models

THIS DOMAIN ENCOMPASSES THE TOTALITY OF THE SECURITY DESIGN FOR A SYSTEM OR APPLICATION. New chapters in this domain address security implemented in UNIX systems as well as the implementation of controls in various network topologies.

In essence, wherever information is stored, processed, or transmitted throughout the n-tier environment, an appropriate control or set of controls must be implemented and managed.

Chapter 21
Introduction to UNIX Security for Security Practitioners

Jeffery J. Lowder

IN AN AGE OF INCREASINGLY SOPHISTICATED SECURITY TOOLS (e.g., firewalls, virtual private networks, intrusion detection systems, etc.), MANY PEOPLE DO NOT CONSIDER OPERATING SYSTEM SECURITY A VERY SEXY TOPIC. Indeed, given that the UNIX operating system was originally developed in 1969 and that multiple full-length books have been written on protecting UNIX machines, one might be tempted to dismiss the entire topic as "old hat." Nevertheless, operating system security is a crucial component of an overall security program. In the words of Anup Ghosh, the operating system is "the foundation for any software that runs on a machine," and this is just as true in the era of E-commerce as it was in the past. Thus, security practitioners who are even indirectly responsible for the protection of UNIX machines need to have at least a basic understanding of UNIX security. This chapter attempts to address that need by providing an overview of security services common to all flavors of UNIX; security mechanisms available in trusted UNIX are beyond the scope of this chapter (but see Exhibit 21-1).

OPERATING SYSTEM SECURITY SERVICES

Summers[7] lists the following security services that operating systems in general can provide:

1. *Identification and authentication.* A secure operating system must be able to distinguish between different users (identification); it also needs some assurance that users are who they say they are (authentication). Identification and authentication are crucial to the other operating system security services. There are typically three ways to authenticate users: something the user *knows* (e.g., a password), something the user *has* (e.g., a smart card), or something the user *is*

Exhibit 21-1. Versions of trusted or secure UNIX.

A1 (Verified Design)	No operating systems have been evaluated in class A1
B3 (Security Domains)	Wang Government Services, Inc. XTS-300 STOP 4.4.2
B2 (Structured Protection)	Trusted Information Systems, Inc. Trusted XENIX 4.0
B1 (Labeled Security Protection)	Digital Equipment Corporation ULTRIX MLS+ Version 2.1 on VAX Station 3100 Hewlett Packard Corporation HP-UX BLS Release 9.09+ Silicon Graphics Inc. Trusted IRIX/B Release 4.0.5EPL
C2 (Controlled Access Protection)	No UNIX operating systems have been evaluated in class C2
C1 (Discretionary Access Protection)	Products are no longer evaluated at this class
D1 (Minimal Protection)	No operating systems have been evaluated in class D1

Note: Various versions of UNIX have been evaluated by the U.S. Government's National Security Agency (NSA) according to the Trusted Computer System Evaluation Criteria. (By way of comparison, Microsoft Corporation's Windows NT Workstation and Windows NT Server, Version 4.0, have both been evaluated at class C2.) The above chart is taken from the NSA's Evaluated Product List.

(e.g., a retinal pattern). Passwords are by far the most common authentication method; this method is also extremely vulnerable to compromise. Passwords can be null, easily guessed, cracked, written down and then discovered, or "sniffed."

2. *Access control.* An operating system is responsible for providing logical access control through the use of subjects, objects, access rights, and access validation. A subject includes a userID, password, group memberships, privileges, etc. for each user. Object security information includes the owner, group, access restrictions, etc. Basic access rights include read, write, and execute. Finally, an operating system evaluates an access request (consisting of a subject, an object, and the requested access) according to access validation rules.

3. *Availability and integrity.* Does the system start up in a secure fashion? Does the system behave according to expectations during an attack? Is the data on the system internally consistent? Does the data correspond with the real-world entities that it represents?

4. *Audit.* An audit trail contains a chronological record of events. Audit trails can be useful as a deterrent; they are even more useful in investigating incidents (e.g., Who did it? How?). Audit trails have even been used as legal evidence in criminal trials. However, for an audit trail to be useful in any of these contexts, the operating system must record all security-relevant events, protect the confidentiality and integrity of the audit trail, and ensure that the data is available in a timely manner.

5. *Security facilities for users.* Non-privileged users need some method for granting rights to their files and changing their passwords. Privileged users need additional facilities, including the ability to lock accounts, gain access to other users' files, configure auditing options, change ownership of files, change users' memberships in groups, etc.

The following pages explore how these services are implemented in the UNIX family of operating systems.

IDENTIFICATION AND AUTHENTICATION

UNIX identifies users according to usernames and authenticates them with passwords. In many implementations of UNIX, both usernames and passwords are limited to eight characters. As a security measure, UNIX does not store passwords in plaintext. Instead, it stores the password as ciphertext, using a modified Digital Encryption Standard (DES) algorithm (crypt) for encryption. The encrypted password, along with other pertinent account information (see Exhibit 21-2), is stored in the */etc/passwd* file according to the following format:

```
username:encrypted password:UserID:GroupID:user's
           full name:home directory:login shell
```

Exhibit 21-2. Sample */etc/passwd* entries.

```
keith::1001:15:Keith Smith:/usr/keith:/bin/csh
greg:Qf@14pL1aqzqB:Greg Jones:/usr/greg/:/bin/csh
cathy:*:1003:15:Cathy Jones:/usr/cathy:/bin/csh
```

(In this example, user keith has no password, user greg has an encrypted password, and user cathy has a shadowed password.)

Unfortunately, the */etc/passwd* file is world-readable, which can place standard, "out-of-the-box" configurations of UNIX at risk for a brute-force password-guessing attack by anyone with system access. Given enough computing resources and readily available tools like Alec Muffet's **crack** utility, an attacker can eventually guess every password on the system. In light of this vulnerability, all current implementations of UNIX now provide support for so-called "shadow" passwords. The basic idea is to store the encrypted passwords in a separate file (*/etc/shadow* to be exact) that is only readable by the privileged "root" account. Also, although vanilla UNIX does not provide support for proactive password checking, add-on tools are available. Finally, password aging is not part of standard UNIX but is supported by many proprietary implementations.

UserIDs (UIDs) are typically 16-bit integers, meaning that they can have any value between 0 and 65,535. *The operating system uses UIDs, not usernames, to track users.* Thus, it is entirely possible in UNIX for two or more usernames to share the same UID. In general, it is a bad idea to give two usernames the same UID. Also, certain UIDs are reserved. (For example, any username with an UID of zero is considered root by the operating system.) Finally, UNIX requires that certain programs like **/bin/passwd** (used by users to change their passwords) and */bin/login* (executed when a user initiates a login sequence) run as root; however, users should not be able to arbitrarily gain root permissions on the system. UNIX solves this problem by allowing certain programs to run under the permissions of another UID. Such programs are called Set UserID (SUID) programs. Of course, such programs can also be risky: if attackers are able to interrupt an SUID program, they may be able to gain root access and ensure that they are able to regain such access in the future.

GroupIDs (GIDs) are also typically 16-bit integers. The GID listed in a user's entry in */etc/passwd* is that user's primary GID; however, in some versions of UNIX, a user can belong to more than one group. A complete listing of all groups, including name, GID, and members (users), can be found in the file */etc/group*.

Once a user successfully logs in, UNIX executes the global file */etc/profile* along with the *.profile* file in the user's home directory using the user's shell specified in */etc/passwd*. If the permissions on these files are not restricted properly, an attacker could modify these files and cause unauthorized commands to be executed each time the user logs in. UNIX also updates the file */usr/adm/lastlog,* which stores the date and time of the latest login for each account. This information can be obtained via the **finger** command and creates another vulnerability: systems with the **finger** command enabled may unwittingly provide attackers with useful information in planning an attack.

ACCESS CONTROL

Standard UNIX systems prevent the unauthorized use of system resources (e.g., files, memory, devices, etc.) by promoting discretionary access control. Permissions are divided into three categories: owner, group, and other. However, privileged accounts can bypass this access control. UNIX treats all system resources consistently by making no distinction between files, memory, and devices; all resources are treated as files for access control purposes.

The UNIX filesystem has a tree structure, with the top-level directory designated as /. Some of the second-level directories are standards. For example, */bin* contains system executables, */dev* contains devices, */usr* contains user files, etc. Each directory contains a pointer to itself (the '.' file) and a pointer to its parent directory (the '..' file). (In the top-level directory, the '..' file points to the top-level directory.) Every file (and directory) has an owner, a group, and a set of permissions. This information can be o btained using the **ls -l** command:

```
drwxr-xr-x   1   jlowder   staff    1024   Feb 21 18:30   ./
drwxr-xr-x   2   jlowder   staff    1024   Oct 28 1996    ../
-rw-------   3   jlowder   staff    2048   Feb 21 18:31   file1
-rw-rw----   4   jlowder   staff    2048   Feb 21 18:31   file2
-rw-rw-rw-   5   jlowder   staff    2048   Feb 21 18:31   file3
-rws------   6   jlowder   staff   18495   Feb 21 18:31   file4
```

In the above example, file1 is readable and writable only by the owner; file2 is readable and writable by both the owner and members of the 'staff' group; file3 is readable and writable by everyone; and file4 is readable and writable by the owner and is a SetUID program.

Devices are displayed a bit differently. The following is the output of the command **ls -l /dev/cdrom /dev/tty02**:

```
br--------   1   root   root   1024   Oct 28 1996   /dev/cdrom
crw-------   2   root   root   1024   Oct 28 1996   /dev/tty02
```

UNIX identifies block devices (e.g., disks) with the letter 'b' and character devices (e.g., modems, printers) with the letter 'c.'

When a user or process creates a new file, the file is given default permissions. For a process-created file (e.g., a file created by a text editor), the process specifies the default permissions. For user-created files, the default permissions are specified in the startup file for the user's shell program. File owners can change the permissions (or mode) of a file by using the **chmod** (change mode) command.

UNIX operating systems treat directories as files, but as a special type of file. Directory "files" have a specified structure, consisting of filename-inode number pairs. Inode numbers refer to a given inode, a sort of record containing information about where parts of the file are stored, file permissions, ownership, group, etc. The important thing to note about the filename-inode number pairs is that *inode numbers need not be unique*. Multiple filenames can (and often do) refer to the same inode number. This is significant from a security perspective, because the **rm** command only removes the directory entry for a file, not the file itself. Thus, to remove a file, one must remove all of the links to that file.

AVAILABILITY AND INTEGRITY

One aspect of availability is whether a system restarts securely after failure. Traditional UNIX systems boot in single-user mode, usually as root. And, unfortunately, single-user mode allows literally anyone sitting at the system console to execute privileged commands. Thus, single-user mode represents a security vulnerability in traditional UNIX. Depending on the flavor of UNIX, the security administrator has one or two options for closing this hole. First, if the operating system supports it, the security practitioner should configure the system to require a password before booting in single-user mode. Second, tight physical controls should be implemented to prevent physical access to the system console.

System restarts are also relevant to system integrity. After an improper shutdown or system crash, the UNIX **fsck** command will check filesystems for inconsistencies and repair them (either automatically or with administrator interaction). Using the **fsck** command, an administrator can detect unreferenced inodes, used disk blocks listed as free blocks, etc.

Although there are many ways to supplement UNIX filesystem integrity, one method has become so popular that it deserves to be mentioned here. Developed by Gene Kim and Gene Spafford of Purdue University, Tripwire is an add-on utility that provides additional filesystem integrity by creating a signature or message digest for each file to be monitored. Tripwire allows administrators to specify what files or directories to monitor, which attributes of an object to monitor, and which message digest algorithm (e.g., MD5, SHA, etc.) to use in generating signatures. When executed, Tripwire reports on changed, added, or deleted files. Thus, not only can Tripwire detect Trojan horses, but it can also detect changes that violate organizational policy.

AUDIT

Different flavors of UNIX use different directories to hold their log files (e.g., */usr/adm, /var/adm,* or */var/log*). But wherever the directory is located, traditional UNIX records security-relevant events in the following log files:

- *lastlog:* records the last time a user logged in
- *utmp:* records accounting information used by the **who** command
- *wtmp:* records every time a user logs in or out; this information can be retrieved using the **last** command.
- *acct:* records all executed commands; this information can be obtained using the **lastcomm** command (unfortunately, there is no way to select events or users to record; thus, this log can consume an enormous amount of disk space if implemented)

Furthermore, most versions of UNIX support the following logfiles:

- *sulog:* logs all su attempts, and indicates whether they were successful
- *messages:* records a copy of all the messages sent to the console and other *syslog* messages

Additionally, most versions of UNIX provide a generic logging utility called *syslog*. Originally designed for the *sendmail* program, *syslog* accepts messages from literally any program. (This also creates an interesting audit vulnerability: any user can create false log entries.) Messages consist of the program name, facility, priority, and the log message itself; the system prepends each message with the system date, time, and name. For example:

```
Nov 7 04:02:00 alvin syslogd: restart
Nov 7 04:10:15 alvin login: ROOT LOGIN REFUSED on ttya
Nov 7 04:10:21 alvin login: ROOT LOGIN on console
```

The *syslog* facility is highly configurable; administrators specify in */etc/syslog.conf* what to log and how to log it. *syslog* recognizes multiple security states or priorities, including emerg (emergency), alert (immediate action required), crit (critical condition), err (ordinary error), warning, notice, info, and debug. Furthermore, *syslog* allows messages to be stored in (or sent to) multiple locations, including files, devices (e.g., console, printer, etc.), and even other machines. These last two options make it much more difficult for intruders to hide their tracks. (Of course, if intruders have superuser privileges, they can change the logging configuration or even stop logging altogether.)

SECURITY FACILITIES FOR USERS

Traditional UNIX supports one privileged administrative role (the "root" account). The root account can create, modify, suspend, and delete user accounts; configure auditing options; administer group memberships; add or remove filesystems; execute any program on the system; shut the system down; etc. In short, root accounts have all possible privileges. This violates both the principle of separation of duties (by not having a separate role for operators, security administrators, etc.) and the principle of complete mediation (by exempting root from access control).

Non-privileged users can change their passwords using the **passwd** command, and they can modify the permissions of their files and directories using the **chmod** program.

MISCELLANEOUS TOPICS

Finally, there are a few miscellaneous topics that pertain to UNIX security but do not neatly fall into one of the categories of operating system security listed at the beginning of this chapter. These miscellaneous topics include *tcpwrapper* and fundamental operating system holes.

Vulnerabilities in Traditional UNIX

Many (but by no means all) UNIX security vulnerabilities result from flaws in its original design. Consider the following examples:

1. *Insecure defaults.* Traditional UNIX was designed for developers; it is shipped with insecure defaults. Out-of-the-box UNIX configurations include enabled default accounts with known default passwords. Traditional UNIX also ships with several services open by default, password shadowing not enabled, etc. Administrators should immediately disable unnecessary accounts and ports. If a default account is necessary, the administrator should change the password.

2. *Superuser and SUID attacks.* Given that UNIX does not have different privileged roles, anyone who compromises the root account has compromised the entire system. When combined with SUID programs, the combination can be disastrous. An attacker need simply "trick" the SUID program into executing an attack, either by modifying the SUID program or by supplying bogus inputs. If the SUID program runs as root, then the attack is likewise executed as root. Given this vulnerability, SUID programs should be prohibited if at all feasible; if not, the system administrator must continually monitor SUID programs to ensure they have not been tampered with.

3. *PATH and Trojan horse attacks.* When a user requests a file, the PATH environment variable specifies the directories that will be searched and the order in which they will be searched. By positioning a Trojan horse version of a command in a directory listed in the search path, such that the Trojan horse directory appears prior to the real program's directory, an attacker could get a user to execute the Trojan horse. Therefore, to avoid this vulnerability in the PATH variable, administrators can specify absolute filepaths and place the user's home directory last.

4. *Trust relationships.* UNIX allows both administrators and users to specify trusted hosts. Administrators can specify trusted hosts in the */etc/hosts.equiv* file and users in a file named *.rhosts* in their home directory. When a trust relationship exists, a user on a trusted (remote) machine can log into the local machine without entering a password. Furthermore, when the trust relationship is defined by an administrator in the */etc/hosts.equiv* file, the remote user can log into the local machine *as any user on the local system*, again without entering a password. Clearly, this is extremely risky. Even if one

trusts the users on the remote machine, there are still two significant risks. First, the trust relationships are transitive. If one trusts person A, then one implicitly trusts everyone who person A trusts. Second, if the remote machine is compromised, the local machine is at risk. For these reasons, trust relationships are extremely risky and should almost always be avoided.

TCP Wrapper

Written by Wietse Venema, *tcpwrapper* allows one to filter, monitor, and log incoming requests for various Internet services (systat, finger, ftp, telnet, rlogin, rsh, exec, tftp, talk, etc.). The utility is highly transparent; it does not require any changes to existing software. The chief advantage of *tcpwrapper* is that it provides a decent access control mechanism for network services. For example, an administrator might want to allow incoming FTP connections, but only from a specific network. *tcpwrapper* provides a convenient, consistent method for implementing this type of access control. Depending on the implementation of UNIX, *tcpwrapper* might also provide superior audit trails for the services it supports.

Login or Warning Banner

UNIX can be configured to display a "message of the day," specified in the file */etc/motd*, to all users upon login. At least part of this message should be a so-called login or warning banner, advising would-be attackers that access to system resources constitutes consent to monitoring and that unauthorized use could lead to criminal prosecution (see Exhibit 21-3).

Exhibit 21-3. Sample warning banner.

WARNING: THIS SYSTEM FOR AUTHORIZED USE ONLY. USE OF THIS
SYSTEM CONSTITUTES CONSENT TO MONITORING; UNAUTHORIZED USE
COULD RESULT IN CRIMINAL PROSECUTION. IF YOU DO NOT AGREE
TO THESE CONDITIONS, DO NOT LOG IN!

CONCLUSION

Traditional UNIX implements some of the components of operating systems security to varying extents. It has many well-known vulnerabilities; out-of-the-box configurations should not be trusted. Furthermore, add-on security tools can supplement core UNIX services. With proper configuration, a UNIX system can be reasonably protected from would-be intruders or attackers.

References

1. Anonymous, *Maximum Security*, Sams.net, New York, 1997.
2. Farrow, Rik, *UNIX System Security: How to Protect Your Data and Prevent Intruders*, Addison-Wesley, New York, 1991.
3. Garfinkel, Simson and Spafford, Gene, *Practical UNIX and Internet Security*, 2nd ed., O'Reilly & Associates, Sebastopol, CA, 1996.
4. Ghosh, Anup K., *E-commerce Security: Weak Links, Best Defenses*, John Wiley & Sons, New York, 1998.
5. Gollmann, Dieter, *Computer Security*, John Wiley & Sons, New York, 1999.
6. National Security Agency, Evaluated Products List Indexed by Rating, <URL: http://www.radium.ncsc.nil/tpep/epl/epl-by-class.html>, January 31, 2000.
7. Summers, Rita C., *Secure Computing: Threats and Safeguards*, McGraw-Hill, New York, 1997.

Domain 7
Operations Security

AT THE TIME OF THIS WRITING, ALMOST EVERY NEWSPAPER AND MAGA-ZINE FEATURE HEADLINES DECRYING THE LATEST HACK ATTACK OR THE MOST VIRULENT OF COMPUTER WORMS INFECTING HUNDREDS OF THOU-SANDS OF COMPUTERS WORLDWIDE. Information security professionals must be armed with data that can assist in understanding how malicious attacks against information assets can be detected and prevented. More-over, they must be armed with information should it be necessary to recover from an attack.

The chapters in this domain speak to the many tools and techniques uti-lized by hackers, and also introduces to the reader valuable methods for controlling malicious code.

Chapter 22
Hacker Tools and Techniques
Ed Skoudis

RECENT HEADLINES DEMONSTRATE THAT THE LATEST CROP OF HACKER TOOLS AND TECHNIQUES CAN BE HIGHLY DAMAGING TO AN ORGANIZATION'S SENSITIVE INFORMATION AND REPUTATION. With the rise of powerful, easy-to-use, and widely distributed hacker tools, many in the security industry have observed that today is the golden age of hacking. The purpose of this chapter is to describe the tools in widespread use today for compromising computer and network security. Additionally, for each tool and technique described, the chapter presents practical advice on defending against each type of attack.

The terminology applied to these tools and their users has caused some controversy, particularly in the computer underground. Traditionally, and particularly in the computer underground, the term "hacker" is a benign word, referring to an individual who is focused on determining how things work and devising innovative approaches to addressing computer problems. To differentiate these noble individuals from a nasty attacker, this school of thought labels malicious attackers as "crackers." While hackers are out to make the world a better place, crackers want to cause damage and mayhem. To avoid the confusion often associated with these terms, in this chapter, the terms "system and security administrator" and "security practitioner" will be used to indicate an individual who has a legitimate and authorized purpose for running these tools. The term "attacker" will be used for those individuals who seek to cause damage to systems or who are not authorized to run such tools.

Many of the tools described in this chapter have dual personalities; they can be used for good or evil. When used by malicious individuals, the tools allow a motivated attacker to gain access to a network, mask the fact that a compromise occurred, or even bring down service, thereby impacting large masses of users. When used by a security practitioner with proper authorization, some tools can be used to measure the security stance of their own organizations, by conducting "ethical hacking" tests to find vulnerabilities before attackers do.

CAVEAT

The purpose of this chapter is to explain the various computer underground tools in use today, and to discuss defensive techniques for addressing each type of tool. This chapter is not designed to encourage attacks. Furthermore, the tools described below are for illustration purposes only, and mention in this chapter is not an endorsement. If readers feel compelled to experiment with these tools, they should do so at their own risk, realizing that such tools frequently have viruses or other undocumented features that could damage networks and information systems. Curious readers who want to use these tools should conduct a through review of the source code, or at least install the tools on a separate, air-gapped network to protect sensitive production systems.

GENERAL TRENDS IN THE COMPUTER UNDERGROUND

The Smart Get Smarter, and the Rise of the Script Kiddie

The best and brightest minds in the computer underground are conducting probing research and finding new vulnerabilities and powerful, novel attacks on a daily basis. The ideas and deep research done by super-smart attackers and security practitioners is being implemented in software programs and scripts. Months of research into how a particular operating system implements its password scheme is being rendered in code, so even a clueless attacker (often called a "script kiddie") can conduct a highly sophisticated attack with just a point-and-click. Although the script kiddie may not understand the tools' true function and nuances, most of the attack is automated.

In this environment, security practitioners must be careful not to underestimate their adversaries' capabilities. Often, security and system administrators think of their potential attackers as mere teenage kids cruising the Internet looking for easy prey. While this assessment is sometimes accurate, it masks two major concerns. First, some of the teenage kids are amazingly intelligent, and can wreak havoc on a network. Second, attackers may not be just kids; organized crime, terrorists, and even foreign governments have taken to sponsoring cyber attacks.

Wide Distribution of High-Quality Tools

Another trend in the computing underground involves the widespread distribution of tools. In the past (a decade ago), powerful attack tools were limited to a core group of elites in the computer underground. Today, hundreds of Web sites are devoted to the sharing of tools for every attacker (and security practitioner) on the planet. FAQs abound describing how to penetrate any type of operating system. These overall trends converge in a world where smart attackers have detailed knowledge of undermining our systems, while the not-so-smart attackers grow more and more plentiful. To address this increasing threat, system administrators and security practitioners must understand these tools and how to defend against them. The remainder of this chapter describes many of these very powerful tools in widespread use today, together with practical defensive tips for protecting one's network from each type of attack.

NETWORK MAPPING AND PORT SCANNING

When launching an attack across a TCP/IP network (such as the Internet or a corporate intranet), an attacker needs to know what addresses are active, how the network topology is constructed, and which services are available. A network mapper identifies systems that are connected to the target network. Given a network address range, the network mapper will send packets to each possible address to determine which addresses have machines.

By sending a simple Internet Control Message Protocol (ICMP) packet to a server (a "ping"), the mapping tool can discover if a server is connected to the network. For those networks that block incoming pings, many of the mapping tools available today can send a single SYN packet to attempt to open a connection to a server. If a server is listening, the SYN packet will trigger an ACK if the port is open, and potentially a "Port Unreachable" message if the port is closed. Regardless of whether the port is open or closed, the response indicates that the address has a machine listening. With this list of addresses, an attacker can refine the attack and focus on these listening systems.

A port scanner identifies open ports on a system. There are 65,535 TCP ports and 65,535 UDP ports, some of which are open on a system, and most of which are closed. Common services are associated with certain ports. For example, TCP Port 80 is most often used by Web servers, TCP Port 23 is used by Telnet daemons, and TCP Port 25 is used for server-to-server mail exchange across the Internet. By conducting a port scan, an attacker will send packets to each and every port. Essentially, ports are rather like doors on a machine. At any one of the thousands of doors available, common services will be listening. A port scanning tool allows an attacker to knock on every one of those doors to see who answers.

Some scanning tools include TCP fingerprinting capabilities. While the Internet Engineering Task Force (IETF) has carefully specified TCP and IP in various Requests for Comments (RFCs), not all packet options have standards associated with them. Without standards for how systems should respond to illegal packet formats, different vendors' TCP/IP stacks respond differently to illegal packets. By sending various combinations of illegal packet options (such as initiating a connection with an RST packet, or combining other odd and illegal TCP code bits), an attacker can determine what type of operating system is running on the target machine. For example, by conducting a TCP fingerprinting scan, an attacker can determine if a machine is running Cisco IOS, Sun Solaris, or Microsoft Windows 2000. In some cases, even the particular version or service pack level can be determined using this technique.

After utilizing network mapping tools and port scanners, an attacker will know which addresses on the target network have listening machines, which ports are open on those machines (and therefore which services are running), and which operating system platforms are in use. This treasure trove of information is useful to the attacker in refining the attack. With this data, the attacker can search for vulnerabilities on the particular services and systems to attempt to gain access.

Nmap, written by Fyodor, is one of the most full-featured mapping and scanning tools available today. Nmap, which supports network mapping, port scanning, and TCP fingerprinting, can be found at http://www.insecure. org/nmap.

Network Mapping and Port Scanning Defenses

To defend against network mapping and port scans, the administrator should remove all unnecessary systems and close all unused ports. To accomplish this, the administrator must disable and remove unneeded services from the machine. Only those services that have an absolute, defined business need should be running. A security administrator should also periodically scan the systems to determine if any unneeded ports are open. When discovered, these unneeded ports must be disabled.

VULNERABILITY SCANNING

Once the target systems are identified with a port scanner and network mapper, an attacker will search to determine if any vulnerabilities are present on the victim machines. Thousands of vulnerabilities have been discovered, allowing a remote attacker to gain a toehold on a machine or to take complete administrative control. An attacker could try each of these vulnerabilities on each system by entering individual commands to test for every vulnerability, but conducting an exhaustive search could take years. To speed up the process, attackers use automated scanning tools to quickly search for vulnerabilities on the target.

These automated vulnerability scanning tools are essentially databases of well-known vulnerabilities with an engine that can read the database, connect to a machine, and check to see if it is vulnerable to the exploit. The effectiveness of the tool in discovering vulnerabilities depends on the quality and thoroughness of its vulnerability database. For this reason, the best vulnerability scanners support the rapid release and update of the vulnerability database and the ability to create new checks using a scripting language.

High-quality commercial vulnerability scanning tools are widely available, and are often used by security practitioners and attackers to search for vulnerabilities. On the freeware front, SATAN (the Security Administrator Tool for Analyzing Network) was one of the first widely distributed automated vulnerability scanners, introduced in 1995. More recently, Nessus has been introduced as a free, open-source vulnerability scanner available at http://www.nessus.org. The Nessus project, which is led by Renaud Deraison, provides a full-featured scanner for identifying vulnerabilities on remote systems. It includes source code and a scripting language for writing new vulnerability checks, allowing it to be highly customized by security practitioners and attackers alike.

While Nessus is a general-purpose vulnerability scanner, looking for holes in numerous types of systems and platforms, some vulnerability scanners are much more focused on particular types of systems. For example, Whisker is a full-feature vulnerability scanning tool focusing on Web server CGI scripts. Written by Rain Forest Puppy, Whisker can be found at http://www.wiretrip.net/rfp.

Vulnerability Scanning Defenses

As described above, the administrator must close unused ports. Additionally, to eliminate the vast majority of system vulnerabilities, system patches must be applied in a timely fashion. All organizations using computers should have a defined change control procedure that specifies when and how system patches will be kept up-to-date.

Security practitioners should also conduct periodic vulnerability scans of their own networks to find vulnerabilities before attackers do. These scans should be conducted on a regular basis (such as quarterly or even monthly for sensitive networks), or when major network changes are implemented. The discovered vulnerabilities must be addressed in a timely fashion by updating system configurations or applying patches.

WARDIALING

A cousin of the network mapper and scanner, a wardialing tool is used to discover target systems across a telephone network. Organizations often spend large amounts of money in securing their network from a full, frontal assault over the Internet by implementing a firewall, intrusion detection system, and secure DMZ. Unfortunately, many attackers avoid this route and instead look for other ways into the network. Modems left on users' desktops or old, forgotten machines often provide the simplest way into a target network.

Wardialers, also known as "demon dialers," dial a series of telephone numbers, attempting to locate modems on the victim network. An attacker will determine the telephone extensions associated with the target organization. This information is often gleaned from a Web site listing telephone contacts, employee newsgroup postings with telephone contact information in the signature line, or even general employee e-mail. Armed with one or a series of telephone numbers, the attacker will enter into the wardialing tool ranges of numbers associated with the original number (for example, if an employee's telephone number in a newsgroup posting is listed as 555-1212, the attacker will dial 555-XXXX). The wardialer will automatically dial each number, listen for the familiar wail of a modem carrier tone, and make a list of all telephone numbers with modems listening.

With the list of modems generated by the wardialer, the attacker will dial each discovered modem using a terminal program or other client. Upon connecting to the modem, the attacker will attempt to identify the system based on its banner information and see if a password is required. Often, no password is required, because the modem was put in place by a clueless user requiring after-hours access and not wanting to bother using approved methods. If a password is required, the attacker will attempt to guess passwords commonly associated with the platform or company.

Some wardialing tools also support the capability of locating a repeat dial-tone, in addition to the ability to detect modems. The repeat dial-tone is a great find for the attacker, as it could allow for unrestricted dialing from a victim's PBX system to anywhere in the world. If an attacker finds a line on PBX supporting repeat dial-tone in the same local dialing exchange, the attacker can conduct international wardialing, with all phone bills paid for by the victim with the misconfigured PBX.

The most fully functional wardialing tool available today is distributed by The Hacker's Choice (THC) group. Known as THC-Scan, the tool was written by Van Hauser and can be found at http://inferno.tusculum.edu/thc. THC-Scan 2.0 supports many advanced features, including sequential or randomized dialing, dialing through a network out-dial, modem carrier and repeat dial-tone detection, and rudimentary detection avoidance capabilities.

Wardialing Defenses

The best defense against wardialing attacks is a strong modem policy that prohibits the use of modems and incoming lines without a defined business need. The policy should also require the registration of all modems with a business need in a centralized database only accessible by a security or system administrator.

Additionally, security personnel should conduct periodic wardialing exercises of their own networks to find the modems before the attackers do. When a phone number with an unregistered modem is discovered, the physical device must be located and deactivated. While finding such devices can be difficult, network defenses depend on finding these renegade modems before an attacker does.

NETWORK EXPLOITS: SNIFFING, SPOOFING, AND SESSION HIJACKING

TCP/IP, the underlying protocol suite that makes up the Internet, was not originally designed to provide security services. Likewise, the most common data-link type used with TCP/IP, Ethernet, is fundamentally insecure. A whole series of attacks are possible given these vulnerabilities of the underlying protocols. The most widely used and potentially damaging attacks based on these network vulnerabilities are sniffing, spoofing, and session hijacking.

Sniffing

Sniffers are extremely useful tools for an attacker and are therefore a fundamental element of an attacker's toolchest. Sniffers allow an attacker to monitor data passing across a network. Given their capability to monitor network traffic, sniffers are also useful for security practitioners and network administrators in troubleshooting networks and conducting investigations. Sniffers exploit characteristics of several data-link technologies, including Token Ring and especially Ethernet.

Ethernet, the most common LAN technology, is essentially a broadcast technology. When Ethernet LANs are constructed using hubs, all machines connected to the LAN can monitor all data on the LAN segment. If userIDs, passwords, or other sensitive information are sent from one machine (e.g., a client) to another machine (e.g., a server or router) on the same LAN, all other systems connected to the LAN could monitor the data. A sniffer is a hardware or software tool that gathers all data on a LAN segment. When a sniffer is running on a machine gathering all network traffic that passes by the system, the Ethernet interface and the machine itself are said to be in "promiscuous mode."

Many commonly used applications, such as Telnet, FTP, POP (the Post Office Protocol used for e-mail), and even some Web applications, transmit their passwords and sensitive data without any encryption. Any attacker on a broadcast Ethernet segment can use a sniffer to gather these passwords and data.

Attackers who take over a system often install a software sniffer on the compromised machine. This sniffer acts as a sentinel for the attacker, gathering sensitive data that moves by the compromised system. The sniffer gathers this data, including passwords, and stores it in a local file or transmits it to the attacker. The attacker then uses this information to compromise more and more systems. The attack methodology of installing a sniffer on one compromised machine, gathering data passing that machine, and using the sniffed information to take over other systems is referred to as an island-hopping attack.

Numerous sniffing tools are available across the Internet. The most fully functional sniffing tools include sniffit (by Brecht Claerhout, available at http://reptile.rug.ac.be/~coder/sniffit/sniffit.html, and Snort (by Martin Roesch, available at http://www.clark.net/~roesch/security.html). Some operating systems ship with their own sniffers installed by default, notably Solaris (with the snoop tool) and some varieties of Linux (which ship with tcpdump). Other commercial sniffers are also available from a variety of vendors.

Sniffing Defenses. The best defense against sniffing attacks is to encrypt the data in transit. Instead of sending passwords or other sensitive data in cleartext, the application or network should encrypt the data (SSH, secure Telnet, etc.).

Another defense against sniffers is to eliminate the broadcast nature of Ethernet. By utilizing a switch instead of a hub to create a LAN, the damage that can be done with a sniffer is limited. A switch can be configured so that only the required source and destination ports on the switch carry the traffic. Although they are on the same LAN, all other ports on the switch (and the machines connected to those ports) do not see this data. Therefore, if one system is compromised on a LAN, a sniffer installed on this machine will not be capable of seeing data exchanged between other machines on the LAN. Switches are therefore useful in improving security by minimizing the data a sniffer can gather, and also help to improve network performance.

IP Spoofing

Another network-based attack involves altering the source address of a computer to disguise the attacker and exploit weak authentication methods. IP address spoofing allows an attacker to use the IP address of another machine to conduct an attack. If the target machines rely on the IP address to authenticate, IP spoofing can give an attacker access to the systems. Additionally, IP spoofing can make it very difficult to apprehend an attacker, because logs will contain decoy addresses and not the real source of the attack. Many of the tools described in other sections of this chapter rely on IP spoofing to hide the true origin of the attack.

Spoofing Defenses. Systems should not use IP addresses for authentication. Any functions or applications that rely solely on IP address for authentication should be disabled or replaced. In UNIX, the "**r**-commands" (**rlogin**, **rsh**, **rexec**, and **rcp**) are notoriously subject to IP spoofing attacks. UNIX trust relationships allow an administrator to manage systems using the **r**-commands without providing a password. Instead of a password, the IP address of the system is used for authentication. This major weakness should be avoided by replacing the **r**-commands with administration tools that utilize strong authentication. One such tool, secure shell (ssh), uses strong cryptography to replace the weak authentication of the **r**-commands. Similarly, all other applications that rely on IP addresses for critical security and administration functions should be replaced.

Additionally, an organization should deploy anti-spoof filters on its perimeter networks that connect the organization to the Internet and business partners. Anti-spoof filters drop all traffic coming from outside the network claiming to come from the inside. With this capability, such filters can prevent some types of spoofing attacks, and should be implemented on all perimeter network routers.

Session Hijacking

While sniffing allows an attacker to view data associated with network connections, a session hijack tool allows an attacker to take over network connections, kicking off the legitimate user or sharing a login. Session hijacking tools are used against services with persistent login sessions, such as Telnet, rlogin, or FTP. For any of these services, an attacker can hijack a session and cause a great deal of damage.

A common scenario illustrating session hijacking involves a machine, Alice, with a user logged in to remotely administer another system, Bob, using Telnet. Eve, the attacker, sits on a network segment between Alice and Bob (either Alice's LAN, Bob's LAN, or between any of the routers between Alice's and Bob's LANs). Exhibit 22-1 illustrates this scenario in more detail.

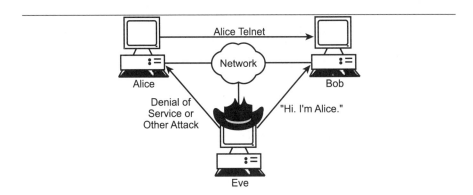

Exhibit 22-1. Eve hijacks the session between Alice and Bob.

Using a session hijacking tool, Eve can do any of the following:

- *Monitor Alice's session.* Most session hijacking tools allow attackers to monitor all connections available on the network and select which connections they want to hijack.
- *Insert commands into the session.* An attacker may just need to add one or two commands into the stream to reconfigure Bob. In this type of hijack, the attacker never takes full control of the session. Instead, Alice's login session to Bob has a small number of commands inserted, which will be executed on Bob as though Alice had typed them.
- *Steal the session.* This feature of most session hijacking tools allows an attacker to grab the session from Alice, and directly control it. Essentially, the Telnet client control is shifted from Alice to Eve, without Bob's knowing.
- *Give the session back.* Some session hijacking tools allow the attacker to steal a session, interact with the server, and then smoothly give the session back to the user. While the session is stolen, Alice is put on hold while Eve controls the session. With Alice on hold, all commands typed by Alice are displayed on Eve's screen, but not transmitted to Bob. When Eve is finished making modifications on Bob, Eve transfers control back to Alice.

For a successful hijack to occur, the attacker must be on a LAN segment between Alice and Bob. A session hijacking tool monitors the connection using an integrate sniffer, observing the TCP sequence numbers of the packets going each direction. Each packet sent from Alice to Bob has a unique TCP sequence number used by Bob to verify that all packets are received and put in proper order. Likewise, all packets going back from Bob to Alice have sequence numbers. A session hijacking tool sniffs the packets to determine these sequence numbers. When a session is hijacked (through command insertion or session stealing), the hijacking tool automatically uses the appropriate sequence numbers and spoofs Alice's address, taking over the conversation with Bob where Alice left off.

One of the most fully functional session hijacking tool available today is Hunt, written by Kra and available at http://www.cri.cz/kra/index.html. Hunt allows an attacker to monitor and steal sessions, insert single commands, and even give a session back to the user.

Session Hijacking Defenses. The best defense against session hijacking is to avoid the use of insecure protocols and applications for sensitive sessions. Instead of using the easy-to-hijack (and easy-to-sniff) Telnet application, a more secure, encrypted session tool should be used. Because the attacker does not have the session encryption keys, an encrypted session cannot be hijacked. The attacker will simply see encrypted gibberish using Hunt, and will only be able to reset the connection, not take it over or insert commands.

Secure shell (ssh) offers strong authentication and encrypted sessions, providing a highly secure alternative to Telnet and rlogin. Furthermore, ssh includes a secure file transfer capability (scp) to replace traditional FTP. Other alternatives are available, including secure, encrypted Telnet or a virtual private network (VPN) established between the source and destination.

DENIAL-OF-SERVICE ATTACKS

Denial-of-service attacks are among the most common exploits available today. As their name implies, a denial-of-service attack prevents legitimate users from being able to access a system. With E-commerce applications constituting the lifeblood of many organizations and a growing piece of the world economy, a well-timed denial-of-service attack can cause a great deal of damage. By bringing down servers that control sensitive machinery or other functions, these attacks could also present a real physical threat to life and limb. An attacker could cause the service denial by flooding a system with bogus traffic, or even purposely causing the server to crash. Countless denial-of-service attacks are in widespread use today, and can be found at http://packetstorm.securify.com/exploits/DoS. The most often used network-based denial-of-service attacks fall into two categories: malformed packet attacks and packet floods.

Malformed Packet Attacks

This type of attack usually involves one or two packets that are formatted in an unexpected way. Many vendor product implementations do not take into account all variations of user entries or packet types. If the software handles such errors poorly, the system may crash when it receives such packets. A classic example of this type of attack involves sending IP fragments to a system that overlap with each other (the fragment offset values are incorrectly set). Some unpatched Windows and Linux systems will crash when they encounter such packets. The teardrop attack is an example of a tool that exploits this IP fragmentation handling vulnerability. Other malformed packet attacks that exploit other weaknesses in TCP/IP implementations include the colorfully named WinNuke, Land, LaTierra, NewTear, Bonk, Boink, etc.

Packet Flood Attacks

Packet flood denial-of-service tools send a deluge of traffic to a system on the network, overwhelming its capability to respond to legitimate users. Attackers have devised numerous techniques for creating such floods, with the most popular being SYN floods, directed broadcast attacks, and distributed denial-of-service tools.

SYN flood tools initiate a large number of half-open connections with a system by sending a series of SYN packets. When any TCP connection is established, a three-way handshake occurs. The initiating system (usually the client) sends a SYN packet to the destination to establish a sequence number for all packets going from source to destination in that session. The destination responds with a SYN-ACK packet, which acknowledges the sequence number for packets going from source to destination, and establishes an initial sequence number for packets going the opposite direction. The source completes the three-way handshake by sending an ACK to the destination. The three-way handshake is completed, and communication (actual data transfer) can occur.

SYN floods take advantage of a weakness in TCP's three-way handshake. By sending only spoofed SYN packets and never responding to the SYN-ACK, an attacker can exhaust a server's ability to maintain state of all the initiated sessions. With a huge number of so-called half-open connections, a server cannot handle any new, legitimate traffic. Rather than filling up all of the pipe bandwidth to a server, only the server's capacity to handle session initiations needs to be overwhelmed (in most network configurations, a server's ability to handle SYNs is lower than the total bandwidth to the site). For this reason, SYN flooding is the most popular packet flood attack. Other tools are also available that flood systems with ICMP and UDP packets, but they merely consume bandwidth, so an attacker would require a bigger connection than the victim to cut off all service.

Another type of packet flood that allows attackers to amplify their bandwidth is the directed broadcast attack. Often called a smurf attack, named after the first tool to exploit this technique, directed broadcast attacks utilize a third-party's network as an amplifier for the packet flood. In a smurf attack, the attacker locates a network on the Internet that will respond to a broadcast ICMP message (essentially a ping to the network's broadcast address). If the network is configured to allow broadcast requests and responses, all machines on the network will send a response to the ping. By spoofing the ICMP request, the attacker can have all machines on the third-party network send responses to the victim. For example, if an organization has 30 hosts on a single DMZ network connected to the Internet, an attacker can send a spoofed network broadcast ping to the DMZ. All 30 hosts will send a response to the spoofed address, which would be the ultimate victim. By sending repeated messages to the broadcast network, the attacker has amplified bandwidth by a factor of 30. Even an attacker with only a 56-kbps dial-up line could fill up a T1 line (1.54 Mbps) with that level of amplification. Other directed broadcast attack tools include Fraggle and Papasmurf.

A final type of denial-of-service that has received considerable press is the distributed denial-of-service attack. Essentially based on standard packet flood concepts, distributed denial-of-service attacks were used to cripple many major Internet sites in February 2000. Tools such as Trin00,

Tribe Flood Network 2000 (TFN2K), and Stacheldraht all support this type of attack. To conduct a distributed denial-of-service attack, an attacker must find numerous vulnerable systems on the Internet. Usually, a remote buffer overflow attack (described below) is used to take over a dozen, a hundred, or even thousands of machines. Simple daemon processes, called zombies, are installed on these machines taken over by the attacker. The attacker communicates with this network of zombies using a control program. The control program is used to send commands to the hundreds or thousands of zombies, requesting them to take uniform action simultaneously.

The most common action to be taken is to simultaneously launch a packet flood against a target. While a traditional SYN flood would deluge a target with packets from one host, a distributed denial-of-service attack would send packets from large numbers of zombies, rapidly exhausting the capacity of even very high-bandwidth, well-designed sites. Many distributed denial-of-service attack tools support SYN, UDP, and ICMP flooding, smurf attacks, as well as some malformed packet attacks. Any one or all of these options can be selected by the attacker using the control program.

Denial-of-Service Attack Defenses

To defend against malformed packet attacks, system patches and security fixes must be regularly applied. Vendors frequently update their systems with patches to handle a new flavor of denial-of-service attack. An organization must have a program for monitoring vendor and industry security bulletins for security fixes, and a controlled method for implementing these fixes soon after they are announced and tested.

For packet flood attacks, critical systems should have underlying network architectures with multiple, redundant paths, eliminating a single point of failure. Furthermore, adequate bandwidth is a must. Also, some routers and firewalls support traffic flow control to help ease the burden of a SYN flood.

Finally, by configuring an Internet-accessible network appropriately, an organization can minimize the possibility that it will be used as a jumping-off point for smurf and distributed denial-of-service attacks. To prevent the possibility of being used as a smurf amplifier, the external router or firewall should be configured to drop all directed broadcast requests from the Internet. To lower the chance of being used in a distributed denial-of-service attack, an organization should implement anti-spoof filters on external routers and firewalls to make sure that all outgoing traffic has a source IP address of the site. This egress filtering prevents an attacker from sending spoofed packets from a zombie or other denial-of-service tool located on the network. Antispoof ingress filters, which drop all packets from the Internet claiming to come from one's internal network, are also useful in preventing some denial-of-service attacks.

STACK-BASED BUFFER OVERFLOWS

Stack-based buffer overflow attacks are commonly used by an attacker to take over a system remotely across a network. Additionally, buffer overflows can be employed by local malicious users to elevate their privileges and gain superuser access to a system. Stack-based buffer overflow attacks exploit the way many operating systems handle their stack, an internal data structure used by running programs to store data temporarily. When a function call is made, the current state of the executing program and variables to be passed to the function are pushed on the stack. New local variables used by the function are also allocated space on the stack. Additionally, the stack stores the return address of the code calling the function. This return address will be accessed from the stack once the function call is complete. The system uses this address to resume execution of the calling program at the appropriate place. Exhibit 22-2 shows how a stack is constructed.

Most UNIX and all Windows systems have a stack that can hold data and executable code. Because local variables are stored on the stack when a function is called, poor code can be exploited to overrun the boundaries of these variables on the stack. If user input length is not examined by the code, a particular variable on the stack may exceed the memory allocated to it on the stack, overwriting all variables and even the return address for where execution should resume after the function is complete. This operation, called "smashing" the stack, allows an attacker to overflow the local variables to insert executable code and another return address on the stack. Exhibit 22-2 also shows a stack that has been smashed with a buffer overflow.

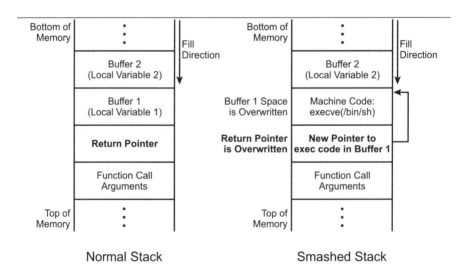

Normal Stack   Smashed Stack

Exhibit 22-2. A normal stack and a stack with a buffer overflow.

The attacker will overflow the buffer on the stack with machine-specific bytecodes that consist of executable commands (usually a shell routine), and a return pointer to begin execution of these inserted commands. Therefore, with very carefully constructed binary code, the attacker can actually enter information as a user into a program that consists of executable code and a new return address. The buggy program will not analyze the length of this input, but will place it on the stack, and actually begin to execute the attacker's code. Such vulnerabilities allow an attacker to break out of the application code, and access any system components with the permissions of the broken program. If the broken program is running with superuser privileges (e.g., SUID root on a UNIX system), the attacker has taken over the machine with a buffer overflow.

Stack-based Buffer Overflow Defenses

The most thorough defenses against buffer overflow attacks is to properly code software so that it cannot be used to smash the stack. All programs should validate all input from users and other programs, ensuring that it fits into allocated memory structures. Each variable should be checked (including user input, variables from other functions, input from other programs, and even environment variables) to ensure that allocated buffers are adequate to hold the data. Unfortunately, this ultimate solution is only available to individuals who write the programs and those with source code.

Additionally, security practitioners and system administrators should carefully control and minimize the number of SUID programs on a system that users can run and have permissions of other users (such as root). Only SUID programs with an explicit business need should be installed on sensitive systems.

Finally, many stack-based buffer overflow attacks can be avoided by configuring the systems to not execute code from the stack. Notably, Solaris and Linux offer this option. For example, to secure a Solaris system against stack-based buffer overflows, the following lines should be added to

```
/etc/system:
```

```
set noexec_user_stack=1
set noexec_user_stack_log=1
```

The first line will prevent execution on a stack, and the second line will log any attempt to do so. Unfortunately, some programs legitimately try to run code off the stack. Such programs will crash if this option is implemented. Generally, if the system is single purpose and needs to be secure (e.g., a Web server), this option should be used to prevent stack-based buffer overflow.

THE ART AND SCIENCE OF PASSWORD CRACKING

The vast majority of systems today authenticate users with a static password. When a user logs in, the password is transmitted to the system, which checks the password to make the decision whether to let the user login. To make this decision, the system must have a mechanism to compare the user's input with the actual password. Of course, the system could just store all of the passwords locally and compare from this file. Such a file of cleartext passwords, however, would provide a very juicy target for an attacker. To make the target less useful for attackers, most modern operating systems use a one-way hash or encryption mechanism to protect the stored passswords. When a user types in a password, the system hashes the user's entry and compares it to the stored hash. If the two hashes match, the password is correct and the user can login.

Password cracking tools are used to attack this method of password protection. An attacker will use some exploit (often a buffer overflow) to gather the encrypted or hashed password file from a system (on a UNIX system without password shadowing, any user can read the hashed password file). After downloading the hashed password file, the attacker uses a password cracking tool to determine users' passwords. The cracking tool operates using a loop: it guesses a password, hashes or encrypts the password, and compares it to the hashed password from the stolen file. If the hashes match, the attacker has the password. If the hashes do not match, the loop begins again with another password guess.

Password cracking tools base their password guesses on a dictionary or a complete brute-force attack, attempting every possible password. Dozens of dictionaries are available online, in a multitude of languages including English, French, German, Klingon, etc.

Numerous password cracking tools are available. The most popular and full-functional password crackers include:

- John-the-Ripper, by Solar Designer, focuses on cracking UNIX passwords, available at http://www.openwall.com/john/.
- L0phtCrack, used to crack Windows NT passwords, is available at http://www.l0pht.com.

Password Cracking Defenses

The first defense against password cracking is to minimize the exposure of the encrypted/hashed password file. On UNIX systems, shadow password files should be used, which allow only the superuser to read the password file. On Windows NT systems, the SYSKEY feature available in NT 4.0 SP 3 and later should be installed and enabled. Furthermore, all backups and system recovery disks should be stored in physically secured locations and possibly even encrypted.

A strong password policy is a crucial element in ensuring a secure network. A password policy should require password lengths greater than eight characters, require the use of alphanumeric *and* special characters in every password, and force users to have passwords with mixed-case letters. Users must be aware of the issue of weak passwords and be trained in creating memorable, yet difficult-to-guess passwords.

To ensure that passwords are secure and to identify weak passwords, security practitioners should check system passwords on a periodic basis using password cracking tools. When weak passwords are discovered, the security group should have a defined procedure for interacting with users whose passwords can be easily guessed.

Finally, several software packages are available that prevent users from setting their passwords to easily guessed values. When a user establishes a new password, these filtering programs check the password to make sure that it is sufficiently complex and is not just a variation of the user name or a dictionary word. With this kind of tool, users are simply unable to create passwords that are easily guessed, eliminating a significant security issue. For filtering software to be effective, it must be installed on all servers where users establish passwords, including UNIX servers, Windows NT Primary and Back-up Domain Controllers, and Novell servers.

BACKDOORS

Backdoors are programs that bypass traditional security checks on a system, allowing an attacker to gain access to a machine without providing a system password and getting logged. Attackers install backdoors on a machine (or dupe a user into installing one for them) to ensure they will be able to gain access to the system at a later time. Once installed, most backdoors listen on special ports for incoming connections from the attacker across the network. When the attacker connects to the backdoor listener, the traditional userID and password or other forms of authentication are bypassed. Instead, the attacker can gain access to the system without providing a password, or by using a special password used only to enter the backdoor.

Netcat is an incredibly flexible tool written for UNIX by Hobbit and for Windows NT by Weld Pond (both versions are available at http://www.l0pht.com/~weld/netcat/). Among its numerous other uses, Netcat can be used to create a backdoor listener with a superuser-level shell on any TCP or UDP port. For Windows systems, an enormous number of backdoor applications are available, including Back Orifice 2000 (called BO2K for short, and available at http://www.bo2k.com), and hack-a-tack (available at http://www.hack-a-tack.com).

Backdoor Defenses

The best defense against backdoor programs is for system and security administrators to know what is running on their machines, particularly sensitive systems storing critical information or processing high-value transactions. If a process suddenly appears running as the superuser listening on a port, the administrator needs to investigate. Backdoors listening on various ports can be discovered using the **netstat –na** command on UNIX and Windows NT systems.

Additionally, many backdoor programs (such as BO2K) can be discovered by an anti-virus program, which should be installed on all users' desktops, as well as servers throughout an organization.

TROJAN HORSES AND ROOTKITS

Another fundamental element of an attacker's toolchest is the Trojan horse program. Like the Trojan horse of ancient Greece, these new Trojan horses appear to have some useful function, but in reality are just disguising some malicious activity. For example, a user may receive an executable birthday card program in electronic mail. When the unsuspecting user activates the birthday card program and watches birthday cakes dance across the screen, the program secretly installs a backdoor or perhaps deletes the users' hard drive. As illustrated in this example, Trojan horses rely on deception — they trick a user or system administrator into running them for their (apparent) usefulness, but their true purpose is to attack the user's machine.

Traditional Trojan Horses

A traditional Trojan horse is simply an independent program that can be run by a user or administrator. Numerous traditional Trojan horse programs have been devised, including:

- The familiar birthday card or holiday greeting e-mail attachment described above.
- A software program that claims to be able to turn CD-ROM readers into CD writing devices. Although this feat is impossible to accomplish in software, many users have been duped into downloading this "tool," which promptly deletes their hard drives upon activation.
- A security vulnerability scanner, WinSATAN. This tool claims to provide a convenient security vulnerability scan for system and security administrators using a Windows NT system. Unfortunately, an unsuspecting user running this program will also have a deleted hard drive.

Countless other examples exist. While conceptually unglamorous, traditional Trojan horses can be a major problem if users are not careful and run untrusted programs on their machines.

RootKits

A RootKit takes the concept of a Trojan horse to a much more powerful level. Although their name implies otherwise, RootKits do not allow an attacker to gain "root" (superuser) access to a system. Instead, RootKits allow an attacker who already has superuser access to keep that access by foiling all attempts of an administrator to detect the invasion. RootKits consist of an entire suite of Trojan horse programs that replace or patch critical system programs. The various tools used by administrators to detect attackers on their machines are routinely undermined with RootKits.

Most RootKits include a Trojan horse backdoor program (in UNIX, the */bin/login* routine). The attacker will install a new Trojan horse version of */bin/login,* overwriting the previous version. The RootKit */bin/login* routine includes a special backdoor userID and password so that the attacker can access the system at later times.

Additionally, RootKits include a sniffer and a program to hide the sniffer. An administrator can detect a sniffer on a system by running the **ifconfig** command. If a sniffer is running, the **ifconfig** output will contain the PROMISC flag, an indication that the Ethernet card is in promiscuous mode and therefore is sniffing. RootKit contains a Trojan horse version of **ifconfig** that does not display the PROMISC flag, allowing an attacker to avoid detection.

UNIX-based RootKits also replace other critical system executables, including **ps** and **du**. The **ps** command, emloyed by users and administrators to determine which processes are running, is modified so that an attacker can hide processes. The **du** command, which shows disk utilization, is altered so that the file space taken up by RootKit and the attacker's other programs can be masked.

By replacing programs like /bin/login, ifconfig, ps, du, and numerous others, these RootKit tools become part of the operating system itself. Therefore, RootKits are used to cover the eyes and ears of an administrator. They create a virtual world on the computer that appears benign to the system administrator, when in actuality, an attacker can log in and move around the system with impunity. RootKits have been developed for most major UNIX systems and Windows NT. A whole variety of UNIX RootKits can be found at http://packetstorm.securify.com/UNIX/penetration/root-kits, while an NT RootKit is available at http://www.rootkit.com.

A recent development in this arena is the release of kernel-level Root-Kits. These RootKits act at the most fundamental levels of an operating system. Rather than replacing application programs such as /bin/login and ifconfig, kernel-level RootKits actually patch the kernel to provide very low-level access to the system. These tools rely on the loadable kernel modules that many new UNIX variants support, including Linux and Solaris. Loadable kernel modules let an administrator add functionality to the kernel on-the-fly, without even rebooting the system. An attacker with superuser access can install a kernel-level RootKit that will allow for the remapping of execution of programs.

When an administrator tries to run a program, the Trojanized kernel will remap the execution request to the attacker's program, which could be a backdoor offering access or other Trojan horse. Because the kernel does the remapping of execution requests, this type of activity is very difficult to detect. If the administrator attempts to look at the remapped file or check its integrity, the program will appear unaltered, because the program's image *is* unaltered. However, when executed, the unaltered program is skipped, and a malicious program is substituted by the kernel. Knark, written by Creed, is a kernel-level RootKit that can be found at http://packet-storm.securify.com/UNIX/penetration/rootkits.

Trojan Horses and RootKit Defenses

To protect against traditional Trojan horses, user awareness is key. Users must understand the risks associated with downloading untrusted programs and running them. They must also be made aware of the problems of running executable attachments in e-mail from untrusted sources.

Additionally, some traditional Trojan horses can be detected and eliminated by anti-virus programs. Every end-user computer system (and even servers) should have an effective and up-to-date anti-virus program installed.

To defend against RootKits, system and security administrators must use integrity checking programs for critical system files. Numerous tools are available, including the venerable Tripwire, that generate a hash of the executables commonly altered when a RootKit is installed. The administrator should store these hashes on a protected medium (such as a write-protected floppy disk) and periodically check the veracity of the programs on the machine with the protected hashes. Commonly, this type of check is done at least weekly, depending on the sensitivity of the machine. The administrator must reconcile any changes discovered in these critical system files with recent patches. If system files have been altered, and no patches were installed by the administrator, a malicious user or outside attacker may have installed a RootKit. If a RootKit is detected, the safest way to ensure its complete removal is to rebuild the entire operating system and even critical applications.

Unfortunately, kernel-level RootKits cannot be detected with integrity check programs because the integrity checker relies on the underlying kernel to do its work. If the kernel lies to the integrity checker, the results will not show the RootKit installation. The best defense against the kernel-level RootKits is a monolithic kernel that does not support loadable kernel modules. On critical systems (such as firewalls, Internet Web servers, DNS servers, mail servers, etc.), administrators should build the systems with complete kernels without support for loadable kernel modules. With this configuration, the system will prevent an attacker from gaining root-level access and patching the kernel in real-time.

OVERALL DEFENSES: INTRUSION DETECTION AND INCIDENT RESPONSE PROCEDURES

Each of the defensive strategies described in this chapter deals with particular tools and attacks. In addition to employing each of those strategies, organizations must also be capable of detecting and responding to an attack. These capabilities are realized through the deployment of intrusion detection systems (IDSs) and the implementation of incident response procedures.

IDSs act as burglar alarms on the network. With a database of known attack signatures, IDSs can determine when an attack is underway and alert security and system administration personnel. Acting as early warning systems, IDSs allow an organization to detect an attack in its early stages and minimize the damage that may be caused.

Perhaps even more important than IDSs, documented incident response procedures are among the most critical elements of an effective security program. Unfortunately, even with industry-best defenses, a sufficiently motivated attacker can penetrate the network. To address this possibility, an organization must have procedures defined in advance describing how the organization will react to the attack. These incident response procedures should specify the roles of individuals in the organization during an attack. The chain of command and escalation procedures should be spelled out in advance. Creating these items during a crisis will lead to costly mistakes.

Truly effective incident response procedures should also be multi-disciplinary, not focusing only on information technology. Instead, the roles, responsibilities, and communication channels for the Legal, Human Resources, Media Relations, Information Technology, and Security organizations should all be documented and communicated. Specific members of these organizations should be identified as the core of a Security Incident Response Team (SIRT), to be called together to address an incident when one occurs. Additionally, the SIRT should conduct periodic exercises of the incident response capability to ensure that team members are effective in their roles.

Additionally, with a large number of organizations outsourcing their information technology infrastructure by utilizing Web hosting, desktop management, e-mail, data storage, and other services, the extension of the incident response procedures to these outside organizations can be critical. The contract established with the outsourcing company should carefully state the obligations of the service provider in intrusion detection, incident notification, and participation in incident response. A specific service-level agreement for handling security incidents and the time needed to pull together members of the service company's staff in a SIRT should also be agreed upon.

CONCLUSIONS

While the number and power of these attack tools continues to escalate, system administrators and security personnel should not give up the fight. All of the defensive strategies discussed throughout this chapter boil down to doing a thorough and professional job of administering systems: know what is running on the system, keep it patched, ensure appropriate bandwidth is available, utilize IDSs, and prepare a Security Incident Response Team. Although these activities are not easy and can involve a great deal of effort, through diligence, an organization can keep its systems secured and minimize the chance of an attack. By employing intrusion detection systems and sound incident response procedures, even those highly sophisticated attacks that do get through can be discovered and contained, minimizing the impact on the organization. By creating an effective security program with sound defensive strategies, critical systems and information can be protected.

Chapter 23
An Introduction to Hostile Code and Its Control

Jay Heiser

VIRUSES AND OTHER FORMS OF HOSTILE CODE, OR "MALWARE," BECAME A UNIVERSALLY EXPERIENCED PROBLEM EARLY IN THE PC ERA, AND THE THREAT CONTINUES TO GROW. *The ICSA Virus Prevalence Survey* reported in 1999 that the infection rate had almost doubled during each of the previous four years. Malware has the potential to subvert firewalls, hijack VPNs, and even defeat digital signature. Hostile code is the most common source of security failure, and it has become so prevalent that its control must be considered a universal, baseline practice. Without an understanding of malware — what it is, what it can do, and how it works — malware cannot be controlled. It is ironic that despite the increasing rate of hostile code infection, the attention given this subject by academics and engineering students is declining. Attack code sophistication and complexity continues to increase, but fortunately, the appropriate response is always good system hygiene and administration.

DEFINITION OF HOSTILE CODE

Hostile code is program data surreptitiously introduced into a computer without the explicit knowledge or consent of the person responsible for the computer. Whatever the purported intent of its creator, code inserted covertly by an outside party can never be considered benign. If it is not approved, it has to be treated as hostile code. Vendors of anti-virus (AV) software have identified approximately 50,000 known viruses. In reality, only about 5 percent of these viruses are ever reported "in the wild," most commonly on Joe Wells's Wild List. (The Wild List is a regularly updated report of malware that has actually been observed infecting real systems. See Exhibit 23-1 for the URL.) Most of these are variations on a few hundred

Exhibit 23-1. Internet resources.

Malware Information Pages	
The Computer Virus Myths Page	http://kumite.com/myths/
IBM's Anti-Virus Online	http://www.av.ibm.com
The WildList Organization International	http://www.wildlist.org/
BackOrifice Resource Center	http://skyscraper.fortunecity.com/cern/600
The BackOrifice Page	http://www.nwi.net/~pchelp/bo/bo.htm
The NetBus Page	http://www.nwi.net/~pchelp/nb/nb.htm
Ports used by Trojans	http://www.simovitz.com/nyheter9902.html
AV Product Test Sites	
Virus Bulletin 100% Awards	http://www.virusbtn.com/100
Virus Test Centre	http://agn-www.informatik.uni-hamburg.de/vtc
Check-Mark certified anti-virus products	http://www.check-mark.com/
ICSA certified anti-virus products	http://www.icsa.net/html/communities/antivirus/certification/certified_products/

well-known examples, and only a small number of viruses account for most attacks. Complicating an understanding of hostile code, simple terms such as "virus" and "Trojan horse" are used imprecisely, blurring a potentially useful distinction between cause and effect. This chapter familiarizes the practitioner with the most common malware terminology, and helps them recognize different contexts in which their meaning changes.

INFECTION AND REPRODUCTION

Analysis of the transmission mechanism for a specific example of hostile code starts by determining two things: (1) if it is self-reproducing, and (2) if it requires the unwitting assistance of a victim. While fear of autonomous attack by self-replicating code is understandable, *manual insertion* is the most reliable way for an attacker to install hostile code. If assailants can gain either physical or remote access to a system, then they have the opportunity to install malware. Many network services, such as FTP, TFTP, and HTTP (and associated poorly written CGI scripts), have been used to upload hostile code onto a victim system. Hacker Web sites contain details on remote buffer overflow exploits for both NT and UNIX, making it possible for script kiddies to install code on many unpatched Web servers. Manual insertion is not very glamorous, but it works.

Cyberplagues, code designed to reproduce and spread itself, takes one of two different forms. A **virus** is hostile code that parasitically attaches to some other code, and is dependent on that code for its transmission. This is completely analogous to a biological virus, which alters the genetic content of its victim, using its victim for reproduction. Unfortunately, the word "virus" has also taken on a secondary meaning as a generic moniker for all forms of hostile code. This meaning is perpetuated by using the term "anti-virus" to describe commercial software products that actually search for a number of forms of malware. A true virus can only spread with the participation of its victim. Host infection occurs when a contaminated file is executed, or when a floppy with an infected boot sector is read. Because users do not log directly into them, servers are less likely to contract viruses than are workstations. However, users who have write access to data on servers, either group configuration files or shared data, will infect files on the server that can spread to all users of the server. If they are write protected, server executables can only be infected when someone with write privilege, such as an administrator, runs a file containing a virus.

A **worm** is self-reproducing hostile code that has its own discrete existence. It is a stand-alone executable that uses remote services to reproduce itself and spread to other systems through a network. This is analogous to a biological bacterium (within the parasite pantheon, some experts distinguish a bacterium from a worm). Worms do not require the victim's participation — they rely on technical vulnerabilities that are the result of bugs or poor configuration. Because they spread by exploiting network vulnerabilities, and do not require a victim's participation, servers are just as vulnerable to worms as workstations are. They are probably more vulnerable, because they typically have more network services running.

A **Trojan horse** is an artifact with an ulterior hostile effect that appears desirable to the victim, tricking the victim into transferring it through a security perimeter so that its hostile intent can be manifested within the protected area. Examples of Trojan horses on computers are e-mailed greeting cards and games that include a hostile payload. The term "Trojan horse" is often applied to any hostile code that is nonreproducing. This secondary usage is imprecise and misleading; it does not explain the infection process, the trigger event, or the effect. This meaning is used in two different contexts. Most recently, it refers to nonreproducing hostile remote control applications, such as Back Orifice and NetBus, which often — but not always — spread as the payload of an e-mailed Trojan horse. NetBus, for example, is often surreptitiously bundled with the Whack-a-Mole video game. More traditionally, and especially on UNIX hosts, the term refers to a manually inserted hostile executable that has the same name as a legitimate program, or as a hostile program that mimics the appearance of a legitimate program, such as a login screen. An effective security practitioner is sensitive to these different meanings for commonly used terms.

Logic bombs are manually inserted, nonreproducing code created by system insiders, usually for revenge. For example, a system administrator might create a utility that is designed to delete all the files on a computer two weeks after that employee leaves a job. There have been cases where software vendors have included logic bombs in their product to encourage prompt payment. These software vendors have usually lost in court.

The term **"backdoor"** most accurately applies to a capability. A backdoor is a hidden mechanism that circumvents existing access controls to provide unauthorized access. Historically, some software developers have left backdoors into their application to facilitate troubleshooting. Backdoors can also be provided through system configuration. If a UNIX system administrator or intruder creates a copy of the shell and sets it to be SUID root, it could also be considered a form of backdoor.

Executable Content

Every new technology brings new risks. The convenience of executable content, data files that have some sort of programming and execution capability, is undeniable, but executable content is also a marvelously convenient mechanism for hostile capability.

Macro viruses are hostile code applications written in the macro language of application software. The ability to automatically launch a macro when a file is opened, and the power to access virtually any system function from within that macro, make some applications particularly vulnerable. Microsoft Word documents are the most widely shared form of executable content, making them an efficient malware vector. In late 1995, Concept was the first macro virus observed in the wild. Within two years, Microsoft Word macro viruses had become the most frequently reported form of malware.

Self-extracting archives include executable zip files, Windows setup files, and UNIX shell archives (shar files). As a convenience to the recipient, a set of files (usually compressed) is bundled into a single executable file, along with a script to extract files into the appropriate directories, and make any necessary changes to system configuration files. When the archive is executed, it extracts its components into a temporary directory; and if an installation script is included, it is automatically launched. A user executing such a self-extracting object must trust the intentions and abilities of the archive's creator. It is a simple matter to modify an existing archive to include a piece of malware, transmogrifying a legitimate file into a Trojan horse.

Mobile code is a form of executable content becoming increasingly prevalent on the Internet. Java, JavaScript, ActiveX, and Shockwave are used to create Web-based objects that are automatically downloaded and locally executed when they are browsed. The environments used to run mobile code reside either within the browser or in downloadable browser plug-ins. The level of system access afforded mobile code interpreters varies, but the user's browser has full access to the user's system privileges — use of mobile code requires a trust in the technical capabilities and configuration of the mobile code execution environment. At the time of this writing, no hostile mobile code exploits have ever been documented in the wild.

Complex Life Cycles

Replicating hostile code has a life cycle, just like biological pathogens, and the increasing sophistication of malware life cycles is enabling malware to take greater advantage of infrastructure opportunities both to evade controls and to maximize infection rate. **Propagation** is the life stage in which malware reproduces itself in a form suitable for the actual **infection**. As described in several examples below, some replicating code has multiple propagation methods. After infection, hostile programs often enter a **dormancy** period, which is ended by a **triggering event**. The trigger may be a specific date and time, a specific user action, the existence of some specific data on the computer, or possibly some combination of any of the above. When the trigger event occurs, an action is taken. The virus code that performs this action is referred to as the **payload**. When the action is performed, it is sometimes referred to as **payload delivery**. The payload may delete data, steal data and send it out, attempt to fool the user with bogus messages, or possibly do nothing at all. Self-replicating hostile code completes its life cycle by propagating itself.

A 1999 attack called Explorezip provides a good example of malware with a complex life cycle. Explorezip is a worm; it does not infect files. It also has a hostile payload that attacks and deletes certain kinds of data files, such as Word documents. It first spreads as a Trojan horse, masquerading as a legitimate message from a known correspondent. Explorezip actually mails itself — the owner of an infected PC does not send the message personally. If the recipient clicks and launches the Explorezip code attached to the phony mail message, their PC becomes infected. The next time their computer starts, the hostile code is activated. It immediately begins to reproduce using a secondary mechanism, spreading across the intranet looking for vulnerable Windows shares so it can copy itself to other PCs. The triggering event for the primary infection mechanism is the reception of mail. Whenever an infected victim receives a new mail message, Explorezip replies with a bogus message containing a copy of itself, potentially spreading itself to another organization. Once an infection has occurred, shutting off the e-mail server may not halt its spread because it can also reproduce through the network using file sharing. This combination of two infection mechanisms complicated the response to Explorezip. Explorezip increases the chance of a successful infection by appropriating its victim's e-mail identity; it is a spoof that takes advantage of correspondent trust to lull recipients into accepting and executing an e-mail attachment that they may otherwise avoid.

EXPLOITS

Autonomous Attacks

Viruses and worms are autonomous. They are self-guided robots that attack victims without direction from their creator. Happy99 spreads as a Trojan horse, purportedly a fun program to display fireworks in a window (sort of a New Year's celebration). While it is displaying fireworks, it also patches WSOCK.DLL. This Winsock modification hooks any attempts to connect or send e-mail. When the victim posts to a newsgroup or sends e-mail, Happy99 invokes its own executable, SKA.DLL, to send a UUEN-CODED copy of itself to the news group or the mail recipients. As illustrated in Exhibit 23-2, Caligula is a Word macro virus that when triggered searches for PGP key rings (a PGP key ring is the data file that includes a user's encrypted private key for Pretty Good Privacy mail and file encryption). If it finds a PGP key ring, it FTPs it to a Web site known to be used for the exchange and distribution of viruses. Caligula is an example of autonomous code that steals data.

Melissa is designed to covertly e-mail infected documents to the first 50 e-mail addresses in a victim's address book. The document — which might contain sensitive or embarrassing information intended only for internal

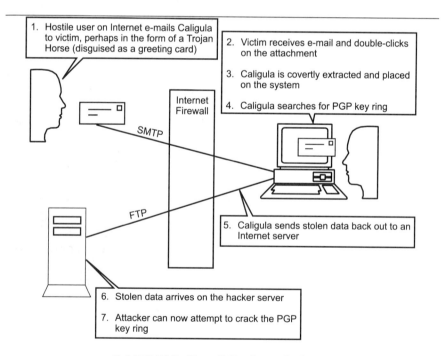

1. Hostile user on Internet e-mails Caligula to victim, perhaps in the form of a Trojan Horse (disguised as a greeting card)

2. Victim receives e-mail and double-clicks on the attachment

3. Caligula is covertly extracted and placed on the system

Internet Firewall

4. Caligula searches for PGP key ring

SMTP

FTP

5. Caligula sends stolen data back out to an Internet server

6. Stolen data arrives on the hacker server

7. Attacker can now attempt to crack the PGP key ring

Exhibit 23-2. How Caligula steals data.

use — will be unwittingly sent to those 50 addresses. While it probably was not designed to steal data, a Melissa infection can easily result in the loss of privacy. At the time of this writing, there are at least 20 different families of mail-enabled hostile code. Caligula, Happy99, Explorezip, and Melissa are all examples of malware that take advantage of network capabilities. As shown in Steps 1 and 5 of Exhibit 23-2, most firewalls are configured to allow all incoming SMTP traffic, and all outgoing FTP connections. Attack code can easily use these protocols to circumvent a firewall and perform its intended task without human direction. However, autonomous attacks lack flexibility. Attackers desiring a more flexible and personal mechanism must use some form of interactive attack.

Interactive Attacks

Fancifully named programs, such as BackOrifice and NetBus, represent a significant change in the use of hostile code to attack computers. If installed on a victim's PC, these programs can serve as backdoors, allowing the establishment of a surreptitious channel that provides an attacker virtually total access to the PC across the Internet. A pun on Microsoft's BackOffice, BackOrifice (or BO) is the first Windows backdoor to be widely spread. Once a BO server has been inserted on a PC, either manually or as a Trojan horse, it can be remotely accessed using either a text or graphical client. The BO server allows intruders to execute commands, list files, silently start network services, share directories, upload and download files, manipulate the registry, list processes, and kill processes. Reminiscent of UNIX attacks, it allows a Windows machine to be a springboard for attacks on other systems. BO supports the use of accessory plug-ins, and several have been developed (continuing the naming convention with catchy puns like Butt Trumpet). Plug-ins allow BO to be wrapped into a self-extracting executable or to ride piggyback on another program. Once it has been installed, another plug-in announces itself on an IRC group. Several dozen surreptitious channel remote control applications are available. These programs can be used as legitimate system administration tools, and their creators steadfastly maintain that this is their purpose. Certainly, attackers also exploit commercial remote control applications, such as pcAnywhere. However, hostile backdoor exploits have special features designed to make them invisible to their victims, and they have other capabilities that facilitate data theft.

Once accidentally installed by the hapless victim, these programs listen for connection attempts on specific ports. Starting in late 1998, CERT reported a high rate of connection attempts on these ports across the Internet. Systems connected to the Internet full-time, such as those using cable modems or DSL, can expect to be scanned several times a week. The appeal of these programs to an attacker should be obvious. Someone motivated to steal or alter specific data can easily do so if they can install a remote control application on a suitable target host and access it over a network. Kiddie scripts are available to piggyback NetBus or BackOrifice onto any executable that an attacker feels a victim would be willing to execute, creating a customized Trojan horse. Attackers too lazy to "trojanize" the remote control server program themselves can just send potential victims a video game that is already prepared as a NetBus Trojan, such as Whack-a-Mole. Once a vulnerable system is created or found, the keystroke recording feature can be used to compromise the passwords, which control access to secret keys, threatening a variety of password-protected security services, including S-MIME, PGP, and SSL. Most VPN clients are only protected by a password. If this password were to be compromised through a surreptitious backdoor's keystroke recording function, someone who later used the backdoor to remotely connect to the infected PC would be able to appropriate the victim's identity and corresponding VPN privileges. This could lead to the compromise of a corporate network.

MEME VIRUSES

Just the threat of a virus is sufficient to impact productivity — **virus hoaxes** can cause more disruption than actual viruses. Typically, a naïve user receives an e-mail message warning them of the dire consequences of some new form of computer virus. This message, full of exclamation points and capital letters, instructs the user to warn as many people as possible of some imminent danger (an example is shown in Exhibit 23-3). Viral hoax creators take advantage of a human need to feel important, and enough users are willing to forward these messages to their friends and co-workers that the deception spreads quickly and widely. Just like actual viruses, some virus hoaxes can live for years, flaring up every six to twelve months in a flurry of unproductive e-mail. When thousands of corporate users receive a bogus warning simultaneously, the effect on corporate productivity can be significant. No e-mail warning from an individual about a new virus should be taken seriously before doing research. Every vendor of anti-virus software has a Web page cataloging known hostile code, and several excellent Web sites are dedicated to the exposure and discussion of viral hoaxes. Virus hoax response can only be accomplished procedurally, and must be addressed in the organizational policy on hostile code or e-mail usage. Users must be instructed to report concerns to the IS department, and not take it upon themselves to inform the entire world. The Internet has proven to be an extraordinarily efficient mechanism for misinformation dissemination, and virus scares are not the only form of disruptive hoax. Well-meaning users are also prone to spreading a variety of similar practical joke messages. Classic e-mail pranks include chain letters, "make a wish" requests for a dying boy who collects business cards, and petitions to the government for some upcoming fictitious decision.

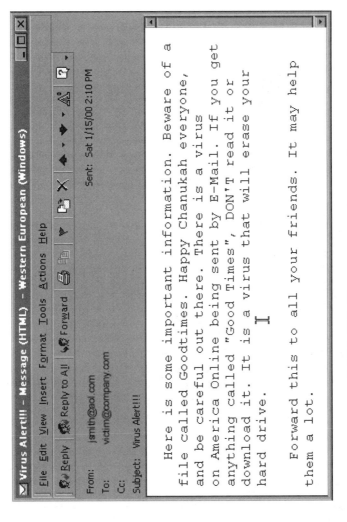

Exhibit 23-3. Hoaxes are easy to recognize.

COUNTERMEASURES

Hostile code control requires a comprehensive program simultaneously addressing both technical and human issues. It is safe to assume that some infections will occur, so prepare a recovery strategy before it is needed.

Policy and Procedure

The first step in computer security is always well-conceived policy establishing organizational priorities and basic security rules. Hostile code infections are prevented through procedural and technical countermeasures; policy must address both. Users need to be aware of the danger associated with the acceptance and use of files from external sources, and trained not to automatically double-click on e-mail attachments. Anti-virus (AV) software must be installed on every desktop and updated regularly. Corporate policy needs to set rules for e-mail. In addition to hostile code, organizational e-mail policy should address chain letters, hoaxes, and other forms of harmful internal communication. Policy must address response and cleanup. A malware response team should be appointed and charged with creating procedures for the rapid response to and recovery from an infection.

Creating policy is just the first step; it must be implemented through guidelines and procedures. Effective implementation involves more than just the publication of a set of rules. If corporate staff understands the nature of the threat, is aware of their role in spreading infection, and is provided with simple but effective behavioral guidelines, they will become the allies of the IS department. Awareness is not a one-time event provided to new hires. Existing staff must be periodically reminded of their responsibility to protect their organization. Media scares about new forms of hostile code can be an opportunity to educate the users and help them understand that security is an ongoing process. Clamp down on hoaxes and chain mail immediately. Remember the fable about the little boy who cried wolf. Users subjected to continuous warnings about dangers that never appear will become inured, and will not respond appropriately when an actual event occurs.

Good Hygiene

Maintaining optimal configuration and following best practices for administration results in robust systems that are resistant to security threats. Effective configuration management ensures that all systems will be appropriately configured for both performance and security, and it facilitates their recovery in case of a disaster or failure. System security should be as tight as practical, protecting sensitive system configuration and corporate data from unauthorized or accidental deletion or change. Excessive use of administrative privileges increases the risk of a failure. Every time someone is logged in with full administrative privileges, the negative consequences of a mistake are increased. Accidentally executing hostile code while logged in as an administrator can be disastrous. UNIX users should not login as root, but should use the **sudo** command to temporarily access root privileges when needed. When NT users read mail or work on documents, they should be logged into an account that is not a member of the administrative group. Human attackers and worms need access to network services in order to compromise systems remotely, so both servers and workstations should avoid running unnecessary network applications.

System and Data Backups. The performance of regular and complete system data backups is the most effective security countermeasure. No security administrator can ever guarantee that a system will not fail, or that some unforeseen attack will not succeed. Having complete restore capability is a last-ditch defense, but it is a reliable defense. Organizational policy should mandate system backups and provide standards for backup storage. Depending on the volume and significance of the information, this policy might direct that some data be backed up on a daily basis or even in real-time, while other data be backed up on a weekly basis. Backups must be stored off-site. While redundant systems, such as RAID, provide a high level of reliability, if a site becomes unusable, the data would probably be inaccessible. Always test restoration capability. While it is helpful to perform a read test whenever data is backed up, this test does not guarantee that the tapes can be used to perform a restore. Develop procedures for periodically testing file restoration. It is inconvenient to back up laptops, but increasingly they contain large amounts of critical corporate data. Requirements for portable computers should be included as part of the data backup policy.

Anti-virus Software

When properly managed, AV software can be highly effective. It uses a variety of mechanisms to identify potentially hostile code; scanning is the most effective. Anti-virus scanning engines methodically search through system executables and other susceptible files for evidence of known malware. A file called the *virus definition* file contains signatures of known hostile code. The signature is a sequence of bits that researchers have identified as being unique to a specific example of hostile code. Searching every executable, Word document, and boot record for each of 50,000 signatures would take an unacceptably long time. Viral code can only be inserted at certain spots within an existing executable, so scanning engines increase performance by only searching specific parts of an executable. Over the years, virus writers have devised several methods to defeat virus scanners. Polymorphic viruses mutate, changing their appearance every time they reproduce; but when they execute, they revert to their original form within system memory. Modern anti-virus software actually runs executables within a CPU simulator first, so that polymorphic viruses can decrypt themselves safely in a controlled environment where their signatures can be recognized. Unfortunately, anti-virus scanners are blissfully unaware of new hostile code until the AV vendors have the opportunity to analyze it and update their definition files. AV software vendors share newly discovered examples of hostile code, allowing each vendor the opportunity to update their own definition files. Most AV vendors update their definitions every four weeks, unless they become aware of some especially harmful virus and provide an interim update. This latency prevents scanning from ever being 100 percent effective, and is the reason why users must be trained to protect themselves. Several techniques have been developed to detect previously unknown hostile code, such as heuristics and behavior blocking, but results have been mixed. It is relatively easy to anticipate certain behaviors that file and boot sector viruses will follow. For example, most AV products can be configured to prevent writing to the master boot record. Monitoring more complex behaviors increases the potential for user disruption from false positives.

AV vendors offer several choices as to when scanning occurs. Scanning can be performed manually, which is a good idea when the virus definition files have been updated, especially if there is reason to believe that a previously undetectable form of hostile code might be present. Scanning can also be scheduled to occur periodically. The most reliable way to prevent the introduction of malware to a PC is to automatically scan files that potentially contain hostile code before accepting them. Before e-mail became a universal means for file exchange, floppy disks with infected boot sectors were the most common infection vector. During the past few years, hostile code has been more likely to spread via e-mail. AV software with real-time capabilities can be configured to scan files for the presence of hostile code whenever a floppy disk is inserted, a file is copied or read, or an e-mail attachment is opened. PC anti-virus software real-time detection capabilities have proven effective at stopping the spread of recognized hostile code attached to e-mail messages. Running AV software in this mode does raise performance concerns, but the cost of faster hardware can be offset against the cost of downtime, cleanup, and loss of system integrity after a significant viral infection.

In addition to running AV software on the desktop, scanners can be server based. The automatic periodic scanning of file servers for hostile code will ensure that even if an individual desktop is misconfigured, malware stored on the server will eventually be discovered. An increasing number of products are available to scan e-mail attachments before the mail is placed in a user's incoming mailbox. It is a common misconception that a firewall is a total solution to Internet security. Firewalls are network perimeter security devices that control access to specific network services — a limited task that they perform well. They are not designed to examine incoming data and determine whether it is executable or what it is likely to do. **Virus walls** are application-level countermeasures designed to screen out hostile code from e-mail. These products can often be run on the firewall or the mail server, but it is usually most practical to use a stand-alone machine for mail filtering, locating it between the firewall and the organizational mail server. Operating as an e-mail proxy, virus walls open each message, check for attachments, unarchive them, and scan them for recognizable hostile code using a commercial AV product. They are efficient at unzipping attachments, but they cannot open encrypted messages. If organizational policy allows incoming encrypted attachments, they can only be scanned at the desktop. E-mail scanners should be considered as an augmentation to desktop control — not as a replacement. Use different AV products on the virus wall and the desktop; the combination of two different products in series provides a better detection rate than either product alone. E-mail scanners can protect both incoming and outgoing mail; unfortunately, most organizations only scan incoming mail. Scanning outgoing mail can double the cost of a virus wall, but this should be balanced against the loss of goodwill or bad publicity that will occur when a customer or partner is sent a virus.

Exhibit 23-4 shows the different locations within an enterprise where hostile code can be controlled. An obvious location for the scanning of incoming content is the firewall, which is already a dedicated security device. However, the primary mission of a firewall is to provide access control at the transport level. From the purist point of view, it is inappropriate to perform application layer functions on a network security device. However, it is becoming common to provide this service on a firewall, and many organizations are doing it successfully. If the firewall has enough processing power to perform scanning in addition to its other duties, adding a scanning upgrade is an easy way to scan mail attachments and downloads. Be aware that the addition of new services to a firewall increases the risk of failure — it is easy to overload a firewall with add-ons. Mail scanning can also be performed on the mail server. This has the minor disadvantage of not protecting HTTP or FTP. The bigger disadvantage is the increased complexity and decreased performance of the mail server. Mail servers are often finicky, and adding additional functionality does not increase dependability. Organizations already using high-end firewall and mail servers should consider one or more dedicated proxy machines, which is the most scalable solution. It can easily be inserted immediately behind the firewall and in front of the mail server. Organizations that want immediate protection but do not have the desire or wherewithal to provide it in-house can contract with an outside provider. Increasingly, ISPs are offering a scanning option for incoming e-mail. Managed security service providers will remotely manage a firewall, including the maintenance of virus wall capabilities. The desktop is

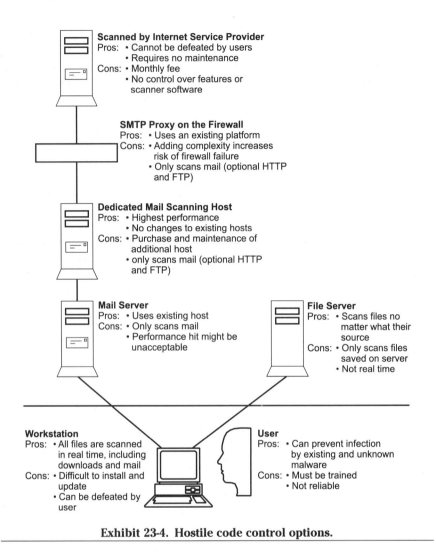

Scanned by Internet Service Provider
Pros: • Cannot be defeated by users
      • Requires no maintenance
Cons: • Monthly fee
      • No control over features or
        scanner software

SMTP Proxy on the Firewall
Pros: • Uses an existing platform
Cons: • Adding complexity increases
        risk of firewall failure
      • Only scans mail (optional HTTP
        and FTP)

Dedicated Mail Scanning Host
Pros: • Highest performance
      • No changes to existing hosts
Cons: • Purchase and maintenance of
        additional host
      • only scans mail (optional HTTP
        and FTP)

Mail Server
Pros: • Uses existing host
Cons: • Only scans mail
      • Performance hit might be
        unacceptable

File Server
Pros: • Scans files no
        matter what their
        source
Cons: • Only scans files
        saved on server
      • Not real time

Workstation
Pros: • All files are scanned
        in real time, including
        downloads and mail
Cons: • Difficult to install and
        update
      • Can be defeated by
        user

User
Pros: • Can prevent infection
        by existing and unknown
        malware
Cons: • Must be trained
      • Not reliable

Exhibit 23-4. Hostile code control options.

the most crucial place to control hostile code. If desktop systems could be reliably updated and users prevented from tampering with the configuration, there would be no need to scan anywhere else in the organization, but desktop scanning is difficult to maintain and the users cannot be trusted.

Cleaning. AV software not only detects hostile code, but also can be used to remove it. Removal of a virus from an executable is not always practical, but the AV vendors work very hard to provide automated cleaning of the hostile code most likely to be encountered in the wild. Although most users are capable of running a wizard and cleaning up their own system, organizational policy should provide them with guidance on what to do when their AV software informs them an infection has been found. Even if users are allowed to clean up their own systems, their AV software should be configured to place a copy of all infected files in a quarantine area to facilitate later diagnosis. When infected, most organizations use their AV software to perform a cleanup; and if the cleanup is successful, the system is returned to production use. Any applications that cannot be repaired must be reinstalled or restored from a backup.

AV Software Configuration Should be Based on Policy. Several policy decisions have to be made in order to control hostile code with an anti-virus product. The most significant decision is whether the desktops will be individually administered or centrally administered. Even the worst product, when properly maintained and updated, outperforms the most effective product available if that product is improperly configured. It is not reasonable to expect users to make appropriate decisions concerning the configuration of their security software; and even when they are provided guidance, they cannot be trusted to reliably configure their own systems. Clearly, the trend is toward central administration, and the AV vendors are trying to accommodate this. Most AV products can be configured to periodically download definition files, automatically updating themselves. Software distribution tools available from Novell, Microsoft, and a number of independent software vendors can be used to push updates to user desktops. Use of a virus wall is also a form of central control. The choice of whether or not incoming files should be scanned before reaching the desktop is a policy decision. Likewise, policy should also address the scanning of outgoing files. Once policy exists that requires the centralized scanning of ingoing or outgoing mail, the choice of whether to scan on the firewall, on a dedicated mail scanning host, or on the existing mail server, is an implementation issue — not a policy decision.

Unless individual users experience problems, such as an unacceptably high number of false positives or a high rate of infection, desktop AV software will probably be configured to use the manufacturer's defaults on every internal system. Anti-virus software typically does not scan every file on the system — this would be a waste of time. On a Windows machine, the choice of files to be scanned is determined by their suffix. The vendor's recommendations for appropriate file types should not be changed unless hostile code has been consistently missed because of its file type. The software should be configured to automatically scan e-mail attachments and files at read time. Hostile code is rarely contracted through FTP or HTTP, but the overhead of scanning individual files is not noticeable, so the cost of scanning all Internet downloads is low.

Choosing a Product. The trade press is ill-equipped to evaluate anti-virus products. Reviews in popular computer magazines are more likely to be misleading than helpful. At best, they tend to dwell on meaningless number games, comparing vendor's inflated claims for the number of recognized viruses. At worst, they concentrate on the attractiveness of the user interface. Only dedicated periodicals, such as *Virus Bulletin*, have the expertise to make valid comparisons between heavily marketed anti-virus products. The industry analyst firms usually have the expertise and objectivity to make useful recommendations on choice of virus control software. Organizations that subscribe to desktop or security bulletins from companies like this should see if they are eligible to receive reports on anti-virus products. Most AV vendors offer free mailing lists. These mailing lists serve a marketing function and tend to exaggerate the danger of newly discovered hostile code examples. Although AV vendor Web sites provide useful reference data on hostile code, their mailing lists are usually not helpful to the security practitioner. Several organizations test AV software and place their results on the Web. See Exhibit 23-1 for the URLs. *Virus Bulletin* (which is owned by an AV vendor), and the ICSA and Check-Mark (which are for-profit organizations) certify AV products and place the results on the Web. The Computer Science Department at the University of Hamburg is the only non-profit organization to methodically test AV products and regularly publish results.

Microsoft Word Macro Virus Control

Word macro viruses are the most prevalent form of hostile code. Microsoft Word documents support a programming language that is a variant of Visual Basic. Virtually anything that can be done on a PC can be done within a Word document using this language, including low-level machine language calls. They can be configured to execute automatically when a document is opened. Macros are a powerful tool for office automation, but they also place Word users at risk. There are several ways to reduce the macro virus risk, but none of them is foolproof. Word can be configured so that it does not automatically execute macros. When so configured, it will prompt the user for a decision whenever encountering a file with an autoexecute macro. Without training, users cannot be expected to make an appropriate decision, and even experienced users can accidentally push the wrong button. Just like executable viruses, macro viruses have become increasingly stealthy over time, and virus writers have developed several techniques for evading this automatic check. Word has the capability of storing documents in several formats. Only Word's native DOC format supports macros, so some organizations have chosen to distribute files in Rich Text Format (RTF). Windows 2000 can also store files in HTML with no loss of formatting, an even more portable format. Unfortunately, it is possible to change the extension on a DOC file to RTF or HTML and Word will still recognize it as a DOC file. Opening a DOC with an autoexecute macro — even when it is disguised with a different extension — will cause the macro to be executed. The safest choice is to use an application that cannot run macros, such as Microsoft's free DOC file viewer. Downloadable from Microsoft's Web site, this utility can be safely used to view a file suspected of containing a macro virus.

Most macro viruses will infect NORMAL.DOT, the Word file containing default styles and macros. If the infection cannot be removed with AV software, remove NORMAL.DOT and Word will recreate it the next time it is started. Note that deleting NORMAL.DOT will result in a loss of all user-defined Word hot keys, macros, and changes to default styles. If this file is shared across the network, all users will contract the virus the next time they start Word. For this reason, a shared NORMAL.DOT file should always be configured as read-only.

Mobile Code Control: Java and ActiveX

Java is an interpreted programming language, while ActiveX is a Microsoft binary format. The two technologies are different, but from the point of view of a Web browser, they are alternate mechanisms for distributing code from a Web page to a user desktop for local execution. Mobile code is a security concern because it allows Web site operators control over what is executed on a user's desktop. It is important to remember that Java and ActiveX have never been exploited in a security-relevant way. The only known mobile code exploits have been demonstrations — there is no recorded example of an actual security failure involving mobile code on a production system. Unlike other more prevalent forms of malware, mobile code security remains a popular area of academic research, ensuring that security-relevant software bugs are identified and reported to the browser vendors.

Because it is a strongly typed language, Java is less susceptible to buffer overruns than C, making Java code more reliable and difficult to exploit. Java executes within a controlled environment called the Java virtual machine (JVM). When running within a browser, the 1.0 version of the JVM enforces its security policy using three different mechanisms. First, the applet class loader assigns a private namespace associated with the network origin of each downloaded applet, maintaining a separate and unique namespace for Java code loaded locally. Second, all applets pass through the applet code verifier, which checks for illegal code constructions. Finally, the Java security manager, a reference monitor, prevents the local reading and writing of files, and prevents applets associated with one host from accessing a different one. Sometimes referred to as the Java sandbox, the security manager only allows applets to do four things: they can run, they can access the screen, they can accept input, and they can connect back to their originating host. Several Java security bugs have been demonstrated in the laboratory by tricking the JVM into allowing applets access to hosts other than the originating host, or allowing them access to the local file system. Both Microsoft and Netscape quickly patched these vulnerabilities. The limitations of Java 1.0 functionality should be clear. While it is an intrinsically safe environment, the lack of file system access limits its utility for transactions. Java 2.0 provides the capability for authorized applets to break out of the Java sandbox. The newer version of Java allows applets to be digitally signed. Compatible browsers will be able to allow controlled access to system resources on behalf of applets signed by approved parties.

ActiveX is Microsoft's trade name for compiled Windows executables that can be automatically distributed across the Internet as part of a Web page. It uses Microsoft's Component Object Module standard (COM). It does not have any form of sandbox, but uses a trust model similar to Java version 2.0. The Microsoft browser, Internet Explorer, checks the digital signature of any ActiveX objects presented to it by a Web server. Microsoft browsers support a hierarchy of security zones, each allowing greater access to system resources. Specific signers can be configured within the browser environment as being authorized for the access level of specific zones. A typical configuration might allow ActiveX originating from within an organization to have full access to a user's resources, but code originating from the Internet would have no special privileges. Unfortunately, if a user encounters an ActiveX object from an unrecognized signer, the default behavior is to ask the user what to do. Because the onus is on the user to determine what code is appropriate to operate, ActiveX has been widely criticized in the security community. For this model to work, users must be trained — which is relatively difficult. Microsoft provides a centralized configuration management tool for Internet Explorer, enabling an organization to centrally configure behavior on all desktops. Effective use of this capability should allow an organization to take full advantage of ActiveX internally without placing users at unnecessary risk.

Although neither Java nor ActiveX has ever been successfully exploited, several commercial products are available that protect desktops for both. Organizations wishing to ensure that mobile code is never activated on employee PCs can also control it at the perimeter. Many Web proxies, including those running directly on a firewall, can be configured to trap Java and ActiveX objects, shielding users from mobile code on the Internet. Security practitioners should be aware of the potential for mobile code failures, and know the countermeasures available in case a problem ever manifests itself. At the time of this writing, only the most sensitive organizations need to be concerned about mobile code risk.

WHY DOES HOSTILE CODE EXIST?

Why is so much malware floating around? The motivations behind the writing of hostile code are complex. In most cases, it is not necessarily an explicit desire to hurt other people, but it is often a form of self-actualization.

It is a hobby — carried to obsessive levels by some of the most successful virus writers. The quest for knowledge and the joy of parenthood are fun and satisfying. Virus creators are driven by Dr. Frankenstein's relentless curiosity on the nature of life itself. Once having created something that appears able to reproduce, it can be difficult to resist the temptation of experimenting in the ultimate laboratory, the Internet. Robert Morris, Jr., the creator of the Internet Worm, is probably not the only programmer who has experienced a sorcerer's apprentice moment and realized that their handiwork has succeeded beyond their wildest dreams — and beyond their sphere of control.

Many writers of self-replicating code belong to an extended virtual community where they socialize, exchanging ideas and code. Virus writers were early users of bulletin board systems, forums that have been transplanted to the Internet. The most desirable virus meeting places are closed, requiring the submission of a functioning virus as an initiation requirement. Created by neophytes, these initial efforts are typically simple variations of existing malware, which explains why such a high percentage of the thousands of identified hostile programs are closely related. Social status within the virus writing community is similar to other hacker subcultures. It is derived from technical prowess, which must be proven repeatedly as community members compete for superiority. Fame and respect derive from recognition within their social group of their superior skills, as demonstrated by clever coding and successfully propagating creations. There is undoubtedly a need on the part of some coders to overcome their inferiority feelings by exerting power of others as digital bullies, but studies of virus writers indicate that the challenge and social aspects are most significant. By attempting to evade AV software, virus writers demonstrate an awareness of the AV industry. Only the most socially obtuse programmer could fail to realize that AV software exists because people fear viruses and wish to avoid them.

Why Windows?

UNIX viruses are possible, but in practice, they are essentially nonexistent. There continue to be a few Macintosh viruses, but the overwhelming majority of malware attacks are aimed at Microsoft Windows systems. That which makes Windows most useful is also its greatest weakness — a characteristic not unique to computer security. Windows represents a monoculture — the majority of user workstations utilize the same operating environment, run the same application (Microsoft Word), and many use Microsoft Outlook for e-mail. As modern agriculture has shown that monoculture provides an opportunity for insects and disease, huge numbers of similar PCs are susceptible to a common infection. Exacerbating the low level of diversity is the high level of both internal and external connectivity, and the privileges granted to their unsophisticated operators make Windows systems vulnerable. Users of Windows 98 are effectively the system administrator. NT is an operating system designed to meet the C2 requirements for access control, but normal users are often granted administrator privileges, effectively bypassing the system's built-in protection. Finally, the widespread use of a macro-enabled word processor means that executable content is pervasive. The combination of ubiquitous e-mail, a powerful word processor, weak access control, and unsophisticated users has resulted in macro viruses quickly becoming a universal threat.

CONCLUSION

While documented cases are low, a risk analyst needs to be aware that remotely inserted hostile code is an ideal way for motivated and skillful attackers to commit computer-based fraud or vandalize information. Malware already exists that steals passwords, and other forms of directed data theft are just as easy to accomplish. As easily customizable hostile code continues to proliferate, and as motivated external attackers become increasingly sophisticated, directed attacks will be carried out through e-mail. Organizations that are subject to either espionage or especially strong and unethical competitive pressure need to be on the lookout for customized attack code. Malware has been present throughout the PC era. While the cost of viral infections remains a matter of debate, despite the millions of dollars spent fighting malware, the rate of hostile code incidents continues to increase. The latest forms of Internet security countermeasures, such as firewalls, VPNs, and PKI, are vulnerable to software attack. Fortunately, control is relatively simple. A well-orchestrated combination of human effort and technical countermeasures has proven effective in maintaining an acceptably low rate of hostile code infection.

Bibliography

1. Cohen, Frederick B., *A Short Course on Computer Viruses*, Wiley, New York, 1994.
2. Denning, Dorothy E., *Information Warfare and Security*, Addison-Wesley, New York, 1999.
3. Gordon, Sarah, The Generic Virus Writer, presented at *The 4th International Virus Bulletin Conference,* Jersey, U.K., September 1994.
4. Gordon, Sarah, Technologically Enabled Crime: Shifting Paradigms for the Year 2000, *Computers and Security*, 1994.
5. Gordon, Sarah, Ford, Richard, and Wells, Joe, Hoaxes & Hypes, presented at the *7th Virus Bulletin International Conference,* San Francisco, CA, October 1997.
   (Sarah Gordon papers can be found at http://www.av.ibm.com/ScientificPapers/Gordon/)
6. Heiser, Jay, Java Security Mechanisms: A Three-sided Approach for the Protection of Your System, *Java Developer's Journal*, 2(3), 1997.
7. Kabay, Michel E., Tippett, Peter, and Bridwell, Lawrence M., *Fifth Annual ICSA Computer Virus Prevalence Survey*, ICSA, 1999.
8. Kephart, Jeffrey O., Sorkin, Gregory B., Chess, David M., and White, Steve R., Fighting Computer Viruses, *Scientific American*, 277(5), 88–93, November 1997.
9. McClure, Stuart, Scambray, Joel, and Kurtz, George, *Hacking Exposed*, Osborne, 1999.
10. Nachenberg, C., Computer Virus-Antivirus Coevolution, *Communications of the ACM*, January 1997.

11. National Institute of Standards and Technology, *Glossary of Computer Security Terminology*, NISTIR4659, 1991.
12. Schneier, Bruce, Inside Risks: The Trojan Horse Race, *Communications of the ACM*, 42(9), September 1999.
13. Slade, Robert, *Robert Slade's Guide to Computer Viruses*, Springer, 1996.
14. Smith, George C., *The Virus Creation Labs*, American Eagle Publications, 1994.
15. Solomon, Alan and Kay, Tim, *Dr. Solomon's PC Antivirus Book*, New Tech, 1994.
16. Spafford, Eugene H., Computer Viruses, *Internet Besieged*, Denning, Dorothy E., Ed., ACM Press, 1998.
17. Whalley, Ian, Testing Times for Trojans, presented at the *Virus Bulletin Conference,* October 1999, http://www.av.ibm.com/ScientificPapers/Whalley/inwVB99.html.

Domain 8
Business Continuity Planning and Disaster Recovery Planning

TO PROTECT AND MANAGE INFORMATION ASSETS, IT IS ESSENTIAL TO HAVE AN INVENTORY OF AN ORGANIZATION'S SYSTEMS AND APPLICATIONS, AND A DEFINITION — BY BUSINESS PRIORITY — OF WHAT SYSTEMS AND APPLICATIONS ARE MOST CRITICAL. This is accomplished by performing a business impact analysis, typically done in partnership between the business information owners and the Information Technology organization.

In this domain, a new chapter on business continuity planning process improvement addresses the continuing efforts in which an organization must participate for a high level of assurance that computing assets will be there when needed.

Chapter 24
The Business Impact Assessment Process

Carl B. Jackson

THE INITIAL VERSION OF THIS CHAPTER WAS WRITTEN FOR THE 1999 EDITION OF THE *HANDBOOK OF INFORMATION SECURITY MANAGEMENT*. Since then, Y2K has come and gone, E-commerce has seized the spotlight, and Web-based technologies are the emerging solution for almost everything. The constant throughout these occurrences is that no matter what the climate, fundamental business processes have changed little. And, as always, the focus of any business impact assessment is to assess the time-critical priority of these business processes. With these more recent realities in mind, this chapter has been updated and is now offered for your consideration.

The objective of this chapter is to examine the business impact assessment (BIA) process in detail and focus on the fundamentals of a successful BIA.

There is no question that business continuity planning (BCP) is a business process issue, not a technical one. While each critical component of the enterprise must participate during the development, testing, and maintenance of the BCP process, it is the results of the business impact assessment (BIA) that will be used to make a case for further action.

Why perform a business impact assessment? The Author's experiences in this area have shown that all too often, recovery strategies, such as hotsites, duplicate facilities, material or inventory stockpiling, etc., are based on emotional motivations rather than the results of a thorough business impact assessment. The key to success in performing BIAs lies in obtaining a firm and formal agreement from management as to the precise maximum tolerable downtimes (MTDs), also referred to in some circles as recovery time objectives (RTOs), for each critical business process. The formalized MTDs/RTOs, once determined, must be validated by each business unit, then communicated to the service organizations (i.e., IT, Network Management, Facilities, HR, etc.) that support the business units.

0-8493-0800-3/00/$0.00+$.50
© 2001 by CRC Press LLC

This process helps ensure that realistic recovery alternatives are acquired and recovery measures are developed and deployed.

There are several reasons why a properly conducted and communicated BIA is so valuable to the organization. These include: (1) identifying and prioritizing time-critical business processes; (2) determining MTDs/RTOs for these processes and associated supporting resources, (3) raising positive awareness as to the importance of business continuity, and (4) providing empirical data upon which management can base its decision for establishing overall continuous operations and recovery strategies and acquiring supporting resources. Therefore, the significance of the BIA is that it sets the stage for shaping a business-oriented judgment concerning the appropriation of resources for recovery planning and continuous operations. (E-commerce — see below).

The Impact of the Internet and E-commerce on Traditional BCP

Internet-enabled E-commerce has profoundly influenced the way organizations do business. This paradigm shift has dramatically affected how technology is used to support the organization's supply chain, and because of this, will also have a significant effect on the manner in which the organization views and undertakes business continuity planning. It is no longer a matter of just preparing to recover from a serious disaster or disruption. It is now incumbent upon technology management to do all it can to avoid any kind of outage whatsoever. The technical disciplines necessary to ensure continuous operations or E-availability include building redundancy, diversity, and security into the E-commerce-related supply chain technologies (e.g., hardware, software, systems, and communications networks) (see Exhibit 24-1).

This framework attempts to focus attention on the traditional recovery planning process components as well as to highlight those process steps that are unique to the continuous operations/E-availability process.

Exhibit 24-1. Continuous availability/recovery planning component framework.

Continuous Operations/Availability Disciplines	Traditional Recovery/BCP Disciplines
Current state assessment	Current state assessment
Business impact assessment	Business impact assessment
Leading practices/benchmarking	Leading practices/benchmarking
Continuous operations strategy development	Recovery strategy development
Continuous operations strategy deployment	Recovery plan development/deployment
Testing/maintenance	Testing/maintenance
Awareness/training	Awareness/training
Process measurement/metrics/value	Process measurement/metrics/value

The BCP professional must become conversant with the disciplines associated with continuous operations/E-availability in order to ensure that organizational E-availability and recovery objectives are met.

THE BCP PROCESS APPROACH

The BIA process is only one phase of recovery planning and E-availability. The following is a brief description of a six-phase methodological approach. This approach is commonly used for development of business unit continuity plans, crisis management plans, technological platform, and communications network recovery plans.

- Phase I — Determine scope of BCP project and develop project plan. This phase examines business operations and information system support services, in order to form a project plan to direct subsequent phases. Project planning must define the precise scope, organization, timing, staffing, and other issues. This enables articulation of project status and requirements throughout the organization, chiefly to those departments and personnel who will be playing the most meaningful roles during the development of the BCP.
- Phase II — Conduct business impact assessment. This phase involves identification of time-critical business processes, and determines the impact of a significant interruption or disaster. These impacts may be financial in terms of dollar loss, or operational in nature, such as the ability to deliver and monitor quality customer service, etc.
- Phase III — Develop recovery/E-availability strategies. The information collected in Phase II is employed to approximate the recovery resources (i.e., business unit or departmental space and resource requirements, technological platform services, and communications networks requirements) necessary to support time-critical business processes and sub-processes. During this phase, an appraisal of E-availability/recovery alternatives and associated cost estimates are prepared and presented to management.
- Phase IV — Perform recovery plan development. This phase develops the actual plans (i.e., business unit, E-availability, crisis management, technology-based plans). Explicit documentation is required for execution of an effective recovery process. The plan must include administrative inventory information and detailed recovery team action plans, among other information.
- Phase V — Implement, test, and maintain the BCP. This phase establishes a rigorous, ongoing testing and maintenance management program.
- Phase VI — Implement awareness and process measurement. The final and probably the most crucial long-term phase establishes a framework for measuring the recovery planning and E-availability pro-

cesses against the value they provide the organization. In addition, this phase includes training of personnel in the execution of specific continuity/recovery activities and tasks. It is vital that they be aware of their role as members of E-availability/recovery teams.

BIA PROCESS DESCRIPTION

As mentioned above, the intent of the BIA process is to assist the organization's management in understanding the impacts associated with possible threats. Management must then employ that intelligence to calculate the maximum tolerable downtime (MTD) for time-critical support services and resources. For most organizations, these resources include:

1. personnel
2. facilities
3. technological platforms (traditional and E-commerce-related systems)
4. software
5. data networks and equipment
6. voice networks and equipment
7. vital records
8. data
9. supply chain partners
10. etc.

THE IMPORTANCE OF DOCUMENTING A FORMAL MTD/RTO DECISION

The BIA process concludes when executive management makes a formalized decision as to the MTD it is willing to live with after analyzing the impacts to the business processes due to outages of vital support services. This includes the decision to communicate these MTD decision(s) to each business unit and support service manager involved.

The Importance of a Formalized Decision

A formalized decision must clearly communicated by senior management because the failure to document and communicate precise MTD information leaves each manager with imprecise direction on: (1) selection of an appropriate recovery alternative method; and (2) the depth of detail that will be required when developing recovery procedures, including their scope and content.

The author has seen many well-executed BIAs with excellent results wasted because senior management failed to articulate its acceptance of the results and communicate to each affected manager that the time requirements had been defined for recovery processes.

BIA INFORMATION-GATHERING TECHNIQUES

There are various schools of thought regarding how to best gather BIA information. Conducting individual one-on-one BIA interviews is popular, but organizational size and location issues sometimes make conducting one-on-one interviews impossible. Other popular techniques include group sessions, the use of an electronic medium (i.e., data or voice network), or a combination of all of these. Exhibit 24-2 is a BIA checklist. The following points highlight the pros and cons of these interviewing techniques:

1. *One-on-one BIA interviews.* In the author' opinion, the one-on-one interview with organizational representatives is the preferred manner in which to gather BIA information. The advantages of this method are the ability to discuss the issues face-to-face and observe the person. This one-on-one discussion will give the interviewer a great deal of both verbal and visual information concerning the topic at hand. In addition, personal rapport can be built between the interviewee and the BIA team, with the potential for additional assistance and support to follow. This rapport can be very beneficial during later stages of the BCP development effort if the person being interviewed understands that the BCP process was undertaken to help them get the job done in times of emergency or disaster. The disadvantages of this approach are that it can become very time-consuming, and can add time to the critical path of the BIA process.
2. *Group BIA interview sessions or exercises.* This type of information-gathering activity can be very efficient in ensuring that a lot of data is gathered in a short period of time and can speed the BIA process tremendously. The drawback to this approach is that if not conducted properly, it can result in a meeting of a number of people without very much useful information being obtained.
3. *Executive management mandate.* While not always recommended, there may be certain circumstances where conducting only selected interviews with very high-level executive management will suffice for BIA purposes. Such situations might include development of continuous operations/E-availability strategies where extremely short recovery timeframes are already obvious, or where times for development of appropriate strategies for recovery are severely shortened (as in the Y2K recovery plan development example). The level of confidence is not as high in comparison to performing many more exhaustive sets of interviews (at various levels of the organization, not just with the senior management group), but it does speed up the process.
4. *Electronic medium.* Use of voice and data communications technologies, video-conferencing, and Web-based technologies and media are becoming increasingly accepted and popular. Many times, the

physical or geographical size and diversity, as well as the structural complexity of the organization, lends itself to this type of information-gathering technique. The pros are that distances can be diminished and travel expenses reduced. The use of automated questionnaires and other data-gathering methods can facilitate the capture of tabular data and ease consolidation of this information. Less attractive, however, is the fact that this type of communication lacks the human touch, and sometimes ignores the importance of the ability of the interviewer to read the verbal and visual communications of the interviewee. *Note:* Especially worrisome is the universal broadcast of BIA-related questionnaires. These inquiries are sent to uninformed groups of users on a network, whereby they are asked to supply answers to qualitative and quantitative BIA questions without regard to the point or nuance of the question or the intent of the use of the result. Such practices almost always lend themselves to misleading and downright wrong results. This type of unsupported data-gathering technique for purposes of formulating a thoughtful strategy for recovery should be avoided.

Most likely, an organization will need to use a mix of these suggested methods, or use others as suited to the situation and culture of the enterprise.

THE USE OF BIA QUESTIONNAIRES

There is no question that the people-to-people contact of the BIA process is *the* most important component in understanding the potential a disaster will have on an organization. People run the organization, and people can best describe business functionality and their business unit's degree of reliance on support services. The issue here, however, is deciding what is the best and most practical technique for gathering information from these people.

There are differing schools of thought regarding the use of questionnaires during the BIA process. The author's opinion is that a well-crafted and customized BIA questionnaire will provide the structure needed to guide the BIA and E-availability project team(s). This consistent interview structure requires that the same questions be asked of each BIA interviewee. Reliance can then be placed on the results because answers to questions can be compared to one another with assurance that the comparisons are based on the same criterion.

While a questionnaire is a valuable tool, the structure of the questions is subject to a great deal of customization. This customization of the questions depends largely on the reason why the BIA is being conducted in the first place.

Exhibit 24-2. BIA do's checklist.

BIA To Do's

- Customize the BIA information gathering tools' questions to suit the organization's customs/culture.
- Focus on time-critical business processes and support resources (i.e., systems, applications, voice and date networks, facilities, people, etc.).
- Assume worstcase disaster (day of week, month of year, etc.).
- Assume no recovery capability exists.
- Obtain raw numbers in orders of magnitude.
- Return for financial information.
- Validate BIA data with BIA participants.
- Formalize decision from senior management so lower-level managers (MTD timeframes, scope, and depth of recovery procedures, etc.) can make precise plans.

Conducting BIA Interviews

- When interviewing business unit personnel, explain that you are here to get the information you need to help IT build their recovery plan. But emphasize that the resulting IT recovery is really theirs, but the recovery plan is really yours. One is obtaining their input as an aid in ensuring that MIS constructs the proper recovery planning strategy.
- Interviews last no longer that 45 minutes to 1 hour and 15 minutes.
- The number of interviewees at one session should be at best one, and at worst two to three. More than that and the ability of the individual to take notes is questionable.
- If possible, at least two personnel should be in attendance at the interview. Each should have a blank copy of the questionnaire on which to take notes.
- One person should probably not perform more than four interviews per day. This is due to the requirement to successfully document the results of each interview as soon as possible and because of fatigue factors.
- Never become confrontational with the interviewees. There is no reason that interviewees should be defensive in their answers unless they do not properly understand the purpose of the BIA interview.
- Relate to interviewees that their comments will be taken into consideration and documented with the others gathered. And that they will be requested to review, at a later date, the output from the process for accuracy and provide their concurrence.

The BIA process can be approached differently, depending on the needs of the organization. Each BIA situation should be evaluated in order to properly design the scope and approach of the BIA process. BIAs are desirable for several reasons, including:

1. initiation of a BCP process where no BIA has been done before, as part of the phased implementation methodology (see "The BCP Process Approach")
2. reinitiating a BCP process where there was a BIA performed in the past, but now it needs to be brought up-to-date

3. conducting a BIA in order to incorporate the impacts of a loss of E-commerce-related supply chain technologies into the overall recovery strategies of the organization

4 conducting a BIA in order to justify BCP activities that have already been undertaken (i.e., the acquisition of a hotsite or other recovery alternative)

5. initiating a BIA as a prelude to beginning a full BCP process for understanding or as a vehicle to sell management on the need to develop a BCP

CUSTOMIZING THE BIA QUESTIONNAIRE

There are a number of ways that a questionnaire can be constructed or customized to adapt itself for the purpose of serving as an efficient tool for accurately gathering BIA information. There are also an unlimited number of examples of BIA questionnaires in use by organizations. It should go without saying that any questionnaire — BIA or otherwise — can be constructed so as to elicit the response one would like. It is important that the goal of the BIA be in the mind of the questionnaire developers so that the questions asked and the responses collected will meet the objective of the BIA process.

BIA Questionnaire Construction

Exhibit 24-3 is an example of a BIA questionnaire. Basically, the BIA questionnaire is made up of the following types of questions:

- *Quantitative questions.* These are the questions asked the interviewee to consider and describe the economic or financial impacts of a potential disruption. Measured in monetary terms, an estimation of these impacts will aid the organization in understanding loss potential, in terms of lost income as well as in an increase in extraordinary expense. The typical quantitative impact categories might include: revenue or sales loss, lost trade discounts, interest paid on borrowed money, interest lost on float, penalties for late payment to vendors or lost discounts, contractual fines or penalties, unavailability of funds, canceled orders due to late delivery, etc. Extraordinary expense categories might include acquisition of outside services, temporary employees, emergency purchases, rental/lease equipment, wages paid to idle staff, and temporary relocation of employees.
- *Qualitative questions.* While the economic impacts can be stated in terms of dollar loss, the qualitative questions ask the participants to estimate potential loss impact in terms of their emotional understanding or feelings. It is surprising how often the qualitative measurements are used to put forth a convincing argument for a shorter recovery window. The typical qualitative impact categories might include loss of customer services capability, loss of confidence, etc.

Exhibit 24-3. Sample BIA questionnaire.

Introduction

Business Unit Name:

Date of Interview:

Contact Name(s):

Identification of business process and/or business unit (BU) function:

Briefly describe the overall business functions of the BU (with focus on time-critical functions/processes, and link each time-critical function/process to the IT application/network, etc.) and understand business process and applications/networks, etc. interrelationships:

Financial Impacts

Revenue Loss Impacts Estimations (revenue or sales loss, lost trade discounts, interest paid on borrowed money, interest lost on float, penalties for late payment to vendors or lost discounts, contractual fines or penalties, unavailability of funds, canceled orders due to late delivery, etc.):

Extraordinary expense impact estimations (acquisition of outside services, temporary employees, emergency purchases, rental/lease equipment, wages paid to idle staff, temporary relocation of employees, etc.):

Operational Impacts

Business interruption impact estimations (loss of customer service capabilities, inability to serve internal customers/management/etc.):

Loss of confidence estimations (loss of confidence on behalf of customers/shareholders/regulatory agencies/employees, etc.):

Technological Dependence

Systems/business functions/applications reliance description (attempt to identify specific automated systems/processes/applications that support BU operations):

Systems interdependencies descriptions:

State of existing BCP measures:

Other BIA-related discussion issues

First question phrased: "What else should I have asked you that I did not, relative to this process?"

Other questions customized to environment of the organization, as needed.

- *Specialized questions.* Make sure that the questionnaire is customized to the organization. It is especially important to make sure that both the economic and operational impact categories (lost sales, interest paid on borrowed funds, business interruption, customer inconvenience, etc.) are stated in such a way that each interviewee will understand the intent of the measurement. Simple is better here.

Using an Automated Tool. If an automated tool is being used to collect and correlate the BIA interview information, then make sure that the questions in the database and questions of the questionnaire are synchronized to avoid duplication of effort or going back to interviewees with questions that might have been handled initially.

A word of warning here, however. This author has seen people pick up a BIA questionnaire off the Internet or from book or periodical (like this one) and use it without regard to the culture and practices of their own organization. Never, ever, use a noncustomized BIA questionnaire. The qualitative and quantitative questions must be structured to the environment and style of the organization. There is a real opportunity for failure should this point be dismissed.

BIA INTERVIEW LOGISTICS AND COORDINATION

This portion of the report will address the logistics and coordination while performing the BIA interviews themselves. Having scoped the BIA process, the next step is to determine who and how many people one is going to interview. To do this, here are some techniques that one might use.

Methods for Identifying Appropriate BIA Interviewees. One certainly is not going to interview everyone in the organization. One must select a sample of those management and staff personnel who will provide the best information in the shortest period. To do that, one must have a precise feel for the scope of the project (i.e., technological platform recovery, business unit recovery, communications recovery, crisis management plans, etc.) and with that understanding one can use:

- *Organizational process models.* Identification of organizational mega and major business processes is the first place to start. Enterprises that are organized along process lines lend themselves to development of recovery planning strategies that will eventually result in the most efficient recovery infrastructure. Use of or development of models that reflect organizational processes will go a long way toward assisting BIA team members in identifying those personnel crucial to determining time-critical process requirements. Exhibit 24-4 attempts to demonstrate that while the enterprise-wide recovery planning/E-continuity infrastructure includes consideration of crisis management, technology disaster recovery, business unit resumption, and E-commerce E-availability components, all aspects of the resulting infrastructure flow from proper identification of time-critical business processes.

- *Organizational chart reviews.* The use of formal, or sometimes even informal organization charts is the first place to start. This method includes examining the organizational chart of the enterprise to understand those functional positions that should be included. Review the organizational chart to determine which organizational structures will be directly involved in the overall effort as well as those that will be the recipients of the benefits of the finished recovery plan.

- *Overlaying systems technology.* Overlay systems technology (applications, networks, etc.) configuration information over the organization chart to understand the components of the organization that may be affected by an outage of the systems. Mapping applications, systems, and networks to the organizations business functions will help tremendously when attempting to identify the appropriate names and numbers of people to interview.

- *Executive management interviews.* This method includes conducting introductory interviews with selected senior management representatives in order to identify critical personnel to be included in the BIA interview process, as well as to receive high-level guidance and to raise overall executive-level management awareness and support.

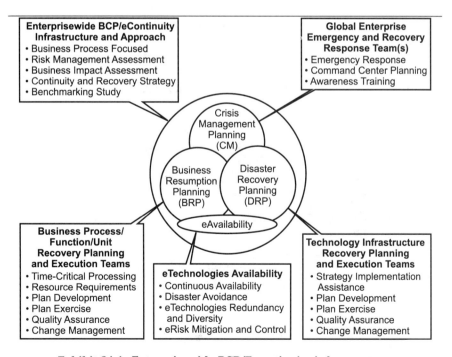

Exhibit 24-4. Enterprisewide BCP/E-continuity infrastructure.

Coordinate with the IT Group. If the scope of the BIA process is recovery of technological platforms or communications systems, then conducting interviews with a number of IT personnel could help shorten the data-gathering effort. While IT users will certainly need to be spoken to, IT personnel can often provide much valuable information, but should not be solely relied on as the primary source of business impact outage information (i.e., revenue loss, extra expense, etc.).

Send Questionnaire Out in Advance. It is a useful technique to distribute the questionnaire to the interviewees in advance. Whether in hardcopy or electronic media format, the person being interviewed should have a chance to review the questions, and be able to invite others into the interview or redirect the interview to others, and begin to develop the responses. One should emphasize to the people who receive the questionnaire in advance to not fill it out, but to simply review it and be prepared to address the questions.

Scheduling of Interviews. Ideally, the BIA interview should last between 45 minutes and 1 hour and 15 minutes. It sometimes can be an advantage to go longer than this; but if one sees many of the interviews lasting longer than the 1 hour, 15 minute window, then there may be a BIA scoping issue that should be addressed, necessitating the need to schedule and conduct a larger number of additional interviews.

Limit Number of Interviewees. It is important to limit the number of interviewees in the session to one, two, or three, but no more. Given the amount and quality of information one is hoping to elicit from this group, more than three people can deliver a tremendous amount of good information that can be missed when too many people are delivering the message at the same time.

Try to Schedule Two Interviewers. When setting up the BIA interview schedule, try to ensure that at least two interviewers can attend and take notes. This will help eliminate the possibility that good information may be missed. Every additional trip back to an interviewee for confirmation of details will add overhead to the process.

Validate Financial Impact Thresholds. An often-overlooked component of the process includes discussing with executive management the thresholds of pain that could be associated with a disaster. Asking the question as to whether a $5 million loss or a $50 million loss impact has enough significance to the long-term bottom line of the organization can lead to interesting results. A lack of understanding on the BIA team's part as to what financial impacts are acceptable, or conversely unacceptable, is crucial to framing BIA financial loss questions and the final findings and recommendations that the BIA report will reflect.

CONDUCTING THE BIA

When actually explaining the intent of the BIA to those being interviewed, the following concepts should be observed and perhaps discussed with the participants.

Intelligent Questions Asked of Knowledgeable People. Based loosely on the concept that if one asks enough reasonably intelligent people a consistent set of measurable questions, one will eventually reach a conclusion that is more or less correct. The BIA questions serve to elicit qualitative results from a number of knowledgeable people. The precise number of people interviewed obviously depends on the scope of the BCP activity and the size of the organization. However, when consistently directing a well-developed number of questions to an informed audience, the results will reflect a high degree of reliability. This is the point when conducting qualitatively oriented BIA: ask the right people good questions and one will come up with the right results.

Ask to Be Directed to the Correct People. As the interview unfolds, it may become evident that the interviewee is the wrong person to be answering the questions. One should ask who else within this area would be better suited to address these issues. They might be invited into the room at that point, or one may want to schedule a meeting with them at another time.

Assure Them that Their Contribution is Valuable. A very important way to build the esteem of the interviewee is to mention that their input to this process is considered valuable, as it will be used to formulate strategies necessary to recover the organization following a disruption or disaster. Explaining to them that one is there to help by getting their business unit's relevant information for input to planning a recovery strategy can sometimes change the tone of the interview in a positive manner.

Explain that the Plan is Not Strictly an IT Plan. Even if the purpose of the BIA is for IT recovery and, when interviewing business unit management for the process of preparing a technological platform recovery plan, it is sometimes useful to couch the discussion in terms of ... "a good IT recovery plan, while helping IT recover, is really a business unit plan"..."Why?" ... Because the IT plan will recover the business functionality of the interviewees business unit as well, and that is why one is there.

Focus on Who Will Really be Exercising the Plan. Another technique is to mention that the recovery plan that will eventually be developed can be used by the interviewees, but is not necessarily developed for them. Why? Because the people being interviewed probably already understand what to do following a disaster, without having to refer to extensive written recovery procedures. But the fact of the matter is that following the disruption, these people may not be available. It may well be the responsibility of the next generation of management to recover, and it will be the issues identified by this interviewee that will serve as the recovery roadmap.

Focus on Time-Critical Business Processes and Support Resources. As the BIA interview progresses, it is important to fall back from time to time and reinforce the concept of being interested in the identification of time-critical functions and processes.

Assume Worst-Case Disaster. When faced with the question as to when will the disruption occur, the answer should be: "It will occur at the worst possible time for your business unit." "If you close your books on 12/31, and you need the computer system the most on 12/30 and 12/31, the disaster will occur on 12/29." Only when measuring the impacts of a disruption at the worst time can the interviewer get an idea as to the full impact of the disaster, and so that the impact information can be meaningfully compared from one business unit to the next.

Assume No Recovery Capability Exists. To reach results that are comparable, it is essential to insist that the interviewee assume that no recovery capability will exist as they answer the impact questions. The reason for this is that when they attempt to quantify or qualify the impact potential, they may confuse a preexisting recovery plan or capability with no impact, and that is incorrect. No matter the existing recovery capability, the impact of a loss of services must be measured in raw terms so that as one compares the results of the interviews from business unit to business unit, the results are comparable (apples to apples, so to speak). Exhibit 24-5 provides an example. In this example, if one allows Interviewees #2 and #4 to assume that they can go somewhere else and use an alternate resource to support their process, the true impact of the potential disruption is

Exhibit 24-5. Comparing the results of the interviews.

Interviewee	Total Loss Impact if Disaster?	Preconceived Recovery Alternative?	Resulting Estimated Loss Potential	No Allowance for Pre-conceived Recovery Alternative
#1	$20K per day	No	$20,000	$20,000
#2	$20K per day	Yes	0	20,000
#3	$20K per day	No	20,000	20,000
#4	$20K per day	Yes	0	20,000
Totals	—	—	$40,000[a]	$80,000[b]

[a] Incorrect estimate, as one should not allow the interviewee to assume a recovery alternative exists (although one may very well exist).

[b] Correct estimate, based on raw loss potential regardless of preexisting recovery alternatives (which may or may not be valid should a disruption or disaster occur).

reduced by one-half ($40K versus $80K). By not allowing them to assume that an appropriate recovery alternative exists, one will recognize the true impact of a disruption, that of $80,000 per day. The $80,000-per day impact is what one is trying to understand, whether or not a recovery alternative already exists.

Order-of-Magnitude Numbers and Estimates. The financial impact information is needed in orders-of-magnitude estimates only. Do not get bogged down in minutia, as it is easy to get lost in the detail. The BIA process is not a quantitative risk assessment. It is not meant to be. It is qualitative in nature and, as such, orders-of-magnitude impacts are completely appropriate and even desirable. Why? Because preciseness in estimation of loss impact almost always results in arguments about the numbers. When this occurs, the true goal of the BIA is lost, because it turns the discussion into a numbers game, not a balanced discussion concerning financial and operational impact potentials. Because of the unlimited and unknown numbers of varieties of disasters that could possibly befall an organization, the true numbers can never ever be precisely known, at least until after the disaster. The financial impact numbers are merely estimates intended to illustrate degrees of impacts. So skip the numbers exercise and get to the point.

Stay Focused on the BCP Scope. Whether the BIA process is for development of technological platforms, end user, facilities recovery, voice network, etc., it is very important that one not allow scope creep in the minds of the interviewees. The discussion can become very unwieldy if one does not hold the focus of the loss impact discussions on the precise scope of the BCP project.

There Are No Wrong Answers. Because all the results will be compared with one another before the BIA report is forwarded, one can emphasize that the interviewee should not worry about wrong numbers. As the BIA process evolves, each business unit's financial and operational impacts will be compared with the others, and those impact estimates that are out of line with the rest will be challenged and adjusted accordingly.

Do Not Insist on Getting the Financial Information on the Spot. Sometimes, the compilation of financial loss impact information requires a little time to accomplish. The author often tells the interviewee that he will return within a few days to collect the information, so that additional care can be taken in preparation, making sure that he does actually return and picks up the information later.

The Value of Pushback. Do not underestimate the value of pushback when conducting BIA interviews. Business unit personnel will, most times, tend to view their activities as extremely time-critical, with little or no downtime acceptable. In reality, their operations will be arranged in some priority order with the other business processes of the organization for recovery priority. Realistic MTDs must be reached, and sometimes the interviewer must push back and challenge what may be considered unrealistic recovery requirements. Be realistic in challenging, and request that the interviewee be realistic in estimating their business unit's MTDs. Common ground will eventually be found that will be more meaningful to those who will read the *BIA Findings and Recommendations* — the senior management group.

INTERPRETING AND DOCUMENTING THE RESULTS

As the BIA interview information is gathered, there is a considerable tabular and written information that begins to quickly accumulate. This information must be correlated and analyzed. Many issues will arise here that may result in some follow-up interviews or information-gathering requirements. The focus at this point in the BIA process should be as follows.

Begin Documentation of the Results Immediately. Even as the initial BIA interviews are being scheduled and completed, it is a good idea to begin preparation of the *BIA Findings and Recommendations* and actually start entering preliminary information. The reason is twofold. The first is that if one waits to the end of the process to start formally documenting the results, it is going to be more difficult to recall details that should be included. Second, as the report begins to evolve, there will be issues that arise where one will want to perform additional investigation, while one still has time to ensure the investigation can be thoroughly performed.

Develop Individual Business Unit BIA Summary Sheets. Another practical technique is to document each and every BIA interview with its own *BIA Summary Sheet.* This information can eventually be used directly by importing it into the *BIA Findings and Recommendations,* and can also be distributed back out to each particular interviewee to authenticate the results of the interview. The *BIA Summary Sheet* contains a summation of all the verbal information that was documented during the interview. This information will be of great value later as the BIA process evolves.

Send Early Results Back to Interviewees for Confirmation. By returning the *BIA Summary Sheet* for each of the interviews back to the interviewee, one can continue to build consensus for the BCP project and begin to ensure that any future misunderstandings regarding the results can be avoided. Sometimes, one may want to get a formal sign-off, and other times the process is simply informal.

We Are Not Trying to Surprise Anyone. The purpose for diligently pursuing the formalization of the BIA interviews and returning to confirm the understandings from the interview process is to make very sure that there are no surprises later. This is especially important in large BCP projects where the BIA process takes a substantial amount of time. There is always a possibility that someone might forget what was said.

Definition of Time-Critical Business Functions/Processes. As has been emphasized, all issues should focus back to the true time-critical business processes of the organization. Allowing the attention to be shifted to specific recovery scenarios too early in the BIA phase will result in confusion and lack of attention toward what is really important.

Tabulation of Financial Impact Information. There can be a tremendous amount of tabular information generated through the BIA process. It should be boiled down to its essence and presented in such a way as to support the eventual conclusions of the BIA project team. It is easy to overdo it with numbers. Just ensure that the numbers do not overwhelm the reader and that they fairly represent the impacts.

Understanding the Implications of the Operational Impact Information Often times, the weight of evidence and the basis for the recovery alternative decision are based on operational rather than the financial information. Why? Usually, the financial impacts are more difficult to accurately quantify because the precise disaster situation and the recovery circumstances are difficult to visualize. One knows that there will be a customer service impact because of a fire, for example. But one would have a difficult time telling someone, with any degree of confidence, what the revenue loss impact would be for a fire that affects one particular location of the organization. Because the BIA process should provide a qualitative estimate (orders of magnitude), the basis for making the difficult decisions regarding acquisition of recovery resources are, in many cases, based on the operational impact estimates rather than hard financial impact information.

PREPARING THE MANAGEMENT PRESENTATION

Presentation of the results of the BIA to concerned management should result in no surprises for them. If one is careful to ensure that the BIA findings are communicated and adjusted as the process has unfolded, then the management review process should really become more of a formality in most cases. The final presentation meeting with the senior management group is not the time to surface new issues and make public startling results for the first time.

To achieve the best results in the management presentation, the following suggestions are offered.

Draft Report for Review Internally First. Begin drafting the report following the initial interviews. By doing this, one captures fresh information. This information will be used to build the tabular tables, graphs, and other

517

visual demonstrations of the results, and it will be used to record the interpretations of the results in the verbiage of the final *BIA Findings and Recommendations Report*. One method for accomplishing a well-constructed *BIA Findings and Recommendations* from the very beginning is to, at the completion of each interview, record the tabular information into the BIA database or manual filing system in use to record this information. Second, the verbal information should be transcribed into a *BIA Summary Sheet* for each interview. This *BIA Summary Sheet* should be completed for each interviewee and contain the highlights of the interview in summarized form. As the BIA process continues, the BIA tabular information and the transcribed verbal information can be combined into the draft *BIA Findings and Recommendations*. The table of contents for a BIA Report might look like the one depicted in Exhibit 24-6.

Exhibit 24-6. BIA report table of contents.

1. Executive Summary
2. Background
3. Current State Assessment
4. Threats and Vulnerabilities
5. Time-Critical Business Functions
6. Business Impacts (Operational)
7. Business Impacts (Financial)
8. Recovery Approach
9. Next Steps/Recommendations
10. Conclusion
11. Appendices (as needed)

Schedule Individual Senior Management Meetings as Necessary. Near the time for final BIA presentation, it is sometimes a good idea to conduct a series of one-on-one meetings with selected senior management representatives in order to brief them on the results and gather their feedback for inclusion in the final deliverables. In addition, this is a good time to begin building grassroots support for the final recommendations that will come out of the BIA process and at the same time provide an opportunity to practice making one's points and discussing the pros and cons of the recommendations.

Prepare Senior Management Presentation (Bullet Point). The author's experience reveals that senior management-level presentations, most often, are better prepared in a brief and focused manner. It will undoubtedly become necessary to present much of the background information used to make the decisions and recommendations, but the formal presentation should be in bullet-point format, crisp, and to the point. Of course, every organization has its own culture, so be sure to understand and comply with the traditional means of making presentations within that environment. Copies of the report, which have been thoroughly reviewed, corrected, bound, and bundled for delivery, can be distributed at the beginning or end of the presentation, depending on circumstances. In addition, copies of the bullet-point handouts can also be supplied so attendees can make notes and for reference at a later time. Remember, the BIA process should end with a formalized agreement as to management's intentions with regard to MTDs, so that business unit and support services managers can be guided accordingly. It is here that that formalized agreement should be discussed and the mechanism for acquiring and communicating it determined.

Distribute Report. Once the management team has had an opportunity to review the contents of the BIA Report and made appropriate decisions or given other input, the final report should be distributed within the organization to the appropriate numbers of interested individuals.

Past Y2K and Current eAvailability Considerations. The author's experience with development of Y2K-related recovery plans was that time was of the essence. Because of the constricted timeframe for development of Y2K plans, it was necessary to truncate the BIA process as much as possible to meet timelines. Modification of the process to shorten the critical path was necessary — resulting in several group meetings focusing on a very selective set of BIA criteria.

Limit Interviews and Focus on Upper-Level Management. To become a little creative in obtaining BIA information in this Y2K example, it was necessary to severely limit the number of interviews and to interview higher-level executives to receive overall guidance, and then move to recovery alternative selection and implementation rapidly.

Truncated BIAs for E-availability Application. Additionally, when considering gathering BIA information during an E-availability application, it is important to remember that delivery of E-commerce-related services through the Internet means that supply chain downtime tolerances — including E-commerce technologies and channels — are usually extremely short (minutes or even seconds), and that it may not be necessary to perform an exhaustive BIA to determine the MTD/RTO only. What is necessary for a BIA under these circumstances, however, is that it helps to determine which business processes truly rely on E-commerce technologies and channels so that they (business unit personnel) can be prepared to react in a timely manner should E-commerce technologies be impacted by a disruption or disaster.

NEXT STEPS

The BIA is truly completed when formalized senior management decisions have been made regarding: (1) MTDs/RTOs, (2) priorities for business process and support services recovery, and (3) recovery/E-availability resource funding sources.

The next step is the selection of the most effective recovery alternative. The work gets a little easier here. One knows what the recovery windows are, and one understands what the recovery priorities are. One must now investigate and select recovery alternative solutions that fit the recovery window and recovery priority expectations of the organization. Once the alternatives have been agreed upon, the actual recovery plans can be developed and tested, with organization personnel organized and trained to execute the recovery plans when needed.

SUMMARY

The process of business continuity planning has matured substantially since the 1980s. BCP is no longer viewed as just a technological question. A practical and cost-effective approach toward planning for disruptions or disasters begins with the business impact assessment. In addition, the rapidly evolving dependence on E-commerce-related supply chain technologies has caused a refocus of the traditional BCP professional upon not only recovery, but also continuous operations or E-availability imperatives.

The goal of the BIA is to assist the management group in identifying time-critical processes, and determining their degree of reliance on support services. Then, map these processes to supporting IT, voice and data networks, facilities, human resources, E-commerce initiatives, etc. Time-critical business processes are prioritized in terms of their MTDs/RTOs, so that executive management can make reasonable decisions as to the recovery costs and timeframes that it is willing to fund and support.

This chapter has focused on how organizations can facilitate the BIA process. See the BCP Route Map in Exhibit 24-7 for a pictorial representation of the BIA process. Understanding and applying the various methods and techniques for gathering the BIA information is the key to success.

Only when executive management formalizes its decisions regarding recovery timeframes and priorities can each business unit and support service manager formulate acceptable and efficient plans for recovery of operations in the event of disruption or disaster. It is for this reason that the BIA process is so important when developing efficient and cost-effective business continuity plans and E-availability strategies.

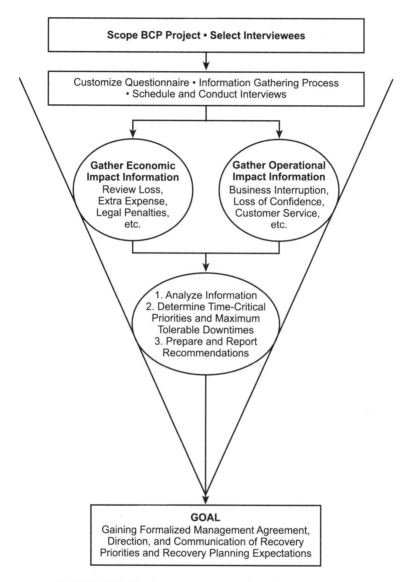

Exhibit 24-7. Business continuity planning route map.

Domain 9
Law, Investigation, and Ethics

THREE NEW CHAPTERS IN THIS DOMAIN ADDRESS DIFFERING ASPECTS OF DETECTING AND RESPONDING TO, COMPUTER CRIME. As computers are increasingly deployed and interconnected, the opportunity for criminal activity using a computer grows. The information security professional must be prepared to defend against attacks, as well as have the tools and processes necessary to detect intrusions before they do harm to the computing environment.

These chapters go into detail about how an organization can prepare itself by implementing an incident response team, tasked with coordinating appropriate responses to numerous types of security breaches. Another new chapter provides timely data on computer crime investigations, forensics, and essential assistance should an organization decide to pursue the criminal perpetrator.

Chapter 25

Computer Crime Investigations: Managing a Process Without Any Golden Rules

George Wade

SECURITY IS OFTEN VIEWED AS AN "AFTER-THE-FACT" SERVICE THAT SETS POLICY TO PROTECT PHYSICAL AND LOGICAL ASSETS OF THE COMPANY. In the event that a policy is violated, the security organization is charged with making a record of the violation and correcting the circumstances that permitted the violation to occur. Unfortunately, the computer security department (CSD) is usually viewed in the same light and both are considered cost-based services. To change that school of thought, security must become a value-added business partner, providing guidance before and after incidents occur.

THE SECURITY CONTINUUM

Each incident can be managed in five phases, with each phase acting as a continuation of the previous phase, and predecessor of the next. Exhibit 25-1 displays the continuum.

Flowing in a clockwise, circular fashion, the security continuum begins with the report of an incident or a request for assistance from the CSD business partner (also known as "the customer"). Strong documentation during this initial report phase is the first building block of an ever-evolving incident response plan. Strong documentation will also be used to determine whether or not an investigation is opened, as not every anomaly requires a full investigation. The report phase flows into the investigative

0-8493-0800-3/00/$0.00+$.50

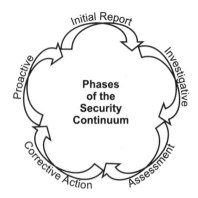

Exhibit 25-1. The security continuum.

phase where intelligence gathering and monitoring begins and documentation continues. At this point, the CSD investigator (CSDI) should understand and be able to define what has occurred so that a determination can be made to begin a full investigation. The investigative phase will flow into the assessment phase, although there may not be a strong demarcation point. The investigative phase and the assessment phase may run concurrently, depending on the incident. Time spent during the assessment phase is dedicated to determining the current state of the business, identifying additional problem areas, and continued documentation. The assessment phase documentation will provide input into the corrective action phase, with this phase beginning as the investigative phase is completed. Intelligence gained during the investigative and assessment phases of the continuum is used to build the corrective action plan. Execution of the correction action plan can be coordinated with the final steps of the investigative phase, in that system holes are plugged as the suspect is being arrested by law enforcement or interviewed by a CSDI. Following the completion of the four previous phases, the proactive phase can begin. This phase should be used to educate management and the user community about incident particulars. Education in the form of security awareness presentations will lead to a greater consciousness of the CSD being a value-added business partner that will generate new reports and lead the CSD back into the report phase.

THE INITIAL REPORT PHASE

Before any investigation can begin, the CSD needs to receive a report of an anomaly. One of the best ways to advertise the services of the CSD is through a comprehensive awareness program that includes the methods to report incidents. The CSD should have the ability to receive reports over the phone, via e-mail, and via the World Wide Web (WWW), and each of these methods should permit anonymous reporting. Additionally, the CSD should make the initial report process as painless as possible for the reporter. Because anomalies in computers and networks do not just occur from 9 to 5, convenient 24-hour coverage should be provided. This may be provided by a well-trained guard staff, an internal helpdesk, an external answering service that receives calls after a designated time, or a simple recording that provides a 24-hour reach number such as a pager. It is important that the CSD personnel designated to receive initial reports be well-versed in the structure of the business, have an understanding of common computer terminology, and have excellent customer service skills. They must also understand that all reports must remain confidential because confidentiality is an important aspect of all investigative issues. Without confidentiality, investigative efforts will be hampered, and employees may be wrongfully accused of policy violation or illicit acts.

The CSD Receives an incident Report

Whether the reports come into the CSD help desk or directly to a CSDI, the same questions need to be asked when receiving the initial report. By asking the "who, what, where, when, why, and how" questions, the CSD trained personnel receiving the initial report should be able to generate a somewhat thorough overview of the anomaly and record this information in a concise, easy-to-read format. An incident is classified as an anomaly at this point because, without initial review, the action or incident may be nothing more than the reporter's misunderstanding of standard business events or practices. The best method to compile and record this information is by using an initial report form (Exhibit 25-2).

Using a form will ensure that each incident is initially handled in the same manner and the same information is recorded. As the types of incidents change, this form can be updated to ensure that the most relevant questions are being asked. It will provide a comprehensive baseline for the CSDI when investigative work begins and can be included as part of the incident case file. Should it be determined during the investigative phase that the anomaly will not be pursued, the form will act as a record of the incident.

An important point to remember is that no question is too trivial to ask. What may seem apparent to CSD personnel may or may not be apparent to the reporter, and vice versa. The person receiving the initial report for the CSD must also be trained to recognize what is and what is not an urgent issue. An urgent issue would be a system administrator calling to report watching an unauthorized user peruse and copy files, versus a customer calling to report a PC, normally turned off at night, was found on in the morning. Asking key questions and obtaining relevant and pertinent information will accomplish this task.

Exhibit 25-2. The Initial Report form.

REPORTER INFORMATION & INITIAL REPORT

FIRST☐_____ MIDDLE☐_____ LASTR/SR☐ _____ ID NUMBER☐ _____

FULL ADDRESS/PHONE☐_____

INCIDENT DATE☐ _____ INCIDENT TIME☐ _____

INCIDENT SUMMARY☐ _____

_____

_____

DISCOVERY DATE:☐ _____ DISCOVERY TIME:☐ _____

STEPS TAKEN: _____

_____

_____

_____

_____

SYSTEM NAME:☐ _____ IP/ADDRESS☐ _____

OPERATING SYSTEM:☐ _____ VERSION/PATCH No.☐ _____

SYSTEM LOCATION☐ _____ SA NAME & PHONE☐ _____

SUPPORTING DATA:☐ _____

CURRENT STATE OF SYSTEM:☐ _____

PURPOSE OF MACHINE:☐ _____

APPLICATION OWNER:☐ _____ PHONE NUMBER:☐ _____

APPLICATION USER:☐ _____ PHONE NUMBER:☐ _____

HOW DID INCIDENT OCCUR:☐ _____

WHY DID INCIDENT OCCUR:☐ _____

ADDITIONAL INFORMATION:☐ _____

ASSIGNED TO:☐ _____ ASSIGNMENT NUMBER:☐ _____

<Company Name >- Proprietary☐

The "who" questions should cover the reporter, witnesses, and victims. The victims will be the application owner, user group, and system administrators. Contact information should be obtained for each. The reporter should also be queried as to who has been notified of the incident. This will help the CSDI determine the number of people aware of the issue.

"What" is comprised of two parts: the "anomaly what" and the "environment what." The "anomaly what" should include a description of the conditions that define the anomaly and the reporter's observations. The "environment what" is comprised of questions that identify the operating hardware and software in the impacted environment. Is the system running a UNIX variant such Linux or Solaris, a DOS variant such as Windows 95/98, or Windows NT? The operating system version number should be obtained, as well as the latest release or software patch applied. The reporter should also be queried about the application's value to business. While all reporters will most likely consider their systems critical, it is important to determine if this is a mission-critical system that will impact revenue stream or shareholder value if the anomaly is confirmed to be a security breech.

The "where" questions cover the location of the incident, the location of the system impacted (these may not be in the same physical location), and the reporter's location. It is very common in logical security incidents that the reporter may be an application user in one location and the system may reside in another location.

"When" should cover the time of discovery and when the reporter suspects the anomaly occurred. This could be the time the system was compromised, a Web page was changed, or data was deleted. If the reporter is utilizing system logs as the basis of the report, the CSD personnel should determine the time zone being used by the system.

"Why" is the reporter's subjective view of the events. By asking why the reporter believes the anomaly occurred, the reporter may provide insight as to ongoing workplace problems, such as layoffs or a disgruntled employee with access to the system. Insight such as this might provide the CDSI with initial investigative direction.

Finally, "how" is the reporter's explanation for how the anomaly occurred. Be sure to ask how the reporter arrived at this conclusion, as this line of questioning will draw out steps the reporter took to parse data. Should the anomaly be confirmed as an incident requiring investigation, these actions would require further understanding and documentation.

When considering logical security incidents, be sure to cover the physical security aspect during the initial report as well. Questions about the physical access to the compromised machine and disaster recovery media (operating system and application data backups) should be covered during the initial report.

The Investigative Phase

Before any monitoring or investigation can take place, the company must set a policy regarding use of business resources. This policy should be broad enough to cover all uses of the resources, yet specific enough so as not to be ambiguous. A policy covering the use of non-company-owned assets (laptop and desktop computers) should also be considered. This will become important during the evidence-gathering portion of the investigative phase. Once the policies are established, thorough disclosure of the corporate policies must take place. Each employee, contractor, and business partner must be required to read the policies and initial a document indicating that the policy was reviewed, and the document should be kept in the employee's personnel folder. A periodic re-review of the policy should also be required.

In addition to the policy on use of resources, a warning banner should be included in the logon process and precede access to all systems. The banner should advise the user that activity must adhere to the policy, that activity can be monitored, and any activity deemed illegal can be turned over to law enforcement authorities. The following is an example of a warning message:

> This system is restricted solely to <company name> authorized users for legitimate business purposes only. The actual or attempted unauthorized access, use, or modification of this system is strictly prohibited by <company name>. Unauthorized users are subject to company disciplinary proceedings and/or criminal and civil penalties under state, federal, or other applicable domestic and foreign laws. The use of this system may be monitored and recorded for administrative and security reasons. Anyone accessing this system expressly consents to such monitoring and is advised that if monitoring reveals possible evidence of criminal activity, <company name> might provide the evidence of such activity to law enforcement officials. All users must comply with <company name> Company Instructions regarding the protection of <company name> information and assets.

This warning banner should precede entry into all corporate systems and networks, including stand-alone (non-networked) computers and FTP sites. When confronted with the banner, the users should be given the option to exit the logon process if they do not agree with the policy.

The investigations undertaken by the CSD can be classified into two broad categories: reactive and proactive. Some of the more common reactive reports include unauthorized or suspected unauthorized access to company resources, non-business use of resources, the release of proprietary material, threatening or harassing activity, and activity that creates a hostile work environment. From the reactive cases being generated, the CSD should identify opportunities for prevention of the reactive cases. For example, if the CSD is receiving a large amount of unauthorized access cases, what are the similarities in each? Can a companywide solution be devised and an awareness campaign started to eliminate the vulnerability? Proactive activities can include intelligence-gathering activities such as the monitoring of company access to WWW and newsgroup sites known to hacking tools, offensive, or illegal material. Monitoring of financial message boards may reveal premature proprietary information release or include anti-company postings that are a precursor to workplace violence. Review and monitoring of traffic to free, WWW-based e-mail sites may identify proprietary information being transferred to a competitor. Periodic review of postings to Internet newsgroups could reveal stolen equipment being resold.

Beyond the Initial Report

From the Incident Report Form, the CSDI can begin developing a plan of action. Each investigation will contain two initial steps; anomaly validation and investigation initiation. The first step determines if the anomaly is actually an incident worth investigating. Not every anomaly is the result of a criminal or dishonest act, and not every anomaly warrants a full-scale investigation. An anomaly that presents itself to be unauthorized access to a system with data deletion, may have been an honest mistake caused by the wrong backup tape being loaded. In this instance, a short report of the incident should be recorded. If several similar reports are received in the same area of the company, steps to initiate better data control should be taken. If a Windows 9x system, in an open area, that does not contain sensitive data or support network access is entered, the CSDI must decide if the action justifies full investigation. In this example, it may be prudent to record the incident without further investigative effort and dedicate resources to more mission-critical tasks. Through proactive review of anomaly report records, a decision might be made to conduct an investigation into recurring incidents.

After it is determined that the anomaly requires further investigation, logs supporting the anomaly or logs that may have been altered at the time of the anomaly need to be collected and analyzed. The CSDI must be careful not to view the anomaly with tunnel vision, thereby overlooking important pieces of information. Additionally, more thorough interviews of the reporter and witnesses need to be conducted. These secondary fact-finding interviews will help the CSDI further document what has occurred and what steps the victim or reporter may have taken during the identification of the anomaly. The CSDI should request and obtain from the reporter, and other witnesses, detailed statements of what steps were taken to identify the anomaly. For example, a system administrator (SA) of a UNIX-based system may have examined system logs from the victim system while logged into the victim system using the root ID. In this example, the CSDI should obtain a detailed written statement from the SA, that describes the steps taken and why they were taken. This statement should clearly state why data might have been added or deleted. In addition to the statement, the CSDI should obtain a copy of the shell history file for the ID used, print a copy of the file, and have the SA annotate the listing. The SA's notes should clearly identify which commands were entered during the review and when the commands, to the best of the SA's recollection, were entered. The written statement should be signed by the SA, and placed, along with the annotated version of the shell history, in an investigative case file.

The written statement and data capture (this will be dealt with in more detail later) should be received by the CSDI as soon as possible after the initial report. It is important that witnesses (in this example, the SA) provide written statements while the steps taken are still fresh in their minds. Should it be determined that the anomaly is actually unauthorized activity, the written statements will help to close potential loopholes in any civil or criminal action that may come at the conclusion of the activity.

Intelligence Gathering

It behooves the CSDI to understand as much as possible about the suspect. Understanding the equipment being used, the physical location from which the suspect is initiating the attacks, the time at which the attacks occur, and human factors such as the suspect's persona, all help the CSDI fully understand the tasks at hand.

Initially, the CSDI will want to gather information about the machine being used. By running commands such as **nbtstat**, **ping**, **trace route**, etc., the CSDI can obtain the IP address being used, userID and machine name being used, and the length of the lease if DHCP is being used.

Following the identification of the machine being used, the CSDI will want to identify where the machine is physically located. If the investigation involves an insider threat, the CSDI could perform physical surveillance on the suspect's office or perform after-business-hours visits to the suspect's office. Before visiting the office, the CSDI should determine the normal business hours at the location, and the ability to gain after-business-hours access. In addition to the physical facility information, the CSDI should determine the type of equipment the suspect utilizes. Once again, if the suspect utilizes a laptop computer to execute the attacks, a late-night visit to the suspect's office may prove fruitless.

If possible, try to gain intelligence about the suspect's work habits in addition to the intelligence gained from the anomalies and initial queries. The suspect may spend the day attacking systems to avoid detection from after-business hours attacks and spend evenings catching up on this work so that management is not aware of his daily activity. In a situation such as this, the CSDI may run into the suspect during a late-night visit. By gathering intelligence, the CSDI can better plan on what equipment will be needed when visiting the suspect's workspace, what actions may need to be taken, and how long the action may take.

NO LONGER AN ANOMALY

From the intelligence gathered during the fact-finding interviews and log review, the CSDI should be able to identify the anomaly as an actual incident of unauthorized activity. One of the most important decisions to make while building the action plans is to decide if the activity will be stopped immediately or monitored while additional evidence is gathered. There are several factors to consider before making this decision — most importantly, the impact to the business should the activity continue. The CSDI must be sure that value of identifying the perpetrator outweighs the potential impact to the business. If the CSDI is assured of being able to accurately monitor the activities of the perpetrator, and there is no potential damage such as additional proprietary information being lost or data deleted, the CSDI should proceed with monitoring and build additional evidence. If the perpetrator cannot be controlled or accurately monitored, the activity should be stopped by shutting down the perpetrator's access. In either case, the CSDI must be sure to obtain CSD management approval of the action plan. The selling point to management for continued monitoring is that it buys the CSDI more time to determine what damage may have been done, identify more areas compromised, record new exploits as they occur, and most importantly, identify areas of entry not yet identified.

Active Monitoring

If the activity will be monitored, the first step in the monitoring process would be to set up a recording device at the point of entry. If the activity is originating from an office within the CSDI's company, monitoring may consist of a keystroke monitor on the computer being used or a sniffer on the network connection. The traffic captured by the sniffer should be limited to the traffic to and from the machine under electronic surveillance. In addition, video surveillance should be considered — if the environment and law permits. Video surveillance will help confirm the identity of the person sitting at the keyboard. If video surveillance is used, the time on the video recorder should be synchronized to match the time of the system being attacked. Synchronizing the time on the video recorder to that of the system being attacked will confirm that the keystrokes of the person at the keyboard are those reaching the system being attacked. While this may seem obvious, the attacker could actually be using the machine being monitored as a stepping stone in a series of machines. To do this, the attacker could be in another office and using something as simple as Telnet to access the system in the office being monitored to get to the system being attacked. It is the task of the CSDI to prove that the system attack is originating from the monitored office.

When using video surveillance, the CSDI needs to be aware that the law only permits video — not audio — and that only certain areas can be monitored. Areas that provide a reasonable expectation of privacy, such as a bathroom, cannot be surveyed. Luckily, there are not that many instances of computing environments being set up in bathrooms. Employee offices do not meet that exception and may be surveyed, although the CSDI should only use video surveillance as a means of building evidence during an investigation.

The next step in the monitoring process is to confirm a baseline for the system being attacked. The goal is to identify how the system looked before any changes occur. If the company's disaster recovery plan requires a full system backup once a week, the CSDI, working with the systems administrator (SA), should determine which full backup is most likely not to contain tainted data. This full backup can be used as the baseline. Because the CSDI cannot be expected to understand each system utilized within the company, the CSDI must rely on the SA for assistance. The SA is likely to be the person who knows the system's normal processes and can identify differences between the last-known good backup and the current system. Ideally, the system backup will be loaded on a similar machine so that subtle differences can be noted. However, this is not usually the case. In most instances, the baseline is used for comparison after monitoring has been completed and the attacker repelled.

While monitoring activity, the SA and CSDI should take incremental backups, at a minimum once a day. The incremental backups are then used to confirm changes to the system being attacked on a daily basis.

As the monitoring progresses, the CSDI and the SA should review the captured activity to identify the attacker's targets and methods. As the activity is monitored, the CSDI should begin building spreadsheets and charts to identify the accounts attacked and the methods used to compromise the accounts. The CSDI should also note any accounts of interest that the attacker was unable to compromise. The CSDI must remember that the big picture includes not only what was compromised, but also what was targeted and not compromised.

THE PROJECT PLAN

In building a picture of the attack, the CSDI should also begin to identify when to begin the assessment, the corrective action phase, when to end monitoring, and when to bring in law enforcement or interview the employee involved. This should be part of the dynamic project plan maintained by the CSDI, and shared with CSD management. As the plan evolves, it is important to get the project plan approved and reapproved as changes are made. While it is always best to keep those who are knowledgeable or involved in the investigation to a minimum, the CSDI may not be able to make informed decisions about the impact of the unauthorized activity to the victim business unit (BU). With this in mind, the CSDI needs to inform management of the BU impacted by the attack and the company legal team, and keep both apprised of project plan changes. The project plan should include a hierarchy of control for the project, with CSD management at the top of the hierarchy providing support to the CSDI. The CSDI, who controls the investigation will offer options and solutions to the victim BU, and the victim BU will accept or reject the project plan based on its level of comfort.

LEGAL CONSIDERATIONS

As the investigation progresses, the CSDI should have a good understanding of which laws and company policies may have been violated. Most states now have laws to combat computer crime, but to list them here would take more room than available for this chapter. However, there are several federal laws defined in the United States Code (USC) with which the CSDI should be familiar. Those laws include:

- *18 USC Sec. 1029.* Fraud and related activities in connection with access devices. This covers the production, use, or trafficking in, unauthorized access devices. Examples would include passwords gleaned from a targeted computer system. This also provides penalties for violations.
- *18 USC Sec. 1030. The Computer Fraud and Abuse act of 1986.* Fraud and related activity in connection with computers. This covers trespass, computer intrusion, unauthorized access, or exceeding authorized access. It includes and prescribes penalties for violations.
- *The Economic Espionage Act of 1996.* Provides the Department of Justice with sweeping authority to prosecute trade secret theft whether it is in the United States, via the Internet, or outside the United States. This act includes:
  - *18 USC Sec. 1831.* Covers offenses committed while intending or knowing that the offense would benefit a foreign government, foreign instrumentality, or foreign agent.
  - *18 USC Sec. 1832.* Covers copyright and software piracy, specifically those who convert a trade secret to their own benefit or the benefit of others intending or knowing that the offense will injure any owner of the trade secret.
- *The Electronic Communications Privacy Act of 1986.* This act covers the interception or access of wire, oral, and electronic communications. Also included is the unauthorized access of, or intentionally exceeded authorized access, to stored communications. This act includes:
  - *18 USC Sec. 2511.* Interception and disclosure of wire, oral, or electronic communications.
  - *18 USC Sec. 2701.* Unlawful access to stored communications.
- *The No Electronic Theft (NET) Act.* The NET Act amends criminal copyright and trademark provisions in 17 USC and 18 USC. Prior to this act,

the government had to prove financial benefit from the activity to prosecute under copyright and trademark laws. This act amended the copyright law so that an individual risks criminal prosecution when there is no direct financial benefit from the reproduction of copyright material. This act is in direct response to *United States v. La Macchia,* 871 F. Supp 535 (D. Mass. 1994), in which an MIT student loaded copyrighted materials onto the Internet and invited others to download this material, free of charge. In *La Macchia,* because the student received no direct financial benefit from his activity, the court held that the criminal provisions of the copyright law did not apply to his infringement.

In addition, those dealing with government computer systems should be familiar with:

- *Public Law 100-235.* The Computer Security Act of 1987. This bill provides for a computer standards program, setting standards for government-wide computer security. It also provides for training of persons involved in the management, operation, and use of federal computer systems, in security matters.

EVIDENCE COLLECTION

Evidence collection must be a very methodical process that is well-documented. Because the CSDI does not know at this point if the incident will result in civil or criminal prosecution, evidence must be collected as if the incident will result in prosecution.

Evidence collection should begin where the anomaly was first noted. If possible, data on the system screen should be captured and a hardcopy and electronic version should be recorded. The hardcopy will provide the starting point in the "series of events" log, a log of activities and events that the CSDI can later use when describing the incident to someone such as a prosecutor, or management making a disciplinary decision. Because CSDIs will be immersed in the investigation from the beginning, they will have a clear picture of the anomaly, the steps taken to verify the anomaly were actually an unauthorized act, the crime committed or policy violated, the actions taken by the suspect, and the damage done. Articulating this event to someone, particularly someone not well-versed in the company's business and who has never used a computer for more than word processing, may be a challenge bigger than the investigation. The series of events log, combined with screen-prints, system flows, and charts explaining the accounts and systems compromised and how compromised, will be valuable tools during the education process.

In addition to screenprints, if the system in which the unauthorized access was noted is one of the systems targeted by the suspect or used by the suspect, photographs should be taken. The CSDI should diagram and photograph the room where the equipment was stored to accurately depict the placement of the equipment within the room. Once the room has been photographed, the equipment involved and all of its components should be photographed. The first step is to take close-up photographs of the equipment as it is placed within the room. If possible, photographs of the screen showing the data on the screen should be taken. Be sure to include all peripheral equipment, remembering it may not be physically adjacent to the CPU or monitor. Peripheral equipment may include a printer, scanner, microphone, storage units, and an uninterrupted power supply component. Bear in mind that with the advent of wireless components, not all components may be physically connected to the CPU. The next step is to photograph the wires connected to the CPU. Photographs should include a close-up to allow for clear identification of the ports being used on the machine. The power supply should also be included.

Once the equipment has been photographed, attention should turn to the surrounding area. Assuming one have permission to search the office, one should begin looking for evidence of the activity. It is important to note the location of diskettes and other storage media in relation to the CPU. Careful review of the desktop may reveal a list of compromised IDs or systems attacked, file lists from systems compromised, printouts of data from files compromised, and notes of the activity. Each of these items should be photographed as they are located.

CONFISCATING AND LOGGING EVIDENCE

After the items have been located, evidence collection should begin. It is important for the CSDI to be familiar with the types of equipment owned and leased by the company. If the CSDI is presented with a machine that is not standard issue, the CSDI must consider the possibility that the machine is privately owned. Without a policy covering privately owned equipment and signed by the employee, the CSDI can not search or confiscate the machine without permission from the owner. Once the CSDI has confirmed company ownership, evidence collection may begin. For each piece of evidence collected, the CSDI needs to identify where and when it was obtained and from whom it was obtained. The best method to accomplish this is a form used to track evidence (Exhibit 25-3).

As the evidence is collected, the CSDI will fill out the form and identify each item using serial numbers and model numbers, if applicable, and list unique features such as scratch marks on a CPU case. Each item should be marked, if possible, with the CSDI's initials, the date the item was collected, and the case number. If it is not possible to mark each item, then each item should be placed in a container and the container sealed with evidence tape. The evidence tape used should not allow for easy removal without breakage.

Exhibit 25-3. The evidence form.

Evidence/Property Custody Document			
District/Office:☐		Serial Number:☐	
Location:☐		Investigator Assigned To:☐	
Name and Title of Person from whom received☐ Owner☐ Other☐		Investigator's Address (include zip code)☐	
Address from where obtained (including zip code)☐		Reason Obtained☐	Date:☐

Item☐ No.☐	Quantity☐	Description of Article(s)☐ (Include model, serial number, condition and unusual marks or scratches)

CHAIN OF CUSTODY☐

Item☐ No.☐	Date☐	Released By☐	Received By☐	Purpose of Change☐ of Custody☐
		SIGNATURE☐ NAME,GRADE OR TITLE☐	SIGNATURE☐ NAME,GRADE OR TITLE☐	
		SIGNATURE☐ NAME,GRADE OR TITLE☐	SIGNATURE☐ NAME,GRADE OR TITLE☐	
		SIGNATURE☐ NAME,GRADE OR TITLE☐	SIGNATURE☐ NAME,GRADE OR TITLE☐	
		SIGNATURE☐ NAME,GRADE OR TITLE☐	SIGNATURE☐ NAME,GRADE OR TITLE☐	

<Company> - Proprietary☐

The CSDI should then sign and date the evidence tape. The CSDI should always mark evidence in the same manner because the CSDI may be asked to testify that he is the person identified by the marking. By marking items in the same fashion, the CSDI can easily identify where the markings were placed.

EVIDENCE STORAGE

After the evidence has been collected, it must be transported to and stored in a secure location. During transport, special care must be taken to ensure that custody can be demonstrated from the point of departure until the evidence arrives at, and is logged into, the storage facility. While in custody of the CSD, the evidence must be protected from damage caused by heat, cold, water, fire, magnetic fields, and excessive vibration. Hard drives should be stored in static-free bags and packed in static-free packaging within the storage container. The CSD must take every precaution to ensure the evidence is protected for successful prosecution and eventual return to the owner. Should the confiscated items be damaged during transport, storage, or examination, the owner of the material may hold the CSD liable for the damage.

EVIDENCE CUSTODIAN

When the evidence arrives at the storage location, it is preferable that an evidence custodian logs it into the facility. It will be the job of the evidence custodian to ensure safe storage for the material as described above. Using an evidence custodian, as opposed to each CSDI storing evidence from their cases, ensures that the evidence, property owned by others until the case is adjudicated, is managed with a set of checks and balances. The evidence custodian will be responsible for confirming receipt of evidence, release of evidence, and periodic inventory of items in evidence. After the case has been adjudicated, the evidence will need to be removed from evidence storage and returned to the owner. The evidence form should then be stored with the case file.

BUSINESS CONTINUITY DURING EVIDENCE COLLECTION

The CSDI must remember that his responsibility is to the company and shareholders. The CSDI must find the balance between performing an investigation and protecting the business, thereby maintaining shareholder value. If the unauthorized activity required the computer be shut down during the length of an investigation, then an attacker need not gain entry and destroy files if the purpose of the attack is to disrupt business. Simply causing a machine to reboot or drop a connection would, in itself, be enough to disrupt the business.

When an investigation requires the CDSI to obtain evidence from a computer's hard drive or from drives that support a network, the CSDI cannot stop the business for an extended period of time by placing the hard drive into evidence. By performing a forensic backup of the hard drives in question, the CSDI can ensure evidence preservation and allow the business to get up and running in a short amount of time. A forensic image of a hard drive preserves not only the allocated file space, but also the deleted files, swap space, and slack space. The forensic image is the optimal answer to gathering evidence. Once a forensic image has been obtained, a new disk can be placed in the target computer and data loaded from a backup. If data loss is a concern, then the forensic image can be restored to the new disk, allowing the business to proceed as the investigation continues.

While it is not recommended, the CSDI may not be able to stop the business long enough for a forensic image to be taken. In situations involving a system that cannot be brought down (for example, a production control systems or systems that accept customer orders), the CSDI may be presented with the task of gathering evidence while the system is continuing to process data. In situations such as these, the CSDI may be able to gather some evidence by attaching removable storage media to the machine and copying pertinent files to the removable media. In these situations, the CSDI must remember that the data gathered is not the best evidence to prosecute the case. However, just because the evidence may not be optimal for prosecution, it should not be overlooked. Evidence such as this may be used to support the CSDI's theories and may provide the CSDI with insight to other unauthorized activities not identified thus far.

Gathering Evidence Through Forensic Imaging

This section provides a cursory overview of forensic imaging. Forensic imaging of a hard drive is a subject deserving a chapter in itself, so this section only attempts to provide the CSDI with an overview of what steps are taken and what equipment is needed to produce a forensic image.

Once the computer has been accurately photographed, the system can be removed to an area where the forensic image will be made or the CPU box opened so that a forensic image can be taken on site. One problem with performing an on-site image is that without an evidence review machine on hand, in which to load and review the forensic image, the CSDI must trust that the image was successful. Assuming removal of the machine would not compromise the investigation, it is best to remove the machine to an examination area. Once in the examination area, a forensic image can be obtained using a DOS boot diskette, forensic imaging software, and tape backup unit. The suspect machine will be booted using the DOS diskette to ensure that no advanced operating system software tools are loaded. The forensic imaging software (there are many packages on the consumer market) is loaded and run from DOS. Output is then directed to the tape backup unit via the system's SCSI port.

In systems without a SCSI port, the hard drive (called the original drive or suspect drive) will have to be removed and installed as a slave drive in another computer. This exercise should not be taken lightly, as there is much opportunity to damage the suspect's drive and lose or overwrite data. In situations such as this, the equipment used to obtain an image may vary; but in all cases, the target for the image must be as large or larger than the original disk. Targets for the image may be either magnetic tape or a second hard drive. The first step in creating the image is to physically access the original drive and remove it from the system housing. Next, the original drive must be connected to a secondary machine, preferably as a slave drive. Once this original drive has been connected to the secondary machine, the data can be copied from the slave drive to the backup media.

As electronics get smaller, laptop computers present challenges that are unique in, and of, themselves. When performing a forensic image of a laptop computer hard drive that does not provide a SCSI port or PCMCIA adapter access, special interface cables are needed to ensure power to the original drive and data connectivity from the original to the imaging media. If a PCM-CIA socket is available, special adapter cards can be obtained to allow the data transfer through the socket to a SCSI device. In this case, drivers for the PCMCIA card are loaded, in addition to the DOS and imaging software.

Once the forensic image has been obtained, the acquired data needs to be reviewed. There are several commercially available packages on the consumer market that support forensic data review. There are also share-ware tools available that claim to perform forensic image review without data alteration. It is best to use a package purchased from a company that has a history of providing expert testimony in court about the integrity of its product. The CSD does not want an investigation challenged in court due to evidence gathering and review methods. Unless a vendor is willing to provide expert testimony as to the technical capabilities of its program, the CSD would be well-advised to steer away from that vendor.

During a review of the acquired hard drive, efforts should be made to recover deleted files, examine slack space, swap space, and temporary files. It is not uncommon for evidence of the unauthorized activity to be found in these areas. Additionally, files with innocuous names should be verified as being unaltered by, or in support of, the unauthorized activity. There are some commercially available products on the market that provide hash values for the more commonly used programs. This will allow the CSDI to automate a search for altered files by identifying those that do not match the hash.

Law Enforcement Now or Later?

Throughout the investigation, the CSDI must continually weigh the options and advantages of involving law enforcement in the investigation. There are several advantages and disadvantages to bringing in law enforce-ment and there is no golden rule as to when law enforcement, should be contacted. While cases involving outsider threats are a little more appar-ent, insider threat cases are not as obvious.

When law enforcement is brought into an investigation, the dynamics of that investigation change. While the CSDI can control information dissem-ination prior to law enforcement involvement, once law enforcement becomes involved, the CSDI no longer has control due to the Freedom of Information Act. Unless the law enforcement agency can prove the need to seal case information, for reasons such as imminent loss of life due to the information release, they do not have the ability to seal the case once arrests have been made. If law enforcement is being brought into an investigation, the CSDI must notify the company's public relations team as soon as possible. Additionally, any steps taken by the CSDI after law enforcement enters the case could be a violation of the Fourth Amendment to the Constitution of the United States. For example, during an insider threat case, the CSDI would normally search the suspect's office for evidence as part of the normal course of the investigation. Because the CSDI is not a sworn law enforcement officer and an employee of the company, the CSDI is permitted by law to conduct the search and not subject to the rules and laws governing search and seizure. However, this does not hold true when:

- the CSDI performs a search in which law enforcement would have needed a search warrant to conduct
- the CSDI performs that search to assist law enforcement
- law enforcement is aware of the CSDI's actions and does not object to them

When the above three are true, the CSDI is acting as an agent of law enforcement and is in violation of the Fourth Amendment.

As stated above, outsider threat cases will not amount to much unless outside assistance through the courts or law enforcement is sought. The most direct way to receive assistance is to contact law enforcement in the event the anomaly can be proven to be intentional and provide them with evidence of the activity. Law enforcement has the power to subpoena business records from Internet service providers (ISPs), telephone companies, etc. in support of their investigation. A less-used tactic is for the CSDI's company to begin a third-party, "John Doe" lawsuit to assist the company in identifying the suspect. These civil remedies will allow the CSDI to gather information not normally available. For example, the anomaly detected was confirmed as unauthorized access from a local ISP known to the CSDI as the ISP utilized by an employee under suspicion. By filing the lawsuit, the company and the CSDI will be able to obtain subscriber information not normally available. The CSDI needs to be aware that some ISPs will inform the user when a subpoena from a lawsuit is received.

Regardless of when the CSDI chooses to bring law enforcement into the investigation, it should not be the first meeting between the CSDI and law enforcement agent. It is important for the CSDI to establish ties with local, state, and various branches of federal law enforcement (FBI, Secret Service, Customs, etc.) before incidents occur. One of the best methods to establish the relationship early is by participating in training offered by professional service organizations such as the American Society of Industrial Security (www.asisonline.org) and the High Technology Crime Investigation Association (www.htcia.org). Both international organizations not only provide training, but also provide important networking opportunities before incidents occur.

ASSESSMENT PHASE

The assessment is the phase where the CSDI knows, or has an idea of what has been done, but needs to determine what other vulnerabilities exist. The assessment phase helps reduce investigative tunnel vision by providing the CSDI with insight as to additional vulnerabilities or changes that may have been made. The assessment phase can run in conjunction with an active investigation and should be run as soon as possible after the unauthorized activity is defined. An exception to this would be when active monitoring and recording of the activity is taking place. There are two reasons for this. First, the attacker is already in the company's system so one does not want the attacker to see processes running that would not normally be run. These new processes might give the attacker insight as to other system vulnerabilities or alert the attacker to the investigation. Second, the CSDI needs to be able to distinguish between the vulnerability tests performed by the automated process and the tests performed by the attacker. Once it is determined safe to execute the test, the automated tools should be run and the results removed from the system immediately.

Closing the Investigation

One of the largest management challenges during a computer-related incident is bringing the investigation to a close when a suspect has been identified. The CSDI must orchestrate a plan that might include the participation of law enforcement, systems administrators, BU management, public relations, and legal departments.

By now, the decision has most likely been made to pursue criminal or civil charges, or handle the incident internally. Aiding in this decision will be the amount of damage done and potential business loss, as quantified by high-level management in the victim BU.

THE INTERVIEW

One of the questions that should be paramount in the CSDI mind is why the suspect engaged in the unauthorized activity. This question can frequently be answered during an interview of the suspect. If involved, law enforcement personnel will usually work with the CSDI to ensure that their questions and the CSDI questions are answered during the interview. If law enforcement is not involved, then it is up to the CSDI to interview the suspect and obtain answers to some very important questions. Other than why the suspect took the actions, the CSDI will want to have the suspect explain the steps taken to perform the unauthorized activity, actions taken before and after the unauthorized activity was noted and reported to the CSD, and what additional unauthorized activity may have occurred. For example, if the unauthorized activity was unauthorized access to a system, the CSDI should have the suspect explain when the access was first attempted, when access was accomplished, what accounts were accessed, and how the system was accessed. The CSDI should have the suspect identify any changes made to the system (i.e., modified data, deleted data, backdoors planted, etc.), and what gains were achieved as a result of the activity. During the interview, the CSDI should not make any promises as to the outcome of the suspect's employment or potential for criminal or civil prosecution, unless first concurring with CSD management and the company legal team. The CSDI should strive for the suspect to detail the discussion in a written statement and sign and date the statement at the completion of the interview. The CSD should utilize a standard form for written statements that includes a phrase about the company being allowed to use the written statement as the company sees fit and that no promises are made in exchange for the written statement. This will ensure that the suspect does not later attempt to say that any employment promises were made in exchange for the written statement or that the suspect was promised the statement would not be used in disciplinary, criminal, or civil proceedings.

The Corrective Action Phase

After the assessment has been completed, the corrective action phase can begin. This phase should be coordinated with investigative efforts so as not to interrupt any final investigative details. Optimally, the corrective action phase begins as the suspect is being arrested by law enforcement or interviewed by the CSDI. Once it has been determined that the phases can run concurrently or the investigative efforts have been completed, the target machines should be brought down and a forensic image should be acquired (see "Forensic Imaging" section). After a forensic image of the machine is acquired, the operating system should be loaded from original disks and all software patches applied. If possible, all userIDs should be verified in writing. If this is not possible, all user passwords should be changed and all users forced to change their passwords at next logon. Careful documentation should be kept to identify those IDs not used within a selected timeframe; for example, 30 days from the time the system is reloaded. Any ID not claimed by a user should be documented and removed from the system. This documentation should be kept as a supplement to the investigative case file in the event it is determined that the unclaimed ID was a product of the attacker's work. The CSDI should note any attempted use of any unclaimed IDs. If a suspect has been identified and either arrested or blocked from the system, attempted use of one of the unclaimed IDs may indicate a further problem not previously identified.

The validity of application programs and user data is at best a shot in the dark, unless the CSDI and system administrator can identify the date the system was compromised. To be absolutely sure backdoors placed by the attacker are not reloaded, BU management may have to fall back to a copy of the last application software load to ensure future system security.

Once the system has been restored and before it is brought back online, a full automated assessment should be run once again to identify any existing vulnerability. Any vulnerability identified should be corrected or, if not corrected, identified and signed off on as an acceptable risk by the BU manager. After all vulnerabilities have been corrected or identified as acceptable risks, the victim system can once again be brought back online.

Proactive Phase. After the investigation and corrective phases have been completed, a post-mortem meeting should be conducted to initiate the proactive phase. Problems encountered, root cause determination, and lessons learned from the incident should be documented in this meeting. The meeting should be led by the CSDI and attended by all company personnel involved in the incident. If the CSDI can show cost savings or recovered loss, these facts should be documented and provided to management. An overview of the incident and the lessons learned should be incorporated into the CSD security awareness presentations and presented to employees throughout the company. Timely reporting of incidents to the CSD should be stressed during the presentations. As this incident and others are presented throughout the company, the CSD is advertised as a value-added business partner, thereby generating more business for the CSD.

SUMMARY

While there are no golden rules to follow when investigating computer crime, following a structured methodology during investigations will provide a means for the CSDI to guarantee thorough investigations. Using the security continuum as a shell for a dynamic project plan, the CSDI will ensure a comprehensive examination of each incident. A strong project plan, coupled with traditional investigative skills and a good understanding of forensics and emerging technology, will provide the CSDI with the tools needed to confront an ever-changing investigative environment.

Chapter 26
CIRT: Responding to Attack

Chris Hare

THIS CHAPTER PRESENTS A NUMBER OF TOPICS AND ISSUES FOR TODAY'S ORGANIZATION WHEN CONSIDERING THE REQUIREMENTS AND IMPACT OF ESTABLISHING A COMPUTER INCIDENT RESPONSE TEAM (CIRT). This article makes no assumptions as to where a CIRT should be positioned from an organizational perspective within an organization, but focuses on why establishing a CIRT is important and what is involved in setting one up.

The term Computer Emergency Response Team, or CERT, is used to identify the government-funded team located at Carnegie Mellon University. The university has trademarked the name CERT (http://www.cert.org). Consequently, incident response teams are known by one of several other names. These include:

- Computer Incident Response Team (CIRT)
- Computer Security Incident Response Team (CSIRT)
- Systems Security Incident Response Team (SSIRT)

Regardless of the nomenclature, the CIRT is typically responsible for the initial evaluation of a computer security incident and providing corrective action recommendations to management. This article explores in detail the prerequisites, roles and responsibilities, and supportive processes necessary for a successful CIRT capability.

HISTORY

Prior to the Morris Internet Worm of 1988, computer security incidents did not really get a lot of attention, as the problem was not well understood. At that time, there was only a fraction of the total network hosts connected today.

The Morris Worm demonstrated to the Internet community, and to the computing world in general, that any determined attacker could cause damage, wreak havoc, and paralyze communication systems by using several commonly known vulnerabilities in UNIX system applications.

0-8493-0800-3/00/$0.00+$.50
© 2001 by CRC Press LLC

The nature of the problem is quite severe. An Internet mailing list known as BUGTRAQ discussed security issues and vulnerabilities in applications and operating systems. This mailing list currently has a volume of more than 1000 messages per quarter, most of which are exploits, bugs, or concerns about commercial applications.

Consider that IBM's mature MVS operating system has 17 million lines of assembly language instructions. Microsoft's Windows NT 5 (Windows 2000) has more than 48 million lines of C and assembly language code. The recognized "bug" factor is one bug for each 1000 lines of code. Windows NT 4 had more than 100,000 validated bugs. This means that there is potential for 48,000 bugs in Windows NT 5.

These bugs provide the perfect opportunity for the attacker to gain access to a system, and either steal, modify, or destroy information or resources from the system owner.

WHO IS ATTACKING WHO?

The nature of the attacker is changing dramatically. Considering the movies of a few years ago, *The Net* and *Sneakers*, computer hackers were portrayed as well-educated adults who knew their way around computer systems. They understood what information they needed, how to get it, and what they had to do once they gained access to a system.

Attacker profiles vary considerably:

- **The Naïve**: These attackers have little real knowledge or experience. They are out to do it for fun, with no understanding of the potential consequences.
- **Brutish** (script kiddies): These attackers also lack little real knowledge, and make heavy use of the various attack tools that exist. This means that they become obvious and visible on attacked systems due to the heavy probing and scanning used.
- **Clueful**: These are more experienced attackers, who use a variety of techniques to gain access to the system. The attacks are generally more subtle and less obvious.
- **Truly Subtle**: These are the computer criminals of the twenty-first century. They know what they want, who will pay for it, how to get access, and how to move around the system once they enter it. These attackers leave few or no traces on a system that they were in fact there.

The Teenage Attacker

The development of more sophisticated tools has lowered the required sophistication level of the attacker. There are reports of attackers who successfully used the tools to gain access to a system, but then did not know what to do once they got in.

Many teenage attackers also make use of the techniques demonstrated by actor Matthew Broderick in the 1980s movie *War Games*. Broderick used a program known as a "war dialer" to locate the modem tones for computer systems. Today's tools provide the naïve or clueful and brutish attackers with the necessary tools to gain access to almost any system. These tools are meant to be stealthy by nature; and while frequently used by the people outside the organization, they are also used from within. Information on common exploits and attacked sites are available at http://www.root-shell.com, among others.

While these tools do provide an easier method to compromise a system and gain access, attackers must still know what to do on the system once they have gained access. Recent attempts, as reported in *Systems Administration and Network Security (SANS)* (http://www.sans.org) bulletins and briefings, show that some successful attacks result in little damage or information loss because the attacker did not know how to interact with the system.

The Insider

Insiders may or may not have malicious intent. Their authorized presence on the network allows them virtually unrestricted access to anything, and may allow them to access information that they would normally not have the authority to access. This makes the distinction between the fact that employees are authorized to access the network and specific information and applications available. It does not imply that an employee has any implicit or explicit authorization to access all of the information available on the network.

Malicious insiders are insidious individuals whose goal is to steal or manipulate information so that the company does not have access to complete and accurate data. They may simply destroy it, provide it to the competition, or attempt to embarrass the company by leaking it to the media. These people have authorized access to the network, and therefore are difficult to trace and monitor effectively.

Insiders who are experiencing personal difficulties (e.g., as financial problems), are targets for recruitment by competitive intelligence agencies.

Even more important, insiders can make copies of the information and leave the original intact, thereby making it more difficult to detect that a theft took place. Those insiders that do cause damage lead to detection of the event, but those that undertake some planning make detection much more difficult — if not impossible

The Industrial Spy

Probably the most feared are the industrial spies. These attackers specifically target a particular company as a place from which to obtain information that they have been hired to collect, or that they believe will be considered valuable to others who would buy it. This is known as industrial or economic espionage. The difference between the two is that industrial espionage is conducted by organizations on behalf of companies, while economic espionage is data collection that is authorized and driven by governments.

These criminals are likely well-trained and will use any means at their disposal to discover and steal or destroy information, including social engineering, dumpster diving, coordinated network attacks, even getting a job as a contractor. The FBI (http://www.fbi.org) states that a typical organization can expect that one in every 700 employees is actively working against the company.

NATURE OF THE ATTACK

The attackers have a variety of tools and an increasing number of vulnerabilities in today's software from which to choose. The nature of the attack and the tools used will vary for each of the attacker types and their intent.

Attack Tools. A very extensive — and for the most part easily obtained — set of attack tools is available to today's attacker. They range from C language files that must be compiled and run against a system, to complex scanning and analysis tools such as *nmap*. A sample *nmap* run against several different hosts is illustrated in Exhibit 26-1.

Exhibit 26-1. Sample Output of nmap of a Linux System.
Log of: ./nmap -O -v -v -o /tmp/log2 192.168.0.4
Interesting ports on linux (192.168.0.4):

Port	State	Protocol	Service
21	open	tcp	ftp
23	open	tcp	telnet
25	open	tcp	smtp
37	open	tcp	time
79	open	tcp	finger
80	open	tcp	http
110	open	tcp	pop-3
111	open	tcp	sunrpc
113	open	tcp	auth
139	open	tcp	netbios-ssn

TCP Sequence Prediction: Class = random positive increments
Difficulty = 4686058 (Good luck!)
Remote operating system guess: Linux 2.2.0-pre6 - 2.2.2-ac5

The output of the various attack tools can provide the attacker with a wealth of information regarding the system platform, and as such is used by many attackers and system administrators alike. For example, the output illustrated in Exhibit 26-1 identifies the network services that are configured and additional information regarding how easy it would be to launch a particular types of attack against the system. Take special note that it was able to correctly guess the operating system.

Viruses and Mobile Code. A virus is program code that is intended to replicate from system to system and execute a set of instructions that would not normally be executed by the user. The impact of a virus can range from simple replication, to destruction of the information stored on the system, even to destruction of the computer itself.

Viruses are quite common on the Windows platform due to the architecture of the processor and the operating system. It is likely that most computer users today have been "hit" by one virus or another. The attacker no longer has to be able to write the World Wide Web (WWW).

Use of the WWW introduces additional threats through "active code" such as Microsoft's ActiveX and Sun Microsystems' Java languages. These active code sources can be used to collect information from a system, or to introduce code to defeat the security of a system, inject a virus, or modify or destroy information.

THE FIRST CERT

The first incident response team was established by the Defense Applied Research Projects Agency (DARPA) (http://www.darpa.mil) in 1988 after the Morris Worm disabled approximately 10 percent of the computer systems connected to the Internet. This team is called the Computer Emergency Response Team (CERT) and is located at the Software Engineering Institute at Carnegie Mellon University.

LEARNING FROM THE MORRIS WORM

The Morris Worm of 1988 was written by Robert Morris, Jr. to demonstrate the vulnerabilities that exist in today's software. Although Morris had contended since his arrest that his intent was not to cause the resulting damage, experts who have analyzed the program have reported that the Morris Worm operated as expected.

There were a large number of reports written in the aftermath of the incident. The U.S. General Accounting Office (GAO) issued a thorough report of the Morris Worm, its impact and the issues surrounding security on the Internet, and the prosecution of this and similar cases in the future.

The GAO report echoes observations made in other reports on the Morris Worm. These observations include:

- The lack of a focal point in addressing Internet-wide security issues contributed to problems in coordination and communication during security emergencies.
- Security weaknesses exist in some sites.
- Not all system managers have the skills and knowledge to properly secure their systems;
- The success of the Morris Worm was through its method of attack, where it made use of known bugs, trusted hosts, and password guessing.
- Problems exist in vendor patch and fix development and distribution.

While these issues were discussed after the Morris Worm incident, they are, in fact, issues that exist within many organizations today.

LEGAL ISSUES

There are many and inconsistent legal issues to be considered in investigating computer crime. It is worth noting, however, that an incident response team (or corporate investigations unit) typically has considerably more leeway in its operations than law enforcement.

As the property being investigated belongs to the company, the company is free to take any action that it deems appropriate. Once law enforcement is notified of the crime, then the situation becomes a law enforcement issue, and the organization's ability to act is significantly curtailed. This is because once law enforcement is informed, the company's investigators become agents for law enforcement and are then bound by the same constraints.

Among the legal issues that must be addressed are the rules of evidence. These vary from country to country due to differences in legal systems. These rules address how evidence must be collected and handled in order for it to be considered evidence by law enforcement agencies and in a court of law.

The exact actions that the CIRT can perform are governed by the appropriate legislation. The team will be advised by Corporate Counsel, at which point appropriate action will be taken with the intent of not jeopardizing the value of collected evidence or interviews.

THREAT ANALYSIS

Threat — and risk analysis in general — is a major proactive role of the CIRT. The CIRT must evaluate every vulnerability report and, based on an analysis of the situation, recommend the appropriate actions to management and who is responsible for completing these actions.

Most often, risk analysis focuses on new exploits or attack methods to determine if there are associated risks within the organizational environment and how such risks can best be mitigated. This is part of the CIRTs ongoing activity, and can include a variety of methods, including research and penetration testing. From this collected information, the CIRT can make recommendations on how to mitigate these risks by making changes to our computing or security infrastructures.

There is, however, the notion of "acceptable" risk. Acceptable risk is that risk which the company is knowingly prepared to accept. For example, if the company can earn $1 million but in the process has an exposure that could cause the loss of $10,000, the company may choose to accept such risk.

These decisions, however, cannot be made by just anyone in the organization. The exact nature of the vulnerability, the threat, and the resulting impact must be clearly evaluated and understood.

- *Threat* is defined as the potential to cause harm to the corporation — intentional or otherwise. Threats include hackers, industrial espionage, and at times, internal employees.
- *Vulnerability* is a weakness or threat to the asset. If there are no vulnerabilities, then a threat cannot put the organization at risk.
- *Impact* reflects degree of harm and is concerned with how significant the problem is, or how much effect it will have on the company.

The threat graph in Exhibit 26-2 illustrates threat, impact, and vulnerability. The risk is lowest when threat and impact are both low. Low impact, low threat, and low vulnerability imply that the *risk* is also low.

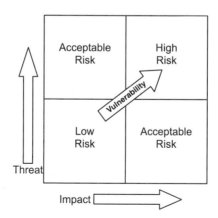

Exhibit 26-2. Threat graph: threat, impact, and vulnerability.

If the threat is low, the impact is high, and the vulnerability is low, the company may accept the risk of information loss. The same is true if the impact is low, the vulnerability low, and the threat high. This may still be an acceptable risk to the organization.

Finally, as the impact, vulnerability, and threat all increase, the issue becomes one of high risk. This is typically the area that most companies choose to address and place their emphasis. This is where the greatest risk is and, consequently, where the greatest return on security investment is found.

CIRT: ROLES AND RESPONSES

Most people think of "Incident Response Teams" as the emergency response unit for computers. The confusing term is "computer." A security incident that involves a computer is only different from a physical security incident in how the event took place. When an unauthorized person gains tactical access to a system or specific information, it should have equivalent importance to unauthorized physical access.

The CIRT must be able to handle a crisis and prevent it from becoming worse than it already is. The CIRT, however, has much more to offer, including a proactive role of vulnerability testing, vulnerability analysis, and awareness.

Obviously, the exact nature of responsibilities that one assigns to a CIRT will depend on the size and nature of the organization, the number of incidents recorded, and how many systems and networks exist. Consequently, some of the suggested activities may not be possible for a CIRT to integrate into its day-to-day tasks.

Incident Response

As mentioned, incident response is the prime reason behind establishing a CIRT. This incident response team puts highly trained people at the forefront of any incident, and allows for a consistently applied approach to resolving the incident. The team handles the investigation from start to finish and makes recommendations to management regarding its findings.

Vulnerability Testing

There are two elements to vulnerability testing. The first is to use automated tools with preconfigured tests to determine if there are vulnerabilities that could be exploited by an attacker. The second element test security implementation is to try it out. A penetration or protection test simulates the various types of attacks — internal and external, blind and informed — against the countermeasures of the network. Essentially, a penetration test attempts to gain access through available vulnerabilities by taking on the mindset of the perpetrator.

As the CIRT is responsible for investigating incidents, over time it will develop a set of skills that can be used to offer penetration or protection testing services to the organization's product developers or IS organization. Vulnerability testing is considered the cornerstone of the effort to improve a security program as it attempts to use vulnerabilities as an attacker would. Protection testing is conducted in a similar manner, but the goal is different.

Types of Penetration Tests. There are essentially three major types of penetration testing, each with its own tools and techniques:

> **Level 1**. Zero-Knowledge Penetration testing: This attempts to penetrate the network from an external source without knowledge of its architecture. However, information that is obtained through publicly accessible information is not excluded.
> **Level 2**. Full-Knowledge Penetration testing: This attempts to penetrate the network from an external source with full knowledge of the network architecture and software levels.
> **Level 3**. Internal Penetration testing: This attempts to compromise network security and hosts from inside one's network.

Penetration testing is interval based, meaning that it is done from time to time and against different target points. Penetration testing is not a real-time activity.

The process consists of collecting information about the network and executing the test. In a level 1 test, the only information available is what is published through open source information. This includes network broadcasts, upstream Internet service providers, domain name servers, and public registration records. This helps simulate an attack from an unsophisticated intruder who may try various standard approaches. This approach primarily tests one's ability to detect and respond to an attack.

A Level 2 penetration test assumes full knowledge of the hardware and software used on the network. Such information may be available to meticulous and determined intruders using whatever means, including social engineering, to increase their understanding of one's networks. This stage of the test assumes the worst-possible scenario, and calls to light the maximum number of vulnerabilities.

A Level 3 penetration test (or acid test) is an attack from within the network. This is the best judge of the quality of the implementation of the company's security policy. A real attack from within a network can come from various sources, including disgruntled employees, accidental attacks, and brazen intruders who can socially engineer their way physically into a company.

Penetration testing should be considered very carefully in the implementation of an overall detection program, but it can lead to the negative side effects that one is trying to prevent. Therefore, it should be used cautiously, but still be used to attempt to locate vulnerabilities and to assess the overall operation of the protection program.

Studying Security Vulnerabilities

When an incident occurs, it is essential to understand what allowed it to happen. Examining the vulnerability used during the incident allows the organization to improve its Security Infrastructure Program to prevent further exploitation.

In addition, security vulnerabilities that are released to the security community need to be assessed for their impact within the organization, and a course of action recommended. The CIRT, with its enhanced skills and knowledge, is capable of reviewing those vulnerabilities and offering the operating system and product groups a method of addressing them.

Publishing Security Alerts

When new issues are found that impact the organization, the CIRT is responsible for the publication of those bulletins and warnings, along with a set of instructions or recommendations regarding how users and systems administrators should react.

Publishing security alerts within the corporation, or new vulnerabilities found, does not include publishing the details of security incidents. The reporting of security incidents is a role for Corporate Security.

Security and Survivability in Wide Area Network-Based Computing

Working from the analysis of incident data, the CIRT is able to make specific recommendations to the systems administrators or applications owners on how to better configure their systems to increase the level of security.

Survivability comes from the application of good administration and consistently applied security techniques to reduce the threat of loss of data from an incident, or the loss of the system. Having to completely rebuild a system is an onerous task that is costly to the business, and one that few people want to repeat frequently.

DEFINING INCIDENTS

An obvious question is, "What is an incident?" Incidents cannot be easily identified without the team. However, an incident can be defined as any unexpected action that has an immediate or potential effect on the organization.

Example incidents include:

- viruses
- unauthorized access, regardless of source
- information theft or loss of confidentiality
- attacks against systems
- denial of service
- information corruption

However, incidents can be further classified based upon the extent to which the incident affects the organization.

The classification of CIRT responses is often based on several factors, including geography, business impact, and the apparent nature of the problem. Business impact includes how many people are affected; how many sites are affected, and will the issue affect stock prices, investor confidence, or damage the organization's reputation.

These classifications are meant to be a guide for discussion purposes — the CIRT may choose to broaden or identify improved characteristics for each.

Class 1: Global. These incidents have the greatest impact on an organization. They have the potential of affecting the entire organization, and they are serious. The uncorrected distribution of a virus can have very significant effects on the organization's ability to function. Other examples include a firewall breach, potential financial loss, customer services, compromise of the corporation's credibility, or the compromise of the organization's external Web site. In these situations, the CIRT is activated immediately, due to the threat to the company.

Class 2: Regional. Regional incidents affect specific areas of the company. They do, however, have the capability of becoming global. Regional threats include logic bombs, and attacks against specific systems in that region. While these can become global in nature, the information systems and security organizations in that region may be able to handle the issue without involvement from the CIRT. In this situation, the CIRT is activated at the request of the region IS or Security Directors.

Class 3: Local. Local incidents are isolated to a specific department and are of low impact. Examples include a virus on a single system, and the building cleaning crew playing solitaire on improperly configured desktop systems. In this situation, the CIRT is not activated unless requested by the department manager.

WHEN DOES THE CIRT RESPOND?

The CIRT responds in one of several situations:

- at the request of a manager when an event is noticed or reported to them
- when the incident requires it, based on sufficient evidence, probability, or due to a pattern of occurrence
- as the result of issues found during vulnerability testing
- on the advice of the help desk personnel who receive problem reports
- on the advice of an external security agency

CIRT response is based on the severity of an issue, as outlined previously. Managers can request CIRT involvement when they suspect unauthorized activity, regardless of whether there has been an incident reported to the CIRT.

If an incident is believed to have occurred based upon evidence (e.g., missing or altered information in a database) or due to alerts from an intrusion detection system, the CIRT is involved to determine the significance, scope, and method of the attack.

It is important to note that help desks can assist in reporting incidents to the CIRT. As employees call their help desks with issues, the help desk may see a pattern emerge that will initiate contacting the CIRT. Consequently, additional training is required for the help-desk staff to inform them of what they should be looking for.

The CIRT then provides a recommendation on how to address the attack and proceed with the investigation of the incident. In some situations, external agencies such as security departments of other organizations may advise of a potential incident and this must be investigated.

RELATIONSHIP TO EXTERNAL AGENCIES

The CIRT operates within the organizational framework and reviews incidents and provides other services as discussed. It is important, however, that the CIRT establish a relationship with external Computer Emergency Response Teams, such as CERT, CANCERT, etc. These teams provide similar services, but focus on incident reporting and advisory capabilities.

In addition, contact with law enforcement and other external teams that may be required must be established early on, so that if an issue arises, the CIRT is not spending valuable time looking for the correct external resource and then contacting them.

CIRT: THE CIRT PROCESS

There is a defined process for creating and establishing the CIRT function. This process is presented in this section. The process consists of six steps. These steps are explained here, but more information on some of the process steps is discussed in other sections.

CIRT is a global process. The team must be available 24 hours a day, 365 days per year. As such, mechanisms to contact the CIRT regardless of where the incident is, must be put into place to allow quick response.

1. Establishing the Process Owner

The *process owner* is responsible for supporting the team, and is the individual to whom the team itself reports. The process owner provides the interface to executive management and ensures that the CIRT is fulfilling its responsibilities effectively.

The process owner is assigned by senior management — not by the reputation or position of a single individual. Many organizations choose the Chief Information Officer (CIO) as the process owner, due to the technical nature of the team. While this is not necessarily incorrect, it is now considered more appropriate to choose either the Chief Financial Officer (CFO) or the Internal Audit Director to avoid any possibility of conflict of interest. The two alternate positions have legally defined fiduciary responsibilities to protect the corporation's assets and their departments often include staff with fraud investigation backgrounds.

2. Establishing the Team

The development of a CIRT is a process that requires full acceptance from the corporation's executives, *and* the groups involved in forming the core team. Specific resources, funding, and authority must be granted for the initiative to be successful and have benefit to the corporation. This section discusses the structure of the CIRT and how it interacts with other internal organizations.

Many organizations consider computer security incidents as an IS problem, while in fact they are a business problem. They are a business problem because any security incident, regardless of how it is caused, has the potential to affect the corporation in many ways, including financial loss, legal or financial liabilities, or customer service.

The very nature of computer involvement means that what is deemed to be an incident may not be when investigated. For example, consider the user who forgets his password and disables it. This may appear like a denial-of-service attack, when in fact it is not. This strains the internal investigative resources, and impacts the company by redirecting resources where they are not needed.

The investigation of an event is a complex process that involves a precise sequence of events and processes to ensure that, should the corporation choose to, it could involve law enforcement and not lose access to the valuable information, or evidence, already collected.

To do this, and for the response to any incident to be effective, people with a wide range of backgrounds and experiences are required. The CIRT ideally would have people from the following areas:

- technical specialists: an understanding of the production aspects of the technology that are relevant to the investigation
- information security specialists: data and systems protection
- auditors and fraud examiners: compliance and fraud
- corporate security: investigations
- human resources: personnel and labor issues
- business continuity specialists: system and data recovery
- legal specialists: protecting the organization's intellectual property
- corporate public relations: press and media interaction
- executive management: the decision-makers
- any other organization- or industry-specific personnel, such as business unit or geographically relevant personnel

The Core Team. For most organizations, it is difficult to rationalize the dedication of such a group of people to the CIRT role and, consequently, it is seen within the industry that the CIRT has two major components: a core team and a support team. The core team is composed of five disciplines, preferably staffed by a single individual from each discipline. These disciplines are:

- corporate security
- internal audit
- information protection
- legal specialists.
- technical specialists, as required

The CIRT core team must:

- determine if the incident is a violation
- determine the cause and advise management on the action required
- if required, establish the appropriately skilled support team
- manage the investigation and report
- all in external agencies as necessary

It is essential that the core team be made up of individuals who have the experience required to determine the nature of the incident and involve the appropriate assistance when required.

Many larger organizations have a corporate security group that provides the investigators who are generally prime for the incident. Smaller organizations may have a need to address their investigative needs with a security generalist. This is because the ultimate recommendation for the CIRT may be to turn the incident over to the corporate security organization for further investigation or to contact law enforcement. Obviously, the correct course of action depends on organization structure, and whether or not to contact law enforcement. In that event, specific rules must have been followed. These rules, while important, are not germane to the discussion here.

Internal Audit Services provide the compliance component. Every organization is required to demonstrate compliance with its policies and general business practices. The internal audit organization brings the compliance component to the team; moreover, it will be able to recommend specific actions that are to be taken to prevent further incidents.

The Information Protection or Information Services security specialist is required because the incident involved the use of a computer. The skills that this person holds will enable rapid determination of the path of the attack from one place to another, or gain rapid access to the information contained on a system.

Legal Specialists are essential to make sure that any actions taken by the CIRT are not in violation of any existing corporate procedures, of any rights of any individuals within the company or country. This is especially important, as there are different laws and regulations governing the corporation and the rights of the individual in many countries.

While team members have these backgrounds in their respective areas, the core team operates in one of two ways:

- dedicated full-time to the role of the CIRT and its additional responsibilities identified previously
- called as needed to examine the incident

In large, geographically dispersed organizations, the CIRT must be capable of deploying quickly and getting the information such as logs, files, buffers, etc., while it is still "fresh," There is no "smoking gun" — only the remnants left behind. Quick action on the part of the CIRT may enable collection of incident-related information that would otherwise be rendered useless as evidence minutes or hours or later.

Selecting the Core Team Members. The selection of the core team members is done based on experience within their knowledge area, their ability to work both individually and as part of a team, and their knowledge of the company as a whole. The process owner, who will select a team leader and then work together to choose the other members of the core team, would conduct the selection process. It is recommended that the team leader be a cooperating member of the team, and that the team leader operate as the point of contact for any requests for assistance.

The Support Team. The support team is used to provide additional resources once the core team has determined what the incident really is, and what other experts need to be called in to assess the situation.

The support team is vital to the operational support of the core team. This is because it is impossible for the core team to have all of the knowledge and expertise to handle every possible scenario and situation. For the core team to be effective, it must identify who the support team members are and maintain contact with and backup information for them over time.

The Support team consists of:

- human resources (HR)
- corporate communications
- platform and technology specialists
- fraud specialist
- others as required, such as business unit specialists or those geographically close to the incident.

Human resources (HR) is a requirement because any issue that is caused by an employee will require HR's involvement up front to assist in the collection of relevant information, and discussion of the situation with the employee's manager and the employee, and recommendations of appropriate sanctions.

If the incident is a major one that might gain public attention, it is recommended that the corporate public relations function issue a press release earlier, rather than take "knocks" from the public press. While any bad news can affect a company, by releasing such information on its own, the company can retain control of the incident and report on planned actions. However, it is essential that any press announcements must be cleared through the appropriate departments within the company, including the legal department and senior management. However, there have been sufficient examples with companies (like Microsoft) that would argue this point both ways.

Additionally, the team must designate an individual who is not actively participating to provide information and feedback to management and employees, as deemed appropriate. By choosing a person who does not have an active part in that particular investigation, that person can focus on the communications aspect and let the rest of the team get the job done.

The platform and technology specialists are used to provide support to the team, as no single individual can be aware of and handle all of the technology-related issues in the company. It is also likely that multiple technical specialists will be required, depending on the nature of the incident.

Fraud specialists provide guidance on the direction and investigation of fraud. In some cases, fraud will be hidden behind other issues to cloud the fraud and throw confusion on the issue.

The core team does the selection of the support team members. The core team must evaluate what types of skills it must have access to and then engage the various units within the organization to locate those skills.

It is essential that the core team conduct this activity to allow establishment of a network of contacts should the identified support team member and his or her backup be unavailable. Support team members are selected based on experience within their knowledge area, their ability to work both individually and as part of a team, and their knowledge of the company as a whole.

A major responsibility of the core team is to maintain this database of support team members to allow for quick response by the team when its involvement is required.

3. Creating the CIRT Operation Process

With the structure of the actual team in mind, it becomes necessary to focus on how the CIRT will operate. This is something that cannot be easily established in advance of core team selection. The process defines the exact steps that are followed each time the team is activated, either by request or due to the nature of the incident.

Aside from some steps that are required to create, establish, and authorize the team, the remaining steps in the process are to be handled by the core team. In addition to training and various other roles, the team must also:

- document its own practices and procedures
- establish and maintain databases of contact names and information
- maintain software and hardware tools required and used during an incident

Several matrices must be developed by the newly formed CIRT. These include an incident matrix and a response matrix. In the incident matrix, the team attempts to discover every possible scenario, and establish the:

- incident type
- personnel required
- financial resources required
- source of resources

With this, the CIRT can establish the broad budget it will need to investigate incidents. The response matrix identifies the incident type, what the team feels is an appropriate response to the incident, what resources it anticipates will be needed, and how it will escalate the incident should that become necessary. Neither of these matrices can be developed without the core team, and even some initial members of the support teams.

With the matrices completed, it is necessary to establish the training and funding requirements for the team.

Training Requirements. With the CIRT formed, it is necessary that the training requirements be determined. At a minimum, all members of the core team will need to be trained in intrusion management techniques, investigations, interviewing, and some level of computer forensics. (There are organizations that can conduct training specifically in these areas.)

Funding Requirements. The CIRT must now establish its requirements for a budget to purchase the needed equipment that will be used on a frequent or daily basis. A contingency budget is also needed to establish spending limits on equipment that is needed in the middle of an incident.

Given the nature and size of the core team, it is easy to establish that personnel budgets within a large organization will include a minimum of $500K for salaries and other employee costs. Training will approximate $50K per year, with an initial training expense of approximately $100K.

4. Policy and Procedures

The operation of the CIRT must be supported through policy. The policy establishes the reasons for establishing a CIRT, its authority, and the limits on its actions. Aside from the issues regarding policy in general, policies that support a CIRT must:

- not violate the law: doing so results in problems should the need for law enforcement result, or if the employee challenges the actions taken by the company as a result
- address privacy: employees must be informed in advance that they have no reasonable expectation of privacy (management has the right to search e-mail, stored files and their on-site workstations during an investigation)
- have corporate counsel review and approve the policy and procedures as being legal and sustainable in the given local areas

The policy itself leaves out the specifics surrounding the CIRT and how it operates. These are written in standards and procedures and describe how the team will react in specific situations, who the team members are, what the organization structure is, etc.

As mentioned, the employee must not have any expectation of privacy. This can only be accomplished effectively by understanding the privacy laws in the different regions, and stating specifically in policy, that this is the case.

CIRT members should operate within a code of ethics specifically designed for them, as they will be in contact and learn information about employees or situations that they would otherwise not know.

5. Funding

Funding is essential to the operation of the CIRT. While it is impossible to know what every investigation will cost, the team will have established a series of matrices identifying possible incidents and the equipment and resources required to handle them. This information is required to establish an operating budget, but contingency funds must be available should an incident cause the team to run over budget, or need a resource that was not planned.

Obviously, not having this information up front affects senior management's decisions to allocate base funding. This means, however, that senior management must believe in the role of the CIRT and the value that it brings to the overall security posture. The CIRT process owner in consultation with the identified CIRT members and external CIRTs, should be able to establish a broad level of required funding and modify it once the matrices are completed.

6. Authority

The CIRT must be granted the authority to act by senior management. This means that during an investigation of an incident, employees — regardless of level in the company — must be directed to cooperate with the CIRT. They must operate with extreme attention to confidentiality of the information they collect. The CIRT's responsibility is to collect evidence and make recommendations — not to determine guilt.

The role of the CIRT, as previously mentioned, is to investigate incidents and recommend appropriate actions to be taken by management to deal appropriately with the issues. The authority for the creation of the CIRT and its ability to get the job done is conveyed through policy.

SUMMARY

In a previous article this author has discussed intrusion detection.[1] Intrusion detection, regardless of the complexity and accuracy of the system, is not effective without an incident response capability. Consequently, any organization — regardless of size — must bear this in mind when deciding to go ahead with intrusion detection.

But incident response goes well beyond. Incident response is a proactive response to an incident. However, the CIRT can assist in the prevention and detection phases of the security cycle, and thereby create a much stronger, more resilient, and more responsive security infrastructure for today's organization.

LAW, INVESTIGATION, AND ETHICS

Note

1. Intrusion detection is the focus of Chris Hare's article in *Data Security Management*, 84-10-31, April – May 2000.

CIRT: References

1. Farrow, Rik, *Intrusion Techniques and Countermeasures*. Computer Security Institute: San Francisco, 1999
2. Icove, David, Seger, Karl, and VonStorch, William, *Computer Crime: A Crime Fighter's Handbook*, O'Reilly & Associates: Sebastopol, CA, 1995.
3. Stephenson, Peter, *How to Form a Skilled Computer Incident Response Team*, Computer Security Institute: San Francisco, 1999.
4. CERT, *Responding to Intrusions*, Carnegie Mellon Software Engineering Institute 1998.
5. Winkler, Ira, *Corporate Espionage*, Prima Publishing: Rocklin, California, 1997.

Chapter 27

Improving Network-Level Security Through Real-time Monitoring and Intrusion Detection

Chris Hare

CORPORATIONS ARE SEEKING PERIMETER DEFENSES WITHOUT IMPEDING BUSINESS. They have to contend with a mix of employees and non-employees on the corporate network. They must be able to address issues in a short time period due to the small window of opportunity to detect inappropriate behavior.

TODAY'S SECURITY PERIMETER: HOW TO PROTECT THE NETWORK

Many companies protect their networks from unauthorized access by implementing a **security program** using perimeter protection devices, including the *screening router* and the *secure gateway*. A screening router is a network device that offers the standard network routing services, and incorporates filters or access control lists to limit the type of traffic that can pass through the router. A firewall or secure gateway is a computer that runs specialized software to limit the traffic that can pass through the gateway. (The term "secure gateway" is used here rather than the more generic term "firewall.")

0-8493-0800-3/00/$0.00+$.50
© 2001 by CRC Press LLC

While on the surface, they seem like they are doing the same thing, and in some respects they are, the router and the secure gateway operate at different levels. The screening router and the secure gateway both offer services that protect entry into the protected network. Their combined operation establishes the firewall as shown in Exhibit 27-1.

Establishing firewalls at the entry points to the corporate network creates a moat-like effect. That means that there is a "moat" around the corporate network that separates it from other external networks.

THE MOAT

While the moat provides good protection, it reduces the ability of the organization to respond quickly to changes in network design, traffic patterns, and connectivity requirements (see Exhibit 27-2). This lack of adaptability to new requirements has been evident throughout the deployment of the secure gateways within numerous organizations.

One of the major complaints surrounds the limited application access that is available to authorized business partner users on the external side of the firewall.

In some situations, this access has been limited not by the authorizations allowed to those users, but to the secure gateway itself. These same limitations have prevented the deployment of firewalls to protect specific network segments within the corporate network.

Many organizations are only connected to the internet and only have a need to protect themselves at that point of entry. However, many others connect to business partners and business partners, who are in turn connected to other networks. None of these points of entry can be ignored.

It is, in fact, highly recommended that today's organizations establish a centralized security team that is responsible for the operation of the various security devices. This places responsibility for the operation of that infrastructure into one group who must do the planning, implement, and take action to maintain it.

THE THREAT OF ATTACK

The threat of attack comes from two major directions: attacks based outside the corporate network and attacks based from within. The moat security model, which is working effectively at many organizations, addresses the "attack from without" scenario. Even then, it cannot reliably provide information on the number of attacks, types of attacks, and their point of origin.

However, the moat cannot address the "attack from within" model, as the attack is occurring from within the walls. Consider the castle of medieval times. The moat was constructed to assist in warding off attacks from

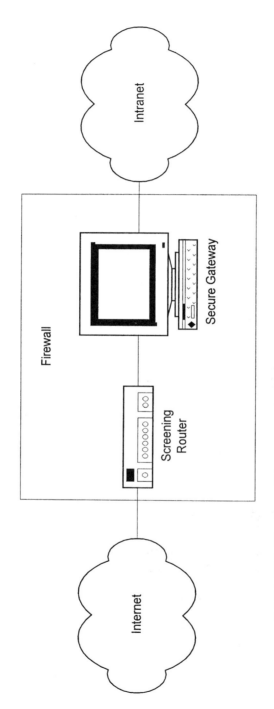

Exhibit 27-1. The firewall is composed of both the screening router and the secure gateway.

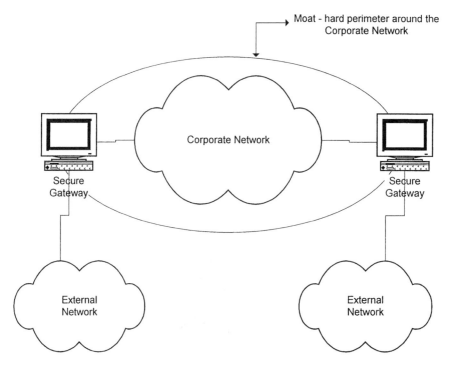

Exhibit 27-2. Establishing firewalls at the entry points to the corporate network creates a moat-like effect.

neighboring hostile forces. However, when fighting breaks out inside the castle walls, the moat offers no value.

The definition of an intrusion attempt is the potential possibility of a deliberate unauthorized attempt to:

- access information
- manipulate information
- render a system unreliable or unusable

However, an attack is a single unauthorized access attempt, or unauthorized use attempt, regardless of success.

UNAUTHORIZED COMPUTER USE

The problem is that the existing perimeter does not protect from an attack from within. The major security surveys continually report that the smallest percentage of loss comes from attacks that originate outside the organization. This means that the employees are really the largest threat to the organization.

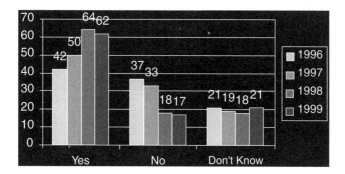

Exhibit 27-3. Computer Security Institute 1999 Survey.

The Computer Security Institute conducts an annual survey of its membership in conjunction with the FBI Computer Crime Unit. In the 1999 survey, the question was asked: "Has your organization experienced an incident involving the unauthorized use of a computer system?" (see Exhibit 27-3). As indicated, there was an overwhelming positive response, which had been climbing over the previous three years, but which saw a slight drop in an affirmative response. Many organizations could answer "Yes" to this question, but there is also a strong element of "I don't know." This element is because the only unauthorized use one is aware of is what is ultimately reported or found as a result of some other factor.

The cost of the information loss is staggering, as illustrated in the following information (also from the CSI Computer Security Survey). From that survey, it is evident that unauthorized insider access and theft of proprietary information has the highest reported cost. Given the potential value of the technical, R&D, marketing, and strategic business information that is available on the network, more and more companies need to focus additional attention to the protection of the data and securing the network.

FINANCIAL LOSSES

The financial impact to organizations continues to add up to staggering figures: a total of over $123 million as reported in the survey (see Exhibit 27-4). The survey identified that there has been a increase in the cost of unauthorized access by insiders, and the cost in other areas has also risen dramatically. The survey also identified that there continues to be an increase in the number of attacks driven from outside the reporting organizations. This is largely due to the increasing sophistication of the network attack tools and the number of attackers who are using them.

Intrusion detection and monitoring systems can assist in reducing the "I don't know" factor by providing a point where unauthorized or undesirable

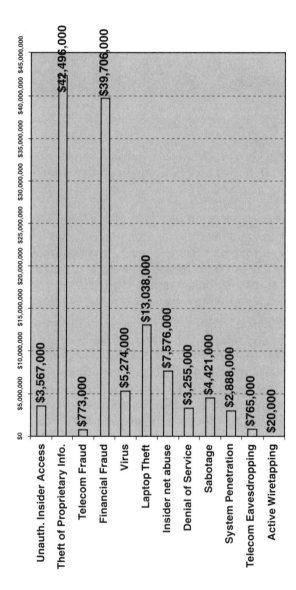

Exhibit 27-4. Dollar amount of losses by type.

use can be viewed, and appropriate action taken either in realtime or after the fact.

OUR EMPLOYEES ARE AGAINST US

An often-quoted metric is that one of 700 employees is actively working against the company. This means that if an organization has 7000 employees, there are ten employees actively working against the organization's best interests. While this sounds like a small number of people, the nature of who they are in an organization will dictate what they have access to and can easily use against the company.

The most recent American Society for Industrial Security (ASIS at http://www.asisonline.org) "Trends in Intellectual Property Loss" survey report suggests that approximately 75 percent of technology losses occur from employees and those with a trusted relationship to the company (i.e., contractors and subcontractors). Computer intrusions involve approximately 87 percent of the insider issue.

While organizations typically have the perimeter secure, the corporate network is wide open, with all manner of information available to every one who has network access. This includes employees, contractors, suppliers, and customers! How does an organization know that their vital information is not being carried out of the network? The truth is that many do not know, and in many cases it is almost impossible to tell.

WHERE IS THE CRITICAL INFORMATION?

The other aspect to this is that many organizations do not know where their critical information is stored. This does not even mean where the source code or technical information is stored. That is important, but one's competitors will be building similar products. The critical information is the strategic business plan, bids for new contracts, and financial information. There are various systems in place to control access to various components, but there are problems with the security components in those systems.

Regardless, the strategic business plan will be scattered throughout the corporation on different desktops and laptops. What is the value of that information? Who has it? Where is it going? In the current environment, few organizations can adequately identify the information, let alone where it is stored within the network.

This situation is even worse in businesses such as government, military, or large corporations where they used to have dozens of filing cabinet to maintain a proper paper trail. Electronic mail has killed the chain of command and the proper establishment of a trail. Information is spread everywhere and important messages simply get deleted when employees leave the company.

The FBI has published a "Top Ten Technology List," which is still current according to the FBI's Awareness of National Security Issues and Response (FBI-ANSIR). This technology list includes:

- manufacturing processes and technologies
- information and communication technologies
- aeronautic and surface transportation systems
- energy and environmental-related technologies
- semiconductor materials and microelectronic circuits
- software engineering
- high-performance computing
- simulation modeling
- sensitive radar
- superconductivity

Many high-tech companies operate within these areas and, as such, are prone to increased incidents of attack and intelligence-gathering operations. Since the primary threat is from internal or authorized users, it becomes necessary to apply security measures within the perimeter.

THE FUTURE OF NETWORK SECURITY

However, the future of network security is changing. The secure gateway will be an integral part of that for a long time. However, implementation of the secure gateway is not the answer in some circumstances. Furthermore, users may be unwilling to accept the performance and convenience penalties created by the secure gateway.

SECURE GATEWAY TYPES

There are two major types of secure gateways — packet filters and application proxy systems — and companies choose one or the other for various reasons. This article does not seek to address the strengths or weaknesses of either approach, but to explain how they are different.

The packet-filter gateway operates at the network and transport levels, performing some basic checks on the header information contained in the packet. (See Exhibit 27-5.) This means that the packet examination and transfer happens very fast, but there is no logical break between the internal and external network.

The application proxy provides a clear break between the internal and external networks. This is because the packet must travel farther up the TCP/IP protocol stack and be handled by a proxy (see Exhibit 27-6). The application proxy receives the packet, and then establishes a connection

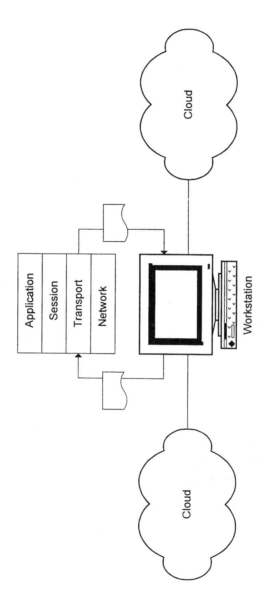

Exhibit 27-5. The packet-filter gateway operates at the network and transport levels, performing some basic checks on the header information contained in the packet.

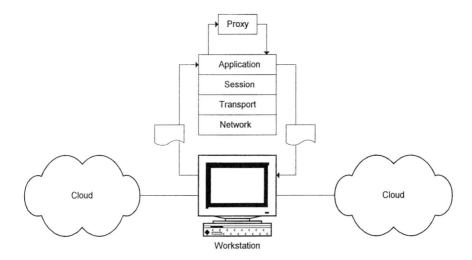

Exhibit 27-6. An application proxy provides a clear break between the internal and external network (this is because the packet must travel farther up the tcp/ip protocol stack and be handled by a proxy).

to the remote destination on behalf of the user. This is how a proxy works. It provides a logical break between the two networks, and ensures that no packets from one network are automatically sent to the other network.

The downside is that there must a proxy on the secure gateway for each protocol. Most secure gateway vendors do not provide a toolkit to build application proxies. Consequently, companies are limited in what services can be offered until the appropriate proxy is developed by the vendor.

The third type of firewall that is beginning to gain attention is the adaptive proxy (see Exhibit 27-7). In this model, the gateway can operate as both an application proxy and a packet filter. When the gateway receives a connection, it behaves like an application proxy. The appropriate proxy checks the connection. As discussed earlier, this has an effect on the overhead associated with the gateway.

However, once the connection has been "approved" by the gateway, future packets will travel through the packet filter portion, thereby providing a greater level of performance throughput. There is currently only one vendor offering this technology, although it will expand to others in the future.

The adaptive proxy operates in a similar manner to stateful inspection systems, but it has a proxy component.

Whenever a firewall receives a SYN packet initiating a TCP connection, that SYN packet is reviewed against the firewall rule base. Just like a router,

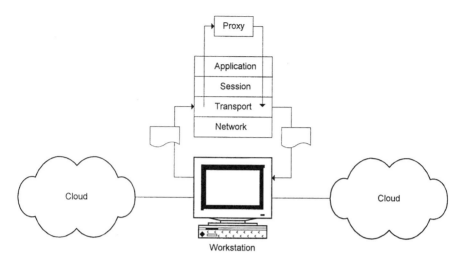

Exhibit 27-7. With an adaptive proxy, the gateway can operate as both an application proxy and a packet filter.

this SYN packet is compared to the rules in sequential order (starting with rule 0). If the packet goes through every rule without being accepted, the packet is denied. The connection is then dropped or rejected (RST is sent back to the remote host). However, if the packet is accepted, the session is then entered into the firewall's stateful connection table, which is located in kernel memory. Every packet that follows (that does not have a SYN) is then compared to the stateful inspection table. If the session is in the table and the packet is part of that session, then the packet is accepted. If the packet is not part of the session, then it is dropped. This improves system performance, as every single packet is not compared against the rule base; only SYN packets initiating a connection are compared to the rule base. All other TCP packets are compared to the state table in kernel memory (very fast).

This means that, to provide increased protection for the information within the corporate network, organizations must deploy security controls within the corporate network that consist of both secure gateways (where there is a good reason) and intrusion and network monitoring and detection. Intrusion detection systems are used in a variety of situations.

SECURITY LAYERING

Security is often layered to provide "defensive depths." This means that at each layer, there are security controls to ensure that authorized people have access, while still denying access to those who are not authorized (see Exhibit 27-8). As seen in this diagram, this layering can be visualized as a series of concentric circles, with the level of protection increasing to the center.

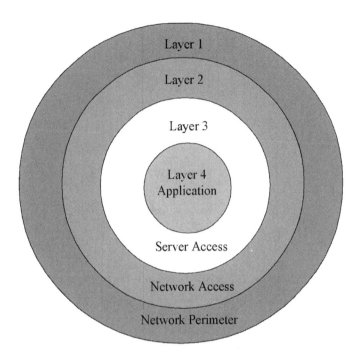

Exhibit 27-8. Security laying provides defensive depths (this means that at each layer, there are security controls to ensure that authorized people have access, while still denying access to those who are not authorized).

Layer 1, or the network perimeter, guards against unauthorized access to the network itself. This would include firewalls, remote access servers, etc. Layer 2 is the network. Some information is handled on the network without any thought. As such, layer 2 addresses the protection of the data as it moves across the network. This technology includes link encryptors, VPN, and IPsec. Layer 3 considers access to the server systems themselves. Many users do not need access to the server, but to an application residing there. However, a user who has access to the server may have access to more information that is appropriate for that user. Consequently, layer 3 addresses access and controls on the server itself.

Finally, layer 4 considers the application-level security. Many security problems exist due to inconsistencies in how each application handles or does not handle security. This includes access and authorization for specific functions within that application.

There are occasions where organizations implement good technology in bad ways, which results in poor implementation. This generally leads to a false sense of security and lulls the organization into complacency.

Consequently, by linking each layer, it becomes possible to provide security that the user does not see in some cases, and will have to interact with at a minimal level with to provide access to the desired services. This corresponds to the goals of the three-year architecture vision.

SECURITY GOALS

Organizations place a great deal of trust in the administrators of computer systems to keep things running first, and then make sure that the needed patches are applied whenever possible. It is very important that the security measures of any system be configured and maintained to prevent unauthorized access. The major threats to information itself are:

- disclosure, either accidental or intentional (confidentiality)
- modification (integrity)
- destruction (availability)

The goal of an information protection program is to maintain the confidentiality, integrity, and availability of information.

Exhibit 27-9 illustrates five essential steps in the information protection arena: protect, detect, react, assess, and correct.

Protection involves establishing appropriate policies procedures and technology implementations to allow for the protection of the corporation's information and technology assets.

Detection is the ability to determine when those assets have been, or are under attack from some source.

To be effective at maintaining the security goals of confidentiality, integrity, and availability, the corporation must be able to **react** to a detected intrusion or attack. This involves establishing a Computer Security Incident Response Team to review the alarm and act.

With the tactical response complete, the **assessment** phase reviews the incident and determines the factors that caused it. From there, a risk analysis is performed to determine:

- the risk of future occurrences
- what the available countermeasures are
- a cost/benefit analysis to determine if any of the available countermeasures should be implemented

The **correct** stage is where the countermeasures or other changes are implemented; or, if the level of risk is determined to be acceptable to the corporation, no action is taken.

Many of today's proactive organizations have the protection side operating well, as it relates to network protection. However, many have no systems in place to protect the internal data and network components.

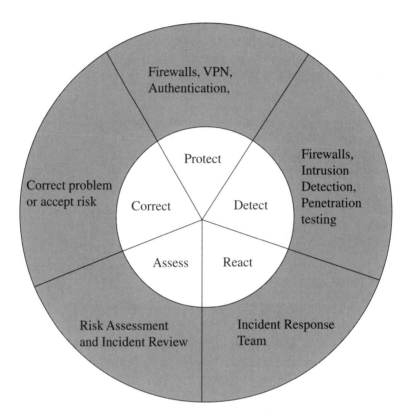

Exhibit 27-9. Five essential steps in the information protection arena: protect, detect, react, assess, and correct.

Likewise, reaction mechanisms may be in place to address and investigate when an incident occurs. This is accomplished by establishing a Computer Incident Response Team to be used when an incident is detected in progress that requires the knowledge of a diverse group of computer and security specialists.

However, for many, their detection abilities are limited, which is the area that intrusion monitoring and detection is aimed at. By improving detection abilities, one can refine both protection strategies and technology, and how one reacts when an incident occurs.

Since today's computer systems must be able to keep information confidential, maintain integrity, and be available when needed, it is highly likely that any expectations of the system being able to completely prevent a security breach is unrealistic.

TYPES OF INTRUSION MONITORING AND DETECTION SYSTEMS

There are two major types of intrusion detection: host and network based. Host-based products are based on the computer system and look for intrusions into its own environment. These host-based systems are capable of examining their own configuration and reporting changes to that configuration or to critical files that may result in unauthorized access or modification. For example, a product such as tripwire can be considered a host-based intrusion detection system. Changes in the configuration of the system or its files are detected and reported by tripwire and then captured at the next report.

Network-based products are those that are not bound to looking at intrusions on a specific host. Rather, they are looking for specific activity on the network may be considered malicious. Network-based tools have the ability to find the attack in progress, while host-based tools can actually see the changes inside the system. In fact, it is recommend that one runs both types of systems.

There are essentially two types of intrusion detection "engines." These are statistical anomaly detection and pattern-matching detection engines. Statistical engines look at deviation from statistical measurements to detect intrusions and unusual behaviours. The baseline established for the statistical variables is determined by observing "normal" activity and behavior. This requires significant data collection over a period of time to establish this "normal" or expected behavior. Statistical anomaly systems are generally not run in real time due to the amount of statistical calculations required. Consequently, they are generally run against logs or other collected data.

Statistical anomaly systems offer some advantages. The well-understood realm of statistical analysis techniques is a major strength so long as the underlying assumptions in the data collection and analysis are valid. Statistical techniques also lend themselves better to analysis dealing with time.

However, the underlying assumptions about the data may not be valid, which causes false alarms and erroneous data reported. The tendency to link information from different variables to demonstrate trends may be statistically incorrect, leading to erroneous conclusions. The major challenge to this technique is establishing the baseline of what is considered expected behavior at the monitored site. This is easier if the users work within some predefined parameters. However, it is well-known that the more experienced users are, the less likely they will operate within those parameters.

One drawback to intrusion detection systems is false-positive alarms. A false positive occurs when the intrusion detection system causes an alarm when no real intrusion exists. This can occur when a pattern, or series of packets, occurs that resemble an attack pattern but are in fact legitimate traffic.

Worth noting is that some of the major issues with statistical engines involve establishing the baseline. For example, how does one know when a user has read too many files?

Pattern-matching systems are more appropriate to run in real- or near-real time. The concept is to look at the collected packets for a "signature," or activities that match a known vulnerability. For example, a port scan against a monitored system would cause an alarm due to the nature of packets being sent. Due to the nature of some of the signatures involved, there is some overlap between the pattern-matching and anomaly-detection systems.

The attack patterns provided by the vendors are compiled from CERT advisories, vendor testing, and practical experience. The challenge is for the vendor to create patterns that match on a more general class of intrusion, rather than being specific to a particular attack.

There are pros and cons to both types, but it is recommended that in the development of the tools, that both forms be run. This means collecting the packets and analyzing them in near-real time and collecting the log data from multiple sources to review it with an anomaly system as well.

In a pattern-matching system, the number and types of events that are monitored are constrained to only those items required to match a pattern. This means that if one is only interested in certain types of attacks, then one does not need to monitor for every event. As previously stated, the pattern matching engine can run faster due to the absence of the floating-point statistical calculations.

However, pattern-matching systems can suffer from scalability issues, depending on the size of the hardware and the number of patterns to match. Even worse is that most vendors do not provide an extensible language to allow the network security administrator to define his own patterns. This makes adding one's own attack signatures a complicated process.

For both systems, neither really has a "learning" model incorporated into it, and certainly none of the commercial intrusion detection systems have a learning component implemented in them.

WHY INTRUSION MONITORING AND DETECTION?

The incorporation of intrusion monitoring and detection systems provides the corporation with the ability to ensure that:

- *protected information is not accessed by unauthorized parties; and if it is, there is a clear audit record.* Organizations must identify the location of various types of information and know where the development of protected technologies takes place. With the installation of an intrusion detection system within the corporate network, one can offer protection to that information without the need for a secure gateway. The intrusion detection system can monitor for connection requests that are not permitted and take appropriate action to block the connection. This provides a clear audit record of the connection request and its origination point, as well as preventing the retrieval of the information. There is no impact to the authorized users.
- *the ability to monitor network traffic without impact to the network.* A secure gateway is intrusive: all of the packets must pass through it before they can be transmitted on the remote network. An intrusion monitoring system is passive: it "listens" on the network and takes appropriate action with the packets.
- *actively respond to attacks on systems.* Many implementations of intrusion monitoring systems have the ability to perform specific actions when an event takes place. Those actions range from notification to a human to automatic reconfiguration of a device and blocking the connection at the network level.
- *information security organizations understand the attacks being made and can build systems and networks to resist those attacks.* As attacks are made against the organization, reviewing the information captured by the intrusion monitoring system can assist in the development of better tools, practices, and processes to improve the level of information security and decrease the risk of loss.
- *metrics reporting is provided.* As in any program, the ability to report on the operation of the program through good quality metrics is essential. Most organizations do not know if there has been a successful penetration into their network because they have no good detection methods to determine this.

IMPLEMENTATION EXAMPLES

As more and more organizations enter the electronic-business (E-biz) forum in full gear, the effective protection of those systems is essential to being able to establish trust with the customer base that will be using them. Monitoring of the activity around those systems will ensure that one responds to any new attacks in an appropriate fashion, and protects that area of the business — both from financial and image perspectives.

Implementing an intrusion monitoring and detection system enables monitoring at specific sites and locations within the network. For example, one should be immediately concerned with Internet access points and the extranets that house so many critical business services on the Internet.

Second, organizations should be working with information owners on the top-ten FBI list, on how to handle corporate strategic information. That venture would involve installing an intrusion monitoring system and identifying the information that people are not allowed to access, and then using that system to log the access attempts and block the network connections to that information.

The following examples are intended to identify some areas where an intrusion monitoring system could be installed and the benefits of each.

Monitoring at the Secure Gateway

In Exhibit 27-10, the intrusion monitoring system is configured to monitor the networks on both sides of the firewall. The intrusion monitoring system is unable to pass packets itself from one side to the other. This type of implementation uses a passive or nonintrusive mode of network data capture.

To illustrate this, first consider the firewall. The firewall must retransmit packets received on one network to the other network. This is intrusive as the packet is handled by the firewall while in transit. The intrusion monitoring system, on the other hand, does not actually handle the packet. It observes and examines the packet as it is transmitted on the network.

This example also lends itself to monitoring those situations where the traffic must be passed through the secure gateway using a local tunnel. As this provides essentially unrestricted access through the secure gateway, the intrusion monitoring system can offer additional support, and improved logging shows where the packet came from, and what it looked like on the other side of the gateway.

Using an intrusion monitoring system in this manner allows metrics collection to support the operation of the perimeter and demonstration that the firewall technology is actually blocking the traffic it was configured to block. In the event of unexpected traffic being passed through anyway, the information provided by the intrusion monitoring system can be used by the appropriate support groups to make the necessary corrections and, if necessary, collect information for law enforcement action.

Monitoring at the Remote Access Service Entry

A second example involves the insertion of an intrusion monitoring device between the RAS access points and their connection to the corporate network (see Exhibit 27-11). In this implementation, the intrusion monitoring system is installed at the remote access point. With the clear realization that most technical and intellectual property loss is through authorized inside access, it makes sense to monitor one's remote access points. It is possible to look for this type of behavior, active attacks against systems, and other misuse of the corporate computing and network services.

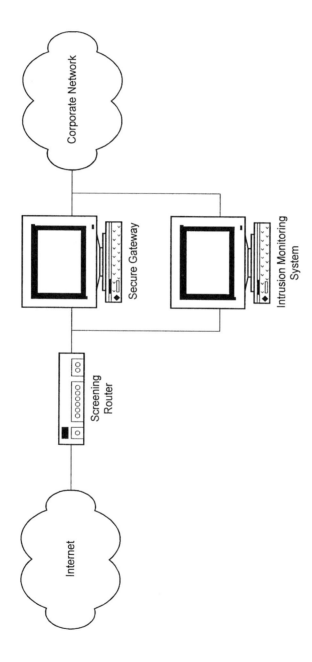

Exhibit 27-10. **An intrusion monitoring system is configured to monitor the networks on both sides of the firewall.**

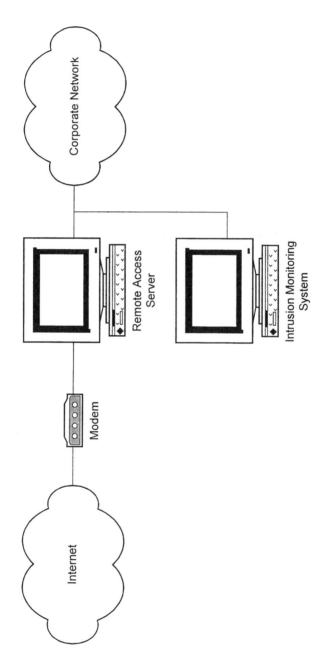

Exhibit 27-11. The intrusion monitoring system is installed at the remote access point.

Monitoring Within the Corporate Network

As mentioned previously, there is no ability to monitor specific subnets within the corporate network where protected information is stored. Through the implementation of intrusion monitoring, it is possible to provide additional protection for that information without the requirement for a secure gateway.

Exhibit 27-12 reveals that the protected servers are on the same subnet as the intrusion monitoring system. When the corporate network user attempts to gain access to the protected servers, the intrusion monitoring server can log and, if configured, intercept the connection attempt. This also means that some guidelines on how to determine where to add an intrusion detection system within the corporate network are required. In many organizations, the corporate network is extensive and it may not be feasible to monitor them all.

Monitoring the Extranet

This will facilitate monitoring attacks against externally connected machines or, in the event that a proper extranet has been implemented, by monitoring any attacks against the systems connected to the extranet. However, in this instance, two IDSs may be required to offer detection capabilities for both the extranet and the firewall, as illustrated in Exhibit 27-13.

In this illustration, all activity coming into the extranet is monitored. The extranet itself is also protected as it is not directly on the Internet, but in a private organizationally controlled network. This allows additional controls to be in operation to protect those systems.

SECURITY IS DIFFICULT TO QUANTIFY

Security is a business element that is often very difficult to quantify. This is because security is a loss prevention exercise. Until something is missing, most people do not bother with it. However, application of an intrusion monitoring system external to network access points can provide valuable information that includes metrics describing the state of the security perimeter.

Aside from the monitoring component, some intrusion detection systems offer the ability to block network sessions where they are deemed inappropriate or undesirable. These systems offer additional opportunities. Deployment of secure gateways can be problematic as the services that are available to users on the external network are reduced due to limitations at the secure gateway. Using the blocking technology, it may be possible to deploy an intrusion monitoring and detection system to monitor the traffic, but also block connection requests to protected information or sites.

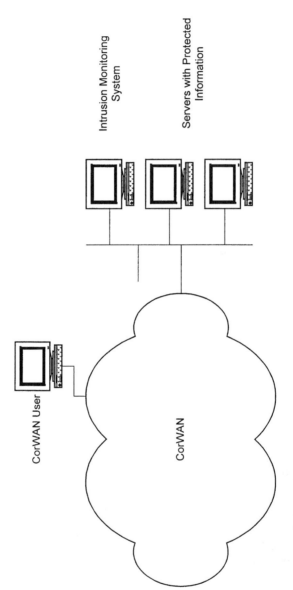

Exhibit 27-12. Protected servers are on the same subnet as the intrusion monitoring system.

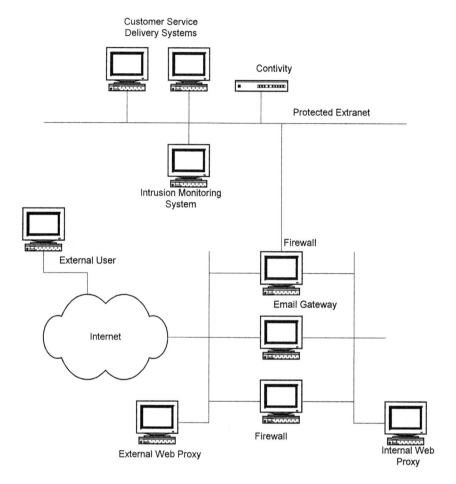

Exhibit 27-13. Two IDS systems may be required to offer detection capabilities for both the extranet and the firewall.

PROACTIVE AND REACTIVE MONITORING

The situations illustrated in Exhibits 27-10 through 27-13 are proactive implementations of an intrusion detection system. The other implementation (not illustrated here) is reactive. A proactive approach calls for the installation and operation of the system in an ongoing mode, as well as ongoing maintenance to ensure that the intrusion monitor is processing information correctly. A reactive mode approach involves having an intrusion monitor system ready for installation, but not actually using it until some event occurs. The operation of an effective intrusion monitoring systems involves both of these elements.

However, there is the concept of realtime and interval-based intrusion detection. Real time implies that the monitoring agent is run on a continuous basis. Interval based means that the monitor is run as needed, or at intervals. Vulnerability scanning is also seen as a form of intrusion detection by exposing holes in an operating system configuration. This is interval-based monitoring, as it cannot be done all the time.

Information security organizations are often focused on the prevention aspect of network security. They operate systems that are intended to limit access to information and connectivity. This is a proactive activity that requires ongoing analysis and corrective action to ensure that the network is providing the services it should, and that is is properly protected.

COMPUTER INCIDENT RESPONSE TEAM

The benefits of the intrusion detection system (i.e., the ability to detect undesirable activities) will be lost without the ability to respond to it. This is done most effectively through the operation of a Computer Security Incident Response Team (or CIRT). Most CIRT teams are modeled after the Carnegie Mellon Computer Emergency Response Team.

The object of the CIRT is to accept alarms from intrusion detection and other sources. Its role is to review the incident and decide if it is a real incident or not.

The CIRT must include personnel from corporate and information security, internal audit, legal, and human resources departments. Other people may be called in as required, such as network engineering and application providers.

Normally, the alarm is provided to a small group of the CIRT to evaluate. If it is agreed that there is an incident, then the entire CIRT is activated. The operation of the CIRT becomes a full-time responsibility until the issue is resolved. There are a variety of potential responses and issues to be resolved in establishing a CIRT. These are well covered in other documents and will not be duplicated here.

The CIRT forms an integral part of the intrusion detection capability by evaluating and responding to the alarms raised by the intrusion detection systems. As such, the personnel involved must have time dedicated to this function; it cannot take a back seat to another project.

Once the tactical response is complete, the CIRT will closely evaluate the situation and make recommendations for review to prevent or reduce the risk of further occurrence. In the protection cycle, these recommendations are used to assess what further action is to be taken.

This being the case, a decision to implement intrusion detection is a decision to implement and support a CIRT. Intrusion detection cannot exist without the CIRT.

PENETRATION AND COMPLIANCE TESTING

The best method to test security implementation is to try it out. A penetration test simulates the various types of attacks — both internal and external, blind and informed — against the countermeasures of the network. Essentially, a penetration test attempts to gain access through available vulnerabilities.

Penetration testing is part of the detection strategy. While intrusion detection capabilities are required to monitor access and network status on an ongoing basis, penetration is an interval-based targeted approach to testing both the infrastructure, and the detection and reaction capabilities.

Penetration testing should be done as part of the network security strategy for several purposes:

- *To provide confidence or assurance of systems integrity:* Vulnerability scans often do not include attempts to exploit any vulnerability found, or any of the long list of known vulnerabilities. This is because many of the systems being tested currently are in production. A successful penetration test could seriously affect normal business operations. However, the integrity of the system can be effectively tested in a non-production role.
- *To verify the impact of the security program:* Penetration testing is used to determine if the security program is performing as it should. There are a number of different products and services that work together to provide this infrastructure. Each can be evaluated on its own, but it is much more complicated to test them as a system.
- *To provide information that can be used in developing and prioritizing security program initiatives:* Any issues found during a penetration test can alter and affect the direction of the security program priorities. Should a major issue be found that requires correction, the security program goals may be altered to provide a timely resolution for the issue.
- *To proactively discover areas of the infrastructure that may be subject to intrusion or misuse:* People do not install an alarm system in their house and never test it. The same is true here. Ongoing evaluation allows for the identification of components in the infrastructure that may be less secure than desired, not operating as expected, or contain a flaw that can be exploited. Taking a proactive stance means that it becomes possible to find and correct problems before they are exploited.

- *To provide information that can be used in developing and prioritizing policy initiatives:* Policy is not cast in stone; it must be updated from time to time to reflect the changing needs of the business. Penetration tests can assist in the testing and development of policies. This is done using the information learned from the testing to evaluate whether one is compliant with the policies, and if not, which is correct — the implementation or the policy.
- *To assess compliance with standards and policies:* It is essential that the infrastructure, once in operation, be compliant with the relevant security policies and procedures. This verification is achieved through penetration testing, or what is also known as protection testing. Protection testing is the same as penetration testing but with a slightly different objective. While penetration testing attempts to find the vulnerabilities, protection testing proves that the infrastructure is working as expected.
- *To provide metrics that can be used to benchmark the security program:* The ability to demonstrate that the security infrastructure is operating as expected, and that improvement is visible, are important parts of the program. Metrics establish what has been *and* what is now. It is also possible from collected to metrics to make "educated guesses" about the future. By collecting metrics, one also gathers data that can be used to benchmark the operation of our infrastructure as compared to the companies.
- *For preimplementation assessments of systems or services:* It is important that appropriate evaluations are performed to ensure that the addition of new services to the infrastructure, or that is dependent on the infrastructure operating correctly, be certified to ensure that no vulnerabilities exist that could be exploited. When a new application is developed that interconnects both internal and external systems, a penetration test against the application and its server is undertaken to verify that neither holds a vulnerability to be exploited. This also ascertains that if the external system is compromised, that the attacker cannot gain access to the corporate network resources.

Types of Penetration Tests

There are essentially three major types of penetration testing, each with their own tools and techniques:

- **Level 1 — Zero Knowledge Penetration Testing:** This attempts to penetrate the network from an external source without knowledge of its architecture. However, information that is obtained through publicly accessible information is not excluded.
- **Level 2 — Full Knowledge Penetration Testing:** This attempts to penetrate the network from an external source with full knowledge of the network architecture and software levels.

- **Level 3 — Internal Penetration Testing:** This attempts to compromise network security and hosts from inside one's network.

Penetration testing is interval based, meaning that it is done from time to time and against different target points. Penetration testing is not a real-time activity.

The process consists of collecting information about the network and executing the test. In a Level 1 test, the only information available is what is published through open source information. This includes network broadcasts, upstream Internet service providers, domain name servers, and public registration records. This helps simulate an attack from an unsophisticated intruder who may try various standard approaches. This approach primarily tests one's ability to detect and respond to an attack.

A Level 2 penetration test assumes full knowledge of the hardware and software used on the network. Such information may be available to meticulous and determined intruders using whatever means, including social engineering, to increase their understanding of your networks. This stage of the test assumes the worst-possible scenario and calls to light the maximum number of vulnerabilities.

A Level 3 penetration test, or acid test, is an attack from within the network. This is the best judge of the quality of the implementation of a company's security policy. A real attack from within a network can come from various sources, including disgruntled employees, accidental attacks, and brazen intruders who can socially engineer their way physically into a company.

Penetration testing should be considered very carefully in the implementation of an overall detection program, but it can lead to the negative side effects one is trying to prevent. Therefore, penetration testing should be used cautiously, but still be used to attempt to locate vulnerabilities and to assess the overall operation of the protection program.

SUMMARY

This article has presented several implementations of secure gateway and intrusion detection techniques, while focusing on the business impact of their implementation. It is essential that the security professional consider the use of both network and host-based intrusion detection devices, and balance their use with the potential for impact within the operating environment.

A key point worth remembering is that the implementation of technology is only part of the solution. There must be a well-thought-out strategy and a plan to achieve it.

Chapter 28
Operational Forensics

Michael J. Corby

THE INCREASED COMPLEXITIES OF COMPUTER SYSTEMS TODAY MAKE IT DIFFICULT TO DETERMINE WHAT HAS HAPPENED WHEN A MALFUNCTION OCCURS OR A SYSTEM CRASHES. Sometimes, it is difficult to even make the basic identification of whether the cause was accidental or intentional. If the cause was intentional, legal action may be in order; if the cause was operational, the reason must be identified and corrected. Both require a planned and measured response.

Unfortunately, with today's emphasis on immediate recovery in the networked environment, and with the obligation to get back online as quickly as possible, determining the cause may be impossible. The tendency to restart, or reboot, may remove information that could be valuable in ascertaining cause or providing evidence of criminal wrongdoing.

Operational forensics is a two-phased approach to resolving this problem. The first phase is the proper collection of operational information such as data logs, system monitoring, and evidence-tracking methods. The appropriate attention to this phase makes it much easier to identify the problem in the second phase, the recovery.

At recovery time, the information at hand can be used to decide whether a formal intrusion investigation needs to be initiated and evidence collected needs to be preserved. By responding in prescribed ways, which can include repair/replacment of the equipment, correction of a software weakness, or identification of human-caused error(s) that resulted in the disruption, the system can be returned to operation with a much reduced probability of the same event occurring in the future.

RELATED BUSINESS REQUIREMENTS

Technology has been more than an efficiency enhancement to the organization. It has become the lifeblood of the successful enterprise and the sole product of the networked application service provider. As such, the maximum availability of this essential resource is critical. When a failure occurs or the system is not operating at expected levels, proper procedures should be used to accurately identify and correct the situation. Failing to do so will result in unpredictable operations, inefficiencies and possibly lost revenue, tarnished image, and failure to thrive. The business case for investing in the time, procedures, and the relatively small cost of computer hardware or software components seems clear.

Why then, do companies not have operational forensics (or the same functions by other names) programs in place? Well, for two reasons: People have started with the assumption that computers are perfectly reliable and therefore will only fail under rare circumstances if programs are well-written. Why waste resources in pointing the finger at something that should never occur? Second, the topic of methodical, procedural investigations is new to other than law enforcement, and only recently has come into the foreground with the advent of computer crimes, cyber terrorism, and the relationship of vengeance and violence linked to some computer "chat rooms," e-mail, and personal private data intrusions.

The good news is that operational forensics is not an expensive option. There is some additional cost needed to properly equip the systems and the process for secure log creation; but unless the need is determined for a full-scale criminal investigation and trial preparation, the process is almost transparent to most operations.

The business objectives of implementing an operational forensics program are threefold:

1. Maintain maximum system availability (99.999% or five-nines "uptime").
2. Quickly restore system operations without losing information related to the interruption.
3. Preserve all information that may be needed as evidence, *in an acceptable legal form*, should court action be warranted.

The acceptable legal form is what calls for the operational forensics process to be rigorously controlled through standard methods and a coordinated effort by areas outside the traditional IT organization.

JUSTIFICATION OPTIONS

The frequent reaction to a request to start an operational forensics program is one of financial concerns. Many stories abound of how forensic investigations of computer crimes have required hundreds or thousands of hours of highly paid investigators pouring over disk drives with a fine-tooth comb — all of this while the business operation is at a standstill. These stories probably have indeed occurred, but the reason they were so disruptive, took so long, or cost so much, was because the operational data or evidence had to be reconstructed. Often, this reconstruction process is difficult and may be effectively challenged in a legal case if not prepared perfectly.

Operational forensics programs can be justified using the age-old 80-20 rule: an investigation cost is 80 percent comprised of re-creating lost data and 20 percent actually investigating. An effective operational forensics program nearly eliminates the 80 percent data re-creation cost.

A second way in which operational forensics programs have been justified is as a positive closed-loop feedback system for making sure that the investment in IT is effectively utilized. It is wise investment planning and prudent loss reduction. For example, an operational forensics program can quickly and easily determine that the cause of a server crashing frequently is due to an unstable power source, not an improperly configured operating system. A power problem can be resolved for a few hundred dollars, whereas the reinstallation of a new operating system with all options can take several days of expensive staff time, and actually solve nothing.

No matter how the program is justified, organizations are beginning to think about the investment in technology and the huge emphasis on continuous availability, and a finding ways to convince management that a plan for identifying and investigating causes of system problems is a worthwhile endeavor.

BASICS OF OPERATIONAL FORENSICS

Operational forensics includes developing procedures and communicating methods of response so that all flexibility to recover more data or make legal or strategic decisions is preserved. Briefly stated, all the procedures in the world and all the smart investigators that can be found cannot reverse the course of events once they have been put into action. If the Ctrl-Alt-Delete sequence has been started, data lost in that action is difficult and expensive, if not impossible to recover. Operational forensics, therefore, starts with a state of mind. That state of mind prescribes a "think before reacting" mentality. The following are the basic components of the preparation process that accompany that mentality.

For all situations:

- definition of the process to prioritize the three key actions when an event occurs:
  — evidence retention
  — system recovery
  — cause identification
- guidelines that provide assistance in identifying whether an intrusion has occurred and if it was intentional

- methods for developing cost-effective investigative methods and recovery solutions
- maintenance of a secure, provable evidentiary chain of custody

For situations where legal action is warranted:

- identification or development of professionally trained forensic specialists and interviewers/interrogators, as needed
- procedures for coordination and referral of unauthorized intrusions and activity to law enforcement and prosecution, as necessary
- guidelines to assist in ongoing communication with legal representatives, prosecutors, and law enforcement, as necessary
- instructions for providing testimony, as needed

Notice that the evidence is collected and maintained in a form suitable for use in cases where legal action is possible, even if the event is purely an operational failure. That way, if after the research begins, it is determined that what was thought initially to be operational, turns out to warrant legal action, all the evidence is available.

Consider the following scenario. A Web server has stopped functioning, and upon initial determination, evidence shows that the building had a power outage and when the server rebooted upon restoration, a diskette was left in the drive from a previous software installation. Initial actions in response include purchasing a new UPS (uninterruptable power supply) capable of keeping the server functioning for a longer time, and changing the boot sequence so that a diskette in the drive will not prevent system recovery. All set? Everybody thinks so, until a few days after the recovery, someone has discovered that new operating parameters have taken effect, allowing an intruder to install a "trap door" into the operating system. That change would take effect only after the system rebooted. Is the data still available to identify how the trap door was installed, whether it posed problems prior to this event, and who is responsible for this act of vandalism?

An operational forensics program is designed to identify the risk of changes to the system operation when it is rebooted and conduct baseline quality control, but also to preserve the evidence in a suitable place and manner so that a future investigation can begin if new facts are uncovered.

BUILDING THE OPERATIONAL FORENSICS PROGRAM

Policy

To start building an operational forensics program, the first key element, as in many other technical programs, includes defining a policy. Success in developing this process must be established at the top levels of the organization. Therefore, a policy endorsed by senior management must be written and distributed to the entire organization. This policy both informs and guides.

This policy *informs* everyone that the organization has corporate endorsement to use appropriate methods to ensure long-term operational stability, and thus ensure that the means to accurately identify and correct problems will be used. It should also inform the organization that methods will be used to take legal action against those who attempt to corrupt, invade, or misuse the technology put in place to accomplish the organization's mission. There is a subtle hint here meant to discourage employees who may be tempted to use the system for questionable purposes (harassing, threatening, or illegal correspondence and actions), that the organization has the means and intent to prosecute violators.

The policy *guides* in that it describes what to do, under what circumstances, and how to evaluate the results. With this policy, the staff responsible for operating the system components, including mainframes, servers, and even workstations, as well as all other peripherals, will have a definition of the process to prioritize the three key actions when an event occurs:

- evidence retention
- system recovery
- cause identification

In general, this policy defines a priority used for establishing irrefutable data that identifies the cause of an interruption. That priority is to first ensure that the evidence is retained; then recover the system operation; and, finally, as time and talent permits, identify the cause.

Guidelines

As a supplement to these policies, guidelines can be developed that provide assistance in identifying whether an intrusion has occurred and if it was intentional. As with all guidelines, this is not a specific set of definitive rules, but rather a checklist of things to consider when conducting an initial response. More detailed guidelines are also provided in the form of a reminder checklist of the process used to secure a site for proper evidence retention. The suggested method for publishing this guideline is to post it on the wall near a server, firewall, or other critical component. Items on this reminder checklist can be constructed to fit the specific installation, but typical entries can include:

Before rebooting this server:

1. Take a photograph of the screen (call Ext xxxx for camera).
2. Verify that the keyboard/monitor switches are set correctly.
3. Record the condition of any lights/indicators.
4. Use the procedure entitled *"Disabling the disk mirror."*
5. ...
6. ...
7. etc.

Accompanying these posted instructions are a series of checklists designed to help record and control the information that can be collected throughout the data collection process.

Log Procedures

Policies and guidelines can help provide people with the motivation and method to act thoughtfully and properly when responding to an event, but they are insufficient by themselves to provide all that is needed. Most operating system components and access software (modem drivers, LAN traffic, Internet access software, etc.) provide for log files to be created when the connection is used, changed, or when errors occur. The catch is that usually these logs are not enabled when the component is installed. Furthermore, the log file may be configured to reside on a system device that gets reset when the system restarts. To properly enable these logs, they must be:

- activated when the service is installed
- maintained on a safe device, protected from unauthorized viewing or alteration
- set to record continuously despite system reboots

Additional third-party access management and control logs can and should be implemented to completely record and report system use in a manner acceptable for use as legal evidence. This includes data that can be independently *corroborated*, *nonrepudiated*, and *chain-of-custody* maintained. These requirements will be discussed more in the next section, "Linking Operating Forensics to Criminal Investigation."

Configuration Planning

The operational forensics program also includes defining methods for maximizing the data/evidence collection abilities while providing for fast and effective system recovery. That often can be accomplished by planning for operational forensics when system components are configured. One technique often used is to provide a form of disk mirroring on all devices where log files are stored. The intent is to capture data as it exists as close as possible to the event. By maintaining mirrored disks, the "mirror" can be disabled and removed for evidence preservation while the system is restarted. This accomplishes the preservation of evidence and quick recovery required in a critical system.

The process for maintaining and preserving this data is then to create a minimum of three copies of the mirrored data:

1. one copy to be signed and sealed in an evidence locker pending legal action (if warranted)

2. one copy to be used as a control copy for evidence/data testing and analysis
3. one copy to be provided to opposing attorney in the discovery phase, if a criminal investigation proceeds

LINKING OPERATIONAL FORENSICS TO CRIMINAL INVESTIGATION

The value of a well-designed operational forensics program is in its ability to have all the evidence necessary to effectively develop a criminal investigation. By far, the most intensive activity in preparing for a legal opportunity is in the preparation of data that is validated and provable in legal proceedings. Three concepts are important to understanding this capacity:

1. evidence corroboration
2. nonrepudiation
3. preservation of the chain of custody

Evidence Corroboration

If one is at all familiar with any type of legal proceeding, from the high profile trials of the 1990s to the courtroom-based movies, television programs, or pseudo-legal entertainment of judicial civil cases, evidence that is not validated through some independent means may by inadmissible. Therefore, to provide the maximum potential for critical evidence to be admitted into the record, it should be corroborated through some other means. Therefore, based on the potential for legal action, several log creation utilities can be employed to record the same type of information. When two sources are compared, the accuracy of the data being reported can be assured. For example, access to a system from the outside reported only by a modem log may be questioned that the data was erroneous. However, if the same information is validated by access to the system from system login attempt, or from an application use log, the data is more likely to be admitted as accurate.

Nonrepudiation

A second crucial element necessary for a smooth legal process is establishing evidence in a way that actions cannot be denied by the suspect. This is called "nonrepudiation." In many recent cases of attempted system intrusion, a likely suspect has been exonerated by testifying that it could not have been his actions that caused the violation. Perhaps someone masqueraded as him, or perhaps his password was compromised, etc. There is no way to definitely make all transactions pass the nonrepudiation test; but in establishing the secure procedures for authenticating all who access the system, nonrepudiation should be included as a high-priority requirement.

Preservation of the Chain of Custody

Finally, the last and perhaps most important legal objective of operational forensics is to preserve the chain of custody. In simple terms, this means that the data/evidence was always under the control of an independent source and that it could not have been altered to support one side of the case. This is perhaps the most easily established legal criterion, but the least frequently followed. To establish a proper chain of custody, all data must be properly signed-in and signed-out using approved procedures, and any chance of its alteration must be eliminated — to a legal certainty. Technology has come to the rescue with devices such as read-only CDs, but there are also some low-technology solutions like evidence lockers, instant photography, and voice recorders to track activity related to obtaining, storing, and preserving data.

For all legal issues, it is wise and highly recommended that the organization's legal counsel be included on the forensic team, and if possible, a representative from the local law enforcement agency's (Attorney General, Prosecutor or FBI/state/local police unit) high-tech crime unit. In the case of properly collecting evidence when and if a situation arises, prior planning and preparation is always a good investment.

LINKING OPERATIONAL FORENSICS TO BUSINESS CONTINUITY PLANNING

What makes operational forensics an entity unto itself is the ability to use the time and effort spent in planning for benefits other than prosecuting criminals. The key benefit is in an organization's ability to learn something from every operational miscue. Countless times, systems stop running because intruders who only partially succeed at gaining access have corrupted the network connections. In most instances, all the information that could have been used to close access vulnerabilities goes away with the Ctrl-Alt-Delete keys. Systems do not crash without cause. If each cause were evaluated, many of them could be eliminated or their probability of reoccurring significantly reduced.

In the current age of continuous availability, maximum network uptime is directly linked to profit or effectiveness. Implementing an operational forensics program can help establish an effective link to business continuity planning risk reduction and can raise the bar of attainable service levels.

Although evidence collected for improving availability does not need to pass all legal hurdles, an effective method of cause identification can help focus the cost of prevention on *real* vulnerabilities, not on the whole universe of possibilities, no matter how remote. Cost justification of new availability features is more readily available, and IT can begin to function more like a well-defined business function than a "black art."

SUMMARY AND CONCLUSION

When a system interruption occurs, operational forensics is a key component of the recovery process and should be utilized to identify the nature and cause of the interruption as well as collecting, preserving, and evaluating the evidence. This special investigation function is essential because it is often difficult to conclusively determine the nature, source, and responsibility for the system interruption. As such, to improve the likelihood of successfully recovering from a system interruption, certain related integral services, such as establishing the data/activity logs, monitoring system, evidence collection mechanisms, intrusion management, and investigative management should be established prior to a system interruptions occurrence. This is the primary benefit of operational forensics. One will see much more of this in the near future.

Index